Navigating Your Way Through the Federal Physician Self-Referral Law

Douglas M. Mancino
Ira J. Coleman
James M. Gaynor, Jr.
Gary B. Gertler
Anita R. Goff
Eric B. Gordon
Jane Lembeck Kuesel
Daniel H. Melvin II

Third Edition

Edited by
David Mlawsky

Atlantic Information Services, Inc.
1100 17th Street, NW, Suite 300 • Washington, D.C. 20036 • (202) 775-9008 • www.aispub.com

Other Health Care Management Books Available from AIS

14 Government-Endorsed Health Care Compliance Plans

1998 Directory of Health Care Management Companies

1998-99 Guide to Patient Satisfaction Survey Instruments

A Guide to Buying Physician Practices

A Guide to Forming Physician Networks

A Guide to Recruiting, Hiring and Training Managed Care Executives

Creating an MSO for Behavioral Health Providers

Designing a Health Care Corporate Compliance Program

Effective Fraud Control Tactics for Insurers and Managed Care Plans

Health Care Executives Guide to Fraud and Abuse

Health Care Report Cards: 1998-99

HMO & PBM Strategies for Pharmacy Benefits

Implementing a Successful Medicare+Choice Plan

Key Strategies and Trends Shaping the Growth of PPMCs

Managed Care Facts, Trend and Data: 1998-99

Managed Medicare and Medicaid Factbook: 1998

Medicare PSOs: Assessing the Market, Risks and Opportunities

Preventing and Detecting Managed Care Fraud

Call 1-800-521-4323 for a catalog of all AIS books, periodicals, training kits, and videos, or visit our web site at www.aispub.com

ISBN: 0-929156-45-5

For information regarding individual or bulk purchases, contact Sharee Wharton at Atlantic Information Services, Inc., 1100 17th Street, NW, Suite 300, Washington, DC 20036 (1-800-521-4323; 202-775-9008).

Table of Contents

Preface

The Omnibus Budget Reconciliation Act of 1989 included the so-called "Stark I" law that banned physician self-referrals of Medicare patients to clinical laboratories in which physicians have a financial interest. While the Stark I ban took effect on Jan. 1, 1992, the Health Care Financing Administration (HCFA) did not issue final regulations to implement the law until Aug. 14, 1995.

The Omnibus Budget Reconciliation Act of 1993 included the far-reaching "Stark II" law that expanded the physician self-referral ban to Medicare and Medicaid patients for 10 additional designated health services. Stark II took effect on Jan. 1, 1995, in the absence of any implementing regulations or regulatory guidance from HCFA. The agency on Jan. 9, 1998, issued proposed Stark II regulations.

Stark II has extremely broad implications for physicians and any health care organization with which physicians do business. The law poses complex compliance problems for virtually any provider or physician who treats Medicare and Medicaid patients.

Because of the law's substantial penalties, including Medicare and Medicaid program exclusions, Stark II presents clear economic and professional exposure for those who fail to comply with the statute's requirements.

This book is meant to be the definitive self-referral guidebook on how to plan for and comply with the Stark laws.

Atlantic Information Services, Inc., is pleased to publish this book, authored by a premier team of legal experts, headed by Douglas Mancino, Esquire, of the national law firm of McDermott, Will & Emery.

About the Authors

Douglas M. Mancino — the leader of the team of authors from the law firm of McDermott, Will & Emery — is a partner in the firm's Los Angeles office. He has represented all types of health care organizations for more than 20 years on tax, business and financial matters. Mr. Mancino has represented a wide range of public and private companies, including physician practice management companies, on corporate, securities and tax matters, and in connection with capital transactions such as mergers, acquisitions, private placements and public offerings. He also advises clients on a wide variety of fraud-and-abuse, self-referral and similar regulatory issues. Mr. Mancino has been named in several editions of *The Best Lawyers in America* and is a past president of the American Health Lawyers Assn.

Ira J. Coleman is the partner-in-charge of McDermott, Will & Emery's Miami office. He serves as counsel to numerous physician practice management companies and advises health care companies on regulatory and strategic acquisition issues.

James M. Gaynor Jr. is the president of James M. Gaynor, Jr., P.C., which is a partner in the Health Law Department of McDermott, Will & Emery's Chicago office. He has significant experience in Medicare issues, including representing clients in reimbursement disputes, Medicare civil fraud investigations, certification issues and Stark law matters. He worked with a group of large physician practices to obtain amendments to the Stark law that protect such practices' long-standing relationships with affiliated hospitals.

Gary B. Gertler is the partner-in-charge of the Health Law Department of McDermott, Will & Emery's Los Angeles office. His practice focuses on the development of hospital-affiliated group practices, emerging primary care and multispecialty group practices, and the structuring of MSOs, PHOs, IPAs, integrated provider networks and related arrangements.

Anita R. Goff is senior vice president and assistant general counsel for Salick Health Care, Inc., which provides diagnostic and therapeutic services to patients with catastrophic illnesses. Prior to joining Salick, she was a partner in the Health Law Department of McDermott, Will & Emery's Los Angeles office, where her practice involved advising hospitals, group practices, other providers and group purchasing organizations in areas of health law including the structuring and implementation of IDSs, MSOs and purchases of physician practices. She is experienced in the Medicare/Medicaid anti-fraud and abuse provisions, the Stark laws and similar state laws.

Eric B. Gordon is a partner in the Health Law Department of McDermott, Will & Emery's Los Angeles office. He represents hospitals, integrated delivery systems, medical groups and academic medical centers on regulatory, compliance and transactional matters with a particular emphasis on fraud-and-abuse and self-referral issues.

Jane Lembeck Kuesel is a partner in the Health Law Department of McDermott, Will & Emery's New York office. Her practice focuses on representation of hospitals, physicians, health plans and health care providers in matters including fraud and abuse, the Stark law and corresponding state laws, the structuring of PHOs and MSOs, contractual and corporate issues, and compliance audits and programs.

Daniel H. Melvin II is an attorney in the Health Law Department of McDermott, Will & Emery's Chicago office. He has considerable experience advising hospitals, physicians, ambulatory care providers and physician practice management companies on physician self-referral issues. His practice is concentrated in the area of health care provider regulation and reimbursement.

CHAPTER 1

Introduction to the Physician Self-Referral Prohibitions

Ethical concerns about physicians making money while treating the sick have been voiced throughout the history of medicine as a profession. These concerns emerge from the vague discomfort with physicians earning a livelihood for treating people who are ill. In a fee-for-service environment, this concern is exacerbated by the possibility that physicians will perform more or even unnecessary services to earn more income. In a managed care environment, this concern is fueled by the possibility that physicians will personally benefit by providing fewer services, delaying referrals for costly tests or otherwise compromising quality by providing substandard care.[1]

In recent years, the ethical concerns over how physicians may profit from services they directly perform, whether in a fee-for-service or managed care environment, have been eclipsed by concerns over how and under what circumstances they should be permitted to earn a profit from diagnostic and therapeutic services they do not administer directly. This is the essential issue presented when physicians acquire an ownership interest in, or enter into an economic relationship with, a facility or organization to which they refer patients for such services. This, too, is the specific conflict addressed by the federal prohibitions against certain self-referrals discussed in detail in this book.

Environmental Factors Stimulating Self-Referral Growth

Hospitals have been owned by physicians almost from the inception of the modern hospital. For example, an early hospital census revealed that physicians owned approximately 36% of the hospitals that reported.[2] Early in this century, many of the nation's smaller hospitals were little more than extensions of physicians' medical and surgical practices. In fact, the growth of physician-owned proprietary hospitals paralleled the transformation of surgery during the 19th century from "a desperate, menial, low-paid aspect of medicine — in Europe it had been relegated to barbers and others outside the organized profession — to the pinnacle of professional esteem and influence."[3] In the 1960s and 1970s, physicians increasingly found it desirable and affordable to provide laboratory and X-ray services in their offices, thus creating a separate profit center while making access to diagnostic tests more convenient for their patients.

During the 1980s, several factors stimulated physician ownership of, and economic relationships with, health care providers to which doctors referred patients and at which the doctors may not have treated patients directly:

■ The enactment of the Medicare prospective payment system in 1983 placed Medicare payments to hospitals on a predetermined- charge basis, rather than on a cost-reimbursement basis. This legislative change caused hospitals to devise means of placing physicians at risk and provide incentives for their efficient behavior. Then, as now, physicians have a direct impact on hospital costs per discharge.

■ The changing economic environment during the 1980s had a detrimental impact on physicians and their personal incomes. This was fueled by the growing number of physicians, the increased costs of medical education and growing competition between specialties, such as radiology and cardiology.

■ The rate of growth of managed care began to accelerate in the 1980s and continues to grow even faster today. This has caused hospitals and physicians to develop new ways of organizing their services through physician-hospital organizations, individual practice associations and other arrangements. This also stimulated the growth of medical group practices as well as group practice structures that are not fully integrated, such as management service organizations and "group practices without walls."

■ The rapid development of diagnostic and therapeutic technology accelerated the shift of many procedures from the inpatient setting to the outpatient setting, and also enabled physicians and others to establish freestanding, nonhospital facilities at which a variety of diagnostic, therapeutic and surgical procedures could be performed. For example, in 1979, about 14% of hospitals' surgical procedures were performed on an outpatient basis. By 1984, that rate had increased to 28%. In 1997, more than 50% of surgical procedures were performed on an outpatient basis, with that percentage continuing to increase.

■ Consumer preferences for a variety of medical services, such as oncology-related services, also began to have an impact on patient and physician decisions. Patients began to select hospitals and physicians on the basis of price, convenience and compatibility with patient expectations of how the care is to be delivered. Further, employers began subjecting their employees to greater deductible, copayment and coinsurance amounts, thereby making workers increasingly accountable for health care expenditures. This growing accountability of patients for the economic consequences of their decisions, as well as the increasing sophistication of patients in the selection of physicians and the making of health decisions, have significantly altered the nature of medical competition, hospital competition and physician-hospital competition.

The changes in the delivery and financing of hospital and medical care have radically altered the way hospitals and physicians do business today. Hospitals have responded to the economic challenges by increasing their emphasis on outpatient services; broadening their markets to provide a wider range of ambulatory and other types of care; developing, acquiring or affiliating with one or more alternative delivery systems; and restructuring into organizations that are capable of assuming financial risk for not only the delivery, but also the financing, of health care services in a vertically integrated manner. Physicians also have responded by becoming more marketing-oriented; expanding the number and scope of services performed on an in-office basis; developing integrated group practices to achieve economies of scale; establishing or affiliating with physician practice management companies; affiliating with managed care and other types of alternative delivery systems; and competing aggressively for many of the same patients for which hospitals are competing.

Early Legislative Responses to the Growth of Self-Referrals

The legislative response to these developments has been incremental. A variety of federal and state laws have been enacted or amended to prohibit kickbacks and other payments made to physicians to induce or reward physicians for patient referrals. These anti-kickback laws have also been directed at a variety of other abusive transactions. In recent years, the number of prosecutions for violations of these laws by joint venture promoters, physicians and hospitals has increased. In addition, these laws are now being used by private parties to terminate contractual, lease and similar arrangements.

A substantial number of states have enacted laws or issued regulations governing the ownership by physicians of interests in health care facilities and businesses that provide ancillary services, such as laboratories, pharmacies and imaging centers. For example, many states require physicians and hospitals to disclose to patients any ownership interest in facilities to which they refer patients.

Disclosure of ownership allows patients to become more aware of physician conflicts of interest and to consider using alternative providers. In a few instances, such as in the case of home health agencies and pharmacies, the extent of physician ownership has been limited to a specific percentage. The apparent rationale is that, if a physician's economic interest is limited, the likelihood that such physician's professional judgment will be compromised is reduced. Finally, most states have decided that the potential conflicts of interest are so great that physician ownership of certain types of health facilities should be flatly prohibited, or that a physician-owned facility should be prohibited from billing a particular program for its services. A large number of states, for example, have made it unlawful for physicians to own interests in pharmacies prior to the federal prohibition. Anti-kickback and state self-referral laws, however, remain generally ill-defined and have not been perceived as totally adequate in addressing the compliance needs.

Stark I — The Laboratory Ownership Prohibition

The original federal bill prohibiting self-referrals, introduced by Rep. Pete Stark (D-Calif.), would have applied to a broad spectrum of health-related goods and services.[4] However, in enacting the original self-referral law (Stark I) as part of the Omnibus Budget Reconciliation Act of 1989 (OBRA '89), Congress decided to apply the ban only to Medicare patient referrals for clinical laboratory services. The limited scope of Stark I reflected Congress' unwillingness at that time to extend the prohibition to any service for which there was no evidence of overutilization resulting from a physician's financial interest. Congress concluded the only evidence of overutilization was with respect to clinical lab services.

The Office of Inspector General of the Department of Health and Human Services issued a report in April 1989 concerning financial arrangements between physicians and other health care businesses.[5] The results were based on a survey of physician ownership of, and utilization patterns associated with, independent clinical laboratories, independent physiological laboratories and durable medical equipment suppliers. OIG found that Medicare patients of referring physicians who own or invest in independent clinical laboratories received 45% more clinical laboratory services than did Medicare beneficiaries in general.[6] OIG also found that Medicare patients of physician owners or investors in independent physiological laboratories received 13% more physiological testing than did Medicare patients in general. OIG found no increased utilization associated with physician owners of, or investors in, durable medical equipment suppliers.

In a separate study, the General Accounting Office surveyed patterns of physician referrals to clinical diagnostic laboratories and diagnostic imaging centers in Maryland and Pennsylvania. In June 1989, GAO testified before Congress that physician owners tended to order more, and more costly, laboratory services. For imaging services, GAO concluded that physician owners tended to order fewer, but more costly, services.[7]

Despite Congress' conclusion that both of these studies supported the proposition that physicians' financial interests could result in overutilization of clinical laboratory services, neither study examined the medical necessity, or lack thereof, of the specific tests ordered. As such, any conclusion with regard to overutilization of services was by implication only.[8]

Additional Challenges to Self-Referrals

In subsequent years, two additional reports fueled Congress' interest in expanding the self-referral prohibition beyond clinical lab services. First, the *New England Journal of Medicine* published a report in December 1990 comparing the frequency and cost of diagnostic imaging examinations performed by primary care physicians who used equipment in their offices with that of physicians who always referred patients to radiologists.[9] This report found that patients of physicians who owned their own equipment received imaging examinations four to four and one-half times more often than did patients referred to radiologists. Ironically, the physicians whom this study found had greater utilization generally are exempt from the self-referral prohibition because they qualify for the in-office ancillary services exception to the referral prohibition discussed in Chapter 4.

A second report was released in 1991 by the Florida Health Care Cost Containment Board.[10] Conducted on behalf of the Florida Legislature, HCCCB found that doctor-owned, full-service clinical labs performed an average of 3.3 tests per patient vs. an average of 1.7 tests per patient at "non-joint venture" laboratories. HCCCB further found that charges at physician-owned laboratories were higher. With regard to diagnostic imaging centers, HCCCB was unable to compare utilization and pricing, because virtually all of these centers in Florida were owned by doctors. With regard to physical therapy and rehabilitation services, doctor-owned facilities were found to have higher charges, use less skilled personnel and offer shorter treatments than non-joint ventures. HCCCB further found that physician ownership had no conclusive effect on utilization of services provided by ambulatory surgical centers, home health agencies, radiation therapy centers or durable medical equipment suppliers.

The American Medical Assn.'s Developing Position on Self-Referrals

The American Medical Assn. has addressed the self-referral issue on many occasions. Its early view was that conflicts of interest were inherent in the practice of medicine, and that the problem of referring patients to outside facilities in which physicians had an investment interest was not significantly different in principle from other conflicts presented by fee-for-service medicine. Subsequently, the AMA acknowledged that some arrangements may present too great a conflict to be appropriate. The AMA prescribed a list of safeguards to help ensure that a patient's interests would not be jeopardized through self-referrals.

As congressional support for more expansive prohibitions against self-referrals increased, and as more studies documented the effects of self-referral on utilization and costs, the AMA began to re-evaluate its original positions on self-referral. Ultimately, the AMA decided it was necessary to strengthen its opinion.

In 1991, the AMA House of Delegates voted to approve specific ethical guidelines that started with the premise that "physicians should not refer patients to a health care facility outside their office practice at which they do not directly provide care or services when they have an investment interest in the facility."[11] The ethical guidelines recognized, however, that there may be appropriate, limited circumstances when physicians should not be prohibited from investing in facilities to which they refer patients. The AMA endorsed a number of situations when physicians may ethically have an ownership interest in a facility when there is a demonstrated community need for the facility and alternate financing is not available. The guidelines, now codified in the AMA's Code of Medical Ethics, clarify that community need exists when there is no facility of reasonable quality in the community or when use of existing facilities is onerous for patients, such as when undue delays in receiving services would compromise the patient's care or affect the curability of the patient's condition. The AMA's Code also says that, to establish that alternative financing is not available, the developer must try to secure funding from banks, other financial institutions and venture capitalists before turning to self-referring physicians. Among other criteria, the ethical guidelines also require that the return on the physician's investment be tied to the physician's equity in the facility rather than to the volume of referrals, and that investment contracts not prevent physicians from investing in other facilities. The AMA's ethical guidelines also prescribe disclosure of ownership interest requirements and call for the establishment of internal utilization review programs to ensure that investing physicians do not exploit their patients in any way, such as by inappropriate or unnecessary utilization.[12]

Stark II — The Broad-Scale Prohibition Against Self-Referrals

Despite the limited evidence of overutilization in health services other than clinical laboratories, Congress enacted a significantly expanded physician self-referral ban (Stark II) as part of the Omnibus Budget Reconciliation Act of 1993. By 1993, Congress' presumption apparently had shifted from affording physicians' the benefit of the doubt to a presumption that physicians would accede to the temptation to overutilize.

Stark II became effective on Jan. 1, 1995. In August 1995 HCFA published the long-awaited final regulations interpreting and implementing the Stark I law.[13] Because the Stark II law maintains the same general prohibitions and some of the exceptions in Stark I, HCFA indicated that a majority of its interpretations in the Stark I rules, which apply to clinical laboratory services, also will apply to the other designated health services subject to Stark II.[14]

In January 1998, HCFA published proposed regulations interpreting and implementing the Stark II law. These proposed regulations and, importantly, their lengthy preamble, offer much-needed guidance concerning the interpretation and application of Stark II to a wide range of arrangements and relationships. In addition, the proposed regulations create new exceptions to Stark II. However, the proposed regulations also propose very restrictive interpretations in many instances. Thus, HCFA has received extensive comments critical of them. This book includes extensive discussion of the proposed regulations and critiques them when appropriate.

In addition, this book refers to the current physician self-referral legislation, which combines Stark I and Stark II, as the "Stark law." Where discussion relates to provisions or policies that relate only to Stark I or Stark II, this book uses the terms "Stark I" and "Stark II," as appropriate.

The ultimate scope and practical impact of the Stark law remains unclear, not only because the implementing regulations are still under development, but also because Congress is considering legislation that would further amend the physician self-referral law in significant ways. References to relevant provisions of pending legislation are made throughout this book.

Overview of this Book

This book has been developed to serve as a useful reference tool for physicians, hospitals, outpatient facilities, suppliers and others who provide services or deal with physicians who provide services to Medicare and Medicaid beneficiaries. The book is organized to allow readers access to information on specific areas of concern without having to read the book from start to finish.

Endnotes

[1] For a general discussion of these ethical concerns, see Fost, "Ethical Considerations of Hospital-Physician Joint Ventures," in L. Burns and D. Mancino, *Joint Ventures Between Hospitals and Physicians* (Aspen 1987).

[2] Steinwald, B., & Neuhauser, D., "The Role of the Proprietary Hospital," 35 *Law & Contemporary Problems 817* (1970).

[3] Rothstein, W., *American Physicians in the Nineteenth Century, 260* (1972); Alexander, J.A., and Amburgey, T.L., "The Dynamics of Change in the American Hospital Industry: Transformation or Selection?" *44 Med. Care Rev. 279, 292-93* (1987).

[4] H.R. 5198, 100th Cong., 2d Sess. Sec. 2(a)(1988).

[5] Office of Inspector General, Department of Health and Human Services, *Financial Arrangements Between Physicians and Other Health Care Businesses* (1989).

[6] Office of Inspector General, supra.

[7] Medicare, Referring Physicians' Ownership of Laboratories and Imaging Centers, Hearings on H.R. 939 before the Subcommittee on Health of the House Committee on Ways and Means, 101st Cong., 1st Sess. 8 (1989).

[8] U.S. General Accounting Office, *Medicare Referrals to Physician-Owned Imaging Facilities Warrant HCFA's Scrutiny*, GAO/HEHS-95-2, 103d Cong., 2d Sess. (1994).

[9] Hillman, B., et.al, "Frequency and Costs of Diagnostic Imaging in Office Practice, a Comparison of Self-Referring and Radiologist-Referring Physicians," *323 New. Eng. J. Med. 1604* (Dec. 6, 1990).

[10] State of Florida Health Care Cost Containment Board, *Joint Ventures among Health Care Providers in Florida, Volume II* (September 1991).

[11] American Medical Assn., *Report of the Council on Ethical and Judicial Affairs*, pg. 6 (1991).

[12] *American Medical Assn. Code of Medical Ethics*, Sec. 8.032 (1994 ed.). See also "Conflict of Interest: Physician Ownership of Medical Facilities." *267 J Amer. Med. Assoc. 2366* (May 6, 1992).

[13] 60 *Fed. Reg.* 41914.

[14] 60 *Fed. Reg.* 41914, 41916.

CHAPTER 2

Prohibited Referrals and Other Practices

The Stark law generally prohibits physicians from referring Medicare patients to an entity for the furnishing of "designated health services" when the physician or an immediate family member of the referring physician has a "financial relationship" with that entity. The Stark law also prohibits the entity from billing Medicare for services rendered as a result of a referral prohibited by the statute. In addition, the Stark law prevents states from receiving federal Medicaid matching payments for designated health services that are provided as a result of a prohibited referral. Many financial relationships that are quite common and appropriate trigger the Stark prohibition against referrals. For referrals to be made where these common relationships exist, an applicable exception to the Stark law must be identified. This method of defining a prohibition broadly and then carving out exceptions as necessary and appropriate is troublesome. First, the drafters of the law did not provide for all of the necessary exceptions to deal with nonabusive transactions and relationships. Second, ambiguities in the drafted exceptions create uncertainty.

The scope of and terms contained in the Stark law are discussed in this chapter. Later chapters define the term "designated health services" and describe and analyze in detail the numerous exceptions to and ambiguities in the Stark law's prohibitions.

The Scope of the Stark Law's Prohibitions

Stark I prohibited physicians from making referrals for clinical laboratory services "for which payment otherwise may be made under [the Medicare title]".[1] No claims arising out of such prohibited referrals may be presented by an entity to the Medicare program, nor may bills be rendered "to any individual, third-party payor or other entity" for payment of services provided under a prohibited referral.[2] Stark II expanded the list of services for which referrals are prohibited. These services for which Stark II prohibits Medicare referrals are discussed in Chapter 3.

In addition, Stark II extended the referral prohibition to Medicaid in an indirect manner. Rather than prohibiting physician self-referrals of Medicaid patients, the Medicaid prohibition applies to the states, not to the individual practitioners and entities that make and receive the referrals and bill state Medicaid programs. Stark II prohibits federal matching payments to a state under the Medicaid title for "expenditures for medical assistance under the State plan consisting of a designated health service...furnished to an individual on the basis of a referral that would result in the denial of payment for the service under [the Medicare program] if [Medicare] provided for coverage of such service to the same extent and under the same terms and conditions as under the State plan...."[3]

Before a state can deny payments to entities providing designated health services to Medicaid recipients, however, it must enact a state law applicable to physicians that is at least as restrictive as the Stark law, and which prohibits physicians from billing the state Medicaid plan for the types of referrals prohibited by the Stark law. While a significant number of states have enacted prohibitions against self-referrals, generally these laws either are not as restrictive as the Stark law, or they do not cover the same designated health services. For example, the current New York physician self-referral law does not cover as many designated health services as does the Stark law.[4] In addition, the New York law has certain definitions and exceptions that could give rise to discrepancies from the Stark law's provisions.[5] Legislation is pending in a number of states to remedy these discrepancies, but generally the legislation was not in effect in time to address this issue by Jan. 1, 1995, when Stark II took effect. Other states may not have even acted yet to address the issue. As a result, many states are in a position where they cannot deny payment to a physician under the Stark law, but cannot obtain from the federal government any portion of amounts paid to a physician.

Referrals Prohibited by the Stark Law

The Stark law divides prohibited referrals into two categories. First, in the case of items or physician services for which payment may be made under Part B of the Medicare program, a referral is defined as "the request by a physician for the item or service."[6] This has been interpreted by the proposed Stark II regulations to include the ordering by a physician of any designated health service covered under Medicine Part B, or the certifying or recertifying of the need for any designated health service.[7] A referral includes "the request by a physician for a consultation with another physician," as well as "any test or procedure ordered by, or to be performed by (or under the supervision of) that other physician."[8] According to the preamble to the Stark II proposed regulations, a "consultation" occurs whenever a physician requests that a patient see another physician but the original physician retains control over the patient's care.[9] The preamble to the proposed Stark II regulations further clarifies that any item or service that may be covered under Medicare is considered a referral, "regardless of whether Medicare would actually pay for this particular service, at the time, for the particular eligible individual who has been referred."[10] For anything other than items and physician services payable by Medicare Part B, a referral is broadly defined as "the request or establishment of a plan of care by a physician which includes the provision of the designated health service."[11] The proposed Stark II regulations again expand the definition to include "the certifying or recertifying of the need for such a designated health service."[12]

A "plan of care" has been defined in the proposed Stark II regulations as "the establishment by a physician of a course of diagnosis or treatment (or both) for a particular patient, including the ordering of services."[13] As with the Part B services, HCFA interprets this referral definition as applying only to those designated health services that "may be" covered under Medicare.[14]

For a Medicaid service, HCFA interprets the Stark law to mean that a state should apply the Medicare rules to a referral for a Medicaid service, even if the service is not covered under Medicare.[15] Similarly, the test for coverage is whether an item or service "may be" covered, not whether the particular individual in question is covered for the item or service.[16] Because Medicaid does not categorize services into Part A and Part B, the definition of referral is simply "a comparable service covered under the Medicaid State plan."[17]

The Stark law creates a limited exception to the definition of "referral" that is available to pathologists, radiologists and radiation oncologists. If a pathologist requests clinical diagnostic laboratory tests or pathological examination services, if a radiologist requests diagnostic radiology services, or if a radiation oncologist requests radiation therapy, such requests are not "referrals" for purposes of the Stark law.[18] For the request not to be considered a prohibited referral, the services must be furnished by, or under the supervision of, the requesting pathologist, radiologist or radiation oncologist in response to a consultation requested by another physician.[19] The preamble to the proposed Stark II regulations clarifies that the level of supervision for a pathologist is that ordinarily required under Medicare coverage rules, payment rules, and health and safety standards, not the "direct supervision" required for the in-office ancillary services exception.[20]

Any entity, such as a hospital, diagnostic imaging center or reference laboratory, receiving referrals for designated services must also take steps to ensure it does not bill for any referrals that are made in violation of the Stark law. The Stark law prohibits an entity from presenting or causing to be presented a claim or bill under Medicare for a prohibited referral to any "individual, third-party payer or other entity."[21] Therefore, the burden of complying with the law is shared by both the referring physician and the entity receiving the referral, although the financial consequences of billing for a service rendered under a prohibited referral fall only on the entity providing the designated health service (see Chapter 8).

The sanctions provisions of the Stark law impose civil money penalties and exclusion from the Medicare program on persons who present a bill or claim "that such person knows or should know" is for services provided pursuant to prohibited referral.[22] In the absence of final implementing rules to Stark II, the "knows" or "should-have-known" standard for impermissible billing will undoubtedly prove difficult to apply and currently leaves parties to certain arrangements unsure of potential liability exposure. While the final Stark I regulations and the proposed Stark II regulations provide some guidance on HCFA's likely interpretation of the Stark law, many ambiguities remain to be addressed by the final Stark II regulations. Accordingly, whether a party should have known a referral was prohibited by the Stark law will depend on the facts and circumstances of each arrangement.

'Physician' and 'Immediate Family Member' Defined

The Stark law prohibits a physician from making a referral if the physican or an immediate family member of that physcian has a financial relationship.[23] The terms "physician" and "immediate family member" are not defined in the law. However, the Stark I regulations and the proposed Stark II regulations state that enforcers will use the definition of "physician" already contained in federal law and regulations, which includes doctors of medicine or osteopathy, doctors of dental surgery or dental medicine, doctors of podiatric medicine, doctors of optometry, and certain chiropractors.[24] Under the Stark I final regulations and the proposed Stark II regulations, "immediate family member or member of a physician's immediate family" is defined as "husband or wife; natural or adoptive parent, child or sibling; stepparent, stepchild, stepbrother or stepsister; father-in-law, mother-in-law, son-in-law, daughter-in-law, brother-in-law or sister-in-law; grandparent or grandchild; and spouse of a grandparent or grandchild."[25] This definition is broad and reflects HCFA's view that the self-referral ban should encompass the full range of relatives who could be in a position to influence the pattern of a physician's referrals.

Financial Relationships Covered by the Stark Law

A "financial relationship" is defined in the Stark law as an ownership or investment interest in an entity that provides designated health services, or a compensation arrangement between the referring physician or an immediate family member and the entity providing such services.[26] Each of these terms is discussed below.

The preamble to the proposed Stark II regulations clarifies financial interest.[27] First, HCFA reiterates that a financial relationship can exist even if the relationship does not involve any designated health services or any Medicare or Medicaid referrals. Secondly, HCFA clarifies that ownership interests may be indirect, including through multiple levels of ownership. Finally, HCFA states that payments resulting from an ownership or investment interest, such as dividends, are not compensation.

Ownership or Investment Interest. An ownership or investment interest in an "entity" that provides one or more designated health services may be through "equity, debt or other means."[28] The term "entity" is not defined by the law; however, the Stark I regulations define an "entity" as a "sole proprietorship, trust, corporation, partnership, foundation, not-for-profit corporation or unincorporated association."[29] The proposed Stark II regulations add to the definition of entity "a physician's sole practice or a practice of multiple physicians that provides for the furnishing of designated health services..."[30] As the preamble to the Stark I proposed regulations states, HCFA desired to define the term "entity" in a way that would be used consistently by Medicare contractors. With respect to the Stark I law, the preamble further notes that HCFA did not believe that

Congress intended to limit the term to independent clinical laboratories; thus, HCFA's definition encompasses all suppliers of clinical lab services.[31] Applying this same definition of "entity" for Stark II purposes suggests that the definition encompasses all possible suppliers of designated health services, not just the separate entities formed only to provide such services. The preamble to the Stark II regulations clarifies that an "entity" does not include "any person, business or other organization or association that owns the components of the operation — such as owning the building that houses the entity or the equipment the entity uses — without owning the operation itself."[32]

"Debt" and "equity" also are undefined by the Stark law, the Stark I regulations, and the proposed Stark II regulations. Clearly, ownership of stock in a corporation, or a partnership interest in a general or limited partnership to which the physician could make a referral for a designated health service, would trigger the law. Although not directly discussed in the Stark I regulations, a membership in a limited liability company also is likely to be included within the definition of "equity." The preamble to the proposed Stark II regulations states that a physician has a "debt" interest "anytime the physician or family member has lent money or given other valuable consideration to the entity and the debt is secured (in whole or in part) by the entity or the entity's assets or property."[33] In addition, a "debt" interest can arise "in any other debtor-creditor relationships that have an indicia of ownership" such as "participation in revenue or profits, subordinated payment terms, low or no interest terms, or ownership of convertible debentures."[34] Unsecured loans, nonconvertible loans or a loan "with no other indicia of ownership" by a physician to an entity would be considered a compensation arrangement, not an ownership interest.[35]

Loans to a physician or family member from an entity do not constitute a debt interest, according to HCFA. Instead, a compensation arrangement arises, for which an exception may be available.[36] Membership in a nonprofit corporation also is not considered an ownership interest.[37] Less clear is what would be considered an ownership or investment interest through "other means." There is little guidance in the legislative history, or in the Stark I regulations, on this point. Congress appears to have intended to include any creative arrangements in which ownership or an investment could be obtained, despite not technically being debt or equity. The preamble to the Stark II regulations provides that stock options and nonvested interests constitute "ownership."[38] The potential breadth of this definition indicates that inventive relationships should be carefully reviewed to ensure they would not be considered an ownership or investment interest "by other means."

Stark II broadened the definition of an "ownership or investment interest" to include an interest in an entity that holds an ownership or investment interest in any entity providing the designated health service.[39] For example, an ownership interest or investment in a holding company where one or more of the subsidiaries provide designated health services would be considered an ownership or investment interest under the statute. The preamble to the Stark I final regulations clarifies that a physician has an ownership or investment interest with an entity providing a designated health service whenever the physician owns some portion of an entity that has an ownership interest in the entity providing the designated health service. This would be true regardless of whether the entities are related as parent-subsidiary or brother-sister corporations.[40] For example, if the physician had an ownership interest in a subsidiary of an entity providing a designated health service, the physician would likely be deemed to have an ownership interest in the parent entity, if the subsidiary had an ownership interest, such as through stock or debt instruments, in the parent entity.

Compensation Arrangements

The definition of a "compensation arrangement" is extremely broad. The Stark law provides that a compensation arrangement means "any arrangement involving any remuneration between a physician (or an immediate family member of such physician) and an entity."[41] The proposed Stark II regulations added that remuneration may be direct or indirect.[42] Using a definition that is similar to the federal anti-kickback law, remuneration paid under the Stark law includes any remuneration, "directly or indirectly, overtly or covertly, in cash or in kind."[43] The proposed Stark II regulations broaden the definition further in providing that remuneration means "any payment, discount, forgiveness of debt, or other benefit made directly or indirectly, overtly or covertly, in cash or in kind."[44] Note, too, that remuneration does not necessarily have to be paid by an entity to a physician. Any remuneration between the entity and physician, even if it is the physician paying the entity, constitutes remuneration under the Stark law.

There are three statutory exclusions from the definition of "remuneration."

First, amounts owed for inaccurate or mistakenly performed tests or procedures may be forgiven, and the correction of minor billing errors may be made.[45] The preamble to the proposed Stark II regulations clarifies that this exception applies only to the items forgiven or corrected, not to the overall transaction of generally providing tests or billing services.[46]

Second, items, devices or supplies that are used solely either to "collect, transport, process or store specimens for the entity providing the item, device or supply," or to "order or communicate the results of tests or procedures for such entity," may be provided without the items, devices or supplies being considered in-kind remuneration.[47] The preamble to the proposed Stark II regulations interprets "solely" to mean that "these items are used solely for the purposes listed in the statute."[48] If the item is used for any additional purposes, it does not meet this exception.[49] In addition, the Stark II preamble focuses on the number of items or devices provided, which must be "consistent with the number or amount that is used for specimens that are actually sent to this entity for processing."[50] Computer equipment and fax machines would not meet the "solely" test unless the physician proves that the equipment is integral to, and used exclusively for, performing the outside entity's work."[51]

Third, a payment from an insurer or a self-insured plan to a physician for a fee-for-service claim "for the furnishing of health services by that physician to an individual who is covered by a policy with the insurer or by the self-insured plan" does not constitute remuneration if four conditions are met:

(1) There must be no contract or other arrangement between the insurer or the plan and the physician, under which the services are furnished and payment is made;

(2) "The payment [must be] made to the physician on behalf of the covered individual and would otherwise be made directly to such individual";

(3) The amount of the payment must be set in advance; must not exceed fair market value; and must not take into account, directly or indirectly, the volume or value of any referrals; and

(4) The payment must meet any other requirements imposed by HCFA.[52] To date, there are no other requirements imposed by regulation.[53]

With only three limited statutory exclusions, the term "compensation arrangement" encompasses a wide range of relationships. A compensation arrangement includes any kind of contract, such as employment or independent contractor agreements, a lease of office space or equipment, management services agreements, medical directorships or other consulting arrangements, and services agreements such as EKG readings and interpretive studies. A compensation arrangement encompasses oral and written arrangements. It clearly includes in-kind compensation, and could be extended to such common practices as the provision of free meals, parking or discounts provided by an entity to physicians on its staff, including referring physicians. Even such perquisites provided to the family members of referring physicians could be considered compensation arrangements.

There are a number of exceptions to the compensation arrangement prohibition that are discussed in detail in Chapter 4. In addition, legislation proposed in 1995-1996 would have significantly altered the compensation arrangement prohibitions. Indeed, the Republican-sponsored Balanced Budget Act of 1995, which passed Congress but was later vetoed by President Clinton, would have entirely repealed the ban on referrals where only a compensation arrangement exists.[54] Alternatively, President Clinton has proposed legislation to simplify the Stark law with respect to compensation arrangements and make a generic exception more readily available for referrals involving such arrangements.[55] Two new exceptions set forth in the proposed regulations also simplify compliance with the law. In the absence of legislative changes, however, each relationship or arrangement between an entity and a physician or immediate family member of a physician must be scrutinized carefully to ensure that it is properly structured under the current Stark law. If the relationship or arrangement falls within the scope of the Stark law, it must be determined whether a relevant exception can be utilized. This process is extremely important because intent to violate the Stark law is not necessary to prove a violation of it. Simply having the financial relationship, making a prohibited referral and submitting a claim for that referral is sufficient to constitute a violation and trigger the penalties imposed by the Stark law.

Endnotes

[1] 42 U.S.C. Sec. 1395nn(a)(1)(A).

[2] 42 U.S.C. Sec. 1395nn(a)(1)(B).

[3] 42 U.S.C. Sec. 1396b(s).

[4] N.Y. Pub. Health Law Sec. 238-a.

[5] Id. See also, Tully & Henninger, "Physician Self-Referral Restrictions: An Overview of the Stark Bill and the Physician Ownership and Referral Act of 1993," *14 Cal. Health L. News 89* (1994).

[6] 42 U.S.C. Sec. 1395nn(h)(5).

[7] 63 *Fed. Reg.* 1722 (proposed 42 CFR Sec. 411.351).

[8] 42 U.S.C. Sec. 1395nn(h)(5).

[9] 63 *Fed. Reg.* 1693.

[10] 63 *Fed. Reg.* 1692.

[11] 42 U.S.C. Sec. 1395nn(h)(5)(B).

[12] 63 *Fed. Reg.* 1723 (proposed 42 CFR Sec. 411.351).

[13] 63 *Fed. Reg.* 1722 (proposed 42 CFR Sec. 411.351).

[14] 63 *Fed. Reg.* 1692.

[15] 63 *Fed. Reg.* 1692.

[16] Id.

[17] 63 *Fed Reg.* 1722,1723 (proposed 42 CFR Sec. 411.351).

[18] 42 U.S.C. Sec. 1395nn(h)(5).

[19] Id.

[20] 63 *Fed. Reg.* 1693.

[21] 42 U.S.C. Sec. 1395nn(a)(1)(B).

[22] 42 U.S.C. Sec. 1395nn(g)(3).

[23] 42 U.S.C. Sec. 1396nn(a)(1).

[24] 42 CFR Sec. 410.20(b); 42 CFR Sec. 411.355(a)

[25] 42 CFR Sec. 411.351; 63 *Fed. Reg.* 1721.

[26] 42 U.S.C. Sec. 1395nn(a)(2).

[27] 63 *Fed. Reg.* 1686.

[28] 42 U.S.C. Sec. 1395nn(a)(2).

[29] 42 CFR Sec. 411.351.

[30] 63 *Fed. Reg.* 1721 (proposed 42 CFR Sec. 411.351).

[31] 60 *Fed. Reg.* 41979.

[32] 63 *Fed. Reg.* 1706.

[33] 63 *Fed. Reg.* 1707.

[34] Id.

[35] Id.

[36] Id.

[37] Id.

[38] 63 *Fed. Reg.* 1708.

[39] 42 U.S.C. Sec. 1395nn(a)(2).

[40] 60 *Fed. Reg.* 41914, 41945.

[41] 42 U.S.C. Sec. 1395nn(h)(1)(A).

[42] 63 *Fed. Reg.* 1720 (proposed 42 CFR Sec. 411.351)

[43] 42 U.S.C. Sec. 1395nn(h)(1)(B).

[44] 63 *Fed. Reg.* 1723 (proposed 42 CFR Sec. 441.351)

[45] 42 U.S.C. Sec. 1395nn(h)(1)(C)(i).

[46] 63 *Fed. Reg.* 1693.

[47] 42 U.S.C. Sec. 1395nn(h)(1)(c)(ii).

[48] 63 *Fed. Reg.* 1693.

[49] Id. at 1694.

[50] Id.

[51] Id.

[52] 42 U.S.C. Sec. 1395nn(h)(1)(c)(iii)(I-IV).

[53] This exception was not part of Stark I. Consequently, the Stark I regulations did not address this issue.

[54] H.R. 2491, 104th Cong. 1st Sess., Sec. 8201 (1995).

[55] President's F.Y. 1997 Budget, Sec. 11212(b).

CHAPTER 3

Designated Health Services

The Stark law identifies the "designated health services" subject to the self-referral prohibition as follows:

> Clinical laboratory services; physical therapy services; occupational therapy services; radiology services, including magnetic resonance imaging, computerized axial tomography scans and ultrasound services; radiation therapy services and supplies; durable medical equipment and supplies; parenteral and enteral nutrients, equipment and supplies; prosthetics, orthotics and prosthetic devices and supplies; home health services; outpatient prescription drugs; inpatient and outpatient hospital services.[1]

The Stark law did not define the items and services constituting "designated health services" beyond this listing The proposed Stark II regulations and the accompanying commentary, however, provide some detail regarding the services that are covered by the Stark law and include HCFA's analysis of particular items and services.

Designated Health Services as Components of Other Services

The preamble to the proposed Stark II regulations states HCFA's belief that a designated health service continues to be one, even if it is billed as something else, bundled with other services for billing purposes, or provided in a different setting.[2] The preamble cites designated health services provided at a skilled nursing facility or clinic services billed under Medicaid that would still be considered designated health services.[3] Certain designated health services, however, are considered "peripheral parts of some other major service that a physician has prescribed."[4] The preamble does not describe this exception in any further detail, other than to give the example of an echocardiogram not being considered a designated health service when provided as part of a coronary bypass surgery, because the echocardiogram is incidental to the physician service being provided.[5]

Because the Medicare and Medicaid programs define designated health services in different ways, the preamble states that the definitions for purposes of the Stark law are generally based upon existing definitions in the Medicare program, with certain exceptions.[6] If the definition of a designated health service under a state's Medicaid program differs from the definition under Medicare, HCFA asserts that it will assume that the services under the state's Medicaid program take precedence, even if the definition will include services that are not covered by Medicare.[7] HCFA specifically requests comments regarding this policy, and there may be a change in the final regulations.[8]

Following is a detailed discussion of the scope of services that currently are affected by the Stark law. Note that the commentary to the proposed Stark II regulations includes detailed descriptions regarding the services covered by the Stark law, but the actual proposed definitions generally refer to current Medicare definitions. This chapter will summarize HCFA's significant commentary regarding particular services, but for additional detail, it may also be useful to examine HCFA's actual commentary.

Clinical Laboratory Services

Because clinical laboratory services were included in Stark I, HCFA has already interpreted the term under the federal self-referral law. Specifically, on March 11, 1992, HCFA published proposed regulations to implement Stark I[9], and on Aug. 14, 1995, published final Stark I regulations.[10] In these regulations, HCFA adopted a definition of "clinical laboratory services" that is based on HCFA's regulations to the Clinical Laboratory Improvement Amendments of 1988.[11] Under the Stark I regulations, clinical laboratory services are defined as:

> biological, microbiological, serological, chemical, immunohematological, hematological, biophysical, cytological, pathological or other examination of materials derived from the human body for the purpose of providing information for the diagnosis, prevention or treatment of any disease or impairment of, or the assessment of the health of, human beings. These examinations also include procedures to determine, measure, or otherwise describe the presence or absence of various substances or organisms in the body.[12]

The proposed Stark II regulations do not change this definition of clinical laboratory services.[13] The Stark I regulations define a laboratory as an entity that furnishes such services and clarify that entities only collecting and/or preparing specimens, or only serving as a mailing service and not performing testing, are not considered laboratories.[14] This definition is also not changed by the proposed Stark II regulations.[15]

HCFA notes in the preambles to the Stark I proposed and final regulations that the definition of "clinical laboratory services" includes the furnishing of anatomic laboratory services, but does not include noninvasive tests, such as electroencephalograms or electrocardiograms. This definition also does not include diagnostic imaging services, such as mammograms or computerized axial tomography scans.[16] HCFA indicates that, generally, if a diagnostic test is subject to categorization under CLIA, it will fall within the definition of a "clinical laboratory service."[17]

In the preamble to the final Stark I regulations, HCFA expressly rejected a recommendation that the American Medical Assn.'s Current Procedural Terminology be used as a reference for identifying which laboratory services are subject to Stark I. HCFA indicated its concern that sole use of CPT codes to identify clinical laboratory services would not encompass the full range of test systems, assays and examinations subject to CLIA certification, which HCFA views as the more appropriate reference point for defining "clinical laboratory services" that are subject to the physician self-referral law.

Physical Therapy Services

HCFA defines physical therapy services for the first time in the proposed Stark II regulations. These services are defined as those "outpatient physical therapy services (including speech-language pathology services) described at section 1861(p) of the Act and at section 410.100(b) and (d) of this chapter. Physical therapy services also include any other services with the characteristics described in section 410.100(b) and (d) that are covered under Medicare Part A or B, regardless of who provides them, the location in which they are provided or how they are billed."[18]

Subject to certain exclusions, outpatient physical therapy services are those services provided to an individual under the care of a physician, and for whom a plan of care has been established, either by the physician or the therapist providing the services. If the therapist provides the services, it must be reviewed by a physician.[19] Physical therapy services include "testing and measurement of the function or disfunction of the neuromuscular, musculoskeletal, cardiovascular and respiratory systems, and assessment and treatment related to dysfunction caused by illness or injury, and aimed at preventing or reducing disability or pain and restoring lost function."[20] Establishment of a maintenance therapy program is also covered.

Speech-language pathology services are defined as "such speech, language, and related function assessment and rehabilitation services furnished by a qualified speech-language pathologist as this pathologist is legally authorized to perform under State law (or the State regulatory mechanism) as otherwise would be covered if furnished by a physician."[21] The preamble to the Stark II regulations notes that the Medicare Carriers Manual provides in section 2216 that services to diagnose and treat swallowing disorders, restorative therapy and maintenance programs and group speech pathology services may also be covered and are therefore considered "designated health services."[22]

The preamble to the proposed Stark II regulations reiterates that physical therapy services are not limited to outpatient services, but include all physical therapy services wherever they are provided, however they are billed and whoever they are provided by.[23]

Occupational Therapy Services

As with physical therapy services, HCFA has issued guidance on its definition of "occupational therapy services" only in the proposed Stark II regulations. Occupational therapy is defined with reference to how the term is used for Medicare purposes. The proposed regulation states that occupational therapy services are "those services described at section 1861(g) of the Act and section 410.100(c) of this chapter. Occupational therapy services also include any other services with the characteristics described in section 410.100(c) that are covered under Medicare Part A or B, regardless of who furnishes them, the location in which they are furnished, or how they are billed."[24]

Occupational therapy is medically prescribed treatment to improve or restore functions impaired by illness or injury or, where function has been permanently lost or reduced, to improve the individual's ability to perform those tasks required for independent functioning.[25] As with physical therapy, to be covered under the Medicare Part A program, occupational therapy must be prescribed by a physician, performed by a qualified occupational therapist or qualified occupational therapy assistant, and be reasonable and necessary for the treatment of the individual's illness or injury.[26] Under Medicare Part B, coverage for occupational therapy services is similar to that for physical therapy services.[27] Specifically, these services are covered when furnished by a provider to its outpatients, including when furnished in a therapist's office or the patient's home, if the service in the home is reasonable and necessary. The patient must be under the care of a doctor of medicine, osteopathy or podiatry and the care must be provided under a plan established by such a doctor or by the therapist. If the therapist establishes the plan of care, it must be periodically reviewed by a physician. Further, the services must be provided with the expectation that the patient will improve significantly in a reasonable, and generally predictable, period of time, or must be necessary for a safe and effective maintenance program required in connection with a specific disease state.[28]

Radiology Services and Radiation Therapy and Supplies

This designated health service was revised by Stark law technical amendments enacted in October 1994.[29] As originally enacted, the Stark law applied to "radiology or other diagnostic services." The provider community immediately expressed concern that this provision was too broad. Providers felt this definition could be interpreted to encompass physicians' professional services that are diagnostic in nature, such as endoscopies, as well as EEGs and EKGs, which providers believed were not intended to be included within the law's scope. Within months of Stark's enactment, legislative revisions were introduced that substituted "radiology services, including MRIs, CT scans and ultrasound" for the original language.[30] These revisions were enacted in October 1994.

Despite the clarification of this designated health service, there remains significant controversy as to its scope. In the proposed Stark II regulations, HCFA has defined radiology services and radiation therapy and supplies as "any diagnostic test or therapeutic procedure using X-rays, ultrasound or other imaging services, computerized axial tomography, magnetic resonance imaging, radiation, or nuclear medicine and diagnostic mammography services, as covered under section 1861 (s)(3) and (4) of the Act and sections 410.32(a), 410.34, and 410.35 of this chapter, including the professional component of these services, and including any invasive radiology procedure in which the imaging modality is used to guide a needle, probe or a catheter accurately."[31]

For purposes of Part B reimbursement, the Medicare law establishes that "diagnostic X-ray tests" including diagnostic mammography services are considered covered medical or other health services.[32] The statute also provides that "X-ray, radium and radioactive isotope therapy, including materials and services of technicians" are covered services under Part B.[33] These services are covered by HCFA under the conditions described in sections 410.32(a), 410.34 and 410.35 of the regulations, and in applicable manuals.

Screening mammography services are excluded from this definition of radiology services because HCFA believes there is little risk of overutilization.[34] Diagnostic mammography is still considered a "designated health service." Diagnostic mammography services are defined in section 410.34(a) of the regulations as mammography furnished to a symptomatic patient, while a screening mammography is provided to asymptomatic patients.

The proposed Stark II regulations exclude "any invasive radiology procedure in which the imaging modality is used to guide a needle, probe or catheter accurately." The preamble gives the following examples of such excluded services: percutaneous transluminal angioplasty; the placement of catheters for therapeutic embolization of tumors; arteriovenous malformations, or bleeding sites; the placement of drainage catheters for removal of stones; balloon dilation of strictures; biopsies; arthrograms; and myelograms.[35] Because HCFA actively solicited comments on any other types of services that are designated health services but are incidental to other procedures and perhaps should be excluded services,[36] this list may be expanded in the future.

Durable Medical Equipment and Supplies

The term "durable medical equipment" is defined in the proposed Stark II regulations as having "the meaning given in section 1861(n) of the Act and section 414.202 of this Chapter." Section 1861(n) DME as including "iron lungs, oxygen tents, hospital beds and wheelchairs...used in the patient's home... whether furnished on a rental basis or purchased....With respect to a seat-lift chair, such term includes only the seat-lift mechanism and does not include the chair."[37] The regulations further define DME to include equipment that can withstand repeated use; is primarily and customarily used to serve a medical purpose; generally is not useful to a person in the absence of illness or injury; and is appropriate for use in the home.[38]

HCFA has also clarified that it will consider DME that is provided under an appropriate home health plan of care to be DME for purposes of the Stark law.[39] The definition of DME has also been interpreted to include the supplies necessary for use of the DME.[40] The preamble cites test strips and lancets used with blood glucose monitoring equipment or drugs used with a nebulizer as necessary DME supplies that would be considered DME for purposes of the Stark law.[41]

The preamble to the proposed Stark II regulations sets forth the following general categories of DME: alternating pressure pads and mattresses and miscellaneous support surfaces; bed pans; blood glucose monitors; canes/crutches and walkers; commodes; continuous positive airway pressure; cushion lift power seats; decubitus care equipment; gel flotation pads and mattresses; heating pads; heat lamps; hospital beds and accessories; intermittent positive pressure breathing equipment; infusion pumps, supplies and drugs; lymphedema pumps; manual wheelchair bases; motorized wheelchair/power wheelchair bases; nebulizers; wheelchair options/accessories; oxygen and related respiratory equipment; pacemaker monitors; patient lifts; pneumatic compressors and appliances; power-operated vehicles; restraints; rollabout chairs; safety equipment; support surfaces; suction pumps; traction equipment; transcutaneous electric nerve simulators and supplies; trapeze equipment, fracture frames and other orthopaedic devices; and ultraviolet cabinets.[42] This is not an exhaustive list. The preamble to the proposed Stark II regulations recommends referring to section 60-9 of the Medicare Coverage Issues Manual for additional information.[43]

The proposed Stark II regulations state that an infusion pump may be covered as DME,[44] and thus subject to the Stark law. External infusion pumps may be covered if certain coverage requirements are met, including the requirement that the pump be used in the home. Sections 60-9 and 60-14 of the Medicare Coverage Issues Manual provide for the coverage of infusion pumps. If a DME regional carrier approves an infusion pump as appropriate, it will also be covered. The drugs that are necessary for the infusion would therefore also be considered designated health services.[45]

Infusion pumps that are used in a physician's office to administer therapy are considered services incident to a physician's service and therefore, not DME.[46] Implantable infusion pumps may also be covered DME if the patient meets the criteria set out in the Medicare Coverage Issues Manual.[47] The carrier's medical staff also may verify that an infusion pump and a drug are reasonable and necessary and therefore covered.[48] Additionally, the in-office ancillary services exception may apply if the implantable infusion pump is implanted in a physician's office.

Home dialysis services also have been identified as an area that some might argue should be encompassed under the DME category. However, the Medicare law defines home dialysis supplies and equipment, self-care home dialysis support services and institutional dialysis services and supplies as a discrete category of "medical and other health services."[49] The proposed Stark II regulations clarify that home dialysis is not covered as DME under Medicare.[50]

Other equipment furnished in a physician's office and billed to Medicare as part of the services and supplies incident to a physician's services are not considered DME.[51] Similarly, equipment used in diagnostic testing would not be considered DME even though it is paid for by Medicare. Rather, it is covered as a diagnostic service under section 1861(s)(3) and therefore would not be considered a designated health service.[52]

The proposed Stark II regulations specifically cite dynamic electrocardiograph, or Holter monitoring, as a diagnostic service that would not be considered either DME or a designated health service.[53]

Note that durable medical equipment, other than infusion pumps, is not eligible for the in-office ancillary services exception to the Stark law.[54] The proposed regulations expand the exception to this prohibition to include crutches and infusion pumps.[55]

Parenteral and Enteral Nutrients, Equipment and Supplies

The proposed Stark II regulations define enteral nutrients, equipment and supplies as:

> items and supplies needed to provide enteral nutrition to a patient with a functioning gastrointestinal tract who, due to pathology to or nonfunction of the structures that normally permit food to reach the digestive tract, cannot maintain weight and strength commensurate with his or her general condition, as described in section 65-10 of the Medicare Coverage Issues Manual (HCFA Pub. 6).[56]

The preamble to the proposed Stark II regulations notes that enteral nutritional therapy may be administered by nasogatric, jejunostomy or gastrostomy tubes.[57] Supplies appropriate for the method of administration are also covered.[58]

Similarly, the proposed Stark II regulations define parenteral nutrients, equipment and supplies as:

> those items and supplies needed to provide nutriment to a patient with permanent, severe pathology of the alimentary tract that does not allow absorption of sufficient nutrients to maintain strength commensurate with the patient's general condition, as described in section 65-10 of the Medicare Coverage Issues Manual (HCFA Pub. 6).[59]

As with enteral nutrition, the supplies and equipment needed to furnish the parenteral nutrition therapy would also be covered.[60]

Parenteral and enteral nutrients, equipment and supplies are not considered services that can qualify for the in-office ancillary services exception.[61]

Prosthetics, Orthotics, and Prosthetic Devices and Supplies

The proposed Stark II regulations define prosthetics, orthotics and prosthetic devices and supplies with reference to their coverage under the Medicare Act.

The proposed regulations define prosthetics as "artificial legs, arms, and eyes, as described in section 1861(s)(9) of the Act."[62] Section 2133 of the Medicare Carrier's Manual provides that a physician's order is required for these services to be covered.

The proposed Stark II regulations define orthotics as "leg, arm, back and neck braces, as listed in section 1861(s)(9) of the Act."[63] As with prosthetics, replacements are covered if they are required due to a change in the patient's physical condition.[64]

The proposed Stark II regulations define prosthetic device as "a device (other than a dental device) listed in section 1861(s)(8) that replaces all or part of an internal body organ, including colostomy bags and including one pair of conventional eyeglasses or contact lenses furnished subsequent to each cataract surgery with insertion of an intraocular lens."[65] Prosthetic supplies are defined in the proposed Stark II regulations as "supplies that are necessary for the effective use of a prosthetic device (including supplies directly related to colostomy care)."[66]

The preamble to the proposed Stark II regulations clarifies that HCFA considers an intraocular lens to be a prosthetic device. The preamble discounts the argument that implanted devices should be excluded from the definition of a designated health service because they are only a small part of the surgery needed to implant them and physicians would not prescribe the surgery just to sell the device.[67] HCFA acknowledges the physicians' argument that they would like to be able to prescribe their own choice of device because they have particularized the design or believe the device works better. However, HCFA maintains that such devices are still considered a prosthetic device and therefore subject to the Stark law.[68]

HCFA is soliciting comments on this issue, however, and may change its position when the final Stark II regulations are promulgated.[69]

Note that intraocular lenses that are implanted in an ambulatory surgery center are covered under the ASC payment rate. Proposed section 411.355(d) specifically excludes from the referral prohibition services covered under the ASC payment rate.

The preamble to the proposed Stark II regulations also discusses whether an ophthalmologist who has an optical shop as part of his or her office may refer Medicare patients to the shop. HCFA concludes that the referral would only be permitted if an exception under the Stark law were applicable, such as the in-office ancillary services exception or the rural provider exception.[70]

Some Medicaid programs may reimburse for such eyeglasses or contact lenses as DME, not as prosthetic devices. In such cases, the in-office ancillary services exception may not be available because it expressly does not apply to DME.[71] However, the Stark law does not prohibit the provider's Medicaid self-referral; instead, it authorizes the withholding of federal monies from states that reimburse Medicaid claims submitted pursuant to what Medicare would prohibit as a self-referral.[72] Thus, unless the state has banned self-referrals, the provider's Medicaid referral may remain protected.

Home Health Services

The proposed Stark II regulations define home health services as "the services described in section 1861(m) of the Act and part 409, subpart E of this chapter."[73] To qualify for home health benefits, a beneficiary must be confined to his or her home under the care of a physician. The beneficiary also must be in need of skilled nursing services on an intermittent basis, or need physical or speech therapy.[74] A plan of care must be established and periodically reviewed by a physician. Further, the services must be furnished by a home health agency or by others under an arrangement with a home health agency on a visiting basis. These services do not include home dialysis or home infusion, but rather are focused on nursing care; social services; and physical, occupational or speech therapy.[75]

The preamble to the proposed Stark II regulations states that home health services provided by a home health agency that is owned by another entity are still considered to be provided only by that agency (assuming it meets the conditions of participation and has its own provider agreement with Medicare), not by the entity — such as a hospital —

that indirectly owns the agency.[76] The preamble further states that even if a hospital owns an agency, the Stark exception for services provided by a hospital would not apply.[77]

Current law prohibits a physician who has a "significant ownership interest in, or a significant financial or contractual relationship with, a home health agency" from certifying the need for home health services for a Medicare recipient.[78] In the preamble to the proposed Stark II regulations, HCFA proposes adopting the Stark law definition of and exceptions to "financial relationship " for the above situation.[79] The exceptions for the "significant ownership interest" that are currently in effect will be repealed, and only the exceptions found under the Stark law will be available if there is a financial relationship.[80] Again, HCFA has solicited comments on this interpretation.

Outpatient Prescription Drugs

The proposed Stark II regulations define "outpatient prescription drugs" as "those drugs (including biologicals) that are defined or listed under section 1861(t) and (s) of the Act and part 410 of this chapter that a patient can obtain from a pharmacy with a prescription (even if the patient can only receive the drug under medical supervision) and that are furnished to an individual under Medicare Part B, but excluding erythropoietin and other drugs furnished as part of a dialysis treatment for an individual who dialyzes at home or in a facility."[81]

The preamble to the proposed Stark II regulations points to the explanation of the drug and biological benefit set in section 2049 of the Medicare Carriers Manual for greater detail.[82] The drugs and biologicals specifically covered under Medicare Part B include those furnished in a physician's office incident to the physician's professional services; those furnished as part of outpatient hospital services under the Medicare law; and certain immunizations and antigens covered under the law. Certain drugs that can be self-administered such as certain blood-clotting factors, drugs used in immunosuppressive therapy and certain oral cancer drugs are also covered.[83]

By contrast, federal law expressly authorizes state Medicaid programs to cover "prescribed drugs."[84] This term is defined in regulations as drugs prescribed by physicians and dispensed by licensed pharmacists and authorized practitioners on written prescriptions.[85] Consequently, self-referrals of Medicaid patients for outpatient prescription drugs implicate Stark II in those states that have elected to provide coverage for such drugs. Further, the referral or prescription for such drugs would only be prohibited if the state in which the prescription is written has a relevant physician self-referral prohibition in place. Again, this is because the Medicare self-referral prohibition has not been extended directly to Medicaid providers. Rather, the Stark law only provides that the federal government will not pay a state its federal share of a Medicaid expenditure for a service provided pursuant to a referral that would be prohibited under the Medicare self-referral law.[86] Thus, unless the state has enacted a law that prohibits the provider from making the Medicaid referral, the provider is not subject to any of the Stark law sanctions for doing so. As a general matter, to the extent that outpatient prescription drugs are designated health services under Stark II, HCFA informally has indicated it will consider the writing of a prescription to be a referral for purposes of the Stark law. Accordingly, regardless of whether a physician directs a patient to a pharmacy with which the physician may have a financial relationship, if a referring physician's patient fills a prescription at such a pharmacy, the Stark law would be violated unless the presumption is rebutted. For in-office pharmacies, physicians should be able to avail themselves of the in-office ancillary services exception discussed in Chapter 4.

Inpatient and Outpatient Hospital Services

The proposed Stark II regulations define both inpatient and outpatient hospital services. Inpatient hospital services are "those services defined in section 1861(b) of the Act and Sections 409.10(a) and (b) of this chapter, and include inpatient hospital psychiatric hospital services listed in section 1861(c) of the Act and inpatient rural primary care hospital services as defined in section 1861(mm)(2) of the Act. Inpatient hospital services do not include emergency inpatient services provided by a hospital located outside the United States and covered under the authority in section 1814(f)(2) of the Act and part 424, subpart H of this chapter and emergency inpatient services provided by a nonparticipating hospital within the United States, as authorized by section 1814(d) of the Act and described in part 424, subpart G of this chapter."

These services also do not include dialysis furnished by a hospital that is not certified to provide end-stage renal dialysis services under subpart U of 42 CFR 405.

Inpatient hospital services include services a hospital provides for its patients that are furnished either by the hospital or by others under arrangements with the hospital. They do not encompass the services of other physicians, physician assistants, nurse practitioners, clinical nurse specialists, certified nurse midwives, certified registered nurse anesthetists and qualified psychologists who bill independently.[87]

This definition encompasses the ordinary Part A inpatient services: bed and board, nursing services and other related services, use of hospital facilities, medical social services, drugs, biologicals, supplies, appliances and equipment, diagnostic or therapeutic services (with certain exceptions), and medical or surgical services provided by interns or residents. The regulations clarify that these services are those a hospital provides either directly or by others under arrangements with the hospital, where the hospital bills for the services.

The proposed regulations also clearly state that the services of professionals who bill independently are not considered inpatient hospital services. Skilled nursing facility-type care furnished by a hospital or a rural primary care hospital that has swing-bed approval, or any nursing facility-type care that may be furnished as a Medicaid service also would not be considered inpatient hospital services.[88]

There is an exception for "emergency services" provided at certain hospitals outside of the United States and at nonparticipating hospitals. "Emergency services" are "those services necessary to prevent death or serious impairment of health and, because of the danger to life or health, require use of the most accessible hospital available and equipped to furnish the services."[89] The preamble to the proposed Stark II regulations states that this exception is based on the fact that physicians do not have the opportunity or incentive to overutilize such emergency services.[90] Similarly, HCFA has created an exception for certain emergency dialysis treatment that the agency believes poses little risk of overutilization. Such dialysis would be provided in a hospital that is not certified to provide ESRD services and therefore would provide dialysis in certain emergency situations.[91]

The emergency exception has not been extended to lithotripsy services. The preamble specifically discusses extracorporeal shock wave lithotripsy as a service that may arguably have little risk of overutilization. HCFA concludes, however, that if physicians insist on using certain equipment based on financial incentives, there may be a risk of patient abuse. HCFA specifically requests comments on this issue, however.[92]

HCFA has also amended the definition of "hospital" from that appearing in the final Stark I regulations. This amendment clarifies that inpatient hospital services include inpatient psychiatric hospital services and inpatient rural primary care services. The preamble notes that this does not include emergency inpatient services provided outside the United States or provided by a nonparticipating hospital in the United States.[93] Dialysis provided by a hospital that is not certified to provide ESRD services is also not considered to be an inpatient hospital service.[94]

The proposed Stark II regulations also provide for the first time a definition of "outpatient hospital services." These services are defined as "the therapeutic, diagnostic, and partial hospitalization services listed under section 1861(s)(2)(B) and (C) of the Act; outpatient services furnished by a psychiatric hospital as defined in section 1861(f); and outpatient rural primary care hospital services as defined in section 1861(mm)(3); but excluding emergency services covered in nonparticipating hospitals under conditions described in section 1835(b) of the Act and subpart G of part 424 of this chapter."[95]

The preamble to the proposed Stark II regulations clarifies that HCFA considers all covered services billed by a hospital to Medicare that are performed on hospital outpatients including arranged for services to be outpatient hospital services.[96] As with inpatient services, emergency services that meet certain criteria are excluded, but lithotripter services are not currently excluded.[97] HCFA is soliciting comments on the lithotripsy issue, however, so this position may change in the next draft of the regulations.[98]

Recent Legislative Proposals

The Republican-sponsored Balanced Budget Act of 1995 would have significantly curtailed the number of health services subject to the Stark law. The bill would have eliminated from the ban on self-referrals radiation therapy services and supplies; DME and supplies; prosthetics, orthotics, and prosthetic devices; home health services; outpatient prescription drugs; and inpatient and outpatient hospital services. The bill would have left in place only five designated health services: clinical laboratory services; parenteral and enteral nutrients, equipment and supplies; radiology services, including MRI, CT and ultrasound services; and outpatient physical and occupational therapy services.[99] The GOP-led 105th Congress may continue to advance this narrowing of the Stark law. The Clinton administration has not yet advanced as extensive a narrowing of the scope of the designated health services. Legislative proposals in the administration's fiscal year 1997 budget would have eliminated inpatient and outpatient hospital services from the self-referral ban.[100] This proposal also would exclude from the prosthetic device category, intraocular lenses inserted during or after cataract surgery, eyeglasses and contact lenses.[101]

Endnotes

[1] 42 U.S.C. Sec. 1395nn(h)(6).

[2] 63 *Fed. Reg.* 1673.

[3] Id.

[4] Id.

[5] Id.

[6] Id.

[7] Id.

[8] 63 *Fed. Reg.* 1674.

[9] 57 *Fed. Reg.* 8588 (to be codified at 42 CFR pt. 411).

[10] 60 *Fed. Reg.* 41914.

[11] 42 CFR Sec. 493.2.

[12] 42 CFR Sec. 411.351.

[13] 63 *Fed. Reg.* 1720.

[14] 42 CFR Sec. 411.351.

[15] 63 *Fed. Reg.* 1722.

[16] 57 *Fed. Reg.* 8588, 8595 (to be codified at 42 CFR pt. 411).

[17] 60 *Fed. Reg.* 41914, 41928.

[18] 63 *Fed. Reg.* 1722.

[19] 42 U.S.C. Sec. 1395x(p)

[20] 42 CFR Sec. 400.100(b)

[21] 42 U.S.C. Sec. 1395x(II)(1).

[22] 63 *Fed. Reg.* 1674.

[23] 63 *Fed. Reg.* 1675.

[24] 63 *Fed. Reg.* 1722 (proposed 42 CFR Sec. 411.351).

[25] Medicare Intermediary Manual, supra, Sec. 3101.9; Medicare Carriers Manual, supra, Sec. 2217(A).

[26] Medicare Intermediary Manual, supra, Sec. 3101.9.

[27] 42 U.S.C. Sec. 1395x(g).

[28] Medicare Carriers Manual, supra, Sec. 2210(B)(c).

[29] H.R. 5252, 103rd Cong., 2d Sess., Sec. 152(b) (1994).

[30] S. 1668, 103rd. Cong., 1st Sess., Sec. 152(b)(1) (1993).

[31] 63 *Fed. Reg.* 1722 (proposed 42 CFR Sec. 411.351).

[32] 42 U.S.C. Sec. 1395x(s)(3).

[33] 42 U.S.C. Sec. 1395x(s)(4).

[34] 63 *Fed. Reg.* 1676.

[35] Id.

[36] Id.

[37] 42 U.S.C. Sec. 1395x(n).

[38] 42 CFR Sec. 414.202.

[39] 63 *Fed. Reg.* 1677

[40] Id.

[41] Id.

[42] Id.

[43] Id.

[44] Id.

[45] Id.

[46] Id.

[47] Id.

[48] Id.

[49] 42 U.S.C. Sec. 1395x(s).

[50] 63 *Fed. Reg.* 1677.

[51] Id.

[52] Id.

[53] Id.

[54] 42 U.S.C. Sec. 1395nn(b)(2).

[55] 63 *Fed. Reg.* 1723 (proposed 42 CFR Sec. 411.355(b)).

[56] 63 *Fed. Reg.* 1720-21 (proposed 42 CFR Sec. 411.351).

[57] 63 *Fed. Reg.* 1678

[58] Id.

[59] 63 *Fed. Reg.* 1722 (proposed 42 CFR Sec. 411.351).

[60] 63 *Fed. Reg.* 1678.

[61] 42 U.S.C. Sec. 1395nn(b)(2).

[62] 63 *Fed. Reg.* 1722 (proposed 42 CFR Sec. 411.351).

[63] Id.

[64] 42 CFR Sec. 410.36(a)(3).

[65] 63 *Fed. Reg.* 1722 (proposed 42 CFR Sec. 411.351).

[66] Id.

[67] 63 *Fed. Reg.* 1678.

[68] Id.

[69] Id.

[70] 63 *Fed. Reg.* 1679.

[71] 42 U.S.C. Sec. 1395nn(b)(2).

[72] 42 U.S.C. Sec. 1396b(s).

[73] 63 *Fed. Reg.* 1721 (proposed 42 CFR Sec. 411.351).

[74] 42 U.S.C. Sec. 1395f(a)(2)(C).

[75] 42 U.S.C. Sec. 1395x(m).

[76] 63 *Fed. Reg.* 1679.

[77] Id.

[78] 42 U.S.C. Sec. 1395f(a), 1395n(a).

[79] 63 *Fed. Reg.* 1680.

[80] Id.

[81] 63 *Fed. Reg.* 1722 (proposed 42 CFR Sec. 411.351).

[82] 63 *Fed. Reg.* 1680

[83] Id.

[84] 42 U.S.C. Sec. 1396d(a)(12).

[85] 42 CFR Sec. 440.120.

[86] 42 U.S.C. Sec. 1396b(s).

[87] 63 *Fed. Reg.* 1722 (proposed 42 CFR Sec. 411.351).

[88] 63 *Fed. Reg.* 1681.

[89] 63 *Fed. Reg.* 1682.

[90] Id.

[91] Id.

[92] Id.

[93] Id.

[94] Id.

[95] 63 *Fed. Reg.* 1722 (proposed 42 CFR Sec. 411.351).

[96] 63 *Fed. Reg.* 1683.

[97] Id.

[98] Id.

[99] H.R. 2491, 104th Cong., 1st Sess. Sec., 8202 (1995).

[100] President's F.Y. 1997 Budget, Sec. 11212(c).

[101] President's F.Y. 1997 Budget, Sec. 11212(g).

CHAPTER 4

General Exceptions to Both Ownership and Compensation Arrangement Prohibitions

The Stark law establishes three exceptions that apply generally to both ownership and compensation arrangement prohibitions[1]: "physicians' services," "in-office ancillary services" and "prepaid plans." In the final Stark I regulations, HCFA added an additional exception that applies to services furnished in an ambulatory surgery center, end-stage renal disease facility or hospice. In the proposed Stark II regulations, HCFA indicated its intention to apply this exception to the expanded list of designated health services. The exceptions are discussed in detail below.

Physicians' Services Exception

The first "service-oriented" exception allowed by the Stark law is for "physicians' services."[2] "[P]hysicians' services provided personally by (or under the personal supervision of) [a] physician in the same group practice [other than] the referring physician"[3] are excepted from the application of the Stark law.[4] In other words, the exception applies only when the services are provided, not by the referring physician, but by another physician who is a member of the same group practice or by a nonmember physician who is "under the personal supervision of" a member of the same group practice. "Personal supervision" is defined in the proposed Stark II regulations to mean that the group practice physician is legally responsible for monitoring the results of the designated health service and available to assist the physician performing the service. But there is no requirement that the group practice physician be physically present.[5]

The law's language presents more questions than answers. In fact, even the legislators who authored this exception have had difficulty articulating its purpose and agreeing on its exact meaning. For example, it is not clear why this exception does not also include physicians' referrals to themselves when they practice in another setting, such as an ambulatory surgery center.

In HCFA's Stark I proposed regulations, the agency merely restated the language in the law. In the final Stark I regulations, HCFA clarified that such services do not need to be furnished in the group practice's offices for the exception to apply, as long as the services are furnished by or under the personal supervision of another doctor in the same group practice as the referring physician.[6] As such, the physicians' services could be provided in a laboratory or in an imaging or radiation therapy center owned by another entity with which the group has a financial arrangement. The proposed Stark II regulations clarify that the exception applies only to services personally furnished by a physician — and not to "incident to" services.

Lawmakers have questioned the necessity of retaining this exception in light of the separate exception pertaining to in-office ancillary services provided in a group setting. In fact, unsuccessful health reform legislation reported out of the House Ways and Means Committee in 1994 proposed to eliminate the physicians' services exception.[7] More recently, President Clinton's proposed legislative amendments contained in the administration's fiscal year 1997 budget request would have eliminated the physicians' services exception.[8]

However, this distinct exception is needed in light of HCFA's decision to define "laboratory services" as including physician services, and HCFA's definition of "radiology services and radiation therapy" in the proposed Stark II regulations as including physicians' services.[9] The physicians' services exception is necessary to protect referrals from a member of a group practice to another member who renders physician services in a laboratory or in an imaging or radiation therapy center where the various requirements of the in-office ancillary services exception relating to supervision, location and billing have not been satisfied.

In-Office Ancillary Services Exception

Current Statutory Exception. The second "service-oriented" exception set forth in the Stark law is for "in-office ancillary services." This exception is perhaps the most critical of the three because it is through this exception that all physician practices, including both solo practitioners and group practices, can continue to provide a variety of ancillary services to their patients.[10]

Specifically, the in-office ancillary services exception creates an exclusion:

"In the case of services (other than durable medical equipment (excluding infusion pumps) and parenteral and enteral nutrients, equipment, and supplies) —

(A) that are furnished —

(i) personally by the referring physician, personally by a physician who is a member of the same group practice as the referring physician, or personally by individuals who are directly supervised by the physician or by another physician in the group practice, and

(ii)(I) in a building in which the referring physician (or another physician who is a member of the same group practice) furnishes physicians' services unrelated to the furnishing of designated health services, or

(II) in the case of a referring physician who is a member of a group practice, in another building which is used by the group practice (aa) for the provision of some or all of the group's clinical laboratory services, or

(bb) for the centralized provision of the group's designated health services (other than clinical laboratory services),

unless the [HHS] secretary determines other terms and conditions under which the provision of such services does not present a risk of program or patient abuse, and

(B) that are billed by the physician performing or supervising the services, by a group practice of which such physician is a member under a billing number assigned to the group practice, or by an entity that is wholly owned by such physician or such group practice,

if the ownership or investment interest in such services meets such other requirements as the secretary may impose by regulation as needed to protect against program or patient abuse."[11]

Scope of Designated Health Services Covered. The in-office ancillary services exception is available for most, but not all, designated health services. Parenteral and enteral nutrients, equipment and supplies are excluded from the exception. Additionally, all durable medical equipment is excluded from the exception except for infusion pumps and, in the proposed Stark II regulations, crutches supplied to the patient where the physician realizes no direct or indirect profit.[12]

The proposed Stark II regulations further clarify that the exception does not apply to "any item that is given to a patient but is meant to be used at home or outside the physician's office, or any item that is delivered to the patient's home."[13] Thus, for example, the proposed Stark II regulations would exclude from the exception external infusion pumps used at home, but would include implantable pumps that are implanted in the physician's office. The rule would presumably also render self-administered drugs ineligible for the exception.

Who May Furnish the Service. The first condition, requiring that the service be furnished either personally by the referring physician, by another group-practice physician, or by individuals who are directly supervised by that physician or another group-practice physician, reflects a change included in Stark II.[14] Stark I required that nonphysician individuals furnishing the services be "employed" by the referring physician or group practice. Stark II substituted "supervised" for "employed," reflecting an understanding that, in some cases, physicians contract for certain ancillary services and may not actually employ those who perform the services.

In the preamble to the final Stark I regulations, HCFA further clarified that it no longer regards the provision of clinical laboratory services in a physician's office as subject to the Medicare "incident-to" rules, which require physicians to employ ancillary services personnel in order to bill for services provided by them.[15] HCFA interprets "direct supervision" as meaning that the physician is present in the office suite and immediately available to provide assistance and direction throughout the time the clinical lab services are being performed.[16]

The preamble to the proposed Stark II regulations further clarifies the definition of "direct supervision."[17] First, HCFA explains that "present in the office suite" means that the physician is present in the office suite in which the services are being furnished at the time they are being furnished. HCFA declined to specify what constitutes a single office "suite," noting that contiguous rooms should generally satisfy the definition but that the decision as to other layouts would be left for the local carrier to determine on a case-by-case basis. HCFA proposes to permit both "brief unexpected absences" as well as "routine absences of a short duration" such as for lunch breaks. This exception would not allow in-office ancillary services to be furnished before or after the physician's regularly scheduled office hours, or while the physician is performing nonemergency medical services elsewhere, such as while rounding at the hospital.

Importantly, HCFA clarifies that the "direct supervision" requirement for the in-office ancillary services exception is intended solely to establish that the physician is actively running the practice and is therefore independent from, and does not supersede, the Medicare coverage requirements for a particular service, which may impose a greater level of supervision. For example, despite the liberalization of the "direct supervision" requirement in the proposed Stark II regulations, the physician could not be absent during an "incident to" service, as the Medicare coverage requirements would not be satisfied.

The Billing Requirement. Another condition added by Stark II concerns the billing number that must be used for ancillary services. Stark I provided that ancillary services must be billed either by the physician performing or supervising the service, by a group practice of which the physician is a member, or by an entity wholly owned by the physician or group practice.[18] Because, in many cases, group practices have more than one billing number, such as group practices with locations in multiple states, the law was revised to require that the billing be processed "under a billing number assigned to the group practice."[19] The preamble to the proposed Stark II regulations further clarifies that the group may use any number assigned to the group in cases when it has been issued multiple numbers, and that the group may use a billing agent to bill for the group under the group's name and provider number.[20] Additionally, the proposed Stark II regulations clarify that an entity wholly-owned by the physician or group practice may bill under its own provider number — if otherwise permissible — and need not bill using the group's number.[21]

Finally, the preamble to the proposed Stark II regulations indicates that when a group practice physician bills a service under an individual number, that physician is considered a solo practitioner for purposes of the in-office ancillary services exception. Thus, other group members cannot directly supervise that service. The quantity of these individually-billed services also could affect the group's ability to satisfy the definition of a "group practice," which, as explained in further detail in Chapter 7, requires that substantially all of the services of physician group members be provided through and billed under a number assigned to the group.

In the preamble to the final Stark I regulations, HCFA clarified that self-referrals to physician office laboratories may qualify for the in-office ancillary services exception even if the laboratories accept referrals from outside physicians who do not have financial relationships with the laboratory. However, when billing Medicare for such services, the claims must be submitted under a separate billing number obtained from Medicare for a laboratory independent of the physician group practice.[22] In addition, if a member of the group is either performing or supervising the lab services, the quantity of outside tests could similarly affect the group's ability to meet the "substantially all" test.

The Location Requirement. Stark II also amended the requirements concerning the site of delivery of the ancillary services provided by a group practice. The House-Senate conference report stated Congress' intent that, for all designated health services other than clinical lab services, the ancillary services exception applies only if the services are provided in a central location.[23] However, the law itself still would permit non-clinical laboratory ancillary services to be furnished in satellite locations, as long as either (a) physicians' services unrelated to the furnishing of the designated health service are performed in that building, or (b) the building is used for the "centralized" provision of designated health services.[24]

The preamble to the proposed Stark II regulations would further liberalize the location requirement by broadly construing the term "centralized."[25] First, any location that services two or more group offices and that furnishes one or any combination of designated health services would meet this requirement. Second, a group may have multiple "centralized" locations. For multi-office group practices, the only real requirement is that the location service more than one office. For single-office group practices, however, an off-site location arguably qualifies only if a physician furnishes nondesignated health services there.

In the preamble to the final Stark I regulations, HCFA underscored that group practices don't have to centralize the provision of their laboratory services and may operate multiple satellite laboratory sites at locations where group practice physicians provide services. However, the satellite facility option is not available to solo practitioners. HCFA explained that if solo practitioners refer laboratory testing to another building, such testing ceases to be in-office testing. The same result would apply to all designated health services under the proposed Stark II regulations. However, HCFA clarified that a physician's examination and diagnosis of a patient qualifies as a physician service unrelated to designated health services, even if it results in a referral for a designated health service.[26]

The site-of-service restriction can be traced to a concern with physicians who are establishing so-called "clinics without walls." Specifically, Congress did not want physicians who maintain either financially and/or administratively separate profit centers that operate as "group practices" to obtain a central billing number, and thereby qualify for the in-office ancillary services exception.

Some lawmakers, including Rep. Stark, have asserted that if ancillary services are required to be centralized within a group, physicians would have less of an incentive to form "clinics without walls." Yet, prudent business practice would suggest that physicians forming "clinics without walls" would want to centralize the provision of ancillary services to realize the cost-efficiencies of pooled resources. Indeed, the centralization requirement, if narrowly construed, probably would most adversely affect larger, truly integrated group practices with geographically disparate locations that each provide a range of ancillary services on site. HCFA has addressed this issue in the proposed Stark II regulations, at least in part, by liberally interpreting the centralization requirement and dealing with the "clinic without walls" issue directly in the group practice definition by limiting the use of separate profit and cost centers, as discussed in Chapter 7.

Proposed Legislative Changes to In-Office Ancillary Services Exception. Debate is ongoing over whether any circumstances exist where it would be appropriate for physicians who practice separately to jointly own and/or lease equipment that is used in the delivery of ancillary services. In the final Stark I regulations, HCFA expressly declined to establish an exception for physicians who practice separately but share the overhead of operating a laboratory, even if the physicians practice in the same building. But HCFA noted that, in some instances, the in-office ancillary services exception could apply to such shared laboratories if each physician separately meets the supervision, location and billing requirements. Accordingly, the pooling of resources in a shared laboratory may be acceptable, if each physician whose patient testing is performed in the shared laboratory remains on-site when the testing is performed, directly supervises the personnel and bills for the services under his/her practice number. Each such shared lab may be issued only one CLIA certificate number, and only one of the physicians would have overall responsibility for operating the lab.[27] HCFA reaffirmed this position in the preamble to the proposed Stark II regulations.[28]

Prepaid Plan Exception

A final general exception to both the ownership and compensation prohibitions is provided in the law for "prepaid plans."[29] The law provides an exception for designated health services furnished by an organization:

■ That has a contract under section 1876 to an individual enrolled with the organization;

■ That is described in section 1833(a)(1)(A) to an individual enrolled with the organization;

■ That receives payments on a prepaid basis, under a demonstration project under section 402(a) of the Social Security Amendments of 1967 or under section 222(a) of the Social Security Amendments of 1972, to an individual enrolled with the organization; or

■ That is a qualified health maintenance organization (within the meaning of section 1310(d) of the Public Health Service Act) to an individual enrolled with the organization.

Essentially, this exception covers only federally qualified HMOs, HMOs with Medicare risk or cost contracts, or HMOs with demonstration-project status. Stark II added federally qualified HMOs as exempt entities. But the final Stark I regulations did not further expand the universe of managed care entities that may qualify for the exception. Medicare Select PPOs and Medicaid managed care plans were not addressed, nor was there any exemption for other managed care plans, even though such entities are designed to control, rather than contribute to, overutilization of health services.

In the proposed Stark II regulations, HCFA announced its intention to expand the scope of the exception to include all analogous Medicaid prepaid health plans and Medicare prepaid demonstration contracts.[30] HCFA also interpreted the exception to apply not only to prepaid health plans, but to physicians, suppliers and providers that contract with such plans, directly or under subcontracts.[31] Thus, the exception would protect all referrals along a vertical "chain" between the plan, contractors and subcontractors.

Importantly, the exception only protects services rendered to individuals "enrolled with the organization." However, some HMOs with Medicare risk or cost contracts arrange for designated health services for Medicare beneficiaries who may not be enrolled under the HMO's risk or cost contract, but who are otherwise enrolled in the HMO. It is unclear whether the existence of the Medicare risk or cost contract exempts all services provided by the prepaid plan, regardless of whether the services are provided to Medicare members enrolled under the Medicare risk or cost contract.

As long as Medicare is paying for the designated health services on a prepaid basis, the referrals for such services should remain exempt. However, it is possible that Medicare will reimburse the HMO on a fee-for-service basis for those Medicare beneficiaries for whom the HMO is a Medicare supplemental insurer. Nonetheless, from a policy perspective, even in these instances, the HMO would share the Medicare program's interest in ensuring that services are not overutilized.

In the preamble to the final Stark I regulations, HCFA rejected adding an additional exception for services furnished by an otherwise eligible managed care organization to nonenrollees. Often this occurs when a patient "walks in" to a health care facility run by the managed care plan or when a relative accompanies a plan enrollee. Or, this may occur when a person of retirement age continues working and remains enrolled in his or her current plan, under arrangements where the person is treated as a commercial enrollee rather than a Medicare beneficiary. In such cases, Medicare serves as a secondary payer to the group health plan. HCFA noted that, because secondary payment is reimbursed by Medicare on a fee-for-service basis, an incentive remains to overutilize services.[32]

Similarly, in the preamble to the proposed Stark II regulations, HCFA concluded that when a physician refers fee-for-service Medicare patients to a health plan for designated health services, the prepaid plan exception would not apply and the financial relationship between the physician and the plan would need to meet another exception.[33]

This analysis underscores the fact that the prepaid plan exception applies only to services rendered to enrollees, and does not confer immunity upon the financial relationships between and among a prepaid health plan and its various contractors and subcontractors. A hospital that operates a risk pool for Medicare HMO enrollees in which physicians participate has created a financial arrangement between the hospital and the physicians. The physicians are therefore prohibited from referring fee-for-service Medicare designated health services to the hospital unless another exception applies. Because the proposed Stark II regulations would limit use of the physician incentive plan exception to HMOs and similar entities, significant self-referral issues may be created by such arrangements.

Services Furnished in an Ambulatory Surgical Center, End-Stage Renal Disease Facility or Hospice

The self-referral law allows HHS to create additional general exceptions that do not pose a risk of program or patient abuse. In the Stark I regulations and the proposed Stark II regulations, HCFA exercised this authority to add a new exception for services furnished in ambulatory surgical centers, end-stage renal disease facilities or hospices, as long as the services are reimbursed by Medicare through the ambulatory surgical center rate, the ESRD composite rate or as part of the per-diem hospice charge, respectively.[34] HCFA reasoned that, in such instances, there is no incentive to overutilize the designated health services.

This exception may be rather limited in scope for referrals to ambulatory surgical centers for clinical laboratory services. Generally, clinical lab services are not considered to be services of ASCs. ASC facility services do not include items and services, such as lab and physician services, that are paid for under other provisions of the Medicare regulations.[35]

As a result, only a limited number of diagnostic laboratory tests are considered ASC facility services and are included in the ASC rate. However, many such centers do not bill separately for clinical laboratory services. Thus, the technical problems presented by the exception may not, as a practical matter, pose significant obstacles for providers.

The expansion of the exception to all designated health services renders largely moot the question of whether outpatient endoscopy constitutes a designated health service, as it will typically be performed in an ASC and is reimbursed by Medicare through the ASC payment rate.

Other Permissible Exceptions

As previously noted, the Stark law allows HCFA to create additional general exceptions that do not "pose a risk of program or patient abuse."[36] The proposed Stark II regulations would add a new exception for services "furnished under other payment rates that the [HHS] Secretary determines provide no financial incentive for under or overutilization, or any other risk of program or patient abuse."[37] In the proposed Stark II regulations, HCFA expressly requests comments as to whether there are analogous payment rates under the Medicaid program.[38]

Endnotes

[1] 42 U.S.C. Sec. 1395nn(b)(1).

[2] 42 U.S.C. Sec. 1395nn(b).

[3] 42 U.S.C. Sec. 1395x(q) (defining "physician services" as professional services performed by physicians, including surgery, consultation, and home, office and institutional calls).

[4] In the original proposed legislation, the physicians' services exception included those services provided directly by the referring physician or by another physician in the same group practice. H.R. 5198, 100th Cong. 2d Sess., Sec. 2(b)(1)(1988).

[5] 63 *Fed. Reg.* 1659, 1695.

[6] 60 *Fed. Reg.* 41919, 41947.

[7] H.R. 3600, 103rd Cong., 2d Sess., Sec. 9303(a) (1994).

[8] President's F.Y. 1997 Budget, Sec. 11212.

[9] 63 *Fed. Reg.* 1659, 1722 (to be codified at 42 CFR Sec. 411.351).

[10] In the proposed Stark II regulations, HCFA clearly indicates that a designated health service furnished personally by a solo practitioner constitutes a referral to an entity that must satisfy an exception. 63 *Fed. Reg.* 1659, 1685-6.

[11] 42 U.S.C. Sec. 1395nn(b)(2).

[12] 63 *Fed. Reg.* 1659, 1711, 1723 (to be codified at 42 CFR Sec. 411.355(b)).

[13] 63 *Fed. Reg.* 1659, 1677.

[14] 42 U.S.C. Sec. 1395nn(b).

[15] 60 *Fed. Reg.* 41914, 41949, 41950.

[16] 42 CFR Sec. 411.351.

[17] 63 *Fed. Reg.* 1659, 1684-1685.

[18] H.R. 3299, 101st Cong. 1st Sess., Sec. 6204(b)(2)(B)(1989).

[19] 42 U.S.C. Sec. 1395nn(b)(2)(B).

[20] 63 *Fed. Reg.* 1659, 1696.

[21] Id.

[22] 60 *Fed. Reg.* 41914, 41948.

[23] H.R. Conf. Rep. No. 213, 103rd Cong., 1st Sess., 809-810 (1993).

[24] 42 U.S.C. Sec. 1395nn(b)(2)(A)(ii)(I). In the proposed Stark II regulations, HCFA indicates that a "building" must be a single physical structure with a single address, and not multiple structures connected by tunnels or walkways; furthermore, mobile equipment parked at the building would not qualify as part of the "building" for these purposes. 63 *Fed. Reg.* 1659, 1695, 1723 (to be codified at 42 CFR Sec. 411.355(b)(2)(i)).

[25] 63 *Fed. Reg.* 1659, 1696.

[26] 63 *Fed. Reg.* 1659, 1695.

[27] 60 *Fed. Reg.* 41914, 41961, 41963.

[28] 63 *Fed. Reg.* 1659, 1716.

[29] 42 U.S.C. Sec. 1395nn(b)(3).

[30] 63 *Fed. Reg.* 1659, 1698. The final regulations will need to address Medicare+Choice plans; to the extent they receive a fixed, capitated payment, one would anticipate HCFA will expand the scope of the exception to include them.

[31] 63 *Fed. Reg.* 1659, 1696-7.

[32] 60 *Fed. Reg.* 41914, 41951.

[33] 63 *Fed. Reg.* 1659, 1711-1712.

[34] 42 CFR Sec. 411.355(d).

[35] 42 CFR Sec. 416.61(b).

[36] 42 U.S.C. Sec. 1395nn(b)(4).

[37] 63 *Fed. Reg.* 1646, 1724 (to be codified at 42 CFR Sec. 411.355(d)(2)).

[38] 63 *Fed. Reg.* 1646, 1666.

CHAPTER 5

Permitted Ownership and Investment Interests

As a general rule, if a physician or an immediate family member has a direct ownership or investment interest in an entity, the Stark II law prohibits that physician from making a referral to the entity for a designated health service that may be billed to the Medicare program, and the entity is prohibited from billing the individual, the Medicare program, or any other third-party payer for that designated health service.[1]

Ownership and Investment Interests Defined

The term "ownership or investment interest" is defined briefly and in expansive terms to mean "equity, debt, or other means" of ownership or investment.[2] Equity forms of ownership and investment interests would include the direct ownership of equity interests in separate entities such as common or preferred stock in a business corporation, interests in a general or limited partnership, memberships in a limited liability company, and beneficial interests in a trust. HCFA has stated that a physician's membership in a nonprofit corporation does not constitute an ownership or investment interest in the entity because members of these organizations do not have the same pecuniary incentives as do for-profit investors to maximize their investment interests. This conclusion is based on the fact that the net earnings of nonprofit corporations that are exempt from federal income taxation under sections 50l(c)(3) or (4) of the Internal Revenue Code may not inure to the benefit of any private shareholder or individual. HCFA does not comment on the memberships in nonprofit corporations that are not tax-exempt.[3]

HCFA has interpreted "debt" to include a loan of money or other valuable consideration to the entity where the repayment obligation is secured, in whole or in part, by the entity or its assets. HCFA distinguishes such a secured loan from "an unsecured or nonconvertible loan...or a loan with no other *indicia* of ownership.[4]" The latter type of financial relationship might be regarded as a compensation arrangement and not an ownership interest.

HCFA has further indicated that other types of "debtor-creditor relationships" may constitute ownership interests. Indicia of the existence of an ownership interest could include a creditor's participation in revenues or profits, subordinated payment terms, low or no interest terms, or ownership of convertible debentures.[5] Thus, some service arrangements could be viewed as ownership interests to which Stark's compensation-related exceptions will not apply.

HCFA has stated that a loan from an entity to a physician or family member would not be considered an ownership interest of the physician or family member in the entity. Rather, such a transaction would be regarded as a compensation arrangement.[6]

Significantly, debt interests can be created by nonprofit as well as proprietary providers or suppliers of designated health services. It is unclear whether contractual obligations such as lines of credit or loan guarantees would constitute debt for purposes of Stark II. An argument can be made that the extension of a line of credit or loan guarantee between a physician and an entity that provides designated health services should be treated as debt for purposes of Stark II because the making of a line of credit or an extension of a loan guarantee reduces the debt capacity of the party providing it, and provides an economic benefit to the recipient of it.

Stark II also includes ownership or investment interests that are created through "other means."[7] The types of interests intended to be covered by this catch-all language are not described. However, this language may have been intended to cover contractual equity rights such as stock options, warrants, phantom stock and stock appreciation rights. These contractual provisions create rights to acquire equity interests in the future or to participate in the future growth of the equity of an entity. This catch-all language also may have been intended to cover other forms of contractual arrangements that are called one thing but are, in reality, disguised equity or debt. HCFA has indicated that an option to purchase stock is an inchoate ownership interest that could subject a physician to the self-referral prohibition. The option might be protected by any of the exceptions relating to ownership interests unless it involves securities that may not be purchased on terms generally available to the public.[8]

Indirect Ownership Interests

In addition to direct ownership interests, Stark II applies to an ownership or investment interest in an entity that holds an ownership or investment interest in an entity that provides the designated health services.[9] This extends the ownership or investment interest prohibition to entities that themselves are not direct providers of designated health services, but instead own interests such as stock of a subsidiary or interests in partnerships.

In the proposed Stark II regulations, HCFA discusses in detail physician ownership of entities providing designated health services, particularly when a physician has an indirect referral relationship with the entity, such as when the physician refers patients to an unrelated skilled nursing facility that obtains physical therapy services from a facility in which the physician has an ownership interest. In some situations, depending on which entity is furnishing the designated health services and/or billing for them, the physician's referral might not be prohibited. However, citing the potential for abuse, HCFA proposes to equate the referring physician and the physical therapy facility when the physician has a significant ownership or controlling interest that enables the doctor to determine how and with whom the entity conducts business. Numerous factors will be considered including the amount of stock held and whether the physician is making decisions for the entity on a day-to-day basis.[10] This approach certainly does not constitute the type of "bright-line" guidance under Stark that many in the health care industry had hoped for.

In a particularly important comment, HCFA notes that it "would be illogical to specifically apply the referral prohibition…to any indirect ownership interest, yet deny an exception…that is based on ownership just because the interest is indirect, especially when the exception itself does not require a direct interest."[11] This statement may open the door to a significantly broader interpretation of the Stark II exceptions, consistent with the scope of interpretation applied to the Stark restrictions.

Compensation or Equity?

It is important to distinguish between compensation arrangements and ownership or investment interests because different sets of exceptions to the general referral prohibitions apply to each.

Compensation arrangements generally are defined as arrangements involving any remuneration between a physician or member of his immediate family and an entity.[12] Although the actual definition of "compensation arrangement" is silent on this question, the term cannot have been intended to include distributions from an equity investment such as stock dividends, or distributions of profits from a partnership to its partners or from a limited liability company to its members. Similarly, payments for the use of money in the form of interest generally should be treated as an ownership or investment interest. Yet, it is unclear whether fee income generated in connection with lending transactions such as loan processing fees (points), loan guaranty fees and standby fees would be treated as ownership or investment interests rather than as compensation arrangements, even though they are paid in connection with a debt transaction.

The overlap between the ownership- and investment-interest definition and the compensation-for-services definition presents a special problem for compensation arrangements that are equity-based, such as stock options and restricted stock awarded to employed physicians as compensation for services. Proprietary companies, especially those whose stock is listed on a national securities exchange or traded over the counter, frequently utilize stock options as part of their long-term compensation program. In addition, publicly held and privately owned companies use awards of restricted stock for compensatory purposes as a means of attracting physician executives who also may be in a position to refer patients. In each of these cases, the options or restricted stock are awarded to reward past service and to assure future performance of services. Because they are awarded for services and are not investments, a strong argument can be made that it should only be necessary to comply with the personal service or bona fide employment exceptions for compensation arrangements. A critical element to this argument would be ensuring that the total compensation paid for personal services to the physician, including the equity-based compensation, is reasonable.

On the other hand, an equally compelling argument can be made that options, restricted stock, or other forms of equity-based compensation must be considered ownership or investment interests as well, and thus their use would be permitted only if an ownership or investment exception was met and there was a qualified personal service arrangement or bona fide employment arrangement in place with respect to an entity that provides designated health services.

Permitted Ownership and Investment Interests

Stark II establishes five exceptions to the general ownership prohibition, thus permitting physicians to have ownership or investment interests in entities to which they refer patients that provide designated health services , and bill the government.[13]

Hospital Ownership Exception. Inpatient and outpatient hospital services are designated health services.[14] Thus, absent an exception that would permit a physician to retain an ownership or investment interest in a provider of inpatient and outpatient services, referrals by a physician would be prohibited, and the provider would be barred from billing Medicare or Medicaid for such services.

If two requirements are satisfied, referring physicians may legally maintain ownership and investment interests in providers of inpatient and outpatient hospital services. First, the referring physician must be "authorized" to perform services at the hospital. Second, the ownership or investment interest must be in the hospital itself, not merely in a "subdivision" of the hospital.[15]

HCFA indicates in the proposed Stark II regulations that this exception applies only when designated health services are furnished by the hospital itself, not when services are furnished by any other health care providers that are owned by the hospital, such as a home health agency or a skilled nursing facility. HCFA emphasizes that services must be provided by an entity that qualifies as a hospital under the Medicare conditions of participation. The agency states that the exception covers any designated health services provided by a hospital, not just inpatient or outpatient hospital services.[16]

The hospital ownership exception is extremely important because of the large number of hospitals in the United States that are owned, in whole or in part, by referring physicians. However, when the hospital ownership exception is analyzed carefully, it is fraught with interpretative problems and its requirements may be difficult to meet in less-than-obvious cases.

During the 1980s, creative advisers designed a wide variety of joint ventures that involved some portion but not all of a hospital's operations.[17] Some joint ventures involved departments such as radiology that were leased to the joint venture, which assumed the risk and enjoyed the opportunity for profit of that department.

Some joint ventures involved specific services, such as outpatient surgery or acute dialysis, and the joint venture enjoyed the opportunity for profit and was at risk for losses for such services irrespective of where they were performed within the physical premises of a hospital. For example, outpatient surgical revenues might go to a joint venture whether the services were performed in a dedicated outpatient surgical suite or the hospital's main operating rooms. Other joint ventures allowed physicians to purchase equipment, such as MRI and CT scanners, lease that equipment to the hospital and receive rent in return. Often, the rent was determined on a per-procedure or per-"click" basis.

In other cases, joint ventures were established to own the entire hospital facility and to lease it to an operating company. In these instances, particularly when a partner in the joint venture was an entity such as a real estate investment trust, usually the rent was composed of two components. Fixed rents were paid by the operating company to the joint venture, and contingent or additional rents would be payable if gross or net revenues of the hospital exceeded certain prescribed levels.

Stark II has greatly simplified the allowable structuring of ownership and investment interests in providers of inpatient and outpatient hospital services by requiring that the ownership or investment interest be in the hospital itself, and not merely in a "subdivision," such as a discrete service or department of the hospital.

To meet the ownership requirement of the exception it appears that the ownership or investment interest must be a direct interest in the licensed hospital operating company. Significantly, this exception appears to focus on the hospital operations and not the assets, and thus should permit a third party, such as a real estate investment trust, to own the hospital facilities and equipment. On the other hand, referring physicians would be prohibited from owning an interest in an entity that only owns the hospital facilities and equipment, and does not directly operate the hospital, if the leasing arrangement does not comply with applicable compensation arrangement exceptions.

Also, because of the apparent direct ownership requirement, a referring physician would likely be prohibited from owning an interest in a holding company for a hospital operating subsidiary, unless another exception, such as that applicable to publicly traded companies, were to apply.[18]

Although the entire-hospital-ownership requirement does not speak to the issue, it is reasonable to assume that the ownership or investment interest must allow its owner to participate in profits and losses of the entire hospital to qualify. Thus, special classes of stock that attempt to share profits and losses from specific aspects of the hospital's operations are likely not to qualify.

HCFA further concludes in the proposed Stark II regulations that a physician has an ownership interest in a particular hospital by holding an interest in an entity that owns a chain or network of hospitals. Such a physician could qualify for the exception if the doctor's interest — although indirect — is in the hospital as a whole, not a subdivision, and if the physician is authorized to perform services at the hospital to which the doctor wishes to refer.[19]

The second requirement of the hospital ownership and investment interest exception is that the referring physician must be authorized to perform services at the hospital.[20] Generally, this requirement means that referring physicians must have some type of admitting privileges at the hospital in which they have an ownership interest. Presumably this requires active, consulting, courtesy or temporary privileges, but would not include honorary privileges that do not allow the physician to admit or treat patients.

This authority-to-perform-services requirement presents several potential problems. First, because the definition of "physician" may include dentists and podiatrists, these practitioners may not be able to obtain privileges at some hospitals. In fact, a "physician" is not even required to be on the medical staff in order to refer for some services, such as laboratory tests. Second, if the ownership or investment interest is held by a medical group, there is a question as to whether all members of the group will be required to have privileges at the hospital. This could create problems for an oncology group, for example, that provides services at several hospitals and not all of the medical groups' members are on staff at all of the hospitals the group services. Finally, this requirement may create problems when a single entity partially owned by physicians owns two or more hospitals in the same market, such as where an integrated delivery system has been formed. Physicians who have invested in the entity may not have admitting privileges at all of the hospitals that are part of the system and thus may violate the self-referral prohibition by referring a patient to one of the system's hospitals at which the physician is not permitted to admit patients.

This requirement also creates some anomalous results. For example, a physician could purchase tax-exempt bonds issued strictly for investment purposes and on the same basis as hundreds of other bond purchasers. Assuming the bonds do not qualify under the publicly traded stock exception, the physician would violate the Stark II prohibition by referring a Medicare patient to that hospital. In addition, if the hospital bills for such services, it would violate the Stark II prohibition even if it were not aware that the physician was a bondholder.

Publicly Traded Securities Exception. Stark II provides that the ownership of investment securities in certain publicly traded entities will not be treated as prohibited ownership and investment interests.[21] This exception is intended to allow physicians and members of their immediate families to acquire shares of stock in corporations or interests in publicly traded limited partnerships, as well as bonds, notes, debentures or other debt instruments of publicly traded entities.[22]

The exception to the general ownership and investment interest prohibition applies only to a limited range of public companies that satisfy specific stringent requirements.

First, the securities must be listed on the New York Stock Exchange, the American Stock Exchange or any regional exchange in which quotations are published on a daily basis. In addition, foreign securities listed on a recognized foreign, national or regional exchange in which quotations are published on a daily basis may also satisfy this requirement. This is undoubtedly intended to apply to the stocks listed on the Vancouver Stock Exchange and on many other recognized foreign exchanges.[23]

The exception also applies to investment securities that are traded on an automated interdealer quotation system operated by the National Assn. of Securities Dealers (NASDAQ).[24]

Significantly, however, the exception does not apply to pure over-the-counter stocks and stocks that are traded in what are generally referred to as the "pink sheets."

The second requirement that investment securities must satisfy to qualify for the publicly traded securities exception is that the corporation that has issued the investment securities must have, at the end of the corporation's most recent fiscal year, or on average during the previous three fiscal years, stockholder equity exceeding $75 million.[25]

Stark I originally required a physician's investment to be in a corporation that had total assets exceeding $100 million. In the Stark I proposed regulations, HHS expressed a concern that an entity in which physicians intended to invest could acquire additional assets primarily with the intent of qualifying for this exception. Thus, HHS proposed that, for purposes of establishing the $100 million in assets required by Stark I, the entity would be unable to include any assets that were obtained "primarily for the purpose of meeting the $100 million requirement."

HHS stated that the intention of imposing this requirement was to deny protection to arrangements that were entered into solely to circumvent the referral prohibition and which HHS considered to be "sham transactions."[26]

The change from an "assets test" to a "stockholder-equity test" is less subjective and easier to administer.

The third requirement that must be satisfied is that the physician must acquire the investment securities "on terms generally available to the public." This language represents a slight change from the original Stark I requirement that the securities actually had to be purchased on terms generally available to the public. The new language would seem to focus primarily on the price that is paid by the physician for the investment securities, and does not appear to preclude the use of different types of consideration. Thus, it should be possible for physicians to exchange for stock noncash assets having an equivalent fair market value, as long as stock of the same class is made available for purchase by the general public. An example would be a physician selling his or her medical practice in exchange for stock in a public company. Assuming the other requirements are met, the fact that the physician received stock of the public company in exchange for the practice rather than paying cash for the stock should not disqualify the transaction from this exception.

The preamble to the proposed Stark II regulations clarifies that the exception for investments in securities that "may be purchased on terms generally available to the public" means that, at the time the physician acquired the securities, they could be purchased on the open market, even if the physician did not acquire them that way. HCFA specifically notes, for example, that the exception could cover situations in which the physician inherits the securities.

An interesting problem is raised by stock purchases made through a stock purchase plan by physicians who are employees of a publicly traded company. Employee stock purchase plans are designed to allow employees to purchase their employer's stock at a discount and receive favorable tax treatment upon a qualified disposition of that stock.

To be a qualified employee stock purchase plan, the plan must meet nine requirements prescribed in section 423 of the Internal Revenue Code. Eligibility to participate in the plan is limited to employees and all employees must have the same rights and privileges. However, the amount of stock that may be purchased by an employee may be a uniform percentage of compensation, and the plan may limit the maximum number of shares to be purchased by any one employee. Also, no options may be granted to employees who own 5% or more of the value or voting power of all classes of stock of the employer, its parent or subsidiary, and no employee may purchase more than $25,000 of stock in one year. To be treated as an employee stock purchase plan, the right to participate must be granted to all employees, including part-time employees. But those with less than two years of service, officers, supervisors and highly compensated employees may be excluded from participating.

Because of the requirements in the Internal Revenue Code, an employee stock purchase plan clearly is limited to bona fide employees, is intended to be treated as additional compensation for personal services rendered, and may not discriminate in favor of highly compensated employees like physicians. On the other hand, under a qualified stock option plan, a physician employee may acquire stock of a public company on terms not generally available to the public, such as at a purchase price that is less than 100% but not less than 85% of the fair market value of the stock at the time it was purchased. This type of an arrangement should only have to be tested under the compensation-for-services exceptions discussed in Chapter 6, and should not have to comply with the ownership interest exceptions, although such a conclusion is not made clear by the Stark law.

Regulated Investment Company Exception. Regulated investment companies, commonly known as mutual funds, are corporations that act as investment agents for their shareholders. Typically, mutual funds invest in government and corporate securities and distribute dividend and interest income earned from the investments as dividends to their shareholders. Regulated investment companies may entirely escape corporate taxation if they distribute all of their earnings and profits. This is because, unlike ordinary corporations, they are entitled to claim a deduction for dividend payments against their ordinary income and net capital gain. Regulated investment companies, because of their combination of expert money management, their ability to pool funds with other investors, and their preferred tax treatment, are very attractive. For physicians and immediate family members who own shares of a regulated investment company, Stark II provides an exception to the ownership investment interest prohibition. To qualify for this exception, the regulated investment company in which the physician has an ownership or investment interest must have had, at the end of its most recent fiscal year, or on average during the previous three fiscal years, total assets exceeding $75 million.[27] This exception allows physicians and members of their families to acquire shares in a mutual fund that owns stock or other ownership interests in entities that provide designated health services.

Rural Provider Exception. One of the broadest ownership exceptions to Stark II is the rural provider exception. Stark II provides that a physician's ownership or investment interest in an entity located in a rural area that furnishes "substantially all" of the entity's designated health services to individuals residing in the rural area is not an ownership or investment interest prohibited under Stark II.[28] For a rural area to qualify as such under the provisions of Stark II, the area must be any one outside of a "metropolitan statistical area."[29]

Neither Congress nor HHS has provided an interpretation of the requirement that "substantially all" of the designated health services provided by the entity be rendered to individuals residing within the rural area. It is expected that a clarification will be included in the final Stark II regulations. In other areas, such as the tax laws, "substantially all" generally has meant 85%.

Reviewing some of the legislative proposals may give some insight into what is meant by "substantially all." The House Ways and Means Committee proposed in the summer of 1993 that 85% of designated health services must be provided by the rural entity for the entity to meet the exception.[30]

In the 1994 health-reform debate several proposals addressed the level of designated health services that had to be provided to residents of the rural area to meet the rural provider exception. Two proposed the insertion of "must provide not less than 75%" instead of "substantially all" designated health services to residents of the rural area to satisfy the rural provider exception. On the other hand, Rep. Stark's 1994 proposals and President Clinton's failed Health Security Act proposed to raise the requirement to 85%.

While the proposed changes to Stark II were never enacted, they provide guidance on the level of designated health services that should be provided by the entity to individuals residing in the rural area to qualify for the rural exception. It is generally recommended that an entity that has physician owners should not bill for services provided to Medicare patients referred by those physicians unless historically the entity has provided at least 75% of its designated health services to residents of its rural area until further clarification is issued.

The rural provider exception may prove beneficial to rural hospitals that want to have a financial relationship with physicians. Stark II has, according to some commentators, clearly improved the legal environment for rural entities that wish to enter into joint venture relationships with physicians.[31] Further clarification of the existing anti-kickback law joint venture "safe harbor" for small entity joint ventures and pending additional anti-kickback law "safe harbors" may improve the legal environment even more.[32]

A concern of HHS expressed in the proposed Stark I regulations is that physicians who have an ownership interest in an urban lab may set up a "shell" laboratory with a rural address to gain the benefit of the rural provider exception.[33] Physicians should be aware that arrangements in which urban labs with physician owners set up labs in rural areas for the purpose of providing tests referred by the physician owners for their urban patients, may be closely scrutinized by HHS.

Observers such as former Rep. Fred Grandy (R-Iowa) have stated their concern that quality of care will suffer in rural areas if doctors are not able to invest in rural facilities. The rural area exception contained in Stark II could provide fertile ground for entrepreneurs still looking to joint venture with physicians. As long as a rural area contains the requisite population, joint ventures can be pursued without much limitation.

Exception for Hospitals in Puerto Rico. Stark II, as did Stark I, provides that a physician's ownership or investment interest in a hospital in Puerto Rico, even if the interest is not in the entire hospital, will not be considered a prohibited ownership or investment interest.[34] Therefore, a physician who has an ownership or investment interest in a hospital in Puerto Rico may continue to refer patients to that hospital for the provision of designated health services without violating the self-referral prohibitions of Stark II.

Other Permitted Ownership or Investment Interests. Stark II gives HHS the authority to specify by regulation other forms of permitted ownership and investment interests. The principal criterion is that the ownership or investment interest must not pose a risk of program or patient abuse.[35]

Conclusion

While the five exceptions to the ownership prohibitions provide some leeway in structuring equity arrangements with physicians, it is clear that traditional joint-venture arrangements with physicians are a thing of the past. Aside from transactions involving rural entities or non-hospital based ventures involving facilities that do not provide designated health services, such as dialysis facilities, entire hospital syndications appear to be the last avenue of equity arrangements between physicians and hospitals.

Endnotes

[1] 42 U.S.C. Sec. 1395nn.

[2] 42 U.S.C. Sec. 1395nn(a)(2)(last sentence).

[3] 63 *Fed. Reg.* 1659, 1707.

[4] Id.

[5] Id.

[6] Id.

[7] 42 U.S.C. Sec. 1395nn(a)(2).

[8] 63 *Fed. Reg.* 1713.

[9] 42 U.S.C. Sec. 1395nn(a)(2).

[10] 63 *Fed. Reg.* 1710.

[11] Id. at 1713.

[12] For a detailed discussion of permitted compensation arrangements, please see Chapter 6.

[13] 42 U.S.C. Sec. 1395nn(c)&(d).

[14] 42 U.S.C. Sec. 1395nn(h)(6)(K). For a more detailed discussion of this designated health service, see Chapter 2.

[15] 42 U.S.C. Sec. 1395nn(d)(3).

[16] 63 *Fed. Reg.* at 1698.

[17] For a general discussion and example of the types of arrangements that flourished in the 1980s, see Burns, L., and Mancino, D., *Joint Ventures Between Hospitals and Physicians* (Aspen 1987).

[18] 42 U.S.C. Sec. 1395nn(d)(3)(B); See discussion on publicly traded securities; 42 U.S.C. Sec. 1395nn(c)(1)&(2).

[19] 63 *Fed. Reg.* at 1713.

[20] 42 U.S.C. Sec. 1395nn(d)(3)(A).

[21] 42 U.S.C. Sec. 1395nn(c).

[22] 42 U.S.C. Sec. 1395nn(c)(1).

[23] 42 U.S.C. Sec. 1395nn(c)(1)(A).

[24] 42 U.S.C. Sec. 1395nn(c)(1)(A)(ii).

[25] 42 U.S.C. Sec. 1395(c)(1)(B).

[26] 57 *Fed. Reg.* 8588.

[27] 42 U.S.C. Sec. 1395nn(c)(2).

[28] 42 U.S.C. Sec. 1395nn(d)(2).

[29] As defined by the Office of Management and Budget.

[30] Rosenberg, "Congressional Committees Tackle Medicare Reimbursement Self-Referral Prohibition," *Phys. Lab. Reg. Manual* (July 1993) at 4.

[31] Steiner, John, "Update: Fraud and Abuse and Stark Laws," *J. of Health and Hosp. L.* 274, at 279 (Sept. 1993).

[32] Steiner, at 279.

[33] 57 Fed. Reg. 8593, at 8598

[34] 42 U.S.C. Sec. 1395nn(d)(1).

[35] 42 U.S.C. Sec. 1395nn(b)(4)

CHAPTER 6

Permitted Compensation Arrangements

The Stark law generally prohibits a physician from making referrals for Medicare-covered designated health services to an entity with which the physician or an immediate family member has a "financial relationship," defined as an ownership/investment interest or a "compensation arrangement."[1] In addition, an entity may not bill a patient, the Medicare program or anyone else for services rendered pursuant to a prohibited referral.[2] This general prohibition applies, for example, to referrals for Medicare-covered designated health services made by a physician to any hospital, freestanding imaging center or independent clinical laboratory with which that physician has a compensation arrangement.

The Stark law's broad ban on physician self-referrals is subject to numerous exceptions. The general exceptions, discussed in Chapter 4, apply to certain designated health services provided under specific circumstances, regardless of the type of financial relationship between the referring physician and the entity furnishing the service. The ownership/investment interest exceptions discussed in Chapter 5 only apply to certain ownership/investment interests. Finally, the Stark law provides 10 exceptions for compensation arrangements, including exceptions for remuneration paid under certain employment, personal services, leasing, purchasing and physician recruitment arrangements.[3] This chapter discusses these permitted compensation arrangements in detail and considers how they apply to a broad range of common, recurring transactions in which health care entities and physicians routinely engage. In addition, this chapter describes the new proposed compensation arrangement exceptions in the Stark II proposed regulations.

'Compensation Arrangement' Defined

The Stark law defines the term "compensation arrangement" expansively as: "[A]ny arrangement involving any remuneration between a physician (or an immediate family member of such physician) and an entity...."[4] "Remuneration" means any direct or indirect payment, discount, forgiveness of debt or other benefit.[5]

This broad definition implicates virtually any type of compensation arrangement, whether the compensation is payable in cash, in property or in services, and includes indirect compensation arrangements. While the current definition of "indirect compensation arrangement" is unsettled, HCFA is considering defining "indirect compensation" as any payment to a physician that passes from an entity that provides for the furnishing of designated health services, regardless of how many intervening levels the payment passes through or how often it changes form.[6]

Certain compensation arrangements are excepted from the Stark law ban on self-referrals as long as the arrangement meets specific criteria. The permitted compensation arrangements specified in the Stark law are (a) rentals of office space,[7] (b) rentals of equipment,[8] (c) employment relationships,[9] (d) personal service arrangements,[10] (e) physician incentive plans,[11] (f) remuneration from a hospital unrelated to the provision of designated health services,[12] (g) isolated transactions,[13] (h) physician recruitment,[14] (i) certain arrangements under which group practices provide services to hospital patients,[15] and (j) payments by physicians for items and services.[16] In the Stark II proposed regulations, HCFA proposes three new compensation arrangement exceptions; the fair market value compensation exception,[17] the discounts exception[18] and the de minimis compensation[19] exception.

Key Defined Terms

Certain key terms are used throughout the compensation arrangement exceptions. Virtually all of the compensation arrangement exceptions require that the remuneration paid be consistent with fair market value. The regulations define "fair market value" as "the value in arm's-length transactions, consistent with the general market value...."[20] "General market value" is defined in the Stark II proposed regulations as "the price that an asset would bring, as the result of bona fide bargaining between well-informed buyers and sellers, or the compensation that would be included in a service agreement, as the result of bona fide bargaining between well-informed parties to the agreement, on the date of acquisition of the asset or at the time of the service agreement."[21] The Stark II proposed regulations suggest that the fair market price "is the price at which bona fide sales have been consummated for assets of like type, quality, and quantity in a particular market at the time of acquisition, or the compensation that has been included in bona fide service agreements with comparable terms at the time of the agreement."[22] For purposes of rental property, "fair market value" means the value of rental property for general commercial purposes (not taking into account its intended use), and rent for such property may not be adjusted to reflect the additional value either party may attribute to the proximity or convenience to the lessor when the lessor is a potential source of patient referrals to the lessee.[23]

Several compensation arrangement exceptions require that the remuneration be paid under an agreement that would be commercially reasonable even if there were no referrals between the parties. HCFA interprets "commercially reasonable" as an arrangement that appears to be a "sensible, prudent business agreement, from the perspective of the particular parties involved, even in the absence of any potential referrals."[24]

A number of compensation arrangement exceptions provide that the remuneration may not be determined in a manner that takes into account the volume or value of referrals. HCFA clarifies the definition of "volume or value of referrals" in the preamble to the Stark II proposed regulations. First, HCFA states that the reference to "referrals" means referrals for Medicare-covered *designated health services*. This clears up an ambiguity created by the Stark law definition of "referral," which suggested that "referrals" meant referrals for all Medicare-covered services. Second, certain compensation arrangement exceptions, such as the office space rental, equipment rental and personal services exceptions, prohibit compensation that takes into account the volume or value of referrals *and* any "other business generated between the parties." In other exceptions, "volume or value of referrals" appears without making any reference to "other business." HCFA contends that Congress may not have wanted to except arrangements that include additional compensation for other business dealings between the parties, and, in any event, it is impractical for HCFA to separate the compensation paid for items and services covered by an exception from the compensation paid for "other business generated between the parties." Thus, HCFA interprets "volume or value of referrals" to mean referrals *and* other business generated between the parties, thus banning compensation for business not expressly covered by the exception.[25]

Finally, HCFA states in the preamble to the Stark II proposed regulations that a compensation arrangement can fail to satisfy the "volume or value of referrals" standard even when a physician's compensation is set in advance, but is predicated, either expressly or otherwise, on the physician making referrals to a particular entity.[26] If, for example, a hospital includes as a condition of a physician's employment the requirement that the physician refer only within the hospital's own network of ancillary service providers, this physician's compensation reflects the volume or value of his or her referrals, because the physician will receive no compensation if he or she fails to refer as required by the hospital. In contrast, HCFA indicates that an entity that is at "substantial financial risk" for the items and services rendered is not compensating physicians based on the volume or value of the physicians' referrals when it requires physicians to make referrals for designated health services within a network of providers.[27]

HCFA does not define "substantial financial risk." Nevertheless, this interpretation may afford a measure of relief to certain networks, and, thus, is discussed in more detail in this chapter in connection with physician incentive plans.

Following is a discussion of each compensation arrangement exception.

Office Space and Equipment Rentals. The Stark law has separate exceptions for office space and equipment leases. Because the terms of these two exceptions are substantially similar, they are discussed here together. Payments by a lessee to a lessor for the rental of office space or equipment do not constitute a "compensation arrangement" for purposes of the Stark law if the following six requirements are satisfied:

▌ The lease is set forth in writing, signed by the parties, and specifies the premises or equipment to be covered by the lease;

▌ The office space or equipment rented or leased does not exceed that which is reasonable and necessary for the legitimate business purposes of the lease or rental, and must be used exclusively by the lessee when used by the lessee, except that the lessee may make payments for the use of space consisting of common areas if the lessee's payments do not exceed the lessee's pro rata share of expenses for such space based upon a certain formula;

■ The lease is for a term of at least one year;

■ The rental charges for the term of the lease are set in advance, consistent with fair market value, and not determined in a manner that takes into account the volume or value of referrals or other business generated between the parties;

■ The lease is commercially reasonable even if no referrals would be made between the parties; and

■ The lease meets other requirements imposed by regulation.[28]

These provisions of the office space or equipment rental exceptions of Stark II are retroactive to Jan. 1, 1992, and thus entirely replace the lease provisions of Stark I. Further, a lease is a "compensation arrangement" under the Stark law, irrespective of whether the physician is the lessee or the lessor.

In light of the above requirements, oral leases are not excepted under the Stark law. This could be disruptive to hospitals that have space or equipment leases in which the terms are not set out in writing.

Notably, the text of the exception refers to "premises" and "common areas," both terms used generally in the context of leases for office space or buildings. Accordingly, leases of unimproved real property may not have been contemplated. Even so, it may be argued that ground leases should be permitted compensation arrangements as long as the requirements of the exception are satisfied.

Many leases include provisions that permit one or both parties to terminate the lease "without cause" prior to the end of the lease term, or renew the lease for terms of less than one year. Under Stark I, such agreements were at substantial risk of being deemed out of compliance with the one-year term requirement, because the stated term of such an agreement is arguably not one year if a party may terminate the arrangement sooner, without cause or penalty. In the Stark II proposed regulations, HCFA interprets the one-year requirement to allow early terminations only for good cause, provided that the parties do not, within the same one-year period, enter into a new arrangement.[29] Once a lease expires, it can be renewed only if the agreement provides for a term of at least one year. An agreement renewed on a month-by-month basis does not meet the exception, according to HCFA, because the short renewal term would allow the parties to adjust the economics of the arrangement in response to fluctuations in referrals. While HCFA indicates that the lease exception language of the law does not permit early termination without cause, it suggests that parties entering into a lease for less than one year might find protection in the new fair market value exception, discussed later in this chapter.

The office and equipment lease exceptions require that the rental charges over the term of the lease be *set in advance*. This raises the question of whether per-unit rental arrangements, under which the aggregate rent paid over the term may fluctuate based on usage, qualify for the exceptions. Such provisions are common in equipment and time-share office space leases where the total rent varies depending upon usage.

The Stark law does not include the requirement found in the federal anti-kickback law's safe harbors for equipment and office space leases that the "aggregate" rental charges be set in advance. The omission of such a requirement from the Stark law apparently was intentional. The House-Senate conference report accompanying the Stark II law states that space and equipment leases in which payments are based on units of service furnished will meet the Stark lease exception, as long as the per-unit rates do not fluctuate based on the volume or value of referrals between the parties.[30] In the preamble to the Stark II proposed regulations, HCFA cites with approval the situation in which a physician rents equipment, such as an MRI machine, to a hospital on a "per-click" or per-use rent basis.[31] HCFA concludes that as long as the per-click rate complies with the other requirements of the rental exception and does not fluctuate with, or take into account, the volume or value of any referrals or other business generated between the parties, the arrangement complies with the Stark law. However, HCFA's interpretation will not be of much benefit to physician-lessors whose aggregate rent will vary based on the volume or value of the physician-lessor's referrals to the lessee. In such cases, HCFA's view is that while the compensation is "set in advance," the compensation nevertheless takes into account the volume and value of the physician-lessor's referrals. Thus, the compensation arrangement fails to satisfy the "volume and value of referrals" prong of the office space and equipment rental exceptions.

In the preamble to the Stark II proposed regulations, HCFA makes two additional comments about the office space and equipment rental exceptions. First, HCFA states that these exceptions do not apply to capital leases.[32] Under a capital lease, the rental is treated as property that a lessee has purchased or is in the process of purchasing. HCFA finds this arrangement more comparable to an installment sale than an actual rental, and, thus, beyond the scope of exceptions that apply to payments for *the use of* space or equipment. Second, HCFA takes the position that the office space and equipment rental exceptions do not permit the lessee to sublease the space or equipment. The exceptions require that the space or equipment be used exclusively by the lessee when being used by the lessee. HCFA believes this restriction is intended to prevent sham rentals entered into to facilitate payments between the lessor and lessee without any real intention of using the space or equipment. HCFA interprets this exclusive-use requirement to mean that the lessee may not even sublease the leased space or equipment during the time that the lessee is expected to be using them. However, HCFA points out that such lease/sublease arrangements may nevertheless qualify for the new proposed "fair market value compensation" exception, discussed later in this chapter.

Bona Fide Employment Relationships. One of the broadest and most important compensation exceptions available under the Stark law is for payments made by an employer to a physician, or an immediate family member of a physician, with whom there exists a bona fide employment relationship.[33] Employers may be hospitals, medical foundations, physician groups or other entities. To qualify for this exception, the physician must be considered an "employee" as defined in the Stark law.

The Stark law considers a person to be an employee of an entity if the individual would be considered to be an employee of the entity under the usual common law rules applicable in determining the employer-employee relationship, as applied under section 3121(d)(2) of the Internal Revenue Code.[34] The reference to the IRS definition of "employee" is favorable to those seeking to rely on this exception. Generally, the IRS presumes that an individual who works substantially full time in the facilities of another is that person's employee, unless the individual can prove he or she is not an employee. The IRS has an economic interest in classifying relationships as employer/employee rather than as principal/independent contractor. In part, that is because an employer/employee relationship facilitates the collection of income and employment taxes. Therefore, the Stark law's reliance on the IRS definition favors an employee classification.

The Stark law does not require that the employment arrangement be in writing or for a set term. Presumably, this is in recognition of the fact that employment relationships often are not evidenced by a written contract and often are "at will."

If it is determined that a physician is an employee of an entity, certain other requirements must be met for payment to the employee to qualify for the exception. Specifically, payment by an employer to a physician, or an immediate family member, who has a bona fide employment relationship with the employer for the provision of services will qualify under the exception as long as the following conditions are met:

▮ The employment is for identifiable services;

▮ The amount of remuneration under the employment is (a) consistent with the fair market value of the services, and (b) not determined in a manner that takes into account, directly or indirectly, the volume or value of referrals by the referring physician;

▮ The remuneration is provided under an agreement that would be commercially reasonable even if no referrals were made to the employer; and

▮ The employment meets any other requirements HHS may impose by regulation to protect against program or patient abuse.[35]

The Stark law generally requires that payments made by an employer to a physician pursuant to a "bona fide employment relationship" may not be determined in a manner that takes into account the value or volume of referrals by the referring physician. However, the Stark law plainly provides that this prohibition on compensation based on the volume or value of referrals does not bar productivity bonuses that are based on services performed personally by the referring physician or an immediate family member. This exception for productivity bonuses evokes several significant issues and observations.

First, unlike the exception for productivity bonuses paid to members of a group practice (see Chapter 7), this exception does not include services "incident to" the physicians' services, but rather, is limited to services performed personally by the employee. Second, this exception does not bar the payment to employees of contingent, bonus-type compensation other than productivity bonuses based on services performed personally by the employee. The bona fide employment exception requires only that the compensation (a) be consistent with the fair market value of the services; and (b) not be determined in a manner that takes into account the volume or value of any referrals by the referring physician. The fact that an exception from the volume and value of referrals standard is made for productivity bonuses based on services performed personally by the employee does not mean that such productivity bonuses are the only form of contingent compensation an employee may receive. Nevertheless, it appears that the bona fide employment exception does not protect payments of a share of the employer's overall profits. While group practice members may be paid a share of the overall profits of the group practice (see Chapter 7), Congress considered, and rejected, permitting employees to receive a share of the employer's overall profits under the bona fide employment exception.[36] However, this does not preclude, for example, employee compensation that is structured as a percentage of charges or receipts for services rendered by an employee or the employees of a hospital department or unit, provided the aggregate compensation paid is consistent with fair market value and does not take into account the volume or value of the employee's referrals for designated health services.

Contingent compensation arrangements with employees also raise the issue of whether compensation paid under such arrangements complies with the requirement that remuneration be paid under an agreement that would be "commercially reasonable" even if there were no referrals to the employer. Payment of a productivity bonus or other contingent compensation may not be "commercially reasonable" if the arrangement is not calculated to leave profits for the employer or, worse yet, if the employer continually operates the medical practice at a loss. For example, a hospital may employ physicians in a freestanding clinic, and through a productivity bonus or other contingent compensation arrangement, distribute all of the profits of the clinic, or even operate it at a loss. At some point, such arrangements may only be commercially reasonable because the physicians are generating referrals to the hospital. Thus, contingent compensation arrangements with physician employees should be scrutinized for "commercial reasonableness" as well as fair market value.

Finally, the Stark II proposed regulations would limit productivity bonuses based upon personally performed designated health services for those services the physician did not order. Thus, for example, if a physician-employee refers a patient for an echocardiogram and personally furnishes the professional interpretation, the physician could not receive productivity credit for the professional interpretation, even though the physician personally performed the service.

HCFA's proposed interpretation of the scope of the productivity bonus is inconsistent with the plain language of the Stark law and leads to the absurdity of an employer not being able to compensate a physician for services performed. Hopefully, HCFA will reconsider its interpretation of the productivity bonus exception prior to issuing the final Stark II regulations.

Personal Services Arrangements. The Stark law provides an exception for remuneration paid under a personal services arrangement if:

▌ The arrangement is set out in writing, signed by the parties, and specifies the services covered by the arrangement;

- The arrangement covers all of the services to be provided by the physician or immediate family member, to the entity;

- The aggregate services contracted for do not exceed those that are reasonable and necessary for the legitimate business purposes of the arrangement;

- The term of the arrangement is for at least one year;

- The compensation to be paid over the term of the arrangement is set in advance, does not exceed fair market value, and, except in the case of a physician incentive plan, is not determined in a manner that takes into account the volume or value of referrals or other business generated between the parties;

- The services to be performed under the arrangement do not involve the counseling, promotion, business arrangement or other activity that violates any state or federal law; and

- The arrangement meets any other requirements imposed by HHS regulation.[37]

The personal services exception can be very useful for entities that contract for physicians' services rather than directly employ physicians. However, this exception raises a number of issues, some of which are addressed in the Stark II proposed regulations.

The Stark I final regulations provide that the personal services exception applies to remuneration paid to a physician or an immediate family member of a physician.[38] However, remuneration for personal services is often paid to entities, such as group practices. Thus, the Stark II proposed regulations add to the exception remuneration paid to a group practice.[39] This is consistent with HCFA's view that compensation paid to a group practice or other entity for the personal services of physicians is indirect compensation to the physicians who actually furnish the services.[40] HCFA cites the example of a hospital that pays compensation to a group practice under a personal services arrangement. HCFA believes that the compensation paid to the group practice, which, in turn, is paid out to the physicians who actually furnish the personal services, creates an indirect compensation arrangement between the physicians and the hospital. In such a case, HCFA believes that the indirect compensation paid by the hospital to the physicians is protected by the personal services exception if *the group practice's* personal services arrangement with the hospital satisfies all of the requirements of the personal services exception.[41]

The personal services exception is limited to "services," which are not defined by the law or regulations. In HCFA's view, the personal services exception is limited to business-oriented personal services, excluding any items or equipment.[42] However, an individual physician or immediate family member having a personal services arrangement with an entity does not have to actually furnish the services. The services may be furnished by an employee of the physician or immediate family member hired to perform the services.[43]

As set forth in the Stark law and regulations, the personal services exception applies to a single written arrangement that covers *all* of the services to be provided by the physician or immediate family member to the entity.[44] However, under HHS' statutory authority to create new exceptions for arrangements that HHS determines do not pose a risk of patient or program abuse, HCFA has proposed amendments to the regulations that would extend the exception to *multiple* written arrangements, provided all of the arrangements incorporate each other by reference.[45]

Similar to the office space and equipment rental exceptions, the personal services exception requires that the compensation paid over the term of the arrangement be set in advance. Unfortunately, HCFA has not clarified through regulations whether this means that the aggregate amount of compensation paid over the term of the arrangement must be set in advance. However, the House-Senate conference report accompanying the Stark II law states that the "set in advance" requirement is not intended to prohibit payments to a physician on a per-unit-of-service basis, as long as the other requirements of the personal services exception are satisfied.[46] Furthermore, an OIG official has indicated that it would be acceptable under the Stark law to specify that a physician will be paid $200 per hour for as many hours as the physician works during the coming year, assuming that $200 per hour represents the fair market value of the physician's services.[47] Nevertheless, in the Stark II proposed regulations, only the new fair market value compensation exception, to be discussed later in this chapter, expressly provides that the set-in-advance requirement may be satisfied by setting the compensation *method* in advance.[48] HCFA's failure to even mention the clear legislative history of the set-in-advance requirement creates unnecessary confusion about whether the exception permits per-unit-of-service or other contingent compensation arrangements.[49] Hopefully HCFA will address this issue in the final regulations.

Payments for services based on a percentage of revenues or collections were not addressed in the Stark law or its legislative history. Arguably, percentage compensation is permissible because, as with per-unit-of-service compensation, the payment formula is set in advance, even though the exact dollar amount is not known in advance. This would be an important issue to explore where physicians who are engaged as independent contractors to provide medical services are paid a percentage of revenue or collections derived from their services. However, although compensation calculated on a per-unit-of-service, percentage-of-revenues or percentage-of-collections basis may be "set in advance," if the referring physician's *aggregate* compensation will vary with the volume or value of the physician's referrals, the compensation is unlikely to satisfy the "volume and value of referrals" prong of the personal services exception.

The requirement that the personal services arrangement be for a term of at least one year raises the same concerns about early-termination provisions and renewal options discussed previously under the office space and equipment lease exceptions. HCFA applies its interpretation of the one-year requirement to all of the exceptions that contain such a requirement. Thus, the personal services exception allows early terminations only for good cause, provided that the parties do not, within the same one-year period, enter into a new arrangement.[50] Once an agreement expires, it can be renewed only if it provides for a term of at least one year. An agreement renewed on a month-by-month basis does not meet the exception, according to HCFA, because the short renewal term would allow the parties to adjust the economics of the arrangement in response to fluctuations in referrals. HCFA states that parties that do not need a one-year personal services agreement should try to qualify under the new fair market value exception.

Physician Incentive Plans. The personal services exception generally does not permit compensation that takes into account the volume or value of referrals or other business generated between the parties.[51] However, an exception to this limitation is provided for payments made under so-called "physician incentive plans."

A "physician incentive plan" is defined by the Stark law as any compensation arrangement between an entity and a physician or physician group that may directly or indirectly have the effect of reducing or limiting services provided to individuals enrolled with the entity.[52] In the case of physician incentive plans between a physician and an entity, the compensation provided by the entity to the physician may lawfully take into account, directly or indirectly, the value or volume of referrals or the business generated between the parties, through such mechanisms as a withhold, capitation, bonus or other payment method, if the incentive plan meets certain statutory requirements.[53]

For a physician incentive plan to satisfy the requirements of the Stark law, no specific payments may be made, directly or indirectly, to a physician or physician group as an inducement to reduce or limit medically necessary services with respect to an individual enrolled with the entity.[54] In addition, if a physician incentive plan places a physician or physician group at "substantial financial risk," as defined by HHS in the final physician incentive plan regulations,[55] the plan must comply with any requirements imposed by HCFA for such plans.[56] Finally, the plan must provide HHS with access to descriptive information regarding the plan so HHS can determine whether the plan is in compliance with the Stark law.[57]

The threshold interpretative issues relate to the scope of the physician incentive plan exception. First, in the preamble to the Stark II proposed regulations, HCFA emphasizes that the exception applies only to personal services arrangements and not to any other compensation arrangements.[58] Thus, the arrangement must satisfy the personal services exception. Second, HCFA clarifies that the exception is limited to arrangements between entities that enroll Medicare beneficiaries, such as HMOs, and physicians.[59] In other words, an HMO or other prepaid plan must administer the physician incentive plan. Thus, downstream incentive compensation plans between IPAs and physicians, PHOs and physicians, or hospitals and IPAs do not qualify for the exception. Such arrangements may find relief under the prepaid plan exception discussed in Chapter 4, which HCFA interprets as providing a general exception for services provided by certain prepaid plans *or* their downstream providers to enrollees.[60] However, the prepaid plan exception is limited to Medicare risk-contracting HMOs, health care prepayment plans having a contract with HCFA, plans operated under demonstration projects, and federally quali-fied HMOs.[61] Notably absent from this list are HMOs that are not federally qualified, and discounted fee-for-service arrangements. Thus, for example, if a referring physician is compensated under a physician incentive plan administered by an IPA that is down-stream from a nonfederally qualified HMO, the physician's referrals to the IPA would not be protected by either the physician incentive plan or prepaid plan exception.

This raises the fundamental question of when does a physician *ever* make referrals to an IPA or any other managed care organization for the furnishing of designated health services? Only staff-model HMOs, which directly provide health care services through their own employed physicians and health care facilities, actually *furnish* designated health services. HCFA's view is that the entity that "furnishes" the designated health service is the entity that actually delivers the services *and*, if a different entity, the entity that arranges and bills for the service.[62] HCFA's view is based, in pertinent part, on the fact that the Stark law includes an exception for certain prepaid plans. Observing that such plans "very often" contract with independent suppliers and providers to actually "furnish" services to their enrollees, HCFA infers that a prepaid plan exception would only be logical if Congress deemed prepaid plans to be "furnishing" designated health services, even when such services are provided under contractual arrangements with suppliers and providers. Thus, HCFA believes that when a physician refers a Medicare beneficiary enrolled in a nonfederally qualified HMO to a hospital for hospital services arranged *and* billed for by the physician's IPA, the physician has made a referral to the IPA for a designated health service.

Consequently, not every referral for a Medicare beneficiary enrolled in an HMO will qualify for the prepaid plan or physician incentive plan exception. Intermediary or "downstream" organizations administering physician incentive plans, and the downstream organization's participating physicians, should be aware of the risk of submitting or causing the submission of claims to Medicare for beneficiaries who are not enrolled in HMOs and other plans that qualify for the prepaid plan exception.

There would appear to be no sound policy reasons why the physician incentive plan exception should be limited to direct contractual relationships between the physician and a health plan. Other provisions of federal law impose sanctions on arrangements that provide improper inducements to reduce care to an individual patient. In addition, the physician incentive plan regulations regulate the amount and nature of the financial risk that can be imposed on physicians. These statutory provisions combined with health plan approval of the physician incentive plan should provide adequate protection against Medicare beneficiaries being victimized by inappropriate physician incentive plan arrangements, without the health plans actually having to administer every physician incentive plan. Thus, HCFA will hopefully use its authority to provide additional exceptions to the Stark law in the final Stark II regulations to protect more broadly physician incentive plans.

Physician Recruitment. The Stark law provides an exception for payments provided by "a hospital to a physician to induce the physician to relocate to the geographic area served by the hospital in order to be a member of the medical staff of the hospital," if certain requirements are met.[63] Under the physician recruitment exception, a hospital may not require the physician to refer patients to the hospital, and the amount of payment may not directly or indirectly take into account any referrals by the referring physician.[64] In addition, HHS has the discretion to issue regulations implementing this provision, to prevent program or patient abuse.

The Stark I final regulations add two requirements to those outlined in the statute: (1) physician recruitment arrangements must be set forth in writing and signed by the parties, and (2) a physician must be allowed to establish staff privileges at hospitals other than the one with which an arrangement has been made.[65] The Stark II proposed regulations retain these requirements.[66]

One issue raised by the language of this exception is whether it applies to the recruitment of new physicians who have not previously been in practice, but who reside in the hospital's service area at the time they are recruited. An example would be a resident who is currently working in the hospital's service area, perhaps in the hospital's own residency program, and who does not need to relocate. In the preamble to the Stark II proposed regulations, HCFA states that the terms of the Stark law "dictate" that this exception applies only to situations in which the physician resides outside of the hospital's geographic area and "must actually relocate in order to join the hospital's staff."[67] This narrow interpretation places significant weight on HCFA's pending definition of "geographic area served by the hospital," which HCFA declined to define in the Stark II proposed regulations. Instead, the agency is soliciting comments on how to define the term.

While this interpretation is supported by a literal reading of the statute, which specifically limits the exception to remuneration that is provided "to induce the physician to relocate to the geographic area served by the hospital," the result is curious. The purpose of recruitment payments is typically not solely to defray the costs of relocating to the hospital's service area, but rather, to defray the costs of starting a practice in an area where the physician does not already have a patient base. The recruitment incentives may often be necessary to recruit local physicians, such as residents or employees of another hospital or a group practice who do not have a patient base and require practice start-up assistance. In such cases, there is no risk that the recruitment incentive constitutes a financial incentive for the physician to shift the doctor's patient base from one hospital to another, because the physician does not have a patient base. The OIG's proposed anti-kickback safe harbor for physician recruitment incentives recognizes this fact, permitting incentives to a physician who has been practicing within the doctor's current specialty for less than one year, regardless of whether the physician has relocated to the hospital's service area.[68]

A new physician coming directly out of residency arguably could be "relocating," in the sense that the doctor does not yet have a practice location, and, therefore, is relocating to wherever the physician establishes his or her first permanent practice. However, HCFA does not appear to accept this interpretation, offering hospitals the consolation that recruitment incentives to retain residents who reside in the hospital's service area "might be excepted" under the proposed fair market value compensation exception.[69] An alternative approach is for the hospital to employ the new physician, in which case the recruitment incentives could be treated as compensation protected under the bona fide employee exception.

Finally, many hospitals provide recruitment packages to existing physician groups to recruit new doctors to the practice because many new physicians often do not want to practice on their own. Providing incentives to the new physician through a group practice, even when revenue-neutral to the existing group, does not appear to satisfy the technical requirements of the Stark law's physician recruitment exception. However, HCFA indicates in the preamble to the Stark II proposed regulations that such payments also "might be excepted" under the proposed new fair market value compensation exception.[70] In the meantime, it appears that the physician recruitment exception would permit a hospital to place a recruited physician in an existing group practice, if the arrangement is revenue-neutral to the group practice and the hospital makes incentive payments, such as income-guarantee payments, directly to the recruited physician.

Remuneration Unrelated to the Provision of Designated Health Services. The Stark law provides an exception for remuneration provided by a hospital to a physician that is unrelated to the provision of designated health services.[71] This is a broadly worded exception that, not surprisingly, is narrowly interpreted by HCFA to require that the parties demonstrate that the remuneration does not directly or indirectly involve designated health services, and that the remuneration in no way reflects the volume or value of a physician's referrals for designated health services.[72] In the preamble to the Stark II proposed regulations, HCFA gives the example of a teaching hospital that pays a physician rental payments for the physician's house in order to use the house as a residence for a visiting faculty member. If both parties can demonstrate that the rental payments are based on fair market value and do not reflect the physician's referrals to the hospital, HCFA believes the exception would apply. On the other hand, this exception would not apply, for example, to payments by a hospital to a physician to supply the hospital with a heart valve the physician has perfected.[73] Here, the physician receives payment for an item that will be used by the hospital to provide inpatient hospital services, a designated health service. Thus, the payment relates to the provision of designated health services, even if the remuneration is unrelated to the volume or value of the physician's referrals.

Isolated Transactions. An "isolated transaction," such as a one-time sale of property or a practice, is not considered a compensation arrangement for purposes of Stark if:

■ The amount of remuneration involved in the transaction reflects the fair market value of the property and is not determined in a manner that takes into account the volume or value of referrals by the referring physician;

■ The remuneration is provided under an agreement that would be commercially reasonable even if the physician did not make any referrals; and

■ The transaction meets any other requirements that may be imposed by HHS regulation.[74]

The regulations defining this exception are critical in determining whether a transaction will qualify as an "isolated transaction" under the Stark law. In the Stark I proposed regulations, HCFA indicated it intended to adopt a restrictive interpretation of this exception. Specifically, the Stark I proposed regulations contained the requirement that there must be no financial relationship between the entity and the physician for one year before or one year after the transaction.[75] However, in response to criticisms that the one-year requirement creates substantial problems, HCFA modified this requirement in the final Stark I regulations. The regulations now impose no restriction on excepted financial transactions prior to the transaction, and the parties are only restricted from engaging in additional "isolated transactions" for a period of six months after the transaction.[76]

In the Stark I final regulations, HCFA defines "isolated transaction" as a transaction involving a single payment, and expressly excludes any transaction involving install-ment or long-term payments, such as mortgages. In HCFA's view, installment payments, by definition, mean that the transaction is not isolated.[77] The Stark II proposed regula-tions retain this definition of "isolated transaction."[78]

This narrow definition of "isolated transaction" can create significant obstacles to the purchase of physician practices, because a common methodology is to structure such purchases with installment payments. Purchasers, such as hospitals, that are unwilling or unable to pay the entire purchase price in cash at closing may need to explore other options, such as making partial payments into properly structured escrow or trust accounts at the time of closing, or consider protecting payments for covenants not to compete under another compensation arrangement exception. If finalized, the proposed fair market value compensation exception, discussed later in this chapter, should be very helpful in these situations.

Of course, any transaction with a referring physician that is not conducted on a fair market value basis will not qualify for the "isolated transaction" exception. The first prong of the isolated transaction exception requires that the remuneration be consistent with fair market value. Thus, for example, payments for the good will of a practice that are inflated to disguise a payment for the value of future referrals would not qualify for this exception.

Hospital-Affiliated Group Practice Arrangements. A compensation arrangement be-tween a hospital and a group practice, where the hospital pays the group for designated health services provided to the hospital's patients but billed by the hospital, will satisfy an exception to the referral prohibitions of the Stark law if:

▪ For hospital inpatient services, the arrangement is pursuant to the provision of inpa-tient hospital services;

▪ The arrangement began before Dec. 19, 1989, and has continued without interruption since that date. (This was clarified in the Stark II proposed regulations to mean that the arrangement must have been continuously in effect since Dec. 19, 1989, not the date the arrangement began);[79]

▪ For designated health services covered under the arrangement, substantially all of such services furnished to patients of the hospital are furnished by the group; (The Stark II proposed regulations clarified that "substantially all" means at least 75%);[80]

▪ The arrangement is under a written agreement that specifies the services to be provided by the parties and the compensation for services provided under the agreement;

▪ The compensation paid over the term of the agreement is consistent with fair market value, and the compensation per unit of service is fixed in advance and doesn't take into account the volume or value of referrals or other business generated between the parties;

∎ The compensation is provided under an agreement that would be commercially reasonable even if no referrals were made to the entity; and

∎ The arrangement between the parties meets any other requirements HHS imposes by regulation to protect against program or patient abuse.[81]

This section was included in the Stark law in response to concerns raised by group practices and health care entities that Stark I had created problems in situations where clinical lab services were provided by a group practice "under arrangements" with a hospital.[82] The exception was made retroactive to January 1992, and under the Stark II proposed regulations, applies to any designated health service. Because this exception applies only to group practices that provided designated health services before Dec. 19, 1989, and have provided them without interruption since that date, it has limited application and does not provide planning opportunities for those groups that had no such arrangements.

In the Stark II proposed regulations, HCFA interprets the exception to allow for changes in the services provided and the identity of the individuals in the group practice that provide the services.[83] Further, HCFA clarifies that the "substantially all" requirement means that at least 75% of *whatever portion* of a particular designated health service that is covered by the arrangement must be actually provided by the group. Thus, the agreement may cover less than 100% of the particular designated health service that is the subject of the agreement, such as 35% of the hospital's laboratory services. In such a case, the group practice is only required to provide 75% of that portion of the service covered by the agreement, *e.g*, 75% of 35% of the hospital's laboratory services.[84]

Payments by a Physician for Items and Services. The Stark law provides a broad and often overlooked exception for payments made by a physician to (a) a laboratory in exchange for the provision of laboratory services, or (b) an entity as compensation for other items and services if they are furnished at a price that is consistent with fair market value.[85] HCFA interprets "other items and services" to mean any kind of item or service that a physician might purchase, excluding clinical laboratory services or those items specifically covered by other compensation arrangement exceptions.[86] Thus, for example, a physician's rent payments for office space must be analyzed under the office space rental exception.

Interestingly, the exception requires that a physician pay fair market value for items and services other than clinical laboratory services. HCFA's rationale for this distinction between laboratory and other items and services follows from HCFA's view that items and services purchased at a discount are not purchased at fair market value unless the discount satisfies a number of requirements, including the requirement that the discount be passed on to the patient or the third-party payer.[87] HCFA believes Congress did not require physicians to purchase clinical laboratory services at fair market value, because Medicare generally restricts payment for lab services to the entity that provided the services and pays for lab services under a fee schedule.[88] Thus, in the case of lab services, there is no risk that the physician will profit from discounts at the expense of Medicare beneficiaries and the Medicare program.

A significant implication of HCFA's interpretation is that a physician's purchases of items and services at a discount, other than clinical lab services, will not qualify for this exception unless the discount:

▌ Is offered in an arm's-length transaction;

▌ Is offered to all similarly situated persons, regardless of whether they make referrals to the entity;

▌ Does not reflect the volume or value of referrals the physician has made or will make to the entity; and

▌ Is passed on to Medicare or other insurers.[89]

This means that any discount a physician receives on items or services purchased from an entity that furnishes designated health services other than clinical lab services must be passed through to the patient or third-party payer, if the physician wishes to make referrals to the entity. This issue is limited to situations where the physician is receiving a discount from an entity to which the physician makes referrals for the furnishing of Medicare-covered designated health services. For example, if a physician purchases pharmaceutical drugs at a volume discount from a manufacturer, and furnishes the drugs to patients, the physician would not be required to pass the discount on to patients and third-party payers to qualify for this exception. The purchasing physician does not make referrals to the drug manufacturer *for the furnishing of drugs*. Physicians and other health care suppliers and providers, not manufacturers, "furnish" drugs to patients. Thus, under Stark, a physician does not need to treat discounts on purchases from a drug manufacturer in the same fashion as the physician may need to treat discounts on purchases from entities to which the physician makes referrals for the furnishing of designated health services. HCFA's views on the discount issue are discussed later in this chapter in connection with the new proposed discount exception.

The "payments by a physician for items and services" exception arguably may cover loans made by hospitals to physicians and the repayment by the physician of loaned amounts. However, HCFA has never clarified that a loan would be viewed as the purchase of an "item or service." The proposed fair market value compensation exception may more clearly be applicable to a loan arrangement.

New Compensation Arrangement Exceptions

Fair Market Value Compensation. Under HHS' statutory authority to promulgate new exceptions for financial relationships HHS determines do not pose a risk of program or patient abuse, HCFA proposes a new exception for compensation resulting from an arrangement between an entity and a physician or an immediate family member or any group of physicians, if the arrangement is set forth in an agreement that:

▌ Is in writing, signed by the parties, and covers only identifiable items or services, all of which are specified in the agreement;

■ Covers all of the items and services to be provided by the physician and any immediate family member to the entity or, alternatively, cross-refers to any other agreements for items or services between these parties;

■ Specifies the time frame for the arrangement, which can be for any period of time and can contain a termination clause, provided the parties enter into only one arrangement for the same items or services during the course of a year. If the arrangement is for less than one year, it may be renewed any number of times if the terms of the arrangement and the compensation for the same items or services do not change;

■ Specifies the compensation that will be provided under the arrangement. The compensation or the method for determining the compensation must be set in advance, be consistent with fair market value, and not be determined in a manner that takes into account the volume or value of any referrals, payment for referrals for medical services that are not covered under Medicare or Medicaid, or any other business generated between the parties;

■ Involves a transaction that is commercially reasonable and furthers the legitimate business purposes of the parties; and

■ Meets an anti-kickback law safe harbor or otherwise complies with the federal health care program anti-kickback law.[90]

HCFA proposes the fair market value compensation exception to fill in the gaps left by the other compensation exceptions, which, because of their specificity, do not cover many common compensation arrangements that are based on fair market value or are otherwise commercially reasonable, and do not reflect the volume or value of a physician's referrals.[91] For example, while fair market value payments by a physician for items and services are covered by a Stark exception, fair market payments *to* a physician enjoy no such exception.[92]

This exception will be useful for (a) rental and personal service arrangements with a term of less than one year or that include early "without cause" termination provisions; (b) fair market value remuneration paid by a hospital to a physician that does not qualify for the "remuneration unrelated to designated health services" exception; (c) fair market value remuneration paid by an entity to a physician for the purchase of items; (d) fair market value and commercially reasonable loan arrangements between hospitals and physicians; (e) personal services arrangement between an entity and a group of physicians that do not qualify as a "group practice" under Stark; and (f) recruitment incentives paid to a medical resident or other physician located in the hospital's geographic service area.

Discounts. As discussed above under the "payment by a physician for items and services" exception, HCFA does not believe that a physician's purchase of items or services at a discount reflects fair market value, unless a number of criteria are satisfied. HCFA proposes codifying this view in a new discount exception.[93] Under the proposed regulation, a discount does not create an impermissible compensation arrangement between the entity and the physician if (a) the discount is passed on in full to either the patient or the patient's insurers, including Medicare; and (b) the discount does not inure to the benefit of the referring physician.[94]

Note that the discount exception is only relevant when the discount is granted by an entity to which the physician makes referrals for the furnishing of designated health services. Unfortunately, in an attempt to illustrate the operation of the discount exception in the preamble to the Stark II proposed regulations, HCFA cites the example of a physician who purchases chemotherapy drugs from a manufacturer at a discount and marks up the price when billing Medicare.[95] In such a case, HCFA concludes, the physician's compensation arrangement with the drug manufacturer does not qualify for a compensation exception. Thus, the physicians "referrals" for pharmaceuticals violate the Stark law.

This analysis erroneously assumes that (a) purchases at a discount are not consistent with fair market value; and (b) drug manufacturers "furnish" designated health services within the meaning of Stark. HCFA's assumption that discounts do not reflect fair market value is inconsistent with the anti-kickback law's safe harbor for discounts and common commercial usage. Moreover, as discussed previously, a manufacturer of drugs does not "furnish" a designated health service. It merely manufactures drugs that are sold to others, such as physicians, hospitals and pharmacies, which dispense them. The Stark law only proscribes financial relationships between physicians and entities to which the physician refers a patient for the furnishing of designated health services. Physicians do not refer patients to drug manufacturers. Thus, their compensation arrangements with such manufacturers do not implicate the Stark law.

The proposed discount exception is very controversial, and HCFA has acknowledged that the exception has some problems.[96] Thus, it would not be surprising if HCFA makes substantial revisions to the exception prior to finalizing the Stark II proposed regulations.

De Minimis Compensation. Lastly, HCFA proposes an exception for compensation from an entity in the form of items or services, not including cash or cash equivalents, the value of which does not exceed $50 per payment and an aggregate of $300 per year. To meet this exception, (a) the entity providing the compensation must make it available to all similarly situated individuals, regardless of whether they refer patients to the entity for services, and (b) the compensation cannot be determined in any way that takes into account the volume or value of the physician's referrals to the entity.[97]

For example, a physician might receive free samples of certain drugs or chemicals from a laboratory, or receive training sessions for the physician's staff before entering into an agreement with an entity that furnishes a designated health service. A provider may also furnish a physician with free coffee mugs or note pads. Examples of compensation that are not covered under the exception include gift certificates, stocks or bonds, or airline frequent-flier miles, all of which are deemed by HCFA to be cash equivalents.[98]

Conclusion

The Stark II proposed regulations clarify greatly HCFA's interpretation of the compensation exceptions, which helps to better apply the law to compensation arrangements between physicians and entities that furnish designated health services. Moreover, the proposed new fair market value compensation exception should afford providers of designated health services much-needed flexibility in fashioning compensation arrangements with physicians. However, HCFA has adopted an overly restrictive interpretation of the physician recruitment exception, unnecessarily restricted productivity compensation to employees under the bona fide employment exception, confused the "set in advance" element of the personal services exception, and fashioned a discount exception that is incoherent. Hopefully, the comments that HCFA receives on the Stark II proposed regulations will result in final regulations that will rectify some of these problems.

Endnotes

[1] 42 U.S.C. Sec. 1395nn(a)1(A); 42 U.S.C. Sec. 1395 nn(h)(1).

[2] 42 U.S.C. Sec. 1395nn(a)(1)(B).

[3] 42 U.S.C. Sec. 1395nn(e).

[4] 42 U.S.C. Sec. 1395nn(h)(1).

[5] 42 CFR Sec. 411.351.

[6] 63 *Fed. Reg.* 1659, 1705.

[7] 42 U.S.C. Sec. 1395nn(e)(1)(A).

[8] 42 U.S.C. Sec. 1395nn(e)(1)(B).

[9] 42 U.S.C. Sec. 1395nn(e)(2).

[10] 42 U.S.C. Sec. 1395nn(e)(3)(A).

[11] 42 U.S.C. Sec. 1395nn(e)(3)(B).

[12] 42 U.S.C. Sec. 1395nn(e)(4).

[13] 42 U.S.C. Sec. 1395nn(e)(6).

[14] 42 U.S.C. Sec. 1395nn(e)(5).

[15] 42 U.S.C. Sec. 1395nn(e)(7).

[16] 42 U.S.C. Sec. 1395nn(e)(8).

[17] 63 *Fed. Reg.* 1659, 1699.

[18] 63 *Fed. Reg.* 1659, 1695.

[19] 63 *Fed. Reg.* 1659, 1699.

[20] 63 *Fed. Reg.* 1659, 1721.

[21] Id.

[22] Id.

[23] 42 CFR Sec. 411.351.

[24] 63 *Fed. Reg.* 1659, 1700.

[25] Id.

[26] 63 *Fed. Reg.* 1659, 1699-1700.

[27] 63 *Fed. Reg.* 1659, 1700.

[28] 42 U.S.C. Sec. 1395nn(e)(1)(A)(vi).

[29] 63 *Fed. Reg.* 1659, 1713.

[30] 139 Cong. Rec. H5792, H6005 (daily ed. Aug. 4, 1993).

[31] 63 *Fed. Reg.* 1659, 1714.

[32] Id.

[33] 42 U.S.C. Sec. 1395nn(e)(2). See also the discussion in Chapter 5 regarding employee stock option/purchase plans.

[34] 42 U.S.C. Sec. 1395nn(h)(2).

[35] 42 U.S.C. Sec. 1395nn(e)(2)(D).

[36] H. Conf. Rep. No. 213, 103rd Cong., 1st Sess. (1993) (adopting Senate amendment eliminating House Bill version providing for remuneration in the form of both productivity bonuses and a share of the overall profits).

[37] 42 U.S.C. Sec. 1395nn(e)(3)(A)(vii).

[38] 60 *Fed. Reg.* 41914, 41981.

[39] 63 *Fed. Reg.* 1659, 1724 (to be codified in 42 CFR pt. 411).

[40] 63 *Fed. Reg.* 1659, 1704-05.

[41] 63 *Fed. Reg.* at 1659, 1706.

[42] 63 *Fed. Reg.* at 1659, 1701.

[43] 63 *Fed. Reg.* 1659, 1701, 1725 (to be codified at 42 CFR pt. 411).

[44] 42 U.S.C. Sec. 1395nn(e)(3)(A)(ii); 42 CFR Sec. 411.357(d).

[45] 63 *Fed. Reg.* 1659, 1725 (to be codified at 42 CFR pt. 411).

[46] 139 Cong. Rec. H5792, H6003, (daily ed. Aug. 4, 1993).

[47] Transcript of speech by Sharon M. Johnson, senior attorney in the Inspector General Division of the HHS Office of General Counsel, to the American Institute of Certified Public Accountants on July 26, 1994.

[48] 63 *Fed. Reg.* 1659, 1726 (to be codified at 42 CFR pt. 411).

[49] 63 *Fed. Reg.* 1659, 1724-25 (to be codified at 42 CFR pt. 411).

[50] See 63 *Fed. Reg.* 1659, 1713.

[51] 42 U.S.C. Sec. 1395(e)(3)(v)

[52] 42 U.S.C. Sec. 1395nn(e)(3)(B)(ii).

[53] 42 U.S.C. Sec. 1395nn(e)(3)(B)(i).

[54] 42 U.S.C. Sec. 1395nn(e)(3)(B)(i)(I).

[55] See 60 *Fed. Reg.* 13430, codified at 42 CFR Secs. 417.479, 434.67, 434.70.

[56] 42 U.S.C. Sec. 1395nn(e)(3)(B)(i)(I).

[57] 42 U.S.C. Sec. 1395nn(e)(3)(B)(i)(III).

[58] 63 *Fed. Reg.* 1659, 1701.

[59] Id.

[60] 63 *Fed. Reg.* 1659, 1697.

[61] See 42 U.S.C. Sec. 1395nn(b)(3); 42 CFR Sec. 411.355(c).

[62] 63 *Fed. Reg.* 1659, 1706-07.

[63] 42 U.S.C. Sec. 1395nn(e)(5).

[64] Id.

[65] 42 CFR Sec. 411.356(e).

[66] 63 *Fed. Reg.* 1659, 1725 (to be codified at 42 CFR pt. 411).

[67] 63 *Fed. Reg.* 1659, 1702.

[68] 58 *Fed. Reg.* 49008.

[69] 63 *Fed. Reg.* 1659, 1702.

[70] Id.

[71] 42 U.S.C. Sec. 1395nn(e)(4).

[72] 63 *Fed. Reg.* 1659, 1702.

[73] Id.

[74] 42 U.S.C. Sec. 1395nn(e)(6).

[75] 57 *Fed. Reg.* 8588, 8599 (to be codified at 42 CFR pt. 411) (proposed Mar. 11, 1992).

[76] 42 CFR Sec. 411.357(f).

[77] 42 CFR Sec. 411.351.

[78] 63 *Fed. Reg.* 1659, 1723 (to be codified at 42 CFR pt. 411).

[79] 63 *Red. Reg.* 1659, 1702.

[80] Id.

[81] 42 U.S.C. Sec. 1395nn(e)(5).

[82] 42 U.S.C. Sec. 1395nn(e)(7)(A)(vii).

[83] 63 *Fed. Reg.* 1659, 1702.

[84] 63 *Fed. Reg.* 1659, 1702-03.

[85] 42 U.S.C. Sec. 1395nn(e)(8).

[86] 63 *Fed. Reg.* 1659, 1703.

[87] 63 *Fed. Reg.* 1659, 1694.

[88] Id.

[89] Id.

[90] 63 *Fed. Reg.* 1659, 1725-26 (to be codified at 42 CFR Sec. 411.357(l)).

[91] 63 *Fed. Reg.* 1659, 1699.

[92] Id.

[93] 63 *Fed. Reg.* 1659, 1694, 1725 (to be codified at 42 CFR pt. 411).

[94] 63 *Fed. Reg.* 1725 (to be codified at 42 CFR pt. 411).

[95] 63 *Fed. Reg.* 1659, 1695.

[96] Presentation by Joanne Sinsheimer, HCFA, at the Medicare and Medicaid Institute, American Health Lawyers Assn., Baltimore, Md. (March 26, 1998).

[97] 63 *Fed. Reg.* 1659, 1699 (to be codified at 42. CFR pt. 411).

[98] Id.

CHAPTER 7

Group Practices

During the past decade, a number of physician organizational structures have been developed, including independent practice associations, preferred provider organizations, shared office arrangements, part-time employment arrangements, so-called "group practices without walls" and other partially integrated medical groups, that have resulted in a blurring of the definition of "group practice." This chapter discusses the necessary attributes a group practice must have for Stark law purposes and attempts to set forth the full range of approaches, from aggressive to conservative, with regard to medical group organizations and physician compensation plans that could satisfy this definition. The last part of this chapter attempts to identify a number of factors relevant to developing group practices and the typical issues that need to be resolved.

Physicians' Services Exception

The physicians' services exception is a little understood and often neglected exception to the Stark law as it applies to group practices. As a result, several congressional proposals have sought to eliminate this exception.

The exception states that physician services provided personally or under the personal supervision of another physician in the same group practice as the referring physician are excepted from the self-referral prohibition.[1] The August 1995 final Stark I rule incorporated this provision in the regulations,[2] and the January 1998 proposed Stark II rules retain this provision.[3] While many assume that services performed by the referring physician are also protected, the Stark II proposed regulations made clear that "self-referrals" for designated health services by a physician in a group practice are not protected when incentive compensation is involved.[4]

The definition of "physicians' services" in the Stark law cross-references another provision of the Medicare law that defines physicians' services as professional services performed by physicians, including surgery, consultations, and home, office and institutional care. The Stark law also defines "physicians' services" as an item or service for which payment may be made under Medicare Part B or a request by a physician for a consultation with another physician, or any test or procedure ordered by or to be performed by or under the supervision of the other physician.[5]

One of the purposes of the physicians' services exception is to permit a referral to another physician in the same group for ancillary services traditionally performed by a physician. Without this exception, arguably, a referral outside of the medical group's facilities, of a patient by one physician in a group practice to another physician to perform a designated health service that has a physician component, such as anatomic laboratory services, could violate the Stark law. The Stark II proposed regulations also clarify that the physicians' services cannot be performed by nonphysicians as incident-to services.[6] If this interpretation of the physicians' services exception is correct, congressional proposals to eliminate it would appear to be inappropriate, because the exception would appear to be necessary to protect referrals for certain services.[7]

On the other hand, broader interpretations of the physicians' services exception have suggested that the exception can be used to develop certain joint-venture arrangements where groups of otherwise independent physicians may come together to personally provide, at a location jointly owned by them, a service traditionally performed by doctors. Thus, these interpretations have suggested the physicians' services exception is applicable as an extension of those physicians' practices or workplace. Such an interpretation would be consistent with recent congressional proposals to eliminate the exception and add an additional designated health service for any other service or item not personally provided by the physician or a member of the physician's group practice.[8]

Under this expanded interpretation of the physicians' services exception, for example, a group of independent cardiologists may be able to come together in a joint-venture arrangement to jointly own a diagnostic catheterization lab in a freestanding facility, where permitted by law, and then refer patients for diagnostic catheterization lab procedures personally performed by those physicians. A similar analysis could be made for other physician specialists referring patients to jointly owned facilities, such as OB/GYNs with respect to ultrasound tests, physicians providing in-office drug therapy to AIDS patients, physiatrists for physical therapy services, oncologists for in-office chemotherapy services, or pulmonologists for pulmonary function tests, as long as the services are personally performed by the referring physician. Overall, such a broad interpretation of the physicians' services exception appears to be very aggressive and appears to be somewhat inconsistent with the concept enunciated in the Stark II proposed regulations that self-referrals of designated health services are not protected.

Although HCFA declined to create a new exception for shared laboratories, HCFA noted in the preamble to the final Stark I regulations that referrals to certain shared-laboratory arrangements could meet the requirements of the in-office ancillary services exception. This would require that the services are personally performed or directly supervised by the referring physician or another member of that physician's group practice, and are billed by the referring physician, the group practice or an entity wholly owned by the group practice or referring physician.[9] Accordingly, if each physician whose patient testing is performed in the shared laboratory remains on-site when the testing is performed, directly supervises the personnel, and bills for the services under his/her group practice number, the pooling of resources in such a laboratory may be acceptable.

Physicians contemplating creation of a joint venture through which they would perform physicians' services that may come within the definition of "designated health services" should carefully consider the risks associated with interpreting the physicians' services exception too broadly. Such individuals should also seek competent legal advice to ensure that any joint venture is structured appropriately.

In-Office Ancillary Services Exception

The principal exception to the Stark law self-referral ban for physicians in group practices is the "in-office ancillary services" exception. This exception permits referrals for all designated health services, other than certain DME and home health services that are not typically provided in a physician office setting. To qualify for this exception, several conditions must be met. These conditions define who may perform and bill for the ancillary service and where ancillary services may be rendered. The specific Stark law language is set forth in Chapter 3.

To fall within the in-office ancillary services exception, three tests must be satisfied.

Provider Test — First, the services must be performed personally by the referring physician, by a member of the referring physician's group practice, or by another individual, such as a lab director, who is directly supervised by the referring physician or a member of the referring physician's group. The August 1995 final Stark I rule defined "direct supervision" as supervision by a physician who is present in the office suite and immediately available to provide assistance and direction throughout the time the clinical laboratory services are to be performed.[10]

The January 1998 proposed Stark II rule further clarifies this provision by making clear that the physician must be physically present in the office suite in which the services are being furnished, at the time they are being furnished.[11] Thus, a physician is not present if he is rendering professional services in one suite in a building, while the designated health services are performed in a separate suite in the same building. Nevertheless, the January 1998 proposed Stark II rules permit brief absences under limited conditions such as unexpected emergencies or routine absences of short durations, such as a lunch break.[12]

Location Test — Second, the designated health services must be provided either in a building in which the referring physician or members of his or her group practice medicine, or in another building used by the group for the centralized provision of clinical laboratory or other designated health services. The January 1998 proposed Stark II regulations contain several clarifications. First, a service is performed whenever a procedure is actually performed upon a patient. In addition, the same building means one physical structure, not multiple structures that are connected by tunnels or walkways. For example, a mobile X-ray van would not be considered part of the building. Moreover, the proposed Stark II regulations suggest that furnishing services unrelated to designated health services means a physician's examination and diagnosis of a patient, even if the result of that exam leads the physician to order a designated health service.

Finally, the proposed regulations indicate that a group practice has the option to use another building for the centralized provision of the group's designated health services. Interestingly, the proposed regulations indicate that a group practice can have more than one of these centralized locations as long as each location services more than one of the group's offices. This option still requires direct supervision, but unrelated physician services do not have to be performed at the centralized location.[13]

Billing Test — Third, the designated health service must be billed by the referring physician, or his or her group practice, using a billing number assigned to the group, or by an entity wholly owned by the referring physician. An argument could be made that this billing test requirement would not be satisfied if, for example, a management company, as an agent for the group practice, billed for the group practice's designated health service using the group practice's billing number. However, such an interpretation would be contrary to other Medicare regulations that expressly permit the engagement of a billing agent, and the January 1998 proposed Stark II regulations expressly allow an agent to bill for the group practice. In addition, in situations in which a wholly-owned entity bills for the group practice, the proposed regulations indicate that the group practice has the option of billing under its own provider number or the provider number of its wholly-owned entity.[14]

'Group Practice' Definition

For physician members of group practices, the availability of the in-office ancillary services exception, in most instances, will depend on whether the group meets the Stark law definition of a "group practice."

Background. At the urging of the HHS Office of the Inspector General, preliminary drafts of the Stark II law were designed to prohibit physician owners of loosely organized or nonintegrated groups, known as "clinics without walls," from referring their patients to the group for ancillary services. OIG had expressed concern that some "clinics without walls" were merely "sham" arrangements intended to split ancillary service profits with the physicians who order the services.

These drafts of the Stark II law tried to close this "loophole" by defining a "group practice" in a restrictive manner based on the number of physicians practicing at a particular office location. Proposals included requirements of 10 or more physicians per location, five or more physicians per location, and no more than three locations for groups with 15 or fewer physicians.[15]

These proposals were strenuously opposed by the Medical Group Management Assn. and the American Group Practice Assn., among others. These organizations objected to the proposals because the average size of group practices is four to five physicians, and many of these groups have more than one office location. Thus, a five or 10 physician-per-office requirement would have prohibited a majority of legitimate groups from referring patients to their own group practice facilities for ancillary services. Such a requirement, these associations argued, would disqualify from the in-office ancillary services exception a substantial percentage of legitimate, fully integrated group practices, along with the few loosely organized "sham" groups the law would be attempting to reach. Congress ultimately agreed, and refrained from narrowing the group practice definition in such a way.

The final version of the Stark law abandoned the proposed physician-staffing-ratio test for group practices in favor of other definitional provisions described in this chapter. The January 1998 proposed Stark II regulations indicate that the group practice definition was designed to allow physicians in specific kinds of groups to continue to refer patients within the group practice for designated health services under certain circumstances.[16] The specific definition of "group practice" in the Stark law is set forth below.

Definition of Group Practice. The term "group practice" is defined in the Stark law as a group of two or more physicians legally organized as a partnership, professional corporation, foundation, not-for-profit corporation, faculty practice plan or similar association —

"(i) in which each physician who is a member of the group provides substantially the full range of services which the physician routinely provides, including medical care, consultation, diagnosis or treatment, through the joint use of shared office space, facilities, equipment and personnel,

(ii) for which substantially all of the services of the physicians who are members of the group are provided through the group and are billed under a billing number assigned to the group and amounts so received are treated as receipts of the group,

(iii) in which the overhead expenses of and the income from the practice are distributed in accordance with methods previously determined,

(iv) except as provided in subparagraph (B)(i), in which no physician who is a member of the group directly or indirectly receives compensation based on the volume or value of referrals by the physician,

(v) in which members of the group personally conduct no less than 75% of the physician-patient encounters of the group practice, and

(vi) which meets such other standards as the [HHS] Secretary may impose by regulation."

Legal Structures. The definition of "group practice" includes any group of two or more physicians legally organized as a partnership, professional corporation, foundation, not-for-profit corporation, faculty practice plan or similar association. Not all nonprofit groups have physicians as their original incorporators or corporate members, nor is this always required by state law. In the preamble to the final Stark I regulations, HCFA clarified that physicians don't have to legally organize, operate or control such entities to satisfy the group practice definition. As long as the entity is legally organized to include two or more physicians who have a role in providing the services of physicians, such as a physician-directed clinic organized by a hospital, it can qualify as a group practice, even if it is established, operated, and controlled by a nonphysician group or corporation.[17] The January 1998 proposed Stark II rule retains this interpretation.[18] Similarly, a group of physicians who are not legally organized, but only hold themselves out as a group, would not qualify as a group practice under the statutory definition. As a practical matter, however, any legal structure in which physician members are not full-time employees of or partners in the group practice may be problematic under the various group practice criteria.

For example, the use of the foundation-model group practice structure — a freestanding entity that bills and collects the professional and ancillary charges under its own provider number and contracts with physicians for a fee to provide the service — creates potential issues under the group practice criterion that requires the professional services provided by the group to be billed in the group's name and under its billing number. To meet this criterion, the foundation would need to be considered the group for Stark law purposes. In that event, the contracting physicians would still need to be considered "members" of the group. The contract between the foundation and the physicians also would need to satisfy the personal services exception to the Stark law (see Chapter 6). Some faculty practice plans have similar problems when the medical school directly bills and collects for the professional services instead of the faculty practice plan. Similarly, many integrated delivery systems may not qualify for group practice designation. In the preamble to the final Stark I regulations, HCFA stated that a nonprofit, hospital-affiliated corporation linked with a professional corporation, which is a common arrangement in states with corporate-practice-of-medicine prohibitions, would not be regarded as one group practice. HCFA noted, however, that physicians in the professional corporation could possibly refer lab testing to the nonprofit corporation's laboratory if the arrangement satisfied the personal services exception.[19]

The August 1995 final Stark I regulations took the position that the law requires a group practice to be organized into *one* legal entity. The January 1998 proposed Stark II regulations further clarify that HCFA believes Congress meant that a group must be one legal entity, and that Congress regarded this characteristic as a mark of a true group practice.[20] However, the proposed regulations clarify that HCFA believes a group practice is still "one legal entity" even if it is composed of owners who are individually incorporated for certain tax and pension plan purposes.[21] Despite the fact that such individual professional corporation owners in a group may be independent contractors, the January 1998 proposed Stark II regulations indicate that such persons would nevertheless be considered "members" of the group practice.[22]

Substantial Integration. To qualify as a "group practice" for purposes of the Stark law, each member of the group must provide substantially the full range of services that physicians routinely provide through the joint use of shared office space, facilities, equipment and personnel. Under this provision, office leases, equipment leases and employment agreements should be assigned to the group and be centrally administered by the group for the joint use and benefit of all members. "Clinics without walls" and other loosely organized groups may not qualify as a "group practice" under this definition if the applicable legal documents specify that office space, equipment or personnel remain under the exclusive control of certain physicians or subgroups, rather than under the group as a whole.

The August 1995 final Stark I regulations further defined the "full range of services" by adding the requirement that the physician members of the group furnish the full range of "patient care services."[23] The January 1998 proposed Stark II regulations further revise this language to include any of a physician's tasks that address the medical needs of specific patients or patients in general, or that benefit the group practice, including training of staff or performing other administrative or management tasks on behalf of the group practice.[24] However, time spent on nonpatient care services, such as teaching in a medical school or doing outside research, would not be included in the definition of "patient care services."[25]

Although the integration requirement seems to create the most discussions in connection with group practice development, the requirement is in many respects misunderstood. Although the requirement existed in the Stark I law, it has been perceived as insufficient to cover many potential "sham" arrangements. Accordingly, in the Stark II law, Congress appears to have created its own vision of an integrated group practice. Basically, multiple locations will be permitted as long as they are not the exclusive domain of the individual physicians practicing at that location. Thus, the group practice entity, rather than individual physicians, must have legal control and ultimate direction over each physician's office space, equipment and personnel.[26]

In addition, the "group practice" definition requires that substantially all of the services of group physicians be provided through the group. This requirement will be satisfied if the group practice as a whole devotes at least 75% of its practice time to patients of that group. The measure for this percentage test is time spent by group practice physicians in providing patient care or other physician tasks on behalf of the group. The January 1998 proposed Stark II regulations indicate that a physician's time spent doing work for the group is the most straightforward and least burdensome method for measuring a physician's efforts. To simplify further, a group practice can assume a physician works 40 hours per week.[27] Satisfaction of this test will require a fair degree of integration of group physicians' patient care activities. The August 1995 final Stark I regulations discuss the "substantially all" test in great detail.[28]

To illustrate how a group would determine its satisfaction of the 75% test, consider the following example. Two physician partners spend 100% of their patient care hours through the group. Four part-time physician employees spend 75% each, and one other part-time physician employee spends 25% of his time at the group practice. An independent contractor physician devotes 10%.

Two physicians at 100% = 200%

Four physicians at 75% = 300%

One physician at 25% = 25%

One physician at 10% = 10%

TOTAL: 535% ÷ 8 physicians = 67% (August 1995 final Stark I rules.).

TOTAL: 525% ÷ 7 physicians = 75% (January 1998 proposed Stark II rules.).

Under the August 1995 final Stark I regulations, the group practice would not satisfy the 75% threshold and would not be deemed a group practice. However, under the January 1998 proposed Stark II regulations, the independent contractor physician would be excluded. Thus, the group practice would satisfy the 75% threshold and would be deemed a group practice under these criteria.

Billing Requirement. A second criterion for "group practices" is that all of the services provided by members must be provided through the group and billed in the name of and under the billing number assigned to the group. Also, the amounts received must be treated as receipts of the group. The January 1998 proposed Stark II regulations clarify, however, that a single group may have more than one billing number.[29] This accommodation will assist groups that have many locations or operate in more than one state.

Once again, truly integrated medical groups need not be concerned with such a requirement because they generally bill through and in the name of the integrated group practice. However, sharing arrangements in which otherwise independent physicians come together to provide designated health services typically could not meet this requirement because each physician generally separately bills for his or her own designated health services.

As previously discussed, the foundation structure and some faculty practice plans — where the foundation or medical school bills and collects the professional services and treats such revenues as receipts of the foundation in exchange for a fixed periodic payment to a group practice or faculty practice plan — may be problematic. This is because the January 1998 proposed Stark II regulations indicate that the Stark law does not appear to permit a group to receive payments for designated health services through a separate entity that is not wholly owned by the group, such as a medical foundation that bills in its own right under its own billing number, even if the payments made to the group practice ultimately constitute group revenues.[30]

In addition, any assignment of revenues to a management company must be carefully structured to ensure that the revenues are treated as medical group revenues and the receipts are treated as receipts of the medical group, not receipts of the management company. In this regard, the January 1998 proposed Stark II regulations specifically permit a management services organization or billing agent to bill on behalf of the group's name, using the group's billing number.[31] However, compensation arrangements by several publicly traded management companies appear to assign 100% of the medical group revenues to the management company, to the extent permitted by law. The apparent purpose of such an assignment is to create a larger management company from a financial accounting standpoint. Such compensation arrangements may be problematic under the proposed Stark II regulations because in those instances, the management companies appear to be billing on their own behalf, instead of on behalf of the group practice.

Overhead Expense Allocation. A third criterion for a "group practice" is that the overhead expenses and income be distributed in accordance with methods previously determined. This criterion appears to have been included because many "group practices without walls" use "cost-center accounting" in which overhead expenses and income at each separate location are allocated to a particular physician instead of to the group as a whole.

The January 1998 proposed Stark II regulations indicate that Congress may have feared that ad hoc distribution methods would be more likely to reflect a physician's referrals. Therefore, the proposed regulations have interpreted this provision to require a group to have in place methods for distribution that were determined before the time period within which the group practice has earned the income or incurred the costs.[32] The distribution methods, however, can be determined by any party, not just the members of the group practice.[33] For example, a hospital could determine how to distribute the income from a hospital-affiliated clinic.

The proposed regulations also would require that the overhead expenses of, and the income from, the group practice be distributed according to methods that demonstrate that the group practice is a unified business. Specifically, the distribution methods must reflect centralized decisionmaking, a pooling of expenses and revenues, and a distribution system that is not based on each satellite office operating as if it were a separate enterprise.[34]

A typical compensation methodology used by many fully integrated group practices and by generic "group practices without walls" is as follows: each physician's compensation is equal to that physician's individual professional service fee revenues, including capitated revenues associated with patients choosing that physician as his or her primary care physician, reduced by the overhead expenses attributable directly to that physician, and reduced further by that physician's pro-rata share of the group's common overhead expenses. Designated health service revenues are either (a) divided on a pro-rata basis among all of the physicians, (b) used to defray the group's common overhead expenses, (c) used for contributions to the group practice's pension or profit-sharing plan, (d) divided only among the primary care physicians, a method used sometimes by multispecialty groups as an incentive for primary care physicians to join the group, and/or (e) divided on an unequal percentage basis among the physicians in accordance with an allocation arrangement agreed to in advance. Each of these methodologies appears to be acceptable under the proposed Stark II rules.

The permissibility of several commonly employed compensation methodologies is uncertain under the Stark law. Some groups have allocated designated health service revenues based upon each physician's historical volume of referrals for designated health services. Such allocations should be determined in advance and not varied during the course of the year. Other groups revise the allocation formula annually based upon referral patterns for designated health services in the past year. Recent discussions with HHS staff indicate a willingness to consider annual redetermination clauses in compensation arrangements. However, tying such annual redetermination clauses to a physician's referral patterns for designated health services during the preceding year probably is still unacceptable to the OIG.

One additional compensation issue needs to be addressed. Many "group practices without walls" have placed a percentage, such as 5%, 10%, 20% or more, of all group practice revenues in a separate bonus pool to be redistributed as the group practice's board deems appropriate. Redistribution pools often serve several purposes. To the extent a multispecialty group practice is being developed and the redistribution pool is allocated pro rata among all of the physicians, or in substantial part to the primary care physicians, this arrangement allows for a redistribution of income from higher-earning physicians to lower-earning physicians. This has particular importance in multispecialty groups headed by specialists who want to create incentives for primary care physicians to join the group practice. The use of redistribution pools appears to be consistent with the Stark law because it creates an element of financial integration among the physicians of the group practice. However, the proposed Stark II regulations appear to disfavor such an approach because each physician's compensation is not "previously determined." The better argument may be, however, that the creation of a bonus pool using objective criteria for distributions, determined in advance, is acceptable.

Even if a group practice meets the integration criteria for Stark law purposes, however, it may not necessarily be financially integrated from an antitrust perspective. Accordingly, this redistribution pool concept has been recommended by antitrust lawyers who have concerns that some group practices may not create sufficient financial risk among all members of the group to protect the group from price-fixing and market-allocation challenges under the antitrust laws. Thus, for example, a 10% redistribution pool appears to create adequate financial integration to avoid a claim that the group practice has engaged in unlawful price fixing in violation of antitrust laws.

Compensation Methodology. The fourth criterion for "group practices" is that no member of the group can be compensated directly or indirectly on the basis of his or her volume or value of referrals. The term "referral(s)" is limited in the Stark II proposed regulations to referrals for designated health services.

Thus, the Stark law explicitly permits a group practice to pay its physician members a productivity bonus based on services personally performed by the physician and services incident to those personally performed services, if the bonus is not directly related to the volume or value of referrals made by such physician. Bonuses based upon referrals for services that are incident to a physician's services appear to be appropriate under the Stark law, but the group practice may not pay bonuses based on the same physician's referrals for designated health services to other physicians within the group practice. As a practical matter, this criterion would appear to prohibit "incentive compensation" arrangements where any portion of the physician's pay is based on the amount of revenue generated by ancillary services ordered by the physician.

The January 1998 proposed Stark II regulations make clear that this prohibition against incentive compensation based upon the volume or value of a doctor's own referrals includes "self-referrals" where the physician directly provides or supervises the designated health service.[35] Many commentators had believed that designated health services personally provided by the referring physician were protected under the Stark law because the productivity-bonus clause appeared to permit such a methodology. The proposed Stark II regulations state that "the 'volume or value' standard precludes a group practice from paying physician members for each referral [of designated health services] they personally make or based on the value of the referred services."[36] However, the proposed regulations also make clear that a group practice could, if it so desired, compensate its members based upon the volume or value of referrals for designated health services for non-Medicare and non-Medicaid patients.[37] In such cases, however, the group practice must separately account for revenues and distributions relating to referrals for designated health services for Medicare or Medicaid patients. Moreover, if payments for non-Medicare or non-Medicaid patient referrals appear to be inordinately high or otherwise inconsistent with fair market value, the OIG still could determine that such compensation may actually reflect additional compensation for Medicare and Medicaid referrals.[38]

The Stark law also provides that a member of a group may be paid a share of the overall profits of the group.[39] In the case of overall profits, the January 1998 proposed Stark II regulations make clear that only profits from Medicare and Medicaid designated health service referrals are considered inappropriate to compensate the referring physician. A group practice may distribute profits from services other than designated health services provided to Medicare and Medicaid patients in any way the group practice sees fit, including without limitation, splitting such profits evenly or distributing them based on the value of such other referrals, according to investment in the group practice, seniority, hours spent devoted to the group practice, etc.[40]

With respect to Medicare and Medicaid designated health service referral profits, however, the proposed Stark II regulations suggest that a referring physician can receive a portion of the group practice's overall pooled revenues only if the group practice does not share these profits in a manner that relates directly to who made the referrals to the group practice. Thus, these profits can be shared according to the mechanisms described in the preceding paragraph as long as such payments do not include payments based directly on the number or value of the Medicare or Medicaid designated health service referrals made by a physician member of the group practice, including any self-referrals.[41]

In addition, "overall profits" are described in the proposed regulations as all of a group practice's profits from Medicare and Medicaid designated health service referrals, even if the group is located in two different states or has many different locations in one state. The proposed regulations indicate that "overall profits" cannot be limited to a particular specialty or subspecialty portion of the group practice. The narrower the pooling of profits, the more likely it will be that a physician member would be considered receiving compensation for his or her own referrals of Medicare and Medicaid designated health services.[42]

The January 1998 proposed Stark II regulations also clarify that the productivity bonus a physician member of a group practice can receive for personally performed or incident-to personally performed Medicare and Medicaid designated health services is limited to such services that result from the referral from a physician other than one performing or supervising the service.[43] A physician in that situation is not being compensated based upon his or her own referrals.

Full-Time Status. The fifth criterion for "group practices" is that the physician members of the group must personally conduct no less than 75% of the physician-patient encounters of the group. While this 75% requirement is less than a model of clarity, it appears intended to prohibit a substantial amount of services for which the group bills, including designated health services, from being provided by nongroup members. It also provides a bright-line rule that will enable regulators to differentiate between legitimate group practices and those with "member" owners or investors who are members in name, but who treat few, if any, patients. In such a prohibited scenario, nonmember physician contractors could be hired to treat most of the group practice's patients, while the "outside" physician owners of the group practice could limit their involvement in the group practice to the referral of Medicare and Medicaid designated health services to the group practice.[44]

The Stark I proposed regulations would have required that 85% of all revenues, rather than patient encounters, be generated by the physician members of the group.[45] However, this criterion would have created problems where a group had a part-time independent-contractor relationship with certain physician specialists that provide very high-cost services like cardiovascular surgery or transplants. Under Stark I, the revenue test might have resulted in a large number of small group practices not meeting this definition. The Stark law's patient-encounter test appears to be directed at resolving the medical group integration issue because the physician members must provide 75% of the group practice's patient encounters.

The final Stark I regulations define group practice members as physician partners, and full-time and part-time physician contractors and employees during the time they furnish services to patients of the group that are furnished through the group and are billed in the group's name.[46] While this interpretation would help group practices with independent contractors more easily satisfy the 75% requirement, it would render the encounter requirement superfluous.

Thus, the January 1998 proposed Stark II regulations exclude independent contractors from the definition of a "member" in a group practice. However, included as members would be not only physician partners, but also physicians with any other form of ownership in the group practice. In addition, any administrative services furnished on behalf of a group practice by a physician member would be included as physician member time.[47] In this regard, a group practice should note, however, that an independent-contractor physician cannot supervise the provision of a Medicare or Medicaid designated health service on behalf of a group practice, because that physician contractor would not be considered a physician member of the group practice.

The Stark law is silent on the time frame to be used for calculating the patient-encounter percentage. Patient encounters could be measured on a daily, weekly, monthly, quarterly or annual basis, or could be determined based upon the patient encounters in the prior year for established medical groups.

Calculating patient encounters on a daily basis would seem to cause significant problems. That's because it would effectively prohibit a medical group from bringing on part-time physicians for vacation or illness coverage, because all referrals for designated health services on those days likely would be found to violate the law. On the other hand, to make calculations on an annual basis also may not be reasonable or practical because a medical group would not know if it is meeting the patient-encounter requirement until the end of the year, except that established medical groups could base their patient encounter calculation on the prior year.

Thus, the August 1995 final Stark I rules require a group practice to submit annually a written statement to its carrier attesting that, during the most recent 12-month period, 75% of the total patient care services of the group practice members were furnished through the group practice, were billed under a billing number assigned to the group practice, and the amounts so received were treated as receipts of the group practice.[48] Moreover, a newly formed group practice would need to attest that it expects to meet the 75% standard during the next 12-month period, and that the group practice will take measures to ensure that the standard is met.[49] Finally, if a newly formed group practice does not meet the 75% standard, any Medicare payments made to the group practice that were conditioned on the group practice meeting the standard would be considered overpayments, and the Stark law would require repayment to Medicare, in addition to other penalties described in the next chapter.[50] Whatever 12-month period a group practice chooses must be adhered to in the future, and the attestation must be signed by an authorized representative of the group practice.[51]

Congress did not enact specific provisions banning self-referrals to "clinics without walls" and other loosely integrated group practices. However, the definition of "group practice" in the Stark law poses compliance problems for groups whose members do not share office space, equipment and personnel, or that compensate their physicians on any productivity basis that takes into account designated health service revenues generated by the physicians. Such problems will exist with respect to legitimate established groups as well.

Group Practice Formation Issues

The following is a step-by-step analysis of the significant issues that need to be addressed and resolved in connection with the formation of a group practice in the post-Stark law era.

Reason to Integrate. Whenever a physician or group of physicians indicates a desire to integrate or reorganize into a medical group, the first step is to have what is usually characterized as a preorganizational meeting. Attendance at this meeting should include a group of four to six of the leading physicians, or all of the physicians, if the group in formation is approximately six physicians or less. At this meeting the first order of business, after introductions, is to get a working understanding as to why this particular group of physicians has decided to come together to form a group. Typically, there are several different reasons put forth by the various physicians.

The most common reason expressed is the belief that to maintain or increase market share, these physicians need to consolidate into larger entities to capture managed care contracts and, in particular, capitated contracts. This reason seems to dominate, whether the group will be comprised entirely of primary care physicians, a multispecialty group or a single-specialty group.

Another factor that drives group formation, especially among single-specialty groups, is the desire to consolidate into a group of four to eight physicians to address scheduling, on-call and coverage issues. Many solo-practice specialists have found difficulties in obtaining coverage that have been exacerbated by the continued penetration of managed care contracts and the requirements on participating providers to offer specified levels of coverage in the evenings and on weekends. Specialists are also concerned that managed care contracting has caused significant reductions in referrals from primary care physicians. These specialists are looking to create multispecialty group practices with a large number of primary care physicians and only a few specialists to recapture or retain a significant referral base for their particular specialties. In addition, most physicians have considered the formation of a group practice to capture ancillary service revenue streams that were previously referred to third parties.

Finally, an important reason for the formation of primary care groups has been the belief that large primary care groups can capture significant capitated patient lives, resulting in increased compensation. These physicians believe that their position as "second cousins" to specialists is coming to an end and that specialists are going to become less important in the new health care paradigm. Basically, these physicians feel that primary care physicians will become the access and control points for the entire health care delivery system, resulting in increased stature and compensation for them.

Organizational Structure. Assuming that the objectives of the physicians cannot be met through other less intrusive means than through the formation of a group, such as through a single-specialty independent practice association, shared-facility arrangement or other joint venture, the next step is to generally decide upon the organizational structure of the new medical group. While various structures may be technically possible, such as partnerships, unincorporated associations, etc., the recommended structure under the Stark law is the professional medical corporation or in some states professional associations, or, where permitted, a limited liability company. This structure would appear to offer the best opportunity to satisfy the Stark law definition of "group practice."

Under a professional corporation structure, the medical group would be governed by a board of directors elected by the shareholders. The board also typically appoints the corporate officers, although in some groups, the shareholders elect the corporate officers. Each physician would become a full-time employee of the medical group. In this regard, each physician would sell or transfer for stock all or substantially all of his or her assets to the new medical group, and assign all of his or her space and equipment leases to the medical group. The physicians would enter into a shareholder agreement in which each physician would agree to restrict the sale or transfer of his or her stock in the medical group, permit the repurchase of that stock upon certain enumerated events, and agree to certain nonsolicitation and restrictive covenants on competing with the medical group. Finally, each physician's existing pension plan would need to be frozen or terminated, and a new pension plan established for the group. Working capital to finance the start-up costs also would need to be borrowed from a third party or contributed by each of the physicians.

By the end of the preorganization meeting, most physicians understand the basic Stark law issues. Harder to convey is an understanding that resolving these issues in a group practice setting is difficult, especially where each person previously made his or her own decisions without second guessing from any other person.

Governance Issues. In forming new medical groups, governance issues are typically significant because most physicians previously were their own bosses and have had no prior experience delegating authority to others. For Stark law purposes, centralized management is an important factor to satisfy the group practice criteria.

The first issue is typically the number of members to be elected to the board of directors. The answer is a function of the size of the group. If the group has eight or fewer physicians, permitting all of them to serve on the board usually makes sense. For larger medical groups, five or seven directors is typically appropriate. An odd number of directors is recommended to avoid potential deadlocks.

It is also advisable to create a staggered board, meaning that one-half or one-third of the directors are elected in any one year, and each director serves for a two- or three-year term. Unless contrary reasons are indicated, re-election of directors for a definite number of successive terms also is typical.

With smaller groups, supermajority voting for certain significant actions is typically required to protect the interests of physicians who have minority ownership interests in the new medical group. In this regard, a requirement of supermajority attendance at meetings in which action will be taken is sometimes prudent.

One issue that deserves special mention is the composition of the board of directors for multispecialty groups. With the explosion of managed care, a growing number of payers want to see multispecialty group boards in which primary care physicians have majority representation. Accordingly, it is strongly recommended that a majority of the directors be comprised of family practice, general practice, internal medicine or pediatric physicians. On occasion, it is advisable that the remaining board seats be delegated exclusively for specialists.

Another issue is the removal of directors. Typically, a board member can be removed for cause by a majority of the board, or without cause by either two-thirds of the board (other than the board member being removed) or two-thirds of the shareholders. Because the officers typically serve at the pleasure of the board, they may be removed with or without cause by a majority of the board or by two-thirds of the shareholders.

The shareholders of the medical group typically reserve certain actions for themselves, such as the approval of any amendments to the governing documents like articles of incorporation and bylaws, the termination of any physician owner/employee, or the approval or ratification of certain significant strategies and financial decisions such as annual operating and capital budgets or marketing or strategic plans.

Ownership Issues. When appropriate, the fairest division of ownership is where each physician owns an equal share of the new medical group. However, this ownership interest must be restricted through the execution of a shareholders' agreement among the shareholders of the medical group. One of the important issues that should be addressed in the shareholders' agreement is the valuation of a physician's stock in the medical group in the event that the physician retires, dies, becomes totally disabled, voluntarily or involuntarily withdraws as an employee of the medical group, or upon any other relevant repurchase event. Typically, the valuation formulas differ depending upon the type of event. In addition, the shareholders' agreement typically restricts any transfer of ownership to a third party without the prior consent of the board of directors of the medical group.

The shareholders' agreement also may set forth criteria for determining when and how many new physicians will be added to the medical group in the future. The agreement also may include standards these physicians will need to meet, a buy-in formula, and how the buy-in will dilute any existing physician interests in the medical group.

Another issue to be addressed in the shareholders' agreement is whether to include a covenant not to compete and/or other restrictive covenants to prevent physicians who leave the group practice from competing with the group. The inclusion of the covenant not to compete serves two purposes. First, it helps to create a cohesive group of physicians practicing together for a common goal. Second, from a Stark law perspective, a covenant helps to demonstrate a degree of integration that would be looked upon favorably by the OIG.

Transfer of Assets. The consolidation of previously separate physician practices into one new medical group raises a number of legal issues regarding the transfer of assets and assignment of liabilities from the individual physician practices to the new group practice. The successful completion of this task is also an important factor from a Stark law perspective. First and foremost is the ability to transfer any and all assets on a tax-free basis to the extent possible.

Also, for Stark law purposes, it is important that the physicians' tangible assets be transferred to the new medical group. Typically, this transfer represents a physician's capital contribution to the new medical group. The physician makes this contribution by receiving stock in the medical group in exchange for these assets. Because most physicians have assets of different values, some physicians typically would receive an installment note for a portion of his or her assets so that all physicians will have an equal ownership interest in the new medical group. Another methodology would be to require physicians with less valuable assets to contribute cash or services in addition to the assets so their capital contributions to the new medical group will equal those of all the other physicians.

In addition to the physicians' assets, their medical office, equipment lease and managed care contracts should be assigned to and assumed by the new medical group as soon as reasonably possible. As many of the assignments as possible should be completed prior to the commencement of operation of the new medical group. However, lessors and landlords on occasion have been hesitant or unwilling to consent to such transfers. Thus, some assignments typically require a transition period and a subleasing arrangement during the first six to 12 months of a new medical group's existence. If the landlord refuses to consent to an assignment or even a sublease, the group should agree to indemnify the physician who is liable on the lease.

One additional issue to be addressed is the determination of which nonphysician employees of the independent physician practices will be offered the opportunity to continue employment with the new medical group. This is often a personal issue among the physicians, who each want his or her own nonphysician employees to continue to have a job. If the group is large enough, the best approach is for the physicians to hire an administrator to determine the proper level of full-time, nonphysician personnel who will be needed and make the final determination of which such personnel will be hired, based upon experience and need. If a physician demands that a particular person be employed in his or her office, such a request can be granted if that physician understands that any additional costs associated with that extra employee will be the sole responsibility of that physician; that is, the physician's compensation will be diminished.

Physician Employment. Each physician owner of the new medical group also needs to become a full-time employee of the group and thereby enter into an employment agreement with the group. An initial term of three to five years is typical. However, many new group practices include a six- to 12-month "honeymoon" period during which any physician who becomes part of the group may leave and receive a return of his or her practice assets if the new group practice is "not what the doctor ordered." In addition to a replication of the covenant not to compete and other restrictive covenants contained in the shareholders' agreement, a physician employment agreement typically contains (a) representations of the physicians' status and ability to practice medicine, (b) the professional and administrative service requirements of each physician, and (c) the events that may lead to the termination of each physician.

Most important are the compensation provisions contained in the employment agreement. Some new medical groups utilize compensation formulas as simple as a fixed salary for each physician, plus a bonus at the end of the year to be determined by the board of directors. As previously discussed, the proposed Stark II regulations suggest that bonuses paid in this manner may violate the Stark law. On the other hand, most new medical groups utilize more sophisticated compensation plans. Most typically have a productivity-based compensation formula which, as discussed previously in this chapter, may raise Stark law issues. In connection with compensation issues, some medical groups also provide for severance payments upon the termination or withdrawal of a physician from the medical group for reasons other than good cause.

In addition to compensation, employee welfare, fringe and retirement benefits also need to be addressed. Not only must the separate malpractice policies of the various physicians be merged, but group health, disability, life insurance, workers' compensation and other benefits issues also must be addressed. In this regard, the single biggest issue is often the freezing or termination of each physician's existing qualified pension or profit-sharing plan, and the design of a new medical group pension plan that addresses the needs and concerns of all physicians in the group. These concerns are more easily addressed when the new medical group is comprised of all primary care physicians or is a single-specialty group. This is because each member's compensation level in such groups typically is comparable. However, in multispecialty groups, the large disparity of incomes among the physicians often require sophisticated pension and profit-sharing advice to meet the needs and concerns of both the lower- and higher-earning physicians.

Affiliated Property Companies. Some group practices have arrangements with companies that are owned by members of the group and that lease facilities or equipment to the group. In some groups, such companies serve as the vehicle for creating retirement income for equity partners in the group practice. Such arrangements could present self-referral problems. That's because the group practice physicians who own the company have a financial relationship with the company. In addition, payments by the group to the property company for renting the equipment creates a compensation arrangement. However, in the preamble to the final Stark I regulations, HCFA stated that it did not view group practice physicians' financial relationships with an affiliated property company as a relationship with an entity furnishing clinical laboratory services. In such arrangements, the financial relationships are with an entity that only rents equipment to the group practice.[52] As a result, relationships with affiliated property companies should not affect the group physicians' ability to refer to the group's laboratory, provided the arrangement otherwise qualifies for the in-office ancillary services exception.

Conclusion

The last portion of this chapter has attempted to set forth some of the significant issues that must be addressed and resolved when forming a new medical group. Only by engaging a qualified consultant or lawyer can the many issues that need to be addressed by new medical groups be resolved in a reasonable manner. In this regard, numerous filings with state and federal agencies also must be made.

Accordingly, care should be taken to engage a person who has significant experience in addressing these issues with other medical groups, and who has a personality that is consistent with the personalities of the physicians in the group practice. The process of forming a new medical group typically takes from six to 12 months and will require many meetings with the consultant or lawyer. Therefore, this "intangible" relationship between the consultant or lawyer and the physicians forming the new medical group is very important to the orderly development of, and ultimately to the successful formation of, the new medical group.

Endnotes

[1] 42 U.S.C. Sec. 1395nn(b)(1)

[2] 42 CFR Sec. 411.355(a)

[3] 63 *Fed. Reg.* 1659, 1665, Jan. 9, 1998.

[4] 63 *Fed. Reg.* 1659, 1721.

[5] 42 U.S.C. Sec. 1395nn(h)(5)(A)

[6] 63 *Fed. Reg.* 1659, 1695.

[7] Please see Chapter 3 for another interpretation of the physicians' services exception.

[8] Sec. 9302 of H.R. 3600 adopted by the House Ways and Means Committee and included in the House Majority Leader's 1994 health reform bill (not enacted).

[9] 60 *Fed. Reg.* 41914, 41964, Aug. 14, 1995.

[10] 42 CFR Sec. 351

[11] 63 *Fed. Reg.* 1659, 1684.

[12] 63 *Fed. Reg.* 1659, 1685.

[13] 63 *Fed. Reg.* 1659, 1695-1696.

[14] 63 *Fed. Reg.* 1659, 1696.

[15] See, e.g., 1993 House Ways and Means Committee proposed amendment and public hearing related thereto.

[16] 63 *Fed. Reg.* 1659, 1687.

[17] 60 *Fed. Reg.* 41914, 41937.

[18] 63 *Fed. Reg.* 1659, 1687.

[19] 60 *Fed. Reg.* 41914, 41936.

[20] 63 *Fed. Reg.* 1659, 1687.

[21] 63 *Fed. Reg.* 1659, 1721.

[22] 63 *Fed. Reg.* 1659, 1687.

[23] 42 CFR Sec. 411.351.

[24] 63 *Fed. Reg.* 1659, 1722.

[25] 63 *Fed. Reg.* 1659, 1688.

[26] Proposals contained in some of the health care reform legislation considered in 1994 and adopted by the House Ways and Means Committee would have imposed additional requirements on group practices to promote further integration, such as requiring that all equipment used in delivering designated health services be owned or leased exclusively by the group. Other proposals adopted in 1994 by the House Ways and Means Committee to promote group practice integration included a prohibition on group practice physicians entering into separate managed care contracts and a requirement that all group practices have a governing body responsible for employment and compensation decisions. See Sec. 9303 of H.R. 3600 adopted by the House Ways and Means Committee and included in the House Majority Leader's 1994 health reform bill (not enacted).

[27] 63 *Fed. Reg.* 1659, 1689.

[28] 60 *Fed. Reg.* 41914, 41931-41933.

[29] 63 *Fed. Reg.* 1659, 1689.

[30] Id.

[31] Id.

[32] 63 *Fed. Reg.* 1659, 1721.

[33] 63 *Fed. Reg.* 1659, 1690.

[34] 63 *Fed. Reg.* 1659, 1721.

[35] Id.

[36] 63 *Fed. Reg.* 1659, 1690.

[37] Id.

[38] 63 *Fed. Reg.* 1659, 1690.

[39] 42 U.S.C. Sec. 1395nn(h)(4)(B)(i)

[40] 63 *Fed. Reg.* 1659, 1690.

[41] 63 *Fed. Reg.* 1659, 1721.

[42] 63 *Fed. Reg.* 1659, 1691.

[43] 63 *Fed. Reg.* 1659, 1721.

[44] 63 *Fed. Reg.* 1659, 1689.

[45] See e.g., 57 *Fed. Reg.* 8588, 8602, March 11, 1992 (to be codified at 42 CFR pt. 411).

[46] 42 CFR Sec. 411.351.

[47] 63 *Fed. Reg.* 1659, 1689.

[48] 42 CFR Sec. 411.360(a).

[49] 42 CFR Sec. 411.360(b)(1).

[50] 42 CFR Sec. 411.360(b)(2).

[51] 42 CFR Sec. 411.360(c) and (d).

[52] 60 *Fed. Reg.* 41914, 41968.

CHAPTER 8

Sanctions for Violations Of the Self-Referral Prohibitions

The Stark law establishes a number of sanctions for violations of its provisions. These sanctions range from denial of payment, required refunds to patients, civil monetary penalties of up to $15,000 for each violation, exclusion from further participation in the Medicare and Medicaid programs, civil money penalties of up to $100,000 for "sham" arrangements, and civil money penalties of up to $10,000 for each day in which an entity fails to report required information.[1] The August 1995 final Stark I rules incorporated this provision into the regulations,[2] and the January 1998 proposed Stark II rules retain those provisions.[3] This chapter describes the potential liabilities and sanctions that may result from violations of the Stark law.

Payment Penalties

The Stark law provides that no payment may be made by Medicare, or by the federal government for its portion of Medicaid payment, for a designated health service that is provided as a result of a prohibited referral, such as when an entity presents or causes to be presented a claim for that designated health service furnished through a prohibited referral.[4] The August 1995 final rule incorporated this provision as it relates to clinical laboratory services into the regulations,[5] and the January 1998 proposed rules would extend the ban to other designated health services.[6] Of course, the denial of payment assumes that an applicable exception to the Stark law, as described elsewhere in this book, does not apply.

In addition, if either the physician or the entity collects any amounts that were billed in violation of the Stark law, that person or entity will be liable for, and be required to refund on a timely basis, any amounts collected from an individual or third party.[7]

Improper Claims

Any person that presents or causes to be presented a bill or claim for a service that the person knows or should know is for a designated health service provided as a result of a prohibited referral in violation of the Stark law will be subject to a civil money penalty of up to $15,000 for each such claim.[8] In addition to the monetary penalty, exclusion from the Medicare program also may be initiated. A rule published by the HHS Office of Inspector General addresses this civil money penalty.[9]

Circumvention Schemes

Congress is aware that some physicians and suppliers may attempt to circumvent the provisions of the Stark law. For this reason, the Stark law imposes civil monetary penalties of up to $100,000 for any arrangement or scheme that the physician or entity knows or should know has a principal purpose of assuring referrals by the physician to the particular entity which, if the physician directly made referrals to the entity, would violate the Stark law.[10] In addition, the Stark law also imposes exclusion from the Medicare program as an additional penalty for entering into a circumvention scheme. A rule published by the OIG addresses this civil money penalty.[11]

Failure to Report Information

Any physician or entity that fails to meet the reporting requirements of the Stark law is subject to a civil money penalty of up to $10,000 for each day that the required reporting does not occur, as well as possible exclusion from the Medicare program.[12] However, the penalty will not commence until the group practice is given at least 30 days from the date the carrier or intermediary asks the group practice to provide the initial information.[13] Thereafter, the group practice must report annually any changes that occurred during the preceding 12-month period. The $10,000 penalty will commence on the day following the applicable deadline established by the carrier or intermediary.[14]

Initiation of Exclusion or Civil Monetary Penalty Proceeding

The decision to initiate a proceeding to impose a civil money penalty or assessment, or to seek exclusion from the Medicare program, may only be made by HHS in accordance with procedures agreed upon by the U.S. Attorney General. An action may not be initiated for any claim, request for payment or other occurrence later than six years after the date the claim was presented, the request for payment was made, or the occurrence took place.[15]

The OIG has indicated that the imposition of a civil monetary penalty or assessment is not a prerequisite to being excluded from the Medicare program. Rather, exclusion is an alternative remedy to be used instead of or in conjunction with a civil money penalty, assessment or criminal proceeding, depending upon the circumstances.[16] In determining the length of an exclusion imposed for a circumvention scheme, the OIG will consider the following factors: (1) the nature and circumstances surrounding the actions that are the basis for liability, including the period of time over which the acts occurred, the number of acts, any evidence of a pattern, and the amount claimed; (2) the degree of culpability; (3) the individual's or entity's prior criminal, civil or administrative sanction record (the lack of any prior record is to be considered neutral); and (4) such other matters as justice may require.[17]

Even though the imposition of a civil money penalty is not a predicate to OIG imposing a Medicare exclusion, OIG has indicated that, if a person or entity successfully defends against the imposition of a civil monetary penalty, OIG would not then impose a Medicare exclusion sanction based on the conduct at issue in the civil money penalty case.[18]

Generally, HHS will not make a final determination that is adverse to any person or entity until that person or entity has been given written notice of the allegations and an opportunity for a determination to be made on the record at a hearing. At the hearing, the person is entitled to be represented by counsel, and to present and cross-examine witnesses.[19]

Any person or entity will be stopped from denying the essential facts leading to an exclusion or civil money penalty if the facts are a part of a criminal offense for which the person or entity has been convicted of or pleaded guilty to.[20]

State Exclusion

An exclusion order will apply both to the Medicare and Medicaid programs. OIG may only exclude an individual or entity from Medicare. Then OIG must direct each state agency administering the Medicaid program to exclude the individual or entity for the same period.[21] In the case of an individual or entity not eligible to participate in Medicare, the exclusion will still be effective on the date and for the period established by OIG.

No payment will be made by Medicare or Medicaid for any item or service furnished on or after the effective date of the exclusion.[22] In addition, an excluded individual or entity may not take assignment of an enrollee's claim on or after the effective date of the exclusion.

Unless HHS determines that the health and safety of beneficiaries warrants immediate exclusion, Medicare payment can continue for up to 30 days after the effective date of an exclusion for either (1) inpatient institutional services furnished to an individual who is admitted to an excluded institution before the date of the exclusion, and (2) home health services and hospice care furnished under a plan of care established before the effective date of the exclusion.[23]

In addition, payment may be made under the Medicare or Medicaid programs for certain emergency items and services furnished by an excluded individual or entity during the period of the exclusion. However, claims for these items or services must be accompanied by a sworn statement of the person furnishing the items or services specifying the nature of the emergency, and why the items or services could not have been furnished by an individual or entity eligible to furnish or order such items or services.[24] That statement will not apply to a claim for emergency items or services provided by an excluded individual who, through an employment, contractual or other arrangement, routinely provides emergency health care items or services.

Notice Procedure

If OIG proposes to exclude an individual or entity, OIG will send notice of its intent and the basis of the proposed exclusion. Within 30 days of receiving the written notice, the affected individual or entity may submit documentary evidence and a written argument against the proposed action, and a written request to present evidence and argue orally to OIG.[25]

If OIG determines that exclusion is warranted after considering the information received, it will send written notice to the affected individual that the exclusion will be effective 20 days from the date of the written notice. The notice also will explain the basis for and length of the exclusion, the factors considered in setting its length, the effect of the exclusion, the earliest date by which OIG will accept a request for reinstatement, and the appeal rights available.[26]

The affected individual has 60 days to file a written request for a hearing. The request must set forth the specific issues or statements in the notice with which the individual or entity disagrees, the basis for that disagreement, the defenses intended to be relied on, any reasons why the proposed length of exclusion should be modified, and any reasons why the health and safety of Medicare and Medicaid beneficiaries does not warrant the exclusion going into effect prior to completion of a proceeding before an HHS administrative law judge.[27]

If the individual or entity does not make a written request within 60 days, the OIG's determination will be final, and notice will be sent. If the individual timely requests a hearing and OIG determines the health and safety of Medicare and Medicaid beneficiaries does not warrant the exclusion going into effect prior to completion of an administrative hearing, the exclusion will not go into effect unless an ALJ upholds the decision of the OIG to exclude.[28] If, however, the health and safety of Medicare and Medicaid beneficiaries may be at risk, the exclusion will take effect prior to completion of the administrative proceeding.

Reinstatement

Excluded individuals or entities may submit to the OIG an early written request for reinstatement, but only after the date specified in the notice of exclusion. This process does not apply if the excluded entity can demonstrate that (a) it has reduced to below 5% the ownership or controlling interest of the individual whose conviction or civil monetary penalty was the basis for the entity's exclusion, and the individual is no longer an officer, director, agent or managing director of the entity; or (b) it has been reinstated into the Medicare program retroactively because its conviction has been reversed or vacated on appeal.[29]

Burden of Proof

The ALJ will conduct a hearing on the record to determine whether the individual or entity should be excluded from Medicare and/or be subject to civil monetary penalties.[30]

The individual or entity bears the burden of presenting affirmative defenses and any mitigating circumstances. The OIG bears the burden of proof with respect to all other issues. The burden of persuasion will be judged by a preponderance of the evidence.[31] The hearing will be open to the public unless otherwise ordered by the ALJ for good cause.

Unless the ALJ permits written testimony, testimony at the hearing will be given orally by witnesses under oath.[32] The ALJ will exercise reasonable control over the mode and order of interrogating witnesses and the presenting of evidence. However, the parties will be entitled to cross-examination as may be required for a full and true disclosure of the facts. In this regard, the ALJ may exclude witnesses so they cannot hear the testimony of other witnesses.

The ALJ will determine the admissibility of evidence and, while not bound by the federal rules of evidence, may apply them where appropriate to exclude unreliable evidence.[33] The hearing will be recorded and transcribed. The ALJ will issue an initial decision based only on the written and oral evidence submitted at the hearing, and the decision will contain findings of fact and conclusions of law.[34]

The ALJ's decision may be appealed to HHS' Departmental Appeals Board by filing a notice of appeal within 30 days of the issuance of the initial decision.[35] There is no right to appear personally before the Appeals Board. The Appeals Board may decline to review the case, or may affirm, increase, reduce, reverse or remand any penalty, assessment or exclusion determined by the ALJ. The Appeals Board's standard of review on a disputed fact is whether the initial decision is supported by substantial evidence on the whole record.

Court Review

Any person or entity that has received a final determination from the ALJ or the Appeals Board imposing a civil money penalty and/or exclusion from the Medicare program may obtain a review of that determination in the U.S. Court of Appeals for the circuit in which the person resides, or in which the claim was presented, by filing in that court a written petition requesting that the determination be modified or set aside.[36] A petition for review must be filed within 60 days following the date the person is notified of the adverse determination.

Upon such a filing, the appeals court will have the power to affirm, modify, remand for further consideration, or set aside, in whole or in part, the decision of the administrative agency.[37] Nevertheless, the factual findings of the ALJ, as affirmed by the Appeals Board, if supported by substantial evidence on the record considered as a whole, will be conclusive with respect to the accuracy of those factual findings. Either party may request in writing to submit additional evidence, and such evidence will be considered if the party requesting the consideration of the additional evidence demonstrates that it is material, and that the failure to submit it in the hearing before the ALJ was for reasonable cause.

Settlements; Recovery of Penalties; Notifications

Settlements. Civil monetary penalties and assessments may be compromised and settled by HHS when appropriate.[38] In addition, the OIG has the authority to grant or deny a request from a state Medicaid program that an exclusion from that program be waived for an individual or entity. Such a request will only be considered if the individual or entity is the sole community physician or the sole source of essential specialized services in a community.[39] If the basis for the waiver ceases to exist, the waiver will be rescinded. Moreover, even if a waiver is granted, it applies only to the Medicaid program that requested the waiver. The decision to grant, deny or rescind the waiver is not subject to administrative or judicial review.

Recovery of Penalties. HHS may also bring a civil action in the name of the United States to recover any amounts assessed by HHS under the Stark law.[40] All amounts recovered arising from a claim under the Medicaid program will be divided between the state and the federal government. The state's proportion of the recovery will equal its proportion of contribution to the Medicaid program. The other portion of any recovery under a Medicaid claim and all amounts recovered with respect to Medicare claims will be deposited as miscellaneous receipts of the U.S. Treasury.

Notifications. If the person or entity does not appeal HHS' decision within 60 days of receiving the notice of an assessment or exclusion, HHS' determination becomes final.[41] After a final adverse determination against an individual or entity, HHS will promptly notify each appropriate state agency of the facts and circumstances of each exclusion, and the period for which the state agency must exclude the individual or entity.[42] In addition, HHS will promptly notify appropriate state and local agencies responsible for the licensing or certification of an excluded individual or entity of the facts and circumstances surrounding the exclusion. HHS also will give notice of the exclusion and its effective date to the public, beneficiaries, other appropriate agencies such as state Medicaid fraud control units, peer review organizations, hospitals, medical societies, professional organizations, HMOs and other affected agencies and organizations.[43]

Timing of Sanctions

It is clear that the Stark law contains many ambiguities that must be resolved through reasoned court decisions. Until final regulations resolve the numerous ambiguities contained in the Stark law, HHS has indicated a concern about imposing sanctions with respect to any ambiguous provisions. Accordingly, the parties to many transactions that raise issues under the ambiguous provisions of the Stark law are moving forward, believing that their interpretations of these provisions are reasonable and will ultimately be validated through the regulations. The parties to such transactions, however, generally include buy-out or "blow-up" provisions in their contracts so that these transactions may be easily unwound if final Stark II regulations indicate that the ongoing activity would be prohibited.

Parties must be careful, however, to distinguish between ambiguous provisions and aspects of the Stark law that are clear from the law or Stark I final regulations. As noted previously, the Stark law prohibits an entity from billing for services rendered as a result of referrals that the parties should have known were prohibited by the Stark law. This could subject parties to retroactive sanctions as enforcement activities increase.

Endnotes

[1] 42 U.S.C. Sec. 1395nn(g)(5).

[2] 42 CFR Sec. 411.361(f).

[3] 63 *Fed. Reg.* 1659, 1671.

[4] 42 U.S.C. Sec. 1395nn(g)(1).

[5] 42 CFR Sec. 411.353(d).

[6] 63 *Fed. Reg.* 1659, 1671.

[7] 42 U.S.C. Sec. 1395nn(g)(2).

[8] 42 U.S.C. Sec. 1395nn(g)(3).

[9] 60 *Fed. Reg.* 16580, 16589.

[10] 42 U.S.C. Sec. 1395nn(g)(4).

[11] 60 *Fed. Reg.* 16580, 16584.

[12] 42 U.S.C. Sec. 1320a-7a(c)(1).

[13] 42 CFR Sec. 411.361(e).

[14] 42 CFR Sec. 411.361(f).

[15] 42 CFR Sec. 1001.901(a).

[16] 42 CFR Sec. 1001.901(b), also 42 U.S.C. Sec. 1320a-7a(d).

[17] 57 *Fed. Reg.* 3298, 3308.

[18] 42 U.S.C. Sec. 1320a-7a(c)(2).

[19] 42 U.S.C. Sec. 1320a-7a(c)(3).

[20] 42 CFR Sec. 1001.1901(a).

[21] 42 CFR Sec. 1001.1901(b).

[22] 42 CFR Sec. 1001.1901(c)(3).

[23] 42 CFR Sec. 1001.1901(c)(4).

[24] 42 CFR Sec. 1001.2001(a).

[25] 42 CFR Sec. 1001.2002.

[26] 42 CFR Sec. 1001.2003(a).

[27] 42 CFR Sec. 1001.2003(b).

[28] 42 CFR Secs. 1001.3001(a)(2) and 1001.3002(c).

[29] 42 CFR Sec. 1005.15(a).

[30] 42 CFR Sec. 1005.15(d).

[31] 42 CFR Sec. 1005.16.

[32] 42 CFR Sec. 1005.17.

[33] 42 CFR Sec. 1005.18.

[34] 42 CFR Sec. 1005.21.

[35] 42 U.S.C. Sec. 1320a-7a(e).

[36] 42 U.S.C. Sec. 1320a-7a(e).

[37] 42 U.S.C. Sec. 1320a-7a(f).

[38] 42 CFR Sec. 1003.105(a).

[39] 42 U.S.C. Sec. 1320a-7a(f).

[40] 42 U.S.C. Sec. 1320a-7a(g).

[41] 42 CFR Sec. 1001.2004.

[42] 42 CFR Sec. 1001.

[43] 42 CFR Sec. 1001.2006.

CHAPTER 9

Reporting Requirements

General Requirements

The Stark law mandates that each entity providing covered items or services for which payment may be made by Medicare or Medicaid must provide HHS with certain information. When Stark I was originally implemented, this reporting requirement extended only to the entity's ownership arrangements. As a result of technical amendments Congress enacted in October 1994, each entity must also provide information concerning investment and compensation arrangements.[1]

The information that must be furnished includes the covered items and services provided by the entity and the names and unique physician identification numbers of all physicians having an ownership or investment interest or a compensation arrangement with the entity, or whose "immediate relatives" have such an interest or arrangement.[2]

The reporting requirements of the law explicitly refer to the general statutory sections defining "ownership interests" or "compensation arrangements." From this language, it is not clear whether an arrangement or interest that is included within the scope of those definitions, but is eligible for an exception under later provisions of the law, is excluded from the reporting requirements.

The required information must be provided in the "form, manner and at such times as the [HHS] Secretary shall specify."[3] HHS formulated a draft disclosure form that appeared to require information only for financial interests for which there is no exception. The form also required a certification from the chief financial officer of the reporting entity listing physicians with an ownership or investment interest or a compensation arrangement and stating that the entity will not present any claims or bills for designated health services provided as a result of a prohibited referral. The entity is further required to obtain from each physician with a financial relationship a statement that the physician will not refer Medicare patients for designated health services to the entity or present claims or bills for such services.

The final version of the form has not been released and the early draft is obsolete in light of subsequently published proposed regulations.

Compliance with reporting requirements relating to financial relationships with physicians and their immediate family members could be difficult and burdensome, particularly in light of the definition of "immediate family member" or "member of a physician's immediate family" in the final Stark I regulations. As previously discussed, the term applies to parents, grandparents, spouses, children, grandchildren, siblings, fathers-in-law, mothers-in-law, sons-in-law, daughters-in-law, brothers-in-law, sisters-in-law, spouses of grandparents or grandchildren, and certain step-relatives.[4] An entity like a hospital may find it nearly impossible to identify those individuals with whom the hospital has a financial relationship, who also have familial relationships with referring physicians.

For example, certain relatives of a referring physician may have purchased tax-exempt bonds that were issued by the hospital. Such an ownership interest, through debt, would be attributed to the physician.

The reporting requirements do not apply to designated health services provided outside the United States.[5] No definition of "United States" is provided in this section. The Social Security Act defines the United States, however, to include the District of Columbia and the Commonwealth of Puerto Rico, and for purposes of the Medicare title, to also include the U.S. Virgin Islands and Guam.

In addition, HHS has the discretion to waive the reporting requirements for entities that infrequently provide services for which payment may be made under the Social Security Act.[6] The final Stark I regulations clarify that this exempts entities providing 20 or fewer Medicare Part A and Part B items and services during a calendar year.[7] No waivers have yet been granted.

Penalty for Failure to Report

Physicians and entities are not currently required to report because HCFA is still developing a procedure for implementing the reporting requirements. In the interim, however, HCFA is continuing to modify the regulations and their interpretation in certain ways. The proposed regulations are less restrictive in that entities will have to report on an annual basis changes in information, rather than 60 days after a change occurs.[8]

On the other hand, the proposed regulations could become significantly more onerous because regulations are being amended to require that entities provide information on all financial relationships covered by Stark II. Previously, entities would not have to report arrangements that met any of the statutory exceptions, except those for physician services, in-office ancillary services, and services furnish under certain prepaid plans. HCFA claims it has changed the rule to prevent the potential for abuse that occurs when entities can prevent HCFA from evaluating the facts by claiming there is no need to report because the arrangement meets an exception.

Recognizing that a publicly traded corporation could find it extremely difficult to comply with the reporting requirements, such as having to identify all its owners and their relatives, determine which of these are physicians, and identify physician-owners when shares of the corporation are held by mutual funds that may have thousands of additional owners, HCFA indicates that it will develop a streamlined process that will not require the entity to retain and submit large quantities of data. Entities will be required to acquire, retain and submit only those records with information that the entity "knows or should know about, in the course of prudently conducting business," including records required by the Internal Revenue Service, the Securities and Exchange Commission, and Medicare and Medicaid.[9] The new HCFA form required for submitting information will be published as a proposed notice soliciting public comment. However, HCFA is currently soliciting comments on this proposed approach.[10]

The penalty for failure to report is a civil money penalty of up to $10,000 for each day that reporting is required to have been made, and possible exclusion from the Medicare program (see Chapter 8). Certain provisions of the Medicare and Medicaid civil monetary penalty law also apply to a civil money penalty imposed under this section.[11]

The applicable provisions of the civil money penalty law also provide for extensive hearing and evidentiary rights.[12]

In light of the severe penalty for failure to report or even for delayed reporting, it is important to adhere strictly to the timing and content of the information requested by HHS.

Medicaid providers of designated health services "for which payment may be made under [Medicaid]" must also comply with the reporting provisions or face penalties.[13] A Medicaid provider would have to report, or be penalized for failure to report, in the same manner as required under the Medicare law. Thus, the reporting sanctions, unlike the self-referral prohibitions, apply directly to both Medicare and Medicaid providers.

Endnotes

[1] 42 U.S.C. Sec. 1395nn(f).

[2] Id.

[3] Id.

[4] 42 CFR Sec. 411.351.

[5] Id.

[6] Id.

[7] 42 CFR Sec. 411.361(b).

[8] 63 *Fed. Reg.* 1659, 1703.

[9] Id.

[10] Id. at 1703-4

[11] 42 U.S.C. Sec. 1395nn(g)(5); 42 U.S.C. Sec. 1320a-7a.

[12] 42 U.S.C. Sec. 1320a-7a. (See Chapter 8 for a detailed discussion of such hearing and evidentiary rights.)

[13] 42 U.S.C. Sec. 1396b(s).

CHAPTER 10

Advisory Opinions and Compliance Issues

Advisory Opinions

Background. Health care providers and health lawyers for many years have argued that the Stark law's complexities and ambiguities, coupled with the severe financial penalties for violations, created the need for a mechanism to obtain formal rulings from the government as to whether a particular arrangement complied with the law's requirements. Responding to those concerns, Congress mandated in the Balanced Budget Act of 1997 that HCFA issue written advisory opinions as to whether a referral relating to designated health services other than clinical laboratory services is prohibited under the Stark law.[1] HCFA published a final rule with comment implementing the advisory opinion process on Jan. 9, 1998.[2] By law, the Stark advisory opinion process sunsets on August 21, 2000.[3]

The regulations are generally patterned on those adopted for advisory opinions regarding the applicability of the anti-kickback law. Those advisory opinions were created by the Health Insurance Portability and Accountability Act of 1996.[4] While the advisory opinion process is likely to help clarify some of the more vexing issues under the Stark law, providers may find the procedure cumbersome, time-consuming, restrictive and, in some cases, legally risky.

Scope of Issues Addressed. The regulations place a number of important restrictions on the scope of issues that may be addressed through the advisory opinion process. First, the law itself precludes the issuance of opinions relating to referrals of clinical laboratory services.[5] The regulations mirror the anti-kickback law advisory opinion process by also excluding determinations of fair market value and bona fide employment.[6]

HCFA will not issue advisory opinions on matters that depend upon a party's knowledge or intent.[7] For example, HCFA will not opine as to whether a particular arrangement constitutes a circumvention scheme.

Additionally, HCFA will not accept an advisory opinion request if (a) the request is not related to a named individual or entity; (b) HCFA is aware that the same or a similar arrangement is under investigation or has been the subject of a governmental proceeding; or (c) HCFA believes it could not make an informed opinion or could only do so after extensive investigation, clinical study, testing or collateral inquiry.[8]

Finally, and perhaps most importantly, HCFA will not issue advisory opinions relating to general questions of interpretation, hypothetical situations, or the activities of third parties. Rather, the request must involve an existing arrangement or one into which the requestor, in good faith, specifically plans to enter.[9] Thus, for example, the advisory opinion process does not allow for a simple inquiry as to whether a particular CPT code constitutes a designated health service. Rather, to obtain that advice on a formal basis, the requestor would need to identify all the material facts of a particular arrangement.

Procedure for Submitting a Request. The regulations detail the process for submitting a request.[10] The request must include the name, address, telephone number and taxpayer identification number of the requestor; the names and addresses of all other actual and potential parties to the arrangement; and a contact person who will be available to discuss the request with HCFA.[11] The requestor is required to provide complete information on the identity of all entities involved, either directly or indirectly, including names, addresses, legal form, ownership structure, nature of business, and, if relevant, Medicare and Medicaid provider numbers.[12] Additionally, the request must include a narrative description of the arrangement — including its purpose — and of any other arrangements that may affect the analysis.[13] The requestor must include copies of all relevant documents or portions of documents.[14]

The requestor must include a discussion of the specific issues it wishes HCFA to address, including, if possible, a discussion of why the requestor believes the Stark law is not or would not be violated and the exception(s) the requestor believes might apply.[15] The requestor must also indicate whether the parties involved in the request have asked for an advisory opinion from the HHS Office of Inspector General as to the arrangement's legality under the anti-kickback law and whether the arrangement is, to the requestor's best knowledge, the subject of an investigation.[16] Finally, the requestor must include a certification that the statements contained are true and correct and that the arrangement is one into which the requestor, in good faith, plans to enter.[17] This latter statement may be made contingent upon obtaining a favorable advisory opinion from HCFA, or from HCFA and the OIG.

HCFA strongly advises requestors to contact the agency before submitting a request so HCFA can provide a preliminary indication as to the scope of information required.[18]

Fees. The regulations require an initial nonrefundable payment of $250.[19] The requestor will also be charged user fees equal to the actual costs incurred in processing the request, including the costs of salaries, benefits and overhead, and administrative and supervisory support. HCFA estimates this charge to be approximately $75 per hour.[20] If outside experts are required, there will be a separate charge; the requestor will need to pay in advance the estimated costs of the expert.[21]

Similar to the OIG's advisory opinion process for the anti-kickback law, the requestor may designate a triggering dollar amount. HCFA will notify the requestor if it estimates that costs have reached, or are likely to exceed, this triggering dollar amount, and the requestor will then have the choice to continue or withdraw the request.[22]

HCFA will not release the advisory opinion until all costs are paid.[23] If a request is withdrawn, the requestor is still obligated to pay all costs incurred up to that point.[24] Additionally, HCFA may retain a withdrawn request and any accompanying documents and information, and use them for any governmental purposes permitting by law.[25]

Timing Issues. Under the regulations, HCFA will either request additional information or formally accept or decline a request within 15 working days of receipt.[26] Once a request is accepted, HCFA will generally issue an opinion within 90 days. However, if the request presents complex legal issues or highly complicated fact patterns, HCFA will issue the opinion "within a reasonable period of time."[27] The 90-day period is also tolled while HCFA waits for additional information, payments or expert advice.[28]

Legal Effect of Advisory Opinions. Advisory opinions may only be relied upon by the parties requesting the opinion.[29] Additionally, HCFA may rescind an advisory opinion "if it determines that it is in the public interest."[30] HCFA will not proceed against a requestor who relied in good faith on an advisory opinion before its rescission, as long as the requestor presented a full, complete and accurate description of all relevant facts and promptly discontinued the action upon rescission, or, in the discretion of HCFA, within a reasonable "wind-down" period.

Thus, even if the parties to an arrangement have sought and obtained a favorable advisory opinion, HCFA may commence an action against the parties based on that arrangement, if, for example, the requestor "has failed to disclose a material fact." Additionally, the issuance of a favorable advisory opinion does not preclude enforcement activity with respect to that arrangement by any other governmental agency. The regulations expressly provide that the issuance of a favorable advisory opinion does not limit the investigatory or prosecutorial authority of the OIG, the Department of Justice, or any other government agency, and that in connection with a request, HCFA, the OIG, or the Department of Justice may conduct whatever independent investigation it believes appropriate.[32] In particular, HCFA expressly notes that it plans to routinely exchange information with the OIG on requests HCFA receives.[33]

Thus, a requestor must carefully consider whether to obtain a concurrent advisory opinion from the OIG with respect to the anti-kickback law, as the arrangement is likely to be closely scrutinized.

Conclusion. The advisory opinion process is likely to provide important clarifications in many areas of the Stark law.[34] For example, the process may help clarify the contours of permissible multi-site group practice arrangements. However, entities considering use of the advisory opinion process must carefully consider the time, expense and risk involved.

Those who are not parties to the advisory opinion may rely on HCFA's pronouncements only at their own peril. HCFA repeatedly indicates in the regulations that seemingly identical fact patterns may produce a different result based on additional elements. On the other hand, where HCFA publishes a negative opinion, it will be difficult to argue that the issues in question remained ambiguous.

Although third parties who are not a part of an arrangement are precluded from seeking an advisory opinion, this does not necessarily preclude its use for strategic competitive purposes. The anti-kickback law advisory opinion process has, for example, been used by a physician's attorney seeking to curtail the activities of physician practice management companies.[35]

Compliance Issues

For any health care provider that maintains financial arrangements with physicians, compliance with the Stark law is critical. For example, the OIG's Compliance Program Guidance for Hospitals indicates that hospitals should have policies and procedures in place with respect to compliance with the Stark law. The current status of the Stark law creates particularly difficult compliance issues, however.

First, it is important to note that the Stark law is self-implementing in the absence of final regulations. Thus, an entity cannot defer its compliance efforts until final Stark II regulations are published.

Second, the proposed Stark II regulations modify the prior regulatory framework in a number of respects. In some instances, the proposed Stark II regulations purport to merely clarify or emphasize existing rules. For example, the statement in the proposed Stark II regulations that "incident to" services cannot be taken into account for purposes of the bona fide employment exception arguably merely restates a rule that has been in effect since the law's effective date.[36]

Other elements of the proposed Stark II regulations clearly create new policy, such as the proposed "fair market value" exception.[37] It is not clear whether providers may rely on this exception during the period before the publication of the final rule. The exception is merely proposed and does not appear in the law. On the other hand, the preamble to the proposed rules suggests that certain of HCFA's restrictive interpretations of the law — for example, excluding locally based residents from the scope of the recruitment exception — were made with the understanding that certain of the relationships in question could nevertheless satisfy the fair market value exception.[38]

Finally, some aspects of the proposed regulations are clearly changes to HCFA's positions in the final Stark I regulations. For example, HCFA expressly reverses its position on imputing the financial relationship of one member of a group practice to all the other members.[39] Similarly, HCFA indicates that it has rethought its position on whether independent contractors may qualify as members of a group practice.[40] In the former case, it would seem reasonable to rely on HCFA's new, more expansive interpretation. On the other hand, it is not at all clear whether independent-contractor relationships need to be restructured in the absence of final regulations.

In conclusion, while compliance with the Stark law must be a primary element of any provider's compliance plan, the law remains in a highly fluid state.

Endnotes

[1] 42 U.S.C. Sec. 1395 nn(g)(6).

[2] 42 CFR Secs. 411.370-411.389.

[3] HCFA has interpreted this statutory provision as requiring that requests be submitted by the sunset date; apparently, opinions relating to those requests may be issued after that time. 42 CFR Sec. 411.370(a).

[4] 42 U.S.C. Sec. 1320a-7d(b).

[5] 42 U.S.C. Sec. 1395 nn(g)(6).

[6] 42 CFR Sec. 411.370(c).

[7] 63 *Fed. Reg.* 1646, 1648, Jan. 9, 1998.

[8] 42 CFR Sec. 411.370(e).

[9] 42 CFR Sec. 411.370(b)(1).

[10] 42 CFR Sec. 411.372.

[11] 42 CFR Sec. 411.372(b)(1)-(3).

[12] 42 CFR Sec. 411.372(b)(5).

[13] 42 CFR Sec. 411.372(b)(i), (iv).

[14] 42 CFR Sec. 411.372(b)(4)(ii).

[15] 42 CFR Sec. 411.372(b)(6).

[16] 42 CFR Sec. 411.372(b)(7).

[17] 42 CFR Sec. 411.373.

[18] 63 *Fed. Reg.* 1646, 1650.

[19] 42 CFR Sec. 411.375(a).

[20] 63 *Fed. Reg.* 1646, 1650.

[21] 42 CFR Sec. 411.375(d).

[22] 42 CFR Sec. 411.375(c)(2), (3).

[23] 42 CFR Sec. 411.375(c)(5).

[24] 42 CFR Sec. 411.375(c)(4).

[25] 42 CFR Sec. 411.378.

[26] 42 CFR Sec. 411.379.

[27] 42 CFR Sec. 411.380(c)(1).

[28] 42 CFR Sec. 411.380(c)(3).

[29] 42 CFR Sec. 411.387.

[30] 42 CFR Sec. 411.382. HCFA indicates that it may rescind an opinion, if it learns after issuing it "that the arrangement in question may lead to fraud and abuse." 63 *Fed. Reg.* 1646, 1652.

[31] 63 *Fed. Reg.* 1646, 1653.

[32] 42 CFR Sec. 411.370(f).

[33] 63 *Fed. Reg.* 1646, 1650.

[34] Advisory opinions will be made available for public inspection at HCFA headquarters and will also be posted on the HCFA website at http://www.hcfa.gov/regs/aop/.

[35] See OIG Advisory Opinion 98-4.

[36] 63 *Fed. Reg.* 1659, 1701.

[37] 63 *Fed. Reg.* 1659, 1725-1726 (to be codified at 42 CFR Sec. 411.357(l)).

[38] 63 *Fed. Reg.* 1659, 1702.

[39] 63 *Fed. Reg.* 1659, 1709.

[40] 63 *Fed. Reg.* 1659, 1689.

'Stark Law' Banning Physician Self-Referrals To Designated Health Services (42 U.S.C. Sec. 1395nn)

TITLE 42--THE PUBLIC HEALTH AND WELFARE

CHAPTER 7--SOCIAL SECURITY

SUBCHAPTER XVIII--HEALTH INSURANCE FOR AGED AND DISABLED

Part C--Miscellaneous Provisions

Sec. 1395nn. Limitation on certain physician referrals

(a) Prohibition of certain referrals

(1) In general

Except as provided in subsection (b) of this section, if a physician (or an immediate family member of such physician) has a financial relationship with an entity specified in paragraph (2), then--
(A) the physician may not make a referral to the entity for the furnishing of designated health services for which payment otherwise may be made under this subchapter, and
(B) the entity may not present or cause to be presented a claim under this subchapter or bill to any individual, third party payor, or other entity for designated health services furnished pursuant to a referral prohibited under subparagraph (A).

(2) Financial relationship specified

For purposes of this section, a financial relationship of a physician (or an immediate family member of such physician) with an entity specified in this paragraph is--
(A) except as provided in subsections (c) and (d) of this section, an ownership or investment interest in the entity, or
(B) except as provided in subsection (e) of this section, a compensation arrangement (as defined in subsection (h)(1) of this section) between the physician (or an immediate family member of such physician) and the entity.

An ownership or investment interest described in subparagraph (A) may be through equity, debt, or other means and includes an interest in an entity that holds an ownership or investment interest in any entity providing the designated health service.

(b) General exceptions to both ownership and compensation arrangement prohibitions

Subsection (a)(1) of this section shall not apply in the following cases:

(1) Physicians' services

In the case of physicians' services (as defined in section 1395x(q) of this title) provided personally by (or under the

personal supervision of) another physician in the same group
practice (as defined in subsection (h)(4) of this section) as the
referring physician.

(2) In-office ancillary services

In the case of services (other than durable medical equipment
(excluding infusion pumps) and parenteral and enteral nutrients,
equipment, and supplies)--
    (A) that are furnished--
        (i) personally by the referring physician, personally by
    a physician who is a member of the same group practice as
    the referring physician, or personally by individuals who
    are directly supervised by the physician or by another
    physician in the group practice, and
        (ii)(I) in a building in which the referring physician
    (or another physician who is a member of the same group
    practice) furnishes physicians' services unrelated to the
    furnishing of designated health services, or
        (II) in the case of a referring physician who is a
    member of a group practice, in another building which is
    used by the group practice--
            (aa) for the provision of some or all of the group's
        clinical laboratory services, or
            (bb) for the centralized provision of the group's
        designated health services (other than clinical
        laboratory services),

    unless the Secretary determines other terms and conditions
        under which the provision of such services does not present
        a risk of program or patient abuse, and

    (B) that are billed by the physician performing or
supervising the services, by a group practice of which such
physician is a member under a billing number assigned to the
group practice, or by an entity that is wholly owned by such
physician or such group practice,

if the ownership or investment interest in such services meets such
other requirements as the Secretary may impose by regulation as
needed to protect against program or patient abuse.

(3) Prepaid plans

In the case of services furnished by an organization--
    (A) with a contract under section 1395mm of this title to an
individual enrolled with the organization,
    (B) described in section 1395l(a)(1)(A) of this title to an
individual enrolled with the organization,
    (C) receiving payments on a prepaid basis, under a
demonstration project under section 1395b-1(a) of this title or
under section 222(a) of the Social Security Amendments of 1972,
to an individual enrolled with the organization, or
    (D) that is a qualified health maintenance organization
(within the meaning of section 300e-9(d)   of this title) to
an individual enrolled with the organization.

(4) Other permissible exceptions

In the case of any other financial relationship which the
Secretary determines, and specifies in regulations, does not pose a
risk of program or patient abuse.

(c) General exception related only to ownership or investment prohibition for ownership in publicly traded securities and mutual funds

Ownership of the following shall not be considered to be an ownership or investment interest described in subsection (a)(2)(A) of this section:

(1) Ownership of investment securities (including shares or bonds, debentures, notes, or other debt instruments) which may be purchased on terms generally available to the public and which are--

(A)(i) securities listed on the New York Stock Exchange, the American Stock Exchange, or any regional exchange in which quotations are published on a daily basis, or foreign securities listed on a recognized foreign, national, or regional exchange in which quotations are published on a daily basis, or

(ii) traded under an automated interdealer quotation system operated by the National Association of Securities Dealers, and

(B) in a corporation that had, at the end of the corporation's most recent fiscal year, or on average during the previous 3 fiscal years, stockholder equity exceeding $75,000,000.

(2) Ownership of shares in a regulated investment company as defined in section 851(a) of the Internal Revenue Code of 1986, if such company had, at the end of the company's most recent fiscal year, or on average during the previous 3 fiscal years, total assets exceeding $75,000,000.

(d) Additional exceptions related only to ownership or investment prohibition

The following, if not otherwise excepted under subsection (b) of this section, shall not be considered to be an ownership or investment interest described in subsection (a)(2)(A) of this section:

(1) Hospitals in Puerto Rico

In the case of designated health services provided by a hospital located in Puerto Rico.

(2) Rural provider

In the case of designated health services furnished in a rural area (as defined in section 1395ww(d)(2)(D) of this title) by an entity, if substantially all of the designated health services furnished by such entity are furnished to individuals residing in such a rural area.

(3) Hospital ownership

In the case of designated health services provided by a hospital (other than a hospital described in paragraph (1)) if--

(A) the referring physician is authorized to perform services at the hospital, and

(B) the ownership or investment interest is in the hospital itself (and not merely in a subdivision of the hospital).

(e) Exceptions relating to other compensation arrangements

The following shall not be considered to be a compensation arrangement described in subsection (a)(2)(B) of this section:

(1) Rental of office space; rental of equipment

(A) Office space

Payments made by a lessee to a lessor for the use of premises if--
    (i) the lease is set out in writing, signed by the parties, and specifies the premises covered by the lease,
    (ii) the space rented or leased does not exceed that which is reasonable and necessary for the legitimate business purposes of the lease or rental and is used exclusively by the lessee when being used by the lessee, except that the lessee may make payments for the use of space consisting of common areas if such payments do not exceed the lessee's pro rata share of expenses for such space based upon the ratio of the space used exclusively by the lessee to the total amount of space (other than common areas) occupied by all persons using such common areas,
    (iii) the lease provides for a term of rental or lease for at least 1 year,
    (iv) the rental charges over the term of the lease are set in advance, are consistent with fair market value, and are not determined in a manner that takes into account the volume or value of any referrals or other business generated between the parties,
    (v) the lease would be commercially reasonable even if no referrals were made between the parties, and
    (vi) the lease meets such other requirements as the Secretary may impose by regulation as needed to protect against program or patient abuse.

(B) Equipment

Payments made by a lessee of equipment to the lessor of the equipment for the use of the equipment if--
    (i) the lease is set out in writing, signed by the parties, and specifies the equipment covered by the lease,
    (ii) the equipment rented or leased does not exceed that which is reasonable and necessary for the legitimate business purposes of the lease or rental and is used exclusively by the lessee when being used by the lessee,
    (iii) the lease provides for a term of rental or lease of at least 1 year,
    (iv) the rental charges over the term of the lease are set in advance, are consistent with fair market value, and are not determined in a manner that takes into account the volume or value of any referrals or other business generated between the parties,
    (v) the lease would be commercially reasonable even if no referrals were made between the parties, and
    (vi) the lease meets such other requirements as the Secretary may impose by regulation as needed to protect against program or patient abuse.

(2) Bona fide employment relationships

Any amount paid by an employer to a physician (or an immediate family member of such physician) who has a bona fide employment relationship with the employer for the provision of services if--
    (A) the employment is for identifiable services,
    (B) the amount of the remuneration under the employment--
        (i) is consistent with the fair market value of the services, and
        (ii) is not determined in a manner that takes into account (directly or indirectly) the volume or value of any referrals by the referring physician,

   (C) the remuneration is provided pursuant to an agreement which would be commercially reasonable even if no referrals were made to the employer, and
   (D) the employment meets such other requirements as the Secretary may impose by regulation as needed to protect against program or patient abuse.

Subparagraph (B)(ii) shall not prohibit the payment of remuneration in the form of a productivity bonus based on services performed personally by the physician (or an immediate family member of such physician).

   (3) Personal service arrangements

(A) In general

   Remuneration from an entity under an arrangement (including remuneration for specific physicians' services furnished to a nonprofit blood center) if--
      (i) the arrangement is set out in writing, signed by the parties, and specifies the services covered by the arrangement,
      (ii) the arrangement covers all of the services to be provided by the physician (or an immediate family member of such physician) to the entity,
      (iii) the aggregate services contracted for do not exceed those that are reasonable and necessary for the legitimate business purposes of the arrangement,
      (iv) the term of the arrangement is for at least 1 year,
      (v) the compensation to be paid over the term of the arrangement is set in advance, does not exceed fair market value, and except in the case of a physician incentive plan described in subparagraph (B), is not determined in a manner that takes into account the volume or value of any referrals or other business generated between the parties,
      (vi) the services to be performed under the arrangement do not involve the counseling or promotion or a business arrangement or other activity that violates any State or Federal law, and
      (vii) the arrangement meets such other requirements as the Secretary may impose by regulation as needed to protect against program or patient abuse.

(B) Physician incentive plan exception

(i) In general

   In the case of a physician incentive plan (as defined in clause (ii)) between a physician and an entity, the compensation may be determined in a manner (through a withhold, capitation, bonus, or otherwise) that takes into account directly or indirectly the volume or value of any referrals or other business generated between the parties, if the plan meets the following requirements:
      (I) No specific payment is made directly or indirectly under the plan to a physician or a physician group as an inducement to reduce or limit medically necessary services provided with respect to a specific individual enrolled with the entity.
      (II) In the case of a plan that places a physician or a physician group at substantial financial risk as determined by the Secretary pursuant to section 1395mm(i)(8)(A)(ii) of this title, the plan complies with any requirements the Secretary may impose pursuant to such section.

(III) Upon request by the Secretary, the entity provides the Secretary with access to descriptive information regarding the plan, in order to permit the Secretary to determine whether the plan is in compliance with the requirements of this clause.
(ii) ``Physician incentive plan'' defined

For purposes of this subparagraph, the term ``physician incentive plan'' means any compensation arrangement between an entity and a physician or physician group that may directly or indirectly have the effect of reducing or limiting services provided with respect to individuals enrolled with the entity.

(4) Remuneration unrelated to the provision of designated health services

In the case of remuneration which is provided by a hospital to a physician if such remuneration does not relate to the provision of designated health services:

(5) Physician recruitment

In the case of remuneration which is provided by a hospital to a physician to induce the physician to relocate to the geographic area served by the hospital in order to be a member of the medical staff of the hospital, if--
(A) the physician is not required to refer patients to the hospital,
(B) the amount of the remuneration under the arrangement is not determined in a manner that takes into account (directly or indirectly) the volume or value of any referrals by the referring physician, and
(C) the arrangement meets such other requirements as the Secretary may impose by regulation as needed to protect against program or patient abuse.

(6) Isolated transactions

In the case of an isolated financial transaction, such as a one-time sale of property or practice, if--
(A) the requirements described in subparagraphs (B) and (C) of paragraph (2) are met with respect to the entity in the same manner as they apply to an employer, and
(B) the transaction meets such other requirements as the Secretary may impose by regulation as needed to protect against program or patient abuse.

(7) Certain group practice arrangements with a hospital

(A)   In general

An arrangement between a hospital and a group under which designated health services are provided by the group but are billed by the hospital if--
(i) with respect to services provided to an inpatient of the hospital, the arrangement is pursuant to the provision of inpatient hospital services under section 1395x(b)(3) of this title.
(ii) the arrangement began before December 19, 1989, and has continued in effect without interruption since such date,

(iii) with respect to the designated health services covered under the arrangement, substantially all of such services furnished to patients of the hospital are furnished by the group under the arrangement,

(iv) the arrangement is pursuant to an agreement that is set out in writing and that specifies the services to be provided by the parties and the compensation for services provided under the agreement,

(v) the compensation paid over the term of the agreement is consistent with fair market value and the compensation per unit of services is fixed in advance and is not determined in a manner that takes into account the volume or value of any referrals or other business generated between the parties,

(vi) the compensation is provided pursuant to an agreement which would be commercially reasonable even if no referrals were made to the entity, and

(vii) the arrangement between the parties meets such other requirements as the Secretary may impose by regulation as needed to protect against program or patient abuse.

(8) Payments by a physician for items and services

Payments made by a physician--
(A) to a laboratory in exchange for the provision of clinical laboratory services, or
(B) to an entity as compensation for other items or services if the items or services are furnished at a price that is consistent with fair market value.

(f) Reporting requirements

Each entity providing covered items or services for which payment may be made under this subchapter shall provide the Secretary with the information concerning the entity's ownership, investment, and compensation arrangements, including--
(1) the covered items and services provided by the entity, and
(2) the names and unique physician identification numbers of all physicians with an ownership or investment interest (as described in subsection (a)(2)(A) of this section), or with a compensation arrangement (as described in subsection (a)(2)(B) of this section), in the entity, or whose immediate relatives have such an ownership or investment interest or who have such a compensation relationship with the entity.

Such information shall be provided in such form, manner, and at such times as the Secretary shall specify. The requirement of this subsection shall not apply to designated health services provided outside the United States or to entities which the Secretary determines provides services for which payment may be made under this subchapter very infrequently.

(g) Sanctions

(1) Denial of payment

No payment may be made under this subchapter for a designated health service which is provided in violation of subsection (a)(1) of this section.

(2) Requiring refunds for certain claims

If a person collects any amounts that were billed in violation of subsection (a)(1) of this section, the person shall be liable to the individual for, and shall refund on a timely basis to the individual, any amounts so collected.

(3) Civil money penalty and exclusion for improper claims

Any person that presents or causes to be presented a bill or a claim for a service that such person knows or should know is for a service for which payment may not be made under paragraph (1) or for which a refund has not been made under paragraph (2) shall be subject to a civil money penalty of not more than $15,000 for each such service. The provisions of section 1320a-7a of this title (other than the first sentence of subsection (a) and other than subsection (b)) shall apply to a civil money penalty under the previous sentence in the same manner as such provisions apply to a penalty or proceeding under section 1320a-7a(a) of this title.

(4) Civil money penalty and exclusion for circumvention schemes

Any physician or other entity that enters into an arrangement or scheme (such as a cross-referral arrangement) which the physician or entity knows or should know has a principal purpose of assuring referrals by the physician to a particular entity which, if the physician directly made referrals to such entity, would be in violation of this section, shall be subject to a civil money penalty of not more than $100,000 for each such arrangement or scheme. The provisions of section 1320a-7a of this title (other than the first sentence of subsection (a) and other than subsection (b)) shall apply to a civil money penalty under the previous sentence in the same manner as such provisions apply to a penalty or proceeding under section 1320a-7a(a) of this title.

(5) Failure to report information

Any person who is required, but fails, to meet a reporting requirement of subsection (f) of this section is subject to a civil money penalty of not more than $10,000 for each day for which reporting is required to have been made. The provisions of section 1320a-7a of this title (other than the first sentence of subsection (a) and other than subsection (b)) shall apply to a civil money penalty under the previous sentence in the same manner as such provisions apply to a penalty or proceeding under section 1320a-7a(a) of this title.

(h) Definitions and special rules

For purposes of this section:

(1) Compensation arrangement; remuneration

(A) The term ``compensation arrangement'' means any arrangement involving any remuneration between a physician (or an immediate family member of such physician) and an entity other than an arrangement involving only remuneration described in subparagraph (C).

(B) The term ``remuneration'' includes any remuneration, directly or indirectly, overtly or covertly, in cash or in kind.

(C) Remuneration described in this subparagraph is any remuneration consisting of any of the following:

(i) The forgiveness of amounts owed for inaccurate tests or procedures, mistakenly performed tests or procedures, or the correction of minor billing errors.

(ii) The provision of items, devices, or supplies that are

used solely to--
      (I) collect, transport, process, or store specimens for
the entity providing the item, device, or supply, or
      (II) order or communicate the results of tests or
procedures for such entity.

      (iii) A payment made by an insurer or a self-insured plan to
a physician to satisfy a claim, submitted on a fee for service
basis, for the furnishing of health services by that physician
to an individual who is covered by a policy with the insurer or
by the self-insured plan, if--
      (I) the health services are not furnished, and the
payment is not made, pursuant to a contract or other
arrangement between the insurer or the plan and the
physician,
      (II) the payment is made to the physician on behalf of
the covered individual and would otherwise be made directly
to such individual,
      (III) the amount of the payment is set in advance, does
not exceed fair market value, and is not determined in a
manner that takes into account directly or indirectly the
volume or value of any referrals, and
      (IV) the payment meets such other requirements as the
Secretary may impose by regulation as needed to protect
against program or patient abuse.

(2) Employee

    An individual is considered to be ``employed by'' or an
``employee'' of an entity if the individual would be considered to
be an employee of the entity under the usual common law rules
applicable in determining the employer-employee relationship (as
applied for purposes of section 3121(d)(2) of the Internal Revenue
Code of 1986).

(3) Fair market value

    The term ``fair market value'' means the value in arms length
transactions, consistent with the general market value, and, with
respect to rentals or leases, the value of rental property for
general commercial purposes (not taking into account its intended
use) and, in the case of a lease of space, not adjusted to reflect
the additional value the prospective lessee or lessor would
attribute to the proximity or convenience to the lessor where the
lessor is a potential source of patient referrals to the lessee.

(4) Group practice

(A) Definition of group practice

    The term ``group practice'' means a group of 2 or more
physicians legally organized as a partnership, professional
corporation, foundation, not-for-profit corporation, faculty
practice plan, or similar association--
      (i) in which each physician who is a member of the group
provides substantially the full range of services which the
physician routinely provides, including medical care,
consultation, diagnosis, or treatment, through the joint use
of shared office space, facilities, equipment and personnel,
      (ii) for which substantially all of the services of the
physicians who are members of the group are provided through
the group and are billed under a billing number assigned to
the group and amounts so received are treated as receipts of
the group,
      (iii) in which the overhead expenses of and the income

from the practice are distributed in accordance with methods previously determined,

    (iv) except as provided in subparagraph (B)(i), in which no physician who is a member of the group directly or indirectly receives compensation based on the volume or value of referrals by the physician,

    (v) in which members of the group personally conduct no less than 75 percent of the physician-patient encounters of the group practice, and

    (vi) which meets such other standards as the Secretary may impose by regulation.

(B) Special rules

(i) Profits and productivity bonuses

    A physician in a group practice may be paid a share of overall profits of the group, or a productivity bonus based on services personally performed or services incident to such personally performed services, so long as the share or bonus is not determined in any manner which is directly related to the volume or value of referrals by such physician.

(ii) Faculty practice plans

    In the case of a faculty practice plan associated with a hospital, institution of higher education, or medical school with an approved medical residency training program in which physician members may provide a variety of different specialty services and provide professional services both within and outside the group, as well as perform other tasks such as research, subparagraph (A) shall be applied only with respect to the services provided within the faculty practice plan.

            (5) Referral; referring physician

(A) Physicians' services

    Except as provided in subparagraph (C), in the case of an item or service for which payment may be made under part B of this subchapter, the request by a physician for the item or service, including the request by a physician for a consultation with another physician (and any test or procedure ordered by, or to be performed by (or under the supervision of) that other physician), constitutes a ``referral'' by a ``referring physician''.

(B) Other items

    Except as provided in subparagraph (C), the request or establishment of a plan of care by a physician which includes the provision of the designated health service constitutes a ``referral'' by a ``referring physician''.

(C) Clarification respecting certain services integral to a
        consultation by certain specialists

    A request by a pathologist for clinical diagnostic laboratory tests and pathological examination services, a request by a radiologist for diagnostic radiology services, and a request by a radiation oncologist for radiation therapy, if such services are furnished by (or under the supervision of) such pathologist, radiologist, or radiation oncologist pursuant to a consultation requested by another physician does not constitute a ``referral'' by a ``referring physician''.

(6) Designated health services

The term ``designated health services'' means any of the following items or services:
(A) Clinical laboratory services.
(B) Physical therapy services.
(C) Occupational therapy services.
(D) Radiology services, including magnetic resonance imaging, computerized axial tomography scans, and ultrasound services.
(E) Radiation therapy services and supplies.
(F) Durable medical equipment and supplies.
(G) Parenteral and enteral nutrients, equipment, and supplies.
(H) Prosthetics, orthotics, and prosthetic devices and supplies.
(I) Home health services.
(J) Outpatient prescription drugs.
(K) Inpatient and outpatient hospital services.

Section 1877(g) (42 U.S.C. 1395nn(g)) is amended by adding at the end the following new paragraph:

"(6) ADVISORY OPINIONS.—

"(A) IN GENERAL.—The Secretary shall issue written advisory opinions concerning whether a referral relating to designated health services (other than clinical laboratory services) is prohibited under this section. Each advisory opinion issued by the Secretary shall be binding as to the Secretary and the party or parties requesting the opinion.

"(B) APPLICATION OF CERTAIN RULES.—The Secretary shall, to the extent practicable, apply the rules under subsections (b)(3) and (b)(4) and take into account the regulations promulgated under subsection (b)(5) of section 1128D in the issuance of advisory opinions under this paragraph.

"(C) REGULATIONS.—In order to implement this paragraph in a timely manner, the Secretary may promulgate regulations that take effect on an interim basis, after notice and pending opportunity for public comment.

"(D) APPLICABILITY.—This paragraph shall apply to requests for advisory opinions made after the date which is 90 days after the date of the enactment of this paragraph and before the close of the period described in section 1128D(b)(6).".

HCFA Final Rules on the 'Stark I' Clinical Laboratory Self-Referral Ban (60 *Fed. Reg.* 41914-41982, Aug. 14, 1995)

41914   Federal Register / Vol. 60, No. 156 / Monday, August 14, 1995 / Rules and Regulations

DEPARTMENT OF HEALTH AND HUMAN SERVICES

Health Care Financing Administration

42 CFR Part 411

[BPD–674–FC]

RIN: 0938–AF40

Medicare Program; Physician Financial Relationships With, and Referrals to, Health Care Entities That Furnish Clinical Laboratory Services and Financial Relationship Reporting Requirements

AGENCY: Health Care Financing Administration (HCFA), HHS.

ACTION: Final rule with comment period.

SUMMARY: This final rule with comment period provides that, if a physician or a member of a physician's immediate family has a financial relationship with an entity, the physician may not make referrals to the entity for the furnishing of clinical laboratory services under the Medicare program, except under specified circumstances. It contains revisions to our proposal of March 11, 1992, based on comments submitted by the public. Further, it incorporates the new expansions and exceptions created by the Omnibus Budget Reconciliation Act of 1993 and the amendments in the Social Security Act Amendments of 1994 (SSA '94), that are related to referrals for clinical laboratory services and have a retroactive effective date of January 1, 1992.

In addition, we are responding to comments received on the interim final rule with comment period (published on December 3, 1991) that set forth Medicare reporting requirements for the submission by certain health care entities of information about their relationships with physicians. That document implemented the reporting requirements of section 1877(f) of the Social Security Act. This rule revises those requirements to incorporate the amendments to section 1877(f) made by SSA '94, to apply to any further reporting we may require.

EFFECTIVE DATES: The regulations are effective September 13, 1995.

Comment Date: Comments on the new provisions added by the Omnibus Budget Reconciliation Act of 1993 and any changes in section 1877 that resulted from the Social Security Act Amendments of 1994 will be considered if we receive them at the appropriate address, as provided below, no later than 5 p.m. on October 13, 1995.

ADDRESSES: Mail written comments (1 original and 3 copies) to the following

address: Health Care Financing Administration, Department of Health and Human Services, Attention: BPD–674–FC, P.O. Box 26688, Baltimore, MD 21207.

If you prefer, you may deliver your written comments (1 original and 3 copies) to one of the following addresses: Room 309–G, Hubert H. Humphrey Building, 200 Independence Avenue, SW., Washington, DC 20201, or Room C–5–09–26, 7500 Security Boulevard, Baltimore, MD 21244–1850.

Because of staffing and resource limitations, we cannot accept comments by facsimile (FAX) transmission. In commenting, please refer to file code BPD–674–FC. Comments received timely will be available for public inspection as they are received, generally beginning approximately 3 weeks after publication of a document, in Room 309–G of the Department's offices at 200 Independence Avenue, SW., Washington, DC, on Monday through Friday of each week from 8:30 a.m. to 5 p.m. (phone: (202) 690–7890).

For comments that relate to information collection requirements, mail a copy of the comments to: Allison Herron Eydt, HCFA Desk Officer, Office of Information and Regulatory Affairs, Room 3001, New Executive Office Building, Washington, DC 20503.

Copies: To order copies of the **Federal Register** containing this document, send your request to the Government Printing Office, ATTN: New Orders, P.O. Box 371954, Pittsburgh, PA 15250–7954. Specify the date of the issue requested and enclose a check or money order payable to the Superintendent of Documents, or enclose your Visa or Master Card number and expiration date. Credit card orders can also be placed by calling the order desk at (202) 512–1800 or by faxing your Visa or Master Card number and expiration date to (202) 512–2250. The cost for each copy is $8.00. As an alternative, you may view and photocopy the **Federal Register** document at most libraries designated as U.S. Government Depository Libraries and at many other public and academic libraries throughout the country that receive the **Federal Register**.

FOR FURTHER INFORMATION CONTACT: Betty Burrier, (410) 786–0191.

SUPPLEMENTARY INFORMATION: To assist readers in referencing sections contained in this final rule, we are providing the following table of contents:

Table of Contents

I. Legislation and Regulations— Chronological Background

In section 6204 of the Omnibus Budget Reconciliation Act of 1989 (OBRA '89) (Public Law 101–239, enacted on December 19, 1989), the Congress added a provision to the Social Security Act (the Act) that governs whether physicians who have financial relationships (or who have immediate family members with financial relationships) with a health care entity can refer Medicare patients to that entity for clinical laboratory services. This provision was amended by section 4207(e) of the Omnibus Budget

Reconciliation Act of 1990 (OBRA '90) (Public Law 101–508, enacted on November 5, 1990); section 13562 of the Omnibus Budget Reconciliation Act of 1993 (OBRA '93) (Public Law 103–66, enacted on August 10, 1993); and section 152 of the Social Security Act Amendments of 1994 (SSA '94) (Public Law 103–432, enacted on October 31, 1994). As discussed below, we published an interim final rule in 1991 concerning financial relationship reporting requirements, and we published a proposed rule in 1992 concerning physician referrals to clinical laboratories.

A. OBRA '89

Section 6204 of OBRA '89 added section 1877, "Limitation on Certain Physician Referrals," to the Act. (Unless otherwise indicated, all references below to various sections of the law are references to the Act.) In general, section 1877 as added by OBRA '89 prohibits a physician with a financial relationship with an entity that furnishes clinical laboratory services (or a physician with an immediate family member who has such a relationship) from making a referral to that entity for clinical laboratory services for which Medicare would pay. It also prohibits the entity from billing Medicare, an individual, a third-party payor, or other entity for an item or service furnished as a result of a prohibited referral. Additionally, it requires a refund of any amount collected from an individual as the result of a billing for an item or service furnished under a prohibited referral. The statute provides for certain exceptions to the prohibition.

B. OBRA '90

Section 4207(e) of OBRA '90 amended certain provisions of section 1877 to clarify definitions and reporting requirements relating to physician ownership and referral and to provide an additional exception to the prohibition.

C. Federal Register Documents

On December 3, 1991, we published an interim final rule in the **Federal Register**, at 56 FR 61374, that set forth reporting requirements under the Medicare program for health care entities furnishing clinical laboratory services (and certain other services as discussed below) to submit information about their relationships with physicians. On March 11, 1992, we published a proposed rule in the **Federal Register**, at 57 FR 8588, that proposed regulations concerning the provisions of section 1877, as amended by OBRA' 90, concerning physician

referrals to clinical laboratories. Although we summarize the provisions of the interim final rule and proposed rule in section II of this document, readers may want to refer to the interim final rule and proposed rule for additional information on the statutory provisions as amended by OBRA '90 and for the specifics of our proposals.

D. OBRA '93 and SSA '94

Section 13562 of OBRA '93 included extensive revisions to section 1877. Some of the revisions simply elaborate on or amend existing law, while others institute entirely new provisions. With regard to referrals for clinical laboratory services, some of the provisions of OBRA '93 have a prospective effective date of January 1, 1995, while others have a retrospective effective date of January 1, 1992. Most dramatically, section 13562 extends section 1877 to cover 10 additional designated health services, beginning with referrals made after December 31, 1994.

In addition, section 13624 added paragraph (r) to section 1903. This section extends certain provisions of section 1877 to the Medicaid program effective on or after December 31, 1994. That is, this section prohibits Medicaid payments to a State for designated health services furnished on the basis of a referral that would result in the denial of payment under Medicare if Medicare provided for coverage of the service to the same extent and under the same terms and conditions as under the State plan. This section also provides that the reporting requirements under 1877(f) and the civil money penalty provisions for failure to report information under section 1877(g)(5) apply to entities that furnish services covered under the Medicaid program in the same manner as they apply to entities that furnish Medicare covered services.

SSA '94 amended the reporting requirements that entities providing Medicare (and now Medicaid) items and services have to meet for purposes of the referral prohibition, changed some of the designated health services, and altered the effective date provisions in OBRA '93. The changes in the effective date provisions have altered the dates on which some of the provisions relating to referrals for clinical laboratory services go into effect prior to January 1, 1995. These changes have been reflected in this final rule.

A separate notice of proposed rulemaking will be published to address those provisions of OBRA '93 that relate to designated health services (including clinical laboratory services) and that become effective January 1, 1995. In other words, the discussion in this

41916 Federal Register / Vol. 60, No. 156 / Monday, August 14, 1995 / Rules and Regulations

preamble and the regulations established as a result of the publication of this final rule with comment period are in the context of referrals for clinical laboratory services and address only those provisions of section 1877 that are effective as of January 1, 1992.

Even though we will cover the designated health services under a separate proposed rule, this final rule with comment will affect how we review referrals involving any of the designated health services. The statute groups clinical laboratory services together with all other designated health services beginning on January 1, 1995. Generally, the prohibition in the statute and the exceptions are drafted so that they apply equally to situations involving referrals for any of the designated health services, including referrals for clinical laboratory services. As a result, we believe that a majority of our interpretations in this final rule with comment will apply to the other designated health services.

Until we publish a rule covering the designated health services, we intend to rely on our language and interpretations in this final rule when reviewing referrals for the designated health services in appropriate cases. We believe appropriate cases are those in which our interpretations of the statute clearly apply equally to referrals for clinical laboratory services and other designated health services. For example, we have defined the term "immediate family member" for purposes of this final rule with comment. We will be guided by this definition when we review referrals for the designated health services.

The following discussion covers the basic prohibition in section 1877 and fundamental concepts and definitions, while it highlights the changes to section 1877 made by OBRA '93, as amended by SSA '94, that relate to clinical laboratory services and that became effective on January 1, 1992.

1. General Prohibition

The prohibition of certain referrals is contained at section 1877(a)(1) of the Act. The provisions of that section remained unchanged by OBRA '93 until January 1, 1995. With certain exceptions, section 1877(a)(1)(A) prohibits a physician from making a referral to an entity for the furnishing of clinical laboratory services, for which Medicare would otherwise pay, if the physician (or a member of the physician's immediate family) has a financial relationship with that entity. ("Financial relationship," as described by the Act, is discussed under I.D.4. below.) Further, section 1877(a)(1)(B)

prohibits an entity from presenting or causing to be presented a Medicare claim or bill to any individual, third party payor, or other entity for clinical laboratory services furnished under a prohibited referral.

2. Definition of Referral

The definition of "referral," as it relates to clinical laboratory services, was not changed by OBRA '93. Section 1877(h)(5) specifies that the following requests constitute a referral:
• For physicians' services, the request by a physician for an item or service for which payment may be made under Medicare Part B, including the request by a physician for a consultation with another physician (and any test or procedure ordered by, or to be performed by (or under the supervision of) that other physician).
• For other items, the request or establishment of a plan of care by a physician that includes the furnishing of clinical laboratory services.

Under section 1877(h)(5)(C), however, a referral does not include a request by a pathologist for clinical diagnostic laboratory tests and pathological examination services if the services are furnished by (or under the supervision of) the pathologist as a result of a consultation requested by another physician.

3. Definitions of Compensation Arrangement and Remuneration

The predecessor provision of section 1877(h)(1) (that is, section 1877(h)(1) as it read before the enactment of OBRA '93) defines a "compensation arrangement" as any arrangement involving any remuneration between a physician (or an immediate family member) and an entity. It defines "remuneration" to include any remuneration, directly or indirectly, overtly or covertly, in cash or in kind. OBRA '93 amends section 1877(h)(1) by adding paragraph (h)(1)(C) to enumerate certain exceptions to the above definition of compensation arrangement. Paragraph (h)(1)(C) specifies that a compensation arrangement does not include the following types of remuneration:
• The forgiveness of amounts owed for inaccurate tests or procedures, mistakenly performed tests or procedures, or the correction of minor billing errors.
• The provision of items, devices, or supplies that are used solely to—
+ Collect, transport, process, or store specimens for the entity providing the item, device, or supply; or
+ Order or communicate the results of tests or procedures for the entity.

• A payment made by an insurer or a self-insured plan to a physician to satisfy a claim, submitted on a fee-for-service basis, for the furnishing of health services by that physician to an individual who is covered by a policy with the insurer or by the self-insured plan, if—
+ The health services are not furnished, and the payment is not made, under a contract or other arrangement between the insurer or the plan and the physician;
+ The payment is made to the physician on behalf of the covered individual and would otherwise be made directly to the individual;
+ The amount of the payment is set in advance, does not exceed fair market value, and is not determined in a manner that takes into account directly or indirectly the volume or value of any referrals; and
+ The payment meets other requirements the Secretary may impose by regulation as needed to protect against Medicare program or patient abuse.

4. Financial Relationships

Under OBRA '93, section 1877(a)(2) continues to describe a financial relationship between a physician (or an immediate family member of a physician) and an entity as being an ownership or investment interest in the entity or a compensation arrangement between a physician (or immediate family member) and the entity. The statute also continues to provide that an ownership or investment interest may be established through equity, debt, or other means. (Note that effective for referrals made on or after January 1, 1995, OBRA '93 provides that an ownership or investment interest also includes an interest in an entity that holds an ownership or investment interest in any entity furnishing the clinical laboratory service or other designated health service.)

5. General Exceptions to the Prohibition on Physician Referrals

Section 1877(b) provides for general exceptions to the prohibition on referrals. (General exceptions are exceptions that apply to both ownership/investment and compensation.) Because these exceptions frequently refer to a "group practice," we begin our discussion of the exceptions by describing "group practice" as defined by the statute at section 1877(h)(4).

Until January 1, 1995, OBRA '93 continued to define "group practice" as a group of two or more physicians legally organized as a partnership,

Federal Register / Vol. 60, No. 156 / Monday, August 14, 1995 / Rules and Regulations **41917**

professional corporation, foundation, not-for-profit corporation, faculty practice plan, or similar association, that meets the following conditions:

• Each physician member of the group furnishes substantially the full range of services that the physician routinely furnishes, including medical care, consultation, diagnosis, or treatment, through the joint use of shared office space, facilities, equipment, and personnel.

• Substantially all of the services of the physician members of the group are furnished through the group, are billed in the name of the group, and amounts so received are treated as receipts of the group.

• The overhead expenses of and the income from the practice are distributed in accordance with methods previously determined. (OBRA '93 eliminates the requirement that the methods be previously determined by members of the group.)

• The group practice complies with all other standards established by the Secretary in regulations.

In addition, OBRA '93 amended section 1877(h)(4). The predecessor provision of section 1877(h)(4) provided that, in the case of a faculty practice plan associated with a hospital with an approved medical residency training program in which physician members may furnish a variety of different specialty services and furnish professional services both within and outside the group, as well as perform other tasks such as research, the conditions contained in the definition of "group practice" apply only with respect to the services furnished within the faculty practice plan. OBRA '93 added, as an addition to a faculty practice plan associated with a hospital, a faculty practice plan associated with an institution of higher education or a medical school.

(Note that OBRA '93 makes other changes to the definition of group practice that will become effective January 1, 1995.)

a. Exception—Physicians' Services

Section 1877(b)(1) continues to specify that the prohibition does not apply to services furnished on a referral basis if the services are physicians' services, as defined in section 1861(q), furnished personally by (or under the personal supervision of) another physician in the same group practice (as defined in section 1877(h)(4)) as the referring physician.

b. Exception—In-Office Ancillary Services

Section 1877(b)(2) continues to specify that the prohibition does not

apply to referrals for certain in-office ancillary services. Both the predecessor provisions and current provisions of section 1877(b)(2) contain requirements that must be met in order for the exception to apply. These requirements concern who may furnish the services, where the services are furnished, and how the services must be billed.

Who May Furnish the Services

Under the predecessor provisions of section 1877(b)(2)(A)(i), the services had to be personally furnished by the referring physician, a physician who was a member of the same group as the referring physician, or individuals employed by the physician or group practice and who were personally supervised by the physician or by another physician in the group practice. OBRA '93 amends this provision to require that the individual performing the service be *directly* supervised by the physician or by another physician in the group practice and dropped the employment requirement.

Where the Services May Be Furnished

The predecessor provision of section 1877(b)(2)(A)(ii) required that the services be furnished in either of the following:

• A building in which the referring physician (or another physician who is a member of the same group practice) furnishes physicians' services unrelated to the furnishing of clinical laboratory services.

• In the case of a referring physician who is a member of a group practice, in another building that is used by the group practice for the centralized provision of the group's clinical laboratory services.

OBRA '93 amended this provision to require, in the group practice situation, that the building be used for the provision of some or all of the group's clinical laboratory services. That is, this provision no longer requires that the provision of laboratory services be centralized at that site.

The statute contains an undesignated paragraph at the end of the group practice location requirements that reads as follows: "unless the Secretary determines other terms and conditions under which the provision of such services does not present a risk of program or patient abuse. * * *"

We believe that, because of the way the paragraph is indented, how it applies to the in-office ancillary services exception is ambiguous. It could apply to all of paragraph (b)(2)(A)(ii) or apply to only paragraph (b)(2)(A)(ii)(II). If it applies to all of paragraph (b)(2)(A)(ii), it would affect both solo and group

practitioners. If it applies to only paragraph (b)(2)(A)(ii)(II), it would affect only group practices.

The Conference Report that accompanied OBRA '93 (H. Rep. No. 213, 103rd Cong., 1st Sess. 810 (1993)) points out that the conference agreement includes an exception for clinical laboratory services provided by a group practice that has multiple office locations. The Report also says that the conferees expect that the Secretary will publish regulations specifying other terms and conditions under which group practices may qualify for a group practice exception to the general prohibition. Arguably, the Congress had only group practices in mind in drafting the provision at issue. Therefore, we believe that the undesignated paragraph applies to only paragraph (b)(2)(A)(ii)(II), which concerns the site requirements as they relate to a group practice.

In addition, this paragraph could be read to mean that the Secretary is allowed to *liberalize* the circumstances in paragraph (b)(2)(A)(ii)(II) (the building/location requirements) if she determines that there are other, additional "terms and conditions" under which an entity can provide services without presenting a risk of program or patient abuse. In this case, the interpretation would not appear redundant with the undesignated paragraph that follows at the end of section 1877(b)(2)(B), which authorizes the Secretary to impose additional "requirements" for application of the in-office exception.

We could also interpret "other terms and conditions" as including any different terms or conditions, whether they are more restrictive or more liberal, that the Secretary may add to the list in paragraph (b)(2)(A)(ii) or in (b)(2)(A)(ii)(II). However, more restrictive conditions could make the two undesignated paragraphs redundant.

Alternatively, the paragraph following section 1877(b)(2)(A)(ii)(II)(bb) could be read to mean that the circumstances in (b)(2)(A)(ii) must be met for the exception to apply unless the Secretary determines *other* terms and conditions under which there will be no patient or program abuse, and which should be substituted for the list of conditions in (b)(2)(A)(ii). We do not believe that this reading would conflict with the paragraph that follows section 1877(b)(2)(B), because the Secretary could then still add more requirements to the list of those in paragraph (b)(2)(A)(ii) (with (b)(2)(A)(ii) now consisting of the Secretary's substitutions). Therefore, it is our

41918 Federal Register / Vol. 60, No. 156 / Monday, August 14, 1995 / Rules and Regulations

interpretation that this paragraph is intended to provide for the possibility of a liberalization of the conditions as described in section 1877(b)(2)(A)(ii)(II). At this time, we are not imposing any additional terms or conditions for the application of this provision, and we solicit comments on this issue.

Billing

Section 1877(b)(2)(B) continues to require that the ancillary services be billed by one of the following:
• The physician performing or supervising the services.
• A group practice of which the performing or supervising physician is a member.
• An entity that is wholly owned by the physician or group practice.
(Note that, effective January 1, 1995, the statutory definition of group practice requires that a group practice bill under a billing number assigned to the group.)

c. Exception—Certain Prepaid Health Plans

Section 1877(b)(3) continues to specify that the prohibition on referrals does not apply to services furnished to their enrollees by Medicare-contracting health maintenance organizations (HMOs), Medicare-contracting competitive medical plans (CMPs), and prepaid health care organizations under a contract or agreement with us. OBRA '93 expands the exception to apply it to services furnished to their enrollees by Federally-qualified HMOs. (The Federally-qualified HMOs are not required to have a contract or agreement with us in order for the exception to apply.)

d. Exception—Hospital Financial Relationship Unrelated to the Provision of Clinical Laboratory Services

Before the enactment of OBRA '93, section 1877(b)(4) provided a general exception to the prohibition in the case of a financial relationship with a hospital if the financial relationship did not relate to the provision of clinical laboratory services. OBRA '93 omitted this general exception, replacing it with section 1877(e)(4). Section 1877(e)(4) provides that remuneration from a hospital to a physician that is unrelated to the provision of clinical laboratory services does not constitute compensation that would trigger the prohibition on referrals. However, SSA '94 revised the effective date provision in section 13562(b)(2)(B) of OBRA '93. This effective date provision now states that section 1877(b)(4) continues to apply until January 1, 1995 as it was in effect before OBRA '93.

e. Other Exceptions

Section 1877(b) (currently at (b)(4)) continues to authorize the Secretary to provide in regulations for additional exceptions for financial relationships, beyond those specified in the statute, if she determines they do not pose a risk of Medicare program or patient abuse.

6. Exceptions Applicable Only to Financial Relationships Consisting of Ownership or Investment Interests

OBRA '93 continues to provide that certain ownership or investment interests do not constitute a "financial relationship" for purposes of the section 1877 prohibition on referrals.

a. Exception—Certain Investment Securities and Shares

Before OBRA '93, section 1877(c) contained an exception for ownership of investment securities, provided they were purchased on terms generally available to the public and were in a corporation that was (1) listed for trading on various specified stock exchanges and (2) had, at the end of the corporation's most recent fiscal year, total assets exceeding $100 million. These provisions were reflected in the proposed rule.

OBRA '93 has modified this provision in several ways. First, investment securities no longer have to be those purchased on terms generally available to the public; they must only be those which "may be purchased" on terms generally available to the public. Second, the securities can be those listed on additional exchanges, including any regional exchange in which quotations are published on a daily basis, or foreign securities listed on a recognized foreign, national, or regional exchange in which quotations are published on a daily basis.

Third, the investment securities no longer have to be in a corporation with $100 million in total assets at the end of a fiscal year; now the holdings of the corporation must be measured in terms of "stockholder equity," and the amount has been modified from $100 million to $75 million. This amount can now either be measured at the end of the most recent fiscal year or based on the corporation's average during the previous 3 fiscal years.

Finally, OBRA '93 extends the exception to apply to mutual funds, exempting ownership of shares in a regulated investment company as defined in section 851(a) of the Internal Revenue Code of 1986, if the company had, at the end of its most recent fiscal year, or on average during the previous 3 fiscal years, total assets exceeding $75 million.

Under the effective date provisions of OBRA '93, the amended version of section 1877(c) was not effective until January 1, 1995. SSA '94 revised the effective date provision to make the amended version of section 1877(c) effective retroactively to January 1, 1992; however, the revised effective date provision states that, prior to January 1, 1995, the amended section 1877(c) does not apply to any securities of a corporation that meets the requirements of section 1877(c)(2) as they appeared prior to OBRA '93. Section 1877(c)(2), prior to OBRA '93, contained the requirement that a corporation have $100 million in total assets. This final rule reflects the amended version of section 1877(c). It also specifies that, until January 1, 1995, ownership of investment securities in a corporation with $100 million in total assets can also qualify for the exception.

b. Exception—Ownership or Investment Interest in Certain Health Care Facilities

Section 1877(d) continues to provide additional exceptions to the prohibition on physician referrals for an ownership or investment interest of a physician (or an immediate family member of the physician) in three types of facilities:
• A hospital located in Puerto Rico.
• A laboratory located in a rural area (that is, an area outside of a Metropolitan Statistical Area as defined in section 1886(d)(2)(D)).
• A hospital outside of Puerto Rico if the referring physician is authorized to perform services at the hospital and the ownership or investment interest is in the hospital itself (and not merely in a subdivision of the hospital).
(Note that OBRA '93 contains changes to the above provisions that became effective on January 1, 1995. These extend the exceptions to designated health services and modify the exception for rural providers. Before OBRA '93, the exception applied if the laboratory furnishing the services is in a rural area (as defined in section 1886(d)(2)(D)). The statute now provides that the exception applies in the case of designated health services furnished in a rural area (as defined in section 1886(d)(2)(D)) by an entity, if substantially all of the designated health services furnished by the entity are furnished to individuals residing in the rural area.

7. Exceptions Applicable Only to Financial Relationships Consisting of Certain Compensation Arrangements

Section 1877(e) continues to provide that certain compensation arrangements are not considered a "financial relationship" for purposes of the prohibition on physician referrals.

a. Exception—Rental of Office Space

OBRA '93 amends the exception in section 1877(e)(1) for payments made by a lessee to a lessor for the use of office space, but delayed the effective date of the amendments until January 1, 1995. Section 152(c) of SSA '94 amends the effective date provision for OBRA '93 to eliminate this delay. The amended version of this exception now contains a requirement that the rented space not exceed that which is reasonable and necessary for the legitimate business purposes of the lease and that the space be used exclusively by the lessee during the lease. In addition, the exception now allows a lessee to pay for common areas shared with other occupants. Specifically, this provision states that payments made by a lessee to a lessor for the use of a premises do not constitute a compensation arrangement that would trigger the prohibition on referrals if the following conditions are met:

• The lease is set out in writing, signed by the parties, and specifies the premises covered by the lease.

• The space rented or leased does not exceed that which is reasonable and necessary for the legitimate business purposes of the lease or rental and is used exclusively by the lessee when being used by the lessee, except that the lessee may make payments for the use of space consisting of common areas if these payments do not exceed the lessee's pro rata share of expenses for that space based upon the ratio of the space used exclusively by the lessee to the total amount of space (other than common areas) occupied by all persons using the common areas.

• The lease provides for a term of rental or lease for at least 1 year.

• The rental charges over the term of the lease are set in advance, are consistent with fair market value, and are not determined in a manner that takes into account the volume or value of referrals or other business generated between the parties.

• The lease would be commercially reasonable even if no referrals were made between the parties.

• The lease meets any other requirements the Secretary may impose by regulation as needed to protect against program or patient abuse.

b. Exception—Rental of Equipment

OBRA '93 added a new provision, section 1877(e)(1)(B), effective January 1992, that excepts from the definition of compensation arrangements payments made by a lessee of equipment to the

lessor of the equipment for the use of the equipment if the following conditions are met:

• The lease is set out in writing, signed by the parties, and specifies the equipment covered by the lease.

• The equipment rented or leased does not exceed that which is reasonable and necessary for the legitimate business purposes of the rental or lease and is used exclusively by the lessee when being used by the lessee.

• The lease provides for a term of rental or lease of at least 1 year.

• The rental charges over the term of the lease are set in advance, are consistent with fair market value, and are not determined in a manner that takes into account the volume or value of any referrals or other business generated between the parties.

• The lease would be commercially reasonable even if no referrals were made between the parties.

• The lease meets any other requirements the Secretary may impose by regulation as needed to protect against Medicare program or patient abuse.

c. Exception—Bona Fide Employment Relationship

The predecessor provision of section 1877(e)(2) provided that an arrangement between a hospital and a physician (or the physician's immediate family member) for the employment of the physician (or family member) or for the provision of administrative services would not trigger the prohibition on referrals if certain conditions (detailed in the March 1992 proposed rule) were met. OBRA '93 amended this exception to make it applicable to any bona fide employment relationship with any employer that meets the same conditions.

d. Exception—Personal Service Arrangements

The predecessor provision of section 1877(e)(3) provided that remuneration from service arrangements with entities (other than hospitals) does not constitute a compensation arrangement for purposes of the prohibition on referrals if certain conditions (detailed in the March 1992 proposed rule) are met. This exception was limited to an arrangement for one of five specific types of services. OBRA '93 amended this provision to specify that remuneration from any entity under any kind of personal service arrangement (including remuneration for specific physicians' services furnished to a nonprofit blood center) would not constitute compensation that would

trigger the prohibition on referrals if the following conditions are met:

• The arrangement is set out in writing, signed by the parties, and specifies the services covered by the arrangement.

• The arrangement covers all of the services to be furnished by the physician (or immediate family member of the physician) to the entity.

• The aggregate services contracted for do not exceed those that are reasonable and necessary for the legitimate business purposes of the arrangement.

• The term of the arrangement is for at least 1 year.

• The compensation to be paid over the term of the arrangement is set in advance, does not exceed fair market value and, except in the case of a physician incentive plan (as described below), is not determined in a manner that takes into account the volume or value of any referrals or other business generated between the parties.

• The services to be performed under the arrangement do not involve the counseling or promotion of a business arrangement or other activity that violates any State or Federal law.

• The arrangement meets any other requirements the Secretary may impose by regulation as needed to protect against Medicare program or patient abuse.

Section 1877(e)(3)(B) provides that, in the case of a physician incentive plan between a physician and an entity, the compensation may be determined in a manner (through a withhold, capitation, bonus, or otherwise) that takes into account, directly or indirectly, the volume or value of any referrals or other business generated between the parties if the plan meets the following requirements:

• No specific payment is made (directly or indirectly) under the plan to a physician or a physician group as an inducement to reduce or limit medically necessary services provided with respect to a specific individual enrolled with the entity.

• If the plan places a physician or a physician group at substantial financial risk as determined by the Secretary under section 1876(i)(8)(A)(ii), the plan complies with any requirements the Secretary may impose under that section.

In addition, section 1877(e)(3)(B)(i)(III) requires the entity, upon request by the Secretary, to provide access to descriptive information regarding the plan, in order to permit the Secretary to determine whether the plan is in compliance with the requirements listed above.

41920   Federal Register / Vol. 60, No. 156 / Monday, August 14, 1995 / Rules and Regulations

Section 1877(e)(3)(B)(ii) defines a "physician incentive plan" as any compensation arrangement between an entity and a physician or physician group that may directly or indirectly have the effect of reducing or limiting services provided with respect to individuals enrolled with the entity.

On December 14, 1992, we published, at 57 FR 59024, our proposed rule on physician incentive plans. Because there may be entities that were not affected by the proposed rule at the time it was published but are now affected, we plan to publish the final rule with a 60-day comment period so that these newly-affected entities have an opportunity to comment.

As the result of section 152(c) of SSA '94, until January 1, 1995, the provisions in section 1877(e)(3) do not apply to any arrangements that meet the requirements of subsection (e)(2) or (e)(3) of section 1877 of the Act before they were amended by OBRA '93.

e. Exception—Remuneration Unrelated to Provision of Clinical Laboratory Services

Before OBRA '93, section 1877(b)(4) provided an exception for financial relationships (ownership/investment interests or compensation arrangements) with a hospital unrelated to the provision of clinical lab services. OBRA '93 omits this exception, but replaces it with section 1877(e)(4), which excepts remuneration provided by a hospital to a physician if it is unrelated to the provision of clinical laboratory services. Section 152(c) of SSA '94 amends section 13562(b)(2)(B) of OBRA '93 to reinstate, until January 1, 1995, section 1877(b)(4) as it appeared before OBRA '93.

f. Exception—Physician Recruitment

OBRA '93 retains, at section 1877(e)(5), the provision previously at section 1877(e)(4). The provision provides that remuneration from a hospital to a physician to induce the physician to relocate to the area serviced by the hospital in order to be a member of the hospital's medical staff does not constitute a compensation arrangement for purposes of the prohibition on referrals if certain conditions (detailed in the March 1992 proposed rule) are met.

g. Exception—Isolated Transaction

OBRA '93 retains, at section 1877(e)(6), the provision previously at section 1877(e)(5). The provision provides that an isolated financial transaction, such as a one-time sale of property or (as added by OBRA '93) a practice, is not considered to be a compensation arrangement for purposes of the prohibition on referrals if certain conditions (detailed in the March 1992 proposed rule) are met.

h. Salaried Physicians in a Group Practice

OBRA '93 removed, effective January 1, 1992, the provision previously at section 1877(e)(6). That provision had specified that a compensation arrangement involving payment by a group practice of the salary of a physician member of the group practice did not constitute a compensation arrangement that would trigger the prohibition on referrals.

i. Exception—Certain Group Practice Arrangements With a Hospital

OBRA '93 added a new section 1877(e)(7) that provides, effective January 1, 1992, that an arrangement between a hospital and group under which clinical laboratory services are furnished by the group but are billed by the hospital does not constitute a compensation arrangement for purposes of the prohibition on referrals if the following conditions are met:

• With respect to the services furnished to a hospital inpatient, the arrangement is in accordance with the provision of inpatient hospital services under section 1861(b)(3).

• The arrangement began before December 19, 1989, and has continued in effect without interruption since that date.

• With respect to the clinical laboratory services covered under the arrangement, substantially all of these services furnished to patients of the hospital are furnished by the group under the arrangement.

• The arrangement is set out in a written agreement that specifies the services to be furnished by the parties and the amount of compensation.

• The compensation paid over the term of the agreement is consistent with fair market value, and the compensation per unit of services is fixed in advance and is not determined in a manner that takes into account the volume or value of any referrals or other business generated between the parties.

• The compensation is provided under an agreement that would be commercially reasonable even if no referrals were made to the entity.

• The arrangement between the parties meets any other requirements the Secretary may impose by regulation as needed to protect against Medicare program or patient abuse.

j. Exception—Payments by a Physician for Items and Services

OBRA '93 added a new section 1877(e)(8), which provides that the following do not constitute compensation arrangements for purposes of the prohibition on referrals:

• Payments made by a physician to a laboratory in exchange for the provision of clinical laboratory services.

• Payments made by a physician to an entity as compensation for items or services other than clinical laboratory services if the items or services are furnished at fair market value.

8. Sections 1877(f) and 1877(g)

SSA '94 amends the provisions of section 1877(f), which concern reporting requirements. This section requires each entity providing covered items or services for which payment may be made under Medicare to provide the Secretary with information concerning the entity's ownership, investment, and (as added by SSA '94) compensation arrangements including (1) the covered items and services furnished by the entity and (2) the names and unique physician identification numbers of all physicians with an ownership or investment interest (as described in section 1877(a)(2)(A)) in or a compensation arrangement (as described in section 1877(a)(2)(B)) with the entity, or whose immediate relatives have such an ownership or investment interest in or who have such a compensation relationship with the entity. OBRA '93 retained the provisions of section 1877(g), which concern sanctions.

9. Other Definitions

OBRA '93 amended section 1877(h)(5) and (6) to remove the definitions for "investor" and "interested investor, disinterested investor," effective January 1, 1992.

II. Published Federal Register Documents

A. Provisions of the Proposed Rule—Physician Ownership of, and Referrals to, Health Care Entities That Furnish Clinical Laboratory Services

As stated earlier, on March 11, 1992, we published in the Federal Register a proposed rule that set forth our proposal for establishing in regulations the provisions of section 1877, as amended by OBRA '90, that relate to physician referrals to clinical laboratories. Section 1877 is very specific. For the most part, we believed the definitions set forth in section 1877(h) were detailed and therefore did not require extensive elaboration in regulations. Accordingly,

133

Federal Register / Vol. 60, No. 156 / Monday, August 14, 1995 / Rules and Regulations   **41921**

we proposed to adopt some of the statutory definitions, as well as some other provisions of section 1877, virtually unchanged from what the statute provided. To establish these rules in our regulations, we proposed to create a new subpart J under 42 CFR part 411 and to make conforming changes as discussed below.

1. Scope

We proposed to cite section 1877 as the statutory authority for the rule.

2. Definitions

In section 411.351, we proposed to establish definitions of certain terms based on definitions or descriptions given in section 1877: compensation arrangement, employee, fair market value, financial relationship, group practice, interested investor, investor, referral, and remuneration. In addition, we proposed to add other definitions: entity, immediate family member or a member of a physician's immediate family, practice, and referring physician.

For purposes of identifying financial relationships that may trigger the statutory prohibition on referrals under Medicare, we proposed to adopt the description of ownership and investment interests and compensation arrangements contained in sections 1877(a)(2) and (h)(1). We also proposed to include indirect financial relationships in the statutory prohibition on referrals under Medicare.

3. General Prohibition on Referrals

In section 411.353(a), we proposed that, unless permitted under an exception, a physician who has a financial relationship with an entity (or who has an immediate family member who has a financial relationship with an entity) may not make a referral to that entity for the furnishing of clinical laboratory services covered under Medicare beginning January 1, 1992. (Note that we are providing a 30-day delay of the effective date for the provisions of this final rule with comment. However, this does not delay the effective date for any of the provisions in the final rule that only reiterate the language in section 1877 of the Social Security Act. These provisions are effective according to their statutory effective dates. The effective date for this final rule with comment is, in essence, the effective date for those parts of the rule that interpret the statute.)

To inform the public of what entities we would consider entities that perform clinical laboratory services and, therefore, subject to the provisions of

section 1877 and to the regulation, we referenced existing section 493.2, which defines a "laboratory."

We proposed, in section 411.353(b), that an entity that furnishes clinical laboratory services under a prohibited referral may not bill the Medicare program or any individual, third party payer, or other entity.

In section 411.353(c), we provided that we would not pay for a clinical laboratory service that is furnished under a prohibited referral, and we proposed, in section 411.353(d), to require an entity that collects payment for a laboratory service performed under a prohibited referral to refund all collected amounts on a timely basis.

4. Exceptions That Apply to Specific Services

In accordance with section 1877(b), we proposed, in section 411.355, that the prohibition on clinical laboratory referrals would not apply in the following circumstances:

• If a physician service is provided personally by (or under the direct personal supervision of) another physician in the same group practice as the referring physician.

• If an in-office ancillary service is performed personally by the referring physician, a physician who is a member of the same group practice as the referring physician, or a nonphysician employee of the referring physician or group practice who is personally supervised by the referring or group practice physician and—

+ The in-office ancillary service is performed either in a building where the referring physician (or another physician who is a member of the same group practice) furnishes physicians' services unrelated to the furnishing of clinical laboratory services; or in a building that is used by the group practice for centrally furnishing the group's clinical laboratory services; and

+ The in-office ancillary service is billed by the physician who performed or supervised the laboratory service; by the group practice in which the physician is a member; or by an entity that is wholly owned by the physician or physician's group practice.

• If the services are furnished to prepaid health plan enrollees by one of the following organizations: (1) A health maintenance organization or a competitive medical plan in accordance with a contract with us under section 1876; (2) a health care prepayment plan in accordance with an agreement with us to furnish the services to Medicare beneficiaries under section 1833(a)(1)(A); or (3) an organization that is receiving payments on a prepaid basis

for the enrollees under a demonstration project under section 402(a) of the Social Security Amendments of 1967 (42 U.S.C. 1395b–1) or under section 222(a) of the Social Security Amendments of 1972 (42 U.S.C. 1395b–1 note).

We also proposed, in section 411.355(a), to use an existing definition of "physicians' services" but cited an incorrect cross reference to that definition. The cross-reference should have been to section 410.20 rather than section 411.20(a). Existing section 410.20 describes physicians' services and specifies the professionals who are considered to be "physicians" if they are authorized under State law to practice and if they act within the scope of their licenses.

5. Exceptions for Certain Ownership or Investment Interests

a. Publicly Traded Securities

We proposed, in section 411.357(a), that the prohibition on referrals would not apply to a physician's referrals if the financial relationship between the physician (or the physician's immediate family member) and the entity results from the ownership of certain investment securities. We proposed that the securities must be purchased by the physician (or immediate family member) on terms generally available to the public and be in a corporation that meets specific criteria.

b. Specific Providers

In section 411.357(b)(1), we proposed that the prohibition on referrals would not apply to a laboratory that is located in a rural area if certain criteria are met.

To supplement the statutory provision excepting services furnished in a rural laboratory, we proposed two requirements intended to address the possibility that this exception would be misused. First, we proposed to require, when physician owners or investors make referrals to a laboratory located in a rural area, that the tests be performed directly by the laboratory on its premises. We stated that, if referral to another laboratory is necessary, the test must be billed by the laboratory that performs the test. Second, we proposed to require that the majority of the tests referred to the rural laboratory be referred by physicians who have office practices in a rural area. (For this purpose, as indicated earlier, we proposed a definition of "practice.")

We proposed, in section 411.357(b)(2) and (b)(3), that the prohibition on referrals would not apply if the ownership or investment interest is in—

A hospital located in Puerto Rico; or

41922   **Federal Register** / Vol. 60, No. 156 / Monday, August 14, 1995 / Rules and Regulations

A hospital located outside of Puerto Rico if one of two specified conditions is met concerning the nature of the ownership.

6. Exceptions Related to Compensation Arrangements

We proposed to add section 411.359 to specify that, for purposes of the referral prohibition, certain compensation arrangements (as defined in the proposed rule) would not constitute a financial relationship if they involve—

• Rental or lease of office space;
• Certain employment and service arrangements with hospitals;
• Certain arrangements connected with physician recruitment;
• Certain isolated financial transactions;
• Certain service arrangements with entities other than hospitals;
• Salaried physicians in a group practice; and
• Other arrangements with hospitals if the arrangement does not relate to furnishing clinical laboratory services.

B. Provisions of the Interim Final Rule With Comment Period—Reporting Requirements for Financial Relationships Between Physicians and Health Care Entities That Furnish Selected Items and Services

The interim final rule with comment period (published December 3, 1991) listed reporting requirements under the Medicare program for the submission by certain health care entities of information about their financial relationships with physicians. It implemented section 1877(f), which includes the requirement that entities furnishing Medicare covered items or services provide us with information concerning their ownership or investment arrangements. (The rule extended the reporting to include compensation arrangements, not just ownership and investment interests.) The December 1991 interim final rule also provided notice of our decision to waive the requirements of section 1877(f) with respect to certain entities that do not furnish clinical laboratory services.

The information submitted was to include at least the name and unique physician identification number (UPIN) of each physician who had a financial relationship with the entity, the name and UPIN of each physician who had an immediate relative who had a financial relationship with the entity and, with respect to each physician identified, the nature of the financial relationship (including the extent and/or value of the ownership or investment interest or the

compensation arrangement, if we requested it).

Any person who, although required to, failed to submit the required information was subject to a civil money penalty of not more than $10,000 for each day of the period beginning on the day following the applicable deadline established until the information was submitted.

In addition, the interim final rule discussed our decision to waive the reporting requirements for all entities (other than those providing clinical laboratory services) in States other than the minimum number of 10 specified in the statute. In the 10 States we selected, the reporting requirements were waived for entities other than the 6 types enumerated in the statute and section 411.361(c). The waiver represented a balance between our need to obtain sufficient ownership information for meaningful use in developing a statistical profile required by the Congress in section 6204(f) of OBRA '89, as amended by section 4207(e)(4) of OBRA '90, and in evaluating the need for future legislative, policy, or operational actions, and the need to minimize the administrative time and cost involved in collecting and analyzing the information. We believe that by collecting the information from the enumerated entities in the minimum number of 10 States, we satisfied these congressional and administrative needs.

In determining the States in which a blanket waiver would not be granted, we selected 10 States that represented approximately 42 percent of the physicians who bill the Medicare program for items and services furnished to beneficiaries. Medicare contractors servicing all providers and suppliers in the 10 selected States process approximately 40 percent of all Medicare claims. Services provided by the six types of entities specified in the statute account for a significant proportion of Medicare expenditures and represent a cross-section of Medicare covered services. Therefore, we decided to waive the requirements of section 1877(f) with respect to entities (other than those providing clinical laboratory services) in all States except the following: Arkansas, California, Connecticut, Florida, Michigan, Ohio, Pennsylvania, South Carolina, Texas, and West Virginia. These States were selected because they represent: A mix of rural (West Virginia), urban (Florida), and mixed urban/rural States (Ohio, Texas); a variety of claims/bills volume, from very small (Arkansas) to very large (Pennsylvania); and, a geographic spread from north (Michigan) to south

(South Carolina) as well as both coasts (from California to Connecticut).

Note that while the effect of section 1877(f) of the Act and section 6204(f) of OBRA '89 was to require the Secretary to submit to the Congress a statistical profile within 90 days after each calendar quarter, section 4207(e)(4) of OBRA '90 amended OBRA '89 to require only one statistical profile, which was due by June 30, 1992. Clinical laboratory entities reported information about financial relationships with physicians as part of a survey conducted in the fall of 1991, and we used this data in the required statistical profile.

Section 1877(f) authorizes the Secretary to gather information from any entity providing covered items or services in such form, manner, and at such time as she specifies. Thus, the Secretary can again require entities to report whenever she deems it appropriate for purposes of enforcing the referral prohibition in section 1877. Section 152(a) of SSA '94 amended section 1877(f), altering the rules for future reporting. The provision now requires entities to report not only their ownership arrangements with physicians, but also their investment and compensation arrangements. Section 152(a) also eliminated the Secretary's authority to waive the reporting requirements for certain states or services. The Secretary, however, continues to have the right to determine that an entity is not subject to the reporting requirements because it provides Medicare-covered services very infrequently. In addition, the reporting requirements still do not apply to designated health services furnished outside the United States. The effective date of the amendments to section 1877(f) is the date of enactment of SSA '94, that is, October 31, 1994.

III. Principles for Developing This Final Rule With Comment Period

In this final rule with comment, we are adopting the provisions of our March 1992 proposed rule, changed as appropriate to address the comments on the proposed rule and the new requirements relating to clinical laboratory services contained in OBRA '93, as amended by SSA '94, that have a retroactive effective date of January 1, 1992. OBRA '93 provides several exceptions that were not in previous legislation. In some cases, these new exceptions address suggestions received through public comment on the March 1992 proposed rule. It is our intention that this final rule with comment reflect, to the extent possible, the comments on the proposed rule and the new, but retroactive, requirements of OBRA '93.

Federal Register / Vol. 60, No. 156 / Monday, August 14, 1995 / Rules and Regulations   **41923**

as amended by SSA '94. This final rule with comment also revises the provisions of the December 1991 interim final rule to incorporate the amendments to section 1877(f) made by SSA '94, to apply to any future reporting that we require.

To address the provisions of section 1877 that are effective on January 1, 1995, as provided by OBRA '93, we plan to publish regulations in addition to this one. We will publish a proposed rule to interpret any retroactive provisions contained in OBRA '93 that we believe allow us to exercise discretion in their implementation. In this final rule, we have, in general, only reiterated the new, but retroactive, statutory provisions, incorporating them into our proposals. We have interpreted the new provisions only in the few instances in which it was necessary to do so in order to allow the statute to be implemented at all.

The proposed rule will also cover those provisions of section 1877 concerning physician referrals for clinical laboratory services that became effective on January 1, 1995, as well as those covering the other designated health services (all of which are effective for referrals made on or after January 1, 1995). Finally, we plan to publish a final rule that will address any comments received on this final rule with comment and the new proposed rule.

We are including in this final rule the OBRA '93 provisions related to the following:

• The in-office ancillary services exception.

• The rental of equipment exception.

• The rental of office space exception.

• The bona fide employment relationships exception.

• The personal services and physician incentive plan exception.

• The exception concerning remuneration unrelated to the provision of clinical laboratory services.

• The change in the isolated transactions exception.

• The exception concerning certain group practice arrangements with a hospital.

• The exception for payments by a physician for items and services.

• All changes in definitions in 1877(h) that have a retroactive effective date (compensation arrangement, remuneration, group practice).

IV. Analysis of and Responses to Public Comments on the Proposed Rule—Physician Ownership of, and Referrals to, Health Care Entities That Furnish Clinical Laboratory Services

In response to the publication in the **Federal Register** of the proposed rule on March 11, 1992, we received 299 timely public comments. The comments came from a wide variety of correspondents including professional associations and societies, health care workers, law firms, third party health insurers, hospitals, and private individuals. We screened each commenter's letter and grouped like or related comments. Some comments were identical, indicating that the commenters had submitted form letters. After associating like comments, we placed them in categories based on subject matter or based on the portion of the regulations affected and then reviewed the comments. All comments relating to general subjects, such as the format of the regulations, were similarly reviewed.

This process identified areas of the proposed regulation that we needed to review in terms of their effect on policy, consistency, or clarity of the rules.

We have presented all comments and responses in, for the most part, the order in which the issues appeared in the March 1992 proposed rule.

Note: We have found it necessary to change the designation of some sections from what was proposed. We have prepared a table, which appears at the end of this preamble, that relates the requirements in this final rule to the correlative proposed sections from which they evolved. If OBRA '93 provisions resulted in significant change, we so identify OBRA '93 as the source. This table is intended merely to assist parties who may be interested in comparing specific provisions as proposed or as contained in OBRA '93 to those of the final rule with comment. It does not supplant the more detailed discussion in this preamble. Unless otherwise indicated, citations in the responses that follow are to the sections as they are designated by this final rule with comment.

A. General

1. Purpose of Final Rule

Comment: One commenter requested that the Secretary ensure that the final rule is cast so that its purpose is clear; that is, the rule should be presented so as to support the idea that the ethical delivery of quality, medically necessary care is fundamental to preserving the integrity of medical practice in general as well as the Medicare program in particular.

Response: We share the commenter's view. We believe that section 1877 was enacted out of concern over the findings of various studies that physicians who

have a financial relationship with a laboratory entity order more clinical laboratory tests for their Medicare patients than physicians who do not have a financial relationship. There have been at least 10 studies conducted over the past few years that concluded that patients of physicians who have financial relationships with health care suppliers receive a greater number of health care services from those suppliers than do patients generally.

To the extent that section 1877 and this final rule protect against this practice, the Medicare program and its beneficiaries are well served. Therefore, to the extent that physicians and providers of clinical laboratory services change their financial relationships and behavior to comply with provisions of section 1877 and, in turn, reduce overutilization of laboratory services, we believe that this change will have a positive effect on other health insurance programs. One of our prime goals is to ensure that our rules carry out the Congress' mandate in a manner that is in the best interest of all individuals who may be affected by the rules.

2. Delay of Effective Date

Comment: Several commenters requested that we delay the effective date of the final rule. One commenter recommended a 60-day delay, another recommended not less than 90 days, and yet another commenter requested not less than 120 days from the date of publication in the **Federal Register** and that application of the regulation should be prospective only.

Response: We usually provide for a 30-day delay in the effective date of a final rule. This delay is offered so that affected parties have the opportunity to change their practices, if necessary, to comply with the requirements of the final rule. While we understand that the goal behind the commenters' suggestions is to provide sufficient time for parties affected by this final rule to make arrangements to comply with its requirements, we do not believe that an additional delay in the effective date would be beneficial. This is so primarily because, in this rule, we are establishing additional exceptions from the prohibition on referrals based upon public comments. In addition, we plan to publish a subsequent final regulation that will address any comments received on this regulation.

3. Delay of Enforcement Provisions

Comment: One commenter requested that the Secretary indicate that the enforcement of the prohibition on referrals begin no earlier than the effective date of this rule. As a result of

41924   Federal Register / Vol. 60, No. 156 / Monday, August 14, 1995 / Rules and Regulations

this suggestion, any physician who is out of compliance with section 1877 before that effective date would be held harmless under the final rule.

Another commenter requested that we postpone the implementation of sanctions, at the very least, until 90 days after the final rule has been issued.

Response: Section 1877(g) of the Act sets forth several enforcement provisions that apply to prohibited referrals for clinical laboratory services and to prohibited claims for payment for these services.

• Section 1877(g)(1) provides for denial of Medicare payment for a clinical laboratory service furnished as the result of a prohibited referral.

• Under section 1877(g)(2), if a person collects any amounts that were billed for services furnished under a prohibited referral, a timely refund of each amount is required.

• Section 1877(g)(3) authorizes the imposition of civil money penalties of not more than $15,000 for each such service and possible exclusion from the Medicare and other programs for any person that presents, or causes to be presented, a bill or a claim for a clinical laboratory service that the person knows or should know was unlawfully referred or for which a refund has not been made.

• Under section 1877(g)(4), civil money penalties of not more than $100,000 for each arrangement or scheme and possible exclusion from participation in the Medicare and other programs are authorized in cases in which a physician or an entity enters into a circumvention arrangement or scheme (such as a cross-referral arrangement) that the physician or entity knows or should know has a principal purpose of ensuring referrals by the physician to a particular entity that would be unlawful under section 1877 if made directly. (See the final rule with comment published by the Office of Inspector General on March 31, 1995 (60 FR 16580) for further information. That rule addresses sections 1877(g)(3) and (g)(4).)

The first commenter appears to be suggesting that these statutory enforcement provisions should not be applied until the effective date of this final rule and that a physician who is not in compliance with the provisions of the statute at the time the final rule is published should be held harmless until the effective date of the final rule. The second commenter suggested a 90-day delay in application of any sanctions following publication of the final rule.

We disagree with these suggestions. First, many of the provisions of section

1877 of the Act were effective on January 1, 1992, by operation of law. These provisions are, for the most part, self-implementing. This rule incorporates into regulations statutory requirements that are already in effect, clarifying or interpreting certain provisions, and exercising the Secretary's authority to promulgate additional exceptions through regulations. Even though the requirements of this final rule are effective later than the effective date of the statute, we cannot postpone the statutory effective date. Nonetheless, any sanctions that can be applied only as a result of the clarification or interpretation of the statute specified in this rule will, of course, be applied prospectively, beginning with the effective date of this rule.

Section 1877(f) of the Act sets forth certain reporting requirements with which entities were to comply by October 1, 1991. Under this authority, we conducted a survey in the fall of 1991 concerning physician ownership in, and compensation arrangements with, entities furnishing clinical laboratory services. Based on data gathered from that survey, Medicare carriers have already been denying some claims for laboratory services furnished by a laboratory that is independent of a physician's office and that are furnished in violation of the prohibition on referrals. Similarly, the Office of the Inspector General could impose sanctions if, for example, a clinical laboratory has failed to refund an amount that it collected for a service furnished as the result of a referral if the laboratory knew the referral was prohibited.

4. Good Faith Standard

Comment: One commenter suggested that the final rule have either a good faith standard or a provision that the statute will not be violated unless the physician or the laboratory has actual knowledge of a prohibited referral. The commenter requested that the final rule specify the scope of the inquiry required and define the extent of the duty imposed upon laboratories and physicians to determine the relationship of persons that would affect their ability to refer laboratory work or to accept a referral.

Response: It is important to emphasize that the statute and this rule do not prohibit financial relationships that exist or might be established between physicians and entities providing clinical laboratory services. What is prohibited are certain referrals for clinical laboratory testing of Medicare patients. The statute itself, at

section 1877(a)(2), describes "financial relationship" for purposes of determining whether a referral is prohibited. And, as discussed above, section 1877(g) specifies several sanctions that may be applied if a physician or an entity billing for a Medicare covered clinical laboratory service violates the statute's requirements. Thus, unless an exception applies, the statute operates automatically under its own terms to prohibit referrals for Medicare-covered clinical laboratory services to be performed by an entity with which the physician or an immediate family member of the physician has a financial relationship.

We understand that this commenter is advocating adoption of a policy that would hold harmless a physician or laboratory if there is no intention on the part of either to seek an advantage from an ownership interest or compensation arrangement. The commenter is also concerned that a physician or a laboratory may be unintentionally involved in a relationship that would call the physician's referrals into question. Similarly, a laboratory may be unaware that it has a relationship with a referring physician's relatives that would cause the prohibition to apply. However, the statutory prohibition against referrals in such situations applies because of the existence of the financial relationship, not because of the intent of the physician or laboratory or because there is actual knowledge of the relationship. It is the responsibility of physicians and laboratory entities to take whatever steps are necessary to ensure that they do not violate Federal law.

5. Physician Ownership of Health Care Facilities

Comment: One major national medical organization indicated that it believed ownership of health care facilities by referring physicians is an issue that should be addressed, and it supported the proposed rule. It believed there is increased evidence that, when physicians have a financial relationship with an entity, the relationship adversely affects patient care and adds to the cost of health care in the United States. Therefore, the organization believed that physicians should not have a direct or indirect financial interest in diagnostic or therapeutic facilities to which they refer patients, and it indicated support for legislation and regulations that would eliminate this conflict of interest by prohibiting such ownership arrangements in health care.

Response: We agree with this commenter. As stated earlier, recent studies have concluded that there is a higher level of utilization of services when physicians refer patients to entities with which they have a financial relationship. As mentioned in the preamble to the proposed rule (57 FR 8589), a report from the Office of the Inspector General to the Congress established that at least 25 percent of the nearly 4500 independent clinical laboratories are owned in whole or in part by referring physicians. The same report found that Medicare patients of referring physicians who own or invest in independent clinical laboratories received 45 percent more clinical laboratory services than all Medicare patients. ("Financial Arrangements Between Physicians and Health Care Businesses," May 1989, page 18). A study published in "Medical Care" (Vol. 32, No. 2) in February 1994 found that a review of clinical laboratory practices in Florida lends support to the contentions of critics that physician joint ventures (health care businesses that physicians own, but where they do not practice or directly provide services) result in increased use of services and higher charges to consumers. Utilization, measured as the number of billable laboratory procedures per patient, is significantly higher in facilities owned by referring physicians. Although the study reported only negligible differences in charges per procedure (compared to nonphysician-owned facilities), it found that higher utilization rates resulted in significantly higher gross and net revenue per patient. Furthermore, the study found that differences in average production costs per patient in physician-owned and nonphysician-owned facilities were not significant. The net result is that physician joint ventures are far more profitable than comparable nonphysician joint ventures. The study results, which included laboratory services furnished to both private and publicly insured patients, corroborate previous evidence of higher use of laboratory procedures among Medicare and Medicaid patients treated by referring physician investors.

Many States have enacted or are considering regulations that would affect physician referrals to entities with which the physicians have financial relationships. For example, New Jersey implemented regulations that effectively prohibit physicians from referring patients to facilities they own. Physicians who do not comply with the regulations are subject to sanctions under the State's physicians practice

law. Furthermore, in OBRA '93 the Congress has extended application of the prohibition on referrals to other types of health care services and health care entities.

6. Process for Amending Regulations

Comment: One commenter indicated that we should maintain an expedited process for amending the regulations and issuing clarifications. The commenter pointed out that, despite a careful review of the proposed regulations, it is not possible to identify all of the unintended consequences of applying the proposed regulations to particular laboratory arrangements. The commenter believed that unless we respond quickly to issue clarifications and correct such problems when identified, inappropriate regulations can disrupt the delivery of, and limit patient access to, quality clinical laboratory services.

Response: We understand and appreciate the commenter's desire to feel secure about the requirements of the law. We make all possible efforts to publish final rules as quickly as possible and to amend the regulations expeditiously if clarifications or changes are needed and can be accomplished through rulemaking. In addition, we keep our regional offices and the Medicare contractors informed through manual instructions of technical changes that can be made without rulemaking. The contractors, in turn, advise the physicians and laboratory entities in their service areas of such changes. In regard to inquiries about particular laboratory arrangements, our regulations do not provide for the issuance of formal advisory opinions of any kind pertaining to section 1877 or any other section of the law for which we are responsible. We receive a large volume of correspondence from the public, and we do respond to general questions about the contents of our regulations and manuals. We, however, do not have the authority and will not attempt to interpret the applicability of these physician self-referral provisions to situations posed in correspondence. Our advice must, of necessity, continue to be general.

7. Evolution of Group Practices

Comment: Before the enactment of section 1877 of the Act, the Medicare program did not have a statutory definition of "group practice," nor any detailed body of law developed through regulations or manual instructions to define or otherwise recognize a group practice as a provider entity. One commenter indicated that we should recognize the significance of this

rulemaking to the development and evolution of group practices in this country.

The commenter expressed hope that regulations will recognize the diversity of business structures within the group practice field and accommodate nonabusive arrangements for the provision of clinical laboratory services based on the substance of the arrangements, not merely their form.

The commenter also indicated that we should be mindful of the significance of this rule to the competitive "playing field" in health care. It was stated that, as medical group practices evolve into larger and more full-service providers of a wide range of physician ancillary and other health care products and services, they are furnishing many items and services that have traditionally been furnished by inpatient institutions or independent suppliers. The commenter also expressed hope that nothing in the final rule will prohibit group practices from performing services for other physicians' patients or other providers assuming, of course, that the referring source does not have a prohibited financial arrangement with the group. The commenter applauded us for proposing a rule that does not force groups to choose between serving their own patients and those of otherwise unrelated physicians.

Response: In publishing these final regulations, it is not our intent to obstruct the efforts of an association of physicians to qualify as a group practice under the definition in section 1877(h)(4) and therefore qualify for the in-office ancillary services exception set forth in section 1877(b)(2) of the Act and described in § 411.355(b). If a group of physicians meets the definition of a "group practice" under section 1877(h), it could also be eligible for the exception for physicians' services in section 1877(b)(1) and possibly the exception in section 1877(e)(7) for certain arrangements between a hospital and a group practice. Further, we believe that, to the extent possible, we have accommodated various group practice configurations given the statutory parameters.

The point made in the last sentence of the comment, as we understand it, endorses the adoption of a policy that would enable group practice laboratories to continue to perform laboratory tests for their own patients as well as to accept laboratory referrals from physicians in the community who do not have a financial relationship with the group practice. In the responses to various comments presented below, we have clarified that the provisions of section 1877 prohibit

41926 Federal Register / Vol. 60, No. 156 / Monday, August 14, 1995 / Rules and Regulations

laboratory referrals only if a financial relationship exists between the referring physician (or an immediate family member) and the laboratory entity. In other words, the law does not prohibit a laboratory from accepting referrals from a physician who does not have a financial relationship with it. Therefore, in all situations, a group practice will be permitted to accept referrals for laboratory services from physicians in the community who do not have, or do not have an immediate family member who has, a financial relationship with the group practice or the laboratory.

8. Use of Diagnosis Code for Laboratory Billing

Comment: One commenter believed the government is being misled about the need for certain diagnostic testing. The commenter noted that self-referrals could be used by unscrupulous physicians as a means to generate income. The commenter believed a major check on this practice would be the requirement of an appropriate diagnosis code for each service billed. The commenter believed it should be the role of the Medicare carriers to monitor unnecessary testing and then to take appropriate actions so that no testing is paid for if the diagnosis code does not suggest medical need.

Response: Section 202(g) of the Medicare Catastrophic Coverage Act of 1988 (Public Law 100–360), enacted July 1, 1988, added paragraph (p) to section 1842 of the Act. Under the provisions of section 1842(p)(1), each bill or request for payment for physicians' services under Medicare Part B must include the appropriate diagnosis code "as established by the Secretary" for each item or service the Medicare beneficiary received. We fully explain the conditions and requirements of this provision in a final rule published on March 4, 1994 (59 FR 10290).

The conference report that accompanied Public Law 100–360 explained clearly the purpose of the requirement for physician diagnostic coding. After rejecting a Senate provision that would have required the use of diagnostic codes on all prescriptions, because they believed that the requirement would have been unduly burdensome on Medicare suppliers of services, the conferees agreed to require diagnostic coding for physicians' services under Part B. They explained their reasons for this requirement as follows: "This information would be available for immediate use for utilization review of physician services * * *." (H.R. Conf. Rep. No. 661, 100th Cong., 2nd Sess.

191 (1988)) The new coding requirement does not apply to bills from laboratories, except for physician laboratory services, which are described in section 405.556.

Claims submitted directly to the Medicare carrier by a clinical laboratory that is not part of a physician's office are not subject to the above requirement. The Medicare carriers, however, review claims submitted for payment to ensure that, to the extent possible, only services that are reasonable and necessary for the treatment of an illness or injury or to improve the functioning of a malformed body member are approved for payment. We agree that it would be easier for a Medicare carrier to make a medical necessity determination if the claim contained an appropriate diagnosis coding. It is clear, however, that the Congress intended to limit diagnosis coding to physicians' services. Therefore, at this time, we are unable to accept the suggestion the commenter made.

9. Referrals That Are Not Abusive

Comment: One commenter indicated that it would appear that relationships between a practitioner and an entity would not pose a risk of patient or program abuse if the relationships do not result in a return to the practitioner of monies beyond those that would be received if the physician directly furnished such laboratory tests (or other Medicare outpatient services).

The commenter suggested that it would be helpful if an exception could be established for referrals, from a physician to an entity, that are medically necessary (that is, represent legitimate claims on the Medicare program) and are not motivated by direct or indirect financial benefits that exceed fair market value accruing to the physician.

Response: The commenter appears to argue that the prohibition should not apply to a referral that is made by a physician to an entity with which he or she has a financial relationship if the service being performed is determined to be medically necessary and the physician does not realize an unacceptable financial gain as a result of the laboratory referral. The financial gain could not be larger than the fair market value of what he or she would realize if the service was performed, for example, in his or her own office and would have qualified for the in-office ancillary services exception.

Section 1862(a)(1) states, in part, that, notwithstanding any other provision of title XVIII of the Act, no payment may be made under Part A or Part B of the Medicare program for any expenses

incurred for items or services that are not reasonable and necessary for the diagnosis or treatment of an illness or injury or to improve the functioning of a malformed body member. In exercising their contractual responsibilities, Medicare carriers enforce this overriding coverage criterion through the use of claims screens, medical review, and other procedures. The commenter appears to believe that, because these carrier safeguards are in place, a "reasonable and necessary" exception could be established. The problem with this commenter's approach is twofold. First, section 1877 prohibits certain referrals to entities with which the referring physician or an immediate family member has a financial relationship regardless of whether the service furnished is found by a carrier to be medically necessary. Second, assessing whether a physician's referrals result in a financial gain from the relationship with a laboratory would be a very difficult and burdensome administrative process. Carriers process approximately 4 million claims for clinical laboratory services each year. It would be very costly to determine whether each claim called into question by certain referrals results in a cost benefit to the referring physician.

10. Contractor Implementation

Comment: One commenter, a Medicare contractor, indicated it had concerns with the administration of the prohibition on referrals along with the numerous exceptions that have been granted for specific services, certain ownership or investment interests, and certain compensation arrangements. The commenter anticipates that the monitoring of these various provisions will be complex and will greatly affect post-pay and systems areas.

Response: It is not clear, at this time, how significant a workload the provisions will create for carrier claims processing and fraud units. However, once this rule is published, the carriers will start performing compliance audits based on specified criteria. We do not expect that these audits will result in much increase in the carrier's workload. We do not believe that there will be any significant effect on either post-pay or systems areas.

B. Scope of Regulations

Comment: One commenter indicated that the preamble section of the proposed rule explaining what the agency believes is the regulatory scope (57 FR 8593) should be omitted. The commenter contended that it imparts no specific guidance and defines no regulatory requirement. Furthermore, this commenter objected to the preamble reference to violations of other Federal or State law and stated that it is gratuitous to advise the regulated entity or person that compliance with section 1877 of the Act, or regulations promulgated thereunder, does not foreclose citation and adjudication under another Federal or State statutory requirement or regulation.

Response: We disagree. Sections 411.1 and 411.350, as described in the preamble of the proposed rule and as set forth in the proposed regulation, conform to regulation drafting guidelines in explaining the general content of 42 CFR part 411, subpart J. Our intent in including this information, something that is routinely done in any new HCFA regulation, is to provide the public with an outline of the regulation's substantive content.

In this case it is important as well to state what the new regulation does not provide for. Before the proposed rule was published, we received numerous inquiries indicating that the provisions of section 1877 were being confused with the anti-kickback safe harbors specified in the final rule published on July 29, 1991 (56 FR 35952). In fact, the Medicare anti-kickback statute (section 1128B(b) of the Act) and section 1877, while similar in that they address possible abuses of Medicare, are different in scope and application and, therefore, need to be distinguished. The conference report for OBRA '89 includes the following statement:

The conferees wish to clarify that any prohibition, exemption, or exception authorized under this provision in no way alters (or reflects on) the scope and application of the anti-kickback provisions in section 1128B of the Social Security Act. The conferees do not intend that this provision should be construed as affecting, or in any way interfering, [sic] with the efforts of the Inspector General to enforce current law, such as cases described in the recent Fraud Alert issued by the Inspector General. In particular, entities which would be eligible for a specific exemption would be subject to all of the provisions of current law. (H.R. Conf. Rep. No. 386, 101st Cong., 1st session 856 (1989).)

Furthermore, we believe it is our duty to inform the public that lawful conduct under sections 1128B and 1877 of the Act may not be lawful under other Federal statutes or State law or regulations. Conversely, conduct that is lawful under those other authorities may be prohibited under section 1877 and these final regulations.

C. Definitions

1. Clinical Laboratory Services

Under the proposed rule (section 411.353), "laboratory services" are considered to be any services provided by the entities described in section 493.2. The preamble to the proposed rule pointed out at 57 FR 8595 that this would include anatomical laboratory services but would not include noninvasive tests that are not considered clinical laboratory services, such as electroencephalograms or electrocardiograms. Nor would it include x-rays or diagnostic imaging services, such as mammogram and computerized axial tomography scans.

Comment: A few commenters recommended that a definition of "clinical laboratory" be included in the regulations. They suggested that, if the definition used for purposes of the Clinical Laboratory Improvement Amendments of 1988 (CLIA '88) is to be adopted, that it should be repeated in section 411.351.

One commenter indicated that the definition of clinical laboratory should state the following:

"Clinical laboratory means a facility for the examination of materials derived from the human body for the purpose of providing information for the diagnosis, prevention, or treatment of any disease or impairment of, or the assessment of the health of, human beings, as described in section 493.2. Such examinations include screening procedures to determine the presence or absence of various substances or organisms in the body. Such examinations do not include noninvasive tests, such as electroencephalograms, electrocardiograms, x-rays or diagnostic imaging services, such as mammogram and computerized axial tomography services."

Response: We agree that this final regulation should contain a definition of clinical laboratory. Thus, based on the definition at section 493.2, which defines a laboratory for CLIA purposes, we are including the following in section 411.351:

Laboratory means an entity furnishing biological, microbiological, serological, chemical, immunohematological, hematological, biophysical, cytological, pathological, or other examination of materials derived from the human body for the purpose of providing information for the diagnosis, prevention, or treatment of any disease or impairment of, or the assessment of the health of, human beings. These examinations also include procedures to determine, measure, or otherwise describe the presence or absence of various substances or organisms in the body. Entities only

collecting or preparing specimens (or both) or only serving as a mailing service and not performing testing are not considered laboratories.

Comment: One commenter urged that the definition of laboratory services should include a statement that what are considered clinical laboratory services for current procedural terminology (CPT) code purposes are also considered clinical laboratory services for the purpose of these regulations. Thus, in this commenter's opinion, there would be no question about what constitutes clinical laboratory services.

Response: As mentioned in the response to the previous comment, we have defined a clinical laboratory as meaning any laboratory entity that is required to satisfy the CLIA standards in order to perform tests on human beings for "* * * the purpose of providing information for the diagnosis, prevention, or treatment of any disease or impairment of, or the assessment of the health of, human beings." Therefore, for the purposes of the prohibition on physician self-referral, we are defining "clinical laboratory services" at section 411.351 as follows:

Clinical laboratory services means the biological, microbiological, serological, chemical, immunohematological, hematological, biophysical, cytological, pathological, or other examination of materials derived from the human body for the purpose of providing information for the diagnosis, prevention, or treatment of any disease or impairment of, or the assessment of the health of, human beings. These examinations also include procedures to determine, measure, or otherwise describe the presence or absence of various substances or organisms in the body.

Given this position, the American Medical Association (the organization responsible for CPT) and the CPT publication would not be the references to define the kind of services that are regulated by the physician referral legislation. If individuals want to know what specific tests and test systems are subject to CLIA certification, they may contact the Center for Disease Control and Prevention (CDC), Public Health Service, Attention: CLIA, 1600 Clifton Road, Atlanta, GA 30333. CDC has categorized approximately 12,000 test systems, assays, and examinations for complexity using the criteria at 42 CFR 493.17. CDC publishes notices periodically in the **Federal Register** to announce additional test systems, assays, or examinations that have been categorized or recategorized since the preceding publication.

For these reasons, we do not support the sole use of CPT codes to identify

41928　Federal Register / Vol. 60, No. 156 / Monday, August 14, 1995 / Rules and Regulations

clinical laboratory services for physician referral purposes.

Comment: One commenter suggested that it would be helpful to define further what type of anatomical laboratory services are covered by the statute and which specific tests we consider to be noninvasive and not subject to the prohibition on referrals.

Response: We agree with this commenter. As mentioned in the preamble to the proposed rule (57 FR 8595), anatomical laboratory services are subject to the prohibition on physician referrals. Anatomical laboratory services (and anatomical pathology services) involve the examination of tissue, often tissue removed during surgery. As such, it appears to us that anatomical laboratory services are always invasive (that is, they involve the examination of materials derived from the human body, as described in 42 CFR 493.2). Therefore, we believe that these tests would always be subject to CLIA and section 1877. Consequently, any physician who refers patients for these kinds of tests to a laboratory with which he or she (or a family member) has a financial relationship could be in violation of section 1877. In such a case, any of the many exceptions in section 1877 might exempt that physician's referral from the prohibition.

The commenter has also suggested that we specify which noninvasive testing is exempt from the prohibition on referrals. As mentioned in the response to the previous comment, we believe that the most appropriate way for a physician or clinical laboratory to determine if Medicare considers a diagnostic test to be a clinical laboratory test subject to the requirements of section 1877, is to find out if the test is subject to categorization under CLIA. The Medicare carriers are available to provide this information to individuals and physicians if it is not clear to a physician, other supplier, or provider of services and if they do not have available the latest compiled list of clinical laboratory test systems, assays, and examinations categorized by complexity and published by the CDC. If a test does not appear on a compiled list, a physician or laboratory should contact the CDC at the address we mentioned in the last response in order to be certain, since the lists are not yet complete.

2. Compensation Arrangement

Under the proposed rule (§ 411.351), a compensation arrangement would be any arrangement that involves any remuneration between a physician or a member of his or her immediate family

and an entity. The definition of compensation arrangement was amended by OBRA '93 to exclude certain types of remuneration (identified in section I.D.1.c. of this preamble).

Comment: One commenter indicated that the final regulations need to give a specific definition for the phrase "compensation arrangement," not simply repeat the words that the Congress has provided.

Response: The commenter did not explain why the proposed definition was perceived as insufficient. The words of the definition are specific, and we do not believe they are susceptible to misinterpretation. The definition is broad, because it covers any remuneration between a physician (or an immediate family member) and an entity, and it may be this aspect of the definition that concerned the commenter. We believe, however, that it was the intent of the Congress to include all arrangements (direct and indirect) between physicians and laboratories involving any remuneration. We believe that the statutory definition accomplishes this purpose. In the OBRA '93 amendments, the Congress retained the broad definition of "remuneration" in section 1877(h)(1)(B), but did specifically except from the term "compensation arrangement" a very limited list of arrangements involving the kinds of remuneration listed in section 1877(h)(1)(C). These changes are reflected in this final regulation.

Comment: One commenter indicated that laboratories often must enter into arrangements with physicians, who are not employed by the laboratory, for necessary services. The commenter believed that as long as certain safeguards, comparable to those applicable to arrangements between physicians and hospitals, are met, these arrangements should not be considered compensation arrangements that would prohibit the physicians from making referrals. Examples of such arrangements are (1) an arrangement to review abnormal test results when further medical consultation is required, and (2) a contract with a physician to provide various consultation services, such as reviewing anatomic pathology specimens, interpreting holter monitors or electrocardiograms, and reviewing Pap tests.

Another commenter indicated that, because of the breadth of the self-referral law, any time a laboratory makes a payment to a physician, a compensation arrangement is created. Thus, for example, if a laboratory maintains a self-insured group medical plan and pays physicians directly for

the medical services provided to its employees, it would, in this commenter's view, have a compensation arrangement with those physicians and should not accept Medicare referrals from them. The commenter suggested that these types of legitimate arrangements should not be considered compensation arrangements as long as safeguards are put into place to ensure nonabuse.

Response: What these commenters are asking for is an exception for an arrangement under which a referring physician furnishes services to a laboratory (or, alternatively, that the term compensation arrangement be defined in a manner so as not to include that arrangement). Section 1877(e)(3), as amended by OBRA '93, provides an exception for a compensation relationship in which a laboratory entity pays a physician for personal services furnished under an arrangement. Such an arrangement does not result in the physician being prohibited from making referrals to that entity if certain specific conditions (detailed in section I.D.6.d. of this preamble) are met.

In addition to the exception in section 1877(e)(3), section 1877(e)(2), as amended by OBRA '93, provides that, if a laboratory makes payments to a physician as the result of a bona fide employment relationship with the physician, that physician's referrals would not be prohibited, providing certain criteria are met.

Comment: One commenter stated that in many situations laboratories are required by State or Federal law to have particular arrangements with physicians. For example, under the new CLIA regulations (42 CFR part 493), laboratories may be required to have physicians in a number of different positions in the laboratory. The commenter believed these types of arrangements should not be considered compensation arrangements that would prohibit referrals by the physicians.

Response: As mentioned in an earlier response, it is our belief that most of these arrangements could qualify for either the exception found in section 1877(e)(2) for bona fide employment relationships or, when the physicians are not employed, section 1877(e)(3) for personal service arrangements.

Accordingly, a compensation arrangement between a laboratory and a referring physician for specific identifiable services that has all of the elements required for the subject exceptions would not cause that physician's referrals to be prohibited.

Comment: One commenter noted that laboratories routinely sell services directly to physicians who then

Federal Register / Vol. 60, No. 156 / Monday, August 14, 1995 / Rules and Regulations   **41929**

reimburse the laboratory for those services before marking them up to patients. The commenter did not believe that those payments should constitute a compensation arrangement.

Response: As set forth in OBRA '93, section 1877(e)(8)(A) of the Act provides a compensation-related exception for physicians who pay a laboratory in exchange for the provision of clinical laboratory services (see section 411.357(i)(1)).

The commenter has made the point that physicians routinely reimburse laboratories for services and then mark them up to patients. Under section 1833(h)(5)(A), Medicare payment for a clinical diagnostic laboratory test may be made only to the person or entity that performed or supervised the performance of the test. (This rule is subject to certain exceptions involving services furnished or supervised by a physician when payment is made to another physician in the same group practice, services performed by a laboratory at the request of another laboratory, and tests performed under arrangements made by a hospital.) As a result, physicians should generally not be able to pay a laboratory in exchange for Medicare covered laboratory services, and then mark them up to patients.

Comment: One commenter noted that many laboratories are part of large, diversified corporations (which themselves may be related to other large, diversified corporations) that provide a number of different services to physicians. These services may include pharmaceutical, billing, and waste transport services. The commenter believed that, so long as these services are provided at fair market value, there is no reason that an entity should not provide these services to physicians and also accept their Medicare referrals.

Response: As mentioned previously, if a physician is paying fair market value to the supplier entity for whatever nonlaboratory services he or she is purchasing, referrals by the physician to the laboratory should not be prohibited. However, the arrangement must meet the conditions found in new § 411.357(i).

Comment: One commenter indicated that the regulations should be clarified to expressly prohibit any arrangement under which the referring physician bills patients for clinical laboratory or anatomic pathology services that are not personally performed or supervised by the billing physician or the group practice. In particular, the commenter suggested that the prohibition should apply to arrangements under which the referring physician requires the

pathologist or independent laboratory to bill the referring physician, rather than the patient or third party payer, for any services provided by the pathologist or independent laboratory on referral by the physician. The commenter pointed out that, at the present time, the Medicare payment rules prohibit a physician from billing for certain clinical diagnostic laboratory tests performed by an independent laboratory for Medicare patients (section 1833(h)(5)(A)) but, the commenter maintained, this payment prohibition does not apply to anatomic pathology services or to clinical laboratory services performed for non-Medicare patients. Thus, the commenter concluded that the referring physician would not be prohibited from marking up the costs of anatomical tests to Medicare and for clinical laboratory and anatomical testing billed to other third party payers.

The commenter believed that an arrangement under which the referring physician charges payers for the services of a separate laboratory constitutes a compensation arrangement within the meaning of the law. The commenter added that "compensation arrangement" is defined as any arrangement "involving any remuneration." Further, the term "remuneration" is defined broadly to include direct or indirect, overt or covert, and in-cash or in-kind arrangements. The commenter believed, therefore, that an arrangement under which the referring physician can receive payment for services not personally performed or supervised by himself or herself, including payment for services for non-Medicare patients, should be found to be a compensation arrangement within the broad language of the law.

Specifically, the commenter recommended that the final regulation make clear that the definition of "compensation arrangement" encompasses any arrangement under which a referring physician bills and collects for laboratory services that are not personally performed or supervised by the physician.

Response: This commenter raised several issues: first, whether anatomical pathology services are diagnostic laboratory tests and, thus, subject to the billing requirements of section 1833(h)(5)(A); second, whether the billing requirements of that section can be applied to clinical diagnostic laboratory tests performed for non-Medicare patients; and third, whether the definitions of compensation and remuneration at section 1877(h)(1) can be broadly interpreted to include payments made to the physician for any

laboratory services he or she did not personally perform or supervise, including payment for services for non-Medicare patients. We will address each of these issues in order.

Under Medicare, the term "medical and other health services" includes, under section 1861(s)(3), the broad category of "diagnostic laboratory tests." Under section 1861(s)(16), such diagnostic laboratory tests include only those diagnostic tests performed in a laboratory that meets CLIA requirements. Anatomical pathology services are tests involving tissue examination, such as that done during surgery. We believe that any anatomical pathology tests would be diagnostic in nature and would have to be performed in a laboratory that meets CLIA requirements. As such, the tests fall squarely within the category of "diagnostic laboratory tests" and would therefore be subject to the payment rules in section 1833(h)(5)(A).

Under section 1833(h)(5)(A), payments for clinical diagnostic laboratory tests are subject to mandatory assignment. That is, with certain narrow exceptions, payment may be made only to the person or entity that performed or supervised the performance of the test. Further, under section 1842(b)(6), a carrier generally may pay assigned benefits only to the physician or other supplier that furnished the service. Thus, unless physicians are billing Medicare within the conditions found in these provisions of the law, they are billing in error.

In regard to the second issue, the language of section 1833(h)(5)(A) applies specifically to services for which payment may be made under Medicare Part B. Therefore, we agree with the commenter that the billing requirements found in the Medicare statute do not extend to non-Medicare patients.

In regard to the third issue, under section 1877(e)(8)(A), payments by a physician to a laboratory for clinical laboratory services do not constitute compensation that triggers the referral prohibition.

3. Entity

In the proposed rule (§ 411.351), we defined "entity" as a sole proprietorship, trust, corporation, partnership, foundation, not-for-profit corporation, or unincorporated association.

Comment: One commenter indicated that the statute does not define "entity" and the definition in the proposed regulations could prohibit certain nonabusive arrangements because it covers trusts, foundations, and not-for-

41930 Federal Register / Vol. 60, No. 156 / Monday, August 14, 1995 / Rules and Regulations

profit corporations. For example, a physician might own stock in a not-for-profit corporation or be a trustee of a charitable trust that operates a laboratory. The commenter suggested that this definition either be modified to contain an exception for nonabusive business entities or that the trust, foundation, and not-for-profit corporation criteria be deleted.

Response: We do not agree with this commenter. Under section 1877, unless an exception applies, any referral for clinical laboratory services is prohibited if the referring physician or a member of the physician's immediate family has a financial relationship with the entity to which the referral is made. This is so because the statute does not, in any way, limit the types of organizations covered by the referral prohibition as long as they provide clinical laboratory services. Therefore, our proposed definition of "entity" was meant to include all possible organizations and associations that provide laboratory testing. As was stated in the proposed rule, we believe that we need to define the term "entity" to ensure that the term is understood by all affected parties. Note, however, that if a trustee takes no compensation from and has no ownership interest in an entity, he or she would not have a financial relationship as defined in section 1877. Therefore, the physician would not be prohibited from referring Medicare patients to that entity. Finally, we are not aware of any situations in which a not-for-profit entity would issue stock.

4. Fair Market Value

Under the proposed rule (section 411.351), fair market value is defined to mean the value in arm's-length transactions, consistent with the general market value. With respect to rentals or leases, "fair market value" means the value of rental property for general commercial purposes (not taking into account its intended use). In the case of a lease of space, this value may not be adjusted to reflect the additional value the prospective lessee or lessor would attribute to the proximity or convenience of the lessor when the lessor is a potential source of patient referrals to the lessee. This definition is based on the definition in the statute. (OBRA '93 did not change the statutory definition.)

Comment: One commenter indicated that the statute makes it clear that lease and rental values may not be adjusted to reflect proximity to referral sources. The commenter was concerned about our statement in the preamble to the proposed rule at 57 FR 8599 that certain rental payments could be construed to

induce referrals, even if there is no explicit or implicit understanding regarding referrals. These arrangements would typically involve rental payments either substantially above or below the fair market value of the rental space. The commenter believed that there is still no adequate means to determine when an increase (or decrease) in value will be considered "substantial" and therefore viewed as suspect. The commenter agreed that an example of an abusive arrangement occurs when a physician rents space to a health care entity at a rate above what the market would ordinarily bear, and the entity agrees to the high rent because of an understanding that the physician will refer his or her patients to that entity.

The commenter pointed out that many factors influence what may be considered as "fair market value" in a normally functioning real estate market. For example, the principle that site rents vary inversely with increased travel time pervades the real estate industry. Thus, the commenter concluded, a facility that is convenient to places in which health care services are furnished, such as a laboratory adjacent to a medical building, will command higher rents than one across town.

The commenter suggested that the final rule should reflect some means of differentiating between rent and lease payments that have inherently greater values based on traditional economic factors and those that are "artificially" inflated.

Response: In using the term "substantially" in excess of or below fair market value, we were describing an example of how a rental or lease agreement could be an influence on referrals. Such an agreement could take many forms and incorporate a myriad of possible financial incentives depending on local factors that could influence the rental or lease price. We want to emphasize, however, that the definitions in the statute (section 1877(h)(3)) and regulations (§411.351) state that fair market value means that a rental or lease of property must be consistent with the value of the property for general commercial purposes and that a rental or lease of space may not be adjusted to reflect any additional value a lessee or lessor would attribute to the proximity or convenience of a potential source of referrals. Therefore, if the economic factor to which the commenter referred, that is, that site rents vary inversely with increased travel time, plays a part in determining the level of rent agreed to by a physician and a laboratory entity, the fair market value test set forth in the statue would

not be met. This would be the case even if the factor is a "traditional economic factor" that "pervades the real estate industry." In other words, if rent is inflated either artificially or because of its proximity to a referral source, the fair market standard would not be met and the exception would not apply.

5. Financial Relationship

In the proposed rule (section 411.351), we defined a "financial relationship" as either a direct or indirect relationship between a physician (or a member of a physician's immediate family) and an entity in which the physician or family member has—

(1) An ownership or investment interest that exists through equity, debt, or other similar means; or

(2) A compensation arrangement.

The OBRA '93 amendments added that, in addition to equity, debt, or other means, an ownership interest includes an interest in an entity that holds an ownership or investment interest in any entity providing clinical laboratory services. This expanded provision, however, is not applicable until January 1, 1995.

Comment: One commenter expressed strong support for the proposed policy that the prohibition would extend to physicians who are the previous owners of a laboratory, if they are paid by the new owners under an installment sales agreement that extends past January 1, 1992. The commenter indicated that such arrangements can easily be abused; that is, they raise the possibility that the previous owners would make referrals for the purpose of ensuring that the new owners continue to pay off their debt. Similarly, the commenter agreed with our statement that, if an organization related to the laboratory agrees to pay the laboratory's debt to the physician, a financial relationship is still created.

On the other hand, another commenter indicated that we should permit specific debt relationships if the following criterion is met: The debt interest is manifested by a written note that has a fixed repayment schedule unrelated in any fashion to the productivity of the debtor or any entity owned by the debtor, and the debt-equity relationship of the debtor does not exceed 4 to 1.

Another commenter recommended that physicians who remain interested investors through a debt relationship in a laboratory that they once owned not be penalized. That is, the physicians should not be subsequently regarded as having a nonexempt financial relationship with that laboratory.

Response: We agree with the first commenter. A financial relationship may exist in the form of an ownership or investment interest, which, according to the language in section 1877(a)(2), "may be through equity, debt, or other means." We did not propose any exceptions addressing situations involving debt. That is because we do not believe that there would be no risk of program or patient abuse in such circumstances. Obviously, the continued financial viability of an entity that is in debt to a potential referring physician could be of great concern to that physician. Therefore, we are not providing the exception requested.

Comment: Two commenters indicated that the term "indirect relationship," which is used to define financial relationships in proposed § 411.351, should be itself defined or deleted since there is no statutory definition of indirect relationships. According to the discussion at page 8595 of the proposed rule's preamble, "a physician would be considered to have an indirect financial relationship with a laboratory entity if he or she had an ownership interest in an entity which in turn has an ownership interest in the laboratory entity." The commenter stated that, if this is the definition we adopt, that definition should appear in § 411.351 of the final regulations; otherwise, the term should be deleted from the regulation entirely.

Response: We agree with the commenter that our interpretation of indirect ownership or investment interest should appear in the regulation. Therefore, we include it in section 411.351 of this final rule. As specified at section 1877(a)(2), financial relationships that could cause a referral to be prohibited are of two kinds. The first is an ownership or investment interest, which may be through equity, debt, or other means. The second is a compensation arrangement, which, as defined at section 1877(h)(1)(A), is any arrangement involving any remuneration (with certain narrow exceptions added by OBRA '93). "Remuneration" is defined in section 1877(h)(1)(B) as including *any remuneration,* direct or indirect, overt or covert, in cash or in kind. This is a broad concept that, we believe, encompasses compensation/ remuneration obtained through an indirect financial arrangement. We further believe that an indirect relationship can occur in the ownership/investment situation as well as under a compensation arrangement. The term "indirect" appears specifically only in the definition of remuneration in section 1877(h)(1)(B), which applies

in the context of compensation arrangements. However, an ownership or investment interest as defined in section 1877(a)(2) may be through equity, debt, or *other means.* We believe that the term "other means" is broad enough to encompass an infinite variety of direct and indirect ownership or investment interests. As a result, we included the concept of an indirect ownership or investment interest in the proposed rule.

It was also our opinion that the Congress intended to cover all forms of financial relationships that may exist between a physician and a laboratory. Any other reading would allow physicians to easily circumvent the statute; they could hold ownership interests in entities furnishing clinical laboratory services by simply establishing and owning shares in holding companies or shell corporations that, in turn, own the laboratories.

The Congress has demonstrated its intention to cover situations involving indirect ownership and investment interests. As amended by OBRA '93, the language at the end of section 1877(a)(2) provides that "[a]n ownership or investment interest may be through equity, debt, or *other means, and includes* an interest in an entity that holds an ownership or investment interest in any entity providing the designated health service." [Emphasis added.] This provision became effective January 1, 1995. However, we believe the amended provision demonstrates that, prior to OBRA '93, an ownership or investment held through "other means" could be interpreted to *include* indirect interests.

In addition, in proposing this amendment, the Committee on Ways and Means explained that "[t]he definition of financial relationship would be modified to include *explicitly* that an interest in an entity (i.e., holding company) that holds an investment or ownership interest in another entity is a financial relationship for purposes of the referral prohibition." [Emphasis added.] (H. Rep. No. 111, 103d Cong., 1st Sess. (1993).) In other words, we believe the intent of this amendment was to explicitly list a concept that was already implicitly included in the scope of the provision. The Conference Report for OBRA '93 reveals that the House Ways and Means provision was enacted without changes. (H. Rep. No. 213, 103d Cong., 1st Sess. (1993).) For these reasons, we decline to delete the term "indirect" and intend that it be considered in determining whether particular referrals are prohibited.

6. Group Practice

Under the proposed rule (§ 411.351), a group practice means a group of two or more physicians legally organized as a partnership, professional corporation, foundation, not-for-profit corporation, faculty practice plan, or similar association that meets the following conditions:

• Each physician who is a member of the group furnishes substantially the full range of patient care services that the physician routinely furnishes including medical care, consultation, diagnosis, and treatment through the joint use of shared office space, facilities, equipment and personnel.

• Substantially all of the patient care services of the physicians who are members of the group (that is, at least 85 percent of the aggregate services furnished by all physician members of the group practice) are furnished through the group and are billed in the name of the group and the amounts received are treated as receipts of the group. The group practice must attest in writing that it meets this 85 percent requirement.

• The practice expenses and income are distributed in accordance with methods previously determined by members of the group.

In the case of faculty practice plans associated with hospitals that have approved medical residency programs for which plan physicians perform specialty and professional services, both within and outside the faculty practice, this definition applies only to those services that are furnished to patients of the faculty practice plan.

"Group practice" as defined in section 1877(h)(4)(A), as it reads under OBRA '93, is discussed in section II.D.1.c.4. of this preamble.

a. Threshold for "Substantially All"

Comment: A few commenters suggested that the threshold for what is "substantially all" of the services of physician members should be lowered from 85 percent to 75 percent because rural group practices would have difficulty in meeting the higher percentage. The same commenters noted that, if the threshold for group practices is not lowered, there should be a special threshold for rural group practices that may not be able to meet the 85 percent standard.

Response: The comments we received on the proposed rule have identified group practices that have partners, full and part-time physician employees, and physician contractors, who may also be either full- or part-time. All configurations of physicians must be

41932 Federal Register / Vol. 60, No. 156 / Monday, August 14, 1995 / Rules and Regulations

able to show that the statutory requirements are met and, specifically, that substantially all of the services of the members are furnished through the group. (We discuss in a later comment which physicians qualify as "members" of a group practice.) As we have mentioned previously in this preamble, it is not our intention to unnecessarily impede associations of physicians from qualifying as a group practice, and we recognize that groups that have part-time physicians may have a more difficult time qualifying than groups that have all full-time physicians.

We agree that the 85 percent criterion should be reduced to 75 percent, and we have made that change in the definition of group practice (§ 411.351). Before deciding to make this change, we considered the implications for group practices that have part-time and contractual physicians and the possibility of establishing separate standards for rural and urban locations and the changes that will be made by the OBRA '93 provision on January 1, 1995. (Beginning on January 1, 1995, members of the group must personally conduct no less than 75 percent of the physician-patient encounters of the group practice.) We accept the point of view that a standard higher than 75 percent would be difficult for many rural group practices to meet. That is because the scarcity of physicians in rural areas generally imposes varying responsibilities that cause these physicians to devote less time to a group practice than might be the case in other areas. In order to be consistent and to eliminate whatever administrative confusion might result from different standards for rural and urban areas, we are adopting the 75 percent standard for all areas.

Comment: One commenter indicated that group practices should be allowed to select the methodology for determining the 85 percent threshold; that is, 85 percent of total physician time, or 85 percent of total group income (calculated on the basis of allowed charges, etc.), or 85 percent of all physicians' services delivered—whatever method they prefer to use and are able to document.

Another commenter recommended that the Medicare allowed charges or fee schedule amounts be used as the measurement criterion for the following reasons: (1) By using such a measure, the necessary data would be readily available to Medicare carriers in the Medicare databases; (2) these measures would not impose any new record keeping obligations on physicians and group practices; and (3) if alternative measures, such as time, patients,

service, or total revenue were used, physicians and group practices would be subjected to additional burdensome record keeping requirements.

A third commenter suggested that the following conditions indicate that the criteria are met: All Medicare allowed charges or fee schedule amounts for the services furnished by all physician members of the group are furnished through the group, and billed in the name of or under a number or numbers assigned to the group practice, and the amounts received are treated as receipts of the group.

Finally, another commenter recommended that we consider (1) excluding from the formula any part-time physician who does not refer work to the laboratory for Medicare patients, and (2) revising the current 85 percent formula to provide that, so long as 85 percent of Medicare laboratory work is attributed to full-time physicians (a full-time physician being a person who bills at least 85 percent of his or her services through the group), the group practice would then be able to meet the exception.

Response: As noted, we proposed that, to meet the "substantially all" criterion, a group practice would have to be able to show that at least 85 percent of the aggregate patient care services furnished by all physician members of the group practice are furnished through the group practice. In addition, as stated in section 1877(h)(4)(B), these services must be billed in the name of the group, and receipts for the services must be treated as receipts of the group. After carefully considering the language of the statute and these comments, we decided to adopt the following approach:

We are continuing to provide that to meet the "substantially all" criterion, in the aggregate, a specific percentage of patient care services furnished by all physician members must be furnished through the group practice. As we noted in an earlier response, we are changing the percentage from 85 percent to 75 percent. The comments have revealed that there is confusion about what constitutes "patient care services" and how to measure them. To remedy this, we are clarifying in the regulation that patient care services include any tasks performed by a group practice member that address the medical needs of specific patients, whether or not they involve direct patient encounters. As a result, patient care services can involve the work of pathologists and radiologists who do not directly treat patients or a physician's time spent consulting with another physician when the patient is

not present or time spent reviewing laboratory tests.

We are also clarifying that a practice must measure patient care services by calculating the total patient care time each member spends on patient care services. We believe that this method of measuring services is an equitable one that will capture most accurately a group practice member's commitment to providing services through the practice. For example, if a member furnishes only a few services through the practice during the course of a week, but these services are surgical procedures that consume most of the physician's time that week, this fact will be reflected in the calculations.

As to the first comment, we do not believe that leaving this matter entirely to the discretion of each group practice would be feasible. It is our goal to accomplish fairness and evenhandedness across group practices by establishing a consistent and uniform approach. Leaving the matter to the discretion of each group practice would also put an additional burden on the Medicare carriers. The carriers could very well be involved in audits of group practices in the future. If we adopted the commenter's suggestion, a carrier would, on the occasion of each audit, first have to determine whether a particular method employed by a group practice is appropriate before determining whether the standard is met. Thus, we are clarifying that, to meet the substantially all criteria, 75 percent of total patient care services (measured as patient care time) of group practice physicians must be provided through the group.

It is not clear to us how using a method employing Medicare allowed charges or physician fee schedule amounts would satisfy the statutory requirements. The carriers would have this information, as the commenter stated, but section 1877(h)(4) does not say that only substantially all of a group practice's Medicare business be considered. The reference is to "* * * substantially all the services of the physicians who are members * * *." Accordingly, we believe that all services, both Medicare and non-Medicare, must be considered.

Here is an example of how our uniform total patient care time approach would work:

Ten physicians deliver services through a group practice. Eight of them devote 100 percent of their patient care time to the group practice. One devotes 80 percent, and one 10 percent. This can be illustrated as follows:

Federal Register / Vol. 60, No. 156 / Monday, August 14, 1995 / Rules and Regulations   **41933**

8 physicians at 100% each =	800%
1 physician at 80% =	80%
1 physician at 10% =	10%
	890% divided by 10 = 89%

Thus, in this example, 89 percent of the total of the time spent by these physicians is devoted to services billable by the group practice. The issues of group practice billing numbers and part-time physicians are discussed below.

Comment: One commenter suggested that the calculations for substantially all services be made, at the election of the practice group, with respect to either the previous fiscal year of the practice group or the previous 12-month period, which is the approach used by the safe harbor regulations. The commenter believed that a 12-month period is appropriate for this purpose in order to avoid short term fluctuations that might otherwise distort the determination.

Response: We agree that a 12-month period is appropriate for use in determining compliance with the "substantially all" criterion. We will allow a group practice (as defined in section 1877(h)(4)) to elect whether to use the calendar year, its fiscal year, or the immediately preceding 12-month period to determine whether it complies with the standard. Furthermore, we will allow any new group practice (one in which the physicians have only recently begun to practice together) or any other group practice that has been unable in the past to meet the requirements of section 1877(h)(4) (including the "substantially all" criterion) to initially look forward 12-months, as described below, to determine compliance with the standard. These groups would also be able to elect whether to use the calendar year, fiscal year, or the next 12-months. Finally, once any group has chosen whether to use its fiscal year, the calendar year, or another 12-month period, the group practice must adhere to this choice.

In new 411.360, each group practice must submit to its carrier an initial attestation that the group has met the "substantially all" criterion (75 percent of patient care time) in the 12-month period it has chosen. New group practices or other groups that wish to initially use future months to meet the "substantially all" criterion must attest that they plan to meet the criterion within whatever upcoming 12-month period they have chosen and will take

measures to ensure the standard is met. After this 12-month period is over, the group must attest that it did meet the standard during that period.

The attestation must contain a statement that the information furnished in the attestation is true and accurate and must be signed by a representative for the group. It must be mailed to the carrier within 90 days after the effective date of this final rule, that is, 120 days after the date of publication of this rule in the **Federal Register**. We are requiring this initial attestation so the carriers will be able to determine whether payment for laboratory services should be continued. After their initial attestation (whether it is retroactive or prospective), group practices must submit updated attestations to the carrier each year at the end of the period they have chosen to use to measure this standard.

If a group practice using an initial prospective period does not meet the "substantially all" criterion at the end of its chosen 12-month period, the group would not qualify as a group practice. As such, an overpayment could exist from the beginning of the period in which the group has claimed that it would meet the "substantially all" standard.

This approach does have paperwork burden implications for group practices. However, we do not believe that the burden is significant. It should be a relatively easy task for most group practice physicians to assess the amount of their patient care time that is spent on services that can be billed in the name of the group.

b. Member of a Group

Comment: Several commenters indicated that we should define more precisely what is meant by a "member" of a group practice because the "substantially all" criteria apply to physicians who are "members" of a group practice. For example, one commenter suggested that for part-time members of a group practice, only that percentage of time/services/income devoted by the member to the group should be assigned to the group for the purpose of calculating the total time/services/income of the group.

Several commenters indicated that the term "member" of the group practice should have a restrictive definition, such as one that is limited to principals of the practice, for example, shareholders, partners, or officers.

Another commenter indicated that the term "member" can be broadly interpreted to include all physician employees or even independent contractor physicians of the group

practice, and that how the term is defined can have significant impact. Yet another commenter recommended that the term "member" be defined to include physician owners as well as full- and part-time employed physicians.

One commenter recommended that the definition exclude any physician who is not a shareholder, partner, or employee of the group, or an independent contractor providing more than a certain number of hours of service per week (for example, 20 hours) for the group. The commenter stated that such a rule is supported by common sense, as it is doubtful that physicians who furnish services on a sporadic basis would consider themselves to be members of a group or qualify for the various benefits associated with being a member of the group.

On the other hand, another commenter stated that, if the term "member" is given a restrictive definition, limited to principals of the group practice, the practice will be able to circumvent the 85 percent aggregate services requirement simply by ensuring that no physician who provides substantial services outside the group becomes a principal of the group. The commenter believed that limiting the definition, however, might restrict the numbers of physicians who may supervise laboratory testing under the in-office ancillary services exception because it applies to only services furnished by or supervised by physicians who are "members" of the same group practice. The commenter also suggested that it might affect where that testing may take place. Under section 1877(b)(2)(A)(ii), testing may be done in a building in which the referring physician (or another physician member of the group practice) has a practice or in another building which is used for the centralized provision of the group's clinical laboratory services. Particularly in multi-site group practices, the referring physicians could be physician-employees or independent contractors who would not be "members." Thus, their laboratory tests would have to be performed in a building in which a member personally supervises the laboratory services. This, however, would not seriously impede the group practice, in this commenter's view, as most group practices could readily set themselves up in a manner that allows for at least one principal to be available for supervision. This commenter further stated that a broader definition of the term "member" that includes all physician employees and/or

41934 Federal Register / Vol. 60, No. 156 / Monday, August 14, 1995 / Rules and Regulations

independent contractors leads to different results. That is, it might make it more difficult for the group practice to satisfy the 85 percent aggregate services requirement in the definition, depending on the number of part-time employees and contractors. However, it would allow for almost any associated physician to make referrals and supervise the performance of laboratory services.

Response: As evidenced by the range of comments we received concerning this group member issue, whatever approach we select may not address all of the concerns raised by the commenters. Essentially, we agree that the issue of who qualifies as a "member" of a group practice raises a number of complex questions. As we understand it, group practices typically have partners, full-time physician employees, part-time physician employees, and physician contractors.

We take the position that all of these physicians can be members of a group for purposes of the group practice provisions of section 1877. We consider physician partners and full-time and part-time physician employees and contract physicians to be members during the time they furnish services to patients of the group practice that are provided through the group and are billed in the name of the group. Thus, their services would be considered in determining whether the group practice as a whole meets the requirement that substantially all of the services of physician members be furnished through the group.

Examples are as follows:

• A group practice consists of two physician partners, five full-time physician employees, two part-time physician employees, and a contractor physician who spends one morning a week at the group practice delivering specialty services. The two partners and the full-time employees practice only through the group. The two part-time employees devote 50 percent of their time to the group, and the contractor physician spends 10 percent of his or her time with the group.

7 physicians at 100% =.	700%
2 physicians at 50% =.	100%
1 physician at 10% =.	10%
	———
	810% divided by 10 = 81%

• In another group practice, two physician partners spend 100 percent of their patient care hours through the

group. Five part-time physician employees spend 70 percent each, and two other part-time physician employees spend 25 percent of their time at the group practice. A contractor physician devotes 10 percent.

2 physicians at 100% =.	200%
5 physicians at 70% =.	350%
2 physicians at 25% =.	50%
1 physician at 10% =.	10%
	———
	610% divided by 10 = 61%

In these examples, using 75 percent as the threshold, the first group practice would qualify, but the second would not.

On balance, we believe this approach is the most appropriate and is neither overly restrictive nor overly permissive. It will eliminate problems that might arise for many group practices that employ physicians or contract for the services of physician specialists on a part-time basis. Because this approach is not overly restrictive, we do not believe it will obstruct rural group practices. On the other hand, as demonstrated in the above example, the inclusion of part-time physicians may cause some group practices to fail to meet the 75 percent aggregate requirement.

To clarify our position about this issue, we have included the following definition under section 411.351 ("Definitions"):

Members of the group means physician partners and full-time and part-time physician employees and physician contractors during the time they furnish services to patients of the group practice that are furnished through the group and are billed in the name of the group.

c. Individual Billing by a Group Practice Physician

Comment: A few commenters indicated that some group practices permit the physicians of the group to bill Medicare under their unique physician identification number. Under the proposed rule, they do not meet the definition of a group practice because services furnished by the group physicians are not billed in the name of the group. The commenters requested an exception for a few group practices that actually practice medicine as a group but do not qualify because of this element of the new definition of group practice.

One commenter indicated that many group practices have made a decision to have each physician bill independently and reassign benefits to the group rather than for services to be billed under the group's provider number. This decision is based on the desire of some physicians within the group to be nonparticipating physicians but only for the services billed by the group as group services. (As nonparticipating physicians, they can bill the beneficiary directly and charge for the part of the bill that is more than the Medicare approved amount, with certain limitations.) According to the commenter, the physicians would agree to bill under a group provider number except for an informal, nonregulatory position that all physician members of a group practice must make a joint decision to be either participating or nonparticipating physicians. The commenter recommended that the final rule clarify that billing in the name of the group allows for physician members of a group to make individual choices about participating or not participating in Medicare. It was suggested that such a decision could be made at a "department level" within the group practice by differentiating between specialty categories.

Response: The definition of a group practice set forth in section 1877(h)(4)(A) requires that substantially all of the services of physicians who are members of the group be provided through the group and be billed in the name of the group. (Beginning January 1, 1995, services must be billed under a billing number assigned to the group.) Under this language, an organization whose individual physicians bill in their own name does not constitute a group practice. Additionally, the services of a physician who does not bill in the group's name cannot be counted in determining whether the group practice satisfies the substantially all criteria.

We recognize that, under the in-office ancillary services exception found in section 1877(b)(2)(B), the physician who performs or supervises the performance of the services may also bill for those services. As mentioned above, however, when a physician bills in this manner, he or she is doing so as a solo practitioner and not as a member of a group practice.

Finally, when a bill is submitted in the name of the group on an assignment-related basis, it is the group that accepts assignment. A Medicare participation agreement under section 1842(h)(1) is an agreement to accept assignment in all cases. Therefore, any participation agreement with respect to services furnished by a group must be entered into by the group and must apply to all services that the physicians furnish as members of the group.

d. Structure of a Group Practice

Comment: One commenter stated that the definition of "group practice" applies not only to professional corporations and other single entities but also to "similar associations." The commenter believed that, when a group practice is organized into two separate entities that are organizationally interrelated through common ownership, administration, or similar substantial and ongoing connections (more than merely their joint ownership of a clinical laboratory), the two entities together should qualify as a similar association under the statute, thus allowing the two entities to satisfy the group practice criteria in the aggregate.

The commenter believed that if such entities are not aggregated for purposes of the group practice definition, then the primary care entity that has the laboratory must qualify separately as a group practice. Further, under the group practice definition, as set forth in the proposed rule, this may be impossible. The commenter described a situation involving a primary care entity and a specialty care entity. These two entities share certain office space, facilities, equipment, and personnel that physicians practicing in both entities jointly use. Thus, as stated by the commenter, there are two group practices sharing a laboratory facility. The commenter believed that each physician member of these entities does furnish the full range of his or her services through the joint use of space, facilities, equipment, and personnel, and the entities allocate the costs of this use on a formulaic basis. The commenter believed the organizational structure described in this situation should meet the conditions in the statute. The commenter pointed out that the preamble to the proposed rule states that each member of the group must individually furnish substantially the full range of services he or she routinely furnishes *through the group practice.* The commenter argued that this language is contradictory to the statute, which requires that each physician who is a member furnish the full range of services *through the joint use of shared space,* etc.—not furnish the full range through the group practice. The commenter suggested that the final rule state the actual requirements.

Response: It appears to us that what the commenter is describing is a situation in which two interrelated group practices share a laboratory. The

physicians' services exception under section 1877(b)(1) allows members of the same group practice to refer Medicare patients to each other for clinical laboratory services, as long as one of the physicians either personally performs the services or personally supervises the provision of the services. Thus, section 1877(b)(1) clearly contemplates physicians *within the same* group practice, but not physicians in different group practices. The in-office ancillary exception in section 1877(b)(2) allows members of the same group practice to refer to each other as long as the physician providing or supervising the services meets the tests in section 1877(b)(2) (A) and (B) for personal performance or direct supervision, location, and billing.

To qualify for the in-office ancillary services exception, an organization of physicians must meet the definition of a "group practice" under section 1877(h)(4). Under the definition, a group practice "means a group of two or more physicians legally organized as a partnership, professional corporation, foundation, not-for-profit corporation, faculty practice plan, or similar association." We agree that, in including a "similar association" in the list, the Congress has provided some flexibility for different kinds of entities to qualify as group practices. Nonetheless, we also believe that the statutory definition clearly contemplates only single legal entities. We do not view two independent group practices as a single practice, just because they are organizationally interrelated through common ownership or other substantial and ongoing connections.

We believe that the statute would have explicitly allowed for a "common ownership" or "substantial connection" configuration as part of the group practice definition had the Congress intended to include it. Also, it appears to us that using the premise of common ownership or substantial connection to combine individuals and entities could lead to far-reaching exceptions to the referral prohibition that we do not believe the Congress ever intended. For example, two solo practitioners could state that they are interrelated through shared administrative services and their common ownership of a shared laboratory, thus qualifying them as a similar association.

As we explain throughout this preamble, we do not believe that a clinical laboratory that is shared by associations of physicians who do not meet the definition of a single group practice will generally qualify for the in-office ancillary services exception. However, each individual physician in

these groups might qualify separately for the exception by meeting the requirements in section 1877(b)(2). That is, the physician must personally furnish the services or directly supervise the individual(s) that are furnishing the services. Further, the services must be furnished in a building in which the referring physician furnishes physicians' services unrelated to clinical laboratory services, and the services must be billed by the physician or an entity wholly owned by the physician.

Comment: One commenter indicated that we should address the issue of group practices that may include more than one legal entity as long as the entities either are in parent-subsidiary relationships or are under common ownership and control. The commenter stated that the proposed definition of group practice requires an entity to be legally organized, and gives multiple examples of the types of legal entities typically used in group practices. The commenter believed the definition is silent on the question of whether a group practice may have more than one such legal entity under a common umbrella. For example, a "parent" professional corporation or partnership might own subsidiary entities for real estate and/or equipment ownership or for billing or ancillary services. Alternatively, rather than having a parent/subsidiary relationship, these same types of separate entities might operate jointly under the common ownership and control of a core group of physicians. These separate structures have been highly desirable for reasons related to taxation, benefits, liability, debt service capacity, etc.

Response: This commenter was concerned about groups of physicians who furnish services through a "group practice" that is composed of several legal entities. The commenter believed that such a group practice should be able to take advantage of the in-office ancillary services exception as long as the entities are in either parent-subsidiary relationships or are under common ownership and control. The commenter specifically mentioned examples in which a professional corporation might own subsidiaries for providing equipment, for billing, or for ancillary services.

The definition of "group practice" in section 1877(h)(4)(A) means a group of 2 or more physicians, legally organized as a partnership, professional corporation, foundation, not-for-profit corporation, faculty practice plan, or similar association. As we have said elsewhere in this preamble, we believe that the statute contemplates a group

41936 **Federal Register** / Vol. 60, No. 156 / Monday, August 14, 1995 / Rules and Regulations

practice that is composed of one single group of physicians who are organized into one legal entity. In short, we do not believe that a group practice can consist of two or more groups of physicians, each organized as separate legal entities.

However, we do not believe the statute precludes a single group practice (that is, one single group of physicians) from owning other legal entities for the purpose of providing services to the group practice. Thus, a group practice could wholly own a separately incorporated laboratory facility which provides laboratory services to group practice or other patients. However, because the group practice physicians have an ownership interest in the laboratory, they could be prohibited from referring to the laboratory, unless an exception applies.

The physicians could qualify for the in-office ancillary services exception, provided they meet the requirements for supervision, location, and billing. This exception does not appear to dictate any particular ownership arrangements between group practice physicians and the laboratory in which the services are provided. In fact, the billing requirement in section 1877(b)(2)(B) allows the services to be billed by the referring physician, the group practice, or an entity wholly owned by the group practice. The exception appears to anticipate that a "group practice," as defined in section 1877(h)(4), may wholly own separate legal entities for billing or for providing ancillary services.

e. Corporate Practice of Medicine

Comment: Two commenters indicated that there are legitimate physician group practice structures and relationships that may not satisfy the definition of a group practice as set forth in the proposed rule. A specific concern is with group practice organizations affiliated with hospitals that are organized in compliance with State corporate practice of medicine statutes.

In States that have these statutes, according to the commenters, only a validly-organized professional corporation or professional association can enter into employment arrangements with physicians.

One of the commenters presented an example of a group practice that is organized as a nonprofit hospital affiliated corporation that owns a clinical laboratory. The nonprofit hospital-affiliated corporation will be unable to employ the physicians; that is, a separate professional corporation must be established to employ the physicians in accordance with applicable State law. Typically, this commenter claimed,

nonprofit corporations will not qualify as the appropriate vehicle for a for-profit professional corporation or association.

The commenters believed that entities such as those described above (joint not for profit/for profit structures) that meet certain specific standards should qualify under the "similar association" language of the group practice definition. They believed that, so long as all other requirements established by the Secretary relating to appropriate standards for group practices (including the performance of services, billing practices, location of facilities, and income distribution provisions) are met, these entities do not pose a threat of abuse to the Medicare program and, as a result, they should be considered as a single group practice under the definition. To ensure that only appropriate entities qualify, one commenter suggested that (1) the separate professional corporation be organized for the sole purpose of providing medical services to the nonprofit corporation/group practice and be obligated to furnish those services exclusively to the nonprofit corporation, and (2) that the nonprofit corporation perform all other services associated with a group practice (including laboratory, billing, etc.) and employ all nonphysician staff.

Response: We believe the commenters are asking that we regard a joint structure, such as a nonprofit hospital-affiliated corporation linked with a professional corporation or association, as one group practice. This designation would allow the physicians in the professional corporation or association to refer to the nonprofit corporation's laboratory under the physicians' services or in-office ancillary services exceptions in section 1877(b).

In order to meet the definition of a group practice, there must be one identifiable legal entity. As we understand it, the clinical laboratory is owned by a nonprofit hospital-affiliated corporation but, because of the corporate practice of medicine requirements, that nonprofit corporation is unable to directly employ the physicians. As a result, the physicians are members of a separate professional corporation or association. The hospital-affiliated corporation and the professional corporation or association are separate legal entities that cannot qualify as one group practice. Also, because the hospital-affiliated corporation cannot directly employ the physicians, the exception in section 1877(e)(2) does not apply. (This exception allows referrals by a physician when there is a compensation arrangement between an entity and a

physician for the employment of the physician.)

We see one possible exception for a nonprofit corporation that is affiliated with physicians who perform certain physician services. Under section 1877(e)(3), as amended by OBRA '93, there is an exception from the prohibition on physician referrals in the case of a personal service arrangement involving remuneration from an entity to a physician, or to an immediate family member of a physician, providing—

• The arrangement is set out in writing, is signed by the parties, and specifies the services covered by the arrangement;

• The arrangement covers all of the services to be furnished by the physician (or an immediate family member of the physician) to the entity;

• The aggregate services contracted for do not exceed those that are reasonable and necessary for the legitimate business purposes of the arrangement;

• The term of the arrangement is for at least 1 year;

• The compensation to be paid over the term of the arrangement is set in advance, does not exceed fair market value, and, except in the case of a physician incentive plan, is not determined in a manner that takes into account the volume or value of any referrals or other business generated between the parties;

• The services to be performed under the arrangement do not involve the counseling or promotion of a business arrangement or other activity that violates any State or Federal law; and

• The arrangement meets any other requirements the Secretary imposes by regulation to protect against Medicare program or patient abuse.

If the nonprofit corporation (that owns the laboratory) and the professional corporation or association (that has physician investors) have such an arrangement, the physicians would not be prohibited from referring laboratory testing to the nonprofit corporation's laboratory.

f. Not-For-Profit Corporations

Comment: One commenter asked about the provision that permits group practices to be legally organized as not-for-profit corporations. The proposed rule defines a "group practice" as "a group of two or more physicians legally organized as * * * a not-for-profit corporation * * *." The commenter, however, stated that not all group practices organized as not-for-profit groups have physicians as their original incorporators or corporate members, nor

Federal Register / Vol. 60, No. 156 / Monday, August 14, 1995 / Rules and Regulations   **41937**

is this required by State law. As an example, the commenter stated that tax-exempt hospitals often have affiliated group practices, and the group practice's operating entity (to which the commenter referred as a "physician-directed clinic") might be a not-for-profit corporation separate from the tax-exempt hospital entity that employs the physicians. This arrangement does not present a potential for abuse, in the commenter's view, although it is unclear whether a not-for-profit physician-directed clinic organization affiliated with a not-for-profit hospital in this manner meets the definition of a group practice. Therefore, the commenter recommended that the final regulation recognize the arrangements.

Response: As we understand the commenter's example, a tax-exempt hospital employs physicians who are part of an affiliated not-for-profit physician-directed clinic that was originally organized by the hospital. (Under Medicare, a physician-directed clinic is one in which (1) a physician (or a number of physicians) is present to perform medical (rather than administrative) services at all times the clinic is open; (2) each patient is under the care of a clinic physician; and (3) the nonphysician services are under medical supervision. (See Medicare Carriers Manual, section 2050.4.)) Further, we understand the commenter to be making the following suggestions:

• That an entity attempting to qualify as a group practice need not have been organized (or incorporated) by physicians; that is, as long as the entity is one in which two or more physicians have been brought together as a group practice, it does not matter that the initial organizing was done by nonphysicians.

• That an entity that, in fact, is a physician-directed clinic, organized by an affiliated hospital, be permitted to qualify as a group practice.

As to the first suggestion, the commenter referred to only the regulations, but the definition of "group practice" at section 1877(h)(4) also requires that there be "two or more physicians legally organized" as a not-for-profit corporation or as one of several other specified associations. Because the statute is silent about who must actually legally organize the association or operate or control it, we believe that any individuals or entities can assume these tasks, as long as the group practice meets all of the other specific requirements in section 1877(h)(4). Thus, if a clinic (or other facility) is legally organized to include two or more physicians and provides the services of physicians, it is a group

practice, even if it is established, operated, and controlled by a nonphysician group or corporation. This would be so regardless of who employs the physicians (in the scenario presented by the commenter, the clinic physicians were employed by the hospital that established the clinic).

g. Individual Pathology Services

Comment: One commenter suggested that the proposed regulations may preclude arrangements under which a group practice retains the services of an independent pathologist to direct the group's laboratory or otherwise assist in improving the quality of laboratory services available. The commenter wrote that the group practice may not be able to satisfy the definition of a group practice laboratory for purposes of section 1877(b)(2) if it retains the services of an independent pathologist who is not considered a member of the group, but who provides medical direction to the laboratory. Second, according to the commenter, an independent pathologist affiliated with a reference laboratory may be unwilling to provide consulting services to a group practice laboratory unless the consulting arrangement is specifically excepted by the regulations. Therefore, the commenter requested that the final regulations provide that (1) a pathologist retained by a group practice on a regular, part-time basis to direct, supervise, and otherwise assist in the performance of laboratory services be considered to be a member of the group practice; and (2) the services of a pathologist serving as a laboratory consultant be included within the category of exceptions set forth in proposed Section 411.359(e)(1)(i) (that is, service arrangements with nonhospital entities).

Another commenter requested that we develop an additional exception relating to compensation arrangements involving the provision of consulting services, as opposed to the furnishing of actual testing services. The commenter suggested that the arrangement would have to be: in writing, consistent with fair market value for the consulting services provided, and not conditioned on referral of laboratory services from one party to the other or otherwise related to the volume or value of referrals for laboratory services.

Response: First, part-time or contract physicians, including independent pathologists, may be considered members of a group practice if they meet the conditions in the "member" definition in § 411.351. As indicated by the commenter, a group practice can hire a pathologist to direct, supervise, or

otherwise assist in performing laboratory tests. We agree that this is an important point because the most significant advantage of a practice meeting the group practice definition is that it qualifies the group for the in-office ancillary services exception in section 1877(b)(2). This exception applies if the referring physician or *another member* of the same group practice either performs or directly supervises the performance of the laboratory services. A group practice would not be able to use the section 1877(b)(2) in-office exception if it is a group practice member who is referring patients to the group's laboratory, but it is a nonmember pathologist who is performing or supervising the laboratory services.

The second concern of the first commenter involves an independent pathologist, who is somehow "affiliated" with an outside laboratory, who might be unwilling to provide consultation services to a group practice laboratory unless the consulting arrangement is specifically excepted from the prohibition by the regulations. Following is our analysis of such a situation.

First, the group practice laboratory is itself a laboratory entity that is compensating a pathologist (physician) for certain services the physician is providing and that relate to the group's laboratory services. We believe the pathologist could refer to the group practice laboratory if this arrangement fits within the exception in section 1877(e)(3). Section 1877(e)(3) excepts from the term "compensation arrangement" payments *from an entity to a physician* for personal services provided by the physician under an arrangement. The arrangement must meet certain criteria (for example, the arrangement must list the specific services in writing, be signed, be reasonable and necessary, and compensation must be for fair market value).

Section 1877(e)(3) does not appear to differentiate between physicians receiving compensation on the basis of whether they are independent contractors who also service other outside laboratories or whether they are employees or owners of outside laboratories.

The group practice could also be regarded as a group of physicians who may be purchasing services from an outside laboratory (if the pathologist is employed by or owns the outside laboratory). If this is the case, the compensation could instead be excepted under section 1877(e)(8). This provision excepts payments *made by a physician*

41938   Federal Register / Vol. 60, No. 156 / Monday, August 14, 1995 / Rules and Regulations

to an entity as compensation for items or services other than clinical laboratory services if they are furnished at a price that is consistent with fair market value.

If the pathologist is considered a member of the group practice and makes referrals to the outside laboratory, whether the referrals would be prohibited depends upon the nature of the pathologist's relationship with the laboratory. The referrals might not be prohibited if the pathologist is the employee of the outside laboratory. In that situation, the payment the pathologist receives from the outside laboratory would not be "compensation" under section 1877(e)(2), which exempts any amount paid by an employer to a physician who has a bona fide employment relationship with the entity for the provision of services if certain standards are met.

If the pathologist is independent but contracts with the outside laboratory, the compensation that flows from the outside laboratory to the pathologist could be excepted under section 1877(e)(3). This provision excepts remuneration from an entity under a personal service arrangement if certain standards are met.

If the pathologist owns the outside laboratory though, his or her referrals would be prohibited. That is because the pathologist would be referring to a laboratory in which he or she has an ownership interest (the section 1877(e) provisions except only compensation arrangements). Finally, if the pathologist is a member of the group practice, none of the group practice members can refer to the laboratory that is owned by the pathologist. That is because, in Section 431.351 of the proposed rule, we defined "referring physician" as a physician (or group practice) who makes a referral. Thus, any referral by one group practice member is imputed to the entire group practice.

7. Immediate Family

Under the proposed rule (§ 411.351) an "immediate family member" of a physician means husband or wife; natural or adoptive parent; child or sibling; stepparent, stepchild, stepbrother, or stepsister; father-in-law, mother-in-law, son-in-law, daughter-in-law, brother-in-law, or sister-in-law; grandparent or grandchild; and spouse of a grandparent or grandchild.

Comment: Two commenters recommended that we adopt what they believed to be a more manageable definition of immediate family member. They recommended eliminating, at the very least, the references to

grandparents, grandchildren, and assorted in-laws.

One of the two commenters recommended that the definition include "natural or adoptive parent, child or sibling" and exclude the remainder of the identified relatives. In this commenter's view, the definition of immediate family reaches beyond what is intended by the statute.

Response: As we stated in the proposed rule, our proposed definition is a longstanding definition used (in § 411.12) by the Medicare program to implement section 1862(a)(11), which excludes from Medicare coverage services furnished by an immediate relative. We also explained that, in our view, the definition encompasses the range of relatives who could be in a position to influence the pattern of a physician's referrals. These commenters simply stated their opinion that the definition is overreaching, without explaining why.

For these reasons, we are retaining the definition as proposed.

Comment: One commenter suggested that when an allowable clinical laboratory service is performed as part of a medical consultation by a family member of the referring physician, we should not prohibit that referral solely because the consulting physician is related to the referring physician.

Response: Under the definition of referral in section 1877(h)(5)(A), the request by a physician for an item or service covered under Part B, including the request by a physician for a consultation with another physician, and any test or procedure ordered by, or to be performed by (or under the supervision of) that other physician, constitutes a "referral" by a "referring physician." The first physician has, in sending his patient to the family member, made a referral under the statute.

If the family member performs or supervises the performance of the laboratory test, it is likely that the family member has either an ownership interest in the entity that performed the test and/or is compensated by the entity for supervising or performing the test. As a result, the first physician has referred a patient for laboratory tests to an entity with which his or her immediate family member has an ownership or compensation relationship. If no exceptions apply, this makes the referral a prohibited one. If the consultant family member merely orders the laboratory test from a laboratory in which neither he or she nor the first physician has a financial interest, the referral would not be prohibited.

We also point out that section 1877(h)(5)(C) provides that if a pathologist performs a laboratory test or supervises the performance of a test that is part of a consultation requested by another physician, the furnishing of the test by the pathologist or his or her request that the test be completed (under the pathologist's supervision) is not a referral. In other words, a self-referral by a pathologist as a result of a consultation does not constitute a referral for purposes of section 1877.

Comment: One commenter is a solo practitioner whose office is located in a building owned by herself and six other physicians, one of whom is her husband. In the building, there is an independent laboratory that is owned by the group practice to which her husband belongs. The laboratory was established by the physicians in the building for the practices in the building. The commenter did not think it is right that, because her husband has an ownership interest in the laboratory, her patients should not have access to it.

Response: Unless an exception applies, it appears, on the face of it, that the commenter is correct in stating that her referrals to the independent clinical laboratory would be prohibited. Her relationships with the laboratory appear to be as follows:

• She may have been an investor in the laboratory, because she was one of the "physicians in the building" who set the laboratory up "for the practices in the building."

• She is the spouse of a member of the group practice that now owns the laboratory.

• She is part owner of the building that houses not only the laboratory, but her solo practice and her husband's group practice as well.

It appears, therefore, that this physician, in addition to being an immediate family member of what may be a partial owner of the laboratory, may also be an investor in the laboratory herself (depending on the nature of her initial involvement in setting up the laboratory and any current financial interest) and may have a compensation arrangement with the laboratory based on rentals she presumably receives as a part owner of the building. We believe, however, that her family relationship generally controls to prohibit her referrals if her husband has an ownership or investment interest in the group practice or its laboratory or if he receives unexcepted forms of compensation from the group practice.

The physician's referrals would not be prohibited on the basis of her husband's ownership interest if the laboratory qualifies as a rural laboratory under

Federal Register / Vol. 60, No. 156 / Monday, August 14, 1995 / Rules and Regulations **41939**

§ 411.356(b)(1). Note that, as discussed elsewhere in the preamble, unless the group practice that owns the laboratory satisfies the definitional requirements, referrals by group practice physicians to the laboratory might also be called into question.

8. Practice

In the proposed rule (411.351), we defined a "practice" to mean an office in which the physician, as a matter of routine, sees patients for purposes of diagnosis and treatment and where patient records are kept.

Comment: One commenter indicated that many group practices provide medical services in satellite facilities where only limited medical services are offered and that the medical records of the group practice are kept in a centralized location. Thus, the commenter recommended that we clarify in the final rule that the definition of "practice" is not incorporated into the definition of "group practice."

Another commenter stated that some physicians maintain a medical practice without being tied to a particular location, such as certain hospital-based physicians and those who treat nursing home patients. These physicians use office space only to receive mail and for other administrative support functions. Such a practice, be it group or individual, does not have an office for purposes of diagnosis and treatment, or even to keep substantial amounts of medical records. The commenter believed this fact is not taken into account in the definition.

Response: We acknowledge that the commenters have raised some legitimate problems with the proposed approach and how difficult it is to determine where someone has a "practice." We are responding to these comments by creating a new, more equitable standard that is not based on the concept of a physician's "practice" (and thus eliminate the definition from the rule). We are using the new standard required by OBRA '93, which states that to qualify as a rural provider, substantially all of the clinical laboratory services furnished by the entity must be furnished to individuals residing in the rural area. As part of this standard, we are defining "substantially all" as meaning that 75 percent of the individuals to whom services are furnished reside in the rural area. Although the effective date of this provision for rural providers is January 1, 1995, we believe it is reasonable to incorporate it into this final rule.

9. Referral

In the proposed rule (§ 411.351), a "referral" means either of the following:
- The request by a physician for, or ordering of, any item or service for which payment may be made under Medicare Part B, including a request for a consultation with another physician other than a pathologist, and any test or procedure ordered by or to be performed by (or under the supervision of) that physician; or
- If a plan of care includes the performance of clinical laboratory testing, the request or establishment of the plan of care by a physician. When a pathologist, in responding to another physician's request for a consultation, furnishes or supervises the furnishing of clinical diagnostic laboratory tests and pathological examination services, the services are not considered to have been furnished on a referral basis.

a. Pathology Referrals

Comment: Two commenters wanted the definition of "referral" to be clarified so as to exclude circumstances in which a pathologist providing professional services to one laboratory sends specimens ordered by the attending physician to a second laboratory in which the pathologist has a financial interest.

One commenter indicated that the definition should also exclude circumstances in which a pathologist recommends to an attending physician appropriate follow-up laboratory services.

Response: Under the definition of "referral" in section 1877(h)(5), a request by a pathologist for clinical diagnostic laboratory tests and pathology examination services will not be considered a referral if such laboratory services are furnished by (or under the supervision of) the pathologist as a result of a consultation requested by another physician. Thus, if the pathologist described in the first comment either performs or directly supervises the performance of the laboratory testing in the second laboratory, the request for services would not be considered a referral by the pathologist. The answer is different, however, if the pathologist sends laboratory work to a laboratory with which he or she has a financial relationship and the services are not performed by the pathologist or under his or her direct supervision. The services in this situation would be considered to have been furnished as a result of a prohibited referral, unless one of the exceptions applies. Similarly, if the pathologist sends tests to a

laboratory with which the first referring physician has a financial relationship, the referral would be prohibited, unless an exception applies. Because we recognize that there are situations in which a physician's request for a consultation with a pathologist could constitute a referral, this final rule revises the proposed definition of "referral" by removing the phrase "other than a pathologist".

We do not consider a pathologist's recommendation to the attending physician for additional testing to be a referral. That is because it is the attending physician who ultimately decides whether such testing is necessary and whether to order the additional testing and from what laboratory.

b. Plan of Care and End-Stage Renal Disease (ESRD) Patients

Comment: One commenter indicated that the proposed rule is ambiguous with regard to the "plan of care" element within the definition of "referral." At one level, the commenter believed, the language is simply unclear in that, with regard to "a plan of care that includes the performance of clinical laboratory tests," it is difficult to understand what is meant by the "request or the establishment of the plan of care by a physician." According to the commenter, this might mean that when a physician establishes a plan of care that entails laboratory testing and the facility or other individual implementing the plan of care orders those tests from a laboratory, the physician shall be considered to have made the laboratory referral. If this interpretation is correct, the commenter believed there are some issues specific to chronic hemodialysis facilities and referrals that require clarification.

The commenter wrote that hemodialysis patients receive three different classes of clinical laboratory tests:

1. Tests ordered on a patient-specific basis on account of particular clinical signs and symptoms and referred by the dialysis facility to an independent or hospital-based clinical laboratory that bills Medicare. These tests pose no interpretive problems, as the physician does, in fact, order each one individually.

2. Routine monthly testing applicable to every patient and for which payment is incorporated into the facility's dialysis composite rate.

3. Testing integral to monitoring the patient during the dialysis treatment itself, performed in the facility and not billed separately.

41940   Federal Register / Vol. 60, No. 156 / Monday, August 14, 1995 / Rules and Regulations

The commenter pointed out that every time a patient is referred to a facility for chronic renal dialysis, clinical laboratory testing from categories 2 and 3 is required on an ongoing basis as part of the overall care of the patient. If the physician's plan of care for dialysis is deemed to include these tests for purposes of this rule, the commenter believed that the practical result would be to prohibit physicians from making referrals for tests to dialysis facilities in which they have an ownership interest.

A second commenter stated that the ESRD program includes in its composite rate payment methodology most items and services related to the treatment of patients with ESRD, including hematocrit and hemoglobin tests, clotting time tests, routine diagnostic tests, and routine diagnostic laboratory tests. Thus, the commenter pointed out, the determination of whether an item or service is included under the composite rate payment is presumptive and in no way depends on the frequency with which a dialysis patient requires the item or service. The commenter recommended that the final rule, or the preamble to the final rule, explicitly exclude clinical laboratory referrals covered by ESRD from its application.

Response: Section 1877(h)(5)(B) says that "the request or establishment of a plan of care by a physician which includes the provision of [clinical laboratory services] constitutes a "referral" by a "referring physician." The commenter has pointed out that this provision, carried over into the proposed rule, is ambiguous and unclear. The statute could mean (1) that there is a referral when a physician establishes a plan of care or requests that one be established that includes laboratory services or (2) that a request by a physician that includes the provision of laboratory services or the establishment of a plan of care by a physician that includes the provision of laboratory services constitutes a referral. Because the comments reveal that this provision has caused confusion, we have decided to adopt the latter interpretation and have incorporated it into the regulation.

We also agree that it is not clear what technically constitutes a "plan of care." We believe that any time a physician orders any item, service, or treatment for a patient, that order is pursuant to a plan of care. If a plan of care entails laboratory testing and the facility or other individual implementing the plan orders those tests from a laboratory, the physician who established the plan of care is considered to have made the laboratory referral. In addition, as we mentioned in a previous response, the

prohibition could also apply if the individual implementing some or all of the plan of care is a consulting physician. We agree, however, that, under certain circumstances, this may cause problems when those laboratory tests are included in the ESRD composite rate. Thus, as we discuss below, we are including those laboratory tests that are paid under the ESRD composite rate as part of a new exception. We agree that the application of the composite rate constitutes a barrier to either Medicare program or patient abuse because the Medicare program will pay only a set amount to the facilities irrespective of the number and frequency of laboratory tests that are ordered.

c. Consultation Referrals

Comment: A few commenters believed that it was unnecessary for us to include in the preamble the discussion about consultations (57 FR 8595) and the responsibility of a consulting physician to not engage in a cross-referral arrangement. They believed there is no corresponding statutory or regulatory provision and that, except for a small number of truly "bad apples" practicing medicine, physicians have not and will not engage in the complicated and tortuous process of directing referrals.

One commenter was concerned that the proposed rule suggests that physicians who refer to consultants have some obligation to tie the consultant's hands when it comes to which clinical laboratories the consultant can use. The commenter believed such an obligation runs afoul of the principle of medical ethics that requires a physician to refer patients to the entity that furnishes the most efficacious service, regardless of other considerations. The commenter indicated that, in a managed care setting, it may be impossible for the attending physician to even know who the consulting physician is, much less be in a position to dictate which laboratory is selected. In sum, this commenter believed that it will be difficult in practice for physicians to determine where the prohibition ends.

Response: We do not agree with these commenters. In response to the first comment, the discussion in the proposed rule was based on the statute at section 1877(g)(4). This provision says that "any physician or other entity that enters into an arrangement or scheme (such as a cross-referral arrangement) which the physician or entity knows or should know has a principal purpose of assuring referrals by the physician to a particular entity

which, if the physician directly made referrals to such entity, would be in violation of [section 1877], shall be subject to a civil money penalty * * *."

Because the provision applies to physicians who make referrals and to "other entities," we believe that it can apply to consulting physicians who help a physician indirectly make prohibited referrals. In the preamble of the proposed rule (57 FR 8595) we stated that, if a consulting physician deems it necessary to order clinical laboratory services, those services may not be ordered from a laboratory in which the referring physician has a financial interest. We included this explanation to give the reader an example of the kinds of referrals that are prohibited under the statutory definition of "referral." Under section 1877(h)(5)(A), a request by a physician for a consultation with another physician (and any test or procedure ordered by, or to be performed by or performed under the supervision of that other physician) constitutes a referral. Thus, it is necessary for the consulting physician to be aware of any financial relationships the referring physician may have with a laboratory, in order for the referral not to be prohibited. Finally, the consulting physician is also obligated not to refer laboratory testing to an entity with which he or she has a financial relationship, unless an exception applies.

Concerning services furnished in a managed care setting, section 1877(b)(3) provides a general exception for services provided to patients enrolled in the prepaid health plans listed in that provision and in the regulations at § 411.355(c).

d. Statutory Authority

Comment: One commenter noted that the statutory definition of referral encompasses requests for any item or service for which payment may be made under Medicare Part B, but the prohibition contained in the statute is aimed at referrals for clinical laboratory services and not other referrals. Thus, in the commenter's view, the statute makes the rule somewhat confusing. That is, the behavior that the statute seeks to restrict, referrals for clinical laboratory services, is narrower in scope than the behavior of "referring" itself. Therefore, the commenter suggested that the final rule clarify that the prohibited behavior is related to clinical laboratory services.

Response: We agree that the definition of "referral" under the statute at section 1877(h)(5) is broad. In section 1877(h)(5)(A), for physicians' services, it covers a physician's request for any item or service covered under Part B of

Federal Register / Vol. 60, No. 156 / Monday, August 14, 1995 / Rules and Regulations   **41941**

Medicare. For other items, section 1877(h)(5)(B) covers a physician's request or establishment of a plan of care that includes furnishing clinical laboratory services. However, section 1877(a)(1)(A) specifically narrows the scope of section 1877 by describing the subset of referrals that are prohibited. Physicians were originally prohibited from making referrals to an entity for the purpose of providing clinical laboratory services. As of January 1, 1995, physicians are prohibited from making a much broader range of referrals to entities furnishing the other designated health services listed in section 1877(h)(6).

e. Hospitals and Group Practice Laboratory

Comment: One commenter believed that, if there is an "under arrangement" agreement between a hospital and a group practice for the group practice to provide laboratory services to hospital patients under section 1861(w)(1), it is the hospital and not the group practice physicians that is making a referral for the purposes of the section 1877 self-referral proscription. The commenter pointed out that, for the most part, as recognized in the proposed regulation, a physician's request for a service is tantamount to a referral to a particular service provider. If services are being furnished to hospital inpatients and outpatients, however, the commenter indicated that it is the hospital's obligation to ensure that the services be performed and to direct that the services be performed by a particular party. Thus, in the commenter's opinion, it is the hospital that is making the referral to the group practice laboratory. Consequently, the commenter recommended clarification of the definition of "referral" and "referring physician" so that it is clear that a physician's ordering of clinical laboratory services for hospital patients does not constitute a "referral" within the meaning of section 1877.

Response: The commenter believed that we should revise the definitions of "referral" and "referring physician" to make it clear that, in the situation described in the comment, it is the hospital that makes a referral to a group practice laboratory and not the group practice physicians. We disagree with this interpretation. Every referral for clinical laboratory services must originate with a physician, and the general rule in section 1877(a)(1)(A) prohibits a *physician* from making a referral to an entity with which the physician (or an immediate family member) has a financial relationship. A "referral" need not even indicate a

specific laboratory. Section 1877(h) defines a "referral" as any request by a physician for an item or service or the establishment of a plan of care that includes the provision of laboratory services.

We do not believe that the Congress intended to allow physicians to circumvent the referral prohibition by imputing their referrals to an operating entity such as a clinic, hospital, or other institution. We believe that "referring physicians" and "referrals" involve only individual physicians or groups of physicians who send a Medicare patient or specimen to a laboratory for services.

Although, in our opinion, the general prohibition applies to the situation described by the commenter, there are exceptions within the statute that could apply to allow the group practice physicians to continue to refer.

The commenter has described a situation in which group practice physicians apparently provide patient care services to hospital patients. They refer hospital patients to the group practice's laboratory; the group practice laboratory provides laboratory services for the hospital under arrangements; and Medicare pays the hospital. The referring physicians in this case are referring to a laboratory that receives compensation from the hospital (the hospital buys laboratory services under arrangements). The hospital is also apparently compensating the group physicians for patient care services. The physicians, in addition, are likely to be receiving compensation from the group practice that owns the group practice laboratory and/or they have an ownership interest in the group practice and its laboratory.

We believe that the exception in section 1877(e)(7) could apply to allow referrals based on part of this scenario. This provision says that there is no "compensation arrangement" that would trigger the prohibition in section 1877, for arrangements between a hospital and a group practice under which the group practice provides laboratory services but the hospital bills for the services, if certain criteria are met. If the arrangement meets the criteria, the group practice should be able to refer to the hospital's laboratory without violating section 1877. That is because the underlying compensation passing between the hospital (which, in essence, is purchasing services from the group practice laboratory) and the group does not trigger the prohibition.

There is, however, a complicating factor in the commenter's scenario. That is, the group practice physicians are referring to their own group practice laboratory. It is likely that these

physicians are receiving compensation from the group practice that owns the laboratory or that they own some portion of the group practice and the laboratory. The compensation or ownership interests involved here would require a separate exception in order to allow the group practice physicians to refer. The services could, for example, be excepted under the in-office ancillary services exception in section 1877(b)(2), which allows a group practice to refer to its own laboratory if certain criteria are met.

In addition, the hospital may be separately compensating the group practice physicians for patient care services, compensation that is independent of the compensation the hospital pays the group to purchase laboratory services. The compensation from the hospital, however, could be excepted under section 1877(e)(2), if there is a bona fide employment relationship between the hospital and the physicians, or section 1877(e)(3) if the hospital is paying the physicians for personal services furnished to the hospital.

10. Referring Physician

We proposed, in § 411.351, to define a "referring physician" as "a physician (or group practice) who makes a referral as defined in this section."

Comment: One commenter believed that the definition of referral is not necessary because the statute is clear as written.

Response: We incorporated this definition in the rule to make the regulations as complete and clear as possible. Furthermore, this definition interprets the statutory term to include referrals made by an individual physician as well as referrals made by a group practice.

Comment: A commenter raised the issue of a physician who owns or manages a clinic but does not function as a physician by providing care to clinic patients. The physician also owns an interest in a clinical laboratory to which clinic patients or samples are sometimes referred. The commenter believed the physician-owner should not be considered a referring physician within the meaning of the regulation when he or she does not function as a physician. The commenter also believed that, if a clinic owner is only incidentally a physician, that professional degree should play no role in setting his or her legal obligations. In the commenter's view, to include physicians who are mere owners/ managers of clinics within the definition of referring physician would be arbitrary and prejudicial to them. The

41942   Federal Register / Vol. 60, No. 156 / Monday, August 14, 1995 / Rules and Regulations

commenter added that such a physician should be compared to nonphysician clinic owners or managers who are not covered by the statute or its implementing regulations. Clearly, according to the commenter, clinic owners or managers with medical degrees should have the same legal status as nonphysician owners or managers. Thus, the commenter recommended that the final regulation, or its preamble, explicitly exclude from the definition of referring physician, physician-owners who neither practice medicine nor make direct referrals to clinical laboratories.

Response: Section 1877 prohibits referrals by "physicians" and does not qualify "physicians" to exempt any subset of these individuals. Since section 1877 does not define who is a physician for purposes of that section, the usual Medicare definition of that term applies. "Physician" is defined in the statute, at section 1861(r), as a doctor of medicine or osteopathy legally authorized to practice medicine and surgery by the State in which he or she performs that function or action (including osteopathic practitioners within the scope of their practice as defined by State law). The definition also includes a doctor of dental surgery or dental medicine, a doctor of podiatric medicine, a doctor of optometry, and a chiropractor. These additional individuals qualify as "physicians" only when they are performing within the scope of their license or providing items and services that they are legally authorized to perform within their specialty. The Medicare regulations define "physicians' services" at 410.20 as those furnished by one of these individuals who is legally authorized to practice by the State and "who is acting within the scope of his or her license." Arguably then, a physician who owns or manages a clinic but does not provide any of the items or services authorized within the scope of his or her license would not be a "physician" for purposes of section 1877. However, if such an individual refers clinic patients to a particular laboratory or attempts to influence a clinic physician to make such referrals, that individual's status changes. That is, he or she has become involved in the care of particular patients and is therefore acting in the role of a physician. As a result, the provisions of section 1877 (including the provision prohibiting circumvention schemes and indirect referrals) would apply.

11. Remuneration

We proposed, in section 411.351, to define "remuneration" as "any

payment, discount, forgiveness of debt, or other benefit made directly or indirectly, overtly or covertly, in cash or in kind."

a. Discounts

Comment: Some commenters supported the concept of including discounts in the definition of remuneration. They indicated that it is not unusual for a physician with substantial Medicare business to obtain a larger discount than a physician who has no Medicare business. Discounts, in the view of these commenters, can therefore influence a physician to use a particular laboratory and, in an extreme case, the prospect of a deeper discount may even induce a physician to order unnecessary tests.

One commenter offered the opinion that the intent of the legislation is clear from the definition of "compensation arrangement," which is defined to include all forms of remuneration, direct or indirect, overt or covert, in cash or in kind.

Another commenter indicated that the existence of a discount arrangement has a strong potential to result in excessive laboratory testing, which contributes to the distressing rise in health care costs in this country. One commenter believed that a compensation arrangement, for the purpose of section 1877, should be created only whenever the following situation occurs: (1) Some remuneration passes from a laboratory to a physician; and (2) the prospect of remuneration gives the physician an incentive to order increased testing.

One commenter indicated that, to a certain extent, physicians receive a lower price than other payers because of the legitimate cost savings associated with physician billing.

Two commenters stated that there is nothing inherently abusive about discounts. One of the commenters believed that what gives the physician an incentive to increase his or her utilization of testing is not the discount; it is his or her ability to mark up the testing and thereby derive a profit from the transaction. The other commenter suggested that discounts be permitted if the laboratory can meet the following conditions:

• The discount is not tied to the referral of Medicare specimens to the laboratory.

• The discount is related to verifiable cost differences in handling specimens that satisfy the conditions for the discount, including cost differences due to such factors as economies of scale, lower billing and collection costs, prompt and regular payment, or reduced bad debt cost.

• The discount is available to anyone who can satisfy the requirements for the discount, for example, type of test or other objective requirement; and

• The discount is not provided to any referring physician. (We assume by this that the commenter meant that discounts a laboratory entity would make to providers of services, such as hospitals, would be permissible under these guidelines.)

Response: As discussed earlier, section 1877(e)(8)(A), as added by OBRA '93, provides that a physician may make payments to a clinical laboratory in exchange for furnishing clinical laboratory services and continue to refer Medicare patients to that laboratory. There is no requirement that the payments meet any particular pricing standards. However, when a laboratory provides a physician with a discount, it may in some cases be providing that physician with a benefit (that is, remuneration) that is separate from the payment that the physician has made to the laboratory to purchase laboratory services. Since we are not interpreting the OBRA '93 provisions in this rule, but merely reiterating them, we have not yet taken a position on how this new provision will affect discounts. We will interpret section 1877(e)(8)(A) and how it applies to discounts in the context of the proposed rule covering all of the designated health services.

In regard to discounts for items and services other than clinical laboratory services, a physician may purchase other things from a clinical laboratory besides clinical laboratory services. Section 1877(e)(8)(B) allows a physician to purchase from any entity items and services, other than laboratory services, as long as they are purchased at fair market value. Section 1877(h)(3) defines fair market value as the value in arm's-length transactions, consistent with the general market value, which would not include discounts. In light of section 1877(e)(8)(B), we are keeping "discounts" in the definition of "remuneration." As a result, discounts would remain "compensation arrangements" for discounts on items or services such as supplies or personnel or consulting services purchased by a physician from a clinical laboratory or other entity.

Comment: One commenter indicated that providing a discount to physicians

Federal Register / Vol. 60, No. 156 / Monday, August 14, 1995 / Rules and Regulations **41943**

is not necessarily a means of providing them compensation. As an example, the commenter pointed out that in New York, a State that has long had a direct billing law and related regulations, discounts are passed directly on to the patient or insurance carrier. It is a market mechanism that, in the commenter's view, actually works to hold down the cost of health care. The commenter considered discounts a goal to be aimed for, not a practice to be precluded. The commenter indicated that a simple way to help hold down the cost of health care is to follow the direct billing practices established in New York or to exempt those States that already have such laws.

Response: This commenter made a good point. Nonetheless, the Medicare statute generally does not currently authorize us to impose the "direct billing" requirement found at section 1877(h)(5)(A) for laboratory services other than those furnished to Medicare patients. As we noted in an earlier response, we will address the discount issue in our proposed rule covering the designated health services.

Comment: A commenter stated that physician groups often contract with HMOs to provide medical care for HMO members and described the following situation: The physician group is paid a predetermined monthly rate per enrollee as payment in full for all outpatient medical services, including laboratory services furnished to covered enrollees. To ensure that the physician group can furnish all necessary services in an efficient and cost effective manner, the physician group typically enters into discount agreements with providers not affiliated with the group to furnish services to the HMO's patients at a discounted rate. These arrangements include laboratory services at a discounted rate.

In the commenter's view, this type of discount arrangement would not pose any risk of Medicare program or patient abuse under the following conditions:

1. The HMO does not bill the Medicare program for any Medicare patient laboratory tests performed by an outside laboratory.

2. The physician group does bill commercial insurance for tests performed but does not mark up the cost of the test; that is, the group bills the exact amount charged by the outside laboratory.

3. The discount arrangement is not, in any way, influenced by the volume of Medicare patient laboratory tests sent to the laboratory facility.

4. The discount arrangement is based upon the volume of laboratory services purchased for HMO patients.

5. An agreement to provide laboratory services to HMO patients at a specified fee or discount that is not based upon volume of Medicare referrals is revenue neutral as far as the Medicare program is concerned. In other words, the fixed discount or specified fee is established completely independently of the volume of Medicare referrals and certainly independently of the Medicare program itself.

Response: We believe that the exception set forth in sections 1877(b)(3) and section 411.355(c) applies in this situation, at least in part. Under those provisions, the prohibition on referrals does not apply to referrals for services furnished by an organization with a contract under section 1876 to an individual enrolled with the organization. (Also see 42 CFR part 417, subpart C.) This exception also applies to referrals for services furnished by organizations with health care prepayment plans that have agreements with us under section 1833(a)(1)(A) to an individual enrolled in the plan (see 42 CFR part 417, subpart D) and by organizations receiving payments on a prepaid basis for their enrollees in accordance with the terms of a demonstration project authorized under section 402(a) of the Social Security Amendments of 1967 (42 U.S.C. 1395b–1) or under section 222(a) of the Social Security Amendments of 1972 (42 U.S.C. 1395b–1 note). Also, as added by OBRA '93, this exception applies to referrals for services furnished by a qualified HMO (within the meaning of section 1310(d) of the Public Health Service Act) to its enrollees. Thus, the exception no longer requires that all HMO plans contract with Medicare in order to qualify for the exception. The exception in section 1877(b)(3) applies to all services furnished by the organizations listed in that provision, including those services furnished to enrollees by outside physician groups, which have contracted with the organizations. As we noted in earlier responses, we will address the issue of how to treat discounts under section 1877 in the proposed rule covering the designated health services.

b. Forgiveness of Debt; Other Benefits

Comment: One commenter indicated concerns with the inclusion of the term "forgiveness of debt" in the definition of remuneration. According to the commenter, there are a number of legitimate reasons why a laboratory might forgive a debt owed by a physician. For example, there might be a dispute over the correctness of a bill or over whether the physician had in fact ordered certain tests. In such instances, a laboratory might decide to write off the debt. In contrast, the laboratory might decide to furnish services to a physician who had previously owed money to the laboratory, which the laboratory had written off. This same commenter recognized that forgiveness of debt in such a situation might be an abuse; that is, the laboratory might simply forgive an obligation owed in order to obtain continued referrals. Thus, the commenter agreed that the forgiveness of debt should be considered remuneration within the meaning of the statute, but added that the definition should distinguish between the atypical situation and routine types of write-offs.

One commenter believed that the inclusion of "other benefit" in the definition of remuneration is very broad. The commenter believed the definition could reach a variety of services that are integral to the provision of laboratory services and that enhance the quality of the services furnished. Examples of "other benefits" that might be exchanged between a physician and laboratory mentioned by the commenter are test tubes and other laboratory testing supplies, telecommunications equipment such as stand-alone printers, courier services, and educational or consultation services.

Another commenter recommended that the definition of remuneration be amended to exclude from the prohibited category those items or services that are enhancements to the quality of laboratory services and that have no value independent of the laboratory service, such as courier pickup of samples, increased frequency of pick up of samples, and electronic transmission of results.

One commenter recommended that the definition of remuneration be amended to exclude "discount, forgiveness of debt, or other benefit" and that we retain the statutory definition.

Response: Section 1877(h)(1) as amended by OBRA '93 specifies that a "compensation arrangement" does not include arrangements involving only the following kinds of remuneration:

• The forgiveness of amounts owed for inaccurate tests or procedures, mistakenly performed tests or procedures, or the correction of minor billing errors.

• The provision of items, devices, or supplies that are used solely as follows:

+ To collect, transport, process, or store specimens for the entity providing the item, device, or supply.

41944   **Federal Register** / Vol. 60, No. 156 / Monday, August 14, 1995 / Rules and Regulations

+ To order or communicate the results of tests or procedures for the entity.

This provision also excepts payments made by an insurer or self-insured plan to a physician for the physician's claims under certain circumstances.

Thus, we believe that, when a laboratory writes off a debt to essentially correct the records between the parties, the exception described above would apply. However, if a laboratory has a continual pattern of disposing of the debt of its referring physicians in this manner, we might scrutinize the situation under the circumvention scheme provision (section 1877(g)(4).) Negotiations between parties about the correct amount of money owed for services delivered, resulting in a balancing of accounts, would also qualify under this exception, as well as the exchange of certain laboratory supplies, telecommunications equipment, and courier services.

One commenter mentioned that "other benefits" exchanged between a physician and a laboratory could be educational or consultation services. Section 1877(e)(3) provides that a physician who has a personal services arrangement (or an immediate family member with a personal services arrangement) with a laboratory entity (for example, to furnish consultations or educational services) may refer patients to that entity if certain conditions are met. Also, section 1877(e)(8)(B) allows a physician to make payments to any entity (including a laboratory) for items and services, other than clinical laboratory services, if the purchase is consistent with fair market value.

Because of these facts, we are retaining the proposed definition of remuneration but are explaining that certain day-to-day business transactions as listed in the statute are not included in this definition.

c. Payments

Comment: One commenter objected to including the term "payment" in the definition of remuneration. This commenter pointed out that payments frequently occur between laboratories and physicians and, in many instances, these payments do not create incentives for physicians to order increased laboratory testing. For example, in the commenter's opinion, the following situations do not create incentives for physicians to increase their laboratory referrals.

• The laboratory *pays* a physician who furnishes interpretation or consultation services such as Pap test interpretation, tissue pathology

consultations, or EKG holter monitor readings.

• A laboratory *pays* a physician a refund as a result of an overpayment or to settle a disputed claim.

• A laboratory that maintains a self-insured group medical plan for its employees *pays* a physician who furnished services to a laboratory employee.

• A laboratory *pays* a physician to be on call to come to its blood-drawing station in case of an emergency, as required by State law.

• A physician *pays* the laboratory for the provision of a nonlaboratory service that it furnishes or that is furnished by a subsidiary or related corporation, for example, billing, management or consultation services, or the provision of some other medical product or service.

Response: As stated above in response to a similar comment, section 1877(h)(1)(B) provides that, for purposes of determining whether a compensation arrangement exists, the term remuneration includes "any remuneration, directly or indirectly, overtly or covertly, in cash or in kind." One of the definitions found in the American Heritage Dictionary of the English Language for "remuneration" is "payment." Therefore, we believe we are correct in concluding that, in general, payments between a laboratory and a physician are a form of remuneration. Arrangements involving remuneration between these parties can, in turn, be characterized as "compensation arrangements." Most, if not all, of the examples provided by the commenter could now fall within specific statutory exceptions. Examples one, three, and four could be excepted under section 1877(e)(3), which excepts certain situations in which an entity pays a physician under a personal service arrangement. The second example could be remuneration that is excepted from the definition of a "compensation arrangement" under section 1877(h)(1)(A) and (C), and the fifth example could be excepted under section 1877(e)(8)(B), which excepts payments by a physician to an entity in exchange for items or services other than clinical laboratory services.

We realize that many legitimate transactions occur between laboratories and physicians. We believe that most of these will qualify for the exceptions listed above. But, in the case of continuing arrangements that provide for payment between laboratories and physicians that do not qualify for the exceptions, the prohibition applies.

D. Prohibition on Certain Referrals by Physicians and Limitations on Billing

1. Medicare Only

Comment: One commenter indicated that the final regulation concerning the prohibition should include a statement that a physician's referrals for non-Medicare patients to receive clinical laboratory services, which are not reimbursable under Medicare, are not affected by section 1877 or this rule.

Another commenter requested that the final rule confirm that the statute and the proposed rule do not apply to State Medicaid programs.

Response: In the preamble to the proposed rule (57 FR 8595), we stated that the general prohibition on referrals applies only to referrals for clinical laboratory services that would otherwise be covered by the Medicare program. Therefore, referrals for clinical laboratory services to be furnished to a physician's non-Medicare patients are not affected by section 1877. This concept is reflected in section 411.353(a) of this rule. As a result of section 13624 of OBRA '93, however, section 1877 will have an effect on the Medicaid program beginning with referrals made on or after December 31, 1994. (We plan to address this matter in a separate proposed rule.)

2. Related Parties

Comment: The preamble to the proposed rule (57 FR 8596) states that a financial relationship between a physician and an organization related to an entity that furnishes clinical laboratory services (for example, a parent or subsidiary corporation of the laboratory entity) is to be considered an indirect financial relationship with the entity.

One commenter believed that this concept needs clarification and that it would be helpful to have some "bright line" rules for what constitutes a related entity. The commenter asked several sets of questions, which, as we understand them, are as follows:

• Is the related entity concept limited to a parent/subsidiary model or will brother/sister corporations be included?

• Is the relationship between the entities to be defined in terms of a stock ownership requirement and, if so, will a threshold percentage of ownership be required?

In this regard, the commenter suggested that we may want to review the control group concepts set out in sections 414(b) and 414(c) of the Internal Revenue Code of 1986 (IRC) and to consider adopting a similar approach.

Federal Register / Vol. 60, No. 156 / Monday, August 14, 1995 / Rules and Regulations   **41945**

Furthermore, the commenter asked questions involving the following situations and suggested that it would be helpful to have specific examples presented in the final rule.

• Twenty-five percent of a clinical laboratory is owned by a professional corporation (P.C.) that, in turn, is owned by five physicians as equal shareholders. The P.C. also employs physicians who are not owners.

—Would a referral to the laboratory by a physician employed by the P.C. be prohibited?

—Would referrals by any of the owners of the P.C. be prohibited?

• Two of the five physician-owners of the P.C. separately own the 25 percent interest in the laboratory rather than the entire P.C.

—Would a referral to the laboratory by a physician employed by the P.C. be prohibited?

—Would a referral by one of the remaining three owners of the P.C. be prohibited?

• A company that is a general partner in a surgery center limited partnership also owns a clinical laboratory. The surgery center has as other limited partners a number of physicians. Can physicians who are limited partners refer patients to the company's laboratory?

Response: First, we want to state that it is not possible to provide specific answers to cover every possible variation of financial relationship. As noted elsewhere in this preamble, we receive a large volume of correspondence. To the extent that there is some uncertainty or confusion concerning a particular provision of the statute or regulation, we are ready to discuss the matter by telephone or in writing. We can, however, only provide our views about general questions; as mentioned previously, we cannot provide formal advisory opinions on specific circumstances.

In regard to the first set of questions, the commenter was concerned about indirect financial relationships with entities. As we explained in an earlier response, we believe that the language of the statute is intended to support indirect, as well as direct, financial relationships, as was specified in proposed section 411.351. In the preamble to the proposed rule, we stated that this would cover financial relationships with an organization related to an entity that furnishes clinical laboratory services. We gave as an example an interest in a parent or subsidiary corporation of the laboratory entity. The commenter's first question was whether the related entity concept

was limited to parent/subsidiary situations or whether brother/sister corporations would also be included.

Although the preamble gave the example of a parent or subsidiary relationship between entities, we believe that a physician can have an indirect financial relationship with a laboratory entity under any circumstances in which that physician owns some portion of an entity that has an ownership interest in the laboratory entity. This would be true regardless of whether the entities are related as parent/subsidiary or brother/sister corporations. In other words, these relationships are not the determining factor. For example, a physician's ownership interest might be in a nonlaboratory subsidiary of a parent laboratory corporation. If the physician has an ownership interest in the subsidiary without owning any portion of the parent laboratory, the physician will not be considered to have an ownership interest in the laboratory. The physician would have an ownership interest in the laboratory only if the nonlaboratory subsidiary had an ownership interest (for example, through stock or debt instruments) in the parent laboratory.

We believe the analysis is similar for brother/sister corporations or entities. Subsidiary entities that are related via a common parent may or may not have any ownership interest in each other. If a physician has an ownership interest in a subsidiary that, in turn, has an ownership interest in a brother laboratory, the physician could be regarded as having an indirect ownership interest in the laboratory. However, this would not be the case if the brother/sister corporations have no ownership relationship.

The commenter also asked whether the relationship between entities depends upon stock ownership and, if so, what threshold percentage of ownership is required. The statute in section 1877(a)(2) defines as a financial relationship any ownership interest, regardless of the manner in which the interest is held or the amount of the interest. We believe this rule applies to all ownership interests, whether they are direct or indirect.

Our analysis of corporate relationships would also involve any compensation aspects of the relationships. As we said in the preamble to the proposed rule, any financial relationship between a physician and an organization related through ownership to a laboratory entity could be covered as an indirect financial relationship with the laboratory entity. In addition, even if a physician has an

ownership interest in a corporation that has no ownership interest in a laboratory entity, the physician may gain certain financial advantages from the relationship between the nonlaboratory entity and a laboratory that could constitute compensation to the physician from the laboratory. For example, if corporations file as one affiliated company, they may pool their gains and losses for tax purposes. As a result, a physician owner could receive some benefits from the affiliation.

The commenter recommended that we adopt an approach for related entities that is similar to that of the control group concept under the IRC. Generally, under section 414(b) of the IRC, employees of all corporations that are members of a controlled group of corporations (within the meaning of section 1563(a) of the IRC) are treated as employed by a single employer. Under 414(c) of the IRC, all employees of trades or businesses (whether or not incorporated) that are under common control are treated as employed by a single employer. Furthermore, under section 1563(a) of the IRC, a controlled group of corporations generally means the following:

• A parent-subsidiary controlled group is one in which one or more chains of corporations are connected through stock ownership with a common parent corporation.

• A brother-sister controlled group is one in which two or more corporations have five or fewer persons (individuals, estates, or trusts) owning certain levels of stock and controlling certain levels of voting power of all classes of stock entitled to vote.

Since we believe that the statutory language is very broad and encompasses both direct and indirect financial relationships, we cannot accept the commenter's suggestions to use the concept of a control group. Such a concept would narrow the scope of the provisions and would, thus, be inconsistent with the statute.

The commenter raised questions about several specific scenarios. In the first, a P.C. that is owned by five physicians owns 25 percent of a clinical laboratory. The P.C. also employs physicians. Referrals by physician-owners of the P.C. to the laboratory that is owned, in part, by the P.C. would be prohibited, unless an exception applies. Clearly, these five physicians have an ownership interest in the laboratory, even though it is indirectly held through their ownership of the P.C. We also believe that referrals by physician-employees of the P.C. may be prohibited depending upon the following facts. If the P.C. is not a group practice and

41946   **Federal Register** / Vol. 60, No. 156 / Monday, August 14, 1995 / Rules and Regulations

employee-physicians are receiving remuneration from the owner physicians for their services as bona fide employees of the P.C., then, under section 1877(e)(2), the remuneration would not constitute a "compensation arrangement" if the (e)(2) requirements are met. The remuneration, therefore, would not subject the employee-physicians to the prohibition.

If the P.C. is a group practice, the employee physicians could be considered "members of the group." If so, the referrals of any one member of the group are imputed to the entire group. Because members who are owner physicians in the example may not be able to refer, then neither can the employees, unless an exception applies. If the P.C. is a group practice, the arrangement would need to be evaluated under the in-office ancillary services exception in section 1877(b)(2). That exception does not appear to dictate any particular ownership arrangements between group practice physicians and the laboratory in which the services are furnished. A group practice can take advantage of this exception, and members can refer to each other in the laboratory provided that the group meets the definition of a group practice under section 1877(h)(4). Under the exception in section 1877(b)(2), the services must be furnished by the referring physician or a group member or must be directly supervised by a group practice member. In addition, the services must be billed by the referring physician, the group practice, or an entity wholly owned by the group practice.

In the second scenario involving a P.C., the facts are different. Here two of the five physician-owners of the P.C. have an ownership interest in the laboratory, and this laboratory interest is separate from their ownership of the P.C. Obviously, referrals by those two physicians to the laboratory are prohibited, unless an exception applies. While additional facts surrounding this situation might lead to a different conclusion, it appears that referrals by the remaining three physician-owners of the P.C. and by physician-employees of the P.C. would probably not be prohibited. This is so because, in this case, the P.C. has no ownership interest in the laboratory and the other physicians have no ownership interest. Although the employees are perhaps indirectly compensated by the two owners, their referrals would not be prohibited if their employment arrangement meets the requirements in section 1877(e)(2). If the P.C. is a group practice, however, referrals of any member of a group practice (including

owners and employees of the practice) would be precluded, unless an exception applies, such as that in section 1877(b)(2). We stress that this conclusion is based on a minimal amount of information; the conclusion could change if it became apparent that any of the three physician owners or physician employees were receiving any income or compensation, directly or indirectly, from the laboratory. We also stress that sanctions could apply if this turns out to be a circumvention scheme.

Concerning the last question, our analysis of this situation indicates that referrals by limited partner physicians would not be prohibited as long as these physicians do not have a financial relationship with the laboratory or with the company that is a partner in the surgery center. That is, the physicians cannot have an ownership or investment interest in the laboratory itself or the company that owns the laboratory. In addition, there can be no compensation passing between the physicians and the laboratory or between the physicians and the company. When physicians and a company are partners in an enterprise such as a surgery center, their joint ownership does not necessarily mean that there is compensation or payment passing between them; they may simply both be investors. If the arrangement, however, is structured so that there is any compensation passing between the physicians and the company or the physicians and the laboratory, the physician's referrals to the laboratory would be prohibited, provided no exception applies.

Finally, we again remind the commenter that section 1877(g) sets forth sanctions that may be imposed if certain requirements of section 1877 are not met. For example, any physician who enters into an arrangement or scheme that the physician knows or should know has the principle purpose of ensuring referrals by the physician to a particular entity that, if they were made directly, would be in violation of the prohibition, would be subject to the sanctions imposed by section 1877(g).

3. Identical Ownership

Comment: One commenter suggested that group practices may own and operate a laboratory that has been set up as a separate entity. The commenter believed that this arrangement did not appear to be addressed in the proposed regulation. The commenter pointed out that often a group practice will own and operate a clinical laboratory as a separate entity for various financial, liability, and other legal reasons. This commenter believed that there does not

appear to be any potential for abuse with these arrangements as long as the separate entity is wholly owned by the group practice or as long as there is identical overlap in ownership. Consequently, the commenter requested that the final rule clarify this point.

Response: As mentioned throughout this preamble, section 1877(a) prohibits a physician who has (or whose immediate family member has) a financial relationship with an entity furnishing clinical laboratory services from referring Medicare patients to that entity unless an exception applies. The statute does not contain a specific exception for wholly-owned entities. The commenter has not provided any evidence to convince us that any entity wholly owned by a group practice is free from program or patient abuse. Thus, we disagree with the conclusion reached by this commenter.

Concerning the commenter's reference to an identical overlap in ownership, we assume the commenter means that the same physicians who own the group practice also own the laboratory. As mentioned above, we do not believe that the Congress intended to except entities that are either wholly-owned or that have an identical overlap in ownership from the referral prohibition. Therefore, unless an exception applies, the physician or group practice owners would be prohibited from referring to a laboratory in which they have an ownership interest.

We believe that in many cases the in-office ancillary services exception in section 1877(b)(2) would apply. For example, physicians in a group practice, as defined in section 1877(h)(4), can refer to a laboratory as long as the laboratory services are furnished personally by the referring physician or by another physician in the same group practice, or under the direct supervision of a physician in the same group practice; in a building that is used by the practice to furnish some or all of the group's laboratory services; and that are billed by the group practice or by an entity that is wholly owned by the group. We believe that this exception applies to any group practice that meets these requirements, regardless of who owns the laboratory, or the manner in which it is owned. Also, services furnished by a rural laboratory would be exempted, regardless of the circumstances of ownership.

4. Technical Change

Comment: One commenter recommended that the phrase "under that referral" at the end of proposed § 411.353(b) be changed to "under that

Federal Register / Vol. 60, No. 156 / Monday, August 14, 1995 / Rules and Regulations **41947**

referral that is prohibited by paragraph (a)."

Response: We do not agree that this change is necessary, since "that referral" refers back to the earlier part of the sentence, which says "that is prohibited by paragraph (a) * * *."

5. Refunds

Comment: One commenter indicated that it is not unreasonable for an "entity that collects payment" to be required to make refunds in accordance with these regulations. The commenter believed, however, that the regulations provide no ability for the "entity that collects payment" to obtain the information needed to determine whether it is required to make a refund. The commenter suggested that the regulations either explicitly provide the means for the entity that collects payment to obtain the requisite referral information from the physician ordering the service or hold it harmless for refunds it does not make because it does not have the needed information.

Response: We do not agree with this comment. A laboratory is responsible for knowing with whom it has a financial relationship. Under section 1877(f) and our rule at § 411.361, laboratory entities are required, as specified by us, to provide us with information concerning their financial relationships, including ownership and compensation arrangements and including the names and unique identification numbers of all physicians with financial relationships or whose immediate relatives have financial relationships. Additionally, under the CLIA rules at § 493.634, laboratories are required to provide and update ownership information.

E. General Exceptions to Referral Prohibitions Related to Ownership and Compensation

1. Physicians' Services

We proposed that the prohibition on referrals does not apply to physicians' services that are furnished personally by (or under the direct personal supervision of) another physician in the same group practice as the referring physician.

Comment: One commenter indicated that the proposed rule states that exempt physicians' services would have to be performed in the group practice's office. The commenter questioned whether the exception should be so limited. The commenter believed that if physicians' services, as that term is defined in the proposed rule, are performed in another entity furnishing clinical laboratory services for a group

practice, the exception should apply as long as the physician performing the physicians' services and the referring physician are members of the same group practice. In other words, in the commenter's opinion, the physicians' services exception should apply regardless of whether the clinical laboratory is a group practice laboratory or a laboratory owned by another entity with which the group practice has a financial arrangement.

Response: We agree, in part, with this commenter. This exception applies to a limited number of services, that is, clinical laboratory services that are treated as physicians' services for Medicare purposes in the context of a group practice. We believe that the services can be performed anywhere and under any circumstances as long as they qualify as "physicians' services" and are personally performed or personally supervised by another group practice member and do not otherwise result in a prohibited referral. Thus, physicians' services furnished by group practice physicians do not need to be furnished in group practice offices, provided they meet the other requirements in the statute.

2. In-Office Ancillary Services

Based on the provisions of OBRA '89, we explained in the proposed rule that the prohibition on referrals would not apply to in-office ancillary services if the following conditions were met:

• The services are furnished personally by one of the following:
  + The referring physician.
  + A physician who is a member of the same group practice as the referring physician.
  + Nonphysician employees of the referring physician or group practice who are personally supervised by the referring physician or by another physician in the group practice.
• The services are furnished in one of the following locations:
  + In a building in which the referring physician (or another physician who is a member of the same group practice) furnishes physicians' services unrelated to the furnishing of clinical laboratory services.
  + In the case of a referring physician who is a member of a group practice, in another building that is used by the group practice for centrally furnishing the group's clinical laboratory services.
• The services are billed by one of the following:
  + The physician performing or supervising the services.
  + The group practice of which the referring physician is a member.

+ An entity that is wholly owned by the physician or the physician's group practice.

(As discussed later in this preamble, OBRA '93 made significant changes to the in-office ancillary services exception (section 1877(b)(2).)

a. Referrals From Physicians Who Do Not Have a Financial Relationship With the Physician or Group Practice

Comment: One commenter suggested that a significant loophole is created in the proposal by exempting from the referral prohibition certain services provided by the referring physician, under his or her direction, or under the direction of others in the same group practice. The commenter suggested that, under this proposal, a group practice could establish a laboratory in its own office and accept referrals from outside physicians not associated with the group practice. The commenter believed that the acceptance of such referrals from physicians outside the group should result in that laboratory being considered an independent clinical laboratory owned by the physicians in the group. Therefore, the commenter believed that, under the terms of section 1877, the laboratory should no longer be permitted to accept referrals from outside.

Some other commenters believed that the exemption for in-office ancillary services was adopted with the understanding that clinical laboratory services would be limited to the physicians' or group practices' own patients. According to these commenters, the regulations implementing the legislation should reflect this intent and specifically require that the exception apply only to physician office laboratories that do not accept referrals from physicians outside of the practice.

Another commenter believed that exempted group practice laboratories should meet the following two conditions:

First, the group practice laboratory should be fully financially integrated with the group practice, such that all group members and only group members share in laboratory expenses and income, and those expenses and income are distributed among group members in precisely the same manner and proportion as professional fees and expenses.

Second, the group practice laboratory should not be allowed to accept referrals of any tests from nongroup members. This commenter believed that these restrictions would guarantee that the laboratory is in fact an extension of the group practice and not a distinct

41948 Federal Register / Vol. 60, No. 156 / Monday, August 14, 1995 / Rules and Regulations

business operating under the protection of the group practice.

On the other hand, another commenter recommended that we definitively state in the final rule that furnishing laboratory services on referral from outside sources will not disqualify a group practice laboratory from the in-office ancillary services exception if the laboratory meets all of the performance standards set forth in the definition of "group practice" in the statute and the proposed rule.

Response: There are two distinct issues that need to be addressed in responding to these comments. The in-office ancillary services exception in section 1877(b)(2) provides that the prohibition on referrals will not apply to those services that are furnished personally by the referring physician, a physician in the same group practice as the referring physician, or by individuals who are (as amended by OBRA '93 and effective on January 1, 1992) directly supervised by the physician or another physician in the same group practice. This exception further contains location and billing criteria. It is our belief that this exception was provided for those clinical laboratory services that are performed as an adjunct to the patient care services of the attending physician. As such, the solo physician, the group practice, or an entity that is wholly owned by the physician or group practice must bill for the services.

On the other hand, the general prohibition on referrals applies only to referrals for clinical laboratory services made by a physician to an entity with which he or she or an immediate family member has a financial relationship. Section 1877 does not prohibit either a solo practitioner's laboratory or group practice laboratory from accepting referrals from outside physicians who do not have a financial relationship with the laboratory. When the solo practitioner or group practice, however, accepts referrals from sources outside of its office practice, the office laboratory is also acting as an independent laboratory because these services are not performed as an adjunct to the patient care services of the attending physician. As a result, the laboratory must have a billing number from the Medicare carrier and directly bill for the services that are performed on referral.

A physician or group practice cannot bill for the laboratory services furnished to the patients of another physician as if they were the physician's or group's own patients, under the physician's or group's provider number.

To summarize, we do not find anything in section 1877 that would prohibit a physician or group practice office laboratory from accepting referrals from physicians who do not have a financial relationship with the laboratory, physician, or group. However, if such referrals are accepted, they cannot be billed by the physician or group practice. Rather, billing must be done under a billing number that is assigned by the Medicare carrier to the laboratory itself.

We would also like to point out that, if a member of the group is either performing or supervising the laboratory services, the quantity of outside tests could affect the group's ability to qualify as a "group practice" under the definition in section 1877(h)(4). Under (h)(4)(A)(ii), substantially all of the services of physician members (who now include any physicians during the time they work for the group) must be provided through the group and be billed in the name of the group (beginning January 1, 1995, these services must be billed under a billing number assigned to the group). If group practice members spend too much time supervising laboratory tests that are billed under the laboratory's separate number, the group practice could fail to meet the "substantially all" test.

b. Independent Group Practice Laboratories

Comment: One commenter indicated that, while the point was not addressed in the proposed rule, we issued guidance to the carriers to deal with situations in which a group practice laboratory is also certified as an independent laboratory. The commenter wrote that we stated that the services must be billed differently depending on whether the test was referred for a patient of the group, or the test was referred from outside the group. The commenter suggested that it would be simpler for the groups and the government to have all services (physician, laboratory, and otherwise) billed to Medicare under one group billing number, regardless of the origin of the patient.

Response: We do not agree with this commenter. It has been an established Medicare policy that a laboratory a physician or group practice maintains solely for performing diagnostic tests for its own patients is not considered an "independent" laboratory. This means that the solo practicing physician or group practice can bill for in-office laboratory testing using the physician's or group practice's own billing number. Conversely, a physician providing clinical laboratory services to patients of other physicians is considered not to be furnishing "in-office ancillary" services

and is, therefore, doing business as an independent laboratory. Since this policy has been in effect for over a decade, we believe that physicians or group practices that have been accepting referrals from outside physicians have already established that the laboratory is a separate entity for those tests and they are familiar with the billing rules.

Furthermore, as previously explained, section 1833(h)(5)(A) indicates that payment may be made only to the person or entity that performed or supervised the performance of the tests. There are several exceptions to this rule, including one in which, if a physician performed or supervised the performance of the test, payment may be made to another physician with whom he or she shares a practice. This would apply, for example, if the two members are members of a group practice. Taking these factors into consideration, we affirm that physicians and group practices can bill, under their provider number, for clinical laboratory services performed only for their own patients. If the physicians' or group practices' in-office laboratory also provides reference work for patients of other physicians, that laboratory entity must bill for the services directly under its own number.

c. Furnishing of Tests

Comment: One commenter indicated that the final regulations should provide further guidance regarding the scope of the term "furnished." For instance, the commenter understood that we take the position that consulting services designed to assist a physician in interpreting test results are not considered a part of the furnishing of the clinical laboratory test; rather, these services are considered to be physicians' services. The commenter further understood that we take this position even though interpretation services are included in the Medicare payment for the laboratory service and Medicare makes no other payment for the physician's interpretation services.

Response: At § 411.353(a) in the proposed rule, we defined clinical laboratory services for purposes of section 1877 as those services described in the CLIA regulations at § 439.2. Thus, a service would be covered under section 1877 as a "clinical laboratory service" only if the service is considered a clinical laboratory service under CLIA. Some services may be billed as, for example, physician's services but they would still be subject to CLIA (and, as a result, to section 1877) if they fall within the scope of services described in § 493.2. This is so regardless of how they are billed. Under § 493.2, a laboratory means a facility for "the

Federal Register / Vol. 60, No. 156 / Monday, August 14, 1995 / Rules and Regulations   **41949**

biological, microbiological, serological, chemical, immunohematological, hematological, biophysical, cytological, pathological, or other examination of materials derived from the human body for the purpose of providing diagnosis, prevention, or treatment of any disease or impairment of, or assessment of the health of, human beings." In short, the services covered under CLIA and section 1877 are those conducted by these facilities and involving the examination of materials derived from the human body.

The commenter has asked specifically about consulting services designed to assist a physician in interpreting test results. We believe that CLIA covers the actual examination of materials, their analysis, and any interpretation and reporting of the results which are performed by a facility that qualifies as a laboratory, as defined in § 493.2. If a laboratory interprets certain test results or hires a consultant who takes the responsibility to interpret them in lieu of laboratory personnel, we believe the interpretation would qualify as a clinical laboratory service. (If a consultant only offers input or information which the laboratory will use in making its own interpretation, the input would not qualify as a clinical laboratory service.)

However, if a laboratory sends test results to an independent physician, any interpretation performed by the physician would not be performed by the laboratory facility. As a result, since the services would not constitute part of the clinical laboratory test. If a physician hires a consultant to help interpret the results, the same rule would apply: the consultant's services would not constitute clinical laboratory services if the consultant is performing outside the auspices of a laboratory facility. The services would not be subject to CLIA or section 1877.

If, on the other hand, a physician or group practice hires a consultant to perform, analyze or interpret test results that are performed in the physician's or group's own laboratory, the interpretation would qualify as part of the services performed by a laboratory. These interpretive services would be subject to CLIA and, as a result, to section 1877. If the physician or group practice wishes to qualify under the in-office ancillary services exception, the physician or member of the group practice must supervise any non-physician consultant when he or she performs clinical laboratory services. In addition, the tests must meet the section 1877(b)(2) location and billing requirements.

d. Services an Outside Laboratory May Provide to a Physician's Office Laboratory

Comment: One commenter had concerns about services a laboratory outside the physician's office may provide a physician's office laboratory. The commenter wrote that the final CLIA regulations contain personnel standards that require laboratories performing moderately complex testing to have a laboratory director, a technical consultant, a clinical consultant, and testing personnel who meet certain standards. (See 42 CFR part 493.) In physician office laboratories, for the most part, one of the practice's physicians will function as the laboratory director and also may function in one or more other roles. In some circumstances, however, physicians have asked an independent laboratory entity to serve in, or assist the physician in carrying out the duties of, one of the required positions to the extent permitted under CLIA. For example, an independent entity might serve as the clinical consultant for a number of its physician customers as well as assist a physician in carrying out the duties of the technical consultant. The commenter requested a clarification in the final regulations that such services would not defeat a physician office laboratory's qualification for the in-office ancillary services exception, since the independent contractors will not be employees of the physician.

The commenter believed that, since all laboratories, including physicians' office laboratories, must meet the CLIA standards, the laboratory testing performed in these laboratories is covered under the provisions found in section 1861(s)(3). Since section 1861(s)(3) does not have an employment requirement, the commenter concluded that the physician does not have to employ the personnel as he or she would if the laboratory services were billed and covered as services performed incident to the professional services of the physician under section 1861(s)(2)(A).

Response: Regardless of the setting in which it is performed, if a service involves laboratory tests on human specimens by a laboratory as defined in § 493.2, the CLIA provisions apply. So we agree that the CLIA requirements apply to in-office laboratories of solo-practicing physicians and of group practices. It appears that the commenter is concerned about the requirement in the predecessor provision at section 1877(b)(2) that, in order for the in-office ancillary services exception to apply, services, when not furnished by a

member physician, must be performed by individuals who are *employed* by the physician or the group practice. The employment requirement was eliminated by OBRA '93 retroactively to January 1, 1992. Therefore, under amended section 1877(b)(2), referrals for services to be furnished by any individuals who are directly supervised by the referring physician or, in the case of group practices, by another physician in the same group practice, are excepted. In other words, the in-office ancillary services exception applies to a physician or group practice that has outside contractors furnishing laboratory services, as long as the physician or group practice physicians directly supervise these individuals. In addition, as mentioned previously, a contracting physician may be considered a "member" of a group practice. As a member, the contractor could perform the services without supervision or directly supervise other individuals who perform clinical laboratory services.

Also, in this regard, we have taken the position in the past that clinical laboratory testing performed in physicians' offices is covered only if furnished by the physicians or if the requirements are met for coverage of services incident to the professional services of the physicians under section 1861(s)(2)(A) (see section 2070 of the Medicare Carriers Manual (MCM)). One of the requirements has been that persons performing services incident to the services of a physician must be employed by the physician. However, section 1861(s)(3) states, in pertinent part, that "medical and other health services" covered by Medicare include "diagnostic laboratory test[s]." Section 1861(s)(3) does not exclude diagnostic tests performed in physicians' offices or clinics. The only restriction on coverage under section 1861(s)(3) is set forth in the language following section 1861(s)(14), which states that "[n]o diagnostic tests performed in any laboratory * * * shall be included within paragraph (3) unless such laboratory" meets the CLIA certification requirements or has a certificate of waiver. Because section 1861(s)(3) relates more specifically to laboratory testing than section 1861(s)(2)(A), and because most laboratory testing performed in a physician's office is subject to CLIA, we now take the position that it would be appropriate to provide coverage of these services under section 1861(s)(3). (We are in the process of changing the MCM to reflect this position.) This means that the employment requirement does not have

41950 Federal Register / Vol. 60, No. 156 / Monday, August 14, 1995 / Rules and Regulations

to be met for purposes of coverage or for purposes of application of the in-office ancillary services exception.

Furthermore, we note that section 1877(e)(8)(B) provides an exception for physicians who contract with an entity outside of their office for items or services, providing the items or services are furnished at a price that is consistent with fair market value. Fair market value is defined in section 1877(h)(3) as meaning the value in arm's-length transactions, consistent with the general market value.

We believe this exception permits a physician to contract with a laboratory outside of his or her office for certain services and to continue to refer testing to that laboratory, providing the services meet the requirements for fair market value. Therefore, an independent laboratory entity will be able to provide personnel to assist a physician in carrying out the CLIA requirements.

Accordingly, from the circumstances described by the commenter, the following conclusions emerge:

• In order to comply with the CLIA requirements, a physician or group practice may contract with a laboratory for the services of various physicians or other personnel. In these cases, as long as the direct supervision requirement is met, application of the in-office ancillary services exception is not jeopardized by the fact that the personnel performing the CLIA-related activities are not employed by the physician or group practice.

• Physicians' referrals to the laboratory with which they contract for the performance of CLIA-related activities will not be prohibited if the contract meets the "fair market value" requirement of the exception found in section 1877(e)(8)(B).

e. Location

Comment: One commenter believed the location requirements of the in-office ancillary services exception arbitrarily distinguish between group practices and solo practitioners. The commenter stated that a referring solo physician, as well as a group practice, should be able to qualify under this exception if the laboratory is located in a building used for centrally furnishing clinical laboratory services. The commenter believed there is no remedial purpose served by requiring that a laboratory with which a solo practitioner has a financial relationship be in the same building as his practice, while permitting a laboratory with which a group practice has a financial relationship to situate the laboratory in a separate building.

Response: We believe that, in creating the exception in section 1877(b)(2) and entitling it "in-office ancillary services," the Congress meant to except situations in which a physician refers patients to the practice's own laboratory located in the physician's practice office, or nearby. As a result, the statute requires that the services be furnished in a building in which the referring physician furnishes physician's services unrelated to clinical laboratory services. Congress, however, has apparently always regarded the same building requirement as too restrictive for a group practice. Before the enactment of OBRA '93, section 1877(b)(2)(A)(ii)(II) allowed a group practice to refer to a laboratory in another building that was used by the group practice for the centralized provision of the group's clinical laboratory services. OBRA '93 liberalized this provision even more, amending it to allow a group practice to refer to another building that is used for some or all of the group's clinical laboratory services, no longer requiring that the services be performed in a "centralized" laboratory. This provision is effective retroactively to January 1, 1992.

Because group practices can have practice offices in many locations, the Congress appears to believe that it could be difficult to locate the group's laboratory close to all of them. The legislative history for the OBRA '93 amendment points out that a number of group practices own and operate satellite facilities in communities other than the community in which the main clinic facility is located. (H.R. Rep. No. 111, 103d Cong., 1st Sess. 545 (1993))

We have not created an exception under section 1877(b)(4) for solo practitioners who refer to laboratories that are located in buildings other than the ones in which they practice. That is so because we believe the services would cease to be in-office ancillary services if they are referred to an outside location and the solo practitioner might be less likely to directly supervise the services. Also, we have seen no evidence that such an exception would be free from any risk of patient or program abuse.

3. Prepaid Health Plan Enrollees

Under §411.355(c) of the proposed rule, the prohibition on referrals does not apply to services furnished by one of the following organizations to its enrollees:

• An HMO or a CMP that has a contract with us under section 1876 and 42 CFR part 417, subpart C.

• A health care prepayment plan that has an agreement with us under section

1833(a)(1)(A) and 42 CFR part 417, subpart D.

• An organization that is receiving payments on a prepaid basis for enrollees through a demonstration project under section 402(a) of the Social Security Amendments of 1967 (42 U.S.C 1395b–1) or under section 222(a) of the Social Security Amendments of 1972 (42 U.S.C. 1395b–1 note).

OBRA '93 amended section 1877(b)(3) to also include services furnished by a qualified HMO (within the meaning of section 1310(d) of the Public Health Service Act) to an individual enrolled with the organization.

Comment: One commenter indicated that the HMO exemption appears to be available only for a narrowly defined group of HMOs. The commenter recommended broadening this exemption because HMOs employ utilization review criteria and these criteria serve as a disincentive to overutilize services.

Response: As mentioned above, OBRA '93 provided an exception for referrals to qualified HMOs for the provision of services to enrollees of the HMO. This exception would apply to referrals for Medicare beneficiaries to Federally-qualified health maintenance organizations (FQHMOs) without requiring the FQHMO to enter into a contract under section 1833 or 1876.

Comment: One commenter indicated that the final regulation should permit staff physicians of a Medicare-contracting HMO or competitive medical plan (CMP), or a health care prepayment plan (HCPP) operated under an agreement with HCFA, to refer Medicare beneficiaries to their affiliated clinical laboratories, regardless of whether the beneficiary is enrolled as a member of the HMO/CMP/HCPP.

This commenter presents the case of an entity that contracts with us to furnish covered services to Medicare beneficiaries as an HCPP under section 1833(a)(1)(A). Medical services furnished by the HCPP are predominantly provided at clinic locations by employee and independent contractor physicians. The commenter believed that the proposed regulation would require the clinics to establish two different protocols for their laboratory services: one for their HCPP enrollees and one for Medicare eligible patients who are not enrolled as members of the HCPP, and on whose behalf Medicare pays on a fee-for-service basis ("fee-for-service patients"). The commenter believed this distinction is artificial and could result in different levels of care for certain classes of Medicare beneficiaries. The distinction

Federal Register / Vol. 60, No. 156 / Monday, August 14, 1995 / Rules and Regulations   **41951**

should, in the commenter's opinion, be eliminated.

Additionally, the commenter believed that providing a broader exception for referrals by HMO, CMP, or HCPP staff physicians is consistent with the statutory exemptions for services furnished by these organizations. The HMO, CMP, or HCPP exception recognizes that managed care plans may properly organize and operate their own clinical laboratories in the interest of serving their patients efficiently and economically. Those organizations may require their physicians to refer certain clinical laboratory services for both enrolled members and fee-for-service patients to their affiliated laboratories.

Even HMOs, CMPs, and HCPPs that engage physicians to practice in facilities owned and operated by the HMO, CMP, or HCPP may furnish services to Medicare beneficiaries who are not enrolled as members. Often this occurs when a patient "walks in" to the HMO, CMP, or HCPP clinic or when a relative accompanies a person who is enrolled in the plan.

The commenter believed that no purpose would be served by requiring physicians in HMOs, CMPs, or HCPPs that operate clinical laboratories to refer services for Medicare beneficiaries who are not enrollees to another laboratory. The commenter stated that these nonenrollee patients should be entitled to expect the same level of care as enrollees.

Response: As we have noted earlier, OBRA '93 added to the list of prepaid plans in the section 1877(b)(3) exception an organization that is a qualified HMO (within the meaning of section 1310(d) of the Public Health Service Act). The statute specifically excepts from the physician referral prohibition only services furnished by the listed organizations *to their enrollees.* Our proposed and final regulation reflect this statutory limitation. We decline to add services furnished to non-enrollees as an additional exception under section 1877(b)(4). When HMOs, CMPs, and HCPPs are reimbursed by Medicare on a fee-for-service basis, we believe that there still exists an incentive for these organizations to overutilize services. The Secretary cannot create an additional exception unless she determines that there is *no* risk of patient or program abuse.

However, physicians who are employed by HMOs, CMPs, and HCPPs may still be able to refer non-enrolled patients to the laboratories that are affiliated with these organizations under other exceptions in the statute. For example, if the physicians only receive compensation from these organizations under an employment agreement or personal services contract, they can refer to the organizations' laboratory if they meet the requirements in section 1877(e)(2) or (e)(3).

F. Exceptions to Referral Prohibitions Related to Ownership or Investment Interest

1. Publicly-Traded Securities

In proposed § 411.357(a), we provided that physicians who hold an ownership or investment interest in certain entities may make referrals to those entities if the following requirements are met:

• The physician purchased ownership of the entity in the form of investment securities (including shares or bonds, debentures, notes or other debt instruments) on terms generally available to the public.

• The ownership or investment interest is in a corporation that meets the following conditions:

+ It is either listed for trading on the New York Stock Exchange or the American Stock Exchange or is a national market system security traded under an automated interdealer quotation system operated by the National Association of Securities Dealers.

+ It had, at the end of its most recent fiscal year, total assets exceeding $100 million. These assets must have been obtained in the normal course of business and not for the primary purpose of qualifying for this exception.

As we have discussed elsewhere, OBRA '93 modified section 1877(c) in several ways. First, investment securities no longer have to be those purchased on terms generally available to the public; they must only be those which "may be purchased" on terms generally available to the public. Second, the securities can be those listed on additional exchanges. Third, the investment securities no longer have to be in a corporation with $100 million in total assets at the end of a fiscal year; now the holdings of the corporation must be measured in terms of "stockholder equity," and the amount has been modified from $100 million to $75 million. This amount can now either be measured at the end of the most recent fiscal year or be based on the corporation's average during the previous 3 fiscal years. Finally, OBRA '93 extends the exception to apply to certain mutual funds.

Under the effective date provisions of OBRA '93, the amended version of section 1877(c) was not effective until January 1, 1995. SSA '94 revised this effective date provision to make the amended version of section 1877(c) effective retroactively to January 1, 1992; however, the revised effective date provision states that, prior to January 1, 1995, the amended § 1877(c) does not apply to any securities of a corporation that meets the requirements of § 1877(c)(2) as they appeared prior to OBRA '93. Section 1877(c)(2), prior to OBRA '93, contained the requirement that a corporation have $100 million in total assets.

Comment: One commenter supported our proposed requirements. The commenter believed that the additional requirement concerning the purpose in obtaining assets will help eliminate certain obvious sham transactions that followed the passage of section 1877. The commenter suggested the inclusion of additional language requiring that these entities have $50 million in shareholder equity. Such a threshold, according to the commenter, could help to ensure that the company has actual, hard assets, rather than simply "phantom" assets that are offset by significant liabilities.

Response: After consideration of the comments we received on this issue (see below), we have decided that it would be extremely difficult to prove exactly what a corporation intended when it decided to acquire assets; that is, to sort through a corporation's financial records to try to separate business purposes from nonbusiness purposes. We further believe that it would be difficult to define what is meant by "acquiring assets during the normal course of business." Therefore this final rule does not specify that the assets must have been obtained in the normal course of business and not for the primary purpose of qualifying for the exception.

We agree that the commenter's suggestion for "shareholder equity" is a good one, but we do not believe that the Congress meant to refer to this concept when it included the term "total assets" in the statute. That is so because the OBRA '93 amendments specifically replaced the concept of "total assets" with "stockholder equity," a change the legislative history describes as a modification of the law and not a clarification or explicit expression of what was already implicitly present in the law. Also, the fact that SSA '94 appears to make the $100 million-total-asset-standard and the $75 million-stockholder-equity- standard apply simultaneously until January 1, 1995 suggests that they are two different concepts. Beginning on January 1, 1995, the "stockholder equity" standard will prevail.

41952   **Federal Register** / Vol. 60, No. 156 / Monday, August 14, 1995 / Rules and Regulations

Comment: Another commenter wished to emphasize the requirement that, in order to qualify for the exception, the general public must have the same opportunity to buy and sell the entity's stock as physician-investors. As noted in the proposed rule, physician-partners in a laboratory should not be permitted to exchange their partnership shares for stock in a new corporation, which is then publicly traded at some later date. The commenter was aware of one entity that has purchased physician-owned laboratories in just this manner. Therefore, the commenter believed that we should emphasize that such conduct is a clear violation of the regulation.

Response: The requirement at issue in the regulation was derived from section 1877(c), as it appeared prior to OBRA '93. Section 1877(c) used to require that investment securities be those *which were purchased* on terms generally available to the public. OBRA '93 amended this provision (the amendment is now retroactively effective as a result of SSA '94) to say that the investment securities are those which *may be purchased* on terms generally available to the public. We will interpret the amended provision and other provisions in OBRA '93 in a proposed rule covering all of the designated health services.

Comment: A few commenters indicated that they disagree with the proposed requirement that the $100 million in assets must have been obtained in the normal course of business and not for the primary purpose of qualifying for this exception. The commenters believed there is no evidence that the Congress intended to deny protection to entities that meet the $100 million asset test in part or in whole by acquiring assets for the purpose of qualifying for the exception spelled out explicitly in section 1877(c). The commenters suggested that the purchase of an independent clinical laboratory by a corporation intending to include the purchase in the total assets needed to qualify for this exception is not clearly an example of a corporation trying to circumvent the law through a sham transaction. One commenter went on to state that any corporation and physician involved in a good faith purchase and sale of a clinical laboratory in order to comply with the law would be unfairly penalized by the proposed language.

A few commenters urged that we eliminate the statement in the preamble advising the OIG to treat as a circumvention scheme any effort by an entity to obtain $100 million principally for the purpose of meeting the "$100 million in total assets" test.

Response: As mentioned in a previous response, we are withdrawing this interpretation and requiring that the corporation meet one of the following criteria: (1) it has, at the end of its most recent fiscal year or, on average during the previous 3 fiscal years, stockholder equity exceeding $75 million or (2) until January 1, 1995, it had, at the end of its most recent fiscal year, total assets exceeding $100 million, irrespective of how those assets were obtained.

The statement that the commenters have asked us to eliminate appears in the preamble to the proposed rule at 57 FR 8600 in the discussion on OIG regulations. Since we are not including a requirement about how the assets are obtained, we are not including language related to this issue in the final rule.

Comment: One commenter indicated that a major ambiguity appears in this exception when one considers how to treat physician investors who have acquired shares prior to the time the laboratory was publicly traded. As written, the statutory exemption might be interpreted not to protect such previously acquired shares since, by definition, they were not acquired in a transaction involving the general public.

The commenter requested that the final regulations specify that, once the laboratory meets both of the exemption's tests (that is, the stock exchange listing and the level of assets criteria), physicians who acquired their shares before this time be permitted to refer patients under certain conditions. That is, physicians can refer provided they own only shares with rights identical to those generally available to the public through trading on one of the specified exchanges.

Response: As we have pointed out in earlier responses, the requirement in the proposed regulation has been modified to reflect the statute, as amended by OBRA '93. OBRA '93 amended this provision (the amendment is now retroactively effective as the result of SSA '94) to say that the investment securities are those which *may be* purchased on terms generally available to the public.

Comment: One commenter requested that we use the same definition of public company that it believes is used by the Securities and Exchange Commission (SEC); that is, the definition used under General Accepted Accounting Principles. The commenter believed that use of this commonly accepted definition is in accord with the "public company" intent of the legislation and will maintain the "bright line" between referrals that can and cannot be influenced by ownership position.

Response: The American Institute of Certified Public Accountants, Inc., defines a public enterprise as a business enterprise—
• Whose debt or equity securities are traded in a public market on a domestic stock exchange or in the domestic over-the-counter market (including securities quoted only locally or regionally); or
• That is required to file financial statements with the SEC.

An enterprise is considered to be a public enterprise as soon as its financial statements are issued in preparation for the sale of any class of securities in a domestic market. (Commerce Clearing House, Professional Standards, AC Section 1072, 024(h).)

We do not believe that this definition adds any clarity to the very specific requirements found in the law; that is, for purposes of section 1877(c), a corporation is an entity that is listed for trading on the New York Stock Exchange or on the American Stock Exchange, or any regional exchange in which quotations are published on a daily basis, or foreign securities listed on a recognized foreign, national, or regional exchange in which quotations are published on a daily basis, or is a national market system security traded under an automated interdealer quotation system operated by the National Association of Securities Dealers.

Comment: One commenter suggested we allow the use of a consolidated balance sheet to show that the $100 million asset test is met.

Response: A consolidated balance sheet is used for financial reports for a group of affiliated corporations, eliminating intercorporation debts and profits and showing minority stockholders interest. It also is used when, under certain circumstances, multiple related entities must report balances in a combined fashion instead of separately.

Since the statute excepts investment interests in a corporation with a minimum amount of assets (or, under OBRA '93, stockholder equity), we do not believe it is appropriate to aggregate the assets of multiple corporations on a consolidated balance sheet.

In the preamble to the proposed rule (57 FR 8597), we stated that the $100 million in assets requirement applies only to the corporate entity that furnished the clinical laboratory services, and it does not include assets of any related corporations. This statement is misleading in that it applies only when the stock ownership giving rise to the financial relationship is held in the corporate entity that furnishes clinical laboratory services; it is

Federal Register / Vol. 60, No. 156 / Monday, August 14, 1995 / Rules and Regulations **41953**

incorrect when applied to stock ownership in a corporation that does not itself furnish clinical laboratory services. In the latter case, the assets requirement would apply to the parent corporation (the corporate entity in which the stock is held), not to the subsidiary laboratory corporation.

Therefore, we are clarifying that only the assets of the corporation in which the physician or immediate family member's stock is held may be counted to determine whether the $100 million asset requirement (or $75 million in stockholder equity requirement) is met under section 1877(c)(1).

Comment: One commenter indicated that we should permit the grandfathering of financial transactions that were entered into to meet the intent of the legislation with regard to the $100 million asset test if they were entered into before the effective date of the regulations. The commenter believed that such grandfathering would ease accounting and reporting requirements. Further, the commenter suggested that the final regulations should apply to an organization's fiscal year beginning after the effective date of the rule.

Response: As discussed earlier in this preamble, we are withdrawing our interpretation concerning how a corporation had to have obtained its assets.

In regard to the commenter's suggestion that the final regulations should apply to an organization's fiscal year beginning after the effective date of the rule, we disagree. Section 1877(c)(2), prior to its amendment by OBRA '93, required that a corporation have, at *the end of the corporation's most recent fiscal year*, total assets exceeding $100 million. The amended version of this provision requires that a corporation have, *at the end of the corporations' most recent fiscal year, or on average during the previous 3 fiscal years*, stockholder equity exceeding $75 million. These statutory provisions require an assessment of a corporation's assets or equity based upon a past year or years. These provisions were effective retroactively to January 1, 1992. We do not believe they can be interpreted to require compliance in the fiscal year occurring subsequent to the publication of this final regulation.

2. Rural Laboratories

In proposed section 411.357(b), we stated that an ownership or investment interest in a laboratory that is located in a rural area will not prohibit the physician owners from making referrals if the following criteria are met:
• The laboratory testing that is referred by a physician who has an

ownership or investment interest in the rural laboratory must either—
+ Be performed on the premises of the rural laboratory; or
+ If not performed on the premises, the laboratory performing the testing must bill the Medicare program directly for the testing.
• The majority of tests referred to the rural laboratory must be referred by physicians who have office practices located in a rural area.

As mentioned in response to a previous comment, we have amended the standards for this exception by eliminating the requirement that a majority of tests referred to the rural laboratory must be referred by physicians who have office practices located in a rural area. Instead, we are adopting the standard required by OBRA '93 that substantially all of the clinical laboratory services furnished by the entity are furnished to individuals residing in such a rural area.

a. General

Comment: One commenter indicated support for our formulation of the exception applicable to laboratories located in a rural area. The commenter was aware of a number of laboratories that were established in rural areas but that serve physician-owners and patients located in large metropolitan areas.

Another commenter stated that this exception protects against abuses by laboratories in rural areas, such as the setting up of a "shell" laboratory with a rural address. This commenter also supported the proposed rule's mandate that at least 51 percent of the tests referred to a rural laboratory be referred by rural doctors. The commenter believed this requirement should help to ensure that the laboratory is in fact serving rural beneficiaries.

On the other hand, a third commenter proposed that the final rule adopt an expanded definition of rural area that would include towns or similar State governmental subdivisions if the population is below 10,000 people and a laboratory located in the area meets the 2 additional requirements set out in the proposed rule. As an additional criterion, the commenter suggested that governmental subdivisions meeting this population standard could be defined as "rural" only if the number of outpatient laboratories in the area was no more than two. The commenter believed that this additional criterion would identify those laboratories that are clearly essential to serving the patient needs of the community.

Response: We agree with the first two commenters and believe that the OBRA

'93 amendment imposing the requirement that "substantially all" of a rural laboratory's services be performed for residents of the rural community indicates that the Congress is aware of and is concerned about the potential for abuse in this area.

What the third commenter urges is recognition of a laboratory entity as a rural provider, despite the fact that the entity is located within a metropolitan statistical area (MSA), if the suggested conditions are met. While we recognize that there may be some laboratory entities located in MSAs that, by virtue of being located in small towns within an MSA, have experiences similar to laboratories located in rural areas, we believe that it would be difficult in any given case to prove that the laboratory's situation actually parallels the situation in a rural area. In addition, it would be difficult and burdensome to make these determinations on a case-by-case basis. Further, at this time, we have no evidence that opening this exception to "nonrural" laboratories would be free of any risk of program or patient abuse, the standard that must be met under section 1877(b)(4).

b. Percentage of Tests and Direct Billing

Comment: One commenter argued that the exception for clinical laboratories in rural areas is too stringent. The commenter was concerned that the proposed requirement that more than 50 percent of the tests performed be referred by physicians whose practices are located in rural areas may present an undue burden on already existing rural laboratories. Those rural laboratories may be forced to close because their viability comes from nonrural business. Thus, the commenter recommended grandfathering existing rural laboratory practices.

Response: Although we have changed the proposed rule, the rule still requires that "substantially all" of a laboratory's services be furnished as rural business. As we explained previously, we believe to meet this standard that at least 75 percent of the clinical laboratory services must be furnished to individuals who reside in a rural area. Section 1877 does not contain an overall "grandfather" clause which would allow laboratory facilities that existed prior to its effective date to continue to accept prohibited referrals just because the laboratories predate the statutory provision. In addition, the statute does not routinely excuse certain referrals because it would be a burden for a facility to alter its business practices in order to fit within an exception. We believe that, instead, the specific

41954 Federal Register / Vol. 60, No. 156 / Monday, August 14, 1995 / Rules and Regulations

purpose of the statute is to require laboratory facilities to alter their practices in order to avoid abusive or potentially abusive financial relationships. Our approach in the proposed and final regulation for this provision reflects that purpose.

Furthermore, we do not believe that we can specifically except from the prohibition rural laboratories whose viability depends on non-rural business. We do not know at this time how many rural laboratories would have extreme difficulty meeting the requirements in the proposed regulation. Also, as described in previous comments, the situation described by the commenter can result in "shell" laboratory arrangements or otherwise be subject to patient and program abuse.

Comment: One commenter recognized the need to prohibit circumvention schemes by urban laboratories through the rural exemption, but thought that the proposed criteria may have a negative impact on a legitimate rural laboratory as follows: The criteria require laboratory testing referred by an investor physician to be performed on the premises or, if referred to another laboratory, that the testing be billed to Medicare directly by the laboratory performing the tests. This provision would prohibit rural laboratories from referring a limited number of tests to other laboratories and billing for the tests, in accordance with present statutory and regulatory requirements concerning shell laboratories.

One commenter indicated that, if a rural laboratory is not able to bill for reference work, it will be forced to collect patient information and forward it to the reference laboratory. This is necessary to enable the reference laboratory to bill Medicare. The rural laboratory will still be collecting the specimens for forwarding to the reference laboratory, but without compensation. The commenter also maintained that the rule will threaten the ability of small rural laboratories to maintain investment and employment while, on the other hand, the rule rewards large laboratories that already have the advantage of lobbying strength that can affect legislation. Also, the rule will not save the taxpayer any money, as good diagnostics for both treatment and preventive medicine are not a function of who bills Medicare for the tests.

This commenter suggested the following alternatives:

• Eliminate the condition that rural laboratories must perform in-house laboratory testing in order to bill Medicare directly.

• Revise the conditions to read: "if all tests are not performed on the premises, 80 percent of referrals must be made by physicians who have office practices in rural areas and 67 percent of all tests must be performed on the premises, otherwise the laboratory performing the testing must bill the Medicare program directly."

Response: We agree that the requirements we proposed for ownership in a rural laboratory are different from those found in the so called "shell laboratory" provision (section 1833(h)(5)(A)). Under the shell laboratory provision, payment may be made to a referring laboratory for the services of a reference laboratory in any of the following circumstances: the referring laboratory is located in, or is part of, a rural hospital; the referring laboratory is wholly owned by the reference laboratory; the referring laboratory wholly owns the reference laboratory; both the referring laboratory and the reference laboratory are wholly owned by the same entity; or not more than 30 percent of the clinical diagnostic laboratory tests for which the referring laboratory (other than a laboratory described in the "wholly owned" provision) receives requests for testing during the year in which the test is performed are performed by another laboratory. These provisions apply to the payment of Medicare-covered clinical diagnostic laboratory services generally. Section 1877 and these regulations contain additional specific requirements that apply to referrals for clinical laboratory services by physicians who have a financial relationship with the laboratory.

In the proposed rule, we stated that laboratory testing that is referred by a physician who has an ownership or investment interest in the rural laboratory must either be performed on the premises of the rural laboratory or, if not performed on the premises, the laboratory performing the testing must bill the Medicare program directly for the testing. Section 1877(d)(2) specifically provides the exception for referrals for clinical laboratory services if the laboratory furnishing the service is in a rural area. We do not believe the exception is satisfied if the rural laboratory in turn refers the work to a laboratory in a nonrural area.

In addition, we do not see this requirement as conflicting with the more general shell laboratory provision, because our requirement applies specifically to the testing ordered by a physician who has a financial relationship with the laboratory. Thus, all other testing referred to the rural laboratory would be subject to the more lenient provisions of section 1833(h)(5)(A) mentioned above. We continue to support this position. It is our firm belief that the Congress provided the rural provider exception in order that beneficiaries living in rural areas would have access to clinical laboratory services that might not be available without the financial investments of local physicians. Without the safeguards included in this regulation, we believe it would be possible to defeat the purpose of the exception.

c. Future Reclassification of Rural Areas

Comment: One commenter indicated that the final rule should provide that laboratories that currently qualify under the rural exception will not be disqualified in the future based on metropolitan statistical area (MSA) reclassification. This clarification will provide stability to legitimate rural laboratories and avoid future uncertainty and future "fireside" sales.

Response: We do not believe the language in section 1877(d)(2) is susceptible to the suggested "clarification." The statute specifically requires that a rural provider be located in a rural area as defined in section 1886(d)(2)(D).

Thus, a provider must be located in such an area, even if the MSAs are at some point reclassified for prospective payment purposes. In addition, we do not believe we should provide an additional exception for a rural provider whose area has ceased to be rural, since we have no evidence that the exception would be free from all risk of program or patient abuse.

3. Hospitals Outside of Puerto Rico

The OBRA '93 amendments to section 1877 substantially changed the provisions that directly concern physician/hospital relationships. Listed below is a table explaining the provisions prior to OBRA '93 and after OBRA '93, as they are in effect until January 1995; the table also reflects amendments made by SSA '94.

Federal Register / Vol. 60, No. 156 / Monday, August 14, 1995 / Rules and Regulations **41955**

Before OBRA '93	OBRA '93
Exceptions for Ownership/Investment and Compensation	
1877(b)(4) exception relating to hospital financial relationships (ownership/investment and compensation) unrelated to provision of laboratory services.	OBRA '93 omitted, but SSA '94 reinstated until 1/95. But see 1877(e)(4) below.
1877(d)(3) exception for hospital ownership	1877(d)(3) unchanged.
Exceptions for Compensation Arrangements	
1877(e)(2) exception for employment and service arrangements with hospitals.	Omitted by OBRA '93; SSA '94 reinstated until 1/1/95
	1877(e)(2) exception for bona fide employment only, with any employer
	1877(e)(3) exception for personal service arrangements with remuneration from any entity.
	1877(e)(4) exception for remuneration from a hospital to a physician if not related to provision of clinical laboratory services.
1877(e)(4) exception for physician recruitment by a hospital	Still present, as 1877(e)(5).
	1877(e)(7) exception for compensation between a group practice and a hospital for services furnished under an arrangement.

Generally, the prohibition in section 1877(a)(1) on physician referrals excepts physicians who furnish services in certain situations or settings described in section 1877(b) (for example, in-office or HMO settings). In addition, under section 1877(a)(2), a financial relationship with an entity is defined as an ownership or investment interest in the entity except for such interests described in sections 1877(c) and (d). A financial relationship is also defined as a compensation arrangement between a physician (or immediate family member) and an entity, except for the arrangements described in section 1877(e). Of these provisions, the following exceptions directly concern physician/hospital relationships if the hospital either is not located in Puerto Rico or is not a rural provider.

• Under section 1877(d)(3), an exception is provided for referrals for clinical laboratory services to be furnished by a hospital located outside of Puerto Rico, even if the referring physician (or immediate relative) has an ownership or investment interest in the hospital, provided the referring physician is authorized to perform services at the hospital and the ownership or investment interest is in the hospital itself and not merely in a subdivision of the hospital.

• Under section 1877(e)(2), a physician who receives payment from any employer, including a hospital (or who has an immediate relative who receives such payment) will not be prohibited from making referrals to the hospital for clinical laboratory services on the basis of this payment if the employment of the physician or family member is bona fide and for identifiable services. In addition, the terms of the employment must be for fair market value with no ties to the volume or value of referrals, and be commercially reasonable. Finally, the arrangement must meet any additional requirements imposed by the Secretary.

• Under section 1877(e)(3), a physician who receives (or whose immediate family member receives) remuneration from any entity, including a hospital, under a personal service arrangement will not be prohibited, on the basis of this remuneration, from making referrals to the entity for clinical laboratory services if the arrangement meets the following conditions:

+ The arrangement is for at least 1 year, set out in writing, signed by the parties, and specifies the services covered.

+ The arrangement covers all of the services to be furnished by the physician (or immediate family member) to the entity.

+ The aggregate services contracted for do not exceed those that are reasonable and necessary for the legitimate business purposes of the arrangement and the compensation to be paid over the term of the arrangement is set in advance, does not exceed fair market value and, except in the case of certain physician incentive plans, is not determined in a manner that takes into account the volume or value of any referrals or other business generated between the parties.

+ The services to be performed under the arrangement do not involve the counseling or promotion of a business arrangement or other activity that violates any State or Federal law.

+ The arrangement meets any other requirements imposed by the Secretary.

• Under section 1877(e)(4), a physician who receives remuneration from a hospital will not be prohibited from making referrals to the hospital on the basis of that remuneration if the remuneration does not relate to the provision of clinical laboratory services.

• Under section 1877(e)(5), a physician who receives remuneration from a hospital that is intended to induce the physician to relocate to the geographic area served by the hospital in order to be a member of the medical staff of the hospital will not be prohibited from making referrals to the hospital if the following conditions are met:

+ The physician is not required to refer patients to the hospital.

+ The amount of remuneration under the arrangement is not determined in a manner that takes into account (directly or indirectly) the volume or value of any referrals by the referring physician.

+ The arrangement meets any other requirements imposed by the Secretary by regulation.

• Under section 1877(e)(7), certain group practices may have an arrangement with a hospital to furnish clinical laboratory services that are billed by the hospital. The physicians may make referrals to the hospital for the furnishing of clinical laboratory services, as long as the following conditions are met:

+ Services provided to a hospital inpatient are furnished under an arrangement under section 1861(b)(3).

+ The arrangement began before December 19, 1989, and has continued in effect without interruption since that date.

+ With respect to the clinical laboratory services covered under the arrangement, substantially all of these services furnished to patients of the

41956   Federal Register / Vol. 60, No. 156 / Monday, August 14, 1995 / Rules and Regulations

hospital are furnished by the group under the arrangement.

+ The arrangement is set out in writing, specifies the services to be provided, and the compensation for the services under the agreement.

+ The compensation paid over the term of the agreement is consistent with fair market value and the compensation per unit of services is fixed in advance and is not determined in a manner that takes into account the volume or value of any referrals or other business generated between the parties.

+ The compensation provided is under an agreement that would be commercially reasonable even if no referrals were made to the entity.

+ The arrangement meets any other requirements imposed by the Secretary by regulation.

a. Joint Ventures Not Related to the Hospital Laboratory

Comment: One commenter suggested that the condition found in proposed § 411.357(b)(3)(ii) concerning "ownership or investment in * * * a hospital that * * * does not relate (directly or indirectly) to the furnishing of clinical laboratory services" could be construed as precluding a physician who has a financial interest in another hospital/physician joint venture that is unrelated to the clinical laboratory from referring to the hospital laboratory. This commenter recommended that the final rule clarify that physicians with financial interests in other hospital-physician joint ventures will not be precluded from making referrals to the hospital laboratory.

Response: The proposed provision that the commenter asked us to clarify was based on the predecessor provision of section 1877(b)(4), which excepted a physician's financial relationship (ownership/investment interest or compensation arrangement) with a hospital if the relationship did not relate to furnishing clinical laboratory services. This provision was eliminated from the statute by section 13562 of OBRA '93, but was reinstated until January 1, 1995 by section 152(c) of SSA '94. The amended section 1877 also contains, in paragraph (e)(4), a new provision which excepts remuneration from a hospital to a physician if the remuneration does not relate to the provision of clinical laboratory services. Section 1877(e)(4) is retroactively effective beginning January 1, 1992, and remains in effect after January 1, 1995.

As for joint ventures, an exception for an ownership or investment interest held *with* a hospital may not be necessary. That is because section 1877(a)(2) defines a prohibited financial

relationship of a physician *with an entity* as an ownership or investment interest *in the entity*. In the case of a joint venture held with a hospital, if the physician has no ownership or investment interest *in* the hospital, a prohibition based on ownership would not apply at all. That is, even though a physician may own a venture with a hospital, as separate partners, that does not mean that the physician actually owns any part of the hospital.

To determine whether a physician has an ownership interest in a hospital, we must define what constitutes a "hospital" for purposes of section 1877. Under the Medicare statute, section 1861(e) defines a "hospital" as an institution, but we have never specifically defined what constitutes an "institution." Although section 1861 dictates what services and functions a "hospital" must provide to qualify as one, it does not appear to mandate any requirements relating to a hospital's corporate structure.

Hospitals often are structured in complex configurations as the result of tax laws and in response to a variety of business concerns. These configurations make defining a "hospital" almost impossible to do on a case-by-case basis. As a result, we are establishing a test that we believe will be relatively easy to apply. For purposes of section 1877, we are defining a "hospital" as any separate legally-organized operating entity plus any subsidiary, related, or other entities that perform services for the hospital's patients and for which the hospital bills. A "hospital" does not include entities that perform services for hospital patients "under arrangements" with the hospital. We believe these arrangements, by their very nature, involve situations in which hospitals contract with outside entities because they cannot or do not wish to provide the services themselves.

For example, a hospital might be a parent corporation that provides administrative services but that furnishes patient care primarily through a variety of subsidiaries such as a home health agency, a laboratory, or a radiology unit, each of which is independently incorporated. If the hospital bills Medicare for services provided by a subsidiary, then we regard the subsidiary as part of the hospital. A physician, as a result of this structure, could own a part of the hospital if he or she owns some of the remaining interest in the laboratory or other subsidiary, even if the physician does not own any of the parent corporation.

If a physician owns part of the hospital by virtue of owning some

portion of a separately incorporated subsidiary, then the physician's referrals to the hospital's laboratory could be prohibited (absent some exception). However, if the physician owns part of the hospital by virtue of owning some portion of a separate corporation that provides services other than clinical laboratory services, the exception in section 1877(b)(4) could apply until January 1, 1995. That is, the physician would have a financial relationship with the hospital (an ownership interest in the hospital) that does not relate to the provision of clinical laboratory services.

If, in contrast, a physician has an ownership interest in the hospital as a whole, we believe that this interest is indirectly related to the provision of clinical laboratory services. That is because, in most cases, a hospital's revenues will reflect the revenues earned by its clinical laboratory. It is for this reason that we included in proposed § 411.357(b)(3)(ii) the concept of ownership or investment interests that relate "directly or indirectly" to the furnishing of laboratory services.

Even if a physician has no ownership interest in the hospital (either in its operating entity or in a subsidiary), referrals to the hospital laboratory might still be prohibited, however, if the joint venture is structured so that there is some compensation passing between the hospital and the physician. If the hospital provides remuneration to the physician, that remuneration will result in prohibited referrals, unless an exception applies. Referrals would not be prohibited under section 1877(e)(4) and § 411.357(g) of this final rule if the remuneration is unrelated to the provision of clinical laboratory services; for example, the hospital and the physician might jointly own a free-standing CAT scanning facility. Any remuneration that flows from the hospital to the physician would be excepted if the remuneration relates only to the CAT scanning operation. This result, however, will change when the prohibition on referrals is extended to other designated health services beginning on January 1, 1995.

Comment: There were several other comments relating to the exceptions that apply to financial relationships between physicians and hospitals. Some commenters maintained that there is a conflict between the exception set forth in section 1877(b)(4) and the proposed regulatory exceptions. The argument is that this section of the law establishes a general exception for financial relationships with a hospital if the relationship does not relate to the provision of clinical laboratory services but that a parallel exception was not included in § 411.355, the title of which is "General exceptions to referral prohibitions related to ownership and compensation." Instead, the commenters pointed out, the proposed rule contains separate exceptions, one for "ownership or investment interests" and one for "compensation arrangements." In the view of these commenters, these regulatory provisions are not consistent with section 1877(b)(4), and they recommended that the regulations be revised so that § 411.355 reflects the content of section 1877(b)(4).

Another commenter had several questions about proposed § 411.357(b)(3)(i) and what is meant by an ownership interest in a distinct part or department of a hospital. The commenter stated that most hospitals are incorporated entities, being either a for-profit or not-for-profit corporation and that parts or departments are assets of the incorporated entity and cannot be owned separately. This being the case, the commenter asked the following:

• How can a physician own an interest in a distinct part of a corporation or was the intention to refer to ownership of entities related to a hospital?

• Why should ownership in an entity related to a hospital cause referrals from a physician to be prohibited if the related entity is not a clinical laboratory (for example, a hospital owns 60 percent of a subsidiary that is not a clinical laboratory and the physician owns 40 percent).

• Why should the facts of this example result in a situation that is any more subject to abuse than one in which a physician has general ownership in the hospital and is authorized to perform patient care services at the hospital?

Response: The first set of commenters maintained that there was a conflict between the exception set forth in section 1877(b)(4) and the proposed regulatory exceptions. We believed that the combination of the provisions at § 411.357(b)(3)(ii) of the proposed rule and § 411.359(g) of the proposed rule effectively incorporated the section 1877(b)(4) provision. We had considered including the content of these two regulatory provisions under one provision in § 411.355, as was suggested in the comment, but that section of the regulation addresses services that can qualify for an exception, whereas section 1877(b)(4) addresses financial relationships that can qualify. Since under section 1877(a) all financial relationships are either ownership/investment interests or

compensation arrangements, we included the section 1877(b)(4) exception under both § 411.357 (which applies to ownership/investment exceptions, and is now § 411.356) and § 411.359 (which applies to exceptions for compensation arrangements, and is now § 411.357).

We believe the commenters' dissatisfaction with our method for incorporating section 1877(b)(4) may stem from the way we drafted the provision in § 411.359(g). We now believe that this proposal deviates from the statute. We discuss this issue and our solution for it in our response to the next comment.

As a result of OBRA '93, as amended by SSA '94, the ownership/investment aspect of section 1877(b)(4) applies only until January 1, 1995. Some aspects of the compensation exception continue in effect, since OBRA '93 incorporated them into section 1877(e)(4).

The second comment asked, in regard to proposed § 411.357(b)(3)(i) and section 1877(d)(3), how a physician can own an interest in a distinct part of a corporation when hospitals are one incorporated entity. As we explained in an earlier response, we believe that a "hospital" can consist of any separate legally-organized operating entity plus a variety of subsidiary, related, or other entities if the hospital bills for the services furnished to its patients by those entities. In drafting section 1877(d)(3), Congress itself perceived that a hospital can consist of separately owned, subdivided parts and that a physician could own an interest in either the hospital itself or only in a subdivision. We are defining "hospital" for purposes of this regulation, to reflect this concept.

The commenter has also asked whether the intention of the exception in section 1877(d)(3) was to refer to ownership of entities related to a hospital. Although the statute does not explicitly say this, it does say that the exception will not apply if a physician's ownership interest is merely in a subdivision of the hospital, rather than in the hospital itself. We believe that a subdivision can be a related entity. We have interpreted such entities, in response to other comments, as parts of a hospital if the hospital bills for services furnished by these entities to hospital patients (excluding situations in which services are furnished for a hospital "under arrangements"). A physician with an interest in a joint or related entity would not have an ownership interest in the hospital at all if the hospital did not bill for the services furnished by the joint or related entity.

The commenter has also asked why ownership in a related entity should cause referrals from a physician to be prohibited if the entity is not a clinical laboratory (for example, if the hospital owns 60 percent of a non-laboratory entity and the physician owns 40 percent). If the entity in this situation is part of the hospital, any referrals by the physician to the hospital laboratory would not qualify for the exception in section 1877(d)(3). To qualify for this exception, the physician's ownership interest must be in the hospital itself and not in a subdivision. However, the physician's referrals could qualify for the exception in section 1877(b)(4) which, until January 1, 1995, excludes any ownership interest in a hospital, provided the ownership interest does not relate to the provision of clinical laboratory services.

Finally, the commenter has asked why the facts in the example should be more subject to abuse than one in which a physician has a general ownership in the hospital and is authorized to perform patient care services there. Section 1877(d)(3) specifically requires that, to take advantage of this exception, a physician must have an ownership interest in the hospital itself, and not in a subdivision. We must reflect this requirement in the regulation, and have incorporated it into the final rule at § 411.356(b)(3). We have not broadened this exception to apply to any other ownership interest in a hospital because we have seen no evidence that such an expanded exception would be free of the risk of program or patient abuse.

Comment: There were two comments relating specifically to proposed § 411.359, which contains exceptions for certain compensation arrangements. One commenter asked under what authority we had limited the broad exception in section 1877(b)(4). Under that exception, the commenter pointed out, *any* financial relationship with a hospital is excepted (ownership/investment interest or compensation arrangement), as long as the relationship does not relate to the furnishing of clinical laboratory services. As such, the commenter questioned why this exception was not included under proposed § 411.355, which covers general exceptions that apply to both ownership/investment and compensation relationships. The commenter believed that, in covering section 1877(b)(4) under § 411.359(g), we had limited the exception so that it no longer constitutes the broad exception, for all financial relationships, included in the statute.

The commenter referred to the fact that the exception in § 411.359(g) is

41958 Federal Register / Vol. 60, No. 156 / Monday, August 14, 1995 / Rules and Regulations

entitled "other arrangements with hospitals" and indicated that the provision is drafted so that this exception applies to compensation arrangements between a hospital and a physician (or family member) other than those arrangements described in §§ 411.359 (a) through (d). (These arrangements in paragraphs (a) through (d) include rental of office space, employment and services arrangements with hospitals, physician recruitment, and isolated transactions. To qualify for these exceptions, physicians and entities must meet a variety of conditions.) The commenter pointed out that, under section 1877(b)(4), the only condition is that a financial relationship cannot be related to the furnishing of clinical laboratory services.

The commenter has read the proposed rule to mean that the exception in § 411.359(g) applies *only if* the compensation arrangement is not one of the ones described under paragraphs (a) through (d). Thus, for example, a hospital may have one or a variety of arrangements with a physician who is performing outpatient surgery on a patient at the hospital. These arrangements could include the rental of office space, employment or service arrangements, physician recruitment arrangements, or isolated transactions. The commenter believed that if a physician had one or more of these arrangements but could not meet the conditions to qualify for an exception, the exception in § 411.359(g) would automatically be foreclosed. That is, if the physician's financial arrangement was one already described in § 411.359 in paragraphs (a) through (d), then it could not be covered by paragraph (g), which applies only to financial arrangements other than those in paragraphs (a) through (d).

The commenter feared that the proposed rule could result in situations in which the hospital's laboratory would refuse to accept the physician's Medicare patient for laboratory work, with the result that the patient could not receive needed medical care at the hospital. The commenter questioned our authority to limit the statutory exception in section 1877(b)(4) and asked that we, at a minimum, add an exception for emergency laboratory work that would apply whenever, in the judgement of the physician, laboratory tests are needed quickly.

Another commenter recommended that the exception addressed in proposed § 411.359(g) be broadened to permit a direct or indirect financial relationship between a physician and a hospital or hospital affiliated organization or entity.

Response: In drafting § 411.359(g), we intended to cover any compensation arrangements that were not described in §§ 411.359 (a) through (d), including those that were the kinds of arrangements described in those provisions but that did not meet the conditions specified in them. We agree with the first commenter that the way we drafted § 411.359(g) is ambiguous and can cause confusion. As a result, we have made § 411.359(g) an independent exception, as it is in the statute.

We have also made several other changes to this provision to reflect amendments to the statute. As we have discussed in other responses, OBRA '93 eliminated section 1877(b)(4), which excepted any ownership/investment interest or compensation arrangement with a hospital that does not relate to the provision of laboratory services. The relationship could be between a physician and a hospital or an immediate family member and a hospital. SSA '94 reinstated section 1877(b)(4) until January 1, 1995. OBRA '93 also added paragraph (e)(4) to section 1877, retroactive to January 1, 1992. This new provision differs somewhat from paragraph (b)(4) in the sense that it retains only the compensation aspect of the exception. In addition, it applies only to remuneration from a hospital to a physician (not to a family member) if the remuneration does not relate to the furnishing of laboratory services.

The commenter also believed that we should provide an exception for referrals by physicians whenever, in the judgment of the referring physician, laboratory tests are needed quickly to treat a patient whose condition will worsen or be put at risk absent prompt laboratory results. We believe that section 1877 and this final regulation provide sufficient exceptions to ensure, in almost all cases, that patients should not be in the position of having their health threatened because of the general referral prohibition. In addition, the commenter's recommendation would give physicians total discretion that could be subject to abuse.

We do not agree with the suggestion that relates to broadening the exception in proposed § 411.359(g) so that it would apply to permit a direct or indirect financial relationship between a physician and a hospital affiliated organization or entity. The current authority in section 1877(e)(4) limits the exception to remuneration provided by a hospital, and not some other entity. We have interpreted the term "hospital" to include related or affiliated organizations or entities in situations in which the hospital bills for services

provided to hospital patients by the organizations or entities (except when the services are provided "under arrangements"). However, we do not believe that expanding the exception to other, non-hospital organizations or entities would necessarily be free of the risk of patient or program abuse.

Comment: One commenter asked that we explain what is meant by the phrase "does not relate to the furnishing of clinical laboratory services," as used in proposed § 411.357(b)(3)(ii) and § 411.359(g). The commenter wanted to know whether a physician who is not authorized to perform patient care services at a for-profit hospital but who has an ownership interest in the hospital is considered to have a financial relationship that is related to the provision of laboratory services. The physician receives dividends based on the business profits earned by the hospital. These dividends may in part depend on the provision of laboratory services.

Response: The commenter has asked about a physician with an ownership interest in a hospital. The commenter has apparently correctly perceived that, because the physician is not authorized to provide patient care services in the hospital, the exception in section 1877(d)(3) and in proposed § 411.357(b)(3)(i) would not apply.

For purposes of the exception in section 1877(b)(4) and proposed § 411.357(b)(3)(ii), the commenter has asked whether the physician's ownership interest in the hospital relates (either directly or indirectly) to the furnishing of clinical laboratory services. We would consider the physician's ownership interest as related to the provision of clinical laboratory services. We base this conclusion on the fact that general ownership in a hospital includes an interest in the hospital laboratory. This exception could apply if the physician had an ownership interest in a subdivision of the hospital which did not provide clinical laboratory services. We would like to point out that, as the result of OBRA '93 (as amended by SSA '94), the exception in section 1877(b)(4) relating to ownership and investment interests is no longer in effect, beginning on January 1, 1995.

b. Ownership and Compensation

Comment: One commenter requested that the final rule clarify that a physician who meets the exception relating to an ownership or investment interest in § 411.357(b)(3) of the proposed rule not also be required to meet the exception relating to compensation arrangements in proposed

§ 411.359(g) in regard to arrangements that are incident to the physician's ownership. Examples of such arrangements are the initial offer to allow the physician to acquire the ownership interest, dividends paid to the physician as an owner, or the opportunity to enter into a stockholders agreement that would provide for the buyout of the physician's ownership on death, disability, retirement, etc., or that provides the hospital with a right of first refusal to buy the physician's ownership interest in a hospital.

Response: We believe that the commenter has asked about compensation arrangements that are inherent in certain ownership/ investment situations for which there are exceptions under the proposed regulation. We believe that a return on equity (for example, dividends) that a physician gets as a consequence of being an owner is not considered a compensation arrangement.

We take this position because section 1877 is designed to prohibit referrals to an entity whenever a physician has a financial relationship with that entity. The purpose is to prevent physicians from realizing a financial gain or some other benefit from making those referrals. The Congress specifically defined "financial relationship" to include two distinct components: an ownership/investment interest and a compensation arrangement. By this, we believe the Congress meant to encompass two mutually exclusive concepts: (1) Investment/ownership interest and whatever potential compensation or value they have or may bring to the owner, and (2) all other arrangements that result in some compensation.

Since we believe that potential compensation from an ownership/ investment interest is already factored into the investment/ownership exceptions, it would make little sense to review the resulting compensation against the exceptions for compensation arrangements. For example, it would make little sense to say that a physician can invest in publicly traded securities under the ownership/investment exception in section 1877(c), yet preclude the physician's referrals because the compensation he or she receives from these investments does not fall within any of the compensation exceptions. As a result, the prohibition on referrals should apply only when a physician has a compensation arrangement that results from something other than an excepted ownership or investment interest. It is to these compensation arrangements, which do not stem from an ownership or

investment interest, that the compensation exceptions apply. Thus, we agree that a physician would not be required to qualify for both exceptions in order to refer laboratory tests to the laboratory in which he or she has an ownership interest.

G. Exceptions to the Referral Prohibition Related to Compensation Arrangements

1. Rental of Office Space

Section 411.359(a) of the proposed rule describes the exception under which the rental of office space does not constitute a financial relationship subject to the prohibition on referrals. The exception applies as long as payment made by a lessee to a lessor is made under the following conditions:

• There is a rental or lease agreement that meets the following requirements:

+ The agreement is set out in writing and is signed by the parties.

+ The agreement identifies the premises covered by the agreement and specifies the space dedicated for the use of the lessee.

+ The term of the agreement is at least 1 year.

+ If the agreement is intended to provide the lessee with access to the premises for periodic intervals of time, rather than on a full-time basis for the term of the agreement, the agreement specifies exactly the schedule of the intervals, their precise length, and the exact rent for the intervals.

+ The agreement provides for payment on a periodic basis of an amount that is consistent with the fair market value of the rented or leased premises in arm's-length transactions.

+ The agreement provides for an amount of aggregate payments that does not vary (directly or indirectly) on the basis of the volume or value of any referrals generated between the parties.

+ The terms of the agreement would be considered to be commercially reasonable even if no referrals were made between the lessee and the lessor.

• If an interested investor (either a physician or immediate family member) has an ownership or investment interest in the rented or leased office space, the arrangement meets the following conditions:

+ The rented or leased office space is in the same building in which the physician's practice or the physician's group practice is located.

+ All of the requirements described in paragraphs (a)(1)(i) through (a)(1)(vii) of § 411.359 are met.

Section 1877(e)(1) as enacted by OBRA '89 was significantly changed by OBRA '93. Section 152(c) of SSA '94 amended the effective date provision for

OBRA '93 so that the amendments to the rental exception are effective retroactively to January 1, 1992. The OBRA '93 provisions for the rental of office space provide that payments made by a lessee to a lessor for the use of a premises shall not be considered a compensation arrangement if—

• The lease is set out in writing, signed by the parties, and specifies the premises covered by the lease.

• The space rented or leased does not exceed that which is reasonable and necessary for the legitimate business purposes of the lease or rental and is used exclusively by the lessee when being used by the lessee, except that the lessee may make payments for the use of space consisting of common areas if such payments do not exceed the lessee's pro rata share of expenses for such space based upon the ratio of the space used exclusively by the lessee to the total amount of space (other than common areas) occupied by all persons using such common areas.

• The lease provides for a term of rental or lease for at least 1 year.

• The rental charges over the term of the lease are set in advance, are consistent with fair market value, and are not determined in a manner that takes into account the volume or value of any referrals or other business generated between the parties.

• The lease would be commercially reasonable even if no referrals were made between the parties, and

• The lease meets such other requirements as the Secretary may impose by regulation as needed to protect against program or patient abuse.

Comment: A number of commenters raised questions about the meaning of the "same building" requirement in section 1877(e)(1)(B). Prior to OBRA '93, section 1877(e)(1)(B) stated that, "in the case of rental or lease of office space in which a physician who is an interested investor (or an interested investor who is an immediate family member of the physician) has an ownership or investment interest, the office space is in the same building as the building in which the physician (or group practice of which the physician is a member) has a practice." Several commenters also questioned the meaning of the terms "investor," "interested investor," and "disinterested investor" in section 1877(h) (5) and (6).

Response: OBRA '93 amended section 1877(h) to eliminate the terms "investor," "interested investor," and "disinterested investor." In addition, OBRA '93 eliminated the "same building" requirement in section 1877(e)(1)(B), effective January 1, 1995.

41960   **Federal Register** / Vol. 60, No. 156 / Monday, August 14, 1995 / Rules and Regulations

SSA '94 amended the OBRA '93 effective date provision so that the revised version of section 1877(e)(1) is retroactively effective to January 1, 1992. As a result, these terms are not reflected in this final rule.

2. Isolated Transactions

Under § 411.359(d) of the proposed rule, referrals by physicians involved in isolated financial transactions, such as the one-time sale of property, qualify for an exception if certain conditions are met and there is no other financial relationship between the entity and the physician for 1 year before and 1 year after the transaction.

Comment: Many commenters believed that the 1 year requirement creates substantial and unnecessary problems.

If a laboratory were to purchase assets from a physician on a one-time basis, it would not be able to accept future Medicare referrals from this physician if there were any previous relationship between the laboratory and the physician.

Response: We attempted in the proposed regulation to quantify and define an "isolated transaction" by adding the 1-year requirement. However, because commenters felt that this requirement creates substantial problems, we have decided to replace it with what we believe is a simpler and clearer standard. To define "isolated," we have eliminated the requirement that there can be no financial relationship between the parties for 1 year before the transaction, and we have shortened the period after the transaction. We have replaced this with the requirement that there can be no other unexcepted financial relationship between the parties for 6 months after the "isolated transaction." That is, if the two parties enter into a compensation arrangement within the 6-month period that qualifies for another exception, such as the employment or personal services exception, or if one of the parties qualifies for one of the ownership exceptions, the original transaction can still qualify as an "isolated" one.

We have also added a definition of "transaction" to make it clear that we regard an isolated transaction as one involving a single payment. If a financial relationship involves long term or installment payments (such as a mortgage), each payment constitutes a separate transaction, and would result in an ongoing financial relationship. (Individual payments between parties generally characterize a compensation arrangement. However, debt, as described in the statute in section 1877(a)(2), can constitute an ownership

interest that continues to exist until the debt is paid off.)

3. Service Arrangements With Nonhospital Entities

Under proposed § 411.359(e), which reflects section 1877(e)(3) before it was amended by OBRA '93, referrals by a physician who has an arrangement to provide specific identifiable services to an entity other than a hospital would not be prohibited if the services are furnished—

• By the physician acting as the medical director or as a member of a medical advisory board of the entity in accordance with a Medicare requirement;

• As physicians' services to an individual receiving hospice care for which Medicare payment may only be made as hospice care; or

• As physicians' services to a nonprofit blood center.

The arrangement must satisfy certain requirements that also apply to employment and service arrangements with hospitals.

As discussed in section I.D.6.d. of this preamble, section 1877(e)(3) was amended by OBRA '93 and now provides that certain personal service arrangements with any entity will not be considered compensation arrangements for purposes of section 1877(a)(2)(B). This provision applies to remuneration paid by any entity to a physician, or to an immediate family member, for furnishing personal services. The exception applies if certain conditions are met. Finally, section 152(c) of SSA '94 amended section 13562(b)(2) of OBRA '93 (the effective date provision for OBRA '93) to create a new paragraph (D). This new effective date provision says that section 1877(e)(3), as amended by OBRA '93, is in effect beginning on January 1, 1992; however, until January 1, 1995, it does not apply to any arrangement that meets the requirements of section 1877(e)(2) or (e)(3) as they were in effect prior to the OBRA '93 amendments.

Comment: One commenter indicated that under the CLIA regulations (42 CFR part 493) laboratories must have physicians who act as laboratory directors, rather than medical directors. Thus, the commenter believed the regulations should be modified so that it is clear that a laboratory does not have a compensation arrangement if it pays a physician to act as the laboratory director of the entity.

Response: Under the revised provision in section 1877(e)(3), remuneration from an entity to a physician for the provision of the physician's personal services will not

prohibit the physician from referring clinical laboratory services to the entity providing the following conditions are met:

• The arrangement is set out in writing, signed by the parties, and specifies the services covered by the arrangement.

• The arrangement covers all of the services to be furnished by the physician (or an immediate family member of the physician) to the entity.

• The aggregate services contracted for do not exceed those that are reasonable and necessary for the legitimate business purposes of the arrangement.

• The term of the arrangement is for at least 1 year.

• The compensation to be paid over the term of the arrangement is set in advance, does not exceed fair market value, and except in the case of a physician incentive plan described in section 1877(e)(3)(B), is not determined in a manner that takes into account the volume or value of any referrals or other business generated between the parties.

• The services to be performed under the arrangement do not involve the counseling or promotion of a business arrangement or other activity that violates any State or Federal law.

• The arrangement meets any other requirements the Secretary imposes by regulations as needed to protect against Medicare program or patient abuse.

Comment: One commenter indicated that there appear to be a number of relationships between clinical laboratories and physicians that are not specifically covered by proposed § 411.359 but would be protected by the fraud and abuse safe harbors. The commenter suggested that the final rule be expanded to specifically state that an arrangement would not violate the physician referral rule if it fits within a safe harbor under the fraud and abuse regulations.

Response: As mentioned in the preamble of the proposed rule and in the response to other comments, the anti-kickback and safe harbor provisions of the law and the section 1877 prohibition are intended to serve different purposes. The safe harbor provisions have been specifically designed to set forth those payment practices and business arrangements that will be protected from criminal prosecution and civil sanctions under the anti-kickback provisions of the statute. Conversely, section 1877 prohibits a physician's Medicare referrals for clinical laboratory services to entities with which the physician (or a family member) has a financial relationship when those referrals are not specifically excepted under section 1877. Because of these distinctions, the provisions of the regulations implementing these laws will not exactly correspond. Additionally, we note that, under the amendments created by OBRA '93 (particularly in the new sections 1877(e)(2) and (e)(3)), many more relationships between physicians and laboratories are now excepted from the effects of the prohibition on referrals.

Comment: One commenter indicated that a justifiable distinction cannot be drawn between the employment of a physician (or family member) by a hospital, which in some cases would be excepted under § 411.359(b) of the proposed rule, and employment of a physician (or family member) by a nonhospital laboratory, which could not be excepted under proposed § 411.359.

Response: Section 1877(e)(2), as amended by OBRA '93, recognizes bona fide employment relationships without drawing a distinction between a hospital laboratory and nonhospital laboratories. Under the new provision, for purposes of section 1877, any amount paid by an employer to a physician (or an immediate family member of the physician) who has a bona fide employment relationship with the employer for the provision of services does not constitute compensation, providing the following conditions, set forth in § 411.357(c), are met:

• The employment is for identifiable services.

• The amount of the remuneration under the employment—

+ Is consistent with the fair market value of the services;

+ Is not determined in a manner that takes into account (directly or indirectly) the volume or value of any referrals by the referring physician (although certain productivity bonuses are allowed); and

+ The remuneration is provided under an agreement that would be commercially reasonable even if no referrals were made to the employer.

H. Additional Exceptions

Under section 1877(b)(4), the Secretary is given the authority to define financial relationships beyond those specified in the law that could be exempt from the prohibition on referrals if the Secretary determines, and specifies in regulations, that they do not pose "a risk of program or patient abuse." (Section 152(c) of SSA '94 amended the effective date provision for OBRA '93 to reinstate section 1877(b)(4), as it appeared prior to the enactment of OBRA '93, until January 1,

1995. The original version of (b)(4) provided an exception for financial relationships with a hospital which are unrelated to the provision of clinical laboratory services. As a result, we believe that there are two versions of section 1877(b)(4) in effect until January 1, 1995.) In the proposed rule, we requested recommendations about financial relationships that do not pose a risk of program or patient abuse. We received suggestions for additional exceptions, all of which are discussed below. In particular, the issue of shared laboratories was raised in the context of various business and practice arrangements, most often with respect to such shared arrangements between physicians.

1. Comments Relating to an Exception for Shared Laboratories

Comment: A few commenters strongly objected to the formulation of any special exception for shared laboratories. The commenters maintained that these arrangements could easily be used as a sham to circumvent the purposes of the law. They believed that a group of physician investors could set up a single laboratory to which they all refer testing. Each physician could then obtain his or her own CLIA number for the laboratory and bill separately for these services, thus making the detection of these schemes extremely difficult. Moreover, the commenters wrote that outside practitioners would also be allowed to refer their testing to any one of these physicians. Such an arrangement, in these commenters' view, is little more than a continuation of the physician-owned laboratory under a different name and is a way for physician-owners to circumvent the terms of section 1877.

Response: We share the concerns raised by these commenters, and we agree that a separate exception cannot be justified. CLIA certifies each laboratory by location. It does not certify individuals. Therefore, a laboratory that registers for CLIA will register once and receive one CLIA registration number. Each shared laboratory location is to have one CLIA certificate regardless of the number of physicians conducting or supervising testing in that laboratory, and only one registration and compliance fee and proficiency testing enrollment and survey is required. Testing performed in the physician's office that contains the shared laboratory may be included under the shared laboratory certificate. Physicians who perform laboratory testing in their own offices, in addition to performing tests in a shared laboratory, must have

a separate certificate for their office laboratory.

As we understand it, there are a variety of circumstances that involve shared office space in general and shared laboratories in particular. Examples of shared laboratories range from laboratories shared by two or more solo practicing physicians to larger laboratories that are shared by hospitals, other health care facilities, and group practices. In effect, these commenters believed that to establish an exception for practicing physicians who share a laboratory would thwart the intent of the statute to end potential and actual overutilization of laboratory services.

In the example presented by the commenters, several physicians set up a laboratory separate from any of their practices, share in the costs of its operation, and bill individually for services furnished to their own patients. (The commenters also stated that physicians who are not owners refer patients for tests.) Since the physicians each appear to have an ownership or investment interest in the laboratory, they would be precluded from referring to the laboratory, unless they qualify for an exception.

It is not clear from the example, but if each physician does not have a practice in the same building as the laboratory and does not directly supervise the laboratory personnel who are performing the services for the physician's patients, the supervision and location requirements of the in-office ancillary services exception in section 1877(b)(2) would not be met. Furthermore, as discussed in greater detail in response to the next comment, we do not believe that it would be possible to develop an exception to accommodate these circumstances that would meet the statutory test contained in section 1877(b)(4); that is, that there be no risk of program or patient abuse.

Nonetheless, we want to clarify that the in-office ancillary exception could apply if each of the individual physicians involved separately met the supervision, location, and billing requirements of section 1877(b)(2). For example, physicians A, B, and C each have their own offices in the same building. Each physician directly supervises the laboratory technician when the technician is performing services for the physician. In addition, each physician bills for services furnished to his or her own patients. We also want to provide an example of a situation that would not qualify for the in-office exception. For example, ten individual physicians each have their own office on different floors in a building and the laboratory they share is

41962 **Federal Register** / Vol. 60, No. 156 / Monday, August 14, 1995 / Rules and Regulations

located in the basement of the building. The physicians do not directly supervise the laboratory technician when the technician is performing services for the physicians. In addition, the laboratory bills for services furnished to the patients of the physicians.

In the first example, as long as the requirements of section 1877(b)(2) and § 411.355(b) are met, it would not matter if the physicians pooled resources to cover the costs of the space occupied by the laboratory or for the cost of the equipment or overhead. We emphasize that the in-office ancillary services exception has been amended by OBRA '93, effective retroactively to January 1, 1992. Before this amendment, the services under this exception had to be furnished by the referring physician or by another physician in the same group practice. Alternatively, services could be furnished by employees of the referring physician or of the physician's group practice, provided the employees were "personally supervised" by the referring physician or another physician in the group practice. This requirement has been changed by OBRA '93 to eliminate the requirement that only a physician's or group practice's employees can furnish services. Also, the term "personally supervised" has been changed to require that a technician's or other individual's services be "directly supervised" by the referring physician or by another physician in the group practice.

For purposes of this exception, we are explicitly defining "direct supervision" using the longstanding Medicare definition of this term. Under this definition, the physician must be present in the office suite and be immediately available to provide assistance and direction throughout the time a technician is performing services. We believe it is appropriate for us to define this term in this final rule with comment period, rather than in a new proposed rule. We have several bases for this conclusion.

First, we believe that the Secretary's definition for this term is interpretive. Interpretive, nonsubstantive agency promulgations fall into the Administrative Procedure Act (APA) exception to notice and comment rulemaking. See 5 U.S.C. 553(b)(A).

In defining "direct supervision," we are merely explicating the Congress' desires rather than adding substantive content of our own. That is, the definition is a clarification of what is implicitly in the statute. A rule that clarifies a statutory term is the classic example of an interpretive rule. Interpretive rules are those that merely

clarify or explain existing law or regulations. They serve an advisory function, explaining the meaning given by the agency to a particular word or phrase in a statute or rule it administers.

The term "direct supervision" is a longstanding term of art with a very particular meaning in the Medicare program. It appears in section 2050.2 of the Medicare Carriers Manual, Part 3—Claims Processing, which describes services that are "incident to" a physician's professional services. This definition has appeared in the manual since the 1970's. It has, over the years, affected the many physicians who bill for services or supplies that are furnished as an integral, although incidental, part of a physician's personal professional services in the course of diagnosis or treatment of an injury or illness. The same definition appears in the regulations at § 410.32(a), which states that, in general, diagnostic x-ray tests are covered only if performed under the "direct supervision" of certain physicians or by certain radiology departments. Congress, in using this term of art, has adopted and ratified the Secretary's definition.

We believe that in changing "personally supervised" to the familiar "directly supervised," Congress was intending to make clear that it wished to incorporate a concept that the agency and the provider community have long understood. For example, physicians are quite familiar with this term because they can only bill for nonphysician services that are "incident to" their own services if the nonphysician services are performed under "direct supervision." As such, we have reiterated in this regulation our long-standing definition for this term. The definition is a clarification of what the Secretary believes "direct supervision" means and has always meant; it does not add to the statute any additional substantive requirements.

We are aware of only one paragraph of legislative history for OBRA '93 that attempts to explain the meaning of the term "direct supervision." The Conference Report for OBRA '93 states that—

[T]he conferees intend that the requirement for *direct supervision by a physician* would be met if the lab is in a physician's office which is personally supervised by a lab director, or a physician, even if the *physician is not always on site.* [Emphasis added.] H.R. Rep. No. 213, 103d Cong., 1st Sess. 810 (1993).

We believe that this explanation provides no insight into the Congress' purpose in using the term "direct supervision." That is, it purports to explain what constitutes direct

supervision, yet defines it by allowing a physician to "directly supervise" without even being present. This appears to us to be at total variance with the Medicare program's longstanding requirements for "direct supervision," and with the statute, which specifically requires that the referring physician or another physician in the same group practice have *direct* involvement with individuals performing laboratory tests. In addition, the statute is very specific about who must directly supervise; it does not say that a laboratory director who is not a group member can provide this supervision instead of a solo or group practice physician.

Also, it appears to us that the legislative history is inconsistent. If "direct supervision" is interpreted to allow a laboratory director to supervise individuals who are furnishing services, this could have the effect of creating an exception for shared laboratories. The very same conference report points out that the House Energy and Commerce Committee introduced a provision that would have added an exception for shared laboratories. The conference agreement, however, specifically rejected this amendment. H.R. Rep. No. 213, 103d Cong., 1st Sess. 810 (1993).

Even without the "interpretive" exception, we believe that there would be good cause to waive notice and comment for this particular term. Title 5 U.S.C. 553(b)(B) authorizes agencies to dispense with certain procedures for rules when they find "good cause" to do so. Under section 553(b)(B), the requirements of notice and comment do not apply when the agency for good cause finds that those procedures are "impracticable, unnecessary, or contrary to the public interest."

We believe that waiting to define "direct supervision" in a future notice of proposed rulemaking would be both impracticable and contrary to the public interest. To begin with, some of the amendments added by OBRA '93 relating to clinical laboratories have a retroactive effective date. The provision containing the "direct supervision" requirement is effective retroactively back to January 1992. The retroactive effective date for some provisions relating to clinical laboratory services, but not others, demonstrates the Congress' desire to expedite their implementation. Although an expedited timeframe alone may not justify a "good cause" exception, we believe it is a crucial factor when considered in conjunction with the entire set of circumstances.

The in-office ancillary services provision establishes an exception to the referral prohibition that is critical to

Federal Register / Vol. 60, No. 156 / Monday, August 14, 1995 / Rules and Regulations   **41963**

the many solo and group practice physicians who wish to be excepted for referrals for their own in-office ancillary services. These physicians have had no way to be certain, from January 1992 until the publication date of this interim final rule, whether they qualify for the in-office ancillary services exception. They cannot know if they do until it is clear that they are "directly supervising" any individuals who perform laboratory tests. In short, a portion of the statute cannot be implemented without interpretation, although some form of "supervision" has been required since January 1992.

Defining "direct supervision" in this interim final rule avoids piecemeal promulgation of the statute for critical provisions such as this one. The in-office ancillary services exception is an important one that affects many physicians in a variety of situations, including those involved in shared laboratories. We have received a tremendous number of inquiries on how shared laboratories fit within the statutory scheme. We cannot provide a definitive answer to many of these inquiries until we define "direct supervision." Without certainty, physicians and entities affected by this provision will continue to be confused about how to handle their highly complicated financial relationships. They may divest themselves unnecessarily of interests that we believe the Congress meant to excuse when it created the in-office ancillary exception.

Any uncertainty over the meaning of "direct supervision" could also damage our ability to enforce section 1877. If we take no action and delay enforcement of the referral prohibition because of uncertainty about the "direct supervision" requirement, we could be allowing over-utilization of services by physicians who have financial relationships with an entity and who continue to make prohibited referrals to that entity.

Finally, we are providing a comment period following publication of this interim final rule. We will carefully consider all comments we receive on the definition of "direct supervision" and publish our responses to these comments in a final rule.

The long-standing definition of "direct supervision" makes the proximity of the laboratory to each physician's office important. That is, in the first example, the laboratory must be situated in a way that each of the three physicians would be able to directly supervise the services of the individual performing the testing when the testing is being performed for the physician's

own patients. This means that it is possible for a physician to have his or her office practice in a location separate from the laboratory as long as the laboratory is in the same building in which the physician practices and he or she fulfills the direct supervision requirement by being in the office suite when the tests are performed.

Finally, the exception in section 1877(d)(2) and §411.356(b)(1) for clinical laboratory services furnished in a laboratory located in a rural area applies to shared laboratories. This exception, however, applies to referrals that would otherwise be prohibited only because of ownership or investment interests. The exception does not apply if the referring physician has a compensation arrangement with the rural laboratory. Therefore, if physicians share ownership in a laboratory located in a rural area but have no compensation arrangements with the laboratory (for example, remuneration between the physicians and laboratories other than return on investment), referrals by the physicians to the rural laboratory would not be prohibited provided the criteria mentioned above are met.

Comment: A majority of commenters regard the absence of a "shared laboratory" exception to be a serious oversight. These commenters indicated that shared clinical laboratories are very common, especially among younger physicians still building their solo practices and among providers in rural or medically underserved areas, whose populations could not otherwise support an independent laboratory testing facility. Other commenters indicated that an exception to permit physicians to make Medicare referrals to their shared laboratories would eliminate the discrimination that exists in the proposed regulations in favor of group practices and individually practicing physicians who can afford to purchase their own laboratory equipment solely for their own use. The commenters suggested that an exception could be added to permit referrals when all of the following factors are present:

• The shared arrangement involves a fixed and limited number of physician practices. The maximum may be specified by the Secretary.

• The arrangement involves only physicians who occupy the same office space or who practice in contiguous offices in the same building.

• The physicians in the arrangement refer only their own patients to their shared laboratory, which would not accept Medicare referrals from other physicians.

• The tests are done by the physicians' employees and are directly supervised by the physicians, or the physician personally performs the laboratory test for his or her own Medicare patients.

• No physician in the arrangement may be required to maintain a specific level or volume of laboratory referrals.

• The services are billed by one of the following:

+ The physician performing or supervising the service.

+ An entity that is wholly owned by the physicians who are parties to the shared office laboratory agreement.

• The shared-office must not loan funds or guarantee a loan for any physicians who share in the costs of the laboratory and who are in a position to refer to the laboratory.

• The agreement under which the shared-office laboratory operates does not contain "noncompetition clauses" that prevent physicians who share in the costs of the laboratory from investing in other laboratories.

• The shared-office laboratory must not furnish its items or services to referring physicians who have an ownership interest in the shared-office laboratory or share in the costs of the laboratory differently from other physicians. (By this, we believe the commenter meant that tests referred by owner physicians are not given priority.)

• Physicians who share in the costs of the shared-office laboratory must disclose their interest to their patients when ordering tests from the laboratory.

• Operation of the laboratory must be the joint responsibility of the physicians and/or practice groups with actual costs shared on a per test basis.

• Shared physician office laboratories must demonstrate that the laboratory simply passes actual costs through to the participating physicians and group practices with no accumulation or distributions of net earnings.

Response: As evidenced by the number of comments concerning this issue and the detail contained in suggestions for an exception, it is clear that there is great concern about this matter. Nonetheless, the Congress, while it was deliberating over the changes it would make in section 1877 by enacting OBRA '93, considered an exception for shared laboratory facilities but chose not to enact it. (See H.R. Rep. No. 213, 103d Cong., 1st Sess. 809–810 (1993)). The Secretary does have the authority to establish a shared laboratory exception if she determines that there would not be a risk of program or patient abuse.

Unfortunately, notwithstanding the arguments for establishing such an

41964   **Federal Register** / Vol. 60, No. 156 / Monday, August 14, 1995 / Rules and Regulations

exception, there is not sufficient basis in the rulemaking record to support an exception that meets the statutory standard. For that reason, we believe that Congress should provide further clarification or specific statutory authority in this area.

• The first suggestion made by the commenters was that a shared laboratory be limited to a fixed number of physicians. In our view, however, any attempt to select a number (three, five, ten, and so on) would be arbitrary. That is because we do not currently have data that would support making a distinction based on the number of physicians involved. We see no rational basis on which to establish or impose a limit.

• The second suggestion is to limit the exception to physicians who occupy the same office space or whose offices are contiguous in the same building. As explained in the response to the last comment, depending on how the physician's office space and the shared laboratory space are physically arranged, the in-office ancillary services exception provided in § 411.355(b) could apply. But we emphasize that the direct supervision and billing requirements must also be met.

• With respect to the remaining points, even if considered cumulatively, they do not clearly describe a situation in which there could be no program or patient abuse. Physicians could still have the opportunity to overutilize services with the possibility of profit that is inherent in any ownership arrangement. We are not suggesting that all physicians who might wish to participate in shared laboratory arrangements would overutilize laboratory tests. We do not believe, however, that there is a basis for concluding that the arrangements pose no risk of patient or program abuse.

Comment: One commenter indicated that, if the Secretary establishes an exception for shared laboratories, physicians involved in shared laboratory arrangements could be required to attest in writing that they meet the criteria required by the Secretary. This requirement would be like the one in the proposed regulation requiring that physicians attest in writing to their Medicare carrier that they meet the group practice exception.

Response: To clarify one point, we required only one attestation in the proposed rule; that is, that a group practice attest in writing, to the appropriate Medicare carrier, that the group complied with the standard we proposed to use to determine whether substantially all of the patient care services of group member physicians are furnished through the group as was

required by section 1877(h)(4)(B) (now section 1877(h)(4)(A)(ii)). There are other standards that a group practice has to meet in order to qualify, but we did not propose that they be the subject of an attestation procedure.

In any case, as explained above, we do not believe that a separate exception for shared laboratories is justifiable.

Comment: One commenter suggested that multiple group practices within the same building be allowed to refer patients to one central laboratory that was created for the patients of the group practices.

Response: What is described here may be a laboratory owned by several group practices that does testing for patients of each group. In effect, the laboratory would be an independent entity that is shared by several group practices in the sense that it does business with each of its group practice owners. (A second possibility is that the laboratory is owned by one group to perform testing for its own patients but also accepts referrals from other groups or other outside sources. This latter situation is discussed elsewhere in this preamble.)

As we have explained in earlier responses to comments, we are not providing a general exception for shared laboratories such as the one described by the commenter. The physicians in the multiple group practices could refer to the laboratory, provided that each referral meets the requirements of the in-office ancillary services exception in section 1877(b)(2). This means that the services must be personally performed by or directly supervised by the referring physician or another member of that physician's own group practice and the services must be billed by the referring physician, the group practice, or an entity wholly owned by the group practice or referring physician.

There is no evidence from the commenter's description that the group physicians personally perform or directly supervise the laboratory services. Also, if this is the case, the group practices cannot individually bill for the services under section 1833(h)(5)(A), which generally allows payment only to the person or entity that performs or supervises the performance of clinical diagnostic laboratory tests. If the laboratory bills, the services will not meet the billing requirement in section 1877(b)(2).

2. Specialized Services Laboratory

Comment: One commenter requested an exception for referrals for "specialized services." This exception would permit the establishment of laboratories by groups of individual

practitioners within a common area of expertise.

The exception would apply when there is a public health need for specialized clinical services not readily available in a geographic region.

According to the commenter, general laboratories may lack the equipment or the expertise to meaningfully analyze samples from patients suffering from particular diseases. The commenter stated that the cost of specialized services could be lowered by making them readily available to patients who would otherwise incur unnecessary costs and delays because samples have to be shipped to laboratories not reasonably close to them. The commenter stated, as an example, that laboratories that usually handle normal blood specimens typically fail to calibrate their laboratory equipment for renal patients who express blood values that depart significantly from the norm. In the commenter's view, the technicians at general laboratories tend to be inexpert at processing these abnormal samples. In turn, this causes dialysis patients to incur unnecessary expense and endure needless delays and incorrect test results. The commenter also stated that laboratories that are not expert in evaluating renal blood samples tend not to report patient values, including cumulative historical laboratory results, to dialysis clinics in the same detailed manner as laboratories that specialize in renal patients.

Response: As mentioned previously, a physician's Medicare referrals to a laboratory owned by that physician will not be prohibited if the laboratory is located in a rural area (as defined in new § 411.356(b)(1)). Therefore, physicians with an ownership interest in a specialized laboratory that is located in a rural area are not prohibited because of that investment from referring Medicare patients to the laboratory. We believe that it is likely to be in rural areas that specialized equipment or technical expertise would be in short supply.

Furthermore, we believe the CLIA certification that is now required for any laboratory that performs tests on human specimens will tend to induce those laboratories that fail to calibrate their equipment or operate in other ineffectual ways to improve their performance or risk going out of business. For example, under CLIA, laboratories are subject to proficiency testing and personnel requirements. Failure to comply with accepted standards can result in serious sanctions. Thus, we do not agree that a special exception is warranted because

Federal Register / Vol. 60, No. 156 / Monday, August 14, 1995 / Rules and Regulations **41965**

some laboratories may not properly conduct tests.

3. Laboratories Shared With Hospitals

Comment: One commenter requested that we create an exception for a shared laboratory facility owned by an organization or hospital that is exempt from taxation under section 501(c)(3) of the Internal Revenue Code if the laboratory is used in common under a written agreement with a group practice and if the group practice constitutes all or substantially all of the staff of the organization or hospital. The commenter stated that the requirement that the entity that owns the laboratory be tax exempt under section 501(c)(3) of the Internal Revenue Code provides significant protection against patient and program abuse. (To qualify for and maintain tax-exempt status, an organization must be a corporation, or a community chest, fund, or foundation, organized and operated exclusively for a community purpose such as for religious, charitable, scientific, public safety, literary, or educational purposes. No part of the net earnings of the organization can inure to the benefit of any private shareholder or other individual. Failure to meet these requirements, or failure to continuously maintain them, results in the denial or loss of tax-exempt status.)

The commenter believed that the conditions associated with tax-exempt status would prevent physicians from having an ownership interest in the laboratory from which they could receive financial benefits in the form of dividends or other distribution of earnings, as a result of their referrals. Consequently, there would be no incentive to order an excessive number of clinical laboratory tests. The commenter pointed out that payment for unreasonable or excessive compensation would also be prohibited by the restriction on private inurement.

Response: It is not clear from this comment exactly what the financial relationship is between the tax-exempt hospital/organization and the group practice physicians. We will first assume that it is the hospital or organization only that owns the laboratory and the physicians receive compensation from the hospital/ organization for providing staff services. This relationship will not prohibit referrals to the hospital's laboratory provided the compensation meets the requirements of one of the exceptions in section 1877. For example, section 1877(e)(2) (for bona fide employment relationships with an entity) or (e)(3) (for personal service arrangements with an entity) could apply. An additional

exception appears in section 1877(e)(7), which exempts certain group practice arrangements with a hospital when a group practice provides services for which the hospital bills.

If, on the other hand, the group practice physicians have an ownership interest in the laboratory, they would be referring to a laboratory in which they have a financial interest under section 1877(a)(2), even if they do not receive dividends or earnings. The physicians could refer to their own laboratory, provided they meet the in-office ancillary services exception in section 1877(b)(2) and § 411.355(b) of this regulation. If the laboratory is rural, then the ownership relationship would be exempt under section 1877(d)(2). If the physicians have an ownership interest in a tax-exempt hospital itself, their relationship could be exempt under several hospital-specific exceptions.

Because there are a number of exceptions available for situations involving compensation between a hospital or other organization and a physician, or for ownership in a hospital, we believe that a specific blanket exception for laboratory facilities associated with a tax-exempt organization or hospital would be unnecessary. Also, we are not convinced that such an exception would be free from any risk of patient or program abuse. For example, a non- profit or tax-exempt organization can own a for-profit laboratory entity. Without further details and evidence, we would not grant such an exception.

Comment: One commenter indicated that an exception should be added for referrals to a laboratory facility that is shared by a hospital and a clinic. The commenter provided the following information. The clinic is a group practice. The shared laboratory is located on hospital premises, and the hospital owns the laboratory space. The clinic leases space from the hospital in an amount proportional to testing on the clinic's patients. Clinic staff manage the laboratory, and the clinic employs all the laboratory personnel. The clinic and hospital each own some of the laboratory equipment. As such, each entity essentially leases from the other entity the equipment needed to perform testing on its own patients. The laboratory is not a separate legal entity, but simply an arrangement that permits the clinic and hospital to work together. The parties entered into this arrangement in 1973 and it has been in effect since that time. Each party is responsible for billing and collecting fees related to laboratory services provided to its respective patients. The

agreement provides that the clinic and hospital would coordinate management, planning, budgeting, and accounting for the laboratory services. The commenter indicated that an exception should be allowed for referrals to a laboratory facility that is shared by a hospital and a clinic (group practice) where the parties divide expenses on a basis that reasonably approximates the costs associated with the tests performed for each party's patients and each party bills for and retains revenues associated with the testing of its own patients.

Response: The commenter has asked for a specific exception for arrangements in which a laboratory facility is shared by a hospital and a group practice clinic. The commenter has described an arrangement which involves a variety of ownership and compensation arrangements, each of which could cause the group practice physicians' referrals to be prohibited. However, as a result of the additional exceptions included in section 1877 by OBRA '93, we believe that most of the relationships described by the commenter could be excepted. As such, a separate exception would be unnecessary.

The commenter first describes several compensation arrangements between the hospital and the group practice. The group practice rents the laboratory space and some equipment from the hospital. (The laboratory is not a separate legal entity and is located on the hospital's premises, so we assume it is part of the hospital.) The hospital, in turn, rents some of the equipment from the group practice. These arrangements should not preclude the physicians' referrals if they meet the exceptions in section 1877(e)(1) (A) and (B), which exempt rental arrangements provided certain conditions are met.

The group practice also provides certain services to the hospital by managing the laboratory and employing the staff. We assume that the group practice is receiving some compensation, in some form, from the hospital for these services. This compensation would not trigger the referral prohibition if the arrangement meets the requirements in the bona fide employment exception in section 1877(e)(2) or qualifies for the exception for personal services arrangements in (e)(3). Alternatively, the relationship might be exempted under the exception in section 1877(e)(7) for certain group practice arrangements with a hospital under which the group provides clinical laboratory services which are billed by the hospital. In this case, the group practice appears to provide most, if not all, of the actual laboratory services while the hospital apparently bills for

41966 Federal Register / Vol. 60, No. 156 / Monday, August 14, 1995 / Rules and Regulations

its own patients. To qualify for this exception, the group must meet the definition of a group practice in section 1877(h)(4) and meet the requirements under section 1877(e)(7).

Finally, there are certain indications that the group practice may have some form of ownership interest in the laboratory entity (although it may not be a separate legal entity). The group pays rent for the space, manages the laboratory, employs all of the laboratory staff, owns some of the equipment, bills for its own patients, and retains the revenues associated with the testing of its own patients. In order for the group practice to refer to its own laboratory, it must qualify as a group practice under the definition in section 1877(h)(4), and meet the requirements of the in-office ancillary services exception in section 1877(b)(2).

Comment: Several commenters indicated that a number of group practices and the hospitals with which they are affiliated have for many years operated a laboratory facility that serves both hospital patients and the group practice's office patients. Under the terms of the agreement between the group and the hospital, the laboratory is operated under a shared services agreement, rather than as a true joint venture or under an "under arrangement" contract. The revenues, costs, profits, and losses resulting from services to hospital patients are attributed to the hospital and the revenues, costs, profits, and losses resulting from services provided to the group practice's office patients are attributed to the group practice. The commenters recommended a new exception that would be limited to teaching hospitals and would apply to clinical laboratory services furnished by a laboratory that is—

• Owned or operated by an organization or hospital that participates in an approved medical training program; and

• Used in common under a written arrangement with a group practice whose physician members constitute all or substantially all of the active medical and teaching staff of the organization or hospital.

Response: This comment is very similar to the previous comment. That is, it involves an arrangement between a hospital or organization and a group practice to share a laboratory facility. The commenters, however, do not address the specifics of the arrangement, so we cannot tell exactly how the situation will be affected by section 1877. In addition, it is not clear why the commenters limited their recommendation for a new exception to

just arrangements between teaching hospitals and group practices. However, as we pointed out in our response to the last comment, we believe that a new exception is unnecessary after OBRA '93 for most situations in which hospitals and other organizations share their laboratories with physicians.

In the commenter's example, for instance, the group practice physicians constitute all or substantially all of the active medical and teaching staff of the hospital or organization. The compensation that these physicians receive from the hospital or organization for their services should not prevent the physicians from referring to the hospital's laboratory, provided the arrangement meets the requirements under section 1877(e)(2) (for bona fide employment relationships) or (e)(3) (for personal services arrangements). The group practice physicians also appear to have some ownership interest in the laboratory, since they refer their own office patients there and the revenues, costs, profits, and losses of the group's office patients are attributed to the group. The group practice physicians can refer their own patients to each other, provided they meet the requirements of the in-office ancillary services exception in section 1877(b)(2).

Comment: One commenter indicated that there are large multi-specialty group practices that own clinics located adjacent to inpatient hospitals and the clinics share certain ancillary facilities, including laboratories, with the hospitals. In some cases, the ancillary services building literally becomes the bridge between the clinic and the hospital, so that a hospital patient enters the ancillary facility from the hospital, and a clinic patient enters the same facility from the clinic. Such a facility would be under the common control of both the clinic and the hospital, and both entities would share in the cost of personnel, space, equipment, supplies, and other operating expenses. The commenter questioned whether the physician group is entitled to treat such a shared facility as "in-office." The commenter believed that if the services furnished at the facility do not qualify for the in-office ancillary exception, the physician group's referrals for those services would be prohibited since the cost sharing agreement between the hospital and clinic would constitute a compensation arrangement under the statute. The commenter requested that we provide an additional exception to accommodate arrangements of this nature that meet all of the following conditions:

• The shared laboratory facility, the group practice, and hospital (or other

entity) are part of the same medical center campus.

• The costs of operation of the shared facility are shared on the basis of utilization originating from each part, so that each party pays only its own costs, and does not subsidize the provision of laboratory services to the other.

• The creation or continuation of such a shared facility arrangement is not conditional or otherwise related to the volume or value of referrals of patients between the clinic and hospital (or other entity) for other, nonlaboratory, covered Medicare services.

Response: The comments we have received on the issue of hospitals or similar organizations which share laboratories with group practices have revealed to us the complexity of many of the financial relationships involved in these arrangements. In some situations, one or both parties actually own the physical facility and/or its equipment, one party may pay rent to the other, and each party may provide the other with certain services both in the laboratory and in a practice context. It is impossible for us to analyze each and every configuration. However, as we pointed out in earlier responses on this issue, OBRA '93 has created additional exceptions which should address many of the interrelationships involved in these situations. We encourage hospitals and other organizations to analyze their own particular circumstances in light of these exceptions.

In regard to the particular situation raised by this commenter, the commenter describes a situation in which a laboratory is under the common control of both a group practice clinic and a hospital, each of which share in the cost of personnel, space, equipment, supplies, and other operating expenses. The commenter appeared to be concerned, primarily, about whether the in-office ancillary services exception would apply to services furnished in the laboratory for the patients of the group practice. The commenter provided few other details about ownership of the hospital or laboratory or whether there is any compensation passing between these parties.

The in-office ancillary services exception in section 1877(b)(2) does not appear to dictate any particular ownership arrangements between group practice physicians and the laboratory in which the services are provided. We believe that the group practice can take advantage of this exception and that members can refer to each other in the laboratory provided that the group meets the definition of a "group practice" under section 1877(h)(4) and

Federal Register / Vol. 60, No. 156 / Monday, August 14, 1995 / Rules and Regulations **41967**

meets the requirements in section 1877(b)(2). Under section 1877(b)(2), the services must be furnished by the referring physician or a group member or must be directly supervised by a group practice member. In addition, the services must be billed by the referring physician, the group practice, or an entity wholly owned by the group practice.

Comment: One other commenter indicated that, if an exception is provided for contracts for services provided "under arrangements" as described in section 1861(w), the language should be broad and not limited only to those circumstances in which the arrangement between the parties meets the safe harbor for personal services and management contracts provided for in the anti-kickback rules (42 CFR part 1001). According to this commenter, this limitation would pose several problems. First, the personal services and management contracts safe harbor would require that the aggregate amount of compensation be set in advance and not vary based on the volume or value of tests performed. This would mean that the parties would have to establish in advance a flat yearly fee for laboratory services. Even a fee schedule would not qualify for the safe harbor. A flat aggregate fee arrangement would be of concern to the hospital because it would place the group practice physicians at risk for the provision of clinical laboratory services that are the hospital's obligation. Under this arrangement, the physicians would have a financial incentive to order too few laboratory services for hospital inpatients and outpatients in order to make the arrangement as profitable as possible. To ensure that hospital patients receive optimum quality health care services, the hospital would not want the physicians to have a financial disincentive to order medically necessary laboratory services. The hospital would also be concerned that this contractual disincentive may have liability implications for the hospital in the event of a misdiagnosis of a hospitalized patient allegedly because the appropriate diagnostic testing was not ordered.

The safe harbor for personal services and management contracts also requires that contracts for less than full-time services be specific about the frequency and timing of the services being furnished. This commenter believed that a hospital in this situation must clearly expect that the group practice laboratory will furnish services for the hospital on an as needed basis when the patient and the patient's attending

physician require the laboratory service for appropriate diagnosis. Thus, the commenter concluded that this safe harbor criterion also could not be met.

Response: The commenter has described a situation in which group practice physicians both order and provide laboratory services to hospital inpatients and outpatients under an arrangement. We believe the commenter is correct in concluding that the section 1877 prohibition applies to both Part A inpatient hospital services as well as to Part B services.

The definition of "referral" found in section 1877(h)(5)(A) applies, by its terms, to items or services for which payment may be made under Part B of the program. Section 1877(h)(5)(A) is entitled "Physicians' Services," which are separate from inpatient hospital services and are always covered under Part B. Section 1877(h)(5)(B), on the other hand, covers "Other Items," and is not limited to Part B items and services. This provision states that, except for specific exceptions listed in (h)(5)(C), "the request or establishment of a plan of care by a physician" that includes clinical laboratory services constitutes a "referral" by a "referring physician." We believe this provision is difficult to decipher. Nonetheless, it appears to contemplate that physicians have made a "referral" in either a Part A or Part B context if they establish a plan of care for an individual that includes clinical laboratory services.

In the "inpatient hospital" context, we believe that most patients will receive clinical laboratory services as part of their "plan of care." We consider that anytime a physician orders anything, it is "pursuant to a plan of care" on the physician's part, even if not formally called that. In addition, we believe that the Congress fully intended to encompass Part A inpatient hospital services within the section 1877 referral prohibition. One of the designated health services that has been added to the prohibition effective January 1, 1995 (by section 1877(h)(6)(K)) is "*inpatient* and outpatient hospital services."

The commenter has asked about a specific exception for services furnished under arrangements. OBRA '93 amended section 1877 to establish such an exception in new paragraph (e)(7). This provision creates a limited exception for compensation that derives from an arrangement between a hospital and a group under which services are furnished by the group but are billed by the hospital. The provision specifies, in (e)(7)(A)(i) that, with respect to services furnished to an inpatient of a hospital, the arrangement is pursuant to the provision of inpatient hospital services

under section 1861(b)(3). Section 1861(b)(3) defines what constitutes "inpatient hospital services," and specifically includes certain services furnished to inpatients "under arrangements." Among other requirements in section 1877(e)(7), the arrangement must have begun before December 19, 1989, and have continued in effect without interruption since that date. Also, the compensation paid over the term of the agreement must be consistent with fair market value and the compensation *per unit* of services must be fixed in advance and not take into account the volume or value of referrals. Therefore, this exception does not present the "aggregate compensation" problem discussed in the comment. Also, there are no additional requirements for details about the frequency or timing of services furnished under a less than full-time service arrangement.

In response to the commenter's concern about the safe harbor for personal services and management contracts, we caution that the anti-kickback safe harbor regulations implement different provisions of the Act than are implemented by these regulations. Therefore, physicians and laboratory entities are obligated to consider the safe harbor requirements separately from the requirements of this rule.

4. Rental of Laboratory Equipment

Comment: One commenter stated that laboratories often rent a variety of equipment to physicians that they need in connection with their practices. For example, a physician may want to rent a blood analyzer in order to perform simple laboratory tests in his or her office. Since laboratories often have extra equipment they rent, the laboratory that the physician uses for his or her reference work will likely be the laboratory from which the physician rents equipment. Laboratories typically charge some rental fee for this equipment if the equipment is not an integral part of the laboratory services furnished. These arrangements could, however, be considered a compensation arrangement that could jeopardize the physician's referrals to the laboratory. The commenter believed that, if the equipment is leased at fair market value and meets other requirements comparable to those set out in the provision related to the lease of office space, there is little risk of patient or program abuse. Thus, this commenter recommended that an additional exception be created for referrals by a physician who has a compensation arrangement with a laboratory through

41968   Federal Register / Vol. 60, No. 156 / Monday, August 14, 1995 / Rules and Regulations

an agreement under which the physician leases or has a role in leasing equipment from or to a laboratory.

Response: We agree with the commenter that, if a physician who is leasing equipment from a laboratory under controlled circumstances refers to that laboratory, this should not lead to program or patient abuse. Section 1877(e)(1)(B), which was added by OBRA '93 retroactive to January 1, 1992, excepts from "compensation arrangements" payments made by a lessee of equipment to the lessor for the use of the equipment if certain conditions (discussed earlier in this preamble at section I.D.7.b.) are met. These conditions are specified in § 411.357(b) of this rule.

5. Group Practice Affiliated Property Companies

In the impact analysis of the proposed rule (57 FR 8601), we discussed group practices with affiliated property companies that are owned by members of the group practice and that lease facilities or equipment to the group. We stated that the group practice would need to restructure if it wanted to continue to make Medicare referrals for clinical laboratory services. Technically, we regarded the lease of equipment by the property company to the group practice that operates a clinical laboratory as a compensation arrangement for which an exception was not provided in the proposed rule. In these cases, it was indicated that the prohibition on referrals would apply, which would require the group physicians to either purchase the equipment from the property company or divest their interests in the laboratory if they intended to continue to make Medicare referrals for clinical laboratory services.

Comment: According to one commenter, in some group practices, affiliated property companies serve as the vehicle for the retirement system for the equity partners in the group practice; that is, as vehicles for creating retirement income. This commenter recommended that we provide an exception for group practices that have affiliated property companies under circumstances in which there is no potential or incentive for program or patient abuse.

Response: What this commenter is concerned about is that the compensation arrangement between the affiliated property company and the group practice might prohibit referrals by the physicians of the group practice to their own in-office laboratory. In this situation, one or more of the group practice physicians who own the property company receive remuneration from the group practice. In the impact analysis of the proposed rule (57 FR 8601), we indicated that a group practice probably would have to divest its interest in an affiliated property company if it intended to refer Medicare patients to its in-office laboratory. After reconsidering the matter, however, we do not believe that our initial interpretation was correct.

Section 1877(a)(1) of the Act prohibits a physician from making referrals to an entity that furnishes clinical laboratory services if the physician or immediate family member has a financial relationship with that entity. In the situation described by the commenter, the group practice physicians appear to have a financial relationship with the affiliated property company which rents equipment to their laboratory, in the form of an ownership interest. We also regarded as a compensation arrangement the payments which the group practice makes to the affiliated property company for renting the equipment. However, the physicians in this case do not have these financial relationships with an entity that furnishes clinical laboratory services; their relationships are with an entity that only rents equipment to the group practice. As a result, these relationships with the affiliated property company should not affect the physicians' ability to refer to their own laboratory.

Instead, the group practice physicians' referrals could be prohibited because they are referring to a laboratory that they own. Section 1877(b)(2) provides an exception for group practices which refer Medicare patients to their own laboratory for in-office ancillary services. These services must be furnished personally by a member of the group practice or an individual who is directly supervised by a member of the group practice, provided these services are furnished in the building where the group practice has its office or a building that is used by the group practice for furnishing some or all of the group's clinical laboratory services. This provision also has certain billing requirements. The conditions in this exception do not place limitations on the origin of the laboratory equipment that is used by the group practice.

Thus, we have determined that, if the in-office laboratory services are furnished in the manner described by section 1877(b)(2) and § 411.355(b), the nature of the physician's financial relationship with the in-office laboratory is irrelevant. As a result, we do not believe that an additional exception is necessary.

6. Faculty Practice Plan Exception

Comment: Several commenters suggested that a separate exception be developed to treat faculty practice plans associated with accredited medical schools as a separate and distinct type of group practice. These commenters indicated that it is not uncommon in a faculty practice plan environment for the physicians to receive their compensation from one entity (the medical school, for example). However, they may conduct their practice through a separate entity that might be a professional corporation, partnership, or simply a contractually organized billing service. In addition they may order their laboratory work from one or more related entities (for example, the teaching hospital, the university's research laboratory for highly specialized testing, in-office laboratories within faculty departments that may or may not be incorporated as professional corporations, etc.). Since there is no consistent organizational arrangement that characterizes a faculty practice plan, these commenters requested that we develop a separate provision that would treat faculty practice plans associated with accredited medical schools as a separate and distinct type of group practice. They have suggested that the definition of a group practice and the separate requirements of the in-office ancillary exception be applied at the level of the umbrella organization. That is, they believed each legal entity within the same academic setting should not be required to satisfy these provisions. In this manner, any physician who is a staff member of the umbrella organization would be permitted to refer Medicare patients to laboratories that are owned or operated by the umbrella organization.

Response: We believe that the amendments made by OBRA '93 make an additional exception unnecessary. We acknowledge that faculty practice plan physicians may be associated with many organizations in an academic setting, in terms of receiving compensation, furnishing patient care, teaching, and doing research. For example, the medical school may pay the plan to teach residents or care for patients. Even though faculty practice plans may operate in a variety of arrangements, the common theme appears to involve physicians or groups of physicians who are compensated by some part of an academic center for providing a variety of services, and who are concerned about whether they can refer patients to laboratories that belong to the academic center.

Federal Register / Vol. 60, No. 156 / Monday, August 14, 1995 / Rules and Regulations **41969**

If the physicians in the plan are directly employed by the academic center, then their referrals should not be prohibited if the employment meets the standards in section 1877(e)(2) and § 411.357(c). If, alternatively, the physicians or group practice members provide services to the academic center under contract, the personal services provided by these physicians would not be compensation if the arrangement meets the requirements in section 1877(e)(3) and § 411.357(d). In short, we cannot see why a separate exception would be necessary.

Comment: One commenter indicated that, in general, faculty practice plans fall under one of three organizational structures, as explained below:

• A single entity: Many faculty practice plans are organized as a single legal entity that submits a single bill for all physician services across specialties using one common Medicare provider number and, thus, clearly meeting the statutory billing requirement for a group practice.

• Multiple entities by specialty, each billing by its own group provider number: Other faculty practice plans within medical schools and teaching hospitals are organized as multiple legal entities, usually professional corporations established by specialty, that submit multiple bills using a provider number for the respective specialty group.

• Multiple entities by specialty, billing by individual physician provider numbers: Still other faculty practice plans are organized by groups but will submit multiple bills for service by specialty, using individual physician provider numbers.

The commenter recommended, therefore, that the final regulations recognize that a variety of faculty practice plan structures associated with a medical school or teaching hospital exist and should be able to qualify for the in-office ancillary services exception at the level of the umbrella organization. The commenter recommended that we not apply the criteria separately to each legal entity within the same academic setting.

Within an academic setting, according to another commenter, physicians may receive compensation from a variety of entities. They may order their laboratory work from one or more of these entities, such as a teaching hospital, a research laboratory for highly specialized testing, or in-office laboratories within faculty departments. Since there are often indirect financial relationships between and among the various entities within an academic setting, the law appears to prohibit referrals by faculty physicians

between and among these entities. The research laboratory may provide a unique situation because, as the commenter pointed out, it generally performs a highly specialized range of laboratory tests that are not available elsewhere. Therefore, the commenter urged us to craft an exception in the final rule that allows these and similar nonabusive arrangements to continue in the academic setting.

Response: We believe that as long as the faculty practice physicians receive remuneration from the academic institution for their bona fide employment or under personal service arrangements that meet the criteria in sections 1877(e)(2) and (e)(3), the physicians should not be prohibited from making referrals to laboratories that are owned by the academic institution.

7. Special Exception for Group Practices

Comment: We stated in our proposed rule that within the definition of "group practice" substantially all (at least 85 percent) of the patient care services of group practice physicians must be furnished through the group and be billed in the name of the group. Further, amounts received for those services must be treated as receipts of the group. One commenter stated that there are situations in which group practices will be unable to meet the "substantially all" requirements of section 1877(h)(4), or whatever percentage of patient care services is adopted in the final regulations. The commenter offered the example of 15 independently practicing physicians who have primary offices in one part of a city and establish a group practice clinic in a medically underserved area in the same city. Each physician spends 1 day a week at the clinic. In this case, only 20 percent of the services of the physicians in the group would be furnished through the group. This would be insufficient to meet the requirement of proposed § 411.351 that at least 85 percent of the aggregate services furnished by all physician members be furnished through the group practice.

The commenter recommended that an exception be added to the regulations that would allow group practices in medically underserved urban areas to furnish clinical laboratory services without being required to meet the "substantially all" requirement. In this commenter's view, this exception would tend to increase the availability of medical care in those urban areas currently deprived of adequate medical services without creating patient or program abuse.

Response: We note that the Congress has determined that there is a shortage of adequate medical care in locations designated as health professional shortage areas (HPSAs) under section 332(a)(1)(A) of the Public Health Service Act. In order to avoid discouraging group practice physicians from providing services in HPSAs, we are redefining the "substantially all" criteria in the definition of a group practice in § 411.351 in two ways. First, we are excluding from the "substantially all" test group practices that are located only in certain HPSAs. We have defined the term HPSA in reference to the definition of the term under the Public Health Service Act. Section 332(a)(1)(A) of the Public Health Service Act defines the term HPSA to include so-called "geographic HPSAs," that is, "an area in an urban or rural area (which need not conform to the geographic boundaries of a political subdivision and which is a rational area for the delivery of health services) which the Secretary determines has a health manpower shortage and which is not reasonably accessible to an adequately served area."

The Secretary has established criteria for designating areas having shortages of a number of types of health professionals, including primary medical care (which includes general or family practice, general internal medicine, pediatrics and OB/GYN), dental, mental health, vision care, podiatric, and pharmacy professionals. For purposes of this regulation, if an area is a primary care HPSA, any group practice located solely in that HPSA (regardless of whether it provides services of the type classified as primary medical care) will be exempt from the "substantially all" test. Since HPSAs do not exist for a number of specialty areas (for example, oncology, dermatology, neurology), if an area is a primary medical care HPSA, we believe that it is likely that there is a shortage of other types of professionals. Therefore, any group practices that are located solely in such an area and provide services of any type will be exempt from the "substantially all" calculation.

In addition, if an area has been designated an HPSA for one of the other types of professional services, such as vision care, any group practice located solely in the HPSA and providing services that are of the type related to the HPSA designation, such as ophthalmology services, will be exempt from the "substantially all" calculation. On the other hand, if an area is an HPSA for vision care professionals (and for no other type of professional services), group practices providing services

41970   **Federal Register** / Vol. 60, No. 156 / Monday, August 14, 1995 / Rules and Regulations

unrelated to vision care in that area will not be exempt from the "substantially all" calculation. There appears to be no justification to exempt such group practices from the "substantially all" calculation in these cases, since there may not be a shortage for such services.

Our second change to the "substantially all" criteria involves group practices located outside an HPSA, but whose members provide services in an HPSA. These outside group practices must continue to meet the "substantially all" test, even if their members provide services in an HPSA. However, we are excluding from the "substantially all" calculation for those groups outside an HPSA any time spent by group members providing the appropriate services in a particular type of HPSA (as described above), whether that time in the HPSA is spent in a group practice, clinic, or an office setting. We have amended § 411.351 ("Definitions") to reflect these concepts. We have also included a definition of "HPSA" in that section.

8. Ambulatory Surgical Center Exception

Comment: One commenter indicated that the Secretary should provide an exception for laboratory services performed in an ambulatory surgical center (ASC). Specifically, the exception should be provided if—

• Any ownership interest of the physician is in the ASC as a whole; and
• Any compensation relationship of the physician with the ASC does not relate to the provision of clinical laboratory services.

Response: We do not entirely agree with this comment. ASC facility services are services that are furnished by an ASC in connection with a covered surgical procedure and that would otherwise be covered if furnished on an inpatient or outpatient basis in a hospital in connection with that procedure. Medicare regulations at § 416.61 describe the scope of facility services. Generally, clinical laboratory services are not considered to be facility services. That is because, under § 416.61(b), ASC facility services do not include items and services for which payment may be made under other provisions in 42 CFR part 405, such as physicians' services, laboratory services, and x-ray or diagnostic procedures (other than those directly related to performance of the surgical procedure). As a result, there are a limited number of diagnostic laboratory tests that are considered ASC facility services and which are included in the ASC rate. We agree with the commenter that referrals for laboratory tests that are performed in

an ASC and included in the ASC rate should be excepted because there is no incentive to overutilize these services.

On the other hand, some ASC's have onsite laboratories that perform and bill for other laboratory testing furnished to ASC patients. Before enactment of CLIA, these laboratories were certified as "independent laboratories" and billed Medicare directly for their services. These laboratory facilities are now required to be certified under CLIA and continue to bill the Medicare program for the laboratory testing performed on the ASC premises, since general laboratory testing is not considered to be part of the ASC facility rate. We believe that, if the onsite laboratory facility is owned or operated by the ASC, referrals to the laboratory for general laboratory testing by a physician who has a financial relationship with the ASC should be prohibited, unless another statutory exception applies.

9. Home Care and Hospice Exception

Comment: One commenter indicated that home health agencies (HHAs) and hospices receive referrals from physicians to provide an array of services in the home. Currently, HHAs and hospices do not bill the Medicare program separately for laboratory services; instead, they bill for a home visit or the per diem hospice charge. The commenter made the following two recommendations:

• The regulations should clearly state that the prohibition does not apply to referrals to entities that do not bill Medicare separately for laboratory testing.
• Another exception should be developed to specify that the Medicare rules governing physician interest in HHAs would also apply to those entities in relation to laboratory services ordered by physicians. Thus, a physician's interest in a clinical laboratory would be permitted if the interest is less than 5 percent.

Response: As discussed earlier, OBRA '93 expanded the list of services subject to the prohibition to include 10 additional services. Because the list of services subject to the prohibition includes home health services, we do not believe an exception for laboratory services provided by home health agencies is warranted.

We agree with the commenter that referrals for laboratory tests that are performed by a hospice and are included in the per diem hospice charge should be excepted because a per diem amount does not reflect the number of tests performed. As a result, we are providing an exception in § 411.355 for laboratory services that are provided by

a hospice and billed as part of the per diem rate.

We disagree with the commenter's second recommendation. Section 1877 prohibits referrals to an entity by a physician who has a financial relationship with that entity. A financial relationship consists of an ownership or investment interest in the entity, regardless of the extent or degree of that ownership interest. Therefore, if a physician owns 5 percent or 95 percent of an entity, he or she is prohibited from making referrals to that entity, unless some exception applies. We will not grant an extra exception for ownership interests that are less than a particular percentage or that involve HHAs. That is because we do not have any evidence upon which to base a percentage or to ensure that the exception would be free from any risk of program or patient abuse.

10. Rural Laboratory Compensation Arrangements

Section 1877(d)(2) provides that ownership or investment by a physician in a rural provider of clinical laboratory services will not prohibit referrals by the physician to that rural provider.

Comment: One commenter stated that the statutory exception for rural laboratories is of little value since it provides only an exception to the ownership or investment interest test and still leaves the rural laboratory subject to the compensation arrangement test. Thus, the commenter recommended that the final rule contain an exception for compensation arrangements between a rural laboratory and a referring physician.

Response: Because of the OBRA '93 amendments to section 1877, we do not believe the exception recommended by the commenter is necessary. Section 1877 now contains exceptions that we believe will cover many compensation arrangements between physicians and laboratories. In addition to the section 1877(d)(2) ownership exception for rural laboratories, section 1877(e)(2) provides an exception if a laboratory compensates a physician as the result of a bona fide employment relationship, and section 1877(e)(3) provides an exception for remuneration from an entity to a physician under a personal services arrangement between the physician and entity. Finally, there are other additional exceptions relating to various other compensation relationships that a physician might have with a laboratory. For example, under section 1877(e)(8), a physician can purchase clinical laboratory services from a laboratory, or other items and services from a laboratory at fair market

183

value, without triggering the prohibition. These exceptions apply to relationships with all laboratory entities, including those located in rural areas, provided the conditions set forth in the statute and this final regulation are met.

11. Case-by-Case Exemptions

Comment: One commenter indicated that we should institute a process by which a laboratory may request an exemption from the law on an individual basis, based upon a determination by the Secretary that enforcement of the prohibition against the laboratory would not be in the public interest. The commenter suggested that narrow guidelines should be established for the types of laboratories that would be eligible to apply for this exemption. Thus, in the commenter's view, the administrative burden would not be prohibitive. The commenter proposed that, in order to be eligible for review, that any one of the following criteria be met:

• The laboratory is wholly owned by one referring physician or one group practice. This requirement would exclude the physician joint venture type laboratories, which this commenter believed are the entities intended to be regulated by the law.

• Referrals to a laboratory by physicians who have financial relationships with the laboratory do not exceed a specified percentage of the total laboratory volume. The commenter suggested that the referrals be limited to 40 percent of the laboratory's total volume, consistent with the Medicare anti-kickback investment safe harbor volume criterion. (See 42 CFR part 1001.)

• A laboratory located in a town or similar-type population center with a population of 10,000 or under should be eligible for exemption review if it is the sole outpatient provider of certain laboratory services within that locality. This would recognize that localities that are within an MSA may, in fact, be small towns lacking adequate outpatient laboratory services.

Response: We do not agree that we should implement such a process. Section 1877(b)(4) specifies that, in addition to the exceptions described in the statute, the section 1877(a)(1) prohibition will not apply with respect to any other financial relationship which the Secretary determines, *and specifies* in *regulations*, does not pose a risk of program or patient abuse (emphasis added). The statute speaks in terms of excepting particular financial relationships according to rules that would apply to any person or entity that

has such a relationship. It does not authorize "case by case" exceptions.

In addition, we do not believe that the guidelines suggested by the commenter to single out those who are eligible for case-by-case review would provide a guarantee against patient or program abuse. It is not clear to us why the review should only be available when a laboratory is wholly owned by one referring physician or one group practice. The commenter's second guideline would allow a laboratory entity to derive 40 percent of its business from referrals by physicians with whom the entity has a financial relationship. We do not believe that this standard would, in any way, satisfy the requirement under section 1877(b)(4) that exceptions beyond those specified in the law pose no risk of program or patient abuse. We simply do not see how a standard excusing any percentage of referrals would guarantee no risk of abuse.

Finally, we understand that it might be possible that a laboratory located within an MSA could have its existence threatened if it cannot accept referrals from physicians with whom it has financial relationships. The commenter did not, however, identify any specific localities, so we cannot tell how likely it is for this to occur. In any case, any such exception must be shown to comply with the "no abuse" criterion, and the commenter has provided us with no evidence that such an exception would be free of abuse. For these reasons, we are not adopting this suggestion.

12. Physician Ownership of Public Companies

Section 411.357(a)(2) of the proposed regulation provided an exception for a physician's or family member's ownership in a publicly owned corporation, provided that the ownership interest met certain requirements. Among these were the requirement that the corporation have, at the end of its most recent fiscal year, total assets exceeding $100 million. This requirement reflected section 1877(c)(2) of the statute. OBRA '93 amended the statute to require, instead, stockholder equity exceeding $75 million at the end of the corporation's most recent fiscal year or on average during the previous 3 fiscal years. SSA '94 made this amendment effective retroactive to January 1, 1992. However, it also provided that, until January 1, 1995, a corporation could still meet the requirement in the exception if it qualified under the pre-OBRA '93 standard.

Comment: One commenter suggested that we create an exception allowing physicians to own shares in clinical laboratories that satisfy the first test of the statutory public-company exception (having publicly-traded securities on the specified national securities exchanges) whether or not the company has $100 million in assets (as required in proposed § 411.357(a)(2)), under certain conditions.

The conditions suggested were that: (1) The total physician ownership of each class of securities of the entity is less than 20 percent, and (2) no one physician's ownership of any class of securities of the entity represents more than 5 percent of the class. The commenter believed that such ownership would not pose a risk of abuse under Medicare. For example, the stock of Laboratory Corporation A, which has assets of $50 million, is owned by the following individuals. Laboratory Corporation A has only one class of stock.

Individual	Percentage
Dr. Abe	5
Mr. Brown	17
Dr. Car	5
Mr. Dorr	17
Dr. Else	5
Mr. Frank	17
Mr. Green	12
Mr. Hann	12
	100

In this example, no one physician owns more than 5 percent of the stock of Laboratory Corporation A and the total physician ownership is 15 percent. The commenter stated that these facts should allow the owner-physicians to refer to Laboratory Corporation A because, in the commenter's view, since the majority of stockholders are nonphysicians, the physicians have no incentive to overutilize laboratory testing to increase the value of their investments. The commenter concluded, therefore, that there would not be the risk of patient or program abuse.

Another commenter suggested that we create an exception for public companies similar to that of the safe harbor for investment interest under the anti-kickback statute. Generally, the commenter suggested that the exception should follow all of the requirements found in 42 CFR 1001.952(a), "Investment interests safe harbor."

Response: The second comment is related to the first, in that one of the requirements found in § 1001.952(a)

41972   **Federal Register** / Vol. 60, No. 156 / Monday, August 14, 1995 / Rules and Regulations

also establishes a percentage limit on the amount of the investment. That is, § 1001.952(a)(2)(i) specifies that, in order to qualify for the safe harbor exception, "[n]o more than 40 percent of the value of the investment interests of each class of investments may be held * * * by investors who are in a position to make or influence referrals to, furnish items or services to, or otherwise generate business for the entity."

While each commenter has made a good suggestion, we do not have any data supporting the first commenter's assumption that a limit of 5 percent ownership of a class of securities by individual physicians and a limit of up to 20 percent ownership of a class of securities by all physicians poses no risk of abuse. We believe that the Congress was very deliberate in establishing the requirements for the exception based on ownership or investment in publicly traded securities that is found in section 1877(c). Further, as pointed out in an earlier response, in order to establish additional exceptions, we must determine that the financial relationship does not pose a risk of program or patient abuse. To adopt the suggested approaches, we would, for example, be required to justify why a total of 20 percent physician ownership in a company would be abusive while a total of less than 20 percent physician ownership in a company would not be abusive. We do not have data to justify such a distinction.

13. Compensation Exception

Comment: One commenter proposed that an additional exception to the prohibition on referrals be added to address certain compensation arrangements between clinical laboratories and physicians. This commenter stated that, under a typical contractual arrangement between a clinical laboratory and a physician, the physician pays a reasonable fee to a laboratory to provide a service in an area in which the physician or his or her office personnel lack expertise. Some examples would be assisting the physician to establish a billing service, providing management services, and hosting educational seminars. The commenter suggested that this exception could contain the following elements:

• The agreement must be in writing and be signed by all of the parties.

• The agreement must be for identifiable services, which must be clearly set forth in the agreement.

• Compensation must be consistent with fair market value for these services.

• The compensation must be considered commercially reasonable even if no referrals were made.

• The amount of compensation for the services must not vary based on the volume or value of any referrals of business by the physician.

• The services must be offered by the clinical laboratory to all physicians.

• There must be no requirement on the part of the physician to refer patients.

As described, this situation involves a payment by the physician to the laboratory under the terms of a contract.

Response: We agree that physicians incur a legitimate cost when they must provide certain services, such as continuing medical education for themselves and their staff members. In addition, the physicians should be able to determine where they can best get these services. The commenter has asked that we add a new exception to the prohibition on referrals to address certain compensation arrangements in which a physician pays a reasonable fee to a laboratory to provide a service in an area in which the physician or his or her office personnel lack expertise. We believe that an additional exception under the authority of section 1877(b)(4) is not necessary. Section 1877(e)(8), as added by OBRA '93, provides an exception for payments made by a physician to any entity as compensation for items and services (other than clinical laboratory services) if the items or services are priced at fair market value. This provision is effective retroactively to January 1, 1992, and is included at § 411.357(i) of this rule.

Comment: A few commenters noted that a laboratory encounters a problem, for the following reasons, if it has an employee who is related to a physician who refers work to the laboratory. The referral prohibition is triggered not only by physicians who themselves have financial relationships with a laboratory entity but also by a physician's immediate relatives who have financial relationships. As a result, the laboratory's payment to an employee can constitute a compensation arrangement and, under the proposed rule, the laboratory would not be permitted to accept referrals from that physician. The commenters suggested that, as long as the employer has a bona fide employment relationship with the employee, there is no reason to question these employment arrangements. The commenters suggested that, with an added exception, the laboratory would be able to avoid the burdensome process of polling its employees to determine if they have a relative who is a referring physician.

Response: Section 1877(e)(2), as amended by OBRA '93, establishes a new exception for bona fide employment situations between an entity and a physician or an immediate family member of a physician. The conditions for the exception are as follows:

• The employment arrangement is for identifiable services.

• The amount of the remuneration under the employment—

+ Is consistent with the fair market value of the services, and

+ Is not determined in a manner that takes into account (directly or indirectly) the volume or value of any referrals by the referring physician.

• The remuneration is provided under an agreement that would be commercially reasonable even if no referrals were made to the employer.

+ The employment meets such other requirements as the Secretary may impose by regulations as needed to protect against program or patient abuse.

Finally, the employees may be paid a productivity bonus based on services they personally performed.

V. Analysis of and Responses to Public Comments on the Interim Final Rule With Comment Period—Reporting Requirements for Financial Relationships Between Physicians and Health Care Entities That Furnish Selected Items and Services

Section 152(a) of SSA '94 amended the reporting requirements in section 1877(f) of the Act. As amended, section 1877(f) specifically applies to not only physicians with an ownership or investment interest in an entity, but to physicians who have a compensation arrangement with an entity as well. SSA '94 also eliminated the Secretary's authority to waive the reporting requirements for certain States or services, although the Secretary continues to have the right to determine that an entity is not subject to the reporting requirements because it provides services covered under Medicare very infrequently. In addition, the reporting requirements continue to not apply to designated health services furnished outside of the United States.

The SSA '94 amendments apply to referrals made on or after January 1, 1995. However, section 1877(f) does not apply to referrals at all, but instead requires providers of Medicare covered items and services to report certain information about their financial relationships with physicians at such times as the Secretary specifies. As such, section 152(d), the effective date provision for the SSA '94 amendments, is silent on when the amendments would apply to a provision that has no nexus with referrals. If section 152 is silent on this issue, we believe that the effective date is the date of enactment of the amendments, which is October 31, 1994. We have incorporated the amendments to section 1877(f) into § 411.361, to apply to any future reporting that we require.

Below we summarize and respond to comments we received in response to the interim final rule with comment period that was published in the **Federal Register** on December 3, 1991 (56 FR 61374). We received timely comments from five organizations.

Near the end of calendar year 1991, we developed a questionnaire titled "Survey of Financial Relationships Between Physicians and Selected Health Care Entities" (form HCFA–95) and forwarded it to selected hospitals, ESRD facilities, suppliers of ambulance services, entities furnishing diagnostic imaging (including magnetic resonance imaging, computerized axial tomography scans, ultrasound, and other diagnostic imaging services), parenteral and enteral suppliers, and entities furnishing physical therapy services. (This survey was also known as the "Ten State Survey.") This process was a collection of information concerning the financial interest arrangements of any entity that furnishes selected items and services for which payment may be made under Medicare. The survey was to be completed by all entities furnishing the above listed covered items and services to Medicare beneficiaries. The scope of the survey was limited to entities in the following 10 States: Connecticut, Pennsylvania, West Virginia, South Carolina, Florida, Michigan, Ohio, Texas, Arkansas, and California.

Surveys were sent to those entities that submitted claims to the Medicare intermediary or carrier for more than 20 items or services in any of the selected categories during calendar year 1990. Originally, an entity was required to return the survey not more than 30 days after the entity received it. Shortly after December 3, 1991, the date contractors were instructed to send the surveys via overnight, certified mail, the response time was extended from 30 days from the date of receipt to 60 days from the date of receipt.

Two commenters applauded our citing the need for the survey because of the potential for abusive behavior in situations where the referring physician has an ownership interest in the facility to which he or she refers patients. A discussion of other comments and our responses to them follow.

Comment: One commenter suggested that requiring the completed survey to be submitted before or at the same time that the comments on the interim final rule were due made the opportunity to comment meaningless.

Response: We agree that the timing of the deadlines for the completed survey and the comments on the interim final rule could be regarded as having had the effect of reducing a commenter's ability to have an impact on that particular survey. As we pointed out in the preamble to the interim final rule, however, section 4207(k) of OBRA '90 authorized the Secretary to issue interim final regulations for the amendments to the Medicare statute. In the preamble, we explained the pressing need for the interim final rule in order for us to fulfill several legislative requirements within their prescribed deadlines. These included carrying out the survey requirements of section 1877(f), as amended by OBRA '90, obtaining adequate information from health care entities in time to apply the payment provisions in section 1877, as amended by OBRA '90, and preparing the statistical profile required by OBRA '89, as amended by OBRA '90.

The purpose of the interim final rule was primarily to notify the public of the decisions the Secretary had made on the few items of discretion left to the Secretary under OBRA '90, such as the selection of the States in which the survey would be administered (the legislation prescribed a minimum of 10 States). In addition, we do not regard the opportunity that was provided to comment on the interim final rule as meaningless. Section 1877 allows the Secretary to collect the survey information in such form, manner, and at such times as she specifies, as long as it is first collected no later than October 1, 1991. The Secretary will take the comments into account if she decides to survey the entities again.

Comment: One commenter suggested that we extend the time for responding to the survey by 60 days and announce the extension publicly.

Response: As noted, we did provide for an automatic extension of 30 days, allowing a total of 60 days for response. We provided 19 representative specialty societies, for example, the American Medical Association, the American Hospital Association, and the American College of Radiology, with this information to alert their members. In addition, we alerted Medicare contractors who, in turn, alerted providers via updates in their routinely distributed bulletins and newsletters.

Comment: One medical specialty association had received several

complaints from its members concerning the question of who must report the ownership interest and what information must be reported. The association stated that the definition of "entity" (physicians, suppliers, or providers) in the instructions was too broad.

Response: The statute at section 1877(f) required, prior to SSA '94, that "*[e]ach* entity providing covered items or services for which payment may be made under [Medicare] shall provide the Secretary with the information concerning the entity's ownership arrangements, * * *." (Emphasis added.) The statute does not define an "entity." Thus, we could include within this concept any individuals or groups that provided Medicare covered items or services. We surveyed every entity, regardless of type, that provided more than 20 services in 1990 from the minimum set of services (hospital services, ambulance services, etc.) covered by the statutory requirement for this study. The use of the terms "physicians, suppliers, or providers" in our survey instructions was meant to cover all types of entities that had provided more than 20 services during 1990 of the types listed in the legislation.

Comment: One commenter wrote that there was no question on the survey that distinguished between those physicians who have an ownership interest in a facility and those who do not, like hospital-based radiologists. The commenter recommended that information relative to hospital-based practices be extracted and excluded from the study as it could produce a flawed database.

Response: We are not certain of the point this commenter wanted to make. Our survey form clearly distinguished between physicians with an ownership interest in an entity and physicians compensated by an entity, such as hospital-based radiologists. After receiving these survey forms, we matched data from the forms to Medicare claims data to determine referral patterns to entities that had submitted these survey forms. Since we also had information for each entity billing the program relating to whether the patient was referred to the entity by a physician with an ownership interest or by a physician compensated by the entity, the study was able to determine the referral patterns to that entity in a totally objective manner.

Comment: Two commenters wrote that the regulations would result in unreasonably burdensome reporting obligations for certain health care entities. The commenters believed that

41974   Federal Register / Vol. 60, No. 156 / Monday, August 14, 1995 / Rules and Regulations

the collection of useless information will thwart, rather than support, legitimate monitoring efforts. Examples of information that the commenters believed was unnecessary was identifying *all* physicians in a teaching hospital, considering the size of the facility, the number of salaried staff and faculty, and the time and effort required to collect, organize, check, and report the required data.

Response: The scope of the data collection activity was expansive in order to ensure that the Congress had sufficient information on utilization rates by physician owned and non-owned entities to consider in its legislative activities. While this may have appeared to be more data than could be effectively used, we believed a more narrow data collection effort would have resulted in the Congress having insufficient facts when considering legislative alternatives. Surveyed entities were expected to make good faith efforts to complete the surveys accurately, completely, and timely. In addition, we granted extensions to the 60-day response period on a case-by-case basis.

Comment: One commenter opposed the requirement that hospitals report compensation/remuneration arrangements, because the requirement exceeds the scope of section 1877(f) of the Act.

Response: Prior to SSA '94, section 1877(f) did not specifically provide us with the authority to require that hospitals report compensation/remuneration arrangements. Section 1877(f) required that entities report only the ownership or investment interests of physicians. As we pointed out in the preamble to the interim final rule, however, we believed that other parts of section 1877, the payment provisions of the Medicare statute, and section 6204(f) of OBRA '89, as amended by OBRA '90, implicitly required us to collect this information.

As we pointed out at 56 FR 61376, we need the information on compensation/remuneration arrangements in order to enforce the general prohibition, in section 1877, against physicians referring to laboratories with which they have a financial relationship, including a relationship based on a compensation arrangement. Without the reporting requirement, we would not have sufficient information to make payment determinations. Also, we would not have had the data we needed to prepare the statistical profile required by section 6204(f) of OBRA '89, as amended by section 4207(e)(4) of OBRA '90. This provision required us to produce a profile that covered all of a physician's

direct or indirect financial interests. As we explained earlier, beginning October 31, 1994, § 152(a) of SSA '94 amended § 1877(f) to explicitly require that a reporting entity provide information concerning the entity's ownership, investment, and compensation arrangements.

Comment: One commenter suggested that the imposition of civil monetary penalties on reporting entities that fail to report compensation/remuneration arrangements in a timely manner exceeds our statutory authority.

Response: Section 1877(g)(5) provides a civil money penalty when a person fails to meet the reporting requirements of section 1877(f). Section 1877(f), prior to OBRA '93, concerned information related to ownership interests only. However, as the result of the changes made in § 1877(f) by § 152(a) of SSA '94, entities are now required to provide information about ownership, investment, and compensation arrangements. As a result, we now have the authority to impose a civil money penalty when an entity fails to provide any of these kinds of information.

Comment: One commenter from California suggested that reporting employee information would place a hospital in jeopardy of violating certain State laws and State regulations.

Response: As we stated in an earlier comment, we have interpreted section 1877, the payment provisions of the Medicare statute, and section 6204(f) of OBRA '89 as requiring that reporting entities provide us with information about all of their financial relationships with a physician or a physician's family member. The statute at § 1877(f) now requires this information for all ownership, investment, and compensation arrangements. If this explicit Federal requirement conflicts with State law or State regulations, the Federal law and Federal regulations prevail.

VI. Provisions of This Final Rule

We have extensively rearranged the regulations from what we proposed and have added numerous OBRA '93 provisions as amended by SSA '94. Because of these many changes, we are including, in section VI.C., a list identifying whether the requirements in this final rule derive from OBRA '93, SSA '94, the proposed rule, or comments on the proposed rule. In addition, we identify below the changes from the December 1991 interim final rule and the March 1992 proposed rule.

A. Proposed Rule—Physician Ownership of, and Referrals to, Health Care Entities That Furnish Clinical Laboratory Services

Based on our analysis of the comments, we are adopting the provisions as set forth in the March 1992 proposed rule, with the following changes. The reason for a change either has been discussed in section IV of this preamble, the change is a result of the provisions of OBRA '93 or SSA '94, or the change merely conforms the regulations to the statute.

• In § 411.1 ("Basis and scope"), we added that section 1877 of the Act sets forth limitations on referrals and payment for clinical laboratory services furnished by entities with which an immediate family member of the referring physician has a financial relationship. This change was made to conform the regulation to the statute.

• As a result of the comments we received, we revised the definition of "compensation arrangement" at § 411.351 ("Definitions") to clarify that it applies to direct and indirect arrangements.

• We revised the definition of "group practice" at § 411.351 as follows:

+ Revised the "substantially all" threshold to 75 percent of the total patient care services of group practice members, measured as "patient care time."

+ Expanded and moved, to a new § 411.360, the requirements related to the group practice attestation statement.

+ Provided an exception to the "substantially all" requirement for those services furnished through a group practice located solely in certain areas designated as HPSAs under § 411.351. Also specified in this section that when members of a group practice that is located outside an HPSA spend time providing services in certain HPSAs, that time is not used to calculate the outside group's "substantially all" standard.

• We removed the definitions of "interested investor" and "investor" from § 411.351.

• We revised the definition of "remuneration" at § 411.351 to provide that forgiveness of debts, certain payments, and the furnishing of certain items, devices, and supplies are not considered remuneration if they meet specified conditions.

• We added a definition of "clinical laboratory services," "direct supervision," "hospital," "HPSA," "laboratory," "members of the group," "patient care services," "physician incentive plan," "plan of care," and "transaction" to § 411.351.

Federal Register / Vol. 60, No. 156 / Monday, August 14, 1995 / Rules and Regulations **41975**

• We revised § 411.355 ("General exceptions to referral prohibitions related to both ownership/investment and compensation") to do the following:

+ For purposes of the in-office ancillary services exception in § 411.355(b), require that individuals furnishing services be "directly" supervised by the referring physician or by another physician in the same group practice. (The proposed rule had required that services be provided by an employee who was "personally" supervised by these physicians.)

+ Include among the locations where the service may be furnished a building that is used by the group practice for the provision of some or all of the group's clinical laboratory services. (The proposed rule had required that the building be used by the group practice for centrally furnishing the group's clinical laboratory services.)

• We added the following services to the general exceptions listed under § 411.355 ("General exceptions to referral prohibitions related to both ownership/investment and compensation"):

+ Services furnished by a qualified HMO (within the meaning of section 1310(d) of the Public Health Service Act) to individuals enrolled in the organization (new § 411.355(c)(4)).

+ Services furnished in an ASC or ESRD facility or by a hospice and included in the ASC rate, ESRD composite rate, or per diem hospice charge, respectively (new § 411.355(d)).

• We revised proposed § 411.357, now designated as § 411.356, ("Exceptions to referral prohibitions related to ownership or investment interests") to—

+ Revise the requirements relating to publicly-traded securities, as specified in section 1877(c) of the Act (as amended by OBRA '93 and SSA '94), to include securities which "may be purchased" on terms generally available to the public, which can be those traded on additional stock markets, and which can be in corporations that had the following:

—Until January 1, 1995, total assets at the end of the corporation's most recent fiscal year exceeding $100 million, or

—Stockholder equity exceeding $75 million at the end of the corporation's

most recent fiscal year, or on average during the previous 3 fiscal years

+ No longer specify, with regard to the corporation's assets, that these assets must have been obtained in the normal course of business and not for the primary purpose of qualifying for the exception;

+ Expand the exception to include mutual funds that constitute ownership in shares in certain regulated investment companies, if the companies had, at the end of their most recent fiscal year, or on average during the previous 3 fiscal years, total assets exceeding $75 million.

+ Until January 1, 1995, retained the exception for a hospital located outside of Puerto Rico based on the condition that the referring physician's ownership or investment interest does not relate to the furnishing of clinical laboratory services.

+ Revise the requirements relating to rural providers, as specified in the proposed rule, to delete paragraph (ii), which added the requirement that the majority of tests referred to the rural laboratory are referred by physicians who have office practices located in a rural area.

+ Revise the requirements relating to rural providers, as specified in the proposed rule, to include the requirement that substantially all of the tests furnished by the entity are furnished to individuals residing in a rural area.

• We revised proposed § 411.359, now designated as § 411.357, ("Exceptions to referral prohibitions related to compensation arrangements") to do the following:.

+ Revise (a)(1) to reflect new requirements specified by OBRA '93 for the rental of space.

+ Remove proposed paragraph (a)(2), which contained requirements related to a physician who has an ownership or investment interest in a laboratory and who also rents or leases space to the laboratory.

+ Add an exception for rental of equipment under certain conditions (new § 411.357(b)).

+ Add an exception for certain group practice arrangements with a hospital (new § 411.357(h).

+ Add an exception for payments by a physician to a laboratory or other

entity in exchange for certain items and services (new § 411.357(i)).

+ Replace proposed § 411.359(b) ("Employment and service arrangements with hospitals") and proposed § 411.359(f) ("Salaried physicians in a group practice") with a new § 411.357(c) ("Bona fide employment relationships"). New § 411.357(c) is based on the exception at section 1877(e)(2) of the Act.

+ Replace proposed § 411.359(e) ("Service arrangements with non-hospital entities") with a new § 411.357(d) ("Personal service arrangements"). New § 411.357(d) is based on the exception at section 1877(e)(3) of the Act.

• We added a new § 411.360 that requires that a group practice submit annually a statement attesting that it met the "substantially all" test set forth, under the definition of "group practice," in § 411.351 of this rule. This section also specifies how a newly-formed group practice meets the "substantially all" criterion.

In addition to the above changes, we have made technical changes. For example, in proposed § 411.355(c)(1), we cross-referenced part 417, subpart C. Subpart C has been redesignated by a new rule. The applicable provisions being cross-referenced are now under subparts J through M. We have also made editorial changes that do not affect the substance of the provisions.

B. Interim Final Rule With Comment Period—Reporting Requirements for Financial Relationships Between Physicians and Health Care Entities That Furnish Selected Items and Services.

The interim final rule with comment published on December 3, 1991, is revised to incorporate the amendments to section 1877(f) made by SSA '94, to apply to any future reporting that we require. However, providers will not be held to the reporting requirements under section 1877(f) until we develop and issue the proper form and accompanying instructions booklet. Until that time, we will use audits and investigations as the primary tools to evaluate compliance with these provisions.

C. Source of Final Regulations.

Final regulations	Source
§ 411.1 Basis and scope	Proposed § 411.1.
§ 411.350 Scope of subpart	Proposed § 411.350, SSA '94.
§ 411.351 Definitions	§ 411.351.
Clinical laboratory services	Comments.
Compensation arrangement	Proposed § 411.352 and comments.
Direct supervision	Comments and OBRA '93.

41976   **Federal Register** / Vol. 60, No. 156 / Monday, August 14, 1995 / Rules and Regulations

Final regulations	Source
Employee	Proposed § 411.351.
Entity	Proposed § 411.351.
Fair market value	Proposed § 411.351.
Financial relationship	Proposed § 411.351.
Group practice	Proposed § 411.351, OBRA '93, and Comments.
HPSA	Comments.
Immediate family member	Proposed § 411.351.
Laboratory	Comments.
Members of a group	Comments.
Patient care services	Comments.
Physician incentive plan	OBRA '93.
Plan of care	Comments.
Referral	Proposed § 411.351 and Comments.
Referring physician	Proposed § 411.351.
Remuneration	Proposed § 411.351 and OBRA '93.
Transaction	Comments.
§ 411.353 Prohibition on certain referrals by physicians and limitations on billing.	Proposed § 411.353.
(a) Prohibition on referrals	Proposed § 411.353(a).
(b) Limitations on billing	Proposed § 411.353(b).
(c) Denial of Payment	Proposed § 411.353(c).
(d) Refunds	Proposed § 411.353(d).
§ 411.355 General exceptions to referral prohibitions related to ownership and compensation ...	Proposed § 411.355.
(a) Physicians' services	Proposed § 411.355(a).
(b) In-office ancillary services	Proposed § 411.355(b) and services OBRA '93.
(c) Services furnished to prepaid health plan enrollees	Proposed § 411.355(c).
(c)(1) HMO or CMP under section 1876	Proposed § 411.355(c)(1).
(c)(2) Prepaid plan under section 1833(a)(1)(A)	Proposed § 411.355(c)(2).
(c)(3) An organization receiving payments through a demonstration project	Proposed § 411.355(c)(3).
(c)(4) A qualified HMO within the meaning of section 1310(d) of the Public Health Service Act.	OBRA '93.
(d) Services furnished in an ASC or ESRD facility	Comments.
§ 411.356 Exceptions to referral prohibitions related to ownership or investment interests	Proposed § 411.357.
(a) Publicly-traded securities	Proposed § 411.357(a) and OBRA '93.
(b) Mutual funds	OBRA '93.
(c) Specific providers	Proposed § 411.357(b).
(c)(1) Rural laboratories	Proposed § 411.357(b)(1) and Comments.
(c)(2) Hospitals in Puerto Rico	Proposed § 411.357(b)(2).
(c)(3) Hospitals outside of Puerto Rico	Proposed § 411.357(b)(3), OBRA '93, SSA '94.
§ 411.357 Exceptions to referral prohibitions related to compensation arrangements	Proposed § 411.359.
(a) Rental of office space	OBRA '93.
(b) Rental of equipment	OBRA '93.
(c) Bona fide employment	OBRA '93.
(d) Personal service arrangements	
(d)(1) General	OBRA '93.
(d)(2) Physician incentive plan exception	OBRA '93.
(e) Physician recruitment	Proposed § 411.359(c).
(f) Isolated transactions	Proposed § 411.359(d), Comments, OBRA '93.
(g) Arrangements with hospitals	OBRA '93.
(h) Group practice arrangements with a hospital	OBRA '93.
(i) Payments by a physician	OBRA '93.
§ 411.360 Group practice attestation	Comments.
§ 411.361 Reporting requirements	Existing § 411.361 and SSA '94.

VII. Collection of Information Requirements

Regulations at § 411.360 contain information collection or recordkeeping requirements or both that are subject to review by the Office of Management and Budget under the Paperwork Reduction Act of 1980 (44 U.S.C. 3501 et seq.). The information collection requirements concern those group practices attempting to meet the definition found in section 1877(h)(4) and require them to attest that, in the aggregate, at least 75 percent of the total patient care services furnished by all physician members are furnished through the group and are billed under a billing number assigned to the group. Public reporting burden for this collection of information is estimated to be 1 hour per response. A document will be published in the **Federal Register** after approval is obtained. Organizations and individuals desiring to submit comments on the information collection and recordkeeping requirements should direct them to the OMB official whose name appears in the **ADDRESSES** section of this preamble.

VIII. Regulatory Impact Statement

A. Introduction

The provisions of this final rule with comment period implement section 6204 of OBRA '89 and section 4207(e) of OBRA '90, which concern a limitation on certain physician referrals. In addition, the rule contains revisions to our March 1992 proposal, based on comments submitted by the public. This final rule also incorporates the new expansions and exceptions created by OBRA '93, as amended by SSA '94, that are related to referrals for clinical laboratory services and have a retroactive effective date of January 1, 1992. This final rule with comment, by prohibiting physician referrals for clinical laboratory services by physicians who have certain ownership, investment, or compensation arrangements with the entity furnishing the service, is meant to eliminate the ordering of unnecessary laboratory tests.

According to the OIG report cited in the March 1992 proposed rule (57 FR 8589), at least 25 percent of the nearly 4500 independent clinical laboratories, at the time of the report, were owned in whole or in part by referring physicians. The same OIG report revealed that Medicare patients of referring physicians who own or invest in these laboratories received 45 percent more clinical laboratory services than all Medicare patients. The OIG estimated in its report that the "increased utilization of clinical laboratory services by patients of physician-owners cost the Medicare program $28 million nationally in 1987." (Financial Arrangements Between Physicians and Health Care Businesses, (May 1989))

We believe the majority of physicians and clinical laboratories do not currently make referrals that are prohibited by this rule. In addition, we believe that, in response to the statutory provisions, many physicians and laboratories took necessary steps, before January 1, 1992, to ensure that their investment and employment activities did not restrict their ability to make referrals. Therefore, any estimate of the aggregate economic impact of this rule will be purely speculative. We believe the statute itself will have a continuing deterrent effect on physicians' aberrant referral patterns and investment interests.

B. Regulatory Flexibility Act

Consistent with the Regulatory Flexibility Act (RFA) (5 U.S.C. 601 through 612), we prepare a regulatory flexibility analysis unless the Secretary certifies that a rule will not have a significant economic impact on a substantial number of small entities. For purposes of the RFA, we consider all hospitals, physicians, and clinical laboratories to be small entities.

In addition, section 1102(b) requires the Secretary to prepare a regulatory impact analysis if a rule may have a significant impact on the operations of a substantial number of small rural hospitals. This analysis must conform to the provisions of section 604 of the RFA. For purposes of section 1102(b), we define a small rural hospital as a hospital that is located outside of a Metropolitan Statistical Area and has fewer than 50 beds.

We expect that a few entities may be affected to varying degrees by this final rule. Relative to the potential impact on these entities, the following discussion is provided.

1. Impact on Physicians and Physician Groups

Physicians reportedly find it inefficient and inconvenient to split their laboratory referral business among multiple laboratories; the physician who uses one laboratory for private-pay patients is likely to use that same laboratory for all of his or her patients. Therefore, it is conceivable that, absent this rule, a physician could seek an ownership or investment interest in a laboratory, or a compensation arrangement with a laboratory, in order for the physician to share in the profits of the laboratory to which he or she makes referrals. In these cases, the prohibition on referrals might apply, which will require the physician to either dispose of his or her interest in the laboratory or stop referring Medicare patients to that laboratory.

As discussed at length earlier in this preamble, some physicians who have independent practices maintain a physician office laboratory with other physicians in shared premises, with shared equipment, shared employees, a shared administrator who has the power to hire and terminate employees on behalf of the physicians, and shared overhead costs. For the most part, these shared office space arrangements are not eligible for the in-office ancillary exception found in section 1877(b)(2) and, therefore, the prohibition on referrals does apply. Thus, the physicians must each separately meet the in-office ancillary services requirements, form a group practice meeting the definition of section 1877(h)(4) of the Act, dispose of their interest in the shared laboratory facility, or stop referring Medicare patients to that laboratory facility.

Also as discussed earlier, in response to OBRA '93 changes, we have added exceptions to the prohibition on referrals that we believe recognize existing medical practice, are reasonable, and will not result in program abuse.

As a result of public comments we received in response to the proposed rule, we are revising the definition of "group practice" (§ 411.351) by lowering the "substantially all" threshold from 85 percent to 75 percent of the total patient care services of group practice members. This change will allow groups of physicians additional flexibility in hiring part-time and temporary physicians, without the

group jeopardizing its standing as a group practice.

2. Impact on Laboratories

As mentioned earlier in this impact statement, the report from the OIG to the Congress indicated that at least 25 percent of the nearly 4500 independent clinical laboratories were owned in whole or in part by referring physicians. The same report found that Medicare "patients of referring physicians who own or invest in these laboratories received 45 percent more clinical laboratory services than all Medicare patients * * *." Other studies found equivalent correlations involving physician self-referrals. However, we are unable to estimate with any degree of accuracy how existing physician laboratory owners will react to the provisions of the law and this rule or how the utilization of laboratory services will change. Nevertheless, given the extensive reach of section 1877 of the Act and these final regulations and the substantial penalties that are provided for violations of the prohibition on referrals, we believe that laboratories and physicians have been restructuring their relationships to ensure compliance with the statute and will continue to do so.

3. Impact on Hospitals

Sections 411.356 (b)(2) and (b)(3) include exceptions related to the prohibition on referrals for ownership or investment interests in certain hospitals. Sections 411.357 (c), (d), (e), (g), and (h) include exceptions related to the prohibition on referrals for compensation for services performed or supervised by physicians. Because we believe that a large number of the financial relationships between physicians and hospitals are covered by these exceptions, we do not believe hospitals will be significantly affected by this rule. In addition, hospitals in Puerto Rico and many hospitals in rural areas are excluded from this rule under § 411.356(c).

For the reasons stated above, we have determined, and the Secretary certifies, that this final rule with comment will not result in a significant economic impact on a substantial number of small entities or on the operations of a substantial number of small rural hospitals. We are, therefore, not preparing analyses for either the RFA or section 1102(b) of the Act.

In accordance with the provisions of E.O. 12866, this regulation was reviewed by the Office of Management and Budget.

41978 Federal Register / Vol. 60, No. 156 / Monday, August 14, 1995 / Rules and Regulations

List of Subjects in 42 CFR Part 411

Kidney diseases, Medicare, Physician referral, Reporting and recordkeeping requirements.

42 CFR part 411 is amended as set forth below:

PART 411—EXCLUSIONS FROM MEDICARE AND LIMITATIONS ON MEDICARE PAYMENT

1. The authority citation for part 411 is revised to read as follows:

Authority: Secs. 1102, 1834, 1842(l), 1861, 1862, 1871, 1877, and 1879 of the Social Security Act (42 U.S.C. 1302, 1395m, 1395u(l), 1395x, 1395y, 1395hh, 1395nn, and 1395pp).

2. In § 411.1, paragraph (a) is revised to read as follows:

§ 411.1 Basis and scope.

(a) *Statutory basis.* Sections 1814(c), 1835(d), and 1862 of the Act exclude from Medicare payment certain specified services. The Act provides special rules for payment of services furnished by Federal providers or agencies (sections 1814(c) and 1835(d)), by hospitals and physicians outside the United States (sections 1814(f) and 1862(a)(4)), and by hospitals and SNFs of the Indian Health Service (section 1880). Section 1877 sets forth limitations on referrals and payment for clinical laboratory services furnished by entities with which the referring physician (or an immediate family member of the referring physician) has a financial relationship.

*   *   *   *   *

3. Section 411.350 is revised to read as follows:

§ 411.350 Scope of subpart.

(a) This subpart implements section 1877 of the Act, which generally prohibits a physician from making a referral under Medicare for clinical laboratory services to an entity with which the physician or a member of the physician's immediate family has a financial relationship.

(b) This subpart does not provide for exceptions or immunity from civil or criminal prosecution or other sanctions applicable under any State laws or under Federal law other than section 1877 of the Act. For example, although a particular arrangement involving a physician's financial relationship with an entity may not prohibit the physician from making referrals to the entity under this subpart, the arrangement may nevertheless violate another provision of the Act or other laws administered by HHS, the Federal Trade Commission, the Securities and Exchange Commission, the Internal Revenue

Service, or any other Federal or State agency.

(c) This subpart requires, with some exceptions, that certain entities furnishing covered items or services under Part A or Part B report information concerning their ownership, investment, or compensation arrangements in the form, manner, and at the times specified by HCFA.

4. New §§ 411.351, 411.353, 411.355 through 411.357, and 411.360 are added to read as follows:

§ 411.351 Definitions.

As used in this subpart, unless the context indicates otherwise:

Clinical laboratory services means the biological, microbiological, serological, chemical, immunohematological, hematological, biophysical, cytological, pathological, or other examination of materials derived from the human body for the purpose of providing information for the diagnosis, prevention, or treatment of any disease or impairment of, or the assessment of the health of, human beings. These examinations also include procedures to determine, measure, or otherwise describe the presence or absence of various substances or organisms in the body.

Compensation arrangement means any arrangement involving any remuneration, direct or indirect, between a physician (or a member of a physician's immediate family) and an entity.

Direct supervision means supervision by a physician who is present in the office suite and immediately available to provide assistance and direction throughout the time services are being performed.

Employee means any individual who, under the usual common law rules that apply in determining the employer-employee relationship (as applied for purposes of section 3121(d)(2) of the Internal Revenue Code of 1986), is considered to be employed by, or an employee of, an entity. (Application of these common law rules is discussed at 20 CFR 404.1007 and 26 CFR 31.3121(d)–1(c).)

Entity means a sole proprietorship, trust, corporation, partnership, foundation, not-for-profit corporation, or unincorporated association.

Fair market value means the value in arm's-length transactions, consistent with the general market value. With respect to rentals or leases, *fair market value* means the value of rental property for general commercial purposes (not taking into account its intended use). In the case of a lease of space, this value may not be adjusted to reflect the

additional value the prospective lessee or lessor would attribute to the proximity or convenience to the lessor when the lessor is a potential source of patient referrals to the lessee.

Financial relationship refers to a direct or indirect relationship between a physician (or a member of a physician's immediate family) and an entity in which the physician or family member has—

(1) An ownership or investment interest that exists in the entity through equity, debt, or other means and includes an interest in an entity that holds an ownership or investment interest in any entity providing laboratory services; or

(2) A compensation arrangement with the entity.

Group practice means a group of two or more physicians, legally organized as a partnership, professional corporation, foundation, not-for-profit corporation, faculty practice plan, or similar association, that meets the following conditions:

(1) Each physician who is a *member of the group*, as defined in this section, furnishes substantially the full range of patient care services that the physician routinely furnishes including medical care, consultation, diagnosis, and treatment through the joint use of shared office space, facilities, equipment, and personnel.

(2) Except as provided in paragraphs (2)(i) and (2)(ii) of this definition, substantially all of the patient care services of the physicians who are members of the group (that is, at least 75 percent of the total patient care services of the group practice members) are furnished through the group and billed in the name of the group and the amounts received are treated as receipts of the group. "Patient care services" are measured by the total patient care time each member spends on these services. For example, if a physician practices 40 hours a week and spends 30 hours on patient care services for a group practice, the physician has spent 75 percent of his or her time providing countable patient care services.

(i) The "substantially all" test does not apply to any group practice that is located solely in an HPSA, as defined in this section, and

(ii) For group practices located outside of an HPSA (as defined in this section) any time spent by group practice members providing services in an HPSA should not be used to calculate whether the group practice located outside the HPSA has met the "substantially all" test, regardless of whether the members' time in the HPSA

Federal Register / Vol. 60, No. 156 / Monday, August 14, 1995 / Rules and Regulations   **41979**

is spent in a group practice, clinic, or office setting.

(3) The practice expenses and income are distributed in accordance with methods previously determined.

In the case of faculty practice plans associated with a hospital, institution of higher education, or medical school that has an approved medical residency training program in which faculty practice plan physicians perform specialty and professional services, both within and outside the faculty practice, as well as perform other tasks such as research, this definition applies only to those services that are furnished within the faculty practice plan.

Hospital means any separate legally organized operating entity plus any subsidiary, related, or other entities that perform services for the hospital's patients and for which the hospital bills. A "hospital" does not include entities that perform services for hospital patients "under arrangements" with the hospital.

HPSA means, for purposes of this regulation, an area designated as a health professional shortage area under section 332(a)(1)(A) of the Public Health Service Act for primary medical care professionals (in accordance with the criteria specified in 42 CFR part 5, appendix A, part I—Geographic Areas). In addition, with respect to dental, mental health, vision care, podiatric, and pharmacy services, an HPSA means an area designated as a health professional shortage area under section 332(a)(1)(A) of the Public Health Service Act for dental professionals, mental health professionals, vision care professionals, podiatric professionals, and pharmacy professionals, respectively.

Immediate family member or member of a physician's immediate family means husband or wife; natural or adoptive parent, child, or sibling; stepparent, stepchild, stepbrother, or stepsister; father-in-law, mother-in-law, son-in-law, daughter-in-law, brother-in-law, or sister-in-law; grandparent or grandchild; and spouse of a grandparent or grandchild.

Laboratory means an entity furnishing biological, microbiological, serological, chemical, immunohematological, hematological, biophysical, cytological, pathological, or other examination of materials derived from the human body for the purpose of providing information for the diagnosis, prevention, or treatment of any disease or impairment of, or the assessment of the health of, human beings. These examinations also include procedures to determine, measure, or otherwise describe the presence or absence of various substances or organisms in the body. Entities only collecting or preparing specimens (or both) or only serving as a mailing service and not performing testing are not considered laboratories.

Members of the group means physician partners and full-time and part-time physician contractors and employees during the time they furnish services to patients of the group practice that are furnished through the group and are billed in the name of the group.

Patient care services means any tasks performed by a group practice member that address the medical needs of specific patients, regardless of whether they involve direct patient encounters. They can include, for example, the services of physicians who do not directly treat patients, time spent by a physician consulting with other physicians, or time spent reviewing laboratory tests.

Physician incentive plan means any compensation arrangement between an entity and a physician or physician group that may directly or indirectly have the effect of reducing or limiting services furnished with respect to individuals enrolled with the entity.

Plan of care means the establishment by a physician of a course of diagnosis or treatment (or both) for a particular patient, including the ordering of items or services.

Referral—

(1) Means either of the following:

(i) Except as provided in paragraph (2) of this definition, the request by a physician for, or ordering of, any item or service for which payment may be made under Medicare Part B, including a request for a consultation with another physician and any test or procedure ordered by or to be performed by (or under the supervision of) that other physician.

(ii) Except as provided in paragraph (2) of this definition, a request by a physician that includes the provision of laboratory services or the establishment of a plan of care by a physician that includes the provision of laboratory services.

(2) Does not include a request by a pathologist for clinical diagnostic laboratory tests and pathological examination services if—

(i) The request is part of a consultation initiated by another physician; and

(ii) The tests or services are furnished by or under the supervision of the pathologist.

Referring physician means a physician (or group practice) who makes a referral as defined in this section.

Remuneration means any payment, discount, forgiveness of debt, or other benefit made directly or indirectly, overtly or covertly, in cash or in kind, except that the following are not considered remuneration:

(1) The forgiveness of amounts owed for inaccurate tests or procedures, mistakenly performed tests or procedures, or the correction of minor billing errors.

(2) The furnishing of items, devices, or supplies that are used solely to collect, transport, process, or store specimens for the entity furnishing the items, devices, or supplies or are used solely to order or communicate the results of tests or procedures for the entity.

(3) A payment made by an insurer or a self-insured plan to a physician to satisfy a claim, submitted on a fee-for-service basis, for the furnishing of health services by that physician to an individual who is covered by a policy with the insurer or by the self-insured plan, if—

(i) The health services are not furnished, and the payment is not made, under a contract or other arrangement between the insurer or the plan and the physician;

(ii) The payment is made to the physician on behalf of the covered individual and would otherwise be made directly to the individual; and

(iii) The amount of the payment is set in advance, does not exceed fair market value, and is not determined in a manner that takes into account directly or indirectly the volume or value of any referrals.

Transaction means an instance or process of two or more persons doing business. An *isolated transaction* is one involving a single payment between two or more persons. A transaction that involves long-term or installment payments is not considered an isolated transaction.

§ 411.353 Prohibition on certain referrals by physicians and limitations on billing.

(a) *Prohibition on referrals.* Except as provided in this subpart, a physician who has a financial relationship with an entity, or who has an immediate family member who has a financial relationship with the entity, may not make a referral to that entity for the furnishing of clinical laboratory services for which payment otherwise may be made under Medicare.

(b) *Limitations on billing.* An entity that furnishes clinical laboratory services under a referral that is prohibited by paragraph (a) of this section may not present or cause to be presented a claim or bill to the Medicare

41980 **Federal Register** / Vol. 60, No. 156 / Monday, August 14, 1995 / Rules and Regulations

program or to any individual, third party payer, or other entity for the clinical laboratory services performed under that referral.

(c) *Denial of payment.* No Medicare payment may be made for a clinical laboratory service that is furnished under a prohibited referral.

(d) *Refunds.* An entity that collects payment for a laboratory service that was performed under a prohibited referral must refund all collected amounts on a timely basis.

§411.355 General exceptions to referral prohibitions related to both ownership/investment and compensation.

The prohibition on referrals set forth in §411.353 does not apply to the following types of services:

(a) *Physicians' services,* as defined in §410.20(a), that are furnished personally by (or under the personal supervision of) another physician in the same group practice as the referring physician.

(b) *In-office ancillary services.* Services that meet the following conditions:

(1) They are furnished personally by one of the following individuals:

(i) The referring physician.

(ii) A physician who is a member of the same group practice as the referring physician.

(iii) Individuals who are directly supervised by the referring physician or, in the case of group practices, by another physician in the same group practice as the referring physician.

(2) They are furnished in one of the following locations:

(i) A building in which the referring physician (or another physician who is a member of the same group practice) furnishes physicians' services unrelated to the furnishing of clinical laboratory services.

(ii) A building that is used by the group practice for the provision of some or all of the group's clinical laboratory services.

(3) They are billed by one of the following:

(i) The physician performing or supervising the service.

(ii) The group practice of which the performing or supervising physician is a member.

(iii) An entity that is wholly owned by the physician or the physician's group practice.

(c) *Services furnished to prepaid health plan enrollees by one of the following organizations:*

(1) An HMO or a CMP in accordance with a contract with HCFA under section 1876 of the Act and part 417, subparts J through M, of this chapter.

(2) A health care prepayment plan in accordance with an agreement with HCFA under section 1833(a)(1)(A) of the Act and part 417, subpart U, of this chapter.

(3) An organization that is receiving payments on a prepaid basis for the enrollees through a demonstration project under section 402(a) of the Social Security Amendments of 1967 (42 U.S.C. 1395b–1) or under section 222(a) of the Social Security Amendments of 1972 (42 U.S.C. 1395b–1 note).

(4) A qualified health maintenance organization (within the meaning of section 1310(d) of the Public Health Service Act).

(d) *Services furnished in an ambulatory surgical center (ASC) or end stage renal disease (ESRD) facility, or by a hospice* if payment for those services is included in the ASC rate, the ESRD composite rate, or as part of the per diem hospice charge, respectively.

§411.356 Exceptions to referral prohibitions related to ownership or investment interests.

For purposes of §411.353, the following ownership or investment interests do not constitute a financial relationship:

(a) *Publicly traded securities.* Ownership of investment securities (including shares or bonds, debentures, notes, or other debt instruments) that may be purchased on terms generally available to the public and that meet the requirements of paragraphs (a)(1) and (a)(2) of this section.

(1) They are either—

(i) Listed for trading on the New York Stock Exchange, the American Stock Exchange, or any regional exchange in which quotations are published on a daily basis, or foreign securities listed on a recognized foreign, national, or regional exchange in which quotations are published on a daily basis; or

(ii) Traded under an automated interdealer quotation system operated by the National Association of Securities Dealers.

(2) In a corporation that had—

(i) Until January 1, 1995, total assets at the end of the corporation's most recent fiscal year exceeding $100 million; or

(ii) Stockholder equity exceeding $75 million at the end of the corporation's most recent fiscal year or on average during the previous 3 fiscal years.

(b) *Mutual funds.* Ownership of shares in a regulated investment company as defined in section 851(a) of the Internal Revenue Code of 1986, if the company had, at the end of its most recent fiscal year, or on average during

the previous 3 fiscal years, total assets exceeding $75 million.

(c) *Specific providers.* Ownership or investment interest in the following entities:

(1) A laboratory that is located in a rural area (that is, a laboratory that is not located in an urban area as defined in §412.62(f)(1)(ii) of this chapter) and that meets the following criteria:

(i) The laboratory testing that is referred by a physician who has (or whose immediate family member has) an ownership or investment interest in the rural laboratory is either—

(A) Performed on the premises of the rural laboratory; or

(B) If not performed on the premises, the laboratory performing the testing bills the Medicare program directly for the testing.

(ii) Substantially all of the laboratory tests furnished by the entity are furnished to individuals who reside in a rural area. Substantially all means no less than 75 percent.

(2) A hospital that is located in Puerto Rico.

(3) A hospital that is located outside of Puerto Rico if one of the following conditions is met:

(i) The referring physician is authorized to perform services at the hospital, and the physician's ownership or investment interest is in the entire hospital and not merely in a distinct part or department of the hospital.

(ii) Until January 1, 1995, the referring physician's ownership or investment interest does not relate (directly or indirectly) to the furnishing of clinical laboratory services.

§411.357 Exceptions to referral prohibitions related to compensation arrangements.

For purposes of §411.353, the following compensation arrangements do not constitute a financial relationship:

(a) *Rental of office space.* Payments for the use of office space made by a lessee to a lessor if there is a rental or lease agreement that meets the following requirements:

(1) The agreement is set out in writing and is signed by the parties and specifies the premises covered by the lease.

(2) The term of the agreement is at least 1 year.

(3) The space rented or leased does not exceed that which is reasonable and necessary for the legitimate business purposes of the lease or rental and is used exclusively by the lessee when being used by the lessee, except that the lessee may make payments for the use of space consisting of common areas if

the payments do not exceed the lessee's pro rata share of expenses for the space based upon the ratio of the space used exclusively by the lessee to the total amount of space (other than common areas) occupied by all persons using the common areas.

(4) The rental charges over the term of the lease are set in advance and are consistent with fair market value.

(5) The charges are not determined in a manner that takes into account the volume or value of any referrals or other business generated between the parties.

(6) The agreement would be commercially reasonable even if no referrals were made between the lessee and the lessor.

(b) *Rental of equipment.* Payments made by a lessee to a lessor for the use of equipment under the following conditions:

(1) A rental or lease agreement is set out in writing and signed by the parties and specifies the equipment covered by the lease.

(2) The equipment rented or leased does not exceed that which is reasonable and necessary for the legitimate business purposes of the lease or rental and is used exclusively by the lessee when being used by the lessee.

(3) The lease provides for a term of rental or lease of at least 1 year.

(4) The rental charges over the term of the lease are set in advance, are consistent with fair market value, and are not determined in a manner that takes into account the volume or value of any referrals or other business generated between the parties.

(5) The lease would be commercially reasonable even if no referrals were made between the parties.

(c) *Bona fide employment relationships.* Any amount paid by an employer to a physician (or immediate family member) who has a bona fide employment relationship with the employer for the provision of services if the following conditions are met:

(1) The employment is for identifiable services.

(2) The amount of the remuneration under the employment is—

(i) Consistent with the fair market value of the services; and

(ii) Except as provided in paragraph (c)(4) of this section, is not determined in a manner that takes into account (directly or indirectly) the volume or value of any referrals by the referring physician.

(3) The remuneration is provided under an agreement that would be commercially reasonable even if no referrals were made to the employer.

(4) Paragraph (c)(2)(ii) of this section does not prohibit payment of remuneration in the form of a productivity bonus based on services performed personally by the physician (or immediate family member of the physician).

(d) *Personal service arrangements—* (1) *General.* Remuneration from an entity under an arrangement to a physician or immediate family member of the physician, including remuneration for specific physicians' services furnished to a nonprofit blood center, if the following conditions are met:

(i) The arrangement is set out in writing, is signed by the parties, and specifies the services covered by the arrangement.

(ii) The arrangement covers all of the services to be furnished by the physician (or an immediate family member of the physician) to the entity.

(iii) The aggregate services contracted for do not exceed those that are reasonable and necessary for the legitimate business purposes of the arrangement.

(iv) The term of the arrangement is for at least 1 year.

(v) The compensation to be paid over the term of the arrangement is set in advance, does not exceed fair market value, and, except in the case of a physician incentive plan, is not determined in a manner that takes into account the volume or value of any referrals or other business generated between the parties.

(vi) The services to be furnished under the arrangement do not involve the counseling or promotion of a business arrangement or other activity that violates any State or Federal law.

(2) *Physician incentive plan exception.* In the case of a physician incentive plan between a physician and an entity, the compensation may be determined in a manner (through a withhold, capitation, bonus, or otherwise) that takes into account directly or indirectly the volume or value of any referrals or other business generated between the parties, if the plan meets the following requirements:

(i) No specific payment is made directly or indirectly under the plan to a physician or a physician group as an inducement to reduce or limit medically necessary services furnished with respect to a specific individual enrolled in the entity.

(ii) In the case of a plan that places a physician or a physician group at substantial financial risk as determined by the Secretary under section 1876(i)(8)(A)(ii) of the Act, the plan complies with any requirements the Secretary has imposed under that section.

(iii) Upon request by the Secretary, the entity provides the Secretary with access to descriptive information regarding the plan, in order to permit the Secretary to determine whether the plan is in compliance with the requirements of paragraph (d)(2) of this section.

(3) Until January 1, 1995, the provisions in paragraph (d) (1) and (2) of this section do not apply to any arrangements that meet the requirements of section 1877(e)(2) or section 1877(e)(3) of the Act as they read before they were amended by the Omnibus Budget Reconciliation Act of 1993 (Public Law 103–66).

(e) *Physician recruitment.* Remuneration provided by a hospital to recruit a physician that is intended to induce the physician to relocate to the geographic area served by the hospital in order to become a member of the hospital's medical staff, if all of the following conditions are met:

(1) The arrangement and its terms are in writing and signed by both parties.

(2) The arrangement is not conditioned on the physician's referral of patients to the hospital.

(3) The hospital does not determine (directly or indirectly) the amount or value of the remuneration to the physician based on the volume or value of any referrals the physician generates for the hospital.

(4) The physician is not precluded from establishing staff privileges at another hospital or referring business to another entity.

(f) *Isolated transactions.* Isolated financial transactions, such as a one-time sale of property or a practice, if all of the conditions set forth in paragraphs (c)(2) and (c)(3) of this section are met with respect to an entity in the same manner as they apply to an employer. There can be no additional transactions between the parties for 6 months after the isolated transaction, except for transactions which are specifically excepted under the other provisions in §§ 411.355 through 411.357.

(g) *Arrangements with hospitals.* (1) Until January 1, 1995, any compensation arrangement between a hospital and a physician or a member of a physician's immediate family if the arrangement does not relate to the furnishing of clinical laboratory services; or

(2) Remuneration provided by a hospital to a physician if the remuneration does not relate to the furnishing of clinical laboratory services.

(h) *Group practice arrangements with a hospital.* An arrangement between a hospital and a group practice under

41982 Federal Register / Vol. 60, No. 156 / Monday, August 14, 1995 / Rules and Regulations

which clinical laboratory services are provided by the group but are billed by the hospital if the following conditions are met:

(1) With respect to services provided to an inpatient of the hospital, the arrangement is pursuant to the provision of inpatient hospital services under section 1861(b)(3) of the Act.

(2) The arrangement began before December 19, 1989, and has continued in effect without interruption since then.

(3) With respect to the clinical laboratory services covered under the arrangement, substantially all of these services furnished to patients of the hospital are furnished by the group under the arrangement.

(4) The arrangement is in accordance with an agreement that is set out in writing and that specifies the services to be furnished by the parties and the compensation for services furnished under the agreement.

(5) The compensation paid over the term of the agreement is consistent with fair market value, and the compensation per unit of services is fixed in advance and is not determined in a manner that takes into account the volume or value of any referrals or other business generated between the parties.

(6) The compensation is provided in accordance with an agreement that would be commercially reasonable even if no referrals were made to the entity.

(i) *Payments by a physician.* Payments made by a physician—

(1) To a laboratory in exchange for the provision of clinical laboratory services; or

(2) To an entity as compensation for other items or services that are furnished at a price that is consistent with fair market value.

§411.360 Group practice attestation.

(a) Except as provided in paragraph (b) of this section, a group practice (as defined in section 1877(h)(4) of the Act and §411.351) must submit a written statement to its carrier annually to attest that, during the most recent 12-month period (calendar year, fiscal year, or immediately preceding 12-month period) 75 percent of the total patient care services of group practice members was furnished through the group, was billed under a billing number assigned to the group, and the amounts so received were treated as receipts of the group.

(b) A newly-formed group practice (one in which physicians have recently begun to practice together) or any group practice that has been unable in the past to meet the requirements of section 1877(h)(4) of the Act must—

(1) Submit a written statement to attest that, during the next 12-month period (calendar year, fiscal year, or next 12 months), it expects to meet the 75-percent standard and will take measures to ensure the standard is met; and

(2) At the end of the 12-month period, submit a written statement to attest that it met the 75-percent standard during that period, billed for those services under a billing number assigned to the group, and treated amounts received for those services as receipts of the group. If the group did not meet the standard, any Medicare payments made for clinical laboratory services furnished by the group during the 12-month period that were conditioned upon the standard being met are overpayments.

(c) Once any group has chosen whether to use its fiscal year, the calendar year, or some other 12-month period, the group practice must adhere to this choice.

(d) The attestation must contain a statement that the information furnished in the attestation is true and accurate and must be signed by a group representative.

(e) A group that intends to meet the definition of a group practice in order to qualify for an exception described in §§411.355 through 411.357, must submit the attestation required by paragraph (a) or paragraph (b)(1) of this section, as applicable, to its carrier by December 12, 1995.

5. Section 411.361 is revised to read as follows:

§411.361 Reporting requirements.

(a) *Basic rule.* Except as provided in paragraph (b) of this section, all entities furnishing items or services for which payment may be made under Medicare must submit information to HCFA concerning their financial relationships (as defined in paragraph (d) of this section), in such form, manner, and at such times as HCFA specifies.

(b) *Exception.* The requirements of paragraph (a) of this section do not apply to entities that provide 20 or fewer Part A and Part B items and services during a calendar year, or to designated health services provided outside the United States.

(c) *Required information.* The information submitted to HCFA under paragraph (a) of this section must include at least the following:

(1) The name and unique physician identification number (UPIN) of each physician who has a financial relationship with the entity;

(2) The name and UPIN of each physician who has an immediate relative (as defined in §411.351) who

has a financial relationship with the entity;

(3) The covered items and services provided by the entity; and

(4) With respect to each physician identified under paragraphs (c)(1) and (c)(2) of this section, the nature of the financial relationship (including the extent and/or value of the ownership or investment interest or the compensation arrangement, if requested by HCFA).

(d) *Reportable financial relationships.* For purposes of this section, a financial relationship is any ownership or investment interest or any compensation arrangement, as described in section 1877 of the Act.

(e) *Form and timing of reports.* Entities that are subject to the requirements of this section must submit the required information on a HCFA-prescribed form within the time period specified by the servicing carrier or intermediary. Entities are given at least 30 days from the date of the carrier's or intermediary's request to provide the initial information. Thereafter, an entity must provide updated information within 60 days from the date of any change in the submitted information. Entities must retain documentation sufficient to verify the information provided on the forms and, upon request, must make that documentation available to HCFA or the OIG.

(f) *Consequences of failure to report.* Any person who is required, but fails, to submit information concerning his or her financial relationships in accordance with this section is subject to a civil money penalty of up to $10,000 for each day of the period beginning on the day following the applicable deadline established under paragraph (e) of this section until the information is submitted. Assessment of these penalties will comply with the applicable provisions of part 1003 of this title.

(g) *Public disclosure.* Information furnished to HCFA under this section is subject to public disclosure in accordance with the provisions of part 401 of this chapter.

(Catalog of Federal Domestic Assistance Program No. 93.774, Medicare—Supplementary Medical Insurance Program)

Dated: January 16, 1995.

Bruce C. Vladeck,

Administrator, Health Care Financing Administration.

Dated: May 10, 1995.

Donna E. Shalala,

Secretary.

[FR Doc. 95–19647 Filed 8–11–95; 8:45 am]

BILLING CODE 4120–01–P

HCFA Proposed Rules on the 'Stark II' Self-Referral Ban Applied to Designated Health Services

(63 *Fed. Reg.* 1659-1728, Jan. 9, 1998)

Federal Register / Vol. 63, No. 6 / Friday, January 9, 1998 / Proposed Rules   1659

DEPARTMENT OF HEALTH AND HUMAN SERVICES

Health Care Financing Administration

42 CFR Parts 411, 424, 435, and 455

[HCFA–1809–P]

RIN 0938–AG80

Medicare and Medicaid Programs; Physicians' Referrals to Health Care Entities With Which They Have Financial Relationships

AGENCY: Health Care Financing Administration (HCFA), HHS.

ACTION: Proposed rule.

SUMMARY: This proposed rule would incorporate into regulations the provisions of sections 1877 and 1903(s) of the Social Security Act. Under section 1877, if a physician or a member of a physician's immediate family has a financial relationship with a health care entity, the physician may not make referrals to that entity for the furnishing of designated health services under the Medicare program, unless certain exceptions apply. The following services are designated health services:

• Clinical laboratory services.
• Physical therapy services.
• Occupational therapy services.
• Radiology services, including magnetic resonance imaging, computerized axial tomography scans, and ultrasound services.
• Radiation therapy services and supplies.
• Durable medical equipment and supplies.
• Parenteral and enteral nutrients, equipment, and supplies.
• Prosthetics, orthotics, and prosthetic devices and supplies.
• Home health services.
• Outpatient prescription drugs.
• Inpatient and outpatient hospital services.

In addition, section 1877 provides that an entity may not present or cause to be presented a Medicare claim or bill to any individual, third party payer, or other entity for designated health services furnished under a prohibited referral, nor may the Secretary make payment for a designated health service furnished under a prohibited referral.

Section 1903(s) of the Social Security Act extended aspects of the referral prohibition to the Medicaid program. It denies payment under the Medicaid program to a State for certain expenditures for designated health services. Payment would be denied if the services are furnished to an individual on the basis of a physician

referral that would result in the denial of payment for the services under Medicare if Medicare covered the services to the same extent and under the same terms and conditions as under the State plan.

This proposed rule incorporates these statutory provisions into the Medicare and Medicaid regulations and interprets certain aspects of the law. The proposed rule is based on the provisions of section 1903(s) and section 1877 of the Social Security Act, as amended by section 13562 of the Omnibus Budget Reconciliation Act of 1993, and by section 152 of the Social Security Act Amendments of 1994.

DATES: Comments will be considered if we receive them at the appropriate address, as provided below, no later than 5 p.m. on March 10, 1998. We will also consider comments that we received in response to the final rule with comment period, "Physician Financial Relationships With, and Referrals to, Health Care Entities That Furnish Clinical Laboratory Services and Financial Relationship Reporting Requirements," which we published in the **Federal Register** on August 14, 1995 (60 FR 41914).

ADDRESSES: Mail written comments (1 original and 3 copies) to the following address: Health Care Financing Administration, Department of Health and Human Services, Attention: HCFA–1809–P, P.O. Box 26688, Baltimore, MD 21207.

If you prefer, you may deliver your written comments (1 original and 3 copies) to one of the following addresses:

Room 309–G, Hubert H. Humphrey Building, 200 Independence Avenue, SW., Washington, DC 20201, or
Room C5–09–26, 7500 Security Boulevard, Baltimore, MD 21244–1850.

Comments may also be submitted electronically to the following e-mail address: hcfa1809p.hcfa.gov. E-mail comments must include the full name and address of the sender and must be submitted to the referenced address in order to be considered. All comments must be incorporated in the e-mail message because we may not be able to access attachments. Because of staffing and resource limitations, we cannot accept comments by facsimile (FAX) transmission. In commenting, please refer to file code HCFA–1809–P. Comments received timely will be available for public inspection as they are received, generally beginning approximately 3 weeks after publication of a document, in Room 309–G of the Department's offices at 200

Independence Avenue, SW., Washington, DC, on Monday through Friday of each week from 8:30 a.m. to 5 p.m. (phone: (202) 690–7890).

Copies: To order copies of the **Federal Register** containing this document, send your request to: New Orders, Superintendent of Documents, P.O. Box 371954, Pittsburgh, PA 15250–7954. Specify the date of the issue requested and enclose a check or money order payable to the Superintendent of Documents, or enclose your Visa or Master Card number and expiration date. Credit card orders can also be placed by calling the order desk at (202) 783–3238 or by faxing to (202) 275–6802. The cost for each copy is $8. As an alternative, you can view and photocopy the **Federal Register** document at most libraries designated as Federal Depository Libraries and at many other public and academic libraries throughout the country that receive the **Federal Register**.

This **Federal Register** document is also available from the **Federal Register** online database through GPO Access, a service of the U.S. Government Printing Office. Free public access is available on a Wide Area Information Server (WAIS) through the Internet and via asynchronous dial-in. Internet users can access the database by using the World Wide Web; the Superintendent of Documents home page address is http://www.access.gpo.gov/su—docs/, by using local WAIS client software, or by telnet to swais.access.gpo.gov, then log in as guest (no password required). Dial-in users should use communications software and modem to call (202) 512–1661; type swais, then log in as guest (no password required).

FOR FURTHER INFORMATION CONTACT: Joanne Sinsheimer (410) 786–4620.

SUPPLEMENTARY INFORMATION: To assist readers in referencing sections contained in this proposed rule, we are providing the following table of contents:

Table of Contents

1660   Federal Register / Vol. 63, No. 6 / Friday, January 9, 1998 / Proposed Rules

Federal Register / Vol. 63, No. 6 / Friday, January 9, 1998 / Proposed Rules **1661**

I. Background

A. Problems Associated With Physician Self-referrals

When a patient seeks medical care, his or her physician has a major role in determining the kind and amount of health care services the patient will receive. Having a financial interest in an entity that furnishes these services can affect a physician's decision about what medical care to furnish a patient and who should furnish the care. In fact, numerous studies have raised serious concerns about the referral patterns of physicians who make self-referrals (referrals to entities with which they or their family members have financial relationships).

In June 1988, Congress mandated that the Office of Inspector General (OIG) of the Department of Health and Human Services conduct a study on physician ownership of and compensation from health care entities to which the physicians make referrals. The OIG reported that patients of referring physicians who owned or invested in independent clinical laboratories received 45 percent more laboratory services than all Medicare patients in general. The OIG found similar effects on utilization associated with the existence of compensation arrangements between laboratories and physicians. Patients of these physicians used 32 percent more laboratory services than all Medicare patients in general. ("Financial Arrangements Between Physicians and Health Care Businesses: Report to Congress," Office of Inspector

General, DHHS, pages 18 and 21 (May 1989)). Based in part on the results of this study, Congress enacted, in November of 1989, section 1877 of the Social Security Act (the Act). (Unless otherwise indicated, references to sections of the law below are to sections of the Act.) We discuss section 1877 in detail below.

Subsequent studies have supported the OIG findings on self-referrals. The studies indicate that other types of services are also associated with higher utilization and increased costs. For example, in 1991 the Florida Cost Containment Board (the Board) analyzed the effect of joint venture arrangements on the following aspects of health care: access, costs, charges, utilization, and quality. A joint venture was defined as any ownership or investment interest or compensation arrangement involving physicians (or any health care professionals who make referrals) and an entity providing health care goods or services.

The Board found that doctor-owned clinical laboratories, diagnostic imaging centers, and physical therapy and rehabilitation centers performed more procedures on a per-patient basis and charged higher prices than nondoctor-affiliated facilities. The Board concluded that there might be referral problems or the results did not allow clear conclusions for ambulatory surgical centers, durable medical equipment suppliers, home health agencies, and radiation therapy centers. The study revealed that little or no impact existed for acute care hospitals and nursing homes. ("Joint Ventures Among Health Care Providers in Florida," State of Florida Health Care Cost Containment Board (Sept. 1991)).

Additionally, in 1994, the General Accounting Office (GAO) released an analysis of 2.4 million diagnostic imaging services ordered by 17,900 physicians in the State of Florida. The GAO found that Florida physicians with a financial interest in joint venture imaging centers had higher referral rates for almost all types of imaging services than other Florida physicians. The differences in the referral rates were greatest for costly high-technology imaging services. For example, owners of joint ventures ordered 54 percent more magnetic resonance imaging scans for patients than did non-owners.

The GAO study also found that Florida physicians, group practices, or other practice affiliations with imaging facilities in their own offices ordered imaging tests more frequently than physicians who referred their patients to imaging facilities outside their practices. The in-practice imaging rates were

about 3 times higher for magnetic resonance imaging scans; about 2 times higher for computed tomograph scans; 4.5 to 5.1 times higher for ultrasound, echocardiography, and diagnostic nuclear medicine imaging; and about 2 times higher for complex and simple X-rays. (GAO Report, "Medicare: Referrals to Physician-owned Imaging Facilities Warrant HCFA's Scrutiny," No. B–253835; pages 2, 3, and 10, October 1994.)

Several other studies, appearing in the New England Journal of Medicine and the Journal of the American Medical Association, have found increased utilization for a variety of services when the physicians have a financial relationship with the entity to which they refer their patients. (See, for example, Bruce J. Hillman, M.D., and others, "Physicians' Utilization and Charges for Outpatient Diagnostic Imaging in a Medicare Population," Journal of the American Medical Association, Vol. 268, No. 15 (Oct. 21, 1992), pp. 2050–2054; Hemenway D., Killen A., and others, "Physicians' Responses to Financial Incentives—Evidence From a For-profit Ambulatory Care Center," New England Journal of Medicine, Vol. 322, No. 15 (April 12, 1990), pp. 1059–1063; Alex Swedlow and others, "Increased Costs and Rates of Use in the California Workers' Compensation System as a Result of Self Referral by Physicians," New England Journal of Medicine, Vol. 327, No. 21 (Nov. 19, 1992), pp. 1502–1506.)

B. Legislation Designed to Address Self-referrals and Similar Practices

1. Legislative History of Section 1877

Section 6204 of the Omnibus Budget Reconciliation Act of 1989 (OBRA '89), Public Law 101–239, enacted on December 19, 1989, added section 1877 to the Social Security Act. In general, section 1877 as it read under OBRA '89 provided that, if a physician (or an immediate family member of a physician) had a financial relationship with a clinical laboratory, that physician could not make a referral to the laboratory entity for the furnishing of clinical laboratory services for which Medicare might otherwise pay. (For the sake of brevity, whenever we refer to "immediate family member" or "family member," this means "a member of the physician's immediate family.") It also provided that the laboratory could not present or cause to be presented a Medicare claim or bill to any individual, third party payer, or other entity for clinical laboratory services furnished under the prohibited referral. Additionally, it required a refund of any amount collected from an individual as a result of a billing for an item or service furnished under a prohibited referral.

The statute defined "financial relationship" as an ownership or investment interest in the entity or a compensation arrangement between the physician (or immediate family member) and the entity. The statute provided a number of exceptions to the prohibition. Some of these exceptions applied to both ownership/investment interests and compensation arrangements, while other exceptions applied to only one or the other of these. Additionally, the statute imposed reporting requirements and provided for sanctions.

Section 4207(e) of the Omnibus Budget Reconciliation Act of 1990 (OBRA '90), Public Law 101–508, enacted on November 5, 1990, amended certain provisions of section 1877 to clarify definitions and reporting requirements relating to physician ownership and referral and to provide an additional exception to the prohibition.

Section 13562 of the Omnibus Budget Reconciliation Act of 1993 (OBRA '93), Public Law 103–66, enacted on August 10, 1993, extensively revised section 1877. It modified the prior law to apply to referrals for ten "designated health services" in addition to clinical laboratory services, modified some exceptions, and added new ones. Section 152 of the Social Security Act Amendments of 1994 (SSA '94), Public Law 103–432, enacted on October 31, 1994, amended the list of designated services, effective January 1, 1995. (Section II of this preamble contains a listing of the designated health services.) It also changed the reporting requirements in section 1877(f) and amended some of the effective dates of the OBRA '93 provisions.

Section 13624 of OBRA '93 extended aspects of the referral prohibition to the Medicaid program. It amended section 1903 of the Act by adding a new paragraph (s). This provision denies Federal financial participation (FFP) payment under the Medicaid program to a State for certain expenditures for designated health services. A State cannot receive FFP for designated health services furnished to an individual on the basis of a physician referral that would result in a denial of payment under the Medicare program if Medicare covered the services to the same extent and under the same terms and conditions as under the State Medicaid plan. Section 13624 also specified that the reporting requirements of section 1877(f) and the civil money penalty provision of section

1877(g)(5) (which relates to reporting) apply to a provider of a designated health service for which payment may be made under Medicaid in the same manner as they apply to a provider of a designated health service for which payment may be made under Medicare.

We describe the provisions of section 1877, as amended, in detail in part A of section II of this preamble. We discuss section 1903(s) in part B of section II.

2. Recent Provisions and How They Relate to Each Other

Congress has enacted into law several provisions governing financial relationships between entities furnishing health care services and those health care professionals who refer patients to them. For example, the "anti-kickback statute" provides criminal penalties for individuals or entities that knowingly and willfully offer, pay, solicit, or receive remuneration to induce the furnishing of items or services covered by Medicare or State health care programs (including Medicaid, and any State program receiving funds under titles V or XX of the Act). (This provision was originally enacted in 1972 as part of the Social Security Amendments of 1972, Public Law 92–603. It was revised in 1977 (in Public Law 95–142) to read as it does today. It was subsequently recodified by the Medicare and Medicaid Program Patient Protection Act of 1987 (Public Law 100–93). It currently appears at 42 U.S.C. 1320a–7b(b)(2) and section 1128B(b) of the Social Security Act.)

Both the anti-kickback statute and section 1877 address Congress' concern that health care decisionmaking can be unduly influenced by a profit motive. When physicians have a financial incentive to refer, this incentive can affect utilization, patient choice, and competition. Physicians can overutilize by ordering items and services for patients that, absent a profit motive, they would not have ordered. A patient's choice can be affected when physicians steer patients to less convenient, lower quality, or more expensive providers of health care, just because the physicians are sharing profits with, or receiving remuneration from, the providers. And lastly, where referrals are controlled by those sharing profits or receiving remuneration, the medical marketplace suffers since new competitors can no longer win business with superior quality, service, or price. Although the purposes behind the anti-kickback statute and section 1877 are similar, it is important to analyze them separately. In other words, to operate lawfully under Medicare and Medicaid, one must comply with both statutes.

Anti-kickback statute: The anti-kickback statute is a criminal statute that applies to those who *knowingly and willfully* offer, pay, solicit, or receive remuneration to induce the furnishing of items or services under Medicare or State health care programs (including Medicaid). The offense is classified as a felony and is punishable by fines of up to $25,000 and imprisonment for up to 5 years. Violation of the statute is also a basis for exclusion from Medicare and Medicaid.

Since the statute on its face is very broad, a number of health care entities expressed concern after its enactment that many relatively innocuous, or even beneficial, commercial arrangements are technically covered by the statute and can therefore lead to criminal prosecution. Congress addressed this fact by enacting section 14 of the Medicare and Medicaid Patient and Program Protection Act of 1987. This provision requires the Department of Health and Human Services to issue "safe harbors," specifying those payment practices that will not be subject to criminal prosecution under the anti-kickback statute and will not provide a basis for an exclusion. The safe harbors are not mandatory in the sense that one is *required* to fit into a safe harbor. The safe harbors exist to provide absolute immunity to those arrangements.

Section 1877: Section 1877 prohibits physicians from referring Medicare patients to certain entities for designated health services if the physician (or an immediate family member) has a financial relationship with the entity, *unless* the relationship fits into an exception. Certain aspects of section 1877 also affect Medicaid referrals. While there are other remedies, section 1877 is primarily a payment ban that is effective *regardless of intent*. Many of the exceptions in section 1877 are similar to the safe harbors under the anti-kickback statute, such as exceptions for certain employees, personal service arrangements, and space and equipment rentals. The exceptions are different in the sense that, under section 1877, a physician is *required* to meet an exception if the physician wants to make an otherwise prohibited referral, while under the anti-kickback statute, a health care provider is not required to meet a safe harbor. That is, if a provider meets a safe harbor, it is automatically protected from prosecution. If a provider does not meet a safe harbor, it may still be in compliance with the anti-kickback statute and therefore be safe from prosecution, but that determination would be based on a case-by-case assessment of the facts.

C. HCFA and OIG Regulations Relating to Section 1877

On December 3, 1991, we issued an interim final rule with comment period (56 FR 61374) setting forth the reporting requirements under section 1877(f). On March 11, 1992, we published a proposed rule (57 FR 8588) setting forth the self-referral prohibition and exceptions to the prohibition in section 1877, as these provisions were amended by OBRA '90, and as they relate to referrals for clinical laboratory services.

On October 20, 1993, the OIG published a proposed rule (58 FR 54096) that would set forth in regulations the penalty provisions specified in sections 1877(g)(3) and (g)(4). The final rule with comment period implementing the civil money penalty provisions was published on March 31, 1995 (60 FR 16580).

On August 14, 1995, we published a final rule with comment period in the **Federal Register** (60 FR 41914) that incorporated into regulations the provisions of section 1877 that relate to the prohibition on physician referrals for clinical laboratory services. The August 1995 final rule contains revisions to the March 11, 1992 proposal based on comments submitted by the public. Further, it incorporates the amendments and exceptions created by OBRA '93 and the amendments in SSA '94 that relate to referrals for clinical laboratory services.

The final rule addresses only those changes that had a retroactive effective date of January 1, 1992; it does not incorporate those modifications made to section 1877 that became effective for referrals made after December 31, 1994. (Even though the August 1995 final rule incorporates OBRA '93 and SSA '94 provisions, it generally only reiterates them without interpreting them. We interpreted the new provisions only in a few instances in which it was necessary to do so in order to implement the statute at all.) The final rule also responds to comments received on the December 1991 interim final rule covering the reporting requirements. In addition, it revises the regulations established by that rule to incorporate the amendments to section 1877(f) made by SSA '94, to apply to any future reporting that we require.

II. Sections 1877 and 1903(s) of the Act and the Provisions of This Proposed Rule

Many of the provisions covered below are discussed in detail in the preamble of either the March 1992 proposed rule

or the August 1995 final rule in the context of referrals for clinical laboratory services. We are proposing, as discussed below, to leave a number of these provisions unchanged except to apply them to the additional designated health services. Readers who desire more background information on these provisions are referred to the earlier documents.

We are also proposing to amend the provisions of the August 1995 final regulation to reflect other changes in section 1877 that were enacted in OBRA '93 or in SSA '94 and became effective on January 1, 1995. In part A of this section, we discuss how we have altered the final regulation to apply it to the additional designated health services, and to reflect the statutory changes in section 1877 that took effect on January 1, 1995. Part B of this section covers the changes made by section 13624 of OBRA '93 to the Medicaid program in section 1903(s) of the Act. Section 13624 applies aspects of the referral prohibition to the Medicaid program for referrals made on or after December 31, 1994. We discuss in part B how we propose to amend the Medicaid regulations to reflect the statutory changes.

In section III of this preamble we discuss in detail how we propose to interpret any provisions in sections 1877 and 1903(s) that we believe are ambiguous, incomplete, or that provide the Secretary with discretion. We also discuss policy changes or clarifications we propose to make to the August 1995 rule. In section IV, we present some of the most common questions concerning physician referrals that we received from the health care community. We include in section IV our interpretations of how the law applies in the situations described to us.

A. Reflecting the Statutory Changes in Section 1877

1. General Prohibition

With certain exceptions, section 1877(a)(1)(A) prohibits a physician from making a referral to an entity for the furnishing of designated health services, for which Medicare may otherwise pay, if the physician (or an immediate family member) has a financial relationship with that entity. This provision as it related to clinical laboratory services was incorporated into our regulations at § 411.353(a) by the August 1995 final rule. We would revise § 411.353(a) to apply the prohibition to referrals for designated health services.

Section 1877(a)(1)(B) prohibits an entity from presenting, or causing to be presented, either a Medicare claim or a

bill to any individual, third party payor, or other entity for designated health services furnished under a prohibited referral. This provision, with regard to clinical laboratory services, was incorporated into our regulations at § 411.353(b) by the August 1995 final rule. We would revise § 411.353(b) to apply it to claims or bills for any of the designated health services.

2. Definitions

For purposes of section 1877, the statute provides definitions of a number of terms. Because they are important to understanding the general prohibition set forth above, we discuss certain of these definitions immediately below. The statutory definitions of other terms are presented elsewhere in this preamble when relevant.

a. Referral, referring physician

As defined by section 1877(h)(5), a "referral" means the following:

• The request by a physician for an item or service for which payment may be made under Medicare Part B, including the request by a physician for a consultation with another physician (and any test or procedure ordered by, or to be performed by (or under the supervision of) that other physician).

• The request or establishment of a plan of care by a physician that includes the furnishing of designated health services.

Section 1877(h)(5)(C), however, provides an exception to this definition in the case of a request by a pathologist for clinical diagnostic laboratory tests and pathological examination services, (and as added by OBRA '93) a request by a radiologist for diagnostic radiology services, and a request by a radiation oncologist for radiation therapy if the services are furnished by (or under the supervision of) the pathologist, radiologist, or radiation oncologist, respectively, as a result of a consultation requested by another physician.

The August 1995 final rule incorporated section 1877(h)(5), with regard to clinical laboratory services, into our regulations by defining "referral" at § 411.351. We interpreted a referral as the request by a physician for, or the ordering of, any item or service covered under Medicare Part B. We interpreted the referral for other items or services as a request by a physician that includes the provision of laboratory services or the establishment of a plan of care by a physician that includes the provision of laboratory services. We also included the statutory exception for certain clinical diagnostic laboratory tests and pathological examination services requested by a pathologist.

This proposed rule would revise the definition of "referral" to apply it to referrals for designated health services. In accordance with section 1877(h)(5)(C), we would also add the exception to the definition described above relating to a request by a radiologist for diagnostic radiology services and a request by a radiation oncologist for radiation therapy. In addition, we would make a technical change in this section. We would remove the phrase "any item or service" and replace it with the phrase "any service." Because the term "services" is defined in our regulations (at § 400.202) to include "items," the phrase "any item or service" contains a redundancy. Hereinafter, unless we specifically state otherwise, we use the term "service(s)" as including "item(s)." We have also made several other changes to the definition that are discussed in section III of this preamble.

Also, in accordance with section 1877(h)(5), the August 1995 final rule at § 411.351 defined "referring physician" as a physician (or group practice) who makes a referral as defined in § 411.351. This proposed rule would retain this definition, but with one amendment that is described in section IV.A.5 of this preamble.

b. Designated health services

Section 1877(h)(6) defines "designated health services" as any of the following services:

- Clinical laboratory services.
- Physical therapy services.
- Occupational therapy services.
- Radiology services, including magnetic resonance imaging, computerized axial tomography scans, and ultrasound services.
- Radiation therapy services and supplies.
- Durable medical equipment and supplies.
- Parenteral and enteral nutrients, equipment, and supplies.
- Prosthetics, orthotics, and prosthetic devices and supplies.
- Home health services.
- Outpatient prescription drugs.
- Inpatient and outpatient hospital services.

This proposed rule would incorporate this definition of "designated health services" into our regulations at § 411.351, except that, for purposes of definition, we would combine radiology services and radiation therapy services and supplies. Also, we propose to define each of these designated health services in § 411.351. We explain our definitions and interpretations in section III of this preamble.

c. Financial relationship

Section 1877(a)(2) describes a financial relationship between a physician (or an immediate family member) and an entity as being an ownership or investment interest in the entity or a compensation arrangement between a physician (or immediate family member) and the entity. (We discuss compensation arrangements in the next section). The statute provides that an ownership or investment interest may be established through equity, debt, or other means. The statute further specifies that an ownership or investment interest includes an interest in an entity that holds an ownership or investment interest in any entity furnishing designated health services.

The August 1995 final rule incorporated this definition into our regulations, with regard to clinical laboratory services, at § 411.351. That section specifies that a financial relationship includes an interest in an entity that holds an ownership or investment interest in any entity providing laboratory services. This proposed rule would revise the definition to specify that a financial relationship includes an interest in an entity that holds an ownership or investment interest in any entity providing designated health services. We have also made certain other changes described in section III of this preamble.

d. Compensation arrangement, remuneration

Section 1877(h)(1)(A) defines a "compensation arrangement" as any arrangement involving any remuneration between a physician (or immediate family member) and an entity, other than an arrangement involving only remuneration described in section 1877(h)(1)(C). Section 1877(h)(1)(B) defines "remuneration" to include "any remuneration, directly or indirectly, overtly or covertly, in cash or in kind." Section 1877(h)(1)(C) provides that a compensation arrangement does not include the following types of remuneration:

- The forgiveness of amounts owed for inaccurate tests or procedures, mistakenly performed tests or procedures, or the correction of minor billing errors.
- The provision of items, devices, or supplies that are used solely to—
+ Collect, transport, process, or store specimens for the entity providing the item, device, or supply; or
+ Order or communicate the results of tests or procedures for the entity.
- A payment made by an insurer or a self-insured plan to a physician to satisfy a claim, submitted on a fee-for-service basis, for the furnishing of health services by that physician to an individual who is covered by a policy with the insurer or by the self-insured plan, if—
+ The health services are not furnished, and the payment is not made, under a contract or other arrangement between the insurer or the plan and the physician;
+ The payment is made to the physician on behalf of the covered individual and would otherwise be made directly to the individual;
+ The amount of the payment is set in advance, does not exceed fair market value, and is not determined in a manner that takes into account directly or indirectly the volume or value of any referrals; and
+ The payment meets any other requirements the Secretary may impose by regulation as needed to protect against Medicare program or patient abuse.

The above definitions of a "compensation arrangement" and "remuneration" were incorporated into our regulations at § 411.351 by the August 1995 final rule. In the definition of "compensation arrangement," we clarified that such an arrangement could be either direct or indirect. This proposed rule would retain that definition. Also, because the statute defines "remuneration" only by referring to how the remuneration might be made (for example, in cash or in kind), we interpreted remuneration to mean any payment, discount, forgiveness of debt, or other benefit. This proposed rule would retain the definition of "remuneration," with one change. We will consider that payments made by an insurer to a physician are not "remuneration" if they meet the requirements in the statute, and if the amount of the payment does not take into account directly or indirectly other business generated between the parties. We explain this change in section III.E.3 of this preamble.

3. General Exceptions to the Prohibition on Physician Referrals

Section 1877(b) provides for general exceptions to the prohibition on referrals. (General exceptions are exceptions that apply to both ownership/investment interests and compensation arrangements.)

Because the first two of these exceptions apply to a "group practice," we begin with a discussion of "group practice" as defined in section 1877. A "group practice," as defined in section 1877(h)(4), is a group of two or more physicians legally organized as a

Federal Register / Vol. 63, No. 6 / Friday, January 9, 1998 / Proposed Rules 1665

partnership, professional corporation, foundation, not-for-profit corporation, faculty practice plan, or similar association, that meets the following conditions:

• Each physician member of the group furnishes substantially the full range of services that the physician routinely furnishes, including medical care, consultation, diagnosis, or treatment, through the joint use of shared office space, facilities, equipment, and personnel.

• Substantially all of the services of the physician members of the group are furnished through the group, are billed under a billing number assigned to the group, and amounts so received are treated as receipts of the group (the "substantially all" test, which we discuss below). (The predecessor provision, that is, the provision as it read before January 1, 1995, required that the services be billed in the name of the group (not that they be billed under a billing number assigned to the group).)

• The overhead expenses of and the income from the practice are distributed in accordance with methods previously determined.

• Except for profits and productivity bonuses that meet the conditions described below, no physician member of the group directly or indirectly receives compensation based on the volume or value of referrals by the physician. (Added by OBRA '93 to be effective January 1, 1995.)

• Members of the group personally conduct at least 75 percent of the physician-patient encounters of the group practice. (Added by OBRA '93 to be effective January 1, 1995.)

• The group practice complies with all other standards established by the Secretary in regulations.

With regard to the above definition, section 1877(h)(4)(B) establishes the following "Special Rules":

• A physician in a group practice may be paid a share of the overall profits of the group, or a productivity bonus based on services personally performed or services incident to the personally performed services, so long as the share or bonus is not determined in any manner that is directly related to the volume or value of referrals by the physician. (Added by OBRA '93 to be effective for referrals made on or after January 1, 1995.)

• In the case of a faculty practice plan associated with a hospital, institution of higher education, or medical school with an approved medical residency training program in which physician members may furnish a variety of different specialty services and furnish

professional services both within and outside the group, as well as perform other tasks such as research, the conditions contained in the definition of "group practice" apply only with respect to the services furnished within the faculty practice plan.

Our August 1995 final rule established a definition of "group practice" at § 411.351 based on the statute as it read effective January 1, 1992. In implementing the statute, we interpreted the provision requiring that "substantially all" of the services of the physician members be furnished through the group as meaning 75 percent of the patient care services of the group practice. (We discuss additional requirements and definitions related to the "substantially all" test in section II.A.6. of this preamble.) As stated above, OBRA '93 made certain revisions to the definition of a group practice, effective January 1, 1995. This proposed rule would revise the definition of "group practice" at § 411.351 to conform with the changes made by OBRA '93. Therefore we would do the following:

• Remove the requirement that substantially all of the services must be billed in the name of the group. We would specify, instead, that substantially all of the services must be billed under a billing number assigned to the group.

• Add the above provisions restricting payments made to physicians based on volume or value of referrals, with the exception for profits and productivity bonuses.

• Add that members of the group must personally conduct at least 75 percent of the physician-patient encounters of the group practice.

In addition, for reasons explained in the August 1995 final rule, the definition would continue to provide that the "substantially all" test does not apply to any group practice that is located solely in a health professional shortage area (HPSA). Also, for group practices located outside of a HPSA, any time spent by group practice members providing services in a HPSA should not be used to calculate whether the group practice located outside the HPSA has met the "substantially all" test. We have also made several other changes to the definition of a group practice, which are discussed later in this preamble.

a. Exception—physician services

Section 1877(b)(1) specifies that the prohibition does not apply to services furnished on a referral basis if the services are physician services, as defined in section 1861(q), furnished personally by (or under the personal

supervision of) another physician in the same group practice as the referring physician. Our August 1995 final rule incorporated this provision at § 411.355(a), covering physician services as we have defined them at § 410.20(a). This proposed rule retains § 411.355(a).

b. Exception—in-office ancillary services

Section 1877(b)(2) specifies that the prohibition does not apply to referrals for certain in-office ancillary services. We consider in-office ancillary services to be all designated health services that can be provided in an in-office setting, except durable medical equipment (excluding infusion pumps) and parenteral and enteral nutrients, equipment, and supplies. (In other words, referrals for infusion pumps can qualify for the exception. However, the exception does not apply to referrals for the in-office provision of other durable medical equipment and parenteral and enteral nutrients, equipment, and supplies.) To qualify for the exception, an ownership or investment interest in the services must meet any requirements the Secretary sets forth in regulations to protect against Medicare program or patient abuse. Additionally, the ancillary services must meet the following requirements:

• The services must be furnished personally by the referring physician, a physician who is a member of the same group practice as the referring physician, or an individual who is directly supervised by the physician or by another physician in the group practice. Also, the services must be furnished in either of the following:

+ A building in which the referring physician (or another physician who is a member of the same group practice) furnishes physician services unrelated to the furnishing of designated health services. (The predecessor provision read "* * * unrelated to the furnishing of clinical laboratory services.")

+ In the case of a referring physician who is a member of a group practice, in another building that is used by the group practice for either of the following:

++ Furnishing some or all of the group's clinical laboratory services.

++ The centralized provision of the group's designated health services (other than clinical laboratory services). (This provision, which was added by OBRA '93, became effective January 1, 1995.) Note that OBRA '93 also contains an undesignated paragraph following this provision that reads as follows: "unless the Secretary determines other terms and conditions under which the provision of such services does not present a risk of program or patient abuse, * * *." As discussed in the August 1995 final rule, it is our interpretation that this paragraph is intended to provide for the possibility of our liberalizing the conditions described in section 1877(b)(2)(A)(ii)(II); that is, the conditions concerning the provision of services in "another building" that is used by a group practice.

• The ancillary services must be billed by one of the following:

+ The physician performing or supervising the services.

+ A group practice of which the physician is a member under a billing number assigned to the group practice. (Prior to January 1, 1995, this provision did not require that the services be billed under a group practice's billing number.)

+ An entity that is wholly owned by the physician or group practice.

The August 1995 final rule incorporated into our regulations an in-office ancillary services exception that was based on the statutory provision, as it was in effect on January 1, 1992, at § 411.355(b). This proposed rule would revise § 411.355(b) to conform it to the current statutory provision. That is, it would—

• Specify that the exception does not apply to durable medical equipment (other than infusion pumps) or to parenteral and enteral nutrients, equipment, and supplies; and

• Revise paragraph (b)(2) of § 411.355 to require that the services be furnished in one of the following locations:

+ A building in which the referring physician (or another physician who is a member of the same group practice) furnishes physician services unrelated to the furnishing of designated health services.

+ A building that is used by the group practice for the provision of some or all of the group's clinical laboratory services.

+ A building that is used by the group practice for the centralized provision of the group's designated health services (other than clinical laboratory services).

• Indicate that when a group practice bills for ancillary services, the services must be billed under a billing number assigned to the group practice.

We have also made several other changes to the in-office ancillary services exception that we discuss in section III of this preamble.

For purposes of the in-office ancillary services exception, the August 1995 final rule also defined "direct supervision" at § 411.351. The rule defines this term as supervision by a

physician who is present in the office suite and immediately available to provide assistance and direction throughout the time services are being performed. This proposed rule would retain that definition, with several changes that are meant to clarify the meaning of the term "present in the office suite." We discuss these changes in section III of this preamble.

c. Exception—certain prepaid health plans

Section 1877(b)(3) specifies that the prohibition on referrals does not apply to services furnished by certain prepaid health plans. To qualify for the exception, the services must be furnished by a Federally-qualified health maintenance organization (within the meaning of section 1310(d) of the Public Health Services Act) to its enrollees or by a prepaid health care organization to its enrollees under a contract or agreement with Medicare under one of the following statutory authorities:

• Section 1876, which authorizes us to enter into contracts with health maintenance organizations and competitive medical plans to furnish covered items and services on a risk-sharing or reasonable cost basis.

• Section 1833(a)(1)(A), which authorizes payment for Medicare Part B services to prepaid health plans on a reasonable cost basis.

• Section 402(a) of the Social Security Amendments of 1967 or section 222(a) of the Social Security Amendments of 1972, both of which authorize us to conduct demonstration projects involving payments on a prepaid basis.

The August 1995 final rule incorporated section 1877(b)(3) into our regulations at § 411.355(c). We are proposing to set forth at § 435.1012(b) an exception for services provided by organizations analogous to those cited above to enrollees under the Medicaid program. We discuss this proposal in section III of this preamble.

d. Other exceptions

Effective January 1, 1995, section 1877(b)(4) authorizes the Secretary to provide in regulations for additional exceptions for financial relationships, beyond those specified in the statute, if she determines that they do not pose a risk of Medicare program or patient abuse. The Secretary determined, based on the rationale explained in the August 1995 final rule, that referrals for certain clinical laboratory services furnished in an ambulatory surgical center or end stage renal disease facility, or by a hospice do not pose a risk of Medicare program or patient abuse. The Secretary

found no risk of abuse when payments for these services are included in the ambulatory surgical center payment rate, the end stage renal disease composite payment rate, or as part of the hospice payment rate, respectively. Therefore, the August 1995 final rule incorporated an exception for those services into our regulations at § 411.355(d). This proposed rule would retain that provision, with a change discussed below. Because this proposed rule covers 10 additional designated health services, this exception would now apply to any of the designated health services provided in the same manner.

As we noted in the August 1995 final rule, we excepted the listed services because they are furnished as part of a composite rate that cannot vary in response to utilization. We are amending § 411.355(d) to allow the Secretary to except services furnished under other payment rates that the Secretary determines provide no financial incentive for either underutilization or overutilization, or any other risk of program or patient abuse. We are specifically soliciting comments on whether there are analogous composite rates under the Medicaid program that are similarly guaranteed not to result in program or patient abuse. Commenters who are interested in this issue should demonstrate why they believe a particular kind of service should qualify for the exception.

4. Exceptions That Apply Only to Certain Ownership or Investment Interests

The statute also provides that certain ownership or investment interests do not constitute a "financial relationship" for purposes of the section 1877 prohibition on referrals.

a. Exception—certain investment securities and shares

Under section 1877(c), the prohibition on referrals does not apply in the case of ownership by a physician (or immediate family member) of the following:

• Investment securities (including shares or bonds, debentures, notes, or other debt instruments) that may be purchased on terms generally available to the public and that are—

• Securities listed on the New York Stock Exchange, the American Stock Exchange, or any regional exchange in which quotations are published on a daily basis, or foreign securities listed on a recognized foreign, national, or regional exchange in which quotations are published on a daily basis, or

- Securities traded under an automated interdealer quotation system operated by the National Association of Securities Dealers, and
- In a corporation that had, at the end of the corporation's most recent fiscal year or on average during the previous 3 fiscal years, stockholder equity exceeding $75 million. (OBRA '93 also included, until January 1, 1995, securities in a corporation that, at the end of the corporation's most recent fiscal year, had total assets exceeding $100 million.)
- Ownership of shares in a regulated investment company as defined in section 851(a) of the Internal Revenue Code of 1986 if the company had, at the end of the company's most recent fiscal year or on average during the previous 3 fiscal years, total assets exceeding $75 million.

The August 1995 final rule incorporated the above provision into our regulations at §§ 411.356 (a) and (b). This proposed rule would remove from § 411.356(a) that portion of the provision that expired on January 1, 1995, and would make certain other changes described in section III of this preamble.

b. Exception—ownership or investment interest in certain health care facilities

Section 1877(d) provides additional exceptions to the prohibition on physician referrals for certain designated health services furnished by three types of facilities if the physician (or immediate family member) has an ownership or investment interest in the facilities:
- Designated health services furnished by a hospital located in Puerto Rico.
- Designated health services furnished in a rural area by an entity if substantially all of the designated health services furnished by the entity are furnished to individuals residing in a rural area. A "rural area" is defined in section 1886(d)(2)(D) as meaning an area outside of a Metropolitan Statistical Area. (Until January 1, 1995, this provision read as follows: "In the case of clinical laboratory services if the laboratory furnishing the services is in a rural area (as defined in section 1886(d)(2)(D)).")
- Designated health services furnished by a hospital outside of Puerto Rico if the referring physician is authorized to perform services at the hospital and the ownership or investment interest is in the hospital itself (and not merely in a subdivision of the hospital).

The August 1995 final rule incorporated section 1877(d), as it

related to clinical laboratory services, into our regulations at § 411.356(c). In establishing the rural provider exception in the regulations, we required that referred laboratory testing be performed on the premises of the rural laboratory (if not performed on the premises, the laboratory performing the testing was required to bill the Medicare program directly). As described in the preamble to the proposed rule covering referrals for clinical laboratory services (57 FR 8598 (March 11, 1992)), we believe that Congress included this exception in order to benefit Medicare beneficiaries who live in rural areas where laboratories may not be available without the financial support of local physicians. We included the additional requirement to prevent situations in which physicians who own an urban laboratory set up a storefront or "shell" laboratory with a rural address in order to use the rural exception. In this scenario, the urban owner could make referrals to the rural laboratory, which would in turn refer the tests to the physician's urban laboratory. Alternatively, urban laboratories with physician owners could set up rural laboratories for the purpose of performing tests referred by the physician owners for their urban patients.

Because section 1877(d)(2) has been amended to apply only to designated health services that are actually furnished in a rural area (they cannot be transferred to an urban provider), and only by providers that provide designated health services to a predominantly rural population, we no longer believe that the extra requirement is necessary. We are therefore proposing to remove it from § 410.356(c).

The August 1995 final regulation adopted the OBRA '93 standard that substantially all of the designated health services furnished by the rural entity are furnished to individuals residing in a rural area. We interpreted "substantially all" as meaning at least 75 percent of the services. In addition, § 411.356(c) provided an exception, until January 1, 1995, for an ownership or investment interest in a hospital if the physician's ownership or investment interest does not relate (directly or indirectly) to the furnishing of clinical laboratory services. This exception was based on section 1877(b)(4) as it read under OBRA '90. OBRA '93, as amended by SSA '94, retained this provision only until January 1, 1995.

This proposed rule would revise § 411.356(c) to reflect the statutory provision as it became effective on January 1, 1995 and to apply § 411.356(c) to entities providing any of

the designated health services. We would change the requirement that a rural entity be located in a rural area to instead except referrals for designated health services furnished in a rural area by an entity that furnishes substantially all of its designated health services to individuals residing in a rural area. We would continue to interpret "substantially all" as being at least 75 percent of the services furnished by the entity. In addition, this proposed rule would remove the exception that expired on January 1, 1995.

5. Exceptions That Apply Only to Certain Compensation Arrangements

Section 1877(e) provides that certain compensation arrangements are not considered a "financial relationship" for purposes of the prohibition on physician referrals.

a. Exception—rental of office space

Section 1877(e)(1)(A) provides an exception for payments made by a lessee to a lessor for the use of premises if the following conditions are met:
- The lease is in writing, signed by the parties, and specifies the premises covered by the lease.
- The space rented or leased does not exceed that which is reasonable and necessary for the legitimate business purposes of the rental or lease. Also, the space is used exclusively by the lessee when being used by the lessee, except that the lessee may make payments for the use of space consisting of common areas under certain conditions. That is, acceptable payments for common areas cannot exceed the lessee's pro rata share of expenses for that space based upon the ratio of the space used exclusively by the lessee to the total amount of space (other than common areas) occupied by all persons using the common areas.
- The lease provides for a term of rental or lease of at least 1 year.
- The rental charges over the term of the lease are set in advance, are consistent with fair market value, and are not determined in a manner that takes into account the volume or value of any referrals or other business generated between the parties.
- The lease would be commercially reasonable even if no referrals were made between the parties.
- The lease meets any other requirements the Secretary may impose by regulation, as needed to protest against Medicare program or patient abuse.

"Fair market value" is defined by section 1877(h)(3) as the value in arm's-length transactions, consistent with the general value market, and, with respect to rentals or leases, the value of rental property for general commercial purposes (not taking into account its intended use) and, in the case of a lease of space by a lessor that is a potential source of patient referrals to the lessee, not adjusted to reflect the additional value the prospective lessee or lessor would attribute to the proximity or convenience to the lessor. (Meeting the fair market value standard is a requirement for several of the other compensation-related exceptions in the statute. We discuss these other exceptions later in this preamble.)

The August 1995 final rule incorporated the provisions of section 1877(e)(1)(A) into our regulations at § 411.357(a), without imposing any additional requirements. This proposed rule would retain § 411.357(a). In addition, the final rule incorporated the definition of "fair market value" in § 411.351. This proposed rule would retain the definition. Also, since the statute requires that fair market value be "consistent with the general market value," we have added to the definition an explanation of "general market value."

b. Exception—rental of equipment

Section 1877(e)(1)(B) provides an exception for payments made by a lessee of equipment to the lessor for the use of the equipment if the following conditions are met:

• The lease is set out in writing, signed by the parties, and specifies the equipment covered by the lease.

• The equipment rented or leased does not exceed that which is reasonable and necessary for the legitimate business purposes of the rental or lease and is used exclusively by the lessee when being used by the lessee.

• The lease provides for a term of rental or lease of at least 1 year.

• The rental charges over the term of the lease are set in advance, are consistent with fair market value, and are not determined in a manner that takes into account the volume or value of any referrals or other business generated between the parties.

• The lease would be commercially reasonable even if no referrals were made between the parties.

• The lease meets any other requirements the Secretary may impose by regulation as needed to protect against Medicare program or patient abuse.

The August 1995 final rule incorporated this provision into our regulations at § 411.357(b), without imposing any additional requirements. This proposed rule would retain

§ 411.357(b), with minor editorial changes.

c. Exception—bona fide employment relationship

Under section 1877(e)(2), any amount paid by an employer to a physician (or an immediate family member of the physician) who has a bona fide employment relationship with the employer for the provision of services does not constitute a compensation arrangement for purposes of the prohibition if the following conditions are met:

• The employment is for identifiable services.

• The amount of the remuneration under the employment is consistent with the fair market value of the services and (except for certain productivity bonuses) is not determined in a manner that takes into account (directly or indirectly) the volume or value of any referrals by the referring physician.

• The remuneration is made in accordance with an agreement that would be commercially reasonable even if no referrals were made to the employer.

• The employment meets any other requirements the Secretary may impose by regulation as needed to protect against Medicare program or patient abuse.

The statute provides that, under this exception, a productivity bonus that is based on services performed personally by the physician (or immediate family member) does not violate the "volume or value of referrals" standard.

"Employee" is defined in section 1877(h)(2) as an individual who would be considered to be an employee of the entity under the usual common law rules that apply in determining employer-employee relationships, as applied for purposes of section 3121(d)(2) of the Internal Revenue Code of 1986.

The August 1995 final rule incorporated the provisions of section 1877(e)(2) into our regulations at § 411.357(c), without imposing any additional requirements. This proposed rule would retain § 411.357(c), but with additional requirements that we describe in section III. The final rule also incorporated the definition of "employee" into our regulations at § 411.351. Again, this proposed rule would retain that definition.

d. Exception—personal service arrangements

Under section 1877(e)(3)(A), remuneration from an entity under an arrangement (including remuneration

for specific physician services furnished to a nonprofit blood center) does not constitute a compensation arrangement for purposes of the prohibition on referrals if the following conditions are met:

• The arrangement is set out in writing, signed by the parties, and specifies the services covered by the arrangement.

• The arrangement covers all of the services to be furnished by the physician (or immediate family member) to the entity.

• The aggregate services contracted for do not exceed those that are reasonable and necessary for the legitimate business purposes of the arrangement.

• The term of the arrangement is for at least 1 year.

• The compensation to be paid over the term of the arrangement is set in advance, does not exceed fair market value, and, except in the case of a physician incentive plan (as described below) is not determined in a manner that takes into account the volume or value of any referrals or other business generated between the parties.

• The services to be performed under the arrangement do not involve the counseling or promotion of a business arrangement or other activity that violates State or Federal law.

• The arrangement meets any other requirements the Secretary may impose by regulation as needed to protect against program or patient abuse.

The August 1995 final rule incorporated section 1877(e)(3)(A) into our regulations at § 411.357(d)(1), without imposing any additional requirements. This proposed rule would retain § 411.357(d)(1), with several changes that we discuss in section III of this preamble.

Section 1877(e)(3)(B)(i) provides that, in the case of a physician incentive plan between a physician and an entity, the compensation may be determined in a manner (through a withhold, capitation, bonus, or otherwise) that takes into account, directly or indirectly, the volume or value of any referrals or other business generated between the parties, if the plan meets the following requirements:

• No specific payment is made (directly or indirectly) under the plan to a physician or a physician group as an inducement to reduce or limit medically necessary services provided with respect to a specific individual enrolled with the entity.

• If the plan places a physician or a physician group at substantial financial risk as determined by the Secretary under section 1876(i)(8)(A)(ii), the plan

Federal Register / Vol. 63, No. 6 / Friday, January 9, 1998 / Proposed Rules **1669**

complies with any requirements the Secretary may impose under that section.

• Upon request by the Secretary, the entity provides the Secretary with access to descriptive information regarding the plan, in order to permit the Secretary to determine whether the plan is in compliance with the requirements listed above.

(Note: Sections 1876(i)(8) and 1903(m)(2)(A) require that physician incentive plans be regulated. On March 27, 1996, we published, at 61 FR 13430, a final rule with comment period that implemented this legislation for purposes of both the Medicare and Medicaid programs by establishing requirements at § 417.479 (for Medicare) and at § 434.70 (for Medicaid). A final rule amending the final rule with comment was published on December 31, 1996 at 61 FR 69034.)

The August 1995 final rule incorporated section 1877(e)(3)(B)(i) into our regulations at § 411.357(d)(2). Because of the establishment at § 417.479 of requirements concerning incentive plans, this proposed rule would revise § 411.357(d)(2). It would replace the reference to requirements established by the Secretary under section 1876(i)(8)(A)(ii) of the Act with a reference to the requirements of § 417.479. We would also reverse the order of paragraphs (ii) and (iii) of § 411.357(d)(2) because we believe this order reflects a more logical progression. In addition, we would delete existing § 411.357(d)(3), which contains a time-sensitive provision related to personal services arrangements that, based on the statute, is now obsolete.

Section 1877(e)(3)(B)(ii) defines a "physician incentive plan" as any compensation arrangement between an entity and a physician or physician group that may directly or indirectly have the effect of reducing or limiting services provided with respect to individuals enrolled with the entity. The August 1995 final rule incorporated this definition into our regulations at § 411.351. This proposed rule would retain that definition.

e. Exception—remuneration unrelated to the provision of designated health services

Prior to OBRA '93, section 1877(b)(4) provided an exception for any financial relationship with a hospital if the financial relationship does not relate to the provision of clinical laboratory services. OBRA '93 eliminated this provision, but SSA '94 reinstated it until January 1, 1995. OBRA '93 also added paragraph (e)(4) to section 1877, retroactive to January 1, 1992. Under

section 1877(e)(4), remuneration provided by a hospital to a physician that does not relate to the furnishing of designated health services does not constitute a compensation arrangement for purposes of the prohibition on referrals. Section 1877(e)(4) differs from the predecessor provision at section 1877(b)(4) in that it retains only the compensation aspect of the exception. In addition, it applies only to remuneration from a hospital to a physician (that is, it does not include remuneration from a physician to a hospital) if the remuneration does not relate to the furnishing of designated health services. Also, the exception does not apply to remuneration from a hospital to a member of a physician's immediate family.

The August 1995 final rule incorporated the provisions of sections 1877(b)(4) and (e)(4) as they were effective on January 1, 1992, and as they relate to compensation, into our regulations at § 411.357(g). This proposed rule would revise § 411.357(g) by removing that portion that was based on the predecessor provision of section 1877(b)(4), since that provision has expired. We would also revise that portion of § 411.357(g) that was based on section 1877(e)(4) by changing the reference to remuneration not related to the furnishing of clinical laboratory services to remuneration not related to the furnishing of designated health services. We have also made several other changes described in section III of this preamble.

f. Exception—physician recruitment

Section 1877(e)(5) provides that remuneration provided by a hospital to a physician to induce the physician to relocate to the area serviced by the hospital in order to be a member of the hospital's medical staff does not constitute a compensation arrangement for purposes of the prohibition on referrals if the following conditions are met:

• The physician is not required to refer patients to the hospital.

• The amount of remuneration under the arrangement is not determined in a manner that takes into account (directly or indirectly) the volume or value of any referrals by the referring physician.

• The arrangement meets any other requirements the Secretary may impose by regulation as needed to protect against program or patient abuse.

The August 1995 final rule incorporated the provisions of section 1877(e)(5) into our regulations at § 411.357(e), with additional requirements. Under our authority to impose additional requirements, we

specified that the arrangement and its terms must be in writing and signed by both parties. We also specified that the physician must not be precluded from establishing staff privileges at another hospital or referring business to another entity. This proposed rule would retain § 411.357(e), with a minor editorial change.

g. Exception—isolated transaction

Section 1877(e)(6) provides that an isolated transaction, such as a one-time sale of property or a practice, is not considered to be a compensation arrangement for purposes of the prohibition on referrals if the following conditions are met:

• The amount of remuneration for the transaction is consistent with fair market value and is not determined, directly or indirectly, in a manner that takes into account the volume or value of referrals by the physician.

• The remuneration is provided under an agreement that would be commercially reasonable even if no referrals were made to the entity.

• The arrangement meets any other requirements the Secretary may impose by regulation as needed to protect against Medicare program or patient abuse.

The August 1995 final rule incorporated the provisions of section 1877(e)(6) into our regulations at § 411.357(f), with additional requirements. Under our authority to impose additional requirements, we specified that there can be no additional transactions between the parties for 6 months after the isolated transaction, except for transactions that are specifically excepted under one of the other exceptions provided in the regulations. This proposed rule would retain § 411.357(f), with a minor editorial change. In addition, we established definitions of "transaction" and "isolated transaction" at § 411.351. We defined a "transaction" as an instance or process of two or more persons doing business. We defined an "isolated transaction" as one involving a single payment between two or more persons. We specified that a transaction that involves long-term or installment payments is not considered an isolated transaction. This proposed rule would retain those definitions, with the clarification that "transactions" can involve persons or entities.

h. Exception—certain group practice arrangements with a hospital

Section 1877(e)(7) provides that an arrangement between a hospital and group under which designated health services are furnished by the group but are billed by the hospital does not constitute a compensation arrangement for purposes of the prohibition on referrals if the following conditions are met:

• With respect to the services furnished to a hospital inpatient, the arrangement is for the provision of inpatient hospital services under section 1861(b)(3).

• The arrangement began before December 19, 1989, and has continued in effect without interruption since that date.

• With respect to the designated health services covered by the arrangement, substantially all of those services furnished to patients of the hospital are furnished by the group under the arrangement.

• The arrangement is set out in a written agreement that specifies the services to be furnished by the parties and the amount of compensation.

• The compensation paid over the term of the agreement is consistent with fair market value, and the compensation per unit of services is fixed in advance and is not determined in a manner that takes into account the volume or value of any referrals or other business generated between the parties.

• The compensation is provided under an agreement that would be commercially reasonable even if no referrals were made to the entity.

• The arrangement between the parties meets any other requirements the Secretary may impose by regulation as needed to protect against Medicare program or patient abuse.

The August 1995 final rule incorporated the provisions of section 1877(e)(7), as they relate to clinical laboratory services, into our regulations at § 411.357(h), without imposing any additional requirements. This proposed rule would revise § 411.357(h) to apply the provisions to the designated health services, and would make certain minor changes described in section III.

i. Exception—payments by a physician for items and services

Section 1877(e)(8) provides that the following do not constitute compensation arrangements for purposes of the prohibition on referrals:

• Payments made by a physician to a laboratory in exchange for the provision of clinical laboratory services.

• Payments made by a physician to an entity as compensation for items or services other than clinical laboratory services if the items or services are furnished at fair market value.

The August 1995 final rule incorporated the provisions of section 1877(e)(8) into our regulations at

§ 411.357(i). This proposed rule would retain § 411.357(i), but clarify that "services" as used in the provision means services of any kind (not just those defined as "services" for purposes of the Medicare program in § 400.202).

6. Requirements Related to the "Substantially All" Test

As mentioned earlier, the definition of "group practice" in section 1877(h)(4) contains a requirement that substantially all of the services of the physicians who are members of the group be furnished through the group. In the August 1995 final rule, we interpreted "substantially all" to mean at least 75 percent of the total patient care services of the group practice members. Further, we defined "members of the group," at § 411.351, as physician partners and full-time and part-time physician contractors and employees during the time they furnish services to patients of the group practice that are furnished through the group and are billed in the name of the group. This proposed rule would revise the definition of "members of the group" to exclude independent contractors, to count physician owners other than partners, and to count physicians as members during the time they furnish "patient care services" to the group. We discuss these changes in section III of this preamble.

The August 1995 final rule defined "patient care services," at § 411.351, as any tasks performed by a group practice member that address the medical needs of specific patients, regardless of whether they involve direct patient encounters. We included, as examples, the services of physicians who do not directly treat patients, time spent by a physician consulting with other physicians, and time spent reviewing laboratory tests. Under § 411.351, "patient care services" are measured by the total patient care time each member spends on these services.

This proposed rule would retain the definition of patient care services, but would broaden the definition to include tasks that benefit patients in general or the group practice. We are also proposing minor changes that we believe are necessary to clarify what tasks qualify under the definition. We describe these changes in section III of this preamble.

The August 1995 final rule also required, at § 411.360, that a group practice submit a written statement to its carrier annually to attest that, during the most recent 12-month period (calendar year, fiscal year, or immediately preceding 12-month period) 75 percent of the total patient

care services of group practice members was furnished through the group, was billed under a billing number assigned to the group, and the amounts so received were treated as receipts of the group.

Section 411.360 also provides that a newly-formed group practice (one in which physicians have recently begun to practice together) or any group practice that has been unable in the past to meet the definition of a group practice as set forth at section 1877(h)(4) must—

• Submit a written statement to attest that, during the next 12-month period (calendar year, fiscal year, or next 12 months), it expects to meet the 75 percent standard and will take measures to ensure the standard is met; and

• At the end of the 12-month period, submit a written statement to attest that it met the 75 percent standard during that period, billed for those services under a billing number assigned to the group, and treated amounts received for those services as receipts of the group. If the group did not meet the standard, any Medicare payments made to the group during the 12-month period that were conditioned on the group meeting the standard are overpayments.

In addition, § 411.360 specifies that—

• Once any group has chosen to use its fiscal year, the calendar year, or some other 12-month period, the group practice must adhere to this choice.

• The attestation must contain a statement that the information furnished in the attestation is true and accurate and must be signed by a group representative.

• Any group that intends to meet the definition of a group practice in order to qualify for one of the exceptions provided in the regulations must submit the required attestation to its carrier by December 12, 1995.

The August 1995 final rule contains a discussion of the rationale for the above provisions. On December 11, 1995, we published in the **Federal Register**, at 60 FR 63438, a final rule that delays the date by which a group of physicians must file an attestation statement. The December final rule amended § 411.360 to require that a group that intends to meet the definition of a group practice must submit an attestation statement to its carrier no later than 60 days after the group receives attestation instructions from its carrier. The preamble to the December rule points out that a group can regard itself as a group practice in the interim period before it receives attestation instructions, provided the group believes that it meets the definition of a group practice under § 411.351.

This proposed rule would retain § 411.360, as amended by the December 1995 final rule. We propose to make several minor changes to clarify that a group is only required to complete an attestation if it wishes to qualify as a group practice for purposes of meeting an exception that requires group status. We are also changing the provision to require that the attestation be signed by an authorized representative of the group practice who is knowledgeable about the group, and to contain a statement that the information furnished in the attestation is true and accurate to the best of the representative's knowledge and belief. The proposed provision also states that any person filing a false statement will be subject to applicable criminal and civil penalties.

7. Reporting Requirements

Prior to SSA '94, section 1877(f) included the requirement that each entity furnishing Medicare covered items or services must provide us with certain information concerning its ownership or investment arrangements. In our December 3, 1991 interim final rule with comment period, published in the **Federal Register** at 56 FR 61374, we extended the rule to include certain information concerning an entity's compensation arrangements for the reasons discussed in the preamble of that rule.

Section 1877(f) also gave the Secretary the option of waiving the reporting requirements, for certain entities that do not furnish clinical laboratory services, in all but 10 States. The interim final rule discussed our decision to waive the reporting requirements for all entities (other than those providing clinical laboratory services) in States other than the minimum 10 States specified in the statute. In the 10 States, we were required to obtain data from at least six specific types of entities. We gathered data from these providers in the fall of 1991.

Section 152 of SSA '94 amended section 1877(f) extensively. It extended the reporting requirements to specifically cover information not only about an entity's ownership or investment interests, but about compensation arrangements as well. SSA '94 also eliminated the Secretary's authority to waive the reporting requirements for certain States or services, although the Secretary continues to have the right to determine that an entity is not subject to the reporting requirements because it provides services covered under Medicare very infrequently. In addition,

the requirements continue to not apply to designated health services furnished outside of the United States. Section 1877(f) allows the Secretary to gather the information in such form, manner, and at such times as she specifies.

We discussed the provisions of section 1877(f), as they relate to clinical laboratories and as they read under OBRA '90, in detail in the December 1991 interim final rule. The August 1995 final rule adopted the provisions of the interim final rule with revisions that reflect the changes made by SSA '94. While the August 1995 final rule reflects the amendments made to section 1877(f), it did not interpret these amendments. This proposed rule retains the reporting requirements as they appear in the August 1995 final rule, subject to certain interpretations we have added in section III of this preamble. These requirements are set forth at existing § 411.361, and we would apply them to any future reporting we may require.

8. Sanctions

Prior to OBRA '93, section 1877(g)(1) required a denial of payment for a clinical laboratory service that was provided in violation of the referral prohibition. Paragraph (g)(2) of section 1877 required the timely refund of amounts collected in violation of the prohibition. OBRA '93 extended these provisions to apply to all of the designated health services, effective January 1, 1995. The August 1995 final rule incorporated these provisions as they relate to clinical laboratory services into our regulations at §§ 411.353(c) and (d), respectively. This proposed rule would revise §§ 411.353(c) and (d) to extend their application to the other designated health services.

Paragraph (g)(3) of section 1877 provides for the imposition of a civil money penalty of $15,000 per service and exclusion from Medicare and any State health care program, including Medicaid, for any person who presents or causes to be presented a bill or claim the person knows or should know is for a service for which payment may not be made under § 1877(a). The same penalty applies for a service for which a person has not made a refund as described in paragraph (g)(2).

Paragraph (g)(4) provides for a $100,000 civil money penalty and the same exclusion penalty for any physician or other entity that enters into a circumvention scheme that the physician or entity knows or should know has a principal purpose of assuring referrals by the physician to a particular entity which, if the physician made the referrals directly, would be in

violation of section 1877. A proposed rule published by the Office of Inspector General on October 20, 1993 (58 FR 54096) addresses sections 1877(g)(3) and (g)(4). That rule became final on March 31, 1995 (60 FR 16580).

Paragraph (g)(5) of section 1877 provides for possible exclusion and a civil money penalty of not more than $10,000 per day for each day in which a person has failed to meet a reporting requirement in section 1877(f). The December 1991 interim final rule covering the reporting requirements incorporated this provision into our regulations at § 411.361(g), and the August 1995 final rule redesignated § 411.361(g) as § 411.361(f). This proposed rule would retain § 411.361(f).

9. Additional Definitions

In implementing provisions of section 1877 as they were effective on January 1, 1992, the August 1995 final rule established definitions of the following terms (which were not discussed above) at § 411.351:

a. *Clinical laboratory services* means the biological, microbiological, serological, chemical, immunohematological, biophysical, cytological, pathological, or other examination of materials derived from the human body for the purpose of providing information for the diagnosis, prevention, or treatment of any disease or impairment of, or the assessment of the health of, human beings. These examinations also include procedures to determine, measure, or otherwise describe the presence or absence of various substances or organisms in the body.

b. *Entity* means a sole proprietorship, trust, corporation, partnership, foundation, not-for-profit corporation, or unincorporated association. For reasons discussed in section III of this preamble, this proposed rule would revise the definition of "entity" to include a physician's sole proprietorship and any practice of multiple physicians that provides for the furnishing of a designated health service.

c. *Hospital* means any separate legally-organized operating entity plus any subsidiary, related, or other entities that perform services for the hospital's patients and for which the hospital bills. However, we have excluded from this definition entities that perform services for hospital patients "under arrangements" with the hospital. We propose to amend this definition to make it clear that "hospitals" include regular hospitals, psychiatric hospitals, and rural primary care hospitals.

d. *HPSA* means, for purposes of the August 1995 final rule, an area designated as a health professional shortage area under section 332(a)(1)(A) of the Public Health Service Act for primary medical care professionals (in accordance with the criteria specified in 42 CFR part 5, Appendix A, Part I— Geographic Areas). In addition, with respect to dental, mental health, vision care, podiatric, and pharmacy services, an HPSA means an area designated as a health professional shortage area under section 332(a)(1)(A) of the Public Health Service Act for dental professionals, mental health professionals, vision care professionals, podiatric professionals, and pharmacy professionals, respectively.

e. *Immediate family member* or "member of a physician's immediate family" means husband or wife; natural or adoptive parent, child, or sibling; stepparent, stepchild, stepbrother, or stepsister; father-in-law, mother-in-law, son-in-law, daughter-in-law, brother-in-law, or sister-in-law; grandparent or grandchild; and spouse of a grandparent or grandchild.

f. *Laboratory* means an entity furnishing biological, microbiological, serological, chemical, immunohematological, hematological, biophysical, cytological, pathological, or other examination of materials derived from the human body for the purpose of providing information for the diagnosis, prevention, or treatment of any disease or impairment of, or the assessment of the health of, human beings. These examinations also include procedures to determine, measure, or otherwise describe the presence or absence of various substances or organisms in the body. Entities only collecting or preparing specimens (or both) or only serving as a mailing service and not performing testing are not considered laboratories.

g. The August 1995 final rule defined a "plan of care" as the establishment by a physician of a course of diagnosis or treatment (or both) for a particular patient, including the ordering of items or services. For reasons discussed earlier, this proposed rule would remove the words "items or" from this definition.

(We explain our rationale for some of these definitions in the March 1992 proposed rule, and we explain the remainder in the August 1995 final rule.) We would extend these definitions to apply to referrals involving any of the designated health services.

We have made some changes to the definitions in addition to those noted above. Any changes in definitions that we have included in this proposed rule do not result from changes in the legislation, but reflect our most recent interpretations of the statute. In section III of this preamble, we discuss in detail how we propose to interpret provisions in section 1877 and in section 1903(s) that we have either not interpreted in the August 1995 final rule or that we believe we must reconsider in the context of the designated health services. In section III, we also define or interpret terms that are present in the statute (such as each of the designated health services) as well as include new definitions that we propose to add to the rule to enable us to implement other parts of the statute.

10. Conforming Changes

We propose to revise existing §§ 411.1(a) and 411.350(a), which set forth the statutory basis for the provisions in part 411, subpart A, and part 411, subpart J, respectively, by changing the reference to "clinical laboratory services" to "designated health services."

11. Editorial Changes

In addition to the proposed changes discussed above, we would also make a number of editorial changes to subpart J of part 411. These changes would not affect the substance of the provisions. As an example of the type of change we would make, in § 411.355(a), we would add the words "of this chapter" after the reference to § 410.20(a).

B. Applying The Referral Prohibition to the Medicaid Program: Section 1903(s) of the Act and the Provisions of This Proposed Rule

Title XIX of the Act authorizes Federal grants to States to establish Medicaid programs to provide medical assistance to needy individuals. Medicaid programs are administered by the States in accordance with Federal laws and regulations. State Medicaid agencies operate their programs in accordance with a Medicaid State plan that is approved by us.

While Medicaid programs are administered by the States, they are jointly financed by the Federal and State governments. The Federal government pays its share of medical assistance expenditures to the State on a quarterly basis according to a formula described in sections 1903 and 1905(b). The amount of the Federal share for medical assistance is called Federal financial participation (FFP). Before the enactment of OBRA '93, there were no statutory or regulatory requirements concerning the availability of FFP for Medicaid services resulting from physician referrals.

Section 13624 of OBRA '93, entitled "Application of Medicare Rules Limiting Certain Physician Referrals," added a new paragraph (s) to section 1903 of the Act. This new provision extends aspects of the Medicare prohibition on physician referrals to Medicaid. Specifically, this provision restricts FFP for expenditures for medical assistance under the State plan consisting of designated health services, as defined under section 1877(h)(6), that are furnished to an individual on the basis of a physician referral that would result in the denial of payment under the Medicare program if Medicare covered the services to the same extent and under the same terms and conditions as under a State's Medicaid plan.

This proposed rule would revise § 435.1002, "FFP for services," to reflect section 1903(s). We would specify in § 435.1002(a) that the availability of FFP for expenditures for Medicaid services is subject to the limitations set forth in new § 435.1012. We would entitle § 435.1012 as "Limitation on FFP Related to Prohibited Referrals." The proposed new provision states that we will deny FFP for designated health services (as defined in § 431.351) furnished under the State plan to an individual on the basis of a physician referral that would result in the denial of payment under the Medicare program if Medicare covered the services to the same extent and under the same terms and conditions as under the State plan. We believe that certain aspects of section 1903(s) require our interpretation, and we discuss these aspects in section III of this preamble.

Section 4314 of the Balanced Budget Act of 1997 established section 1877(g)(6) of the Act. It requires that the Secretary issue written advisory opinions to outside parties concerning whether the referral of a Medicare patient by a physician for designated health services (other than clinical laboratory services) is prohibited under the physician referral provisions in section 1877. Because the Medicare rules can affect whether a State will receive FFP for certain services, States, as well as individuals and entities that provide services under the Medicaid program, may be interested in the advisory opinion process. As a result, we have included in § 435.1012(c) a cross reference to the Medicare regulations that set forth the specific procedures we will use in issuing advisory opinions.

Section 1903(s) also specifies that the reporting requirements of section

Federal Register / Vol. 63, No. 6 / Friday, January 9, 1998 / Proposed Rules **1673**

1877(f) and the penalties for failing to report in section 1877(g)(5) apply to a provider of a designated health service for which payment may be made under Medicaid in the same manner as they apply to a provider that furnishes a designated health service for which payment may be made under Medicare.

This proposed rule would incorporate the provisions of sections 1877(f) and (g)(5) into our Medicaid regulations by adding new §§ 455.108 and 455.109 to part 455 ("Program Integrity: Medicaid"). These two provisions would appear under a new subpart C entitled "Disclosure of Information by Providers for Purposes of the Prohibition on Certain Physician Referrals." Section 455.108, "Purpose," would specify that subpart C implements section 1903(s) of the Act. Section 455.109, "Disclosure of ownership, investment, and compensation arrangements," would list the specific disclosure requirements, and the sanctions for failing to comply. We interpret these disclosure requirements, as we believe they apply to Medicaid providers, in section III of this preamble.

III. Interpretations of Sections 1877 and 1903(s) of the Act

In this section of the preamble, we discuss in detail how we propose to interpret provisions in section 1877 and in section 1903(s) that we either did not interpret in the August 1995 final rule or that we interpreted in the context of referrals for clinical laboratory services, but must reconsider in the context of the additional designated health services. We propose to define or interpret terms that are present in the statute (such as each of the designated health services) or to reinterpret or clarify certain statutory terms that we interpreted in the past. We also propose to add certain new terms and definitions to the rule that we believe are necessary for us to implement parts of the statute. This section is structured in the order we used to present the statutory provisions and our interpretations in the August 1995 final rule. We would like to point out that, in these proposed regulations, we intend to interpret only the provisions of section 1877 of the Act, and not the provisions of any other State or Federal laws, such as the antitrust laws, the anti-kickback statute, or the Internal Revenue Code.

A. Definitions

1. Designated Health Services

As we noted above, OBRA '93 expanded the physician referral prohibition to apply to ten designated

health services in addition to clinical laboratory services. Section 1877(h)(6) lists these services, but does not define them. Because the designated health services are not defined in section 1877, we would define them in § 411.351.

Designated health services as components of other services. We believe that a designated health service remains one, even if it is billed as something else or is subsumed within another service category by being bundled with other services for billing purposes. For example, most services provided by a skilled nursing facility (SNF) are considered SNF services, which are not themselves designated health services. Nonetheless, SNF services can encompass a variety of designated health services, such as physical therapy services or laboratory services.

Similarly under Medicaid, services provided by a clinic are considered "clinic services" under section 1905(a)(9) of the Act, but could encompass a variety of designated health services, such as occupational therapy, physical therapy, or radiology services.

We base our interpretation on the fact that Congress compiled its list of designated health services based on abuses or potential abuses it perceived in regard to a variety of specific kinds of services. The list in section 1877(h)(6), in fact, does not exactly track the service categories as they are defined under either Medicare or Medicaid. In short, we regard the services designated in section 1877 as subject to the requirements of that section regardless of the setting in which they are provided or the payment category under which they are billed.

On the other hand, we are also aware that designated health services are sometimes provided as merely peripheral parts of some other major service that a physician has prescribed. For example, physicians often employ echocardiography (to obtain ultrasound signals from the heart) as a mechanism to intraoperatively view the results of bypass surgery. We do not believe that a physician using echocardiography this way has made a specific referral for a designated health service; instead, we regard the physician as prescribing a physician service that happens to incidentally include echocardiography. In other words, it is our view that a physician is unlikely to over-prescribe bypass surgery in order to enhance his or her investment in an echocardiography machine. Because we believe that Congress meant to include under designated health services specific services that are or could be

subject to abuse, we are proposing to define those services accordingly. Thus, we propose to deviate from standard Medicare or Medicaid definitions of certain services in order to meet the intent of the statute.

How we define designated health services. We have chosen, in general, to base the definitions for the designated health services on existing definitions in the Medicare program. Except for inpatient hospital services and home health services, our definitions are based on how Medicare covers a service under Part B. As noted above, we have chosen to deviate from these definitions when we believe it is appropriate to fulfill the purpose of the statute.

These definitions would apply for purposes of physician referrals that are made for services covered under Medicare and for analogous services covered under the Medicaid program. However, section 1903(s) precludes FFP for medical assistance under a State plan consisting of a designated health service furnished to an individual on the basis of a referral that would result in a denial of payment under Medicare *if Medicare provided for coverage of the service to the same extent and under the same terms and conditions as under the State plan.* We believe that in enacting section 1903(s), Congress was clearly concerned that financial relationships of the kind that would prohibit a referral for services under Medicare may also lead to improper utilization of Medicaid services. However, because Medicaid has its own unique set of coverage requirements, a State can cover and reimburse designated health services very differently from the way these services are covered and reimbursed under the Medicare program. We believe that Congress was aware of these program differences and specifically meant to provide us with some flexibility in applying the Medicare physician referral rules in the Medicaid context. Therefore, we intend to apply this flexibility in the following manner, which we believe will further the goals of the statute:

When the definition of a designated health service is the same under both programs, we intend to use the same definition, as described in this preamble, for both programs. However, when the definition of a designated health service differs under a State's plan from the definition under Medicare, we will assume that the services under the State's plan take precedence, even if the definition will encompass services that are not covered by Medicare. However, we propose not to include Medicaid services as designated health services in situations in which including those services appears to run counter to the underlying purpose of the legislation. Because Medicaid is administered by the States, we do not believe that we are in the best position to determine when including particular services will have this effect. As a result, we are specifically soliciting comments on how to implement our policy in a manner that will achieve the goals of the statute.

We have received a number of inquiries from individuals who were confused about whether a particular service falls under one of the designated service categories listed in section 1877(h)(6). In order to remedy this problem, we have included below general explanations of each of the designated health services, including explanations of how we interpret similar or parallel services under Medicare. In the text of the proposed regulation, however, we have defined designated health services whenever we could by simply cross-referencing existing definitions in the Medicare statute, regulations, or manuals or by including specific language whenever we believe the definitions should deviate from standard Medicare definitions.

a. Clinical laboratory services

We would retain the definition that was incorporated into our regulations at § 411.351 by the August 1995 rule.

b. Physical therapy services (including speech-language pathology services)

Physical therapy services. Sections 1861(s)(2)(D) and 1832 provide for coverage of outpatient physical therapy services under Part B, which are defined in section 1861(p). Under section 1861(p), outpatient physical therapy services may be furnished by a provider of services, a clinic, rehabilitation agency, or public health agency, or by others under arrangements with and under the supervision of one of these entities. The services must be furnished to an outpatient who is under the care of a doctor of medicine or osteopathy, or a doctor of podiatric medicine, under a plan of care established by one of these physicians or by a qualified physical therapist. The plan must be periodically reviewed by the physician and must include the type, amount, and duration of physical therapy services to be furnished. No service is included as outpatient physical therapy if it would not be included as an inpatient hospital service if furnished to an inpatient of a hospital. Outpatient physical therapy may be furnished by a provider to an individual as an inpatient of a hospital or extended care facility if the

individual has exhausted or is otherwise ineligible for benefit days under Medicare Part A.

Outpatient physical therapy services may be furnished by an independent physical therapist in his or her office or in an individual's home. The physical therapist must meet any standards created by the Secretary in regulations, including health and safety standards. Special provisions concerning services furnished by a physical therapist in independent practice are set forth at § 410.60(c).

Under section 1861(p), the term "outpatient physical therapy services" also includes speech-language pathology services. Medicare covers speech-language pathology services if furnished to an outpatient by a provider of services, a clinic, rehabilitation agency, or public health agency, or by others under arrangements with and under the supervision of one of these entities. However, the statute does not provide for coverage of services furnished by speech-language pathologists in independent practice.

Plan of treatment requirements for outpatient physical therapy and speech-language pathology services are set forth in § 410.61. Conditions for outpatient physical therapy services are set forth in § 410.60(a) and (b), and conditions and exclusions for outpatient speech-language pathology services are set forth in § 410.62.

Basically, covered outpatient physical therapy services include three types of services, which are best described in § 410.100(b) (which specifically concerns services provided by a comprehensive outpatient rehabilitation facility). Section 410.100(b) provides that the following are physical therapy services:

• Testing and measurement of the function or dysfunction of the neuromuscular, musculoskeletal, cardiovascular, and respiratory systems.

• Assessment and treatment related to dysfunction caused by illness or injury and aimed at preventing or reducing disability or pain and restoring lost function.

• The establishment of a maintenance therapy program for an individual whose restoration has been reached. (However, maintenance therapy itself is not covered as part of these services. Sections 3101.8 of the Medicare Intermediary Manual (HCFA Pub. 13, Part 3) and 2210 of the Medicare Carriers Manual provide guidelines for coverage of restorative therapy and maintenance programs.)

Speech-language pathology services. These services are defined in section 1861(ll)(1) as such speech, language,

and related function assessment and rehabilitation services furnished by a qualified speech-language pathologist as this pathologist is legally authorized to perform under State law (or the State regulatory mechanism) as would otherwise be covered if furnished by a physician. Section 1877(ll)(3) defines a "qualified speech-language pathologist."

Speech-language pathology services are briefly described in § 410.100(d) as those necessary for the diagnosis and treatment of speech and language disorders that create difficulties in communication. Section 2216 of the Medicare Carriers Manual provides that speech-language pathology services are also services necessary for the diagnosis and treatment of swallowing disorders (dysphagia), regardless of the presence of a communication disability. This section of the manual also discusses restorative therapy and maintenance programs and group speech pathology services under the two main categories of diagnostic or evaluation services and therapeutic services.

Services that are essentially the same as "outpatient physical therapy services" and "outpatient speech pathology services" are also covered by Medicare in other contexts and in different settings, and may be billed under different categories. For example, section 1861(b)(3) lists as "inpatient hospital services" other diagnostic or therapeutic items or services furnished by a hospital or by others under arrangements with the hospital, as are ordinarily furnished to inpatients. We have a longstanding policy of covering physical therapy and occupational therapy as diagnostic or therapeutic "inpatient hospital services." The Medicare regulations in § 482.56, in fact, include conditions of participation for hospitals that provide physical therapy, occupational therapy, or speech pathology services.

Similarly, these services can also be covered as SNF services. Section 1861(h)(3) includes as "extended care services" physical or occupational therapy or speech-language pathology services furnished by the SNF (or by others under arrangements made by the facility), to an inpatient of the facility. These services can also be furnished as "incident to" a physician's services under section 1861(b)(2)(A). This provision covers services and supplies furnished as an incident to a physician's professional service, of kinds that are commonly furnished in physicians' offices and are commonly either furnished without charge or included in the physicians' bills. Physical and occupational therapy can qualify as "incident to" services, as reflected in section 2050.2 of the Carriers Manual, if the physician directly supervises auxiliary personnel who furnish these services and if these personnel are employed by the physician.

Section 1877(h)(6)(B) lists as a designated health service "physical therapy services," rather than the more limited category of "*outpatient* physical therapy services." Therefore, we believe that we can include within our definition of these services any physical therapy or speech-language pathology services that are covered under Medicare, regardless of where they are furnished and by whom, or how they are billed.

For purposes of section 1877, we would define "physical therapy services" as those outpatient physical therapy services (including speech-language pathology services) described at section 1861(p) of the Act and at § 410.100(b) and (d). Physical therapy services also include any other services with the characteristics described in § 410.100(b) and (d) that are covered under Medicare Part A or B, regardless of who provides them, the location in which they are provided, or how they are billed.

c. Occupational therapy services

Sections 1861(s)(2)(D) and 1832 of the Act provide for coverage of outpatient occupational therapy services under Part B. Section 1861(g) defines "outpatient occupational therapy services" by substituting the word "occupational" for the word "physical" each place that it appears in the definition of outpatient physical therapy services in section 1861(p).

Under section 1861(g), outpatient occupational therapy services may be furnished by a provider of services, a clinic, rehabilitation agency, or public health agency, or by others under arrangements with and under the supervision of one of these entities. The services must be furnished to an outpatient who is under the care of a doctor of medicine or osteopathy, or a doctor of podiatric medicine, under a plan of care established by one of these physicians or by a qualified occupational therapist. The plan must be periodically reviewed by the physician and must include the type, amount, and duration of occupational therapy services to be furnished. No service is included as outpatient occupational therapy if it would not be included as an inpatient hospital service if furnished to an inpatient of a hospital. Outpatient occupational therapy may be furnished by a provider to an individual as an inpatient of a hospital or extended care facility if the individual has exhausted or is otherwise ineligible for benefit days under Medicare Part A.

Outpatient occupational therapy services may be furnished by an independent occupational therapist in his or her office or in an individual's home. The occupational therapist must meet any standards created by the Secretary in regulations, including health and safety standards.

Coverage guidelines for occupational therapy services are set forth in sections 3101.9 of the Medicare Intermediary Manual (HCFA Pub. 13, Part 3) and 2217 of the Medicare Carriers Manual. The purpose of occupational therapy services is described generally in section 3101.9 of the Intermediary Manual as follows: "Occupational therapy is a medically prescribed treatment concerned with improving or restoring functions which have been impaired by illness or injury or, where function has been permanently lost or reduced by illness or injury, to improve the individual's ability to perform those tasks required for independent functioning."

Basically, covered outpatient occupational therapy services include the following types of services, which are best described in section 410.100(c), a section that specifically concerns services provided by a comprehensive outpatient rehabilitation facility. For purposes of section 1877, we would use the same services that are described in section 410.100(c). In § 411.351, occupational therapy services would include the following:

• Teaching of compensatory techniques to permit an individual with a physical impairment or limitation to engage in daily activities.

• Evaluation of an individual's level of independent functioning.

• Selection and teaching of task-oriented therapeutic activities to restore sensory-integrative function.

• Assessment of an individual's vocational potential, except when the assessment is related solely to vocational rehabilitation.

As we pointed out in the section covering physical therapy services, services that are essentially the same as "outpatient occupational therapy services" are also covered by Medicare in other contexts and in different settings, and may be billed under different categories. For example, they might be covered as "inpatient hospital services" under section 1861(b)(3) as "other diagnostic or therapeutic items or services" furnished by a hospital or by others under arrangements with the hospital; they might be covered as SNF services under section 1861(h)(3) as part of a patient's "extended care services"; or they might be furnished in a physician's office as services "incident to" the physician's services under section 1861(b)(2)(A).

Section 1877(h)(6)(C) lists as a designated health service "occupational therapy services," rather than the more limited category of "*outpatient* occupational therapy services." Therefore, we believe that we can include within our definition of these services any occupational therapy services which are covered under Medicare, regardless of where they are furnished and by whom, or how they are billed.

For purposes of section 1877, we would define "occupational therapy services" as those outpatient occupational therapy services described at section 1861(g) of the Act and at 42 CFR 410.100(c). Occupational therapy services also include any other services with the characteristics described in § 410.100(c) that are covered under Medicare Part A or B, regardless of who furnishes them, the location in which they are furnished, or how they are billed.

d. Radiology services, including magnetic resonance imaging, computerized axial tomography scans, ultrasound services, and radiation therapy services and supplies

Section 1877(h)(6)(D) identifies "radiology services, including magnetic resonance imaging, computerized axial tomography scans, and ultrasound" as a designated health service. Section 1877(h)(6)(E) identifies "radiation therapy services and supplies" as a designated health service.

Sections 1861(s)(3) and 1832 establish that "diagnostic X-ray tests," including diagnostic mammography services under certain conditions, are considered medical or other health services under Part B. Similarly, section 1861(s)(4) establishes that "X-ray, radium, and radioactive isotope therapy, including materials and services of technicians" are considered medical or other health services under Part B. Even though the statute does not define these terms, the payment provisions in section 1833(a)(2)(E) prescribe rules for paying for outpatient hospital radiology services. These include diagnostic and therapeutic radiology, nuclear medicine, computer assisted tomography (CAT scan) procedures, magnetic resonance imaging, and ultrasound and other imaging services (but excluding screening mammography). We cover these services under the conditions described in §§ 410.32(a) and 410.35 of the regulations and in the Coverage

1676 **Federal Register** / Vol. 63, No. 6 / Friday, January 9, 1998 / Proposed Rules

Issues Manual (HCFA Pub. 6) and in other manuals.

Section 1861(s)(13) includes as medical or other health services screening mammography services, which are defined in section 1861(jj) as a "radiologic procedure" provided to a woman for the purpose of early detection of breast cancer. We believe that screening mammography could qualify as one of the "radiology services" listed in section 1877(h)(6)(D) as a designated health service. However, as we have stated elsewhere, we believe that Congress enacted the physician referral prohibition to limit the tendency of referring physicians to overutilize services because they have a financial incentive to do so. It is our view that screening mammography services cannot be subject to overutilization. We base this conclusion on the fact that the statute specifically limits the frequency with which the Medicare program will cover these services. That is, section 1834(c)(2) specifically prescribes how frequently the screenings will be covered for different age groups. In addition, we never consider the covered level of screenings to be unnecessary services—we believe that all women should receive the screenings that are covered for them under the statute. (We cover these screening services under the conditions described in § 410.34 and in the Coverage Issues Manual.)

We wish to make it clear that the only type of mammography that we would exclude from the definition of "radiology services" listed under section 1877(h)(6)(D) would be screening mammography as covered under section 1861(s)(13) and as defined in section 1861(jj). It is our view that "radiology services" does include diagnostic mammography, which is not subject to the same limits. (Diagnostic mammography services are defined in § 410.34(a) as mammography furnished to a symptomatic patient for the purpose of detecting breast disease, while screening mammography is furnished to asymptomatic patients.)

Although Congress did not set up section 1877(h)(6)(D) and (E) in a manner that parallels section 1861(s)(3) and (4), we believe that paragraphs (D) and (E) of section 1877(h)(6), taken together, cover the same services that are covered as Part B services under section 1861(s)(3) and (4). Therefore, throughout this document the terms "radiology" and "imaging" mean any diagnostic test or therapeutic procedure using X-rays, ultrasound and other imaging services, CT scans, MRIs, radiation, or nuclear medicine, including diagnostic mammography

services, except for the distinctions that follow.

The physician's professional component—Medicare has traditionally considered a physician's professional services related to radiology to in general be covered as physician services under section 1861(s)(1) rather than as radiology services under either paragraph (3) or (4) of section 1861(s). However, we believe that it is appropriate for purposes of section 1877 to consider radiology services as including these physician services. We are proposing to include the professional component because radiology always consists of a technical service combined with a physician's professional service. Whenever a technical radiological service is overutilized, it follows that a physician's radiological service will also be overutilized.

Several studies have found that nonradiologists with imaging facilities in their own offices order imaging tests far more frequently than physicians who refer their patients to imaging facilities outside their practices. We mentioned several of these studies in section I.A of this preamble in the general discussion concerning studies that have raised serious concerns about physicians who make self-referrals. For example, one GAO study found that Florida nonradiologists who were sole practitioners or in group practices or other practice affiliations with imaging facilities in their own offices, when compared to physicians who referred outside their practices, had imaging rates about 3 times higher for MRIs; about 2 times higher for CT scans; 4.5 to 5.1 times higher for ultrasound, echocardiography, and diagnostic nuclear medicine imaging; and about 2 times higher for complex and simple X-rays. (GAO Report, "Medicare: Referrals to Physician-owned Imaging Facilities Warrant HCFA's Scrutiny," No. B–253835, pages 2, 3, and 10 (October 1994).)

Similarly, a study appearing in the New England Journal of Medicine compared the frequency and costs of diagnostic imaging furnished by self-referring physicians to the frequency and costs of these same services when physicians refer patients to an unrelated radiologist. The study covered referrals for four medical conditions. The study determined that the self-referring physicians obtained imaging examinations 4.0 to 4.5 times more often than the physicians who referred to unrelated radiologists. In addition, with respect to three of the four medical conditions, the self-referring physicians charged significantly more than the

radiologists for imaging examinations of similar complexity. The combination of more frequent imaging and higher charges resulted in mean imaging charges per episode of care that were 4.4 to 7.5 times higher for the self-referring physicians. (Bruce J. Hillman, M.D., and others, "Frequency and Costs of Diagnostic Imaging In Office Practice— A Comparison of Self-Referring and Radiologist-Referring Physicians," The New England Journal of Medicine, Vol. 323, No. 23 (Dec. 6, 1990), pp. 1604–1608)

Exclusion for Invasive or Interventional Radiology

We would exclude from the meaning of radiology, for the purposes of section 1877, any "invasive" radiology (also commonly referred to as interventional radiology). Invasive radiology is any procedure in which the imaging modality is used to guide a needle, probe, or a catheter accurately. Examples include percutaneous transluminal angioplasty (PTA); the placement of catheters for therapeutic embolization of tumors, arteriovenous malformations, or bleeding sites; the placement of drainage catheters; removal of stones; balloon dilation of strictures; biopsies; arthrograms; and myelograms.

We are basing this exclusion on the theory that the radiology services in these procedures are merely incidental or secondary to another procedure that the physician has ordered. As we have stated earlier, we believe that Congress meant for the categories listed in the statute as designated health services to encompass services that tend to be subject to abuse. It is our view that physicians do not routinely refer patients for the main procedures listed in the last paragraph, such as angioplasty, in order to profit from unnecessary radiology services. As a result, we are proposing not to include these "secondary" radiology procedures as designated health services. We are also specifically soliciting comments on any other types of services that would qualify as designated health services, but which may actually be incidental to other procedures.

We would include the following definition at § 411.351:

Radiology services and radiation therapy and supplies means any diagnostic test or therapeutic procedure using X-rays, ultrasound or other imaging services, computerized axial tomography, magnetic resonance imaging, radiation, or nuclear medicine, and diagnostic mammography services, as covered under section 1861(s)(3) and (4) of the Act and §§ 410.32(a), 410.34, and 410.35, including the professional

Federal Register / Vol. 63, No. 6 / Friday, January 9, 1998 / Proposed Rules **1677**

component of these services, but excluding any invasive radiology procedure in which the imaging modality is used to guide a needle, probe, or a catheter accurately.

e. Durable medical equipment and supplies

Sections 1861(s)(6) and 1832 establish DME as one of the "medical or other health services" covered under Medicare Part B. Section 1861(n) defines DME as including iron lungs, oxygen tents, hospital beds, and wheelchairs (under certain conditions), used in a patient's home (including certain institutions that can qualify as the patient's home), whether furnished on a rental basis or purchased. The definition of DME is explained further in the Medicare regulations. Section 414.202 defines DME as equipment furnished by a supplier or a home health agency that meets the following conditions:

• Can withstand repeated use.
• Is primarily and customarily used to serve a medical purpose.
• Generally is not useful to an individual in the absence of an illness or injury.
• Is appropriate for use in the home.

Durable medical equipment includes equipment such as wheelchairs, hospital beds, nebulizers, and walkers. We also regard DME that is furnished to a patient under a home health plan under section 1861(m)(5) as DME for purposes of section 1877. The conditions under which we cover DME are described in § 410.38. For the purposes of this proposed rule, we would use the definition of DME set forth in section 1861(n) and in § 414.202.

We have received a number of inquiries concerning Medicare claims processed by the four Durable Medical Equipment Regional Carriers (DMERCs). Many people erroneously believe that all devices, items, or supplies processed by the DMERCs are items of DME. This is not so, because the DMERCs are also responsible for paying claims for other items, such as immunosuppressive drugs, orthotics, prosthetics, and prosthetic devices and related supplies.

We have received requests that we clearly identify in this regulation which items are considered DME and which are not. Because the number of items considered to be DME is so extensive, we cannot in this proposed rule identify each of them. However, in response to these requests, we have provided below the general categories of DME.

We have also listed below the types of supplies used with the DME. We are listing the supplies because when identifying DME as a designated health service, Congress also included the supplies necessary for the effective use of the DME as part of the designated health service. For example, supplies used with DME could include such items as test strips and lancets used with blood glucose monitoring equipment or drugs used with a nebulizer. In general, supplies are items that cannot be reused. We would also like to point out that, effective December 1, 1996, in order for drugs used in conjunction with DME to be covered by Medicare, the entity dispensing the drug must have a Medicare supplier number, must be licensed to dispense the drug in the State in which it will be dispensed, and must bill and receive payment in its own name.

An infusion pump may be covered as DME, in which case the supplies necessary for its effective use are covered as designated health services; these supplies include the drugs and biologicals that must be put directly into the infusion pump.

External infusion pumps—External infusion pumps may be covered as DME under Medicare if certain coverage requirements are met, including use in the home. The Medicare Coverage Issues Manual provides for the coverage of infusion pumps for certain indications and under certain circumstances, as described in sections 60–9 and 60–14. Other uses of external infusion pumps are covered if the DMERC's medical staff verifies the appropriateness of the therapy and of the prescribed pump for the individual patient. Payment may also be made for the drugs necessary for the effective use of an infusion pump as long as they are reasonable and necessary for the patient's treatment.

Section 1877(b)(2) provides an exception for in-office ancillary services "other than durable medical equipment (excluding infusion pumps) and parenteral and enteral nutrients, equipment, and supplies." Section 1877(b)(2) has the effect of specifically excepting infusion pumps from the prohibition on a physician referring durable medical equipment furnished in the physician's own office. External infusion pumps may be used in a physician's office to administer drug therapy, including chemotherapy. However, external infusion pumps (or other drug delivery systems *used in the physician's office* (and not in the patient's home) are covered by Medicare under section 1861(s)(2)(A) as a service incident to the physician's service and not as DME. In addition, we do not believe that the *in-office* ancillary exception applies to external infusion pumps used outside a physician's office. That is, we do not believe that Congress intended for the in-office exception to apply to infusion pumps that are only picked up at a physician's office to be used in the home, or that are delivered to the home.

Implantable infusion pumps—Implantable infusion pumps may also be covered as DME in accordance with the policy described in the Medicare Coverage Issues Manual when they are used for certain indications. Coverage for other uses of implantable infusion pumps is allowed if the carrier's medical staff verifies that the drug and the infusion pump are reasonable and necessary. (Implantable devices are not billed to the DMERC carriers; rather, they are billed to the local carrier.)

If an implantable infusion pump is implanted in the physician's office, but will be used at home and elsewhere, we believe that it qualifies as DME that has been furnished in the physician's office. Hence, the in-office ancillary services exception could apply, since section 1877(b)(2) specifically includes infusion pumps, but not other DME.

End-Stage Renal Disease equipment and supplies—Section 1861(s)(2)(F) includes as covered medical and other health services home dialysis supplies, equipment, and self-care home dialysis support services, as well

as institutional dialysis services and supplies provided to individuals with end-stage renal disease (ESRD). This ESRD benefit is separate from the DME benefit under section 1861(s)(6). Therefore, the equipment, services, and supplies covered under this section of the statute are not covered as DME under Medicare. Examples of home dialysis equipment and supplies include needles and syringes, blood pressure cuffs, dialysate solution, and intermittent peritoneal dialyzers.

Other items of equipment furnished in a physician's office—As mentioned above, Medicare does not cover equipment used in a physician's office as DME but may pay for the equipment under other provisions in the statute. For example, section 1861(s)(2)(A) covers services and supplies furnished incident to a physician's services, and can include the use of any equipment that is needed in order for a physician to provide a covered service.

In addition, we may cover diagnostic testing under the diagnostic services benefit under section 1861(s)(3), which would include equipment used in diagnostic testing irrespective of where the equipment is used. For example, dynamic electrocardiography (EKG), commonly known as Holter monitoring, is a diagnostic procedure that provides a continuous record of the electrocardiographic activity of a patient's heart while he or she is engaged in daily activities. Diagnostic services under section 1861(s)(3) are not themselves included as a designated health service and thus are not specifically covered by this rule.

General Categories of DME—Under certain circumstances (which include use in the patient's home), the following items may be covered as DME. (Readers should refer to section 60–9 of the Medicare Coverage Issues Manual for additional information.)

Alternating pressure pads and mattresses and miscellaneous support surfaces
Bed pans
Blood glucose monitors
Canes/crutches and walkers
Commodes
Continuous positive airway pressure
Cushion lift, power seat
Decubitus care equipment
Gel flotation pads and mattresses
Heating pads
Heat lamps
Hospital beds and accessories
Intermittent positive pressure breathing equipment
Infusion pumps, supplies and drugs
Lymphedema pumps
Manual wheelchair base
Motorized wheelchair/power wheel chair base
Nebulizers
Wheel chair options/accessories
Oxygen and related respiratory equipment
Pacemaker monitor
Patient lifts
Pneumatic compressor and appliances
Power operated vehicles
Restraints
Roll about chairs
Safety equipment
Support surfaces

Suction pumps

Traction equipment

Transcutaneous electric nerve simulators and supplies

Trapeze equipment, fracture frame, and other orthopaedic devices

Ultraviolet cabinets

We would include the following definition at § 411.351:

Durable medical equipment has the meaning given in section 1861(n) of the Act and § 414.202.

f. Parenteral and enteral nutrients, equipment, and supplies

Coverage of enteral and parenteral therapy as a Medicare Part B benefit is provided under the prosthetic device benefit provision in section 1861(s)(8). The regulations cover prosthetic devices in § 410.36(a)(2). Details for enteral and parenteral therapy are set forth in the Medicare Coverage Issues Manual at section 65–10. When the coverage requirements for enteral or parenteral nutritional therapy are met, Medicare also covers related supplies, equipment and nutrients.

Enteral nutrients, equipment, and supplies—Enteral nutrition therapy provides nutrients to an individual with a functioning gastrointestinal tract who, due to pathology to or nonfunction of the structures that normally permit food to reach the digestive tract, cannot maintain weight and strength commensurate with his or her general condition. Enteral nutritional therapy may be administered by nasogastric, jejunostomy, or gastrostomy tubes. This benefit also includes supplies appropriate for the method of administration.

Therefore, at § 411.351, we would define "enteral nutrients, equipment, and supplies" as "items and supplies needed to provide enteral nutrition to a patient with a functioning gastrointestinal tract who, due to pathology to or nonfunction of the structures that normally permit food to reach the digestive tract, cannot maintain weight and strength commensurate with his or her general condition, as described in section 65–10 of the Medicare Coverage Issues Manual (HCFA Pub. 6)."

Parenteral nutrients, equipment, and supplies—Parenteral nutrition therapy provides nutrients to an individual with severe pathology of the alimentary tract that does not allow adequate absorption of sufficient nutrients to maintain weight and strength commensurate with the patient's general condition. Since the alimentary tract of such a patient does not function adequately, parenteral nutrition may be provided through an indwelling catheter placed percutaneously in the subclavian vein and then advanced into the superior vena cava. An example of a condition that may typically qualify for coverage is a massive small bowel resection resulting in a severe inability to absorb nutrition in spite of oral intake.

Parenteral nutritional therapy would include the equipment and supplies necessary to furnish the parenteral nutrition therapy. (Parenteral nutrients are commonly considered as prescription drugs. Effective

December 1, 1996, any entity dispensing drugs that are used in conjunction with a prosthetic device, including parenteral equipment, must meet certain conditions in order for the drugs to be covered under Medicare. These conditions are described in the section covering DME and the supplies used in conjunction with DME.)

At § 411.351, we would define "parenteral nutrients, equipment, and supplies" as "items and supplies needed to provide nutriment to a patient with permanent, severe pathology of the alimentary tract that does not allow absorption of sufficient nutrients to maintain strength commensurate with the patient's general condition, as described in section 65–10 of the Medicare Coverage Issues Manual (HCFA Pub. 6)."

We wish to point out that section 1877(b)(2) specifically excludes parenteral and enteral nutrients, equipment, and supplies as a service that can qualify for the in-office ancillary services exception.

g. Prosthetics, orthotics, and prosthetic devices

Prosthetics—Section 1861(s)(9) provides for inclusion as medical and other health services artificial legs, arms, and eyes, including replacements if required because of a change in a patient's physical condition. Prosthetics are covered in the regulations in §§ 410.36(a)(3) and 414.202. As described in section 2133 of the Medicare Carriers Manual, these appliances are covered when furnished under a physician's order. We also cover adjustments to artificial limbs or other appliances required by wear or by a change in the patient's condition when ordered by a physician.

We would define "prosthetics," at § 411.351, as artificial legs, arms, and eyes, as described in section 1861(s)(9) of the Act.

Orthotics—Orthotics are included as a medical service under section 1861(s)(9) as leg, arm, back, and neck braces. The regulations at § 410.36(a)(3) allow payment for these services to include replacements if required because of a change in the individual's condition. We have interpreted the statute in section 2133 of the Medicare Carriers Manual to cover these items when used for the purpose of supporting a weak or deformed body member or restricting or eliminating motion in a diseased or injured part of the body. In the Carriers Manual, orthotics are covered only when furnished under a physician's order.

Under section 2133D of the Medicare Carriers Manual, orthopedic footwear is covered under the orthotic benefit if the footwear is an integral part of a leg brace. Diabetic shoes are covered under section 1861(s)(12) of the Act in a separate benefit category. Splints, casts, and other devices used for the reduction of fractures and dislocations are covered under section 1861(s)(5). We do not consider diabetic shoes, casts, splints, or these other devices to be included under orthotics, prosthetics, or prosthetic devices.

At § 411.351, we would define "orthotics" as "leg, arm, back, and neck braces, as listed in section 1861(s)(9) of the Act."

Prosthetic devices—Section 1861(s)(8) provides for inclusion as medical and other

health services "prosthetic devices (other than dental) which replace all or part of an internal body organ (including colostomy bags and supplies directly related to colostomy care), including replacement of such devices, and including one pair of conventional eyeglasses or contact lenses furnished subsequent to each cataract surgery with insertion of an intraocular lens." This definition is reflected in the regulations at §§ 410.36(a)(2) and 414.202. The statute specifically excludes dental devices from Medicare coverage as prosthetic devices. (In addition, renal dialysis machines are covered under the end stage renal disease benefit and are discussed elsewhere in this section.)

Under the prosthetic device benefit, Medicare also includes supplies that are necessary for the effective use of a prosthetic device, for example, tape to secure an indwelling catheter. Section 1877(h)(6)(H) includes prosthetic devices as a designated health service and also specifically includes the supplies associated with these devices. (Effective December 1, 1996, any entity dispensing drugs that are used in conjunction with a prosthetic device must meet certain conditions in order for the drugs to be covered under Medicare. These conditions are described in the section covering DME and drugs used in conjunction with DME.) Section 410.100(f)(2) provides that services necessary to design the device, select materials and components, measure, fit, and align the device, and instructions to the patient are also included in this benefit. Examples of prosthetic devices include cochlear implants, cardiac pacemakers, and incontinence control appliances.

We have received many questions concerning whether Medicare considers an intraocular lens to be a prosthetic device. The answer is yes. We have also been asked, for purposes of the designated health services listed in section 1877(h)(6), to define a prosthetic device to exclude any device that is implanted by a physician as part of a surgical procedure. The theory behind this exclusion is that such devices are only a small component of a central procedure, which is the surgery needed to implant them. Physicians would not unnecessarily subject patients to a surgical procedure just to boost profits on intraocular lenses or other implantable devices, and are thus not the kind of services Congress meant to cover. In addition, some physicians believe that it is critical in many cases that they have the freedom to prescribe their own choice of an implantable device because they have particularized the design or find the device better to work with than others.

On the other hand, we have also been advised that only a very small percentage of surgeons "customize" prosthetic devices by developing their own, or by modifying existing devices. In addition, it is not uncommon for physicians to receive compensation from companies that manufacture or supply these devices, sometimes in the form of "consulting fees," perhaps in exchange for the physician's agreement to use that company's device exclusively. Physicians might also have an ownership interest in a supplier or manufacturer, thus realizing a profit every time the device is used.

Federal Register / Vol. 63, No. 6 / Friday, January 9, 1998 / Proposed Rules **1679**

It has also come to our attention that physicians who have some relationship with a manufacturer or supplier are in a position to manipulate a hospital's or an ASC's choice of a prosthetic device in exchange for the physicians' referrals. Although these practices might not lead to the overutilization of services, we believe that they can drive up the cost of certain services that are not subject to a fee schedule, which we would regard as a form of potential program abuse. Such an arrangement might also result in patient abuse, since a physician may choose a prosthetic device based on financial incentives rather than on the best interest of the patient. Because of the controversy surrounding surgically implanted devices, we have not excluded them from the definition of "prosthetic devices," but specifically solicit comments on this issue.

We would also like to point out that intraocular lenses that are implanted in an ambulatory surgical center (ASC) would be covered under the ASC payment rate. We have excluded any services covered under the ASC rate from the referral prohibition under an exception we created in § 411.355(d).

We have also been asked whether, if an ophthalmologist has an optical shop as part of his or her office, he or she can refer Medicare patients to the optical shop for eyeglasses. Medicare coverage of eyeglasses and contact lenses is very limited, covering only those that qualify as "prosthetic devices" used after intraocular lenses are implanted during cataract surgery. Thus, a physician would not be prohibited from referring a Medicare patient to the optical shop for any conventional eyewear that is not covered under the Medicare program. For eyeglasses that are covered by Medicare, the physician could prescribe and fill the eyeglass prescription if an exception applies. For example, the services might meet the in-office ancillary services exception if the optical shop is located in the physician's office suite. Alternatively, the optical shop might qualify as a rural provider so that the exception for rural ownership in section 1877(d)(2) of the Act could apply.

At § 411.351, we would define a "prosthetic device" as a device (other than a dental device) listed in section 1861(s)(8) that replaces all or part of an internal body organ, including colostomy bags and including one pair of conventional eyeglasses or contact lenses furnished subsequent to each cataract surgery with insertion of an intraocular lens. We would define "prosthetic supplies" as "supplies that are necessary for the effective use of a prosthetic device (including supplies directly related to colostomy care)."

h. Home health services

How we will define home health services. Medicare-covered home health services are defined in section 1861(m), and requirements for payment for home health services furnished to eligible beneficiaries are set forth in part 409, subpart E ("Home Health Services Under Hospital Insurance") of our regulations. For purposes of the physician referral prohibition, "home health services" would have the same meaning as the appropriate provisions described in part 409,

subpart E. A brief explanation of the home health benefit follows:

Home health services are items and services furnished to an individual who is confined to the home, under the care of a physician, and in need of at least one of the following skilled services: intermittent skilled nursing services, physical therapy services, speech-language pathology services, or continuing occupational therapy services.

To receive covered home health services, a beneficiary must be under a plan of care established and periodically reviewed by a physician. Home health services are furnished by, or under arrangements made by, a participating home health agency. Home health services are furnished on a visiting basis in a place of residence used as an individual's home. (A patient may not receive home health services in a physician's office.) An individual's home is wherever the individual makes his or her home. This may be his or her own dwelling, an apartment, a relative's home, a home for the aged, or some other type of institution. However, an institution is not considered a patient's home if the institution meets the basic requirements in the definition of a hospital (as defined in section 1861(e)(1)), an SNF (as defined in section 1819(a)(1)), or a nursing facility (as defined in section 1919(a)(1)).

• The following services may be furnished under the home health services benefit if appropriate requirements are met:

• Part-time or intermittent nursing care furnished by or under the supervision of a registered professional nurse.

• Physical therapy, occupational therapy, and speech-language pathology services.

• Medical social services furnished under the direction of a physician.

• Part-time or intermittent services of a home health aide.

• Medical supplies (including catheters, catheter supplies, ostomy bags, and supplies related to ostomy care, and a covered osteoporosis drug, but excluding biologicals and other drugs), the use of durable medical equipment, and appliances suitable for home use.

• The medical services of an intern or resident in training under an approved hospital teaching program if a home health agency is affiliated with or under the common control of the hospital furnishing the medical services.

A beneficiary may also receive home health services on an outpatient basis at a hospital, SNF, or a rehabilitation center under arrangements made by the home health agency if equipment is required that cannot be made available at the beneficiary's home or the services are furnished while the beneficiary is at the facility to receive services requiring equipment that cannot be made available at the beneficiary's home. Home health services do not include transportation of the beneficiary to the facility for these home health services.

Existing § 409.49 identifies services that are excluded from payment under the Medicare home health benefit. Note that included among those services is any service that would not be covered as inpatient hospital services.

Also note that under the Medicare statute, home health services can be provided only

by an HHA. That is, under section 1814(a), payments for services furnished to an individual may be made only to providers of services that are eligible for that payment. To be eligible, an HHA must, among other things, have in effect its own provider agreement with Medicare, as described in section 1866, and meet the specific conditions of participation for HHAs, as described in section 1891. As a result, we regard home health services as services "provided by an HHA" and not as services provided by any other entity, even if the HHA is owned by the other entity or is otherwise financially related to it. (We regard hospital services the same way; that is, they can be provided only by an entity that meets the requirements for participation as a hospital.) Therefore, even if a hospital owns an HHA, the exception for hospital ownership in section 1877(d)(3), which applies to designated health services "provided by a hospital," would not apply to home health services provided by a hospital-based HHA.

At § 411.351, we would include the following definition: "Home health services" means the services described in section 1861(m) of the Act and part 409, subpart E of this chapter."

How We Propose to Reconcile Section 1877 and the Physician Certification Requirements for Home Health Services Under 42 CFR 424.22(d)

Section 903 of the Omnibus Reconciliation Act of 1980 amended sections 1814(a) and 1835(a) of the Act to prohibit the certification of need for home health services, and the establishment and review of a home health plan of care for those services, by a physician who has a significant ownership interest in, or a significant contractual or financial relationship with, the home health agency that provides those services. These amendments were incorporated into the regulations at 42 CFR 405.1633(d) (which was redesignated as section 424.22(d)), by an interim final rule with comment period that we published in the Federal Register on October 26, 1982, at 42 FR 47388, and that became effective on November 26, 1982.

On June 30, 1986, we published a final rule in the Federal Register at 51 FR 23541 that confirmed the provisions of the October 26, 1982 rule and clarified that under the term, "significant ownership interest in or a significant financial or contractual relationship with" the home health agency, we intended to include salaried employment. This clarification was made effective on August 29, 1986.

The only exceptions to the home health regulations were uncompensated officers or directors of an HHA, HHAs operated by Federal, State, or local governmental authority, and sole community HHAs. The home health certification restrictions of sections 1814(a) and 1835(a) and § 424.22(d) have not been significantly updated since 1986.

1680 Federal Register / Vol. 63, No. 6 / Friday, January 9, 1998 / Proposed Rules

On November 5, 1997, we published a notice with comment period in the **Federal Register** (62 FR 59818) that announced our intention to reconcile the statutory prohibitions in sections 1814(a) and 1835(a) concerning physician certification for home health services with the related section 1877 prohibition. In that notice we stated that we had decided to reexamine appropriate provisions of section 1877 and the home health regulations as they pertain to indirect compensation arrangements involving physicians who are compensated by entities that own HHAs. We announced that, pending that evaluation, we had decided to withdraw certain recent interpretations of § 424.22(d), as it applies to certification and recertification or establishment and review of plans of care by physicians who are salaried employees of, or have a contractual arrangement to provide services to, an entity that also owns the HHA. In addition, we stated that we would address the issue of indirect compensation, applicable to the health services designated in section 1877, in this proposed rule.

We believe that sections 1814(a), 1835(a), and 1877 address the same behaviors and are identical in purpose: they each prohibit a physician who has a significant ownership interest in, or a significant financial relationship with, a home health agency from certifying or recertifying a patient's need for home health services. We have defined the concepts of "significant ownership interests and significant financial relationships" in the home health context in § 424.22(d)(1) through (d)(3), based on a fixed percentage of ownership and, for financial or contractual relationships, based on a specific dollar amount of compensation (or, if less, a percent of the agency's operating expenses).

Under section 1877, in contrast, any level of ownership or compensation amounts to a financial relationship unless the arrangement meets any of a number of exceptions. We believe that the provisions we are developing under section 1877 are more effective than the current provisions in § 424.22(d) in accommodating Congress' desire to discourage physicians from overutilizing certain services. Furthermore, section 1877 relates more specifically and in greater detail to the issue of referrals for home health services by physicians who have a financial relationship with the entity providing those services, and reflects Congress' most recent thoughts on that issue.

We believe that it is confusing to have in effect two provisions that address prohibited referrals, each of which includes different criteria, and can lead to different results.

We are therefore proposing to use the section 1877 definition of a "financial relationship," and our interpretations of this definition, for the concept of a "significant ownership interest in, or a significant financial or contractual relationship with, a home health agency" in sections 1814(a) and 1835(a). In order to do this, we are proposing to amend § 424.22(d) to state that a physician cannot certify or recertify a patient's need to receive home health

services from an agency if the physician has a "financial relationship" with that agency, as defined in § 411.351, unless the financial relationship meets one of the exceptions in §§ 411.355 through 411.357. In addition, we will list sections 1814(a) and 1835(a) in § 411.1 as part of the statutory basis for this proposed regulation.

Section 424.22, paragraphs (d)(4), (e), (f), and (g) relate to certain specific exceptions to the prohibition on certification in sections 1814(a) and 1835(a). These paragraphs except physicians who serve as uncompensated officers or directors of an HHA, HHAs that are operated by a Federal, State, or local governmental authority, or HHAs that are classified as sole community HHAs in accordance with our regulations. Even if a physician and an HHA are involved in an arrangement that meets one of these exceptions, the arrangement simultaneously remains subject to the requirements in section 1877. That is, if an exception in § 424.22 is subsumed within the exceptions in section 1877, a physician will be able to refer; if it is not, the arrangement will disqualify the physician from referring in spite of § 424.22. Thus, we believe the exceptions listed in § 424.22 have been superseded by section 1877 and should not be separately listed; we are therefore proposing to eliminate them. We are particularly interested in hearing from the public about these proposed changes.

i. Outpatient prescription drugs

Medicare does not cover a category of services called "outpatient prescription drugs." Without additional direction from Congress on what constitutes "outpatient prescription drugs" for the purposes of section 1877, we believe that it is reasonable to assume that Congress intended to include only drugs furnished to individuals under the Medicare Part B benefit and to exclude drugs furnished by providers under Medicare Part A. We also propose to limit "outpatient prescription drugs" to drugs that a patient would be able to obtain from a pharmacy with a prescription. We consider that this category includes any drugs that a patient could get with a prescription, even if patients generally do not do so. For example, we would include such drugs as oncology drugs that are routinely furnished in a physician's office, under the physician's direct supervision, provided the drugs could be obtained by prescription from a pharmacy.

Coverage for prescription drugs furnished outside of a provider setting is very limited under Medicare Part B. "Drugs and biologicals" are defined in the Medicare statute in section 1861(t) and the coverage of drugs and biologicals is explained in part 410 of our regulations. We consider a "biological" to be a drug product that is derived from a living organism or its products, including, but not limited to, serums, vaccines, antigens, and antitoxins. We apply to biologicals the same rules that we apply to any drugs. Therefore, for purposes of section 1877, we propose to define outpatient prescription drugs to include biologicals.

An explanation of the drug and biological benefit is set forth in section 2049 of the Medicare Carriers Manual. This section of the manual provides general requirements for drugs and biologicals that are covered under Medicare Part B. (These requirements do not apply to certain kinds of drugs that are covered under specific provisions of the statute. We discuss these other provisions below, following the general requirements.) In general, drugs are covered only if all of the following requirements are met:

• The drug or biological is included, or approved for inclusion, in the latest official edition of the *United States Pharmacopoeia*, the *National Formulary*, or the *United States Homeopathic Pharmacopoeia*, unless unfavorably evaluated in *AMA Drug Evaluations* or *Accepted Dental Therapeutics*.

• The drug or biological is furnished incident to a physician's services.

• The drug or biological is reasonable and necessary for the diagnosis or treatment of the illness for which it is administered according to accepted standards of medical practice.

• The drug or biological is not excluded as a preventive immunization.

• The drug or biological has not been determined by the Food and Drug Administration (FDA) to be less than effective. Drugs or biologicals must be approved for marketing by the FDA to be considered safe and effective, for purposes of the Medicare program, when used for indications specified on the labeling.

• Based on the usual method of administration of the form of a drug or biological as furnished by a physician, the drug or biological is of a type that cannot be self-administered.

Drugs and biologicals that are specifically covered under Part B would include those furnished in a physician's office incident to the physician's professional services under section 1861(s)(2)(A); as part of outpatient hospital services under section 1861(s)(2)(B); and, even though they are preventive immunizations, pneumococcal vaccine, influenza vaccine, and hepatitis B vaccine under section 1861(s)(10); and antigens under section 1861(s)(2)(G).

Drugs that are or can be self-administered, such as those in pill form or in a self-injectable form, are not covered by Medicare Part B unless the statute specifically provides this coverage. The statute currently provides for the coverage of the following self-administered drugs under limited conditions: blood clotting factors under section 1861(s)(2)(I), drugs used in immunosuppressive therapy under section 1861(s)(2)(J), erythropoietin (EPO) for dialysis patients under section 1861(s)(2)(O), and certain oral cancer drugs under section 1861(s)(2)(Q). (The statute provides under section 1861(m) for the coverage of certain osteoporosis drugs, defined in section 1861(kk), that can be self-administered but are furnished to a home health patient who is unable to self-administer the drugs. However, these drugs are covered under section 1861(m) as part of the Medicare Part A home health services benefit.)

After much consideration, we believe it would be inappropriate to include as outpatient prescription drugs, for purposes of section 1877, EPO and other drugs furnished as part of dialysis treatment for ESRD patients who dialyze at home or in a dialysis center, even though these drugs are not included in the end stage renal disease composite payment rate, but are billed separately. We base this policy on our perception that what the patient is primarily receiving is the dialysis treatment. EPO and several other drugs are a relatively minor (although important) part of a much larger and more complicated treatment and are inextricably linked to the dialysis service. That is, it would not be possible to provide dialysis safely and effectively without these drugs because they are critical to the overall effectiveness of the treatment and well-being of the patient. In addition, although many dialysis patients self-administer EPO, we believe that the opportunity for program abuse involving EPO is extremely unlikely. That is because section 1881(b)(11)(B)(ii)(I) establishes the payment rate for EPO, regardless of whether the beneficiary purchases the drug for self-administration or it is administered by the dialysis facility. Also, we have recently implemented a claims processing mechanism to ensure that payment is not made for excessive administration. That is, payment will not be made for EPO when a patient's hematocrit reading over a 3-month average exceeds 36.5, the upper limit of the drug labeling indication.

We would define "outpatient prescription drugs" at § 411.351 as "those drugs (including biologicals) defined or listed under section 1861(t) and (s) of the Act and part 410 of this chapter, that a patient can obtain from a pharmacy with a prescription (even if patients can only receive the drug under medical supervision), and that are furnished to an individual under Medicare Part B, but excluding EPO and other drugs furnished as part of a dialysis treatment for an individual who dialyzes at home or in a facility."

j. Inpatient hospital services

Services generally regarded as inpatient hospital services. Inpatient hospital services are a Part A benefit defined under section 1861(b). The definition of these services in section 1861(b) is reflected in § 409.10(a) of our regulations. As defined at § 409.10(a), inpatient hospital services include the following services when furnished to an inpatient of a participating hospital or, in the case of emergency services or services in foreign hospitals, to an inpatient of a qualified hospital (as described below).

- Bed and board.
- Nursing services and other related services.
- Use of hospital facilities.
- Medical social services.
- Drugs, biologicals, supplies, appliances, and equipment.
- Certain other diagnostic or therapeutic services.
- Medical or surgical services provided by certain interns or residents-in-training.

We propose to use the definition in section 1861(b) and § 409.10(a). As a clarification, we would state in the definition that inpatient hospital services include services that a hospital provides for its patients that are furnished either by the hospital or by others under arrangements with the hospital; that is, the hospital bills for these services on behalf of its patients. We would specify that the definition does not encompass the services of other physicians, physician assistants, nurse practitioners, clinical nurse specialists, certified nurse midwives, and certified registered nurse anesthetists and qualified psychologists who bill independently. Also, we would refer to existing § 409.10(b), which states that "inpatient hospital services" do not include SNF-type care furnished by a hospital or an RPCH that has a swing-bed approval, or any nursing facility-type care that may be furnished as a Medicaid service.

Psychiatric hospital and RPCH services. We propose to also include as inpatient hospital services inpatient psychiatric hospital services, which are defined in section 1861(c). These services are defined as "inpatient hospital services" furnished to an inpatient of a psychiatric hospital (defined in section 1861(ff)), which means that they are essentially the same services as those furnished to an inpatient of a regular hospital. In addition, we believe that a psychiatric hospital qualifies as a hospital, for all practical purposes, except that it is primarily engaged in providing

psychiatric services for the diagnosis and treatment of mentally ill persons rather than the more general care and treatment that a regular hospital provides to injured, disabled, or sick persons. Also, a psychiatric hospital must meet all of the nine basic requirements that a regular hospital must meet in order to qualify as a hospital, except that for two of the requirements, it must meet analogous standards that relate particularly to psychiatric care.

We also propose to regard as "inpatient hospital services," for purposes of section 1877, inpatient services provided by a participating rural primary care hospital (RPCH). This term refers to facilities designated as RPCHs by the Secretary under section 1820(i)(2). "Inpatient rural primary care hospital services" are defined in section 1861(mm)(2) as items and services, furnished to an inpatient of an RPCH by such a hospital, that would be inpatient hospital services if furnished to an inpatient of a hospital by a hospital.

Section 1861(e) of the Act states that "the term 'hospital' does not include, unless the context otherwise requires, a rural primary care hospital * * *." While it seems clear from this provision that RPCHs are not to be considered hospitals under the Medicare law for most purposes, we also believe the reference to context in this provision indicates that RPCHs may be classified as hospitals where, in specific contexts, it is consistent with the purpose of the legislation to do so. We base the policy to include inpatient RPCH services as "inpatient hospital services" on our belief that a physician who has a financial relationship with an RPCH is in as much of a position to profit from overutilizing referrals to the RPCH as he or she would be if the financial relationship were with an ordinary hospital. In addition, the RPCH provides services that are very similar to inpatient hospital services.

Because we propose to consider RPCH and psychiatric hospital services as inpatient hospital services, the exception for hospital services included in section 1877(d)(3) could apply. This exception applies to services furnished by a hospital if a physician refers to a hospital in which he or she is authorized to perform services and if the physician has an ownership or investment interest in the hospital as a whole, and not in a subdivision of the hospital.

Emergency hospital services. We propose to not include within the definition of "inpatient hospital services" emergency inpatient services provided by a hospital located outside

1682   Federal Register / Vol. 63, No. 6 / Friday, January 9, 1998 / Proposed Rules

the United States and covered under the authority in section 1814(f)(2) of the Act and part 424, subpart H. We also propose to exclude inpatient hospital services provided by a nonparticipating hospital within the United States under emergency conditions, as authorized by section 1814(d) and described in part 424, subpart G. We are excluding these services because Medicare covers them infrequently and only when they result from an emergency situation.

The regulations define "emergency services" in § 424.101 as only those services necessary to prevent death or serious impairment of health and, because of the danger to life or health, require use of the most accessible hospital available and equipped to furnish the services. In order to receive payment, a physician or the hospital must submit medical information that describes the nature of the emergency and specifies why it required that the beneficiary be treated in the most accessible hospital. Because Medicare covers these services only if they involve a documented emergency situation, we do not believe that physicians have the opportunity or incentive to overutilize them.

For the reasons cited above, we are also proposing to exclude from the definition of "designated health services" any physician services that otherwise qualify as designated health services but are furnished to an individual in conjunction with emergency inpatient hospital services furnished outside of the United States. These physician services are covered by Medicare under the authority in section 1862(a)(4), which permits coverage of inpatient hospital services, accompanying physician services, and ambulance services (which are not designated health services) furnished outside of the United States under certain limited conditions. To reflect this proposal, we are defining "designated health services" for purposes of the referral prohibition to exclude emergency physician services furnished outside of the United States.

Certain dialysis services. We are aware that there are situations in which a physician might own a dialysis machine, rent it to a hospital, and provide the hospital with a technician to run the machine. This arrangement might fail to meet an exception if the physician refers patients for dialysis services, and also receives rental payments based on the volume or value of those referrals. The physician might also fail to meet an exception if he or she owns a part of the dialysis unit in the hospital (rather than owning part of the hospital as a whole, as required

under the "hospital exception" in section 1877(d)(3)).

We believe there are certain unique situations involving dialysis in which there would be no risk of overutilization. We intend to exclude from the definition of "inpatient hospital services" dialysis furnished by a hospital that is not certified to provide end stage renal dialysis (ESRD) services under subpart U of 42 CFR 405. In these circumstances, we do not believe there would be a risk of program or patient abuse because dialysis would be provided only under the following emergency circumstances, when there is no other appropriate treatment:

• A non-ESRD patient needs dialysis because of renal dysfunction or for augmenting clearance of toxins. For example, a patient with acute tubular necrosis or a patient with theophylline overdose requires dialysis.

• The primary reason for a hospital admission for an ESRD patient is not maintenance dialysis. For example, an ESRD patient needs surgery unrelated to his or her kidney condition, and the surgeon has operating privileges only at a participating Medicare, but non-ESRD, certified hospital and the individual receives maintenance dialysis while he or she is an inpatient.

Certain lithotripsy services. We have been asked to consider excluding from the definition of "inpatient hospital services" services involving certain lithotriptors. Specifically, we are referring to services involving lithotriptors that employ extracorporeal shock wave lithotripsy (ESWL) when used to break up upper urinary tract kidney stones. ESWL focuses shock waves generated outside of the body specifically on stones under X-ray visualization, pulverizing them by repeated shocks. (The use of lithotripsy for breaking up kidney stones is discussed in section 35–81 of the Medicare Coverage Issues Manual.)

The theory behind excluding from "inpatient hospital services" services involving ESWL is that there is no risk of overutilization of these services. In general, severe obstruction, infection, intractable pain, or serious bleeding are indications of the need for surgical removal of a stone. Only when a patient requires surgical treatment would a physician prescribe ESWL. When a patient needs additional treatment, there is no alternative available that is less invasive or less expensive than ESWL. In addition, the procedure itself apparently documents the medical necessity to prescribe it. As we understand ESWL, the kidney stone is located, identified, and the progress of

the therapy is recorded as part of the visualization process.

While we agree that it might be unlikely that physicians would overutilize ESWL, we wish to raise some of the same concerns that we raised under our discussion on surgically-implanted prosthetic devices. That is, we believe that these arrangements can potentially lead to patient abuse, with physicians requiring the use of certain equipment based on financial incentives, rather than on the best interests of the patient. Because of the controversial nature of lithotripsy, we have not excluded it from the definition, but specifically solicit comments on this issue.

Inpatient hospital services and the definition of a "hospital." Note that our proposed definition of "inpatient hospital services" would affect in only a limited way the definition of the term "hospital" that we included in the August 1995 final rule. We included the definition of a "hospital" in § 411.351 solely for the purpose of determining ownership of a hospital as an entity, and we did not include as part of the hospital any entities furnishing services under arrangements. However, we would amend the definition of a hospital to make it clear that the entities covered by that definition are those that qualify as a "hospital" under section 1861(e), as a "psychiatric hospital" under section 1861(f), or as a "rural primary care hospital" under section 1861(mm)(1).

We would include the following definition at § 411.351: "Inpatient hospital services" are those services defined in section 1861(b) of the Act and § 409.10(a) and (b) and include inpatient psychiatric hospital services listed in section 1861(c) of the Act and inpatient rural primary care hospital services, as defined in section 1861(mm)(2). "Inpatient hospital services" do not include emergency inpatient services provided by a hospital located outside the United States and covered under the authority in section 1814(f)(2) and 42 CFR part 424, subpart H and emergency inpatient services provided by a nonparticipating hospital within the United States, as authorized by section 1814(d) and described in 42 CFR part 424, subpart G. These services also do not include dialysis furnished by a hospital that is not certified to provide end stage renal dialysis (ESRD) services under subpart U of 42 CFR 405.

Inpatient hospital services include services that a hospital provides for its patients that are furnished either by the hospital or by others under arrangements with the hospital. They do not encompass the services of other physicians, physician assistants, nurse practitioners, clinical nurse specialists, certified nurse midwives, and certified registered nurse anesthetists and qualified psychologists who bill independently.

k. Outpatient hospital services

Sections 1861(s)(2)(B) and (C) and 1832 provide for coverage of outpatient hospital services under Part B. Section 1861(s)(2)(B) provides for coverage of hospital services (including drugs and biologicals that cannot, as determined in accordance with regulations, be self-administered) incident to physician services furnished to outpatients (we consider these "therapeutic services") and partial hospitalization services incident to these services. Section 1861(s)(2)(C) provides for coverage of "diagnostic services which are—(i) furnished to an individual as an outpatient by a hospital or by others under arrangements with them made by a hospital; and (ii) ordinarily furnished by such hospital (or by others under such arrangements) to its outpatients for the purpose of diagnostic study." We describe below the coverage provisions concerning outpatient hospital services under the categories of therapeutic and diagnostic services, and partial hospitalization services. We also discuss briefly the special rules for physical therapy, occupational therapy, and speech pathology services furnished to a hospital outpatient.

We would consider all covered services (either diagnostic or therapeutic) performed on hospital outpatients that are billed by the hospital to Medicare (including arranged for services) as outpatient hospital services. In addition, it should be noted that outpatient hospital emergency services may be therapeutic (furnished incident to a physician's service) or may be diagnostic in nature. Unlike other outpatient hospital services, emergency services may be covered in nonparticipating hospitals subject to the conditions described in section 1835(b) and 42 CFR part 424, subpart G. We propose to exclude these emergency services from the definition of "outpatient hospital services" for the same reasons that we cited above in excluding them from the definition of "inpatient hospital services."

We have also been asked to exclude services involving lithotriptors that employ ESWL when used to break up upper urinary tract kidney stones. We have the same concerns in the outpatient context about the potential for patient abuse that we raised in our discussion about excluding these

services from the definition of "inpatient hospital services." In addition, we have learned of situations in which urologists in a particular geographic area invest in lithotriptors, then require that outpatient departments use the physicians' equipment if they want to receive any urology referrals. Because this kind of manipulation can lead to increases in the cost of services, we regard it as creating the potential for program abuse. Because of the controversial nature of lithotripsy, we have not excluded it as an outpatient hospital service, but specifically solicit comments on this issue.

However, we are proposing to include under the definition of "outpatient hospital services" outpatient services furnished by a psychiatric hospital (as defined in section 1861(f)) and RPCH services, which are included under Medicare Part B by section 1832(a)(2)(H). "Outpatient rural primary care hospital services" are defined in section 1861(mm)(3) as medical and other health services furnished by an RPCH. We are including both of these kinds of services as "outpatient hospital services" for the same reasons that we have included them as "inpatient hospital services," as described in the section above covering inpatient hospital services.

Outpatient hospital services incident to physician services (therapeutic services)—Under sections 1861(s)(2)(B) of the Act and 42 CFR 410.27, these "incident to" services specifically include drugs and biologicals that cannot be self-administered. "Incident to" services must be furnished by or under arrangements made by a participating hospital and as an integral though incidental part of a physician's services. We consider these services as therapeutic services that aid the physician in the treatment of the patient. Under section 230.4 of the Medicare Hospital Manual (HCFA Pub. 10), therapeutic services that hospitals furnish on an outpatient basis are those services and supplies (including the use of hospital facilities) that are incident to the services of physicians in the treatment of patients. These services include clinic services and emergency room services. To be covered as "incident to" a physician's services, the services and supplies must be furnished on a physician's order by hospital personnel under hospital medical staff supervision in the hospital or, if outside the hospital, by hospital-affiliated personnel who are under the direct personal supervision of a physician who is treating the patient.

Diagnostic outpatient hospital services—Under § 410.28, diagnostic

services furnished in a hospital to outpatients, including certain drugs and biologicals required to perform the services (even if those drugs or biologicals are self-administered), are covered if the services meet the following conditions:

• They are furnished by or under arrangements made by a participating hospital.

• They are ordinarily furnished by, or under arrangements made by, the hospital to its outpatients for the purpose of diagnostic study.

• They would be covered as inpatient hospital services if furnished to an inpatient.

• If furnished under arrangements, they are furnished in the hospital or in other facilities operated by or under the supervision of the hospital or its organized medical staff.

Section 230.3 of the Medicare Hospital Manual explains that a service is diagnostic if it is an examination or procedure to which the patient is subjected, or which is performed on materials derived from a hospital outpatient, to obtain information to aid in the assessment of a medical condition or the identification of a disease. Among these examinations and tests are diagnostic laboratory services such as hematology and chemistry; diagnostic x-rays; isotope studies; EKGs; pulmonary function tests; and other tests given to determine the nature and severity of an ailment or injury. Hospital personnel may furnish diagnostic services outside the hospital premises without the direct personal supervision of a physician.

Partial hospitalization services—Partial hospitalization services are included as "medical or other health services" covered by Medicare Part B under section 1861(s)(2)(B) and must be provided "incident to" a physician's services. Partial hospitalization services are defined in section 1861(ff). This definition is reflected in §§ 410.27(d) and 410.43, which provide that partial hospitalization services consist of a variety of outpatient psychiatric services. These services must be prescribed by a physician, who certifies and recertifies the need for the services, and the services must be furnished under a plan of treatment, all in accordance with provisions in subpart B of part 424. Section 424.24(e)(1) requires that a physician certify that an individual would require inpatient psychiatric care if the partial hospitalization services were not provided.

Section 230.5 of the Medicare Hospital Manual further explains the partial hospitalization services benefit. It points out that there is a wide range of services and programs that a hospital may provide to its outpatients who need psychiatric care, ranging from a few individual services to comprehensive, full-day programs. However, payment may be made only for services meeting the requirements of the outpatient hospital benefit. That is, the services must be incident to a physician's service and be reasonable and necessary for the diagnosis or treatment of the patient's condition. This means the services must be for the purpose of diagnostic study or the services must reasonably be expected to improve the patient's condition.

Special rules that apply to physical therapy, occupational therapy, and speech pathology services furnished to a hospital outpatient covered under Part B—The rules for these services appear in sections 241 and 242 of the Medicare Hospital Manual. Sections 210.8, 210.9, and 210.11 of the Medicare Hospital Manual describe these therapies (which do not require direct physician supervision) and set forth the conditions that must be met for the services to be covered as outpatient hospital services.

We would include the following definition at § 411.351: "Outpatient hospital services" means the therapeutic, diagnostic, and partial hospitalization services listed under section 1861(s)(2)(B) and (C); outpatient services furnished by a psychiatric hospital, as defined in section 1861(f); and outpatient rural primary care hospital services, as defined in section 1861(mm)(3); but excluding emergency services covered in nonparticipating hospitals under the conditions described in section 1835(b) and 42 CFR part 424, subpart G.

2. Direct Supervision

Section 1877(b)(2) provides an exception for in-office ancillary services. To qualify as in-office ancillary services, the services must, among other things, be furnished personally by a referring physician or another physician in the same group practice, or be furnished by individuals who are "directly supervised" by one of these physicians.

In the August 1995 final rule, we defined "direct supervision" as supervision by a physician who is present in the office suite and immediately available to provide assistance and direction throughout the time that clinical laboratory services are being performed. We are proposing to apply this definition to referrals for any of the other designated health services that can be excepted under section 1877(b)(2). We also propose to revise this definition to make it clear that

"present in the office suite" means the physician must be present in the office suite in which the services are being furnished, at the time they are being furnished. We believe this clarification is necessary for situations in which a physician might be working in more than one suite in a building, such as when he or she provides services other than designated health services in one suite, while the designated health services are furnished in a separate suite in the same building.

We also wish to clarify that we believe the supervision requirement is meant to establish the services as those that are integral to the physician's own practice, and that are conducted within his or her own sphere of activity: hence the title *in-office ancillary* services. It is our view that Congress did not intend to except referrals made by a physician to a separate, profit-making enterprise in which the physician has invested or from which he or she receives payments. Hence, we do not believe the in-office ancillary exception applies to services that are performed in a location that is separate and distinct from one in which the physician conducts his or her own everyday activities.

Consistent with our interpretation that Congress intended this exception to apply to services that are closely attached to the activities of the referring physician, we used the definition of "direct supervision" that appears in section 2050 of the Medicare Carriers Manual, Part 3—Claims Processing, which describes services that are "incident to" a physician's professional services under section 1861(s)(2)(A). This provision requires that the physician be present in the office suite and immediately available to provide assistance and direction throughout the time the aide or technician is performing services. The very same definition appears in the regulations at § 410.32(a), which states, in general, that diagnostic x-ray tests are covered only if performed under the "direct supervision" of certain physicians or by certain radiology departments. As we stated in the preamble to the August 1995 final rule, we believe Congress was adopting and ratifying the Secretary's longstanding definition of this term.

Nonetheless, since the publication of the August 1995 final rule, we have become aware that many of the ancillary services that physicians and physician groups provide are subject to a range of supervision requirements for coverage purposes, some of which are more stringent than the current "incident to" supervision requirements, and some of which are less stringent. (The requirements for diagnostic services, for

example, currently appear in § 410.32 of the regulations, in various places in the Medicare Carriers Manual, and as part of certain CPT codes. The requirements for physician supervision of diagnostic tests in all settings in which the technical component is payable under the physician fee schedule have been consolidated in a proposed regulation that was published on June 18, 1997 at 62 FR 33158.)

We recognize, in examining supervision requirements that include a physician's presence, that they each have some of the same and some separate purposes. The "incident to" rule is intended to ensure that the physician is at hand when the services are furnished because the law only covers them when they are "incident to a physician's professional services," making the physician's presence essential, for both quality control and billing purposes, as a condition of coverage. In the case of the diagnostic services, the service is explicitly related to a medical need for the personal supervision or involvement of a physician in performing or monitoring the tests. These two sets of coverage-based "supervision" tests have their particular purposes and both remain a condition of coverage and payment for Medicare, in addition to any supervision requirements that appear in the section 1877 referral provisions.

The "direct supervision" requirement in the in-office ancillary services exception appears to us to share with the "incident to" test the need to tie the services directly to the activities of the physician, to ensure that they are part of his or her own medical practice. We continue to believe that Congress intended in including "direct supervision" in the law the concept of "direct supervision" that appears as part of the "incident to" requirements. However, in the context of physician referrals, we believe the physician's presence is necessary for "management" purposes (that is, to demonstrate that the physician is there, actively running the practice), rather than for coverage purposes. Thus, the requirement that the physician be on the premises the entire time that a designated health service is being furnished can have absurd and impractical results, preventing a physician from leaving the office suite for even brief periods when there may be no health and safety standards requiring his presence.

Accordingly, we propose to depart from our interpretation that the definition of "direct supervision" for purposes of the referral prohibition is identical to the definition in the "incident to" context. That is, we

Federal Register / Vol. 63, No. 6 / Friday, January 9, 1998 / Proposed Rules 1685

propose to continue to require that the services in general be performed by aides or technicians only when the physician is present in the office suite so that they are tied to his or her activities, but allow very limited absences from the office. We propose to amend the definition as follows:

Direct supervision means supervision by a physician who is present in the office suite in which the services are being furnished, throughout the time they are being furnished, and immediately available to provide assistance and direction. "Present in the office suite" means that the physician is actually physically present. However, the physician is still considered "present" during brief unexpected absences as well as during routine absences of a short duration (such as during a lunch break), provided the absences occur during time periods in which the physician is otherwise scheduled and ordinarily expected to be present and the absences do not conflict with any other requirements in the Medicare program for a particular level of physician supervision.

Under this definition, a physician must actually be physically present in the office suite at the time designated health services are being furnished, or be absent only under the limited conditions described in the definition. We anticipate that the question of when an absence qualifies as "brief and unexpected" or as a "routine absence of a short duration" will be a determination that only the local carrier can make, based on individual circumstances.

A service will not qualify as an in-office ancillary service during any time period in which the physician is scheduled to be in the office, but in reality is specifically or routinely expected to be somewhere else or during any time period in which the physician is scheduled to be somewhere else. Therefore, laboratory services or other designated health services performed by technicians or aides would not qualify as in-office ancillary services if they are performed during time periods that occur before or after the physician's regularly scheduled office hours. (Aides or technicians can perform other tasks in the absence of the physician, such as setting up equipment or cleaning up, as long as the tasks are not components of designated health services provided to Medicare or Medicaid patients.) Also, a physician's absences to perform medical services outside the office would not be permissible under "direct supervision," such as absences to do hospital rounds or provide care in an outpatient clinic. However, we would allow absences for unexpected medical emergencies.

While this definition for referral purposes would allow a physician to occasionally be absent for short periods, specific coverage requirements for services furnished and billed as "incident to" a physician's services, for diagnostic services, or for any other services with separate supervision requirements would continue to operate to determine whether a specific service is covered. We recognize that this approach will require a physician to pay close attention to the specific coverage requirements that apply to individual services, as well as the supervision requirement in section 1877(b). Nonetheless, most of the coverage rules have been in effect for many years, so physicians have had experience in complying with them. In coordinating the separate supervision requirements with the requirement in section 1877, physicians must only comply with the separate coverage requirement if it is more stringent than the requirement in section 1877, as interpreted in this proposed rule.

We believe that our proposed amendment to the definition of "direct supervision" addresses the concerns of physicians who feel that, as a practical matter, they cannot be in the office every single minute of every day. The amendment will allow physicians who must be called away briefly to avoid the sanctions that could arise from section 1877 if they are not present at the moment when a medical service is furnished, provided there are no health and safety reasons for them to be on the premises.

In line with the "incident to" manual provision, we are also proposing that a physician is directly supervising an individual outside the office suite (such as in an SNF) if the physician is in the room with the technician when the technician is performing services. (We derive this rule from section 2050, which states that direct supervision does not exist if a physician is only available by phone or is only physically present somewhere in the building.) Section 45–15 of the Coverage Issues Manual discusses situations in which a physician establishes an office within an SNF or other institution. Under this provision, a physician's office within an institution must be confined to a separately identified part of the facility that is used solely as the physician's office and cannot be construed to extend throughout the entire institution. (However, to qualify for the in-office ancillary exception in either of these "out of office" situations, the services must meet the additional statutory requirements for location and billing described in section 1877(b)(2).)

We are not proposing that there must be any particular configuration of rooms for an office to qualify as one office "suite." However, direct supervision means that a physician must be in the office suite and immediately available to provide assistance and direction. Thus, a group of contiguous rooms should in most cases satisfy this requirement. We have been asked whether it would be possible for a physician to directly supervise a service furnished on a different floor. We think the answer would depend upon individual circumstances that demonstrate that the physician is close at hand. The question of physician proximity for physician referral purposes, as well as for incident to purposes, is a decision that only the local carrier could make based on the layout of each group of offices. For example, a carrier might decide that in certain circumstances it is appropriate for one room of an office suite to be located on a different floor, such as when a physician practices on two floors of a townhouse.

3. Entity

In-office referrals are referrals to an "entity." Section 1877(a)(1) prohibits a physician from referring Medicare patients for the furnishing of designated health services to an entity with which the physician (or an immediate family member) has a financial relationship, unless an exception applies. The statute encompasses *any* entity that provides designated health services, without qualifications or limits. We attempted to reflect the breadth of the concept in the August 1995 final rule at § 411.351, where we defined an "entity" as a sole proprietorship, trust, corporation, partnership, foundation, not-for-profit corporation, or unincorporated association.

We wish to clarify that we regard an individual physician or group of physicians as referring to an "entity" when they refer to themselves, or among themselves. The concept of a "referral" under section 1877(h)(5)(A) and (B) covers the request by a physician for an item or service under Part B, or the request or establishment of a plan of care by a physician that includes the provision of a designated health service. This statutory definition does not exclude in-office referrals, nor does it specify that a referral occurs only when a physician refers to an outside entity.

In addition, the in-office ancillary services exception in section 1877(b)(2) would not be necessary if in-office referrals were free from the prohibition. Section 1877(b)(2) makes it clear that designated health services that are furnished personally by the referring physician who is a solo practitioner or, in the case of a group practice, by

Federal Register / Vol. 63, No. 6 / Friday, January 9, 1998 / Proposed Rules

another member of the physician's group practice, or by other individuals who are directly supervised by these physicians, are subject to the referral prohibition. Physicians who refer to or among themselves are excepted from the prohibition only if they meet the criteria specified in section 1877(b)(2). Similarly, physician services provided personally by (or under the personal supervision of) another physician in the same group practice as the referring physician are specifically excepted under section 1877(b)(1). To clarify our position on in-office referrals, we propose revising the definition of an "entity" in §411.351 to include any physician's solo practice or any practice of multiple physicians that provides for the furnishing of a designated health service.

4. Fair Market Value

The term "fair market value" appears in most of the compensation related exceptions. These exceptions, among other things, require that compensation between physicians (or family members) and entities be based on the fair market value of the particular items or services that these parties are exchanging. We defined this term in the August 1995 final rule by using the definition in section 1877(h)(3). This provision defines fair market value as the value in arm's-length transactions, consistent with the general market value, with other specific terms for rentals or leases.

We have previously defined the term fair market value in our regulations in part 413, in the context of reasonable cost reimbursement in payments for end stage renal disease services. Section 413.134(b)(2) explains the circumstances under which an appropriate allowance for depreciation on buildings and equipment used in furnishing patient care can be an allowable cost. This provision defines "fair market value" for purposes of determining the costs incurred by a present owner in acquiring an asset. "Fair market value" is defined as "the price that the asset would bring by bona fide bargaining between well-informed buyers and sellers at the date of acquisition. Usually the fair market price is the price that bona fide sales have been consummated for assets of like type, quality, and quantity in a particular market at the time of acquisition."

To be consistent, we are incorporating this definition of what constitutes "fair market value" into this proposed rule to explain, for purposes of those exceptions that involve compensation paid for assets, what we believe constitutes a value that is "consistent with the general market value." However, we are modifying the definition as follows so that it also applies to any arrangements involving items or services, including employment relationships, personal services arrangements, and rental agreements:

General market value is the price that an asset would bring, as the result of bona fide bargaining between well-informed buyers and sellers, or the compensation that would be included in a service agreement, as the result of bona fide bargaining between well-informed parties to the agreement, on the date of acquisition of the asset or at the time of the service agreement. Usually the fair market price is the price at which bona fide sales have been consummated for assets of like type, quality, and quantity in a particular market at the time of acquisition, or the compensation that has been included in bona fide service agreements with comparable terms at the time of the agreement.

The definition of "fair market value" will continue to include the additional requirements in section 1877(h)(3) for rentals or leases. Among other things, the statute defines the fair market value of rental property as its value for general commercial purposes, not taking into account its intended use.

5. Financial Relationship

A referral alone is not a financial relationship. We wish to clarify that when a physician simply refers patients to an outside entity, he or she does not have a financial relationship with that entity. A financial relationship consists of an ownership or investment interest in the entity or a compensation arrangement with the entity. If the physician does not own any portion of the entity, and does not pay the entity or receive any kind of payment from the entity for the referral or for anything else, there is no financial relationship.

A financial relationship can involve more than the Medicare or Medicaid programs. In §411.351 we defined a financial relationship as a direct or indirect relationship in which a physician or immediate family member has an ownership or investment interest in an entity or a compensation arrangement with the entity. We would like to emphasize that a financial relationship can exist between a physician and an entity even if that relationship does not involve designated health services or the Medicare or Medicaid programs. For example, a compensation arrangement is defined in §411.351 as, in general, any arrangement involving any remuneration between a physician (or family member) and an entity. This remuneration can involve payments for anything, such as payments for rent,

payments for nonmedical types of items or services, or for housing or travel expenses.

Ownership interests can be indirect. The statute and the August 1995 final regulation specify that an ownership or investment interest in an entity can exist through equity, debt, or other means and includes an interest in an entity that holds an ownership or investment interest in any entity providing designated health services. We do not regard the last part of this provision as a limiting factor, but rather as an indication that Congress wished to include, in the concept of "ownership," an interest that is at least one level removed from direct ownership. We propose to interpret this provision to apply to interests that are removed by an unlimited number of levels.

This interpretation would cover situations involving multiple levels, such as when a physician has an interest in an entity that has an interest in another entity that in turn holds the ownership interest in the entity that provides designated health services. We believe that this interpretation fulfills the intent of the statute, which was meant to prevent physicians from evading the prohibition by establishing their ownership interests indirectly in "holding companies" rather than in the entities that furnish designated health services. It is our view that the number of layers of ownership is irrelevant, as long as a physician or family member has established an indirect interest. To reflect this interpretation, we would revise the description of ownership in §411.351 (as part of the definition of "financial relationship") as follows: "An ownership or investment interest in an entity that exists in the entity through equity, debt, or other means and includes any indirect ownership or investment interest, no matter how many levels removed from a direct interest; for example, ownership includes situations in which a physician or immediate family member has an interest in any entity that holds an ownership or investment interest in any entity providing designated health services."

Payments that result from an ownership or investment interest are not compensation. We would like to emphasize a point that we discussed at length in the preamble to the August 1995 final regulation. We explained there that when a physician or family member has an ownership or investment interest in an entity, we will not count as compensation any returns on that investment. For example, if a physician has an investment interest in an entity in the form of stock or securities, we will not count any of the dividends or other payments that derive from that ownership or investment interest as a compensation arrangement between the physician and the entity. (However, a physician or family member can receive an ownership interest from an entity in a manner than could constitute a compensation arrangement, such as when a physician receives stock as part of a salary payment or in exchange for the sale of his or her practice.)

6. Group Practice

The value of group practice status under the law. When a group of physicians qualifies as a "group practice" as defined under section 1877(h)(4), the group may qualify for several exceptions in the law that are specifically designed to accommodate groups. For example, section 1877(b)(1) excepts from the referral prohibition physician services provided personally by (or under the personal supervision of) another physician in the same group practice as the referring physician. Similarly, section 1877(b)(2) excepts in-office ancillary services that are furnished personally by or are directly supervised by either the referring physician or by another physician who is a member of the same group practice as the referring physician. However, a group of physicians does not have to meet the definition of a group practice in order to qualify for other exceptions under the law that are based on characteristics other than the referring physician's group practice status.

We wish to also point out that the definition of a group practice in section 1877(h)(4) is particular to the referral rules. That is, it was designed to allow physicians in specific kinds of groups to continue to refer patients for designated health services under certain circumstances. Therefore, the definition may have little or no bearing on which physicians qualify as a group practice for purposes of other Medicare or Medicaid provisions.

Who can organize and control a group practice. The statute defines a "group practice" as a group of two or more physicians legally organized into a partnership, professional corporation, foundation, not-for-profit corporation, faculty practice plan, or similar association. The statute requires that a group practice consist of a legal entity. Thus, a group that is not legally organized, but is instead only holding itself out as a group, would not qualify as a group practice under the statutory definition. Moreover, we believe that the statute specifically requires that a partnership consist of two or more

physicians who are partners and that a professional corporation consist of two or more physicians who are incorporated together.

We believe that more complex business configurations may be involved when two or more physicians are "legally organized" into a foundation, not-for-profit corporation, or a faculty practice plan. As we pointed out in the preamble to the August 1995 final rule, the statute is silent about who must actually legally organize these kinds of associations. As a result, we interpreted this provision in the final rule to allow any individuals or entities to set up legal structures for these kinds of associations, provided two or more physicians have a role in providing services and the physicians meet all of the other specific requirements in section 1877(h)(4). In addition, the statute is silent about who must operate any of the group practice associations. We have interpreted the statute, in the August 1995 final rule, to allow any individuals or entities to do this. For example, a hospital could own and operate a group practice, provided there are no State laws to prevent this.

A group practice as one legal entity. In the August 1995 final rule we took the position that the statute contemplates a group practice that is composed of one single group of physicians who are organized into one legal entity. We stated that a group practice could not consist of two or more groups of physicians, each organized as separate legal entities, although we believed that a single group practice (that is, one single group of physicians) could own other legal entities (such as a billing entity) for the purpose of providing services to the group practice. We based this conclusion on the fact that section 1877(h)(4)(A) defines a group practice as a group of two or more physicians who are legally organized as a partnership, professional corporation, etc. However, we continue to receive numerous inquiries about whether a group can consist of several legal entities that are, in turn, legally organized into the one group.

We believe that Congress meant that a group must be one legal entity, and that it regarded this characteristic as a mark of a true group practice. It is our view that any other interpretation could pose the risk of multiple groups of physicians remaining in many ways separate, but joining together for the sole purpose of taking advantage of the exceptions in section 1877 that apply to group practices. Therefore, we propose to continue to require that a group consist of just one legal entity.

Nonetheless, we would like to clarify that we believe that a group practice is still "one legal entity" even if it is composed of owners who are actually individual professional corporations or is owned by physicians who are individually incorporated. It is our understanding that a group can contain physicians who are individually incorporated as professional corporations, and who provide services to group patients. This kind of configuration is apparently common in group situations and generally results when an individual physician wishes to qualify for certain tax and pension advantages. The physician is employed by the professional corporation, which in turn contracts with the group. We believe that such a group is not a conglomeration of multiple physician groups, but may instead be a true group practice, provided all the other criteria in section 1877(h)(4) are met.

We have also considered the issue of whether individuals who are separately incorporated as individual professional corporations and who contract with the group practice qualify as "members" of the group. We are proposing (in this section under the heading "The requirement for physician-patient encounters") to, in general, eliminate contractors from qualifying as "members" of a group practice, a proposal that a major group practice association asserted would be highly important to its membership. The association believes that many group practices would have difficulty meeting the "substantially all" requirement in the group practice definition if the groups have to consider as members the many specialists with whom they contract to furnish services through the group practice on a part-time basis. Thus, we are proposing to include only owner and employee physicians as "members" of a group practice. However, we are also proposing to consider as owner "members" physicians who belong to individual professional corporations that, in turn, own the group practice.

The "full range of services" test. A "group practice" is defined in some detail in section 1877(h)(4) of the statute. One of the criteria in the statutory definition is that each physician who is a member of the group must furnish substantially the full range of services that the physician routinely furnishes, including medical care, consultation, diagnosis, and treatment through the joint use of shared office space, facilities, equipment, and personnel. We defined the term "group practice" in §411.351 of the August 1995 final rule by using the statutory definition and by adding certain interpretations. In one of these, we required physician members to furnish the full range of "patient care services" that they routinely furnish, rather than just "services." Elsewhere in § 411.351, we defined "patient care services" as any tasks performed by a member that address the medical needs of specific patients, regardless of whether they involve direct patient encounters.

On considering this issue further, we propose revising the definition of "patient care services" to apply to any of a physician's tasks that address the medical needs of specific patients or patients in general, or that benefit the practice.

We believe that the "full range of services" provision, along with most of the other criteria in the group practice definition, was designed to ensure that, as part of the group, a physician is actually practicing medicine as he or she ordinarily would and has not simply joined the group in name only. We realize, however, that a physician member can legitimately furnish other kinds of services to the group, beyond services that benefit only specific patients. For example, a physician member might spend time training staff members, arranging for equipment, or performing administrative or management tasks. As long as these tasks actually benefit the operation of the group practice, we believe they should be counted as part of the test for gauging "substantially the full range of" a physician's services.

The "substantially all" test and the group billing number requirement. The "Substantially All" Test—Effective January 1, 1995, substantially all of the services of the group members must be furnished through the group and be billed under a billing number assigned to the group (the "substantially all" test). We discussed the substantially all test, as it was effective on January 1, 1992, at great length in the August 1995 final rule. We wish to clarify certain aspects of the test, which appears as part of the definition of a group practice in § 411.351.

Section 411.351 requires that substantially all of the "patient care services" of the physicians who are group members (at least 75 percent of the total patient care services of the members) be furnished through the group. The change we have described above in the section on the "full range of services" test, concerning our definition of "patient care services," would affect this test as well. As a result, a group would count any of a physician's tasks that address the medical needs of specific group patients

or group patients in general or that benefit the group practice. The group would not consider in the calculation any time during a physician's week that he or she spent on nonpatient care services, such as teaching in a medical school or doing outside research. For example, if a physician spends 3 days a week furnishing patient care services as part of a group practice and 2 days a week doing research outside the practice, the physician is providing 100 percent of his or her patient care services through the group practice.

The definition in § 411.351 also requires that patient care services be measured in terms of total patient care time that each member spends on patient care services. We wish to clarify that we expect a group practice to look at a physician's total patient care time during a week, furnished both inside and outside of the group practice, to determine what percentage of this time is furnished through the one group. For example, if a physician provides patient care services to a group practice 4 days a week and patient care services in an unrelated clinic 1 day a week, the physician is providing 80 percent of his or her patient care services through the group practice.

Some group practices have informed us that patient care time is not a common measurement of how groups keep track of a physician's contributions to the group. The time standard in the regulation, they claim, will create a whole separate, burdensome administrative process. In light of these comments, we explored alternative options that were suggested to us. These included counting a percentage of the physician's personal income, counting physician-patient encounters, or counting resource-based Relative Value Units (RVUs), a method of assigning resources to CPT codes ([Physicians'] Current Procedural Terminology, 4th edition, 1993 (copyrighted by the American Medical Association)). We found that there is no perfect measure; each of these methods has advantages and disadvantages.

The income option would require that a group determine what percentage of the physician's overall practice income is derived from the group practice. While this would be perhaps the easiest calculation to make, many physicians might consider the data involved to be intensely private. In addition, to the extent that a physician's billing practices differ among settings, an equivalent amount of income derived from within the practice may not account for the same amount of patient care activity that occurs outside the practice. For example, a physician who

works at a clinic for low income patients while outside the group could receive considerably less income for patient care than he or she would receive for equivalent services furnished through the group practice.

We also explored the possibility of counting the number of a physician's patient encounters. However, encounters do not capture the level of intensity involved in any task. For example, a physician might complete one encounter in an entire day, if it involves complex surgery. Another physician could have 30 encounters in the same day, each of which took 15 minutes to complete. In addition, a group would need to gather information about the number of a physician's encounters outside of the group practice to determine the percentage of encounters furnished through the group. One problem with counting the number of patient care encounters and also with counting RVUs, which is discussed immediately below, is that neither method can take into account work that benefits the group in general but is not a service furnished to a patient, for example, time a physician spends training technical personnel.

We next explored the possibility of counting RVUs to determine the share of a physician's efforts furnished through a group practice, since RVUs capture the intensity level of different services. For Medicare purposes, a physician is paid based on the CPT code that is billed for a particular service. Each CPT code has assigned to it a certain intensity level (based on the content of the service and the time the physician has spent), and each intensity level translates into a specified number of RVUs. It is this associated RVU amount that determines a physician's payment for a service. The Medicare billing system can reveal all of the procedures for which a physician has billed, based on the CPT codes, and the value of all of the associated RVUs. There are thousands of CPT codes, many of which can be modified (for instance, to state that a physician acted as an assistant at surgery or co-surgeon, rather than as the surgeon). There is software available that can assign RVUs based on the CPT code and modifiers.

To use this method, it would be necessary for a group to collect all CPT and modifier billing data for the physician both inside and outside the practice, assign RVUs, and compare the totals. There is no "full-time" equivalent RVU amount that a group could use as a proxy to measure the inside RVUs against; therefore, the group would have to collect detailed data about outside practice time. We believe that the RVU method could

Federal Register / Vol. 63, No. 6 / Friday, January 9, 1998 / Proposed Rules **1689**

impose a burden on groups because of the high volume of codes that physicians are likely to submit, especially in large group practices. This method is further complicated by the fact that it is not clear that all insurers use CPT codes in all cases. For example, some HMOs provide a given payment for a particular kind of service and may not collect data on individual office visits or tests.

As a result of our assessment, we believe that measuring a physician's activities by using time spent doing work for the group, as required in the August 1995 final rule, may be the most straightforward and least burdensome method for measuring a physician's efforts, especially because we do not intend to require that physicians keep detailed time sheets to verify their time. Practices should already be able to track the amount of time spent by each member in activities related to the practice. While this data may not be present in billing records, it should be present in appointment databases, personal schedules, and other easily accessible sources. To simplify matters, a group can assume a physician works a standard 40 hour week unless he or she can present evidence of a shorter or longer work week. A practice should be able to maintain records in the form of general schedules that are sufficient to demonstrate its calculations in the event of an audit. Finally, we consulted several group practice associations about their preference for measuring the standard. They informed us that they favor using time in calculating the standard.

As a result of our investigation, we are therefore proposing to use the measure of physician time as the "default" standard. We believe that our carriers can evaluate the "substantially all" test only if we have one, or perhaps a few, standards. Therefore, we are soliciting comments on other possible methods that groups might use, provided these methods will provide verifiable data that demonstrates that a group meets the "substantially all" criteria. We will review all alternative methods, but only include those in the final rule that we believe are both verifiable and administratively feasible.

The Billing Number Requirement— We are interpreting the new billing number requirement in the "substantially all" test to mean that a single group can have more than one billing number, as long as the group bills under a billing number that has been assigned to the group. We do not believe there is anything in the statute to preclude a group practice from having more than one number. This

interpretation will accommodate situations in which one group practice has multiple numbers because it has many locations or operates in more than one State.

It has also come to our attention that there are an increasing number of situations in which a group has another entity (not a wholly-owned entity) bill for it, such as a management services organization (MSO) or billing agent. We propose to allow a group to meet the requirement that services have been "billed under a billing number assigned to the group" if an agent bills for the group, under the group's name, using the group's billing number, provided the arrangement meets the requirements in § 424.80(b)(6). However, because of the specific terms of the statute, we do not believe a group can receive payments for its services through a separate entity (one that is not wholly owned) that bills in its own right, under its own billing number, even if the payments ultimately constitute group revenues.

The requirement for physician-patient encounters and the definition of group "members". Effective January 1, 1995, the group practice definition in section 1877(h)(4)(A)(v) requires that members of the group must personally conduct no less than 75 percent of the physician-patient encounters of the group practice. We believe this provision may have been designed to differentiate between legitimate group practices and those with "member" owners or investors who are members in name, but who treat few, if any, patients. In such a scenario, nonmember physician contractors could be hired to treat most of the group's patients. This arrangement would allow the nonpracticing "outside" physician owners to refer to the "group" for the furnishing of laboratory services or other ancillary types of services that are designated health services.

In § 411.351 of the August 1995 final rule, we defined "members" of a group practice broadly as physician partners and full-time and part-time physician contractors and employees during the time they furnish services to patients of the group practice that are furnished through the group and are billed in the name of the group. This definition would cover all of the physicians who are involved, in some capacity, in a group practice arrangement, while they are furnishing services to group patients. As a result, all group practice patients who have an encounter in the group setting with a physician would be treated by a member of the group practice. Our interpretation would thus render the encounter requirement in section 1877(h)(4)(A)(v) superfluous.

It has come to our attention that group practices generally do not regard independent contractors as members of the group. In addition, when a group practice contracts with a number of independent contractors, the group can experience difficulties in meeting the "substantially all" requirement, especially if the contractors work for the group only on a part-time basis. In order to remedy this problem, and to give meaning to the encounter requirement in section 1877(h)(4)(A)(v), we propose a change in the definition of a member of a group practice. We propose to exclude independent contractors from the definition. In addition, we propose to redefine "members of the group" to include not just physician partners, but physicians with any other form of ownership in the practice (including physicians whose ownership is held by their individual professional corporations). We also propose to count any of the physicians listed under the definition as "members" during the time they furnish "patient care services" to the group rather than just during the time they furnish services to patients of the group that are furnished through the group and are billed in the name of the group. This change reflects our belief that a physician can legitimately be participating as a group member while providing services to the group for which the practice cannot directly bill, such as certain administrative services. We are also proposing to extend this definition to group practices in the context of the additional designated health services.

Group practices should note that under the revised definition of a group "member," independent contractors cannot supervise the provision of designated health services under the in-office ancillary services exception. Under section 1877(b)(2), services must be furnished personally by the referring physician, personally by a physician who is a member of the same group practice, or by individuals who are directly supervised by the referring physician or another physician in the group practice. We will no longer consider independent contractors as physicians who are "in the group practice." An independent contractor may be able to refer to the group practice for the provision of designated health services, provided the physician qualifies for the personal services exception in section 1877(e)(3) of the Act, or the new general compensation exception in § 411.357. We would also like to point out that the definition of who qualifies as a "member of a group practice" in § 411.351 applies only in the context of the referral provisions in section 1877 of the Act. The concept of group membership may be different for purposes of other provisions of the Medicare or Medicaid statutes.

As a result of our change in who constitutes a group practice member, at least 75 percent of all physician-patient encounters must occur between owner or employee physicians and patients. We regard an "encounter" as any appointment during which a group practice patient is actually examined or treated by a physician.

Methods for distributing group costs and revenues. The statute requires that a group distribute its income and overhead in accordance with methods that are "previously determined." We regard this provision as ambiguous, since it is not clear prior to what event these methods must be in place. A method will always be in place just prior to a distribution, since a distribution can occur only if there is some method in place to carry it out.

It is our view that this provision was meant to require that a group have an established plan for its distributions, rather than making ad hoc decisions about distributions just before making them. Congress may have feared that ad hoc disbursements would be more likely to reflect a physician's referrals. To give meaning to this provision, we propose to interpret it so that a group must have in place methods for distribution determined prior to the time period the group has earned the income or incurred the costs. We believe these methods can be determined by any party, and not just members of the group practice. For example, if a hospital has established a group practice to run a hospital affiliated clinic, the hospital might be the party that determines how clinic income will be distributed.

We are also proposing that the overhead expenses of and the income from the practice be distributed according to methods that indicate that the practice is a unified business. That is, the methods must reflect centralized decision making, a pooling of expenses and revenues, and a distribution system that is not based on each satellite office operating as if it were a separate enterprise. We would impose this additional standard under our authority under section 1877(h)(4)(A)(vi) to add standards by regulation to the definition of a group practice.

Volume or value of referrals cannot be reflected in a physician member's compensation. Beginning on January 1, 1995, physicians who are group practice members cannot directly or indirectly receive compensation based on the volume or value of their own referrals.

However, the statute qualifies this rule by allowing physicians to be paid a share of over-all profits of the group, or a productivity bonus, as described under the next two subheadings. (Groups should take note that the following discussion only describes what is appropriate under section 1877. You should be aware of and comply with other applicable statutes, including the anti-kickback statute, when entering into arrangements.)

We believe that the "volume or value" standard precludes a group practice from paying physician members for each referral they personally make or based on the value of the referred services. This standard applies to any of a physician's actions that constitute "referrals," as these are defined in section 1877(h)(5)(A) and (B) of the Act. We include here a brief discussion of what constitutes a "referral" for purposes of the "volume or value" standard:

Section 1877(h)(5)(A) states that referrals include, subject to an exception for certain specialized services, the request by a physician for an item or service for which payment may be made under Part B, including the request for a consultation with another physician (and any test or procedure ordered by, or to be performed by (or under the supervision of) that other physician). We are interpreting this provision to apply not to a physician's requests for any Part B items or services, but only to a physician's requests for designated health services covered under Part B. We explain our rationale for this position in the next section, which discusses the definition of a "referral."

The second part of the statutory definition of "referral" in section 1877(h)(5)(B) covers (subject to an exception for certain specific services) the request or establishment of a plan of care by a physician that includes the provision of a designated health service. Although this second part is not drafted in Medicare-specific terms and could be interpreted to cover situations involving any designated health service, we are interpreting it as applying only to those designated health services covered under Medicare. We discuss this position, and our interpretation of referrals for Medicaid covered services, in more detail in the section dealing with what constitutes a "referral."

Because of our interpretation of what constitutes a "referral," an entity wishing to be considered a group practice in order to use the in-office ancillary services exception cannot compensate its members based on the volume or value of referrals for designated health services for Medicare

or Medicaid patients but could do so in the case of other patients. However, the most straightforward way for a group to demonstrate that it is meeting the requirements for the exception would be for the group to avoid a link between physician compensation and the volume or value of any referrals, regardless of whether the referrals involve Medicare or Medicaid patients. Alternatively, a group that wants to compensate its members on the basis of non-Medicare and non-Medicaid referrals would be required to separately account for revenues and distributions relating to referrals for designated health services for Medicare and Medicaid patients. If a group purports to be making payments to its physicians for nonprogram referrals, but these appear to us to be inordinately high or otherwise inconsistent with the fair market value of those referrals, we could determine that the physicians' compensation does not meet the fair market value standard, and thus may actually reflect additional compensation for Medicare or Medicaid referrals.

A physician member's compensation can reflect over-all profits. Although physician members cannot be compensated directly or indirectly based on their own referrals, under section 1877(h)(4)(A)(iv) and (B)(i), a physician can be paid a share of over-all profits of the group, as long as the share is not determined in a manner that is *directly* related to the volume or value of that physician's own referrals.

In the case of over-all profits, we are interpreting the statute as follows: First, we are taking the position that the statute does not affect a physician's compensation for services other than designated health services. Thus, for purposes of section 1877, a group practice can distribute profits from services other than designated health services in any way it sees fit. For example, a group can distribute profits from the physicians' own nondesignated health services under an even split, based on referrals, or according to the amount of a physician's investment in the group, seniority, hours spent devoted to the practice, or the number or difficulty of services the physician has furnished. The practice can also offer different types of sharing of profits or other kinds of compensation arrangements, or combinations of arrangements, to different physicians or groups of physicians. (Groups should be careful to comply with other statutes, including the anti-kickback statute, when creating compensation arrangements.)

However, when a physician makes a referral for a designated health service for a Medicare or Medicaid patient (for example, orders a laboratory test or occupational therapy), we believe the statute requires a different scheme. That is, the referring physician can receive a portion of the group's overall pooled revenues from these services as long as the group does not share these profits in a manner that relates directly to who made the referrals for them. We believe, for example, that these profits can be shared according to most of the principles described above, such as an even split, a physician's investment in the group, the number of hours a physician in general devotes to the group, or the difficulty of a physician's work. However, each physician's personal compensation cannot include payments based directly on the number or value of the referrals he or she has made.

Since self-referrals are referrals under section 1877, profits should not be pooled and divided between group members so that they relate directly to the number of designated health services for Medicare or Medicaid patients physicians referred to themselves or the value of those self-referrals (such as a value based on the complexity of the service). Thus, a physician should not receive extra, specific compensation from the pooled profits for performing a designated health service he or she has self-referred. We believe that rewarding a physician each time he or she self-refers for a designated health service can constitute an incentive to overutilize services. Nor should a physician's compensation relate directly to the number of referrals for designated health services he or she has made to other group physicians, to the group's nonphysician staff, or to any other entity or individual.

We regard "over-all profits of the group" to mean all of the profits or revenues a group can distribute in any form to group members, even if the group is located in two different States or has many different locations within one State. We would not interpret the concept of "overall profits" as the profits that belong only to a particular specialty or subspecialty group. We believe that the narrower the pooling, the more likely it will be that a physician will receive compensation for his or her own referrals (for example, a subspecialty group or location could contain only one or two physicians).

A physician member's compensation can reflect productivity bonuses. Under section 1877(h)(4)(A)(iv) and (B)(i), a physician's compensation cannot directly or indirectly reflect the volume or value of his or her referrals, except

that the physician can receive a productivity bonus, as long as the bonus is not determined in a manner that is *directly* related to the volume or value of that physician's own referrals. A productivity bonus must be based on services that are personally performed by a physician or incident to personally performed services.

As we have noted above for sharing of profits, we have interpreted section 1877 as imposing no restrictions on productivity bonuses based on revenues that have nothing to do with a physician's referrals for designated health services under Medicare or Medicaid. Thus, for all nondesignated health services, a physician can be compensated under any productivity scheme that a group derives. We understand that group practices use many different measures of a physician's productivity, such as counting patient encounters, charges or collections attributable to the physician, or hours of patient care services, or factoring in the degree of difficulty of a physician's procedures, ways in which the physician has improved his or her professional qualifications, or the amount of time the physician is willing to be on-call. In addition, a group can pay physicians based on a percentage of profits, straight salary, or any combination of base and incentive payments.

In terms of designated health services that a physician refers for Medicare or Medicaid patients, a physician's productivity bonus can only indirectly reflect those services that he or she personally performed or that are incident to those personally performed services. We regard services as "personally performed" by a physician when he or she participates directly in the delivery of the service. As we have noted elsewhere, we believe that a physician has made a "referral" if the physician refers a patient for a designated health service to him or herself, to other physicians in the group, or to the physician's own or the group practice's employees or contractors or to any other entity or individual. Unlike the over-all profit situation, in which amounts can be aggregated, the productivity bonus by its very nature will be based on a physician's individual referrals and performance, and will fluctuate accordingly. However, the statute precludes a productivity bonus for a physician that directly reflects the volume or value of that physician's own referrals.

Thus, we believe a physician's compensation can reflect a bonus for designated health services the physician personally performs or "incident to"

services the physician directly supervises, provided the services result from the referral of a physician other than the one performing or supervising the service. A physician in this situation is not being compensated based on the volume or value of his or her own referrals. A physician can receive compensation for his or her own referrals for designated health services only through the aggregation that occurs as part of over-all sharing of profits.

We regard the reference in section 1877(h)(4)(B)(i) to services performed "incident to a physician's personally performed services" as a reference to the services defined in section 1861(s)(2)(A) of the Act. Here they are listed under "Medical and Other Health Services" as services and supplies (including drugs and biologicals that cannot, as determined in accordance with regulations, be self-administered) furnished as an incident to a physician's professional service, of kinds that are commonly furnished in physicians' offices and are commonly either furnished without charge or included in the physicians' bills.

Our longstanding interpretation of this provision appears in section 2050 of the Medicare Carriers Manual, Part 3— Claims Processing. This provision states that "incident to" services are those that are furnished as an integral, although incidental part, of the physician's personal professional services in the course of diagnosis or treatment of an illness or injury. The services of nonphysicians must be furnished under the physician's direct supervision by employees of the physician.

Because the provision in section 1877(h)(4)(B)(i) on productivity bonuses is a difficult one, and because physicians are now compensated in many ways, we directly solicit comments on our interpretation of this provision.

7. Referral

We have received a number of inquiries about what constitutes a "referral" for purposes of section 1877. The concept of a referral appears in several places: physicians are prohibited from making certain referrals and a number of the compensation-related exceptions require that any payment passing between a physician and an entity not reflect the volume or value of the physician's referrals. We believe that the concept of a "referral" in the statute is a broad one, and that prohibited referrals are a subset of these. Below we discuss our interpretation of what constitutes a "referral."

Under section 1877(h)(5)(A), referrals include, subject to an exception for

1692 Federal Register / Vol. 63, No. 6 / Friday, January 9, 1998 / Proposed Rules

certain specialized services, the request by a physician for an item or service for which payment may be made under Part B, including the request for a consultation with another physician (and any test or procedure ordered by, or to be performed by (or under the supervision of) that other physician).

We believe that "an item or service for which payment may be made under Part B" means a Part B item or service that ordinarily "may be" covered under Medicare (that is, that could be a covered service under Medicare at the present time in the community in which the service has been furnished) for a Medicare-eligible individual, regardless of whether Medicare would actually pay for this particular service, at the time, for the particular eligible individual who has been referred. (For example, Medicare might not pay for a service if the individual has not yet met his or her deductible.)

The second part of the statutory definition of "referral" in section 1877(h)(5)(B) covers (subject to an exception for certain specialized services) the request or establishment of a plan of care by a physician that includes the provision of a designated health service. Although this second part is not drafted in Medicare-specific terms and could be interpreted to cover situations involving any designated health service, we are interpreting it as applying only to those designated health services that "may be" covered under Medicare. We base this position on the fact that the referral prohibition in section 1877(a)(1) applies only to designated health services covered under Medicare.

We are not aware of any rationale for the distinction between the definition for Part B services, in which a physician's request for any Part B item or service constitutes a referral, and the definition for other items or services, in which a referral consists of a physician's request for, or a plan of care providing for, only a designated health service. The broader definition for Part B services has no ramifications in terms of the actual referral prohibition, which encompasses only referrals for designated health services. However, it is significant in terms of the standard that appears in the "group practice" definition and in a number of the compensation-related exceptions that precludes compensation between parties that reflects the volume or value of a physician's referrals.

It is our understanding that section 1877 was designed to prevent physicians from overutilizing the specific health care services designated in the statute, a list Congress derived

based on its sense of which services tend to be subject to abuse. We do not believe the statute was meant to preclude physicians from being compensated for their referrals for totally different Part B services. Thus, we are taking the position that, since the prohibition relates only to referrals for designated health services, the concept of a referral for a Part B service under section 1877(h)(5)(A) should be limited to just referrals for designated health services.

As we explained in the discussion on the definition of an "entity," we believe that the concept of a "referral" covers situations in which physicians refer to themselves or among themselves. (As we noted in that discussion, a physician could be prohibited from referring to him or herself or to other group practice members if the services do not meet the in-office ancillary services exception in section 1877(b)(2) or the physician services exception in section 1877(b)(1) of the Act or some other exception.) We believe that a physician has made a referral under section 1877(h)(5) when he or she requests any designated health service covered under Part A or Part B or establishes a plan of care that includes a designated health service covered under Part A or B, even if the physician furnishes the service personally. We interpret this language to cover a physician's certifying or recertifying a patient's need for a designated health service. For Part B services, a referral can also include a consultation with another physician.

We are interpreting a physician's "request" for an item or service, or the establishment of a plan of care, as a step that occurs after a physician has initially examined a patient or furnished physician services that are not designated health services, or otherwise concluded that the patient needs a designated health service. (We describe our rationale for this interpretation in more detail in section III.C.2 of this preamble, where we discuss the in-office ancillary services exception.)

We are interpreting a "request" as occurring whenever a physician asks for a service in any way or indicates that he or she believes the service is necessary (for example, by verbally stating that the service is necessary, by entering description of the service into the patient's records or onto a medical chart or by writing a prescription).

What constitutes a "referral" for a Medicaid service. Section 1903(s) of the Act applies aspects of the referral prohibition to the Medicaid program for referrals that would result in a denial of payment for the service under Medicare, if Medicare covered the service to the

same extent and under the same terms and conditions as under the State plan. We interpret this provision to mean that a State should apply the Medicare rules in section 1877 to a referral for a Medicaid service, even if the service is not covered under Medicare.

However, the definition of a referral in section 1877(h)(5)(A) and (B) is cast specifically in terms of a request for certain Part B Medicare services and for "other items," which in the Medicare context we have interpreted to mean Part A services. Since Medicaid services are not categorized this way, we propose to interpret this provision by establishing an analogous definition. That is, (subject to an exception for certain specialized services, which we describe below) a physician has made a referral if he or she has requested a Medicaid covered designated health service that is comparable to a service covered under Part B of Medicare (including a request for a consultation with another physician). A physician has also made a referral for any other Medicaid covered item or service if the service is a designated health service and the physician has requested it or has established a plan of care that includes it.

We are also translating a "referral" from the Medicare context to mean a physician's requests for, or plan of care including, a designated health service that ordinarily "may be" covered under the particular State Medicaid program for an individual in the patient's eligibility category, regardless of whether the State Medicaid agency would actually pay for this particular service, at the time, for the particular Medicaid-eligible individual who has been referred.

Prohibited referrals only involve designated health services. It is important to keep in mind that the only referrals that are prohibited under section 1877 of the Act are those that involve the furnishing of a designated health service listed in section 1877(h)(6). As we note in section IV.A.5 of this preamble in our discussion on referrals to immediate family members, a physician is free to make a referral for a service that is not a designated health service (or a service that does not include a designated health service), such as certain physician services. For example, a physician can refer a patient to an obstetrician for general prenatal care. If the obstetrician prescribes ultrasound as part of this prenatal care, it is the obstetrician who has made a referral for a designated health service, and not the original physician.

The statutory exception to the definition of a "referral." Before OBRA

'93, the definition of a "referral" under section 1877(h)(5)(A) was qualified by an exception in section 1877(h)(5)(C) for a request by a pathologist for certain clinical diagnostic laboratory tests and pathological examination services. These services had to be furnished by (or under the supervision of) the pathologist, as the result of a consultation requested by another physician. We incorporated this provision into the August 1995 final rule in § 411.351.

We are also proposing to interpret the level of supervision that a pathologist must provide if another individual, such as a technician, actually furnishes the services. The statute requires "supervision," rather than the "direct supervision" that appears as part of the in-office ancillary services exception. We are interpreting "supervision" to mean the level of supervision ordinarily required under Medicare coverage and payment rules or, when they apply, the health and safety standards, for the particular services at issue in the particular locations in which the services will be furnished.

As the result of OBRA '93, beginning on January 1, 1995, the exception to what constitutes a "referral" in section 1877(h)(5)(C) was expanded to include a request by a radiologist for diagnostic radiology services and a request by a radiation oncologist for radiation therapy, if the services are furnished by (or under the supervision of) the radiologist or radiation oncologist as the result of a consultation requested by another physician. We are incorporating this amendment into the definition of a "referral" in § 411.351. Diagnostic radiology services and radiation therapy are also defined in § 411.351, where we have presented our proposed definitions of the different designated health services.

When a physician has requested a "consultation." The services that are excepted from the "referral definition" under section 1877(h)(5)(C) must result from a consultation requested by a physician other than the pathologist, radiologist, or radiation oncologist who actually performs or supervises the performance of the services listed above. We discussed the concept of a consultation briefly in the preamble to the proposed rule covering referrals for clinical laboratory services at 57 FR 8595. We said that, for purposes of Medicare coverage, a "consultation" is—

a professional service furnished to a patient by a physician (the consultant) at the request of the patient's attending physician. A consultation includes the history and examination of the patient as well as a written report that is transmitted to the attending physician for inclusion in the patient's permanent record ***. Other referrals, such as sending a patient to a specialist who assumes responsibility for furnishing the appropriate treatment, or providing a list of referrals for a second opinion, are not "consultations" or "referrals" that would trigger the laboratory services use prohibition.

We would like to clarify that a consultation occurs whenever a physician requests that a patient see another physician, such as a particular specialist, but the original physician retains control over the care of the patient, including any care related to the condition that prompted the consultation. Section 1877(h)(5)(A) implies that a "consultation" is still a consultation even if the consultant physician takes the initiative to order, perform, or supervise the performance of, tests for the patient. The consultant physician, as we noted in the preamble of the August 1995 rule, must provide the original physician with a report. Nonetheless, we regard this as a consultation as long as it is the original physician who gathers information from the consultant physician about his or her examination of the patient and any test results and then makes a decision about how to proceed with the patient's care.

Conversely, the original physician has not arranged for a consultation, but instead has made a referral, in situations in which the specialist takes over the patient's care for purposes of the condition that prompted the referral. For example, a physician might send a patient to a specific cardiologist, who examines the patient thoroughly, sends a report to the attending physician but is the only one who sees the patient thereafter for the purpose of treating a heart problem.

8. Remuneration

Remuneration that does not result in a compensation arrangement. A compensation arrangement is defined in section 1877(h)(1) as any arrangement involving any remuneration between a physician (or family member) and an entity, *other than* an arrangement involving only remuneration described in section 1877(h)(1)(C). Section 1877(h)(1)(C) lists certain specific kinds of remuneration that do not result in a compensation arrangement, such as the forgiveness of amounts owed for inaccurate tests, mistakenly performed tests, or for the correction of minor billing errors.

We believe there is some ambiguity in section 1877(h)(1) concerning the requirement that excepted remuneration must result *from an arrangement involving only* the remuneration described in section 1877(h)(1)(C). This provision could be read to mean that the items in section 1877(h)(1)(C) are excepted when the arrangement that exists between the physician and entity involves nothing but the excepted forms of payment. As a practical matter, we realize that the kinds of remuneration listed in section 1877(h)(1)(C) seldom occur as isolated transactions, but are often subsets or components of other arrangements. For example, the forgiveness of minor billing errors suggests that the parties transact and exchange services or items for payment when there are no billing errors; those transactions that contain billing errors may be only a small fraction of the parties' overall business dealings.

To clarify this provision, we are interpreting it to mean that the portion of a business arrangement that consists of the remuneration listed in section 1877(h)(1)(C) alone does not constitute a compensation arrangement. Any other forms of remuneration that might accompany these payments are not excepted and could constitute a compensation arrangement, provided they do not otherwise meet one of the other exceptions in this proposed regulation.

Section 1877(h)(1)(C)(ii) excepts from the definition of "remuneration" the provision of items, devices, or supplies that are used *solely* to collect, transport, process, or store specimens for the entity providing the item, device, or supply, or order or communicate the results of tests or procedures for the entity. We believe that some pathology laboratories have been furnishing physicians with materials ranging from basic collection items and storage items (for example, jars for urine samples and vials for blood samples) to more specialized or sophisticated items, devices, or equipment (snares used to remove gastrointestinal polyps, needles used for biopsies or to draw bone marrow or samples of amniotic fluid for amniocentesis, and computers or fax machines used to transmit results).

In order for these items and devices to meet the statutory requirement, they must be used *solely* to collect, transport, process, or store specimens for the laboratory or other entity that provided the items and devices. We interpret "solely" in this context to mean that these items are used solely for the purposes listed in the statute, such as cups used for urine collection or vials used to hold and transport blood to the entity that supplied the items or devices.

We do not believe that an item or device meets this requirement if it is used for any purposes besides these. For example, we do not regard specialized equipment such as disposable or reusable aspiration and injection needles and snares as solely collection or storage devices. Instead, these items are also surgical tools that are routinely used as part of a surgical or medical procedure. For example, the Food and Drug Administration (FDA) regulations in 21 CFR 878.4800(a) define a "manual surgical instrument for general use" as a "non-powered, hand-held, or hand-manipulated device, either reusable or disposable, intended to be used in various general surgical procedures." Surgical instruments listed in the regulation include disposable or reusable aspiration and injection needles, snares, and other similar devices. Snares are also listed in these regulations as components of various specialized surgical devices, such as ear, nose, and throat manual surgical instruments, endoscopic electrosurgical units, and manual gastroenterology-urology surgical instruments and accessories.

In addition, to ensure that items or devices that could qualify for this exception are used solely for the entity that supplied them, the number or amount of these items should be consistent with the number or amount that is used for specimens that are actually sent to this entity for processing. That is, if a physician tends to annually perform 400 blood tests that are sent to a particular laboratory for analysis, we would not expect the physician to accept from that laboratory items, devices, or supplies in excess of an amount that is reasonable for the projected tests. In determining the amount of goods that are reasonable, we would consider not just quantity, but such facts as whether the laboratory packages together a set of items to be used for just *one* tissue collection or one use, or whether an item can be used multiple times, for multiple entities.

If, on the other hand, a physician keeps a particular item or device and uses it repeatedly or could use it repeatedly for any patients or for other uses, we would presume that the item or device is not one that meets the requirement, unless the physician can demonstrate otherwise. For example, if computer equipment or fax machines can be used for a number of purposes in addition to ordering or receiving results from an entity, we would presume that the "solely" requirement is not met, unless the physician can demonstrate that the equipment is integral to, and used exclusively for,

performing the outside entity's work. Detailed records concerning the use of the machine would be necessary to overcome this presumption.

Section 1877(h)(1)(C)(iii) "excepts" from a compensation arrangement situations involving certain payments made by an insurer or a self-insured plan to a physician. The payments must be those that satisfy a claim, submitted on a fee-for-service basis, for the furnishing of health services by that physician to an individual who is covered by a policy with the insurer or by the self-insured plan. The payments must meet certain specified conditions.

We believe that this provision was designed for situations in which an insurer is involved in the delivery of health care services. If the insurer owns a health care facility, a physician might otherwise be precluded from referring to that facility just because the physician receives compensation from the insurer in the form of payments that satisfy claims the physician has submitted. If the physician is seeking fee-for-service payments from an insurer, he or she may not have an arrangement with the insurer that could qualify as a personal services arrangement, or otherwise qualify under any of the other statutory exceptions.

Discounts can be a form of remuneration for some of the designated health services. In the August 1995 final rule, we defined remuneration to include discounts. In the preamble to that rule, we explained that we believe that, for most items or services that a physician might purchase, the statute dictates this result. Section 1877(e)(8)(B) excepts from a compensation arrangement payments made by a physician to an entity as compensation for items or services (other than clinical laboratory services) if the items or services are furnished at fair market value. As a result, any amounts that a physician pays for items or services that do not reflect fair market value, such as certain discounted items or services, would not meet the exception.

We may have implied in the August 1995 final rule that all discounts would fail to meet the fair market value standard. We wish to clarify here that we believe a discount does meet the fair market value standard if it is an arm's-length transaction; an entity offers it to all similarly situated individuals, regardless of whether they make referrals to the entity; the discount does not reflect the volume or value of any referrals the physician has made or will make to the entity; and the discount is passed on to Medicare or other insurers. We are aware of situations in which discounts enure to the benefit of

referring physicians. For example, physicians will sometimes purchase oncology drugs from manufacturers at a discount, yet mark the drugs up to eliminate the discount when billing Medicare. Such arrangements would not meet the standard.

We are also creating a new exception under our authority in section 1877(b)(4), which allows us to except any other financial relationship that we determine does not pose a risk of program or patient abuse. The new exception would allow physicians to receive a discount based on the volume of their referrals to an entity, provided the discount is passed on in full to the patients or their insurers (including Medicare), and does not enure to the benefit of the physicians in any way.

The statute provides a different exception for laboratory services. Section 1877(e)(8)(A) states that there is no compensation arrangement when a physician makes payments to a laboratory in exchange for the laboratory providing clinical laboratory services. This exception does not include a fair market value standard. Congress may not have included this standard based on its belief that, under the Medicare program, physicians cannot purchase laboratory services at a discount, and then bill the Medicare program for them at a marked up rate.

We agree that physicians are precluded from purchasing and marking up laboratory services covered under Medicare under section 1833(h)(5)(A) of the Act. This provision states that, in general, Medicare payment for a clinical diagnostic laboratory test may be made only to the person or entity that performed or supervised the performance of the test. In addition, payment for laboratory tests is made on the basis of a fee schedule.

B. General Prohibition on Referrals

Which designated health services are covered by the prohibition. Section 1877(a)(1)(A) prohibits referrals to an entity for the furnishing of designated health services "for which payment otherwise may be made under [Medicare], * * *." We believe that this means any designated health service that ordinarily "may be" covered under Medicare (that is, that could be a covered service under Medicare in the community in which the service has been provided) for a Medicare-eligible individual, regardless of whether Medicare would actually pay for this particular service, at the time, for that particular individual (for example, the individual may not have met his or her deductible).

We believe that the same principles apply for designated health services under the Medicaid program. Section 1903(s) says that the Secretary cannot make Federal financial participation payments to a State for designated health services, as they are defined under section 1877(h)(6), furnished to an individual on the basis of a referral that would result in a denial of payment under Medicare, if Medicare covered the services to the same extent and under the same terms and conditions as under the State plan. We interpret this provision to mean that the Medicare rules in section 1877 apply to Medicaid services, as if Medicare covered the same items and services as a State's Medicaid program.

As a result, a referral could affect a State's FFP if the designated health service is one "for which payment otherwise may be made" under a State's Medicaid program, regardless of whether a State agency would actually pay for this particular service, at the time, for that particular individual. Therefore, if a State plan could cover the service for a Medicaid eligible individual in the individual's eligibility group, we believe it is a service that is covered by the referral prohibition.

Limitations on billing and refunds on a timely basis. As part of the prohibition on referrals in section 1877(a), the statute also provides that an entity may not present or cause to be presented a Medicare claim or a bill to any individual, third party payor, or other entity for designated health services furnished under a prohibited referral. In the August 1995 final rule, we included in § 411.353(d) the requirement that an entity that collects payment for a laboratory service that was performed under a prohibited referral must refund all collected amounts on a timely basis. We are proposing to apply this provision to such amounts collected for any of the designated health services. We are also proposing to define "timely basis" by cross referring to § 1003.101 in the OIG civil money penalty regulations. While § 1003.101 currently defines this term as "the 60-day period from the time the prohibited amounts are collected by the individual or entity," the OIG is planning to issue shortly revised final regulations that will amend this term. Under the amended version, the 60-day timeframe for a refund will begin when the individual or entity knew or should have known that the amount collected was related to a prohibited referral. We plan to adopt this revised definition as well.

C. General Exceptions That Apply to Ownership or Investment Interests and to Compensation Arrangements

1. Exception for Physician Services

The statute provides that the referral prohibition does not apply in cases involving physician services (as defined in section 1861(q)) provided personally by (or under the personal supervision of) another physician in the same group practice as the referring physician. Physician services are generally defined in section 1861(q) as professional services *performed by* physicians, including surgery, consultation, and home, office, and institutional calls. The Medicare regulations have interpreted this provision in § 410.20(a) to include diagnosis, therapy, surgery, consultations, and home, office, and institutional calls, provided the services are furnished by one of the types of doctors listed in § 410.20(b).

Note that this exception applies to physician services that constitute designated health services, as we would define designated health services in § 411.351. The exception in the Medicare context does not cover services that are performed by nonphysicians but are furnished under a physician's supervision, such as ancillary or "incident-to" services. Under Medicare, physician services can only be performed by a physician. Thus, we believe the exception applies only to services that are provided personally by a physician who is a member of the same group practice as the referring physician or that are provided by a nonmember physician who is personally supervised by a group practice physician. We would interpret "personal supervision" to mean that the group practice physician is legally responsible for monitoring the results of any test or other designated health service and is available to assist the individual who is furnishing the service, even though the member physician need not be present while the service is being furnished.

2. Exception for In-office Ancillary Services

This exception applies to services other than parenteral and enteral nutrients, equipment and supplies and durable medical equipment (although it does apply to infusion pumps) that are referred by a solo practitioner or group practice member within his or her own practice. The exception requires that the services be performed by the referring physician or group practice member, or by another member of the same group practice as the referring physician, or be directly supervised by one of these

physicians (we discussed the direct supervision requirement in section III.A.2 of this preamble), that the services be furnished in certain locations, and that the services be billed in a particular way. We discuss these last two requirements below.

a. The site requirement

Where a service is actually "furnished." Section 1877(b)(2)(A)(ii)(I) requires, for a solo or group practice, that the services be furnished in a building in which the referring physician or another member of the group practice furnishes physician services unrelated to the furnishing of designated health services. It is our view that a service is furnished wherever a procedure is actually performed upon a patient or in the location in which a patient receives and begins using an item.

For example, if a patient receives an MRI (magnetic resonance image) in a physician's office, the service has been furnished there. If a patient is fitted for and receives a brace in the physician's office, the brace has been furnished there. The same rule would apply to a prosthetic device that is implanted in a physician's office. However, any item that is given to a patient but is meant to be used at home or outside the physician's office, or any item that is delivered to the patient's home, has not been "furnished" in the physician's office.

What constitutes the "same building" in which the physician is practicing. We are interpreting "the same building" to mean one physical structure, with one address, and not multiple structures that are connected by tunnels or walkways. In addition, we believe "the building" consists of parts of the physical structure that are used as office or other commercial space. For example, a mobile X-ray van that is pulled into the garage of a building would not be part of that building.

When a physician is furnishing physician services "unrelated to the furnishing of designated health services." To meet this criterion, we believe that a physician must be providing in the same building any amount of physician services (as defined in § 410.20(a)) other than those listed as designated health services as we have defined them in § 411.351. Thus, we would regard as "unrelated to designated health services" a physician's examination of a patient and diagnosis, even if these lead to the physician requesting a designated health service, such as an X-ray or laboratory test.

The location test for group practices. In the case of a group practice, the group has the option of meeting a location test other than the one requiring that the designated health services be provided in the same building in which a group member provides physician services. The group can provide clinical laboratory services in any other building that is used by the group for the provision of some or all of the group's clinical laboratory services.

A group can furnish the other designated health services in another building that is used by the group for the centralized provision of the group's designated health services. We believe that a location meets this "centralized" requirement if it services more than one of a group's offices, and if it furnishes one or any combination of designated health services. It is also our view that a group can have more than one of these centralized locations. To meet the in-office ancillary exception, a group would be required to have a physician member present in the "centralized" location to perform or directly supervise the performance of designated health services, but the physician would not be required to perform physician services that are unrelated to the designated health services in this location.

b. The billing requirement

Section 1877(b)(2)(B) requires that in-office ancillary services be billed by the physician performing or supervising the services, by the referring or supervising physician's group practice under a billing number assigned to the group, or by an entity that is wholly owned by the physician or group practice. For a group practice that bills, we discussed a similar requirement for a group billing number in section III.A.6 of this preamble, where we covered the definition of a group practice. There, as here, we are interpreting this provision to allow a single group to bill under any billing number that has been assigned to the group in situations in which a group has more than one number, and to allow an agent to bill for the group in the group's name, using the group's number, provided the arrangement meets the requirements in § 424.80(b)(6).

In situations in which a "wholly-owned" entity bills for a group, we do not believe the statute requires that the service be billed under the group number, if the wholly owned entity can bill under its own provider number. Also, we are interpreting "a wholly-owned" entity that bills to cover an entity that provides billing or administrative services to a physician or group practice. Alternatively, this entity can be a wholly-owned provider of designated health services, such as a laboratory or radiology facility that is wholly owned by a physician or group, but bills for its own services. However, because the provision refers to an entity that is "wholly owned," we do not believe that it covers billing entities that are owned jointly by a physician or group practice with any other individuals or entities.

We also believe that a group practice member cannot use the in-office ancillary services exception to refer to other group practice members for services he or she intends to bill independently. Section 1877(b)(2)(B) states that the services must be billed *by the physician performing or supervising the services* or by a group practice of which the physician is a member, or by entities wholly owned by the physician or the group. Nonetheless, under the definition of who qualifies as a "member" of a group practice in § 411.351, a group practice physician billing under his or her own provider status would be considered a solo practicing physician for purposes of the in-office ancillary exception.

In § 411.351, we defined who can qualify as a "member" of a group practice broadly in order to accommodate the many part-time and contract physicians who often participate in one or more group practices. The definition of a "member" covered physician partners and full and part-time physician contractors and employees. Physicians under the definition qualify as "members" only *during the time they furnish services to patients of the group practice* that are furnished through the group and are *billed in the name of the group.* Therefore, whenever a physician bills separately for a lab service the physician has personally performed or supervised, he or she is functioning as a solo practitioner and not as a group member. (We are currently proposing to amend the definition of a "member" to exclude independent contractors and to regard a physician as a member during the time he or she furnishes "patient care services" to the group. These changes would not affect our interpretation.)

If a physician bills for a service independently, other group members cannot directly supervise those services for the referring physician. In addition, if a group member bills for too many services independently, the group practice may fail to meet the "substantially all" test under the definition of a group practice in section 1877(h)(4)(A)(ii). That provision requires that substantially all of the services provided by group members be billed under a billing number assigned to the group.

c. Designated health services that do not trigger the in-office exception

The location requirements for this exception specify that designated health services must be provided in a building in which a solo practitioner or a group practice physician also provides physician services unrelated to the furnishing of designated health services or, for group practices, in a building that serves as a centralized location in which a group provides designated health services. Thus, this exception would not cover services provided elsewhere, such as home health services.

If services are furnished in a hospital or skilled nursing facility, we believe they can be covered under this exception if these locations serve as a centralized location in which a group provides designated health services or if the referring physician or a member of the same group practice furnishes unrelated physician services in the building, and the physicians can meet the requirement for direct supervision and billing.

3. Exception for Services Provided Under Prepaid Health Plans

We are aware that the health care world is evolving rapidly, consisting of a broad spectrum that ranges from traditional practices using fee-for-service billing all the way to fully capitated managed care systems, many of which are excepted under the "prepaid" provision in the statute. In between these extremes exist a host of "hybrid" systems that display a mixture of fee-for-service and managed care characteristics. Section 1877 addresses some of these systems directly; most others we believe can continue to function by meeting the exceptions in the statute and in this proposed regulation. We specifically solicit comments on whether our assessment is accurate.

In this section we describe how we propose to interpret the law in a manner that we believe will help to safeguard the Medicare and Medicaid programs from abuse, while facilitating the evolution of integrated delivery and other health care delivery systems. We also discuss how we believe the law affects referrals for designated health services provided under demonstration projects and waivers.

a. Physicians, suppliers, and providers that contract with prepaid organizations

The "prepaid plan" exception covers services furnished by certain specified organizations to their enrollees. Under section 1877(b)(3), these include health maintenance organizations and competitive medical plans that have a contract with Medicare, certain prepaid organizations functioning under a demonstration project, and Federally qualified health maintenance organizations. We have incorporated this exception into the regulations at § 411.355(c). We are aware that a number of these organizations do not furnish services directly but often contract with outside physicians, providers, or suppliers to furnish items or services to their enrollees, for which the organizations bill. The outside physicians, providers, or suppliers may, in turn, contract with other physicians or entities for certain supplies or services. In order to accommodate these situations, we are interpreting this exception broadly to cover not only services furnished by the organizations themselves, but also those furnished to the organization's enrollees by outside physicians, providers, or suppliers under contract with these organizations. The exception would also cover services furnished to enrollees by those with whom the outside physicians, providers, or suppliers have contracted.

b. Managed care organizations under the Medicaid program

We propose to add to the regulation a new exception in § 435.1012(b) for designated health services provided by managed care entities analogous to those listed in section 1877(b)(3) that provide services to Medicaid eligible enrollees under contracts with State Medicaid agencies. We are basing this addition on our analysis of section 1903(s) of the Act. Under section 1903(s), a State can receive no FFP for expenditures for medical assistance under the State plan consisting of a designated health service furnished to an individual on the basis of a referral that would result in a denial of payment for the service under Medicare if Medicare covered the service to the same extent and under the same terms and conditions as under the State plan. We read this provision to mean that the Medicare-based rules in section 1877 must be applied to services furnished under a State's Medicaid program to determine when a referral is a "prohibited" one.

Section 1877(b)(3) excepts from the referral prohibition services furnished to enrollees of certain "prepaid" plans; however, all of the entities listed in that exception provide services to Medicare patients. As a result, the exception for prepaid arrangements has no meaning for physicians who wish to refer in the context of the Medicaid program. In

order to give some meaning to this provision in the Medicaid context, when it is read in conjunction with section 1903(s), we are adding an exception for services furnished by the Medicaid counterparts of the Medicare managed care contracts expressly referenced in section 1877(b).

In section 1877(b)(3), Congress exempted all types of Medicare contracts with prepaid managed care health plans. We propose to extend this exemption to the categories of Medicaid-contracting managed care plans analogous to those exempted for Medicare in section 1877(b)(3). Like the section 1876 Medicare contracts exempted under section 1877(b)(3)(A), section 1903(m) governs Medicaid HMO contracts (specifically, comprehensive risk contracts), and requires that contracting HMOs comply with the physician incentive plan requirements in section 1876(i)(8).

The type of Medicare prepaid health plan exempted under section 1877(b)(3)(B) is an entity with a less than comprehensive contract (involving only Part B, or outpatient, services) under section 1833(a)(1)(A) of the Act and regulations at 42 CFR Part 417, Subpart U. These entities are known as "health care prepayment plans" (HCPPs). The Medicaid equivalent of a Medicare HCPP is a "prepaid health plan," or PHP. Like an HCPP, PHPs generally contract for less than a comprehensive range of services (a PHP can also be a nonrisk comprehensive contract, since section 1903(m) only governs comprehensive risk contracts). Like HCPPs, PHPs are not subject to the full range of requirements that HMOs must satisfy under section 1876 or section 1903(m).

Section 1877(b)(3)(C) exempts entities receiving payment on a prepaid basis under a demonstration project under section 402(a) of the Social Security Amendments of 1967 or section 222(a) of the Social Security Amendments of 1972. The Medicaid counterpart of section 402(a) is section 1115(a) of the Social Security Act. Indeed, several demonstration projects under section 402(a) involving Medicaid-eligible Medicare beneficiaries also involve Medicaid capitation payments under the authority in section 1115(a). We accordingly are proposing to exempt entities receiving payments on a prepaid capitation basis under a demonstration project under section 1115(a) of the Act.

Finally, in order to cover the full range of Medicaid managed care contractors paid on a prepaid basis, as Congress did for Medicare, it is also necessary to exempt "Health Insuring Organizations" (HIOs) if they furnish or

arrange for services as a managed care contractor. We are accordingly proposing to exempt these entities as well.

c. Evolving structures of integrated delivery and other health care delivery systems

As described above, the statute directly excepts from the referral prohibition all of the services provided by "prepaid" entities described in section 1877(b)(3) to the entities' enrollees. We realize that a host of organizations and integrated systems are not specifically excepted under the statute, so the services they provide to Medicare and Medicaid patients may be subject to the referral prohibition. For example, Medicare may provide secondary coverage to patients who participate in employer group health plans and are treated by HMOs that do not have contracts with Medicare or are not Federally qualified. Also, there are nontraditional systems that use both fee-for-service and capitated billing and are not specifically excepted under the law. We can find no grounds to create a blanket exception for these arrangements; we see no guarantee that these "hybrid" structures will all be free from any risk of patient or program abuse.

It is our view that a large percentage of the new and evolving structures will continue to thrive by meeting the exceptions in the statute and in this proposed regulation. For example, entities such as preferred provider organizations (PPOs) and physician hospital organizations (PHOs) that are not excepted under section 1877(b)(3) normally contract with physicians to provide services to the organization's patients, including Medicare or Medicaid patients. These physicians can continue to refer Medicare and Medicaid patients to the organization for designated health services, provided the physicians' arrangements with the organization qualify for the personal services exception in section 1877(e)(3) (and in § 411.357(d) of this proposed regulation).

This exception provides, among other things, that the arrangement must be for at least 1 year, the physician's compensation must be based on fair market value and cannot reflect the volume or value of the physician's referrals, except as allowed under certain physician incentive plans. We have defined "fair market value" in § 411.351 to allow payment that is consistent with the general market value of the services; that is, the compensation that would be included in a comparable service agreement, as the result of bona fide bargaining between well-informed parties, at the time the agreement takes place.

If a physician has contracted with an organization for less than 1 year, the arrangement could meet the new general exception for compensation arrangements that we have added in § 411.357(l). We have added this new exception to accommodate the many complex arrangements that we believe exist between physicians and entities, as described below in section II.E.1. Also, as described in section II.E.3, we have interpreted the "volume or value of referrals" standard (one of the standards in the personal services exception and in many of the compensation-related exceptions) in a manner that we believe will not obstruct physicians who are required to refer for certain services within a network when the entity furnishing the services is at substantial financial risk for their cost. In section IV, in which we answer questions about the law, we present a discussion about physicians who have contracted with HMOs or other prepaid organizations, but who wish to refer fee-for-service patients to the HMO or to other physicians or providers who are affiliated with the HMO.

d. Designated health services furnished under a demonstration project or waiver

We propose to interpret section 1877 in a manner that we believe will allow most Medicare or Medicaid patients to continue to receive designated health services under demonstration projects or waivers. Our analysis of this issue depends upon whether the organization is paid on a prepaid basis under section 1115(a) of the Social Security Act or under one of the demonstration authorities specified in section 1877(b)(3)(C).

Prepaid demonstration contracts. Entities receiving payment on a prepaid basis under section 402(a) of the Social Security Amendments of 1967 or section 222 of the Social Security Amendments of 1972, have been exempted from the referral prohibition by section 1877(b)(3)(C). Entities receiving payment on a prepaid basis under a Medicaid demonstration project under section 1115(a) of the Social Security Act would be exempt under the proposed Medicaid analogue, as discussed earlier in this section.

We would note that the exemption for Medicare prepaid demonstration contractors extends not only to demonstration projects initiated by the Secretary under her discretionary authority in sections 402(a) and 222, but to all demonstrations that incorporate or rely upon section 402 authority,

including such congressionally-mandated demonstrations as the PACE ("Program for All-inclusive Care for the Elderly") demonstration projects, under which a public or non-profit entity contracts to provide comprehensive care to frail elderly Medicare beneficiaries, including dual eligibles who have been certified for skilled nursing facility level care, and the "Social HMO" (SHMO) demonstration projects, including the ESRD SHMO demonstration.

Demonstration projects that are not prepaid. If a demonstration project does not involve an organization receiving payments on a prepaid basis, the Medicare "prepaid" exception in section 1877(b)(3)(C) and the Medicaid analogue we are proposing in this rule would not apply.

We believe that the referral prohibition applies to services furnished under a demonstration project or waiver that does not qualify under section 1877(b)(3)(C) or the Medicaid prepaid demonstration exception proposed in this rule; however, the Secretary can exercise authority to waive or otherwise alter the requirements in sections 1877 or 1903(s). For example, section 402(a) of the Social Security Amendments of 1967 permits the Secretary to conduct demonstrations for a variety of purposes specified in section 402(a)(1)(A) through (K) (for example, to test whether changes in methods of reimbursement and payment for services, or covering additional services, would have the effect of increasing efficiency and economy without adversely affecting quality). Section 402(b) of these amendments permits the Secretary to waive compliance with the requirements of the Medicare statute for such research, insofar as these requirements are related to reimbursement or payment. We have determined that the requirements in section 1877 constitute requirements related to reimbursement and payment and thus may be waived for the kind of demonstration project described above, when there are no prepaid payments.

In the Medicaid context, where a demonstration project does not fall within the general exception proposed in this rule, the Secretary has the authority under section 1115(a)(2) to consider as expenditures under the State plan costs of the demonstration project that would not otherwise be included as expenditures under section 1903, to the extent and for the period prescribed by the Secretary. Hence, section 1115 could allow the Secretary to provide to a State the FFP that would otherwise be precluded under section 1903(s).

D. Exceptions That Apply Only to Ownership or Investment Interests

1. Exception for Ownership in Publicly Traded Securities

To qualify for the securities exception under section 1877(c)(1), the statute originally required that a physician's or family member's investment had to be in securities "which *were* purchased on terms generally available to the public * * *." (Emphasis added.) OBRA '93 amended this provision to require that the securities be those "which *may be* purchased on terms generally available to the public." (Emphasis added.) This amendment went into effect retroactively to January 1, 1992, and is reflected in the August 1995 final rule. We did not, however, interpret this change in the final rule.

We believe the purpose of this exception is to allow physicians or family members to acquire stock in large companies if the transaction does not particularly favor the physicians over other purchasers. In keeping with this purpose, we propose to interpret "may be purchased" to mean that, at the time the physician or family member obtained the securities, they *could* be purchased on the open market, even if the physician or family member did not actually purchase the securities on those terms. For example, the physician or family member may have inherited the securities or otherwise acquired them without actually purchasing them. We have reflected this interpretation in § 411.356(a).

Section 1877(c)(1) also requires that the securities be in a corporation that had, at the end of the corporation's most recent fiscal year, or on average during the previous 3 fiscal years, stockholder equity exceeding $75,000,000. In proposed 411.356(a)(2), we define stockholder equity as the difference in value between a corporation's total assets and total liabilities.

2. Exception for Hospital Ownership

Section 1877(d)(3) excepts designated health services "provided by a hospital" (other than a hospital located in Puerto Rico) if the referring physician is authorized to perform services at the hospital, and the ownership or investment interest is in the hospital itself (and not merely in a subdivision of the hospital). We believe that this exception applies only to designated health services that are furnished by a hospital, and not to services furnished by any other health care providers the hospital owns, such as a hospital-owned home health agency or SNF. It is our view that services "provided by a hospital" corresponds only to those services provided by an entity that qualifies as a "hospital" under the Medicare conditions of participation. We further believe that section 1877(d)(3) covers any "designated health services" provided by a hospital, rather than just "inpatient or outpatient hospital services," because hospitals can provide services to individuals who are neither inpatients nor outpatients (for example, they provide laboratory services to outside patients).

E. Exceptions That Apply Only to Compensation Arrangements

1. A new exception for all compensation arrangements that meet certain standards

Section 1877 of the Act contains a number of exceptions to the referral prohibition that apply only to compensation arrangements. Section 1877(e) contains eight exceptions to the referral prohibition based specifically on various kinds of compensation arrangements, and these are reflected in § 411.357 of the August 1995 final rule. If a physician's (or family member's) arrangement with an entity falls within one of the categories covered by these exceptions, and the arrangement meets the specific criteria listed for that category, the physician is not prohibited from making referrals to the entity.

It has come to our attention that the statutory categories, because of their specificity, do not encompass some compensation arrangements even though they may be common in the provider community, are based on fair market value or are otherwise commercially reasonable, and do not reflect the volume or value of a · physician's referrals. For example, a physician can continue to make referrals to an entity under section 1877(e)(8)(B) even if the physician purchases items from the entity, provided the items are furnished at fair market value. On the other hand, the law does not exempt from the referral prohibition situations in which entities purchase items from a physician, even if the purchase price is comparably fair.

In light of the increase in recent years of integrated delivery systems, and the complex nature of financial arrangements between physicians and entities, it is our view that any compensation arrangements that are based on fair value, and that meet certain other criteria, should be excepted. Therefore, we are proposing to establish a new paragraph (l) in § 431.357 to provide an additional exception for compensation arrangements under the authority of section 1877(b)(4). This provision

allows the Secretary to establish exceptions for any other financial relationship that she determines, and specifies in regulations, does not pose a risk of program or patient abuse. To meet this requirement, we are proposing an exception for any compensation arrangement between a physician (or immediate family member), or any group of physicians (even if the group does not qualify as a group practice) and an entity, provided the arrangement meets the following criteria, which we believe by their terms will prevent program or patient abuse. The arrangement must—

• Be in writing, be signed by the parties, and cover only identifiable items or services, all of which are specified in the agreement;

• Cover all of the items and services to be provided by the physician or immediate family member to the entity or, alternatively, cross refer to any other agreements for items or services between any of these parties.

• Specify the timeframe for the arrangement, which can be for any period of time and contain a termination clause, provided the parties enter into only one arrangement covering the same items or services during the course of a year. An arrangement made for less than 1 year may be renewed any number of times if the terms of the arrangement and the compensation for the same items or services do not change;

• Specify the compensation that will be provided under the arrangement, which has been set in advance. The compensation must be consistent with fair market value and not be determined in a manner that takes into account the volume or value of any referrals (as defined in § 411.351), payments for referrals for medical services that are not covered under Medicare or Medicaid, or other business generated between the parties;

• Involve a transaction that is commercially reasonable and furthers the legitimate business purposes of the parties; and

• Meet a safe harbor under the anti-kickback statute or otherwise be in compliance with the anti-kickback provisions in section 1128B(b) of the Act.

We would advise the parties involved in a compensation arrangement to use this exception if they have any doubts about whether they meet the requirements in the other exceptions listed in § 411.357.

2. A new exception for certain forms of "de minimis" compensation

We are aware that there are a number of situations in which physicians or

their immediate family members receive compensation in the form of incidental benefits that are not part of a formal, written agreement. For example, a physician might receive free samples of certain drugs or chemicals from a laboratory, training sessions for his or her staff before entering into an agreement with a facility that furnishes a designated health service, or training sessions that are not considered part of the agreement. Also, a provider might furnish a physician with free coffee mugs or note pads. We are exercising our authority under section 1877(b)(4) to create a new exception that we believe will allow physicians or their family members to receive de minimis amounts of compensation, without a risk that the compensation will result in any Medicare program or patient abuse.

We have drafted the exception, which would appear at § 411.357(k), to apply to noncash items or services. Items cannot include cash equivalents, such as gift certificates, stocks or bonds, or airline frequent flier miles. We propose to limit the exception to a value of $50 per gift, with a $300 per year aggregate. This exception would apply only in situations in which the entity providing the compensation makes it available to all similarly situated individuals, regardless of whether these individuals refer patients to the entity for services. In addition, any compensation a physician or family member receives from an entity cannot be based in any way on the volume or value of the physician's referrals. We believe the criteria for this exception, by their terms, will prevent patient or program abuse.

3. The "volume or value of referrals" standard

Most of the exceptions in the law covering specific kinds of compensation arrangements state that the compensation involved cannot reflect the volume or value of any referrals. (We have included a similar standard in the two new compensation exceptions described above.) We are applying our interpretation of that standard as it appears in section III.A.6 under our discussion of the criteria a group of physicians must meet to qualify as a "group practice." In that section, we describe what constitutes a "referral" for purposes of the "volume or value" standard.

The volume or value of referrals standard appears in the exceptions for the rental of space or equipment, bona fide employment relationships, personal services arrangements, physician recruitment, isolated transactions, and group practice arrangements with a hospital. It also appears in the definition of "remuneration," which excepts certain payments made by an insurer or self-insured plan to a physician to satisfy a claim, and in the definition of a group practice. The exceptions for the rental of office space, rental of equipment, personal service arrangements, and group practice arrangements with a hospital also state that the compensation cannot reflect, directly or indirectly, the volume or value of referrals *or any other business generated between the parties.*

It is our view that Congress intended to except arrangements in which a physician or family member receives fair market compensation for providing a particular item or service. We believe Congress may not have wished to except arrangements that include additional compensation for other business dealings. We also believe that it would be administratively difficult for us to sort out, from a particular business arrangement, different strands of payment that are meant to compensate an individual for things other than the items or services that qualify for the exception. In sum, we believe that the "or other business generated between the parties" merely clarifies this concept.

As a result of this analysis, we are proposing to interpret the "volume or value" standard that appears in the compensation exceptions and elsewhere as a standard that uniformly is meant to cover (and thus exclude from an exception) other business generated between the parties. We are doing so under our authority, in each of the compensation exceptions and under the definitions, to add other requirements that we may impose by regulation as needed to protect against patient and program abuse. If a party's compensation contains payment for other business generated between the parties, we would expect the parties to separately determine if this extra payment falls within one of the exceptions.

The volume or value standard also varies from exception to exception in terms of simply precluding compensation that takes into account the volume or value of referrals, as opposed to not taking into account, *directly or indirectly,* the volume or value of referrals. We regard these provisions as essentially equivalent, since we believe not accounting for referrals can be interpreted as not accounting for them in any way.

We have been asked whether an arrangement fails to meet the "volume or value" of referrals standard only in situations in which a physician's

payments from an entity fluctuate in a manner that reflects referrals. It is our view that an arrangement can also fail to meet this standard in some cases when a physician's payments from an entity are stable, but predicated, either expressly or otherwise, on the physician making referrals to a particular provider. For example, a hospital might include as a condition of a physician's employment the requirement that the physician refer only within the hospital's own network of ancillary service providers, such as to the hospital's own home health agency. We believe that in these situations, a physician's compensation reflects the volume or value of his or her referrals in the sense that the physician will receive no future compensation if he or she fails to refer as required.

However, we do not intend to include, in this interpretation, situations in which physicians are not required to refer within the entity's network, but choose to on their own. Nor do we believe the volume or value standard is violated in those situations in which physicians refer patients within a network at the patients' own request, rather than under an entity's mandate, even if the entity has encouraged patients to remain within the network through various incentives.

In addition, we do not believe that an arrangement affects the volume or value standard for any designated health services a physician is required to refer within a network, provided the entity itself is, through a risk sharing arrangement, at substantial financial risk for the cost or utilization of items or services that the entity is obligated to provide. In these situations, we believe the requirement that a physician refer within the network addresses the issue of where a physician must refer, rather than whether the physician is encouraged or discouraged from making a referral (resulting in under or overutilization).

4. The commercial reasonableness standard

A number of the compensation-related exceptions in section 1877(e) include the requirement that remuneration provided under an agreement "would be commercially reasonable" even if no referrals were made between the parties. We are interpreting "commercially reasonable" to mean that an arrangement appears to be a sensible, prudent business agreement, from the perspective of the particular parties involved, even in the absence of any potential referrals.

5. The Secretary's authority to create additional requirements

Several of the statutory exceptions (particularly the compensation-related exceptions) permit the Secretary to impose additional conditions if the conditions are needed to protect against program or patient abuse. In promulgating these regulations, the Secretary has taken into account the fact that many of the excepted arrangements are also subject to the Medicare and Medicaid anti-kickback statute. The Secretary believes that the proposed regulatory exceptions, in conjunction with the independent requirements of the anti-kickback statute, are such that in most cases no additional conditions are necessary at this time to protect against program or patient abuse (we have included in this proposed regulation several specific new requirements that we believe are necessary). However, with respect to those exceptions for which the Secretary has authority to impose additional requirements, the Secretary invites comments from interested parties on whether additional conditions are necessary and if so, what conditions would be appropriate.

6. Exception for bona fide employment relationships

Section 1877(e)(2) excepts from a "compensation arrangement" any amount paid by an employer to a physician (or immediate family member) who has a bona fide employment relationship for the provision of services if the employment arrangement meets certain standards (these appear in § 411.357(c)). One standard specifies that remuneration under the employment cannot be determined in a manner that takes into account (directly or indirectly) the volume or value of referrals by the referring physician. Nonetheless, this exception specifically allows remuneration in the form of a productivity bonus based on services performed personally by the physician or an immediate family member. Thus, under the terms of the statute, physician or family member employees can receive payments based on any work they actually personally perform, including designated health services that a physician refers to him or herself. Under such a scheme, the more a physician self-refers, the more profit he or she will make.

Because we regard this provision as an open-ended invitation for physicians to generate self-referrals for designated health services, we are proposing to equalize this provision with the one allowing productivity bonuses under the definition of a group practice in section 1877(h)(4)(B)(i). This provision allows group practices to pay members a productivity bonus only if the bonus is not directly related to the volume or value of a physician's own referrals. We are equalizing the provisions in this regard under the authority in section 1877(e)(2)(D), which allows the Secretary to impose by regulation other requirements as are needed to protect against patient or program abuse. Without this change, we believe that physicians have an incentive to overutilize designated health services, since they can be compensated directly for every self referral they make.

We would like to point out that because we have interpreted the concept of a "referral" to involve only a physician's requests for designated health services covered under Medicare or Medicaid, the new requirement will in no way affect a physician's ability to receive a productivity bonus for any nondesignated health services or noncovered services he or she refers or performs, or designated health services referred by another physician.

The bona fide employment exception does not, by its terms, allow for indirect compensation based on profit sharing and productivity bonuses for a physician's "incident to" services. The group practice definition does allow for such compensation. We do not believe that we can equalize the provisions in this regard, since it is our view that there are situations in which compensating a physician even indirectly for his or her self referrals could encourage overutilization and abuse.

7. Exception for personal services arrangements

Section 1877(e)(3) excepts from the referral prohibition situations involving remuneration from an entity under a personal services arrangement if certain criteria are met. The statute does not specify to whom the remuneration must be paid or for what kinds of services, although we believe the services must be "personal services."

One of the criteria for this exception requires that the arrangement cover all of the services to be furnished to the entity by the referring physician or an immediate family member of the physician. Therefore, we are interpreting this exception as covering services furnished by these individuals. We believe there is nothing in the statute to preclude a physician or family member from having personal services arrangements with several entities. (For example, a physician might have a

contract to serve as a hospital's medical director and another contract with an unrelated group practice to perform surgery.) However, the statute does appear to require, in section 1877(e)(3)(A)(ii), that an excepted arrangement with one entity cover all of the services to be provided by the physician (or family member) to that entity.

We are aware that at times it will not be logical for all of a physician's or family member's contracts for personal services to be in one agreement. However, we are also aware that entities have used multiple contracts, at times, in devising schemes to reward physicians for their referrals. In order to provide physicians and entities with more flexibility than the statutory requirement that all services appear in one agreement, we propose to allow multiple agreements, provided that the agreements each meet all of the requirements described in section 1877(e)(3) and all separate agreements between the entity and the physician and the entity and any family members incorporate each other by reference. We base our proposal on section 1877(b)(4), which allows the Secretary to specify, in regulations, an exception for any other financial relationship that she determines does not pose a risk of patient or program abuse. In this case, because all excepted agreements will be subject to the fair market value and other standards, and because each agreement will make us aware of all other agreements, we see no potential risk for abuse.

It is our view that "personal services" are not simply the generic Medicare services (which are defined in § 400.202 to include "items") but are services of any kind performed personally by an individual for an entity (but *not* including any items or equipment). We are using the broader, more common notion of what constitutes a "service" based on the fact that all kinds of business relationships can trigger the referral prohibition; hence, the exception should be read to apply to business-oriented services in general.

We are also interpreting the exception to mean that the physician or family member can actually perform the services, or that these individuals can enter into an agreement to provide the services through technicians or others whom they employ. A physician or family member cannot, though, include equipment or other items as part of an excepted personal services arrangement. For example, if a hospital contracts with a nephrologist to provide dialysis services to its patients, the physician could have a personal services

arrangement with the hospital even if the dialysis services are actually furnished by technicians whom the physician employs. However, if the physician also provides dialysis equipment to the hospital, this arrangement would have to separately meet the exception for the rental of equipment in section 1877(e)(1), since we do not regard items or equipment as "personal services."

The personal services exception specifies that compensation under an arrangement cannot be determined in a manner that takes into account the volume or value of any referrals or other business generated between the parties. However, this requirement is qualified to allow compensation to reflect these under certain situations in which there is a physician incentive plan between a physician and an entity. We would like to emphasize that the physician incentive plan aspect of section 1877(e)(3) applies only in the context of personal services arrangements, and not to any other compensation arrangements.

"Physician incentive plans" are defined in section 1877(e)(3)(B)(ii) as certain compensation arrangements between an entity and a physician or physician group. We have defined a physician group for purposes of the physician incentive rules more broadly than a group practice under section 1877, so that a group practice is a subset of physician groups. (A final rule with comment period governing physician incentive plans was published on March 27, 1996, at 61 FR 13430. This rule was amended on December 31, 1996, at 61 FR 69034.)

A physician incentive plan is any compensation arrangement between an entity and a physician or physician group that may directly or indirectly have the effect of reducing or limiting services provided with respect to individuals enrolled with the entity. We believe that the incentive plan qualification applies only when the entity paying the physician or physician group is the kind of entity that enrolls its patients, such as a health maintenance organization. Section 1877(b)(3), the exception for prepaid plans, does exempt from the referral prohibition almost all designated health services provided by these entities to Medicare patients who are enrollees. In addition, this regulation proposes to exempt services provided to Medicaid patients by analogous kinds of entities (see our discussion of this issue earlier in this preamble). Nonetheless, the personal services exception, with its physician incentive aspect, is still a viable exception. This exception could apply, for example, to situations in which a physician refers a fee for service patient covered under Medicare to an HMO when he or she also has a contract to provide services to the HMO's enrollees. The physician's contract with the HMO is an underlying financial relationship and, in order for the physician to refer fee-for-service patients to the HMO, the financial relationship must meet an exception. In order to qualify for the personal services exception, the physician's payments from the HMO for treating HMO enrollees cannot vary with the volume or value of his or her referrals, except under a physician incentive plan, as described in section 1877(e)(3)(B).

The personal services exception in section 1877(e)(3) as a whole is silent about to whom an entity must be paying remuneration or with whom it must have an arrangement. As a result, we are interpreting the personal services exception to apply to situations in which an entity has an arrangement with either an individual physician (or family member) or a group practice to provide personal services. For example, a hospital could use the exception if it contracts with a group practice for purposes of having group members serve as the hospital's staff.

8. Exception for remuneration unrelated to the provision of designated health services

Section 1877(e)(4) provides for an exception for remuneration that is provided by a hospital to a physician if the remuneration does not relate to the provision of designated health services. (As we have noted earlier in this preamble, this exception does not apply to remuneration from entities other than hospitals, nor does it apply to payments to a physician's family members.) We are interpreting this provision to except any remuneration that is completely unrelated to the furnishing of designated health services. By this we mean that the parties must be able to demonstrate that the remuneration does not in any direct or indirect way involve these services, and that the remuneration in no way reflects the volume or value of a physician's referrals for designated health services. If a physician is receiving payments from a hospital that appear to be inordinately high for an "unrelated" item or service and is also making referrals to the hospital for designated health services, we will presume that the overpayments relate to the designated health services because they reflect the volume or value of the physician's referrals.

On the other hand, we realize there can be situations in which a hospital's payments are completely unrelated to the provision of designated health services. For example, a teaching hospital might pay a physician rental payments for his or her house in order to use the house as a residence for a visiting faculty member. If the parties involved can demonstrate that the rental payments are based on fair market value and in no way reflect the physician owner's referrals to the hospital, we believe this exception would apply. Similarly a physician might receive compensation for teaching or for providing an entity with general utilization review or administrative services.

We do not intend to apply this exception in any situation involving remuneration that might have a nexus with the provision of, or referrals for, a designated health service. For example, if a hospital pays a physician to supply a heart valve that the physician has perfected, we believe that the exception does not apply. It is our position that the physician is receiving payment for an item that will likely be used by the hospital in furnishing inpatient hospital services, which are a designated health service. Similarly, if a hospital pays for a physician's malpractice insurance or other general costs to enable the physician to provide a designated health service, such as radiology, the payments are related to furnishing a designated health service. Nonetheless, these financial relationships could still be excepted under one of the statutory exceptions or under the new exception we would include in § 431.357(l), which covers any compensation arrangement that meets certain criteria.

9. Exception for a hospital's payments for physician recruitment

Section 1877(e)(5) includes an exception for remuneration provided by a hospital to an individual physician to induce the physician to relocate to the geographic area served by the hospital in order to be a member of the medical staff of the hospital. We believe that the terms of the statute dictate that this exception applies just to those situations in which a physician resides outside the geographic area and must actually relocate in order to join the hospital's staff.

We considered a number of ways to define the concept of a hospital's "geographic area," including mileage requirements or the likelihood that the physician would be able to bring patients along when he or she relocates. Because we believe that what constitutes a hospital's "geographic

area" may depend on a variety of circumstances, we are specifically soliciting comments on how to define this term.

If a hospital makes recruitment payments to physicians who are living in the hospital's geographic area (for example, to retain residents) or to a group practice that intends to employ the physician and contracts with the hospital, these payments might be excepted under the new compensation-related exception that we have included in § 431.357(l).

10. Exception for certain group practice arrangements with a hospital

Under section 1877(e)(7), this exception applies to only a limited number of arrangements; that is, arrangements that began before December 19, 1989, and have continued in effect without interruption since that date. We are interpreting this provision to mean that the arrangement between the hospital and the specific group practice must have been in effect within the timeframe specified in the statute. However, we realize that most agreements do not remain static over time. As a result, it is our view that this criterion may still be met, even if the agreement between the parties has changed over time so that it covers different services or so that the services are provided by different individuals within the same group practice.

We also intend in this provision to make an editorial change that we believe removes an ambiguity in the statutory language. Existing § 411.357(h)(2) states "[t]he arrangement began before December 19, 1989, and has continued in effect without interruption since then." Upon closer consideration, we believe that "since then" is ambiguous. (Does it mean since the actual date before December 19, 1989 on which the arrangement began, or does it mean since December 19, 1989?) We believe that by revising this provision to read "[t]he arrangement began before, and has continued in effect without interruption since, December 19, 1989," we have provided a reasonable interpretation that removes this ambiguity.

Section 1877(e)(7)(A)(ii) requires that, with respect to the designated health services covered under the arrangement, substantially all of the services furnished to patients of the hospital are furnished by the group under the arrangement. We believe this standard means that whatever portion of a particular designated health service the agreement covers, the group must actually provide "substantially all" of that portion. For example, if the group has agreed to provide 35 percent of a hospital's laboratory services, the group must actually provide a substantial part of this percentage.

In keeping with our interpretation of the term "substantially all" in other parts of section 1877, we are interpreting that term here as being 75 percent of all the services at issue.

11. Exception for payments by a physician for items and services

Section 1877(e)(8) excepts payments that a physician makes to a laboratory in exchange for clinical laboratory services (we have discussed this provision in some detail in section III.A.8 of this preamble). In addition, the statute excepts payments that a physician makes to any entity for other items or services if these are furnished at fair market value. We are proposing to interpret "other items or services" to mean any kinds of items or services that a physician might purchase, but not including clinical laboratory services or those specifically listed under the other compensation exceptions. For example, we do not believe that Congress meant for the "items or services" exception to cover a rental agreement as a service that a physician might purchase, when it has already included in the statute a specific rental exception, with specific standards, in section 1877(e)(1).

F. The Reporting Requirements

1. Which financial relationships must be reported

Under section 1877(f), each entity providing Medicare-covered services must provide the Secretary with information concerning the entity's ownership, investment, and compensation arrangements, including the names and UPINs (unique physician identification numbers) of all physicians with an ownership or investment interest (as described in section 1877(a)(2)(A)) in the entity or with a compensation arrangement (as described in section 1877(a)(2)(B)) with the entity, or whose immediate relatives have such a relationship. The information must be provided in such form, manner, and at such times as the Secretary specifies.

Section 411.361 currently states that entities must submit the required information on a HCFA-prescribed form within the time period specified by the servicing carrier or intermediary. Entities are given at least 30 days from the date of the request to provide the information. Thereafter, entities must provide updated information within 60 days from the date of any change in the submitted information.

At this time, we are still developing a procedure for implementing the reporting requirements and plan to notify affected parties about the procedure at a later date. Until that time, physicians and entities are not required to report to us. In addition, we are aware that the 60 day timeframe for updated information could be onerous, especially for large entities that must collect information about their employees, owners, and contractors and who would then have to update that information approximately every two months. As a result, we are proposing to modify § 411.361 to require that entities report to us once a year on all of the changes that have occurred in the previous 12 months.

Under the reporting regulation in § 411.361(d), a "reportable financial relationship" is any ownership or investment interest or any compensation arrangement, as described in section 1877 of the Act. Under section 1877(a)(2), a financial relationship of a physician (or family member) with an entity is defined as an ownership or investment interest in the entity, except as provided in subsections (c) and (d), or a compensation arrangement between the physician (or family member) and the entity, except as provided in subsection (e). Subsections (c) and (d) contain lists of ownership interests that "shall not be considered to be an ownership or investment interest described in subsection (a)(2)(A)." Subsection (e) contains a list of arrangements that are not to be considered as "compensation arrangements described in (a)(2)(B)." Thus, entities must only report their ownership or investment interests, or compensation arrangements, if these relationships do not meet the exceptions in subsections (c), (d), or (e) of section 1877. However, if an entity's financial relationship is excepted under subsection (b) of section 1877 (which contains exceptions for physician services, in-office ancillary services, services furnished under certain prepaid plans, or other new exceptions included by the Secretary) the entity must still report.

As the rule reads now, an entity can decide that it is excepted under (c), (d), or (e) and not report any data. As a result, we will have no opportunity to scrutinize the entity's arrangements to see if its assessment is correct. We believe that the statute allows us to gather a broader scope of data. We base this interpretation on the opening paragraph in section 1877(f), which states that each entity providing any covered items or services for which payment may be made under Medicare

shall provide the Secretary "with the information" concerning the entity's ownership, investment, and compensation arrangements, *including* the names and UPINs of all physicians with an ownership interest (as described in (a)(2)(A)), or with a compensation arrangement (as described in (a)(2)(B)). Thus, we believe the statute allows us to gather any data on financial relationships, *including*, but not necessarily limited to, relationships for which there are no exceptions under (a)(2)(A) or (B). Therefore, we are proposing to amend the rule, at § 411.361(d), to reflect our authority to ask for a broader scope of information than the regulation currently allows.

A number of entities have pointed out to us that the amounts of data they are required to report under the statute will, in some circumstances, be overwhelming and perhaps almost impossible to acquire. In addition, if we require every entity that is subject to the referral rules to report on every financial relationship, excepted or not, the administrative burden could be enormous. For example, a large publicly-held enterprise would be required to report (and hence retain records documenting) all of its owners who are physicians, all owners who are relatives of physicians, all physicians with whom it has compensation arrangements of any kind, and all relatives of physicians with whom it has compensation arrangements.

A publicly traded corporation with thousands of stockholders may find it extremely difficult to identify all of its owners and their relatives, and to identify which of these owners and relatives are physicians. In addition, such a corporation could be owned by mutual funds which in turn have hundreds of thousands of additional owners, some of whom may be physicians or have relatives who are physicians. In order to make the reporting requirements more manageable, we intend to develop a streamlined "reporting" system that does not require entities to retain and submit large quantities of data. However, we believe that entities should retain enough records to demonstrate, in the event of an audit, that they have correctly determined that particular relationships are excepted under the law.

We are proposing to limit the information that an entity must acquire, retain and, at some later point, possibly submit to us. We would include only those records covering information that the entity knows or should know about, in the course of prudently conducting business, including records that the entity is already required to retain to meet Internal Revenue Service and Securities and Exchange Commission rules, and other rules under the Medicare or Medicaid programs. We are circumscribing these records under the Secretary's discretion in section 1877(f) to ask entities to provide information in such form, manner, and at such times as the Secretary specifies. When we develop a form for reporting information to us, we plan to first publish it as a proposed notice in order to receive public comment. If we later find that this plan is inadequate and elect to change the scope of the requirement, we will provide entities with adequate notice to comply. We specifically solicit comments on this proposal.

2. What entities outside the United States must report

Section 1877(f) states that the reporting requirements do not apply to designated health services furnished outside the United States. The reporting requirements in general apply to each entity furnishing services covered under Medicare, and not just to those furnishing designated health services. Arguably, then, the statute relieves an entity from the reporting requirements involved when it furnishes designated health services, but not when it furnishes other covered services. Because we believe that referrals for designated health services are the focus of section 1877, and because Medicare covers only a limited number of services when they are furnished outside of the United States, we are interpreting section 1877(f) to relieve an entity from reporting any Medicare services it has furnished outside of the United States.

G. How the Referral Prohibition Applies to the Medicaid Program

1. Who qualifies as a "physician" for purposes of section 1903(s)

Under the Medicare definition of "physician" in section 1861(r), paragraphs (r)(1) through (r)(5) cover a doctor of medicine or osteopathy, a doctor of dental surgery or of dental medicine, a doctor of podiatric medicine, a doctor of optometry, and a chiropractor. Under the Medicaid statute in section 1905(a)(5)(A), physician services are those furnished by a physician as defined in section 1861(r)(1), which covers only a doctor of medicine or osteopathy.

In determining whether an individual is a "physician" for purposes of section 1903(s), we believe that it is the Medicare definition that would apply. That is because this provision prohibits the Secretary from paying FFP to a State

for services that result from a referral for a designated health service that would be prohibited under Medicare if Medicare covered the service in the same way (to the same extent and under the same terms and conditions) as under the State plan. A referral by any of the "physicians" listed in section 1861(r) could result in a prohibited referral under Medicare.

We believe that a physician is still a physician for purposes of section 1903(s), even if he or she does not participate in the Medicaid program. For example, a provider of designated health services may participate in and bill Medicaid when the referring physician, who has an interest in the entity, does not participate. The rules in section 1877 apply to services furnished under Medicaid in the same manner as they would apply if furnished under Medicare. As a general rule under section 1877(a)(1), if a physician (or immediate family member) has a financial relationship with an entity, then the physician may not make a referral to the entity to furnish designated health services for which payment may otherwise be made under Medicare. This provision appears to apply to all physicians, regardless of whether they participate in either the Medicare or Medicaid programs, as long as the services involved are covered services under Medicare or Medicaid.

2. How the referral prohibition and sanctions affect Medicaid providers

Absent an exception, section 1877(a)(1) in general prohibits a physician from making a referral to an entity with which he or she has a financial relationship for the furnishing of a designated health service covered under Medicare. The entity, in turn, may not present a claim to Medicare or bill any other individual or entity for the service furnished as the result of a prohibited referral. If physicians or entities violate these rules, they are subject to certain sanctions under section 1877(g). However, we do not believe these rules and sanctions apply to physicians and providers when the referral involves Medicaid services. The first part of section 1903(s) prohibits the Secretary from paying FFP to a State for designated health services furnished on the basis of a referral *that would result* in a denial of payment under Medicare *if* Medicare covered the services in the same way as the State plan. This part of the provision is strictly an FFP provision. It imposes a requirement on the Secretary to review a Medicaid claim, *as if* it were under Medicare, and deny FFP *if* a referral would result in the denial of payment under Medicare.

Section 1903(s) does not, for the most part, make the provisions in section 1877 that govern the actions of Medicare physicians and providers of designated health services apply directly to Medicaid physicians and providers. As such, these individuals and entities are not precluded from referring Medicaid patients or from billing for designated health services. A State may pay for these services, but cannot receive FFP for them. However, States are free to establish their own sanctions for situations in which physicians refer to related entities.

3. How the referral rules apply when Medicaid-covered designated health services differ from the services covered under Medicare

The statute specifically provides that a State cannot receive FFP for a designated health service if it is furnished to an individual on the basis of a referral that would result in a denial of payment for the service under Medicare *if Medicare* covered the services to the same extent and under the same terms and conditions as under the State plan. We believe this means that Congress was aware of differences in the two programs and specifically intended to cover under section 1877 designated health services as they are covered under a State's Medicaid plan whenever this coverage differs from coverage under Medicare.

4. How the reporting requirements apply under the Medicaid program

Section 1903(s) states that subsections (f) and (g)(5) of section 1877 shall apply to a provider of Medicaid-covered designated health services in the same manner as these subsections apply to a provider of Medicare-covered designated health services. Section 1877(f) requires that each entity providing Medicare-covered items or services must provide the Secretary with certain information about the entity's ownership, investment, and compensation arrangements. The information must include the covered items and services the entity provides, and the names and UPINs of all physicians who have (or whose immediate relatives have) an ownership or investment interest in or compensation arrangement with the entity. These requirements do not apply to designated health services furnished outside of the United States, or to entities the Secretary determines furnish Medicare-covered services infrequently.

Section 1903(s) could be read to mean that section 1877(f) must apply identically to Medicare and Medicaid providers, so that Medicaid entities must furnish information to the Secretary (that is, to HCFA). However, we are taking the position that the provision allows us to require that entities report directly to the States. Section 1903(s) provides that section 1877(f) applies "in the same manner" in the Medicaid program as it does in Medicare. In Medicare, the reports are made to the Secretary, the official who is responsible for making payment under Medicare. "In the same manner," in the context of the Medicaid program, would mean that the reports would be made to the entity that makes payment; that is, the State, thus maintaining a symmetry between reporting in the two programs.

We have taken this position because, under section 1903(s), it is the States that are at risk of losing FFP for paying improper claims for designated health services submitted by entities that have financial relationships with physicians. Therefore, in order to ensure that FFP will be available, States must determine whether a physician has a financial relationship with an entity that would prohibit referrals under Medicare. Our interpretation will allow States to protect themselves and to avoid any duplication of effort with HCFA.

We are amending the regulations to create a new Subpart C, "Disclosure of Information by Providers for Purposes of the Prohibition on Certain Physician Referrals." In § 455.108, "Basis," we state that, based on section 1903(s), we are applying the reporting requirements of section 1877(f) and (g) to Medicaid providers of designated health services. Section 455.109(a) would state that the Medicaid agency must require that each entity that furnishes designated health services submit information to the Medicaid agency concerning its financial relationships, in such form, manner, and at such times as the agency specifies. Although the statute requires that entities submit information to the Secretary, we believe that the State should receive this information in the Medicaid context, in order to help States ensure that they will receive FFP.

Section 455.109(b) would specify that the requirements of § 455.109(a) do not apply to entities that provide 20 or fewer designated health services under the State plan during a calendar year, or to any entity for items or services provided outside the United States. We have derived the limit of 20 or fewer designated health services from the Medicare regulation interpreting section 1877(f) (§ 411.361).

Section 455.109(c) would specify that the information submitted to the Medicaid agency under § 455.109(a) must include at least the following:

• The name and Medicaid State Specific Identifier (MSSI) of each physician who has a financial relationship with the entity that provides services.

• The name and MSSI of each physician who has an immediate relative (as defined in § 411.351) who has a financial relationship with the entity.

• The covered items and services furnished by the entity.

• With respect to each physician identified above, the nature of the financial relationship (including the extent and/or value of the ownership or investment interest or the compensation arrangement), if requested by the Medicaid agency.

Section 455.109(d) would define a reportable financial relationship as an ownership or investment interest or any compensation arrangement, as defined in § 411.351, including relationships that qualify for an exception described in §§ 411.355 through 411.357.

Section 455.109(e) would specify that—

• Entities that are subject to the reporting requirements must submit the required information on a prescribed form within the time period specified by the Medicaid agency. Similarly, entities must report to the Medicaid agency all changes in the submitted information within a timeframe specified by the State. We believe that States have the discretion to determine these deadlines in line with § 455.109(a), which requires that the Medicaid agency gather information on financial relationships in such form, manner, and at such times as the agency specifies.

• Entities must retain documentation sufficient to verify the information provided on the forms and, upon request, must make that documentation available to the Medicaid State agency, HCFA, or the OIG.

Section 455.109(f) would reflect section 1877(g)(5), specifying that any entity that is required, but has failed, to meet the reporting requirements of § 455.109(a), is subject to a civil money penalty of not more than $10,000 for each day of the period beginning on the day following the applicable deadline until the information is submitted. It would further specify that assessment of the penalty will comply with the applicable provisions of 42 CFR part 1003.

IV. Our Responses to Questions About the Law

In this section of the preamble, we have included some of the most common questions concerning physician referrals that we have received from physicians, providers, and others in the health care community. (Note that, in this section, we are using the term "provider" in the generic sense to include all providers of health care services. That is, we are not using the term with the special meaning given in our regulations at § 400.202.) We summarize these questions below and present our interpretation of how we believe the law applies in the situations that have been described to us. We have organized this section so that the issues raised by the questions appear in the order in which they appear in the regulation.

A. Definitions

1. Compensation Arrangement

What is an "indirect" compensation arrangement? We defined a "compensation arrangement" in the August 1995 final rule, in line with the statute, as any arrangement involving any remuneration, *direct or indirect,* between a physician (or family member) and an entity. This means that a compensation arrangement can result when remuneration flows from an entity to a physician or family member, or from a physician or family member to an entity. We have received a number of inquiries on what constitutes an "indirect" compensation arrangement. We believe that a physician or family member can receive compensation from an entity, even if the payment is "funneled through" a business or other entity or association and even if the payment changes form before the physician actually receives it.

For example, suppose that a hospital has contracted with a group practice for the group to furnish physician services and to otherwise staff the hospital. The hospital pays the group practice, which might be a professional corporation or a similar association or entity, for the physician services under a personal services arrangement, rather than directly compensating the individual physicians. The group practice, in turn, pays the individual physicians a salary that in some way reflects the hospital's payments.

It is our position that, in such a scenario, each physician has been indirectly compensated by the hospital for his or her own services. As a result, the physicians have a compensation arrangement with the hospital. In the absence of an exception, the physicians would be prohibited from referring to the hospital for the furnishing of designated health services.

We believe that a physician has received indirect compensation whether the "intervening" professional association, corporation, or other entity directly receiving payment is a group practice or any other type of physician or nonphysician owned entity. We also believe a physician can receive indirect compensation through a nonprofit enterprise if that enterprise is controlled by an individual who is in a position to influence the physician's referrals. For example, the owner of a clinical laboratory who also serves as the director of a nonprofit research facility could provide a physician with research grants in exchange for referrals to the laboratory. We are considering regarding as indirect compensation any payment to a physician that passes from an entity that provides for the furnishing of designated health services, no matter how many intervening "levels" the payment passes through or how often it changes form. We directly solicit comments on this approach.

We would also like to reiterate a point that we made in the preamble to the August 1995 final rule. Just because a hospital or similar entity is affiliated with a physician or group of physicians does not automatically mean that the hospital or similar entity is compensating the physicians. Physicians and entities can have joint ventures and similar relationships in which the hospital or similar entity and the physicians share profits, but do not compensate each other.

Which exceptions apply in indirect situations? We have also received questions about which exception applies when an indirect payment changes form. For example, in the situation described above, a hospital makes payments to a group practice under a personal services arrangement. The group practice, in turn, passes the payments on in the form of salary payments to its physician employees. We believe that the compensation at issue involves a personal services arrangement between the hospital and the group practice (see the discussion in III.E.6 of this preamble about personal services arrangements between entities and group practices, rather than between entities and individual physicians).

We are interpreting the statute to focus on the payment the entity furnishing designated health services initially makes to determine the appropriate exception. In this case, the hospital is making a payment under a personal services arrangement, and is not in any way making a salary payment to its own employees. Thus, we believe the physicians could make referrals to the hospital if the group practice's personal services arrangement with the

hospital meets the criteria under the personal services exception.

It is our view that the salary payment from the group practice to its physician employees is a payment separate from the remuneration flowing indirectly from the hospital to the physicians. As a result, this payment, as a payment from the group practice, should itself have no additional effect on a physician's ability to refer to the hospital. (The nature of the payment might, however, affect whether the physicians qualify as a group practice. See the discussion in section III.A.6 of this preamble covering the characteristics of a group practice.)

2. Entity

What are the characteristics of an "entity" that provides for the furnishing of designated health services? We have received a number of questions about what constitutes an "entity" involved in the furnishing of designated health services and who owns that entity. For example, a group of individuals asked us whether they own a hospital based solely on the fact that they own the building that houses the hospital. We believe that an "entity" for purposes of section 1877 is the business, organization, or other association that actually furnishes, or provides for the furnishing of, a service to a Medicare or Medicaid patient and bills for that service (or receives payment for the service from the billing entity as part of an "under arrangements" or similar agreement).

An "entity," therefore, does not include any person, business, or other organization or association that owns the components of the operation—such as owning the building that houses the entity or the equipment the entity uses—without owning the operation itself. For example, a physician might own and operate an MRI machine in his or her office. If this physician enters into a lease arrangement for the use of the MRI machine every Tuesday by the physician down the hall, who bills for the services, we believe that the physician down the hall is the entity providing MRI services to his or her patients on Tuesday. This physician could refer patients for MRI services if he or she qualifies for an exception, such as the in-office ancillary services exception.

When is an entity furnishing, or providing for the furnishing of, designated health services? Section 1877(a)(1)(A) prohibits a physician from making a referral to an entity "for the furnishing of designated health services" if the physician or a family member has a financial relationship

with that entity. The health care community has expressed some confusion about when an entity is one involved in the "furnishing of" designated health services.

We have, for example, received questions about which entities are the relevant ones when some entities only bill for services, while others actually directly "furnish" the services. For example in an "under arrangements" situation, a hospital, rural primary care hospital, skilled nursing facility (SNF), home health agency, or hospice program contracts with a separate provider to furnish services to the hospital's, SNF's, or other contracting entity's patients, for which the hospital, SNF or other contracting entity ultimately bills.

The statutory provisions that mention "under arrangements" draw a distinction between services that are actually furnished by the hospital or SNF and those that are actually furnished by the separate, outside entity. (Under section 1861(w)(1), HCFA's payment to the hospital, SNF, or other contracting entity discharges the beneficiary's liability. "Under arrangements" situations are further referenced in sections 1861(b)(3) and 1862(a)(14).) We are aware that there are comparable agreements in the community between entities other than hospitals, SNFs, and the other contracting entities listed above, such as agreements between group practices that furnish services to HMO patients, with the HMO billing for the services.

We believe that, absent an exception, the referral prohibition applies to a physician's referrals to any entity that directly furnishes designated health services to Medicare or Medicaid patients. We believe the prohibition also applies to referrals to any entities that arrange "for the furnishing of" these services to Medicare or Medicaid patients by contracting with other providers, whenever it is the arranging entity that bills for the services.

This interpretation is consistent with the intent of the statute. Congress intended, in enacting section 1877, to prohibit referrals in situations in which a physician has a financial incentive to overutilize the various designated health services and to steer patients toward certain providers of these services. For example, a physician might routinely refer patients to a SNF in which he has a financial interest and prescribe occupational therapy (OT) services. The SNF, in turn, might contract with a separate, unrelated entity to furnish SNF patients with the OT, for which the SNF bills. Even if the physician has no relationship with the separate OT provider, he does have a financial relationship with the SNF that is providing for "the furnishing of" OT to referred patients. As a result, the physician can potentially profit from each referral he or she makes for OT, even if the SNF must first purchase those services from an outside source before passing on the cost to its patients.

If, however, the unrelated OT entity itself bills for the services under Part B, so that the SNF only helps to make these services available to its patients, our conclusion would be different. In this situation, we do not believe that the physician has a financial incentive to overutilize OT services. As a result, we would not regard the SNF as an entity involved in "the furnishing of" a designated health service.

We also believe that a physician can have an incentive to overutilize services if he or she has a financial relationship with the entity that directly furnishes designated health services, even if this is not the entity ultimately billing for the services. In these situations, the physician can potentially recognize a profit from each referral based on the fact that the designated health services will, in essence, be sold to the entity that bills.

For example, a physician who is a member of a group practice might work in a hospital as a staff physician and refer patients to the group's own outside laboratory in which the physician has an ownership interest. The laboratory, in turn, furnishes services to hospital patients under arrangements. The hospital will therefore be billing Medicare for laboratory services furnished by the physician's own laboratory. In this case, the physician is in a position to influence how many services the laboratory will be able to "sell" to the hospital. Thus, the physician should be prohibited from making these referrals, unless one of the exceptions applies.

We believe our policy of including entities that contract for services as those that provide for "the furnishing of" designated health services is consistent with the structure of section 1877 and the way the exceptions are drafted. For example, under section 1877(b)(3), services are excepted if furnished by an organization that functions under a prepaid plan, such as an HMO. It is our understanding that such services are very often made available in a manner that is comparable to "under arrangements" situations; that is, the prepaid organization contracts with a broad range of independent suppliers and providers to furnish services to its enrollees. This exception makes no distinction between services that are furnished directly by the HMO

and those that are furnished under contract by outside providers: all such services appear to be considered as furnished by the HMO, and would be excepted.

Similarly, section 1877(d)(3) excepts certain "designated health services provided by a hospital," but makes no distinctions between services the hospital itself furnishes and those furnished by the hospital under arrangements.

3. Financial Relationship

How do equity and debt qualify as ownership? The statute states that an ownership interest can be through equity or debt. We have received a number of inquiries about what this provision means and what kinds of debt situations constitute a form of ownership. We believe that "ownership through equity" refers to a direct ownership interest that does not involve debt; for example, one in which the physician or family member has actually purchased assets of a business entity with cash or other property. This interest could be in the form of stock in a publicly-held entity or an investment (such as a capital contribution) in a partnership.

We believe that a physician or family member holds an ownership interest in an entity "through debt" anytime the physician or family member has lent money or given other valuable consideration to the entity and the debt is secured (in whole or in part) by the entity or by the entity's assets or property. For example, the physician could hold such an interest by providing the entity with a note, a mortgage or by purchasing bonds. This interpretation is consistent with the definition of an ownership or control interest in section 1124(a)(3) of the Act, which governs which suppliers and providers must disclose these interests to us for purposes other than the referral prohibition. Section 1124(a)(3)(A)(ii) defines a person with an ownership or control interest as a person who is the owner of a whole or part interest in any mortgage, deed of trust, note, or other obligation secured (in whole or in part) by the entity or any of the entity's property or assets, if the interest is worth a certain amount.

We also believe that ownership through debt can exist in any other debtor-creditor relationships that have some indicia of ownership. For example, such indicia could include the creditor's participation in revenue or profits, subordinated payment terms, low or no interest terms, or ownership of convertible debentures (bonds that a physician or family member can convert

into the common stock of the issuer or an affiliate until the convertible feature expires).

However, if a physician or family member has made an unsecured or nonconvertible loan to an entity, or a loan with no other indicia of ownership, we do not believe the loan is an ownership interest. The loan would likely qualify as a compensation arrangement, to which an exception might apply.

We do not believe that a physician or family member has "ownership through debt" when either of them has received a loan *from* an entity. In ordinary business transactions, when a debtor receives a loan, this transaction in no way establishes for the debtor an ownership interest in the creditor. We also assume that in providing the loan, the creditor entity has provided remuneration to the physician or family member, resulting in a compensation arrangement. This kind of compensation arrangement could meet one of the exceptions to the prohibition. For example, the loan might be one form of payment an entity makes to a physician to recruit the physician or as part of the physician's employment contract. The loan would be an excepted arrangement if it met the fair market value and other standards in these exceptions.

Is membership in a nonprofit corporation an ownership or investment interest? We have received a number of inquiries concerning whether membership in a nonprofit corporation constitutes an ownership or investment interest in that corporation. (We are assuming that a "member" is someone who establishes, sponsors, directs, or controls a nonprofit corporation.) Most nonprofit health care corporations that are exempt from Federal income taxation are exempt under section 501(c)(3) or (4) of the Internal Revenue Code. These provisions state that the net earnings of such a corporation cannot inure to the benefit of any private shareholder or individual. Therefore, while members of such a nonprofit corporation may exercise control over the activities of the corporation, they do not have the pecuniary incentive that for-profit investors have to enhance their investment interests. As such, we do not regard being a member of these kinds of nonprofit corporations as an ownership or investment interest analogous to being a shareholder in a for-profit corporation. However, any remuneration that the physician or family member receives from the corporation, such as a salary, would be compensation and must meet an exception.

Do stock options and nonvested interests constitute ownership? We have been asked whether a physician or family member has an ownership interest in an entity if he or she receives an option to purchase the stock of the entity or an affiliate, such as when an employee has a stock option that constitutes part of his or her pay. We have also received questions about retirement funds or similar options that do not vest until a future date. For example, a physician might hold an option to purchase stock at a particular price, but not be able to exercise that option until he or she retires. Similarly, a physician might be entitled to certain retirement funds only after he or she has retired after having worked a specified number of years.

The statute defines an ownership interest in section 1877(a)(2) as an interest held through equity, debt, or other means. It is our view that options and nonvested interests are inchoate or partial ownership interests that qualify as "ownership" for purposes of this law. We base our interpretation on the fact that a physician has a tremendous incentive to refer to an entity in which he or she is invested, whether the interest is a present or future one. For example, if a physician has an option to buy stock at a certain price in a clinical laboratory, the physician will have an interest in generating business for the entity in order to enhance the value of that stock.

4. Group practice

What is the "full range of services" test? One of the criteria in the statutory definition of a group practice is that each member must furnish substantially the full range of services that the physician routinely furnishes, including medical care, consultation, diagnosis, and treatment through the joint use of shared office space, facilities, equipment, and personnel. We have been asked about the meaning and purpose of this provision, and how it will affect a physician's normal practice patterns. only token tasks, for the group. It is our view that this standard should not alter a physician's ordinary schedule or practice habits. For example, one physician described himself as having two specialty areas, which resulted in his providing dermatology services to one group one day a week, and another kind of service to another group on a different day. We believe that different kinds of services such as these on different days can reflect a physician's normal "routine of services." That is, a physician can furnish one type of service that is that physician's "full range of services" on a

particular day, as long as the physician is legitimately practicing medicine for the group practice on that day.

5. Immediate family member or member of a physician's immediate family

How does the prohibition affect a physician's referrals to immediate family members? The referral prohibition in section 1877(a) states that if a physician, or immediate family member, has a financial relationship with an entity, the physician cannot refer a Medicare patient to that entity for the furnishing of designated health services, unless an exception applies. In § 411.351 of the August 1995 final rule, we listed the individuals who qualify as a physician's "immediate" family members. These individuals include, among others, spouses and children of a referring physician.

We have received a number of inquiries from physicians about whether the statute precludes a physician from referring patients to a family member to receive designated health services, if the referring physician has no financial relationship with the entity furnishing the services. We believe the answer to this question depends upon the nature of the family member's financial relationship with the furnishing entity.

If a family member has a compensation arrangement with the entity furnishing the designated health services, the physician cannot refer to the entity, unless the arrangement meets one of the exceptions under the statute. For example, a physician might wish to refer a patient to her husband for occupational therapy services. The husband furnishes OT services as an employee of an occupational therapy facility. The husband, who is an immediate family member of the referring physician, has a compensation arrangement with an entity that furnishes a designated health service (the OT facility pays him a salary). However, the referral would be acceptable if the arrangement meets the requirements in section 1877(e)(2), which excepts bona fide employment relationships between employers and physicians or immediate family members if the relationship meets fair market value and other standards.

The situation is similar if a physician refers a patient to an immediate family member who has an ownership or investment interest in the facility that furnishes the designated health services. For example, the physician may wish to refer a patient to his wife, who is a solo practicing physician who herself furnishes OT. If the wife owns the practice, she would have a financial relationship with the entity that

furnishes the designated health services. The husband's referral would not be prohibited if the wife's relationship qualifies for one of the exceptions under the statute. For example, the wife's practice might qualify as a rural entity, the ownership of which is excepted under section 1877(d)(2) of the Act. However, if an exception does not apply, the referring physician would be precluded from referring to his spouse.

Physicians have also asked us whether the in-office ancillary services exception in section 1877(b)(2) applies to those situations in which a physician refers a patient to an immediate family member who furnishes designated health services outside of the referring physician's practice. The ancillary services exception applies when a physician refers a patient for a service that the referring physician either will personally perform or directly supervise, or that will be personally performed or directly supervised by another member of the referring physician's group practice. As a result, referring physicians can refer patients to and among themselves, within their own practices, if they meet the section 1877(b)(2) requirements. However, the exception does not apply when physicians refer to their spouses or to other close relatives who furnish services outside of the practice.

In creating the in-office ancillary services exception, we believe that Congress made a policy decision not to restrict certain referrals that occur within the confines of one practice. We are not aware of any rationale for extending this "single practice" exception to any outside entities, whether or not those entities have a financial relationship with an immediate family member.

We would also like to point out that a physician may send a patient to an immediate relative without actually "referring" that patient for a designated health service. A referral is defined in section 1877 for purposes of Part B services as, with an exception for certain specialized services, the request by a physician for an item or service, including the request for a consultation with another physician (including any test or procedure ordered by, or to be performed by (or under the supervision of) that other physician). We have interpreted this provision in section III.A.7 of this preamble to apply to just requests by the physician for designated health services covered under Part B, rather than any Part B item or service. For other kinds of items and services, a referral is, with an exception for certain specialized services, the request or establishment of a plan of care by a

Federal Register / Vol. 63, No. 6 / Friday, January 9, 1998 / Proposed Rules **1709**

physician, which includes the provision of a designated health service.

We believe a referral would be acceptable where the referral is not for a designated health service. For example, a physician who is a general practitioner might believe that a patient has a neurological problem, but be unsure of a diagnosis. This physician could refer the patient to his or her neurologist spouse, if the referral is not a "consultation" (see our discussion of "consultations" in section III.A.7 of this preamble). That is because the referring physician has not requested a designated health service or established a plan of care including one, nor has he or she requested a consultation. We believe the referral, in this case, is for physician services, which are generally not designated health services. If the spouse, in turn, determines that the patient requires an MRI, the spouse would be the one making the referral for this designated health service.

If one member of a group practice cannot make a referral to an entity, are all other group practice physicians also precluded? Group practices have informed us that they are concerned about the definition of a "referring physician" in § 411.351, and how it affects a group when one member is precluded from referring to a particular entity that furnishes designated health services. In particular, several groups wondered whether having a physician member whose immediate relative has an unexcepted ownership interest in an entity would preclude all group practice members from referring to that entity. Groups believe that the preamble to the final rule covering referrals to clinical laboratories implied that the referral prohibition would be imputed to all physician members.

Section 411.351 defines a "referring physician" as a physician (or group practice) who makes a referral (as defined elsewhere in the regulations). We interpreted this definition to mean that when an individual group member refers, the entire group has referred. As a result, any member of a group who has an unexcepted financial relationship (or whose relative has such a relationship) with an entity could "taint" the referrals of the entire group.

We have reconsidered this issue and now propose to amend the definition to exclude any reference to the entire group practice. We believe that the statute was drafted to cover the referral behavior of individual physicians and to regulate the entities to which they refer. There does not appear to us to be any clear reason to extend the effects of one physician's relationships and behaviors to other physicians, just because they

are all members of the same group practice. As several practices have pointed out to us, being members of the same group practice does not mean that physicians automatically have the opportunity, power, or incentive to exert pressure on each other to refer to their related entities.

However, in any instance in which a group member is in a position to exert influence or control over the referrals of other group physicians, the prohibition could still apply. For example, group members could be subject to sanctions if their referral patterns reveal a circumvention scheme between them. Similarly, if a group practice owner conditions payment to his or her employee members on referrals to the owner's laboratory, the employment could be a compensation arrangement that triggers the prohibition.

6. Remuneration

Do payments qualify as remuneration only if they result in a net benefit? Certain members of the provider community have requested that we interpret a payment as remuneration only if it is made in exchange for identifiable property or services. Under this theory, if the physician or entity making the payment has no expectation of or entitlement to something of value in return for the payment, there would be no compensation arrangement, even if other physicians or entities might benefit from the exchange.

In the August 1995 final regulation, we defined remuneration as "any payment, discount, forgiveness of debt, or other benefit made directly or indirectly, overtly or covertly, in cash or in kind," except for a narrow list of remuneration excluded from the definition by section 1877(h)(1)(C). We believe that remuneration generally involves any payment of cash, property, or services, whether or not either or both parties receive a net benefit. For example, we would regard as remuneration the repayment of a loan, even if there are no accompanying interest payments.

We base this interpretation on the statute, which excepts from compensation arrangements under section 1877(h)(1)(C) only very limited and specific types of remuneration. Among the list is the forgiveness of amounts for the correction of minor billing errors; that is, small amounts that are excused by one party in order to even out the parties' accounts. However, the statute does not except amounts that are forgiven to even out larger billing errors, nor does it contain a general exception for remuneration that does not result in a net benefit for one or both

of the parties. (The correction of a large billing error might, however, qualify as an "isolated transaction" or qualify for the new exception in § 411.357(l) as part of a fair market value exchange.)

We believe that the statute is designed to prohibit referrals whenever a physician makes a payment to an entity or an entity makes a payment to a physician, regardless of who profits or gains. The statute, in our view, contains a presumption that if there has been a payment of any kind, a physician should not refer. As a result, the agency need not "look behind" each transaction to ascertain whether the physician has gained some benefit as a result of the transaction, has realized little or no net benefit, or has benefitted too much. The law does, however, designate certain very specific compensation arrangements that require that the Secretary "look behind" them and except them if the exchanges of payment meet fair market value and certain other standards.

It is our view that the one-way payments described by the providers are remuneration. If a payment does not reflect an actual fair market value exchange, it could easily serve as the vehicle for referral payments. We believe the law was meant to prevent a physician from referring to an entity if that physician (or a family member) is receiving payments of any kind that cannot be accounted for as part of a fair exchange.

B. General Prohibition—What Constitutes a Prohibited Referral

Does the prohibition apply only if a physician refers directly to a particular related entity? As we mentioned in the section above covering the definition of "entity," section 1877(a)(1) prohibits a physician from making a *referral to an entity* for the furnishing of designated health services if the physician or immediate family member of the physician *has a financial relationship* with that entity. Section 1877(h)(5) defines a referral very broadly: A referral is the request by a physician for a Part B item or service (including certain consultations). In addition, "the request or establishment of a plan of care by a physician that includes the provision of [a] designated health service" constitutes a "referral" by a "referring physician." We have interpreted this provision in § 411.351 of the August 1995 final clinical laboratory rule to mean that a physician has made a referral if he or she has made a request for a Part B item or service or a request for other items or services that includes the provision of laboratory services or if he or she has established a plan of care that includes the provision of laboratory services.

The "referral" provision requires that a physician only request an item or service or include it in a plan of care; it does not require that the physician directly send a patient to a particular entity or specifically indicate in a plan of care that the service must be provided by a particular entity. However, section 1877(h)(5) must be read in conjunction with the prohibition in section 1877(a)(1). The general prohibition applies only when a physician makes a referral *to an entity* for the furnishing of a designated health service if the physician or a family member has a financial relationship *with that entity*.

For example, a physician might have a small noncontrolling ownership interest in a provider of a designated health service, such as a physical therapy (PT) facility. The physician does not directly refer patients to this provider. However, the physician does establish plans of care for patients in a hospital setting, which include PT services. When a particular patient leaves the hospital, the physician may refer the patient to an unrelated skilled nursing facility (SNF) that, in turn, refers the patient to the related PT provider. The PT facility bills the patient separately. As a result, the patient may receive services prescribed by the physician from an entity with which the physician has a financial relationship.

In situations such as this one, the physician has prescribed a plan of care that includes designated health services, an action that constitutes a referral. However, the physician has not made the referral to an entity with which he or she has a financial relationship. Instead, the physician has made the referral to an SNF with which he or she has no financial relationship. As such, the referral prohibition would generally not apply. Nonetheless, if there was any evidence that the physician has an agreement with the SNF that involves the SNF systematically referring the physician's Medicare patients to the physician's PT facility, we would likely investigate the situation as a possible circumvention scheme.

When is the owner of a designated health services provider considered as equivalent to that provider? We have received several comments about when a physician who has an ownership interest in an entity that furnishes designated health services should be equated with that entity. For example, suppose that a physician regularly refers patients to an SNF in which the physician has no investment interest. The SNF, in turn, buys PT services from a PT facility that also provides other noncovered items and services to the SNF and is owned solely by the physician. Arguably the referring physician, as sole proprietor of the PT facility, is related to the SNF because the physician's PT facility sells PT and other, noncovered services to the SNF. We believe that it is likely, in this situation, that the physician is in a position to negotiate or influence the terms of the arrangement, as well as to initiate patient referrals to the SNF.

We believe that there is a potential for abuse in such situations. For example, the physician may be referring as many patients as possible to the SNF in exchange for inflated rates from the SNF for the variety of noncovered items and services that the PT facility furnishes, or for any covered services that are not subject to a fee schedule. Although the SNF may be negotiating with the PT facility as a corporate or other business entity, we would equate the referring physician and the PT facility with each other when the referring physician (or a family member) has a significant ownership or controlling interest that allows him or her to determine how the PT facility conducts its business and with whom. We will consider a number of factors in these situations, such as whether the physician or the physician in combination with his or her immediate family members owns all or a controlling amount of the stock of an entity, and whether the physician and/or the family members are making decisions for the entity, particularly on a day-to-day basis. Our analysis will depend upon the entire record of the interrelationship between the physician and/or immediate family members and the entity, whether the relationships are direct or indirect, and the totality of the circumstances.

We believe the analysis is similar when a referring physician receives compensation from an entity that is owned or controlled by a party that also owns a designated health services provider. For example, suppose that a physician owns a controlling interest in a general practice clinic, and also independently owns a controlling interest in an outside laboratory in which the clinic itself has no interest. The clinic also employs a number of physicians who receive salaries from the clinic corporation.

Arguably, the employee physicians in this situation have no financial relationship with the outside laboratory. That is, they do not themselves own any part of the laboratory, nor do they receive compensation from or pay compensation to the laboratory entity. However, if we were to take the position that there is no financial relationship, and hence no referral prohibition, the physician owner of the laboratory, by controlling the clinic, could arrange to compensate the employee physicians with inflated salaries based directly on the number of referrals they make to the outside laboratory.

In order to avoid this result, we propose to equate the owner physician with the outside laboratory and with the clinic when he or she owns or controls them. Under this interpretation, we would regard the employee physicians as receiving compensation from the laboratory. Although this compensation is indirect, we believe it is covered by the statute. Section 1877(h)(1) defines a "compensation arrangement" as any arrangement involving any remuneration (with certain narrow exceptions). "Remuneration," in turn, is defined as any remuneration paid directly or indirectly.

If the physician, on the other hand, has a noncontrolling interest in the outside laboratory, we would not equate the owner physician with the laboratory. However, we would regard this situation as a potential circumvention scheme. That is, we would regard the physician owner in this situation as referring indirectly, through the employee physicians, to a designated health services provider to which the owner physician cannot personally refer. The inflated salaries of the employee physicians, in fact, could serve as evidence of the existence of such a circumvention scheme.

The analysis would vary somewhat if the referring physicians are compensated by an entity, rather than an individual physician. Suppose, for example, that a hospital hires physicians to serve on its staff. The hospital compensates the physicians for their services, but inflates their salaries to reflect all the referrals they make to a separate MRI subsidiary that is not part of the hospital but is owned by it. If the hospital owns a controlling share of the MRI entity, we would regard the hospital and the entity as equivalent.

The analysis would be different if the hospital owns less than a controlling interest in the MRI facility. Arguably, the physicians are compensated by an entity (the hospital) that is technically separate from the one providing the referred MRI services. The physicians do not own the MRI facility, nor do they receive payment from it. Nonetheless, if the physicians receive payments from the hospital that exceed fair market value for the services they are otherwise providing, we propose to presume that they are being indirectly compensated by the MRI facility, through the hospital, for their referrals.

Has a physician made a referral to a particular entity if another individual directs the patient there?

We have received inquiries about situations in which a physician requests a designated health service, but it is another individual, such as a discharge planner, who follows the physician's plan of care and refers the patient directly to a specific provider. We discussed this issue in the August 1995 final rule. In the preamble to that rule at 60 FR 41941, we stated that a physician who establishes a plan of care or requests an item or service is responsible for the referral, even if it is another individual or an institutional entity that carries out that plan of care for the physician. For example, we stated that we would not allow a hospital physician to avoid the referral prohibition by claiming that it is the hospital that actually makes the referral or selects the provider in his or her place. We took this position in order to prevent a physician from disavowing all referrals by having personnel or employers carry them out.

In light of our analysis in the responses to the last two questions, we would like to refine our position on this issue. That is, we want to qualify our position to "impute" a physician's referrals to others only in those situations in which the physician has the ability to control or influence the individuals who select an entity. We would also "impute" referrals if a physician is him or herself in a position to be compensated for the referrals by those who can control or influence the actions of the person who actually selects the entity.

For example, suppose that a physician works for a hospital and refers a patient to the hospital's discharge planner for laboratory tests. The discharge planner in turn refers the patient to the hospital's laboratory. We would regard the physician's request and referral to the discharge planner as a referral to an agent of the entity that owns the laboratory; that is, to an agent of the entity that furnishes designated health services. We believe that such a referral would be governed by the rules in section 1877. Suppose, on the other hand, that the discharge planner refers the patient to an outside laboratory that happens to be owned by the hospital. The physician in this situation may not be able to compensate the discharge planner or otherwise in any way influence that individual's actions. Nonetheless, if the hospital pays the physician to order as many laboratory tests as possible, and in turn pays the discharge planner to refer patients directly to a hospital-owned provider,

we would impute the referral to the physician.

We can translate these rules into a group practice setting. For example, a group practice member might request a designated health service, but allow a nonphysician employee to direct the patient to a particular provider. If the nonphysician refers the patient to the group's own provider, we would regard the referral as the physician's own referral to an agent of a provider of designated health services. This arrangement, we believe, would be subject to the referral rules. For outside referrals, we would gauge whether the physician member is in any position to control the actions of the nonphysician. In order to gauge whether a physician is in a position to affect a nonphysician's actions, we propose to use the same ownership and control rules that we mentioned above. We would also impute the referral to the physician if the entity compensating the physician is in a position to both compensate the physician for his or her referrals and to control the actions of the individual who selects the provider.

How will HCFA interpret situations in which it is not clear whether a physician has referred to a particular entity?

A physician might request or order a designated health service for a patient without establishing a record of whether he or she referred the patient to a specific provider. If the patient receives the designated health service from an entity with which the physician (or a family member) has a financial relationship, as the result of the referral, we will presume that the service results from the physician referring to that specific entity. We will allow physicians to rebut that presumption by establishing that they mentioned no specific provider or supplier or that the patient was directly referred by some other independent individual or through an unrelated entity.

C. General Exceptions That Apply to Ownership or Investment Interests and to Compensation Arrangements

1. The in-office ancillary services exception

Can a physician supply crutches as in-office ancillary services? The in-office ancillary services exception in section 1877(b)(2) applies to services that meet the requirements for supervision, location, and billing, but not to any parenteral and enteral nutrients, equipment and supplies or to durable medical equipment (DME) (although the exception does apply to infusion pumps). Many physicians have brought to our attention the problems with

excluding crutches from the exception. That is, an orthopaedist might diagnose a patient with a broken leg, set the leg, personally furnish the patient in his or her own office with crutches, and then bill for those crutches. If the patient will use the crutches at home, they qualify as DME. Physicians have pointed out that this exclusion will cause great inconvenience to such patients, who will have to obtain crutches or similar equipment elsewhere.

We agree that excluding crutches from the section 1877(b)(2) exception could cause great inconvenience to patients, and disrupt the efficient delivery of health care services. We regard crutches as different from other DME in that a patient very often needs them immediately after treatment for an injury that has resulted from an unexpected traumatic event. Thus, patients may often be precluded from arranging to receive crutches in advance from other, unrelated entities. Nonetheless, the Secretary does not have the authority to simply create a blanket exception for crutches. The Secretary only has the authority, under section 1877(b)(4), to create new exceptions in the case of any other financial relationship that the Secretary determines, and specifies in regulations, does not pose a risk of program or patient abuse. We have no evidence that allowing physicians a blanket exception to self-refer for crutches will be free from abuse. In the ownership context, for example, each referral will inherently increase a physician's or group practices' profits.

We are thus proposing to create an exception, at § 411.355(e), that we believe will remedy this problem, while meeting the statutory condition. That is, the exception would apply only to situations in which a physician furnishes crutches in a manner that meets the in-office ancillary services requirements in section 1877(b)(2) (and in § 411.355(b)), provided the physician realizes no direct or indirect profit from furnishing the crutches. In other words, Medicare will pay for the crutches if the physician bills only for the cost he or she incurred to acquire and supply the crutches or to create or manufacture the crutches. We believe that there is no threat of abuse in these situations, since physicians will have no incentive to overutilize crutches.

2. Exception for services furnished by organizations operating under prepaid plans

Can a physician refer non-enrollees to a related prepaid organization or to its physicians and providers?

We have been asked about situations in which a physician furnishes services to managed care patients under a personal services contract, but wishes to refer his or her own outside, fee-for-service Medicare patients for designated health services to the managed care entity, or to physicians, suppliers, or providers that are affiliated with the managed care entity. If the physician refers to an otherwise unrelated physician, provider, or supplier that is affiliated with the managed care entity, but is not part of it and accepts the fee-for-service patient independently, the referral prohibition should not apply. That is, the physician would not be referring to the managed care entity with which he or she has a financial relationship.

The analysis would be different, however, if the other physician, provider, or supplier is functioning as part of the managed care entity. For example, a physician might provide services to enrollees of a Federally qualified HMO under a contract arrangement. These services are excepted from the referral prohibition by section 1877(b)(3). However, when the physician wishes to refer a fee-for-service Medicare patient to the HMO's laboratory, the physician is making a referral to an entity with which the physician has a financial relationship. That is, the physician's personal services contract constitutes a compensation arrangement with the HMO.

In order for the physician in this situation to refer, the financial relationship must meet one of the compensation-related exceptions in section 1877 or in this proposed rule. For example, the physician could continue to refer if his or her arrangement meets the criteria in the personal services exception in section 1877(e)(3) and in § 411.357(d) of this proposed rule. The compensation the physician receives from the HMO would have to be, among other things, consistent with fair market value, and could not reflect the volume or value of the physician's referrals (except as allowed under a physician incentive plan). We have proposed to define the concept of a "referral," for purposes of section 1877, as limited to a referral for a designated health service that may be covered under Medicare or Medicaid (see our discussion of the definition in section III.A.7 of this preamble). Thus, the "volume or value" standard would automatically be met if (in the context of the physician's HMO practice) the physician treated and referred only non-Medicare or non-Medicaid HMO enrollees (that is, the physician's HMO

compensation would never reflect the volume or value of Medicare or Medicaid referrals).

If, on the other hand, the physician is compensated by the HMO for treating HMO enrollees who are covered by Medicare or Medicaid, the compensation would be subject to the "volume or value" standard. Hence, the arrangement could still meet the personal services exception if the physician's compensation does not reflect Medicare or Medicaid covered referrals or reflects them only as part of a physician incentive plan, as these plans are described in section 1877(e)(3)(B), and in § 411.351 of this proposed rule.

As noted earlier in this preamble, we believe that, for the most part, physicians working for managed care organizations or as part of an integrated delivery system will be able to refer Medicare and Medicaid patients within these systems, provided their arrangements with these entities meet certain standards. However, we anticipate that there may be some unusual situations in which an exception does not apply. One example of providers in a delivery system who may be adversely affected by the referral prohibition involves providers under Medicaid primary care case management (PCCM) programs.

We are aware that, under certain circumstances, some providers contracting under these managed fee-for-service programs may not be eligible for any of the existing exceptions written into the law or proposed in this rule. Because the Secretary can only create new exceptions for financial relationships which she determines pose no risk of program or patient abuse, we have not created a blanket exception for Medicaid PCCM programs. However, we do not wish, as an unintended consequence of this decision, to discourage the participation of Medicaid providers in PCCM programs, thereby threatening Medicaid beneficiaries' access to care. Therefore, we are soliciting comments from States and others on the potential impact of the referral prohibition on Medicaid PCCM programs and the providers who contract under them.

One example of a situation in which a PCCM provider might be prohibited from making a referral involves HMOs that contract as primary care case managers. While HMO participation in PCCM programs is relatively rare, HMOs in some States have contracted to serve as case managers to the disabled population. Such contracts allow the HMO to gain experience in serving the disabled without having to accept the

financial risk that an HMO would normally accept under a capitation contract. As States move to enroll more of their disabled populations into capitated programs, involving HMOs in PCCM programs could serve as a transitional method of developing a managed care provider network that is experienced in caring for the disabled.

If an HMO physician who is required by contract to refer within the HMO's network wishes to refer a PCCM patient within that network, his or her financial relationship with the HMO would have to meet one of the existing exceptions in the law or in this proposed rule. Because the HMO in the above example is paid on a fee-for-service basis under the PCCM program, none of the exceptions for services furnished by pre-paid risk plans would be appropriate.

The manner in which we have interpreted the volume or value of referrals standard in this proposed rule could prevent the financial relationship from qualifying for one of the compensation-related exceptions. Most of these exceptions can be satisfied only if a physician's compensation does not reflect the volume or value of his or her referrals. Certain provider contracts that require a physician to refer within a defined network of providers could violate that standard. (We discuss our interpretation of this standard in section III.E.3.) That is, regardless of whether the physician's income actually varies based on the volume or value of referrals, the physician's income reflects the referrals because it could be lost entirely if the physician repeatedly refers patients out-of-network. If the financial relationship does not qualify for an exception, there may be no Federal matching funds for any in-network referral of PCCM patients made by this physician.

3. Other permissible exceptions for financial relationships that do not pose a risk of program or patient abuse

Should situations that meet a safe harbor under the anti-kickback statute be automatically excepted? We have received inquiries about the Secretary's authority under section 1877(b)(4) to create additional exceptions for financial relationships which the Secretary determines, and specifies in regulations, do not pose a risk of program or patient abuse. We have had some requests that the Secretary create an exception for any financial relationship that meets a safe harbor under the anti-kickback statute. As we have stated elsewhere in this preamble, the anti-kickback statute in section 1128B(b) and section 1877 are totally independent laws, with separate requirements. In order for a physician who has a financial relationship with an entity to refer to that entity, the arrangement must meet the requirements in both laws. However, we are willing to consider this option and specifically solicit comments on whether meeting a safe harbor would qualify an arrangement as one that involves no risk of program or patient abuse.

D. Exceptions That Apply Only to Ownership or Investment Interests

1. Exception for ownership in publicly traded securities or mutual funds

Does the exception for publicly traded securities apply to stock options? We have been asked whether ownership of an option to purchase stock in an entity that furnishes a designated health service constitutes an excepted ownership interest in the entity. As we stated in section IV.A.3 above, we regard the option to purchase stock in an entity as an inchoate ownership interest that could subject a physician to the referral prohibition. As such, all of the exceptions that ordinarily apply to ownership interests would apply. However, the exception for publicly traded securities would not apply if the stock option involves investment securities that may not be purchased on terms generally available to the public, as required by section 1877(c)(1).

2. Exception for services provided by a hospital in which a physician or family member has an interest

Can a physician or family member own an interest in a chain of hospitals? Section 1877(d)(3) contains an exception for designated health services provided by a hospital (other than a hospital in Puerto Rico) if the referring physician is authorized to perform services there, and the ownership or investment interest is in the hospital itself (and not merely in a subdivision of the hospital). We discussed at some length in the August 1995 final rule how we believe an individual can hold an interest in a subdivision of a hospital.

We have received inquiries about whether this exception applies if a physician or family member holds an interest in a company or network that owns a chain of hospitals, rather than an interest in the one hospital to which the physician makes referrals. It is our view that a physician can have an ownership or investment interest in a hospital that is part of a chain by virtue of holding an interest in the organization that owns the chain. We base our position on the language of the exception, which does not require that the physician have a

direct interest in the hospital. In addition, we believe that the exception in section 1877(d)(3) must be read in conjunction with section 1877(a)(2), which states that a physician's or family member's ownership or investment interest in an entity that provides a designated health service constitutes a financial relationship with that entity. This provision further defines an ownership or investment interest in an entity to include an interest in an entity that holds an ownership or investment interest in any entity providing the designated health services. Thus, by definition, a physician who has an ownership interest in a health system that owns a hospital that provides designated health services has an ownership interest in that individual hospital. If that indirect interest is in the hospital as a whole, and not in a subdivision, then the exception should apply. In fact, we believe that it would be illogical to specifically apply the referral prohibition in section 1877(a)(1) to any indirect ownership interest, yet deny an exception in section 1877(d) that is based on ownership just because the interest is indirect, especially when the exception itself does not require a direct interest.

Nonetheless, in order to meet the hospital ownership exception, we believe the law requires that the physician be authorized to perform services at the hospital to which he or she wishes to refer. We do not believe that this last requirement is met if the physician has these privileges with any one of the other hospitals in the chain, but not with the referral hospital.

We also wish to make the point that any ownership interest a physician or family member has in a hospital could involve a separate compensation arrangement. For example, if a physician acquires an interest in a hospital from a health care network, this acquisition could constitute remuneration from an entity that provides designated health services. Consequently, for the physician to refer to the entity, the arrangement would have to meet a compensation-related exception.

E. Exceptions That Apply Only to Compensation Arrangements

1. Compensation arrangements in general

Can a lease or arrangement for items or services have a termination clause? The lease exceptions for space and equipment and a number of the other compensation exceptions require that, among other things, the arrangement be in writing and provide for a term of at

least 1 year. We believe that this requirement has been met as long as the arrangement clearly establishes a business relationship that will last for at least 1 year. Nonetheless, it is our view that the arrangement can still qualify for the exception even if it also includes a clause allowing the parties to terminate sooner for good cause, provided the parties do not enter into a new arrangement within the originally established 1 year time period.

We believe that Congress included the 1 year requirement with the intention of excepting stable arrangements that cannot be renegotiated frequently to reflect the current volume or value of a physician's referrals. Nonetheless, we do not believe that Congress intended, in creating this requirement, to bind parties to an arrangement once that arrangement has become unsatisfactory to some or all of the parties. Therefore, we are interpreting all of the exceptions with the 1 year requirement to allow terminations for good cause, provided the parties do not, within the 1 year period, enter into a new arrangement. We also believe that a lease or arrangement must be renewed in at least 1 year increments, so that it is always an agreement that provides for a term of at least 1 year. That is, once the first year of an agreement expires, it cannot be converted into, for example, a month-by-month arrangement that could fluctuate with a physician's referrals.

Will a physician's referrals be prohibited if an entity pays for certain incidental benefits? Entities, such as hospitals, often provide physicians with certain incidental benefits, such as their malpractice insurance, or with reduced or free parking, meals, or other incidental benefits. We believe the answer to this question hinges on the nature of any other financial relationship the physician has with the entity. For example, if a physician receives free "extras" such as malpractice insurance, parking, or meals while he or she serves as the entity's employee, then these extras might qualify as part of the compensation that the physician receives under a bona fide employment relationship, provided they are specified in the employment agreement. If the physician or entity can demonstrate that the extras constitute part of the payment that such entities typically provide to physicians, regardless of whether they make referrals to the entity, the extras might constitute payment that is consistent with fair market value and that furthers the entity's legitimate business purposes. If an incidental benefit cannot meet the requirements under a statutory exception or the new general exception for compensation arrangements we have included in § 411.357(l), it might still meet the de minimis exception we have added in § 411.357(k) if it has limited value. We have also been asked about parking spaces that a hospital provides to physicians who have privileges to treat their patients in the hospital. It is our view that, while a physician is making rounds, the parking benefits both the hospital and its patients, rather than providing the physician with any personal benefit. Thus, we do not intend to regard parking for this purpose as remuneration furnished by the hospital to the physician, but instead as part of the physician's privileges. However, if a hospital provides parking to a physician for periods of time that do not coincide with his or her rounds, that parking could constitute remuneration.

2. Exception for agreements involving the rental of office space or equipment

Can a lessee sublet office space or equipment? Section 1877(c)(1) and (2) excepts from compensation arrangements that trigger the referral prohibition, payments made by a lessee to a lessor for the use of premises or equipment if certain criteria are met. We have listed these requirements in the regulation at § 411.357(a) and (b). Among these is the requirement that the office space or equipment be "used exclusively by the lessee when being used by the lessee." We believe Congress included this requirement to ensure that excepted rental agreements are valid ones, rather than "paper" leases that might involve payments passing between the lessor and lessee, when the lessee is not actually using or intending to use the space or the equipment. As a result, we believe that this requirement precludes the lessee from subletting the space or equipment during any portion of a lease during which the lessee is expected to be using them.

A sublease arrangement might nonetheless qualify under the new compensation exception that we are proposing under § 411.357(l). That exception requires, among other things, that the rental payments be consistent with fair market value and not take into account the volume or value of any referrals between the parties. In addition, the lease arrangement must be commercially reasonable and further the legitimate business purposes of the parties. We envision that there could be arrangements in which both the lease arrangement and the sublease would meet all of these criteria.

Does the lease exception apply to any kind of lease covering space or equipment? As we understand general accounting principles, there are differences between operational leases and capital leases that may be relevant to our application of section 1877. Operational leases are basic, simple leases in which the lessee makes rental payments to the lessor in order to use the lessor's property or space. These kinds of leases, we believe, could fall within the exceptions in section 1877(e)(1)(A) and (B) because they constitute payments made by the lessee for the use of space or equipment.

Capital leases, on the other hand, are very much like installment sales purchases. Upon entering into such a lease, the lessee receives all of the benefits and obligations of ownership of the property. That is, the lessee (and not the lessor) can depreciate the property and record it on its books as a capital asset and the long-term capital lease payments as a liability (very much like the way the lessee would record a loan). In most cases, the title to the property at issue will pass to the lessee at the end of the term of the lease. In other words, the property that is covered by capital leases is treated by accountants as property that a lessee has purchased or is in the process of purchasing. We believe that such leases go beyond the section 1877(e)(1) exceptions, which except only payments for *the use* of equipment or space.

Can a lease provide for payment based on how often the equipment is used? We have been asked about situations in which a physician rents equipment to an entity that furnishes a designated health service, such as a hospital that rents an MRI machine, with the physician receiving rental payments on a "per click" basis (that is, rental payments go up each time the machine is used). We believe that this arrangement will not prohibit the physician from otherwise referring to the entity, provided that these kinds of arrangements are typical and comply with the fair market value and other standards that are included under the rental exception. However, because a physician's compensation under this exception cannot reflect the volume or value of the physician's own referrals, the rental payments cannot reflect "per click" payments for patients who are referred for the service by the lessor physician.

3. Exception for personal services arrangements

How does the physician incentive plan exception apply when an enrolling entity contracts with a group practice? The exception for personal services arrangements includes the criteria that any compensation paid by an entity under the arrangement cannot reflect the volume or value of a physician's referrals, unless the compensation is paid under a physician incentive plan, as that term is defined in section 1877(e)(3)(B). A physician incentive plan is defined by this provision as any compensation arrangement between an entity and a physician or physician group that may directly or indirectly have the effect of reducing or limiting services furnished with respect to individuals enrolled with the entity. We have defined "physician group" broadly in our March 27, 1996, final rule (61 FR 13430) interpreting physician incentive plans under section 1876(i)(8), of which group practices as defined under section 1877(h) are a subset.

Although an entity can compensate a physician group to reflect the volume or value of referrals under a physician incentive plan, the definition of a group practice under section 1877(h)(4)(A)(iv) precludes the group, with certain exceptions, from compensating its members based directly or indirectly on the volume or value of their referrals (it does not contain the exception for physician incentive plans). As we have described earlier in this preamble, we believe the volume or value standard applies only to a physician's own referrals for designated health services covered under Medicare or Medicaid.

Several interested parties have asked us whether these provisions contain contradictory standards, which could make it difficult for entities that enroll patients to continue their common practice of contracting with group practices to provide services to the entities' enrollees. We believe that the two provisions need not be read as contradictory. While the group practice definition in general precludes a group from compensating its physician members based on their referrals, it does allow groups to pay physicians a share of the overall profits of the group, or a productivity bonus based on services personally performed or services incident to such personally performed services, so long as the share or bonus is not determined in a manner that is directly related to the volume or value of a physician's own referrals. We have discussed our interpretation of these principles elsewhere in this preamble. In the context of a physician incentive plan, a physician group as a whole could be compensated more by an entity based on providing or referring for fewer services. We believe that the group practice could then pass any additional compensation it receives from a physician incentive plan on to the individual physician members via overall profit sharing, which would only indirectly compensate them for the volume of their referrals. Also, the physicians could receive a productivity bonus for their decreased utilization of any services that are not designated health services covered under Medicare or Medicaid.

V. Regulatory Impact Statement

A. Background

We have examined the impacts of this proposed rule as required by Executive Order 12866 and the Regulatory Flexibility Act (RFA) (Public Law 96–354). Executive Order 12866 directs agencies to assess all costs and benefits of available regulatory alternatives and, when regulation is necessary, to select regulatory approaches that maximize net benefits (including potential economic, environmental, public health and safety effects, distributive impacts, and equity). The RFA requires agencies to analyze options for regulatory relief of small businesses. For purposes of the RFA, most hospitals, and most other providers, physicians, and health care suppliers are small entities, either by nonprofit status or by having revenues of $5 million or less annually.

Section 202 of the Unfunded Mandates Reform Act provides for "Regulatory Accountability and Reform." It requires the agency to engage in certain procedures, including a cost benefit analysis and consultation with affected State and local governments, for proposed and certain final rules that include "Federal mandates" that may result in the expenditure by State, local, and tribal governments, in the aggregate, or by the private sector, of $100 million or more annually. Section 201 of the Unfunded Mandates Reform Act requires this assessment only to the extent that a regulation incorporates requirements other than those specifically set forth in the law.

Section 1102(b) of the Social Security Act requires us to prepare a regulatory impact analysis for any proposed rule that may have a significant impact on the operations of a substantial number of small rural hospitals. This analysis must conform to the provisions of section 603 of the RFA. For purposes of section 1102(b) of the Act, we define a small rural hospital as a hospital that is located outside a Metropolitan Statistical Area and has fewer than 50 beds.

Sections 1877 and 1903(s) of the Act were enacted in order to correct an abuse highlighted by a number of studies: The ordering by some physicians of unnecessary services because they have a financial incentive

do so. (See section I.A. of this preamble for citations to the studies.) The legislation identified those types of services (referred to as "designated health services") where the existence of, or potential for, abuse appeared to be the greatest. The approach taken in the legislation was to assume that, in general, if a financial relationship exists between a physician or a physician's immediate family member and an entity that provides designated health services, an incentive to overutilize those services also exists. The statute defined a financial relationship as an ownership or investment interest in, or compensation arrangement with, an entity. Congress created a number of exceptions to the prohibition in recognition of certain existing business practices. In addition, the legislation provides the Secretary with authority to create new exceptions. However, we must first determine, and specify in regulations, that any new exception will not pose a risk of program or patient abuse.

Because of its exceptions, the current law is complicated. However, the essence of the prohibition in section 1877 is clear: If a physician or a physician's immediate family member has a financial relationship with an entity, the physician cannot refer patients to that entity for the furnishing of a designated health service for which payment otherwise may be made under Medicare. Unlike the anti-kickback statute discussed in the preamble, the law is triggered by the mere fact that a financial relationship exists; the intention of the referring physician is not taken into consideration.

Section 1903(s) denies Federal financial participation payment under the Medicaid program to a State for designated health services furnished to an individual on the basis of a physician referral that would result in a denial of payment under the Medicare program if Medicare covered the services to the same extent and under the same terms and conditions as under the State Medicaid plan.

The goal of this proposed rule is to integrate section 1877 (as amended by OBRA '93 and SSA '94) into the Medicare regulations and section 1903(s) into the Medicaid regulations, and to interpret the statute in accordance with its language and intent.

B. Anticipated Effects and Alternatives Considered

For the reasons described below, we believe any estimate of the individual or aggregate economic impact of the provisions of this proposed rule would be purely speculative. Although the

provisions proposed in this rule do not lend themselves to a quantitative impact estimate, for reasons discussed below and elsewhere in the preamble, we do not anticipate that they would have a significant economic impact on a substantial number of small entities. However, to the extent that our proposals may have significant effects on some health care practitioners or be viewed as controversial, we believe it is desirable to inform the public of what we view as the possible effects of the proposals. This analysis, together with the other sections of the preamble, constitutes a regulatory flexibility analysis and analysis for purposes of section 1102(b) of the Act.

We expect that some kinds of entities could be affected to varying degrees by this proposed rule. Following are the groups we believe are most likely to experience some economic impact:

1. Physicians

A physician can be financially related to an entity either through an ownership or investment interest in the entity, or through a compensation arrangement with the entity. We begin by first discussing ownership/investment interests.

Ownership or investment interests. A physician who has (or whose immediate family member has) an ownership or investment interest in an entity and does not qualify for an exception is prohibited from referring Medicare patients to that entity for the provision of designated health services. Also, when a physician with such an ownership or investment interest makes a prohibited referral, there is a risk that the entity will receive no Medicare payment for those designated health services. Under Medicaid, a State may receive no FFP for services that result from a referral that would be prohibited under Medicare, if Medicare covered the same designated health services as are covered under the State plan. The State may, in turn, choose not to pay the furnishing entity.

The American Medical Association's (AMA) Center for Health Policy Research (hereafter, the Center) reviewed three studies that analyze self-referral: (1) "Financial Arrangements Between Physicians and Health Care Businesses: Report to Congress," Office of Inspector General, DHHS, pages 18 and 21 (May 1989); (2) "Joint Ventures Among Health Care Providers in Florida," State of Florida Health Care Cost Containment Board (Sept. 1991); and (3) "Frequency and Costs of Diagnostic Imagining in Office Practice—A Comparison of Self-Referring and Radiologist-Referring

1716   Federal Register / Vol. 63, No. 6 / Friday, January 9, 1998 / Proposed Rules

Physicians," Bruce J. Hillman and others, The New England Journal of Medicine (December 1990; pp. 1604–1608). As reported in the Journal of the American Medical Association (JAMA, May 6, 1992, Vol 267, No. 17), the Center found that approximately 10 percent of physicians nationwide have ownership interests in health care entities that have been associated with potential self-referral issues. It pointed out, however, that not all of these physicians engage in self-referral. The Center also reported that there was no evidence in the studies they reviewed on the extent to which physicians may profit from self-referrals. Therefore, it concluded that the degree of conflict of interest presented by a physician's investment in entities to which he or she refers patients is unknown.

If we were to assume that the 10 percent figure cited above is currently true, this would mean, based on the number of active physicians in 1995, that approximately 79,000 physicians have an ownership interest in health care entities that furnish designated health services. Note, however, that others cite higher percentages. For example, the 1991 study issued by the Florida Health Care Cost Containment Board found that at least 40 percent of Florida physicians involved in direct patient care had an investment in a health care business to which they could—in the absence of prohibiting legislation—refer patients for services. We would also like to point out that ownership information or information on the investments of physicians and all of their immediate family members in the entities that furnish any of eleven designated health services constitutes an enormous amount of data that is continually subject to change.

In 1991, the AMA's Council on Ethical and Judicial Affairs had concluded that physicians should not refer patients to a health care facility outside their office at which they do not directly provide services if they have an investment interest in the facility. The Council stated that physicians have a special fiduciary responsibility to their patients and that there are some activities involving their patients that physicians should avoid whether or not there is evidence of abuse. In December 1992, the AMA voted to declare self-referral unethical, with a few exceptions. Exceptions are allowed if there is a demonstrated need in the community and alternative financing is not available.

As of October 1994, 27 States had enacted legislation that restricts or qualifies self-referral. There is great variation among the States. Some only require disclosure of the financial relationship to the patient, while others prohibit such referrals.

We believe that this increased examination of self-referral arrangements and enactment of both Federal and State laws prohibiting such arrangements has led to a decline in self-referral activity and financial relationships between physicians and entities. However, we lack the data necessary to either confirm or refute this supposition. We also lack data that would tell us how many of the financial relationships that physicians have with an entity that furnishes a designated health service would be exempted under the statute. We would welcome receiving current relevant data.

One exception that may have broad application is the in-office ancillary services exception. With regard to this exception, which applies to both ownership/investment interests and compensation arrangements, we offer the following discussion.

To qualify as in-office ancillary services, the services must, among other things, be furnished personally by the referring physician or another physician in the same group practice as the referring physician, or be furnished by individuals who are directly supervised by one of these physicians. How we interpret a number of elements in this provision would affect whether certain referrals qualify for the in-office ancillary services exception. These include how we define "group practice," "members of the group," and "direct supervision." We discuss these definitions below.

The in-office ancillary services exception allows physicians who are members of a group practice to supervise designated health services referred by any group member. Paragraph (h)(4)(A) of section 1877 provides a definition of a "group practice." That definition, however, consists of elements that require interpretation—for example, what qualifies a group of physicians as "a legal entity," what is meant by the "full range of a physician's services," which must be furnished through group arrangements, and what constitutes "substantially all" of a physician's services, which must also be furnished through the group. We discuss these elements in section III.A.6 of this preamble. As noted in that discussion, we propose to modify some of the interpretations that we made in the August 1995 final rule. We believe that these modifications, which recognize established business practices that do not pose the risk of program or patient abuse, will enable more physicians to meet the definition of a group practice than would the interpretations in the August 1995 rule. If a group of physicians qualifies as a group practice, services can be furnished by certain individuals other than the referring physician and still qualify for the in-office ancillary services exception. We are unable, however, to make an estimate of the economic impact of these modifications.

Also affecting the in-office ancillary services exception is how we would define "members of the group." Again, this proposed rule would modify the definition we established in the August 1995 final rule. This modification, discussed in detail in section III.A.6 of this preamble, would not regard independent contractors as members of the group. This interpretation may make it easier for a group of physicians to meet the "substantially all" test to qualify as a group practice than would the interpretation in the August 1995 rule. On the other hand, independent contractors could not supervise the provision of designated health services. We are unable to estimate the impact of these opposing effects.

The in-office ancillary services exception provides both solo practitioners as well as group practice physicians with the ability to refer within their own practices. As we discussed in detail in the August 1995 final rule, this provision can except solo practitioners with certain shared arrangements who do not wish to become a group practice. For example, two solo practitioners who share one office and jointly own a laboratory can continue to refer to that laboratory, as long as each physician furnishes physician services unrelated to the designated health services in the office, directly supervises the laboratory services for his or her own Medicare and Medicaid patients while they are being furnished, and bills for the services. If only one of the solo practitioners owns the laboratory in a shared office, the non-owning physician can refer to the laboratory as long as he or she is not receiving compensation from the owner in exchange for referrals. We are aware, however, that this exception may not accommodate the variety of different arrangements physicians have entered into to share facilities or otherwise group together without losing their status as solo practitioners. We directly solicit comments on the effects of the referral prohibition on these arrangements.

The proposed regulation defines the statutory requirement for a physician's "direct supervision" of individuals furnishing designated health services

Federal Register / Vol. 63, No. 6 / Friday, January 9, 1998 / Proposed Rules **1717**

under the in-office ancillary services exception. Under the definition, "direct supervision" requires that a physician be present in the office suite and immediately available to provide assistance and direction during the time services are being performed.

One option for defining "direct supervision" would be to say that it means that the service is furnished under the physician's overall supervision and control but that the physician need not be physically present in the office suite in which the services are performed while they are being performed. This rule would not adopt such a definition, however. We believe that the supervision requirement is meant to establish as "in-office ancillary" services those services that are integral to the physician's own practice and that are conducted within his or her own sphere of activity. We believe Congress intended this exception to apply to services that are closely attached to the activities of the referring physician.

If we were to allow physicians to supervise the furnishing of designated health services from a distance, we believe that we would be creating an opportunity for physicians to refer to entities outside their own practices, for services which are not actually "in-office ancillary" in nature. Although our proposed definition may result in fewer referrals qualifying for the "in-office" exception than a more liberal definition, we believe our definition is necessary to achieve the purposes of the statute. We are not, however, proposing that there must be a particular configuration of rooms for an office to qualify as a "suite," for example, that the rooms be contiguous. As stated in section III.A.2 of this preamble, the question of physician proximity for purposes of meeting the direct supervision requirement is a decision that would be made by the local carrier based on the circumstances. We have also proposed to liberalize the concept of "present in the office suite," as we interpreted it in the August 1995 final rule, to allow brief absences from the office under certain conditions.

Because we do not have data on how many physicians have financial relationships that already qualify for the in-office exception, and how many would have to alter their practices, even given the modifications discussed immediately above, we cannot judge the economic impact of our definition. We specifically solicit information on this issue.

As already stated, we do not have current data on the number of physicians with ownership/investment interests in entities that furnish designated health services. Nor do we know how many of these physicians would qualify for an exception to the referral prohibition. However, even if we were to assume that a substantial number of physicians have nonexcepted ownership interests in entities that furnish a designated health service, we do not believe that, in general, the economic impact on these physicians necessarily has to be substantial, for the following reasons:

If a physician's ownership interest in an entity would lead to a prohibition on his or her referrals to that entity, the physician has three options: First, he or she can stop making referrals to that entity and make referrals to another unrelated entity. Second, the physician can divest him or herself of the interest. Third, the physician can, if possible, position him or herself to qualify for an exception. Below we discuss the economic impact of each of these options.

While the impact on an individual physician may be significant, we do not believe that physicians, in general, will be significantly affected if they have to stop making referrals to an entity in which they have an ownership interest. We come to this conclusion because we assume that the majority of physicians receive most of their income from the services they personally furnish, not from those they refer. In addition, we assume that unless the physician established the entity to serve only his or her own patients, the entity receives referrals from other sources. Thus, the physician may still receive a return on the investment. Further, it is possible that, if physician ownership of entities providing the particular designated health services is prevalent in the area, what may occur is a "shifting" of referrals; that is, the loss of a physician's own referrals to the entity might be offset by other physicians shifting referrals to unrelated entities. These shifts would be acceptable under section 1877, provided they do not result from circumvention schemes.

We do not believe the second option, divesting of the ownership interest, would necessarily have a significant economic effect. However, we assume, that, at least from an economic standpoint, most physicians invest in entities because they are income-producing. If an investment is successful, a physician may not have difficulty finding new investors willing to take over the physician's investment. The physician, in turn, can then invest the monies received in some other investment. We believe the cost of divesting will vary from situation to situation. (A search of the literature on this issue resulted in only anecdotal information that indicated that some physicians sustained a loss in divesting, while others did not.) We do see the possibility of a significant effect in the case of a physician who has, at considerable expense, established an entity to serve only his or her own patients, with the expectation of future return on that investment. We believe, however, that the exceptions in the statute and regulation allowing physicians to refer within their own practices (primarily the in-office ancillary services exception) will greatly reduce the number of physicians otherwise subject to the prohibition.

It is difficult to estimate how many physicians would select the third option of changing the circumstances of their practices in order to meet an exception to the referral prohibition. It is also difficult to estimate the extent of the changes that would be necessary or the potential economic impact of any modifications. As an example of one modification, a physician maintains with other independently-practicing physicians a nonrural facility for furnishing X-rays. The physicians share premises, equipment, employees, and overhead costs. If an individual physician does not meet the requirements for the in-office ancillary exception found in section 1877(b)(2), the physician's Medicare referrals to that entity would be prohibited. In such a situation, as an alternative to options 1 and 2 above (stopping referrals or divesting), the physician could choose to form a group practice with the other physicians in order to qualify for the in-office ancillary services exception. By forming a group practice, the referrals would not be prohibited if the services were furnished personally by the referring physician, personally by another physician who is a member of the same group practice as the referring physician, or if they are furnished personally by individuals who are directly supervised by any of these physicians and the billing and location requirements specified in the in-office ancillary exception are met.

Although we realize that a physician reorganizing his or her practice in this way may be subject to various economic and noneconomic effects, we believe those effects will differ widely from case to case. Some physicians may need to make major alterations in their practices, while others may need only minor changes, with minimal or no help from legal or financial advisors. It is possible that some physicians would profit from reorganizing, while others might suffer losses. Thus, we cannot

1718 Federal Register / Vol. 63, No. 6 / Friday, January 9, 1998 / Proposed Rules

judge whether any particular physician, or physicians in general, will sustain a significant economic impact because they have reconfigured their practices.

Compensation arrangements: The statute defines a compensation arrangement very broadly as any arrangement involving any remuneration between a physician (or an immediate family member) and an entity, with certain narrowly defined exceptions. We believe that this definition involves almost every situation in which a physician or relative receives payment from an entity or makes payments to an entity, including payments under personal services contracts, employment agreements, sales contracts, and rentals or leases. The amount of data we would need to account for every compensation arrangement that might be affected by the law would likely be overwhelming, as well as subject to the constant changes inherent in the business world. As a result, it is difficult for us to assess how many physicians (or their relatives) are currently involved in compensation arrangements.

We believe that most physicians who have compensation, rather than ownership, arrangements with an entity and are receiving fair payments will qualify for one of the many compensation-related exceptions set forth in this proposed rule, especially since we propose to exercise our authority to create several additional exceptions related to compensation. We expect that those who do not will be few in number, and, thus, this rule would not have an impact on a substantial number of physicians whose financial relationships are based on compensation.

2. Entities, Including Hospitals

We lack the data to determine the number of entities that would be affected by this proposed rule. However, even if we were to assume that a substantial number of entities would be affected, we do not believe that, in general, the impact would be significant. In order for the effect on a substantial number of entities to be significant, this rule would have to result in a very significant decline in utilization of the designated health services. The statute was enacted to curb an abusive practice: the ordering by some physicians of unnecessary services because they have a financial incentive to do so. We do not believe, however, that the abuse is so prevalent that the survival of entities would be threatened because a physician's financial incentive to make referrals is removed. It is our view that most health care entities exist because they provide medically necessary services and that these services will continue to be furnished.

In addition, the statute contains a number of exceptions to the referral prohibition that will allow physicians to continue to refer to any entity furnishing designated health services if certain criteria are met. These exceptions are set forth in this proposed rule. For example, § 411.356(c) includes exceptions for ownership or investment interests in certain hospitals or in certain rural entities. Sections 411.357(c) and (d) include relevant exceptions related to compensation arrangements: Paragraph (c) provides an exception for bona fide employment relationships that meet certain conditions, and paragraph (d) provides an exception for remuneration for personal service arrangements that meet certain conditions. Also, this proposed rule would provide an additional exception for any compensation that is, among other things, based on fair market value. We believe many, if not most, of the financial relationships between physicians and entities, including hospitals, are covered by these exceptions.

C. Conclusion

For the reasons stated above, we have determined, and the Secretary certifies, that, based on the limited data currently available to us, this proposed rule would not result in a significant economic impact on a substantial number of small entities or on the operations of a substantial number of small rural hospitals. In addition, for purposes of the Unfunded Mandates Reform Act, we believe that any significant economic results of this proposed rule originate from the general referral prohibition in the statute and not from an agency mandate. We have, in fact, liberalized the requirements in the law by adding new exceptions. In the relatively few instances in which we have added additional requirements, as authorized by the statute, our data is too limited for us to ascertain whether these new provisions alone may result in the expenditure by State, local, and tribal governments, in the aggregate, or by the private sector, of $100 million or more in any one year. In terms of requirements on State governments, it is the statute that applies aspects of the referral prohibition to State Medicaid agencies. This proposed rule does interpret the statute to apply the reporting requirements in section 1877(f) of the Act to States, but does not mandate any action. The proposed rule allows States to collect financial information from Medicaid providers in any form, manner, and at whatever times they choose.

In accordance with the provisions of Executive Order 12866, this regulation was reviewed by the Office of Management and Budget.

VI. Collection of Information Requirements

Under the Paperwork Reduction Act of 1995, we are required to provide 60-day notice in the **Federal Register** and solicit public comment before a collection of information requirement is submitted to the Office of Management and Budget (OMB) for review and approval. In order to fairly evaluate whether an information collection should be approved by OMB, section 3506(c)(2)(A) of the Paperwork Reduction Act of 1995 requires that we solicit comment on the following issues:

• The need for the information collection and its usefulness in carrying out the proper functions of our agency.

• The accuracy of our estimate of the information collection burden.

• The quality, utility, and clarity of the information to be collected.

• Recommendations to minimize the information collection burden on the affected public, including automated collection techniques.

Sections 411.360 and 411.361 of this proposed rule contain information collection requirements that are subject to the Paperwork Reduction Act of 1995. However, we are not requiring the public to comply with these reporting requirements at this time. Instead we are seeking public comment to determine possible methods of implementing these information collection and recordkeeping requirements. Once we have determined how to impose these requirements in the least burdensome method, while meeting program requirements, we will publish a separate 60-day notice in the **Federal Register** seeking comments on the proposed information collection before it is submitted to OMB for review.

Below is a discussion of the information collection requirements referenced in §§ 411.360 and 411.361.

As stated earlier in this preamble, a number of entities have pointed out to us that the amounts of data they are required to report under the statute as reflected in our current regulations will, in some circumstances, be overwhelming and perhaps almost impossible to acquire. Therefore, in order to make the reporting requirements more manageable, we intend to develop a streamlined "reporting" system that does not require entities to retain and submit large quantities of data. We believe, however, that entities should retain enough records to demonstrate, in the event of an audit, that they have correctly determined that particular relationships are excepted under the law.

We are proposing to limit the information that an entity must acquire, retain and, at some later point, possibly submit to us. We would include only those records covering information that the entity knows or should know about, in the course of prudently conducting business, including records that the entity is already required to retain to meet Internal Revenue Service and Security Exchange Commission rules, and other rules under the Medicare or Medicaid programs. We are circumscribing these records under the Secretary's discretion in section 1877(f) to ask entities to provide information in such form, manner, and at such times as the Secretary specifies. As stated above, when we develop a form for reporting information to us, we plan to first publish it as a proposed notice in order to receive public comment. If we later find that this plan is inadequate and elect to change the scope of the requirement, we will provide entities with adequate notice to comply.

While we are not at this time proposing to impose reporting requirements, we do propose to make modifications to the existing information collection requirements referenced in this proposed rule. Existing § 411.361 reflects the reporting requirements in section 1877(f) of the Act. Specifically, § 411.361 requires, with certain exceptions, that all entities furnishing services for which payment may be made under Medicare submit information to us concerning their financial relationships (as described in § 411.361(d)). The requirement does not apply to entities that furnish 20 or fewer Part A and Part B services during a calendar year, or to designated health services furnished outside the United States. Paragraph (a) of § 411.361 requires that all entities furnishing services for which payment may be made under Medicare submit information to us concerning their financial relationships in the form, manner, and at the times we specify. We would revise this to add that this information must be submitted on a HCFA-prescribed form. As stated above, this form would first be published as a proposed notice in order to receive public comment.

Paragraph (c) of § 411.361 requires that the entity submit information that includes at least the following with regard to each physician who has, or whose immediate family member has, a financial relationship with the entity: The name and unique physician identification number (UPIN) of the physician, the covered services furnished by the entity, and the nature of the financial relationship. We now propose to specify that the entity submit information that may include the information described above depending upon the process we select.

Existing § 411.361(d) provides that a reportable financial relationship is any ownership or investment interest or any compensation arrangement, as described in section 1877 of the Act. This proposed, would revise this section to specify that a financial relationship is any ownership or investment interest or any compensation arrangement, as defined in § 411.351, including those relationships excepted under §§ 411.355 through 411.357.

We would also revise existing § 411.361(e) as follows. Currently that paragraph requires that an entity provide updated information within 60 days from the date of any change in the submitted information. We propose to require instead that an entity report to HCFA once a year all changes in the submitted information that occurred in the previous 12 months.

OBRA '93 amended section 1903 of the Act by adding a new paragraph(s) that, among other things, applied the reporting requirements of 1877(f) to a provider of a designated health service for which payment may be made under Medicaid in the same manner as those requirements apply to a Medicare provider. Therefore, at § 455.109(a) of this proposed rule, we would specify that the Medicaid agency must require that each provider of services that furnishes designated health services that are covered by Medicaid submit information to the Medicaid agency concerning their financial relationships in such form, manner, and at such times as the agency specifies. Paragraph (c) of § 445.109 would specify that the entity submit the same information identified with regard to Medicare providers/suppliers except that, instead of the UPIN, the entity would report the Medicaid State Specific Identifier of each physician who has, or whose immediate relative has, a financial relationship with the entity. Paragraph (d) of § 445.109 would establish the same definition of what constitutes a reportable financial relationship as under Medicare, and paragraph (e) would give States the discretion to establish the timeframes within which providers must submit and update information. We solicit comments on these proposed changes to the existing reporting requirements.

This proposed rule would also retain existing § 411.360, which requires that a group practice that wants to be identified as such submit a written statement to its carrier annually to attest that it meets the "substantially all" test, one of the criteria that qualifies a group of physicians as a group practice (the criteria are set forth under the definition of a group practice in § 411.351). This provision would now apply to any group of physicians who refer for or furnish designated health services and who wish to qualify as a group practice. We believe that, since this requirement has already been established by the August 1995 final rule, a significant number of physician groups may already be subject to the reporting requirements. We base this conclusion on the fact that many groups have their own clinical laboratories and will already be prepared to attest for purposes of complying with the final regulation covering referrals for clinical laboratory services. Once a group is identified as a group practice for purposes of laboratory services, it is identified as a group practice for all services. Thus it was the August 1995 final rule that established the burden for those groups. However, we have no way of estimating how many other groups of physicians will want to try to qualify as group practices exclusively for purposes of referring for some or all of the other designated health services. We specifically solicit information on this issue. A group of physicians must submit the attestation required by § 411.360 within 60 days after receiving attestation instructions from its carrier.

If you comment on these information collection and recordkeeping requirements, please mail copies directly to the following:

Health Care Financing Administration, Office of Financial and Human Resources, Management Planning and Analysis Staff, Attention: HCFA–1809–P, Room C2–26–17, 7500 Security Boulevard, Baltimore, MD 21244–1850.

Office of Information and Regulatory Affairs, Office of Management and Budget, Room 10235, New Executive Office Building, Washington, DC 20503, Attn: Allison Herron Eydt, HCFA Desk Officer.

VII. Response to Comments

Because of the large number of items of correspondence we normally receive on a proposed rule, we are not able to acknowledge or respond to them individually. We will, however, consider all comments that we receive by the date specified in the DATES section of this preamble and, if we

Federal Register / Vol. 63, No. 6 / Friday, January 9, 1998 / Proposed Rules

proceed with a final rule, we will respond to the comments in the preamble of the final rule. We will also respond, in that final rule, to comments that we received on the August 1995 final rule with comment covering referrals for clinical laboratory services.

List of Subjects

42 CFR Part 411

Kidney diseases, Medicare, Physician referral, Reporting and recordkeeping requirements.

42 CFR Part 424

Emergency medical services, Health facilities, Health professions, Medicare.

42 CFR Part 435

Aid to Families with Dependent Children, Grant programs-health, Medicaid, Reporting and recordkeeping requirements, Supplemental Security Income (SSI), Wages.

42 CFR Part 455

Fraud, Grant programs-health, Health facilities, Health professions, Investigations, Medicaid, Reporting and recordkeeping requirements.

42 CFR chapter IV would be amended as set forth below:

PART 411—EXCLUSIONS FROM MEDICARE AND LIMITATIONS ON MEDICARE PAYMENT

A. Part 411 is amended as follows:
1. The authority citation for part 411 continues to read as follows:

Authority: Secs. 1102 and 1871 of the Social Security Act (42 U.S.C. 1302 and 1395hh).

2. In § 411.1, paragraph (a) is revised to read as follows:

§ 411.1 Basis and scope.

(a) *Statutory basis.* Sections 1814(a) and 1835(a) of the Act require that a physician certify or recertify a patient's need for home health services, but in general, prohibit a physician from certifying or recertifying the need for services if the services will be furnished by a home health agency in which the physician has a significant ownership interest, or with which the physician has a significant financial or contractual relationship. Sections 1814(c), 1835(d), and 1862 of the Act exclude from Medicare payment certain specified services. The Act provides special rules for payment of services furnished by Federal providers or agencies (sections 1814(c) and 1835(d)), by hospitals and physicians outside the United States (sections 1814(f) and 1862(a)(4)), and by hospitals and SNFs of the Indian Health Service (section 1880). Section 1877 sets

forth limitations on referrals and payment for designated health services furnished by entities with which the referring physician (or an immediate family member of the referring physician) has a financial relationship.

*   *   *   *   *

3. In § 411.350, paragraphs (a) and (c) are revised, and paragraph (b) is republished, to read as follows:

§ 411.350 Scope of subpart.

(a) This subpart implements section 1877 of the Act, which generally prohibits a physician from making a referral under Medicare for designated health services to an entity with which the physician or a member of the physician's immediate family has a financial relationship.

(b) This subpart does not provide for exceptions or immunity from civil or criminal prosecution or other sanctions applicable under any State laws or under Federal law other than section 1877 of the Act. For example, although a particular arrangement involving a physician's financial relationship with an entity may not prohibit the physician from making referrals to the entity under this subpart, the arrangement may nevertheless violate another provision of the Act or other laws administered by HHS, the Federal Trade Commission, the Securities and Exchange Commission, the Internal Revenue Service, or any other Federal or State agency.

(c) This subpart requires, with some exceptions, that certain entities furnishing covered services under Part A or Part B report information concerning their ownership, investment, or compensation arrangements in the form, manner, and at the times specified by HCFA.

4. Section 411.351 is revised to read as follows:

§ 411.351 Definitions.

As used in this subpart, unless the context indicates otherwise:

Clinical laboratory services means the biological, microbiological, serological, chemical, immunohematological, hematological, biophysical, cytological, pathological, or other examination of materials derived from the human body for the purpose of providing information for the diagnosis, prevention, or treatment of any disease or impairment of, or the assessment of the health of, human beings. These examinations also include procedures to determine, measure, or otherwise describe the presence or absence of various substances or organisms in the body.

Compensation arrangement means any arrangement involving any

remuneration, direct or indirect, between a physician (or a member of a physician's immediate family) and an entity.

Designated health services means any of the following services (other than those provided as emergency physician services furnished outside of the United States), as they are defined in this section:

(1) Clinical laboratory services.
(2) Physical therapy services.
(3) Occupational therapy services.
(4) Radiology services and radiation therapy services and supplies.
(5) Durable medical equipment and supplies.
(6) Parenteral and enteral nutrients, equipment, and supplies.
(7) Prosthetics, orthotics, and prosthetic devices and supplies.
(8) Home health services.
(9) Outpatient prescription drugs.
(10) Inpatient and outpatient hospital services.

Direct supervision means supervision by a physician who is present in the office suite in which the services are being furnished, throughout the time they are being furnished, and immediately available to provide assistance and direction. "Present in the office suite" means that the physician is actually physically present. However, the physician is still considered "present" during brief unexpected absences as well as during routine absences of a short duration (such as during a lunch break), provided the absences occur during time periods in which the physician is otherwise scheduled and ordinarily expected to be present and the absences do not conflict with any other requirements in the Medicare program for a particular level of physician supervision.

Durable medical equipment has the meaning given in section 1861(n) of the Act and § 414.202 of this chapter.

Employee means any individual who, under the usual common law rules that apply in determining the employer-employee relationship (as applied for purposes of section 3121(d)(2) of the Internal Revenue Code of 1986), is considered to be employed by, or an employee of, an entity. (Application of these common law rules is discussed at 20 CFR 404.1007 and 26 CFR 31.3121(d)–1(c).)

Enteral nutrients, equipment, and supplies means items and supplies needed to provide enteral nutrition to a patient with a functioning gastrointestinal tract who, due to pathology to or nonfunction of the structures that normally permit food to reach the digestive tract, cannot maintain weight and strength

Federal Register / Vol. 63, No. 6 / Friday, January 9, 1998 / Proposed Rules 1721

commensurate with his or her general condition, as described in section 65–10 of the Medicare Coverage Issues Manual (HCFA Pub. 6).

Entity means a physician's sole practice or a practice of multiple physicians that provides for the furnishing of designated health services, or any other sole proprietorship, trust, corporation, partnership, foundation, not-for-profit corporation, or unincorporated association.

Fair market value means the value in arm's-length transactions, consistent with the general market value. "General market value" means the price that an asset would bring, as the result of bona fide bargaining between well-informed buyers and sellers, or the compensation that would be included in a service agreement, as the result of bona fide bargaining between well-informed parties to the agreement, on the date of acquisition of the asset or at the time of the service agreement. Usually the fair market price is the price at which bona fide sales have been consummated for assets of like type, quality, and quantity in a particular market at the time of acquisition, or the compensation that has been included in bona fide service agreements with comparable terms at the time of the agreement. With respect to the rentals and leases described in § 411.357(a) and (b), *fair market value* means the value of rental property for general commercial purposes (not taking into account its intended use). In the case of a lease of space, this value may not be adjusted to reflect the additional value the prospective lessee or lessor would attribute to the proximity or convenience to the lessor when the lessor is a potential source of patient referrals to the lessee.

Financial relationship means a direct or indirect ownership or investment interest (including an option or nonvested interest) in any entity that exists through equity, debt, or other means and includes any indirect ownership or investment interest no matter how many levels removed from a direct interest (for example, a financial relationship in an entity furnishing designated health services exists if the individual has an ownership or investment interest in an entity that holds an ownership or investment interest in an entity that furnishes designated health services), or a compensation arrangement with an entity.

Group practice means a group of two or more physicians, legally organized as a single partnership, professional corporation, foundation, not-for-profit corporation, faculty practice plan, or similar association, with the exception

that a group can consist of physicians who are also individually incorporated as professional corporations. To qualify as a group practice, a group must meet the following conditions:

(1) Each physician who is a *member of the group*, as defined in this section, furnishes substantially the full range of patient care services that the physician routinely furnishes, including medical care, consultation, diagnosis, and treatment, through the joint use of shared office space, facilities, equipment, and personnel.

(2) Except as provided in paragraphs (2)(i) and (2)(ii) of this definition, substantially all of the patient care services of the physicians who are members of the group (that is, at least 75 percent of the total patient care services of the group practice members) are furnished through the group and billed under a billing number assigned to the group and the amounts received are treated as receipts of the group. "Patient care services" are measured by the total patient care time each member spends on these services (for example, if a physician practices 40 hours a week and spends 30 hours on patient care services for a group practice, the physician has spent 75 percent of his or her time providing countable patient care services).

(i) The "substantially all" test does not apply to any group practice that is located solely in an HPSA, as defined in this section.

(ii) For group practices located outside of an HPSA (as defined in this section) any time spent by group practice members providing services in an HPSA should not be used to calculate whether the group practice located outside the HPSA has met the "substantially all" test, regardless of whether the members' time in the HPSA is spent in a group practice, clinic, or office setting.

(3) The overhead expenses of and income from the practice are distributed according to methods that are determined prior to the time period during which the group has earned the income or incurred the costs.

(4) The overhead expenses of and the income from the practice are distributed according to methods that indicate that the practice is a unified business. That is, the methods must reflect centralized decision making, a pooling of expenses and revenues, and a distribution system that is not based on each satellite office operating as if it were a separate enterprise.

(5) No physician who is a member of the group directly or indirectly receives compensation based on the volume or value of referrals by the physician,

except that a physician in a group practice may be paid a share of overall profits of the group or a productivity bonus based on services he or she has personally performed or services incident to these personally performed services, as long as the share or bonus is not determined in any manner that is directly related to the volume or value of referrals by the physician.

(6) Members of the group personally conduct no less that 75 percent of the physician-patient encounters of the group practice.

(7) In the case of faculty practice plans associated with a hospital, institution of higher education, or medical school that has an approved medical residency training program in which faculty practice plan physicians perform specialty and professional services, both within and outside the faculty practice, as well as perform other tasks such as research, this definition applies only to those services that are furnished within the faculty practice plan.

Home health services means the services described in section 1861(m) of the Act and part 409, subpart E of this chapter.

Hospital means any entity that qualifies as a "hospital" under section 1861(e) of the Act, as a "psychiatric hospital" under section 1861(f) of the Act, or as a "rural primary care hospital" under section 1861(mm)(1) of the Act, and refers to any separate legally-organized operating entity plus any subsidiary, related entity, or other entities that perform services for the hospital's patients and for which the hospital bills. However, a "hospital" does not include entities that perform services for hospital patients "under arrangements" with the hospital.

HPSA means, for purposes of this subpart, an area designated as a health professional shortage area under section 332(a)(1)(A) of the Public Health Service Act for primary medical care professionals (in accordance with the criteria specified in 42 CFR part 5, appendix A, Part I-Geographic Areas). In addition, with respect to dental, mental health, vision care, podiatric, and pharmacy services, an HPSA means an area designated as a health professional shortage area under section 332(a)(1)(A) of the Public Health Service Act for dental professionals, mental health professionals, vision care professionals, podiatric professionals, and pharmacy professionals, respectively.

Immediate family member or member of a physician's immediate family means husband or wife; natural or adoptive parent, child, or sibling; stepparent, stepchild, stepbrother, or stepsister; father-in-law, mother-in-law, son-in-law, daughter-in-law, brother-in-law, or sister-in-law; grandparent or grandchild; and spouse of a grandparent or grandchild.

Inpatient hospital services are those services defined in section 1861(b) of the Act and § 409.10(a) and (b) of this chapter, and include inpatient psychiatric hospital services listed in section 1861(c) of the Act and inpatient rural primary care hospital services, as defined in section 1861(mm)(2) of the Act. "Inpatient hospital services" do not include emergency inpatient services provided by a hospital located outside the United States and covered under the authority in section 1814(f)(2) of the Act and part 424, subpart H of this chapter and emergency inpatient services provided by a nonparticipating hospital within the United States, as authorized by section 1814(d) of the Act and described in part 424, subpart G of this chapter. These services also do not include dialysis furnished by a hospital that is not certified to provide end stage renal dialysis (ESRD) services under subpart U of 42 CFR 405.

Inpatient hospital services include services that a hospital provides for its patients that are furnished either by the hospital or by others under arrangements with the hospital. They do not encompass the services of other physicians, physician assistants, nurse practitioners, clinical nurse specialists, certified nurse midwives, and certified registered nurse anesthetists and qualified psychologists who bill independently.

Laboratory means an entity furnishing biological, microbiological, serological, chemical, immunohematological, hematological, biophysical, cytological, pathological, or other examination of materials derived from the human body for the purpose of providing information for the diagnosis, prevention, or treatment of any disease or impairment of, or the assessment of the health of, human beings. These examinations also include procedures to determine, measure, or otherwise describe the presence or absence of various substances or organisms in the body. Entities only collecting or preparing specimens (or both) or only serving as a mailing service and not performing testing are not considered laboratories.

Members of the group means physician partners and other physician owners (including physicians whose interest is held by an individual professional corporation), and full-time and part-time physician employees. These physicians are "members" during the time they furnish "patient care services" to the group.

Occupational therapy services means those services described at section 1861(g) of the Act and § 410.100(c) of this chapter. Occupational therapy services also include any other services with the characteristics described in § 410.100(c) that are covered under Medicare Part A or B, regardless of who furnishes them, the location in which they are furnished, or how they are billed.

Orthotics means leg, arm, back, and neck braces, as listed in section 1861(s)(9) of the Act.

Outpatient hospital services means the therapeutic, diagnostic, and partial hospitalization services listed under section 1861(s)(2)(B) and (C) of the Act; outpatient services furnished by a psychiatric hospital, as defined in section 1861(f); and outpatient rural primary care hospital services, as defined in section 1861(mm)(3); but excluding emergency services covered in nonparticipating hospitals under the conditions described in section 1835(b) of the Act and subpart G of part 424 of this chapter.

Outpatient prescription drugs means those drugs (including biologicals) defined or listed under section 1861(t) and (s) of the Act and part 410 of this chapter, that a patient can obtain from a pharmacy with a prescription (even if the patient can only receive the drug under medical supervision), and that are furnished to an individual under Medicare Part B, but excluding erythropoietin and other drugs furnished as part of a dialysis treatment for an individual who dialyzes at home or in a facility.

Parenteral nutrients, equipment, and supplies means those items and supplies needed to provide nutriment to a patient with permanent, severe pathology of the alimentary tract that does not allow absorption of sufficient nutrients to maintain strength commensurate with the patient's general condition, as described in section 65–10 of the Medicare Coverage Issues Manual (HCFA Pub. 6).

Patient care services means any tasks performed by a group practice member that address the medical needs of specific patients or patients in general, regardless of whether they involve direct patient encounters, or tasks that generally benefit a particular practice. They can include, for example, the services of physicians who do not directly treat patients, such as time spent by a physician consulting with other physicians or reviewing laboratory tests, or time spent training staff members, arranging for equipment, or performing administrative or management tasks.

Physical therapy services means those outpatient physical therapy services (including speech-language pathology services) described at section 1861(p) of the Act and at § 410.100(b) and (d) of this chapter. Physical therapy services also include any other services with the characteristics described in § 400.100(b) and (d) that are covered under Medicare Part A or B, regardless of who provides them, the location in which they are provided, or how they are billed.

Physician incentive plan means any compensation arrangement between an entity and a physician or physician group that may directly or indirectly have the effect of reducing or limiting services furnished with respect to individuals enrolled with the entity.

Plan of care means the establishment by a physician of a course of diagnosis or treatment (or both) for a particular patient, including the ordering of services.

Prosthetic device and supplies: *Prosthetic device* means a device (other than a dental device) listed in section 1861(s)(8) that replaces all or part of an internal body organ, including colostomy bags and including one pair of conventional eyeglasses or contact lenses furnished subsequent to each cataract surgery with insertion of an intraocular lens. *Prosthetic supplies* are supplies that are necessary for the effective use of a prosthetic device (including supplies directly related to colostomy care).

Prosthetics means artificial legs, arms, and eyes, as described in section 1861(s)(9) of the Act.

Radiology services and radiation therapy and supplies means any diagnostic test or therapeutic procedure using X-rays, ultrasound or other imaging services, computerized axial tomography, magnetic resonance imaging, radiation, or nuclear medicine, and diagnostic mammography services, as covered under section 1861(s)(3) and (4) of the Act and §§ 410.32(a), 410.34, and 410.35 of this chapter, including the professional component of these services, but excluding any invasive radiology procedure in which the imaging modality is used to guide a needle, probe, or a catheter accurately.

Referral—

(1) Means either of the following:

(i) Except as provided in paragraph (2) of this definition, the request by a physician for, or ordering of, or the certifying or recertifying of the need for, any designated health service for which payment may be made under Medicare Part B (or, for purposes of the Medicaid program, a comparable service covered under the Medicaid State plan), including a request for a consultation with another physician and any test or procedure ordered by or to be performed by (or under the supervision of) that other physician.

(ii) Except as provided in paragraph (2) of this definition, a request by a physician that includes the provision of any other designated health service for which payment may be made under Medicare (or, for purposes of the Medicaid program, a comparable service covered under the Medicaid State plan) the establishment of a plan of care by a physician that includes the provision of such a designated health service, or the certifying or recertifying of the need for such a designated health service.

(2) Does not include a request by a pathologist for clinical diagnostic laboratory tests and pathological examination services, by a radiologist for diagnostic radiology services, and by a radiation oncologist for radiation therapy, if—

(i) The request results from a consultation initiated by another physician; and

(ii) The tests or services are furnished by or under the supervision of the pathologist, radiologist, or radiation oncologist.

Referring physician means a physician who makes a referral as defined in this section.

Remuneration means any payment, discount, forgiveness of debt, or other benefit made directly or indirectly, overtly or covertly, in cash or in kind, except that the following are not considered remuneration:

(1) The forgiveness of amounts owed for inaccurate tests or procedures, mistakenly performed tests or procedures, or the correction of minor billing errors.

(2) The furnishing of items, devices, or supplies that are used solely to collect, transport, process, or store specimens for the entity furnishing the items, devices, or supplies or are used solely to order or communicate the results of tests or procedures for the entity.

(3) A payment made by an insurer or a self-insured plan to a physician to satisfy a claim, submitted on a fee-for-service basis, for the furnishing of health services by that physician to an individual who is covered by a policy with the insurer or by the self-insured plan, if—

(i) The health services are not furnished, and the payment is not made, under a contract or other arrangement between the insurer or the plan and the physician;

(ii) The payment is made to the physician on behalf of the covered

individual and would otherwise be made directly to the individual; and

(iii) The amount of the payment is set in advance, does not exceed fair market value, and is not determined in a manner that takes into account directly or indirectly the volume or value of any referrals or other business generated between the parties.

Transaction: A *transaction* is an instance or process of two or more persons or entities doing business. An *isolated transaction* is one involving a single payment between two or more persons or entities. A transaction that involves long-term or installment payments is not considered an isolated transaction.

5. Section 411.353 is revised to read as follows:

§ 411.353 Prohibition on certain referrals by physicians and limitations on billing.

(a) *Prohibition on referrals.* Except as provided in this subpart, a physician who has a financial relationship with an entity, or who has an immediate family member who has a financial relationship with the entity, may not make a referral to that entity for the furnishing of designated health services for which payment otherwise may be made under Medicare.

(b) *Limitations on billing.* An entity that furnishes designated health services under a referral that is prohibited by paragraph (a) of this section may not present or cause to be presented a claim or bill to the Medicare program or to any individual, third party payer, or other entity for the designated health services performed under that referral.

(c) *Denial of payment.* No Medicare payment may be made for a designated health service that is furnished under a prohibited referral.

(d) *Refunds.* An entity that collects payment for a designated health service that was performed under a prohibited referral must refund all collected amounts on a timely basis, as defined in § 1003.101 of Chapter V.

6. Section 411.355 is revised to read as follows:

§ 411.355 General exceptions to the referral prohibition related to both ownership/investment and compensation.

The prohibition on referrals set forth in § 411.353 does not apply to the following types of services:

(a) *Physician services,* as defined in § 410.20(a), that are furnished personally by (or under the personal supervision of) another physician in the same group practice as the referring physician.

(b) *In-office ancillary services.* Services (including infusion pumps and

crutches, but excluding all other durable medical equipment and parenteral and enteral nutrients, equipment, and supplies), that meet the following conditions:

(1) They are furnished personally by one of the following individuals:

(i) The referring physician.

(ii) A physician who is a member of the same group practice as the referring physician.

(iii) Individuals who are directly supervised by the referring physician or, in the case of group practices, by another physician member of the same group practice as the referring physician.

(2) They are furnished in one of the following locations:

(i) The same building in which the referring physician (or another physician who is a member of the same group practice) furnishes physician services unrelated to the furnishing of designated health services. The "same building" means the same physical structure, with one address, and not multiple structures connected by tunnels or walkways.

(ii) A building that is used by the group practice for the provision of some or all of the group's clinical laboratory services.

(iii) A building that is used by the group practice for the centralized provision of the group's designated health services (other than clinical laboratory services).

(3) They are billed by one of the following:

(i) The physician performing or supervising the service.

(ii) The group practice of which the performing or supervising physician is a member under a billing number assigned to the group practice.

(iii) An entity that is wholly owned by the physician or the physician's group practice.

(4) In the case of crutches, the physician realizes no direct or indirect profit from furnishing the crutches.

(c) *Services furnished to prepaid health plan enrollees* by one of the following organizations:

(1) An HMO or a CMP in accordance with a contract with HCFA under section 1876 of the Act and part 417, subparts J through M of this chapter.

(2) A health care prepayment plan in accordance with an agreement with HCFA under section 1833(a)(1)(A) of the Act and part 417, subpart U of this chapter.

(3) An organization that is receiving payments on a prepaid basis for Medicare enrollees through a demonstration project under section 402(a) of the Social Security

Amendments of 1967 (42 U.S.C. 1395b-1) or under section 222(a) of the Social Security Amendments of 1972 (42 U.S.C. 1395b-1 note).

(4) A qualified health maintenance organization (within the meaning of section 1310(d) of the Public Health Service Act).

(d) *Services furnished under certain payment rates.* (1) Services furnished in an ambulatory surgical center (ASC) or ESRD facility or by a hospice if payment for those services is included in the ASC payment rate, the ESRD composite payment rate, or as part of the hospice payment rate, respectively; and

(2) Services furnished under other payment rates that the Secretary determines provide no financial incentive for under or overutilization, or any other risk of program or patient abuse.

7. Section 411.356 is revised to read as follows:

§ 411.356 Exceptions to the referral prohibition related to ownership or investment interests.

For purposes of § 411.353, the following ownership or investment interests do not constitute a financial relationship:

(a) *Publicly-traded securities.* Ownership of investment securities (including shares or bonds, debentures, notes, or other debt instruments) that at the time they were obtained could be purchased on the open market and that meet the requirements of paragraphs (a)(1) and (a)(2) of this section.

(1) They are either—

(i) Listed for trading on the New York Stock Exchange, the American Stock Exchange, or any regional exchange in which quotations are published on a daily basis, or foreign securities listed on a recognized foreign, national, or regional exchange in which quotations are published on a daily basis, or

(ii) Traded under an automated interdealer quotation system operated by the National Association of Securities Dealers.

(2) They are in a corporation that had stockholder equity exceeding $75 million at the end of the corporation's most recent fiscal year or on average during the previous 3 fiscal years. "Stockholder equity" is the difference in value between a corporation's total assets and total liabilities.

(b) *Mutual funds.* Ownership of shares in a regulated investment company as defined in section 851(a) of the Internal Revenue Code of 1986, if the company had, at the end of its most recent fiscal year, or on average during the previous 3 fiscal years, total assets exceeding $75 million.

(c) *Specific providers.* Ownership or investment interest in the following entities, for purposes of the services specified:

(1) A rural provider, in the case of designated health services furnished in a rural area by the provider. A "rural provider" is an entity that furnishes substantially all (not less than 75 percent) of the designated health services that it furnishes to residents of a rural area (that is, an area that is not an urban area as defined in § 412.62(f)(1)(ii) of this chapter).

(2) A hospital that is located in Puerto Rico, in the case of designated health services furnished by such a hospital.

(3) A hospital that is located outside of Puerto Rico, in the case of designated health services furnished by such a hospital, if the referring physician is authorized to perform services at the hospital, and the physician's ownership or investment interest is in the entire hospital and not merely in a distinct part or department of the hospital.

8. Section 411.357 is revised to read as follows:

§ 411.357 Exceptions to the referral prohibition related to compensation arrangements.

For purposes of § 411.353, the following compensation arrangements do not constitute a financial relationship:

(a) *Rental of office space.* Payments for the use of office space made by a lessee to a lessor if there is a rental or lease agreement that meets the following requirements:

(1) The agreement is set out in writing, is signed by the parties, and specifies the premises it covers.

(2) The term of the agreement is at least 1 year.

(3) The space rented or leased does not exceed that which is reasonable and necessary for the legitimate business purposes of the lease or rental and is used exclusively by the lessee when being used by the lessee, except that the lessee may make payments for the use of space consisting of common areas if the payments do not exceed the lessee's pro rata share of expenses for the space based upon the ratio of the space used exclusively by the lessee to the total amount of space (other than common areas) occupied by all persons using the common areas.

(4) The rental charges over the term of the agreement are set in advance and are consistent with fair market value.

(5) The charges are not determined in a manner that takes into account the volume or value of any referrals or other business generated between the parties.

(6) The agreement would be commercially reasonable even if no

referrals were made between the lessee and the lessor.

(b) *Rental of equipment.* Payments made by a lessee to a lessor for the use of equipment under the following conditions:

(1) A rental or lease agreement is set out in writing, is signed by the parties, and specifies the equipment it covers.

(2) The equipment rented or leased does not exceed that which is reasonable and necessary for the legitimate business purposes of the lease or rental and is used exclusively by the lessee when being used by the lessee.

(3) The agreement provides for a term of rental or lease of at least 1 year.

(4) The rental charges over the term of the agreement are set in advance, are consistent with fair market value, and are not determined in a manner that takes into account the volume or value of any referrals or other business generated between the parties.

(5) The agreement would be commercially reasonable even if no referrals were made between the parties.

(c) *Bona fide employment relationships.* Any amount paid by an employer to a physician (or immediate family member) who has a bona fide employment relationship with the employer for the provision of services if the following conditions are met:

(1) The employment is for identifiable services.

(2) The amount of the remuneration under the employment is—

(i) Consistent with the fair market value of the services; and

(ii) Except as provided in paragraph (c)(4) of this section, is not determined in a manner that takes into account (directly or indirectly) the volume or value of any referrals by the referring physician or other business generated between the parties.

(3) The remuneration is provided under an agreement that would be commercially reasonable even if no referrals were made to the employer.

(4) Paragraph (c)(2)(ii) of this section does not prohibit payment of remuneration in the form of a productivity bonus based on services performed personally by the physician (or immediate family member of the physician) if the bonus is not directly related to the volume or value of a physician's own referrals.

(d) *Personal service arrangements*—

(1) *General.* Remuneration from an entity under an arrangement or multiple arrangements to a physician, an immediate family member of the physician, or to a group practice, including remuneration for specific physician services furnished to a

nonprofit blood center, if the following conditions are met:

(i) Each arrangement is set out in writing, is signed by the parties, and specifies the services covered by the arrangement.

(ii) The arrangement(s) covers all of the services to be furnished by the physician (or an immediate family member of the physician) to the entity, and all separate arrangements between the entity and the physician and the entity and any family members incorporate each other by reference. A physician or family member can "furnish" services through employees whom they have hired for the purpose of performing the services.

(iii) The aggregate services contracted for do not exceed those that are reasonable and necessary for the legitimate business purposes of the arrangement(s).

(iv) The term of each arrangement is for at least 1 year.

(v) The compensation to be paid over the term of each arrangement is set in advance, does not exceed fair market value, and, except in the case of a physician incentive plan, is not determined in a manner that takes into account the volume or value of any referrals or other business generated between the parties.

(vi) The services to be furnished under each arrangement do not involve the counseling or promotion of a business arrangement or other activity that violates any State or Federal law.

(2) *Physician incentive plan exception.* In the case of a physician incentive plan between a physician and an entity, the compensation may be determined in a manner (through a withhold, capitation, bonus, or otherwise) that takes into account directly or indirectly the volume or value of any referrals or other business generated between the parties, if the plan meets the following requirements:

(i) No specific payment is made directly or indirectly under the plan to a physician or a physician group as an inducement to reduce or limit medically necessary services furnished with respect to a specific individual enrolled with the entity.

(ii) Upon request by the Secretary, the entity provides the Secretary with access to the information about the plan specified in 417.479(h) of this chapter.

(iii) In the case of a plan that places a physician or a physician group at substantial financial risk as determined by the Secretary under § 417.479(e) and (f) of this chapter, the entity complies with the requirements concerning physician incentive plans set forth at § 417.479(g) and (i).

(e) *Physician recruitment.* Remuneration provided by a hospital to recruit a physician that is intended to induce the physician to relocate to the geographic area served by the hospital in order to become a member of the hospital's medical staff, if all of the following conditions are met:

(1) The arrangement is set out in writing and signed by both parties.

(2) The arrangement is not conditioned on the physician's referral of patients to the hospital.

(3) The hospital does not determine (directly or indirectly) the amount of the remuneration to the physician based on the volume or value of any referrals by the physician or other business generated between the parties.

(4) The physician is not precluded from establishing staff privileges at another hospital or referring business to another entity.

(f) *Isolated transactions.* Isolated financial transactions, such as a one-time sale of property or a practice, if all of the following conditions are met:

(1) The amount of remuneration under the transaction is—

(i) Consistent with the fair market value of the transaction; and

(ii) Not determined in a manner that takes into account (directly or indirectly) the volume or value of any referrals by the referring physician or other business generated between the parties.

(2) The remuneration is provided under an agreement that would be commercially reasonable even if the physician made no referrals.

(3) There are no additional transactions between the parties for 6 months after the isolated transaction, except for transactions that are specifically excepted under the other provisions in §§ 411.355 through 411.357.

(g) *Arrangements with hospitals.* Remuneration provided by a hospital to a physician if the remuneration does not relate, directly or indirectly, to the furnishing of designated health services. To qualify as "unrelated," remuneration must not in any way reflect the volume or value of a physician's referrals.

(h) *Group practice arrangements with a hospital.* An arrangement between a hospital and a group practice under which designated health services are furnished by the group but are billed by the hospital if the following conditions are met:

(1) With respect to services furnished to an inpatient of the hospital, the arrangement is pursuant to the provision of inpatient hospital services under section 1861(b)(3) of the Act.

(2) The arrangement began before, and has continued in effect without interruption since, December 19, 1989.

(3) With respect to the designated health services covered under the arrangement, at least 75 percent of these services furnished to patients of the hospital are furnished by the group under the arrangement.

(4) The arrangement is in accordance with a written agreement that specifies the services to be furnished by the parties and the compensation for services furnished under the agreement.

(5) The compensation paid over the term of the agreement is consistent with fair market value, and the compensation per unit of services is fixed in advance and is not determined in a manner that takes into account the volume or value of any referrals or other business generated between the parties.

(6) The compensation is provided in accordance with an agreement that would be commercially reasonable even if no referrals were made to the entity.

(i) *Payments by a physician.* Payments made by a physician—

(1) To a laboratory in exchange for the provision of clinical laboratory services, or

(2) To an entity as compensation for any other items or services that are furnished at a price that is consistent with fair market value, and that are not specifically excepted under another provision in §§ 411.355 through 411.357. "Services" in this context means services of any kind (not just those defined as "services" for purposes of the Medicare program in § 400.202).

(j) *Discounts.* Any discount made to a physician that is passed on in full to either the patient or the patient's insurers (including Medicare) and that does not enure to the benefit of the referring physician.

(k) *De minimis compensation.* Compensation from an entity in the form of items or services (not including cash or cash equivalents) that does not exceed $50 per gift and an aggregate of $300 per year if—

(1) The entity providing the compensation makes it available to all similarly situated individuals, regardless of whether these individuals refer patients to the entity for services; and

(2) The compensation is not determined in any way that takes into account the volume or value of the physician's referrals to the entity.

(l) *Fair market value compensation.* Compensation resulting from an arrangement between an entity and a physician (or immediate family member) or any group of physicians (regardless of whether the group meets

1726   **Federal Register** / Vol. 63, No. 6 / Friday, January 9, 1998 / Proposed Rules

the definition of a group practice set forth at § 411.351) if the arrangement is set forth in an agreement that meets the following conditions:

(1) It is in writing, signed by the parties, and covers only identifiable items or services, all of which are specified in the agreement. The agreement covers all of the items and services to be provided by the physician and any immediate family member to the entity or, alternatively, cross refers to any other agreements for items or services between these parties.

(2) It specifies the timeframe for the arrangement, which can be for any period of time and contain a termination clause, provided the parties enter into only one arrangement for the same items or services during the course of a year. An arrangement made for less than 1 year may be renewed any number of times if the terms of the arrangement and the compensation for the same items or services do not change.

(3) It specifies the compensation that will be provided under the arrangement. The compensation, or the method for determining the compensation, must be set in advance, be consistent with fair market value, and not be determined in a manner that takes into account the volume or value of any referrals (as defined in § 411.351), payment for referrals for medical services that are not covered under Medicare or Medicaid, or any other business generated between the parties.

(4) It involves a transaction that is commercially reasonable and furthers the legitimate business purposes of the parties.

(5) It meets a safe harbor under the anti-kickback statute or otherwise is in compliance with the anti-kickback provisions in section 1128B(b) of the Act.

9. In § 411.360, paragraphs (a), (b), and (d) are revised to read as set forth below, and paragraphs (c) and (e) are republished.

§ 411.360 Group practice attestation.

(a) Except as provided in paragraph (b) of this section, a group of physicians that wishes to qualify as a group practice (as defined in § 411.351) must submit a written statement to its carrier annually to attest that, during the most recent 12-month period (calendar year, fiscal year, or immediately preceding 12-month period) 75 percent of the total patient care services of group practice members was furnished through the group, was billed under a billing number assigned to the group, and the amounts so received were treated as receipts of the group.

(b) A newly-formed group (one in which physicians have recently begun to practice together) or any group practice that has been unable in the past to meet the requirements of section 1877(h)(4) of the Act or § 411.351, that wishes to qualify as a group practice, must—

(1) Submit a written statement to attest that, during the next 12-month period (calendar year, fiscal year, or next 12 months), it expects to meet the 75 percent standard and will take measures to ensure that the standard is met; and

(2) At the end of the 12-month period, submit a written statement to attest that it met the 75 percent standard during that period, billed for those services under a billing number assigned to the group, and treated amounts received for those services as receipts of the group. If the group did not meet the standard, any Medicare payments made for designated health services furnished by the group during the 12-month period that were conditioned upon the standard being met are overpayments.

(c) Once any group has chosen whether to use its fiscal year, the calendar year, or some other 12-month period, the group practice must adhere to this choice.

(d) The attestation must be signed by an authorized representative of the group practice who is knowledgeable about the group, and must contain a statement that the information furnished in the attestation is true and accurate to the best of the representative's knowledge and belief. Any person filing a false statement will be subject to applicable criminal and/or civil penalties.

(e) A group that intends to meet the definition of a group practice in order to qualify for an exception described in §§ 411.355 through 411.357, must submit the attestation required by paragraph (a) or (b)(1) of this section, as applicable, to its carrier no later than 60 days after receipt of the attestation instructions from its carrier.

10. In § 411.361, paragraphs (a) through (e) are revised to read as set forth below, and paragraphs (f) and (g) are republished.

§ 411.361 Reporting requirements.

(a) *Basic rule.* Except as provided in paragraph (b) of this section, all entities furnishing services for which payment may be made under Medicare must submit information to HCFA concerning their financial relationships (as defined in paragraph (d) of this section), in the form, manner, and at the times that HCFA specifies using an HCFA-prescribed form.

(b) *Exception.* The requirements of paragraph (a) of this section do not apply to entities that furnish 20 or fewer Part A and Part B services during a calendar year, or to any Medicare covered services furnished outside the United States.

(c) *Required information.* The information requested by HCFA can include the following:

(1) The name and unique physician identification number (UPIN) of each physician who has a financial relationship with the entity.

(2) The name and UPIN of each physician who has an immediate relative (as defined in § 411.351) who has a financial relationship with the entity.

(3) The covered services furnished by the entity.

(4) With respect to each physician identified under paragraphs (c)(1) and (c)(2) of this section, the nature of the financial relationship (including the extent and/or value of the ownership or investment interest or the compensation arrangement, if requested by HCFA).

(d) *Reportable financial relationships.* For purposes of this section, a financial relationship is any ownership or investment interest or any compensation arrangement, as defined in § 411.351, including those relationships excepted under §§ 411.355 through 411.357.

(e) *Form and timing of reports.* Entities that are subject to the requirements of this section must submit the required information on a HCFA-prescribed form within the time period specified by the servicing carrier or intermediary. Entities are given at least 30 days from the date of the carrier's or intermediary's request to provide the initial information. Thereafter, an entity must report to HCFA once a year all changes in the submitted information that occurred in the previous 12 months. Entities must retain documentation sufficient to verify the information provided on the forms and, upon request, must make that documentation available to HCFA or the OIG.

(f) *Consequences of failure to report.* Any person who is required, but fails, to submit information concerning his or her financial relationships in accordance with this section is subject to a civil money penalty of up to $10,000 for each day of the period beginning on the day following the applicable deadline established under paragraph (e) of this section until the information is submitted. Assessment of these penalties will comply with the applicable provisions of part 1003 of this title.

(g) *Public disclosure.* Information furnished to HCFA under this section is subject to public disclosure in accordance with the provisions of part 401 of this chapter.

PART 424—CONDITIONS FOR MEDICARE PAYMENT

B. Part 424 is amended as follows:

1. The authority citation for part 424 continues to read as follows:

Authority: Secs. 1102 and 1871 of the Social Security Act (42 U.S.C. 1302 and 1395hh).

2. In § 424.22, paragraph (d) is revised to read as set forth below, and paragraphs (e), (f), and (g) are removed.

§ 424.22   Requirements for home health services.

* * * * *

(d) *Limitation on the performance of certification and plan of treatment functions.* The need for home health services to be provided by an HHA may not be certified or recertified, and a plan of treatment may not be established and reviewed, by any physician who has a financial relationship, as defined in § 411.351 of this chapter, with that HHA, unless the physician's relationship meets one of the exceptions in §§ 411.355 through 411.357 of this chapter.

PART 435—ELIGIBILITY IN THE STATES, DISTRICT OF COLUMBIA, THE NORTHERN MARIANA ISLANDS, AND AMERICAN SAMOA

C. Part 435 is amended as follows:

1. The authority citation for part 435 continues to read as follows:

Authority: Sec. 1102 of the Social Security Act (42 U.S.C. 1302).

2. In § 435.1002, paragraph (a) is revised to read as follows:

§ 435.1002   FFP for services.

(a) Except for the limitations and conditions specified in §§ 435.1007, 435.1008, and 435.1012, FFP is available in expenditures for Medicaid services for all recipients whose coverage is required or allowed under this part.

* * * * *

3. Section 435.1012 is added to subpart K, under an undesignated centered heading, to read as follows:

Limitation on FFP Related to Prohibited Referrals

§ 435.1012   Limitation on FFP related to prohibited referrals.

(a) *Basic rule.* Except as specified in paragraph (b) of this section, no FFP in the State's expenditures for services is

available for expenditures for designated health services (as defined in § 411.351 of this chapter) furnished under the State plan to an individual on the basis of a physician referral that would, if Medicare provided for coverage of the services to the same extent and under the same terms and conditions as under the State plan, result in the denial of Medicare payment for the services under §§ 411.351 through 411.360 of this chapter. (Section 411.353 provides that if a physician (or an immediate family member) has a financial relationship with an entity, the physician may not make a referral to that entity for the furnishing of designated health services for which payment otherwise may be made under Medicare and denies payment for any service furnished under a prohibited referral. Section 411.351 contains definitions, and §§ 411.355 through 411.357 provide exceptions to the prohibition on referrals.) The provisions of this section are based on section 1903(s) of the Act, which applies to Medicaid aspects of the Medicare rules limiting physician referrals.

(b) *Exception for services furnished to enrollees on a predetermined, capitated basis.* The limitation on FFP in paragraph (a) does not apply to services furnished to, or arranged for, an enrollee by an entity with an HMO contract with a State under section 1903(m); a prepaid health plan (PHP) contract with a State under part 434, subpart C; or a health insuring organization (HIO) contract under part 434, subpart D.

(c) *Advisory opinions relating to physician referrals.* Sections 411.370 through 411.389 cover the procedures for obtaining an advisory opinion from HCFA on whether a physician's referrals relating to designated health services (other than clinical laboratory services) are prohibited under section 1877.

PART 455—PROGRAM INTEGRITY: MEDICAID

D. Part 455 is amended as follows:

1. The authority citation for part 455 continues to read as follows:

Authority: Sec. 1102 of the Social Security Act (42 U.S.C. 1302).

2. Section 455.100 is revised to read as follows:

§ 455.100   Basis and Purpose.

(a) *Basis.* This subpart implements sections 1124, 1126, 1902(a)(38), 1903(i)(2), 1903(n), and 1903(s) of the Act.

(b) *Purpose.* This subpart does the following:

(1) Sets forth State plan requirements regarding—

(i) Disclosure by providers and fiscal agents of information concerning ownership and control, investment arrangements, and compensation arrangements; and

(ii) Disclosure of information on a provider's owners and other persons convicted of criminal offenses against Medicare, Medicaid, or the title XX services program.

(2) Specifies conditions under which the Administrator will deny Federal financial participation for services furnished by providers or fiscal agents that fail to comply with the disclosure requirements.

(3) Provides for a civil money penalty for failure to meet certain reporting requirements.

3. Section 455.103 is revised to read as follows:

§ 455.103   State plan requirement.

A State plan must provide that the requirements of §§ 445.104 through 455.109 are met.

4. A new subpart C, consisting of section §§ 455.108 and 455.109, is added to read as follows:

Subpart C—Disclosure of Information by Providers for Purposes of the Prohibition on Certain Physician Referrals

§ 455.108   Basis.

This subpart is based on section 1903(s) of the Act, which, in part, applies the reporting requirements of section 1877(f) and (g) of the Act to Medicaid providers of designated health services (as these services are defined in § 411.351).

§ 455.109   Disclosure of ownership, investment, and compensation arrangements.

(a) The Medicaid agency must require that each provider of services that furnishes designated health services covered by the State plan submit information to the Medicaid agency concerning its financial relationships (as defined in paragraph (d) of this section), in the form, manner, and at the times the agency specifies. The term "designated health services," for purposes of this section, refers to the services listed in § 411.351 of this chapter, as they are defined in that section, or as those services are otherwise defined under the State plan.

(b) *Exception.* The requirements of paragraph (a) of this section do not apply to providers of services that provide 20 or fewer designated health services covered under the State plan during a calendar year, or to designated health services furnished outside the United States.

(c) *Required information.* The information requested by the Medicaid agency can include the following:

(1) The name and Medicaid State Specific Identifier (MSSI) of each physician who has a financial relationship with the provider of services.

(2) The name and MSSI of each physician who has an immediate relative (as defined in § 411.351 of this chapter) who has a financial relationship with the provider of services.

(3) The covered items and services furnished by the provider of services.

(4) With respect to each physician identified under paragraphs (c)(1) and (c)(2) of this section, the nature of the financial relationship (including the extent and/or value of the ownership or investment interest or the compensation arrangement, if requested by the Medicaid agency).

(d) *Reportable financial relationships.* For purposes of this section, a financial relationship is any ownership or investment interest or any compensation arrangement, as defined in § 411.351, including those relationships excepted under §§ 411.355 through 411.357.

(e) *Form and timing of reports.* Providers of services that are subject to the requirements of this section must submit the required information on a prescribed form within the time period specified by the Medicaid agency. Thereafter, a provider must report to the Medicaid agency all changes in the submitted information within a timeframe specified by the Medicaid agency. Providers of services must retain documentation sufficient to verify the information provided on the forms and, upon request, must make that documentation available to the Medicaid State agency, HCFA, or the OIG.

(f) *Consequences of failure to report.* Any provider of services that is required, but failed, to meet the reporting requirements of paragraph (a) of this section is subject to a civil money penalty of not more than $10,000 for each day of the period beginning on the day following the applicable deadline until the information is submitted. Assessment of the penalty will comply with the applicable provisions of part 1003 of this title.

(Catalog of Federal Domestic Assistance Program No. 93.773, Medicare—Hospital Insurance; Program No. 93.774, Medicare—Supplementary Medical Insurance Program; and Federal Domestic Assistance Program No. 93.778, Medical Assistance Program)

Dated: November 10, 1997.

Nancy-Ann Min DeParle,

Administrator, Health Care Financing Administration.

Dated: December 17, 1997.

Donna E. Shalala,

Secretary.

[FR Doc. 98–282 Filed 1–5–98; 8:45 am]

BILLING CODE 4120–03–P

HCFA Final Rules on Issuance of Advisory Opinions Under the 'Stark II' Law (63 *Fed. Reg.* 1646-1658, Jan. 9, 1998)

DEPARTMENT OF HEALTH AND HUMAN SERVICES

Health Care Financing Administration

42 CFR Part 411

[HCFA–1902–IFC]

RIN: 0938–AI38

Medicare Program; Physicians' Referrals; Issuance of Advisory Opinions

AGENCY: Health Care Financing Administration (HCFA), HHS.

ACTION: Final rule with comment period.

SUMMARY: This final rule with comment period incorporates into HCFA's regulations the provisions of section 1877(g)(6) of the Social Security Act (the Act), as added by section 4314 of the Balanced Budget Act of 1997. Section 1877(g)(6) requires that the Secretary issue written advisory opinions to outside parties concerning whether the referral of a Medicare patient by a physician for certain designated health services (other than clinical laboratory services) is prohibited under the physician referral provisions in section 1877 of the Act. Section 1877 not only prohibits certain referrals under the Medicare program, but also affects Federal financial participation payments to States under the Medicaid program for medical assistance consisting of designated health services furnished as the result of certain physician referrals. This final rule sets forth the specific procedures HCFA will use to issue advisory opinions.

EFFECTIVE DATES: The regulations are effective January 9, 1998.

Comment Date: Comments will be considered if we receive them at the appropriate address as provided below, no later than 5 p.m on March 10, 1998.

ADDRESSES: Mail written comments (1 original and 3 copies) to the following address: Health Care Financing Administration, Department of Health and Human Services, Attention: HCFA–1902–IFC, P.O. Box 26688, Baltimore, MD 21207.

If you prefer, you may deliver your written comments (1 original and 3 copies) to one of the following addresses:

Room 309–G, Hubert H. Humphrey Building, 200 Independence Avenue, SW., Washington, DC 20201, or

Room C5–09–26, 7500 Security Boulevard, Baltimore, MD 21244–1850.

Comments may also be submitted electronically to the following e-mail address: hcfa1902ifc.hcfa.gov. E-mail comments must include the full name and address of the sender and must be submitted to the referenced address in order to be considered. All comments must be incorporated in the e-mail message because we may not be able to access attachments. Because of staffing and resource limitations, we cannot accept comments by facsimile (FAX) transmission. In commenting, please refer to file code HCFA–1902–IFC. Comments received timely will be available for public inspection as they are received, generally beginning approximately 3 weeks after publication of a document, in Room 309–G of the Department's offices at 200 Independence Avenue, SW., Washington, DC, on Monday through Friday of each week from 8:30 a.m. to 5 p.m. (phone: (202) 690–7890).

Copies: To order copies of the **Federal Register** containing this document, send your request to: New Orders, Superintendent of Documents, P.O. Box 371954, Pittsburgh, PA 15250–7954. Specify the date of the issue requested and enclose a check or money order payable to the Superintendent of Documents, or enclose your Visa or Master Card number and expiration date. Credit card orders can also be placed by calling the order desk at (202) 783–3238 or by faxing to (202) 275–6802. The cost for each copy is $8. As an alternative, you can view and photocopy the **Federal Register** document at most libraries designated as Federal Depository Libraries and at many other public and academic libraries throughout the country that receive the **Federal Register**.

This **Federal Register** document is also available from the **Federal Register** online database through GPO Access, a service of the U.S. Government Printing Office. Free public access is available on a Wide Area Information Server (WAIS) through the Internet and via asynchronous dial-in. Internet users can access the database by using the World Wide Web; the Superintendent of Documents home page address is http://www.access.gpo.gov/su_docs/, by using local WAIS client software, or by telnet to swais.access.gpo.gov, then log in as guest (no password required). Dial-in users should use communications software and modem to call (202) 512–1661; type swais, then log in as guest (no password required).

FOR FURTHER INFORMATION CONTACT:
Joanne Sinsheimer (410) 786–4620.

SUPPLEMENTARY INFORMATION:

I. Background

A. Legislative history of section 1877

Section 6204 of the Omnibus Budget Reconciliation Act of 1989 (OBRA'89), Public Law 101–239, enacted on December 19, 1989, added section 1877 to the Social Security Act (the Act). (Unless we indicate otherwise, all references in this document are to sections of the law are references to the Act.) In general, section 1877 as it read under OBRA'89 provided that, if a physician (or an immediate family member of a physician) had a financial relationship with a clinical laboratory, that physician could not make a referral to the laboratory for the furnishing of clinical laboratory services for which Medicare might otherwise pay. It also provided that the laboratory could not present or cause to be presented a Medicare claim or bill to any individual, third party payer, or other entity for clinical laboratory services furnished under the prohibited referral. Additionally, it required a refund of any amount collected from an individual as the result of billing for an item or service furnished under a prohibited referral. These provisions were effective for referrals made on or after January 1, 1992.

The statute defined "financial relationship" as an ownership or investment interest in the entity providing clinical laboratory services or a compensation arrangement between the physician (or immediate family member) and the entity. The statute provided a number of exceptions to the prohibition. Some of these exceptions applied to both ownership/investment interests and compensation arrangements, while other exceptions applied to only one or the other of these. Additionally, the statute imposed reporting requirements relating to a physician's (or family member's) financial relationships and provided for sanctions.

Section 4207(e) of the Omnibus Budget Reconciliation Act of 1990 (OBRA'90), Public Law 101–508, enacted on November 5, 1990, amended certain provisions of section 1877 to clarify the definitions in section 1877(h), alter the reporting requirements, and to provide an additional exception to the prohibition.

Section 1877 was extensively revised by section 13562 of the Omnibus Budget Reconciliation Act of 1993 (OBRA'93), Public Law 103–66, enacted on August 10, 1993. It modified the prior law to apply to referrals for ten "designated health services" in addition to clinical

Federal Register / Vol. 63, No. 6 / Friday, January 9, 1998 / Rules and Regulations **1647**

laboratory services, modified some exceptions, and added new ones. Some of the amendments were retroactively effective to January 1, 1992, while others (such as the expansion to the additional designated health services) did not become effective until January 1, 1995. Section 152 of the Social Security Act Amendments of 1994 (SSA'94), Public Law 103–432, enacted on October 31, 1994, amended the list of designated services, effective January 1, 1995. It also changed the reporting requirements in section 1877(f) and amended some of the effective dates of the OBRA'93 provisions. The amended list of designated health services includes:

- Clinical laboratory services.
- Physical therapy services.
- Occupational therapy services.
- Radiology services, including magnetic resonance imaging, computerized axial tomography scans, and ultrasound services.
- Radiation therapy services and supplies.
- Durable medical equipment and supplies.
- Parenteral and enteral nutrients, equipment, and supplies.
- Prosthetics, orthotics, and prosthetic devices and supplies.
- Home health services.
- Outpatient prescription drugs.
- Inpatient and outpatient hospital services.

Section 13624 of OBRA'93 extended aspects of the referral prohibition to the Medicaid program, adding a new paragraph (s) to section 1903 of the Social Security Act. This provision denies Federal financial participation (FFP) payment under the Medicaid program to a State for certain expenditures for designated health services. A State cannot receive FFP for designated health services furnished to an individual on the basis of a physician referral that would result in a denial of payment under the Medicare program if Medicare covered the services to the same extent and under the same terms and conditions as under the State Medicaid plan. Section 13624 also specified that the reporting requirements in section 1877(f) and the civil money penalty provision in section 1877(g)(5) (which relates to reporting) apply to a provider of a designated health service for which payment may be made under Medicaid in the same manner as they apply to a provider of a designated health service for which payment may be made under Medicare. Section 1903(s) applies to a physician's referrals made on or after December 31, 1994.

B. Regulations relating to section 1877

On March 11, 1992, we published a proposed rule (57 FR 8588) setting forth the self-referral prohibition and exceptions to the prohibition in section 1877, as enacted by OBRA' 89 and amended by OBRA '90, relating to a physician's referrals for clinical laboratory services.

On August 14, 1995, we published, at 60 FR 41914, a final rule with comment period that incorporated into the Medicare regulations the provisions of section 1877 that relate to the prohibition on physician referrals for clinical laboratory services. The August 1995 final rule contains revisions to the March 11, 1992, proposal based on comments submitted by the public. Further, it incorporates the amendments and exceptions created by OBRA '93 and the amendments in SSA '94 that relate to referrals for clinical laboratory services. It addresses only those changes that had a retroactive effective date of January 1, 1992; it does not incorporate those modifications to section 1877 that became effective for referrals made on or after January 1, 1995. (Even though the August 1995 final rule incorporates OBRA '93 and SSA '94 provisions, it generally only reiterates them without interpreting them. We interpreted the new provisions only in a few instances in which it was necessary to do so in order to implement the statute at all.)

We are publishing elsewhere in this same issue of the **Federal Register** a proposed rule that interprets the OBRA'93 and SSA '94 provisions described above and incorporates and interprets the provisions of section 1877 that became effective on January 1, 1995, and concern the other designated health services. This proposed rule also addresses the application of sections 1877 and 1903(s) to the Medicaid program.

C. Advisory Opinions: Section 4314 of Public Law 105–33

Section 4314 of the Balanced Budget Act of 1997, Public Law 105–33, enacted on August 5, 1997, added section 1877(g)(6) to the Act. This provision requires that the Department provide additional formal guidance to outside parties regarding the application of the physician referral statute.

Section 1877(g)(6)(A) requires that the Secretary issue written advisory opinions concerning whether a referral relating to designated health services (other than clinical laboratory services) is prohibited under the provisions in section 1877. This paragraph states that each advisory opinion issued by the Secretary will be binding on the

Secretary and the party or parties who requested the opinion.

Section 1877(g)(6)(B) requires the Secretary, in issuing physician referral advisory opinions, to apply the rules in paragraphs (b)(3) and (4) of section 1128D of the Act, to the extent practicable. Section 1128D was added to the Act by section 205 of the Health Insurance Portability and Accountability Act of 1996, Public Law 104–191, effective August 21, 1996. It requires the Secretary, in consultation with the Attorney General, to issue written advisory opinions to particular parties on certain specified matters involved in applying the anti-kickback statute in section 1128B(b) of the Act, the safe harbor provisions in 42 CFR 1001.952, as well as other health care fraud and abuse sanctions handled by the Office of Inspector General (OIG).

Section 1128D(b)(3)(A) prohibits the OIG in its advisory opinions from addressing whether fair market value will be or was paid or received for any goods, services, or property. Section 1128D(b)(3)(B) prohibits the OIG from addressing whether an individual is a bona fide employee within the requirements of section 3121(d)(2) of the Internal Revenue Code of 1986. As noted above, HCFA is required to apply these provisions "to the extent practicable." We are incorporating these provisions in their entirety into our own advisory opinion rules.

Section 1128D(b)(4)(A) states that the OIG advisory opinions are binding on the Secretary and the party or parties requesting the opinion. Section 1128D(b)(4)(B) provides that if a party fails to seek an advisory opinion, this fact may not be introduced into evidence to prove that the party intended to violate the provisions of sections 1128, 1128A, or 1128B. We are also required to apply these provisions "to the extent practicable." We are incorporating section 1128D(b)(4)(B) in its entirety. However, we are not incorporating section 1128D(b)(4)(A) because we believe that it is redundant with our own advisory authority in section 1877(g)(6)(A). This provision states that each advisory opinion issued by the Secretary will be binding on the Secretary and on the party or parties requesting the opinion.

Section 1877(g)(6)(B) also requires us to take into account the regulations promulgated by the OIG to cover advisory opinions, issued by the OIG under the authority of section 1128D(b)(5). We believe that "take into account" means that we should use the OIG regulations as our model, but that we are not bound to follow them. We have attempted to follow the OIG

1648 Federal Register / Vol. 63, No. 6 / Friday, January 9, 1998 / Rules and Regulations

regulations as closely as possible in each instance in which we believed that it was reasonable to do so.

Section 1128D(b)(5)(A) states that the OIG's regulations must provide for—
• The procedure to be followed by a party applying for an advisory opinion;
• The procedure to be followed by the Secretary in responding to a request for an advisory opinion;
• The interval in which the Secretary will respond;
• The reasonable fee to be charged to the party requesting an advisory opinion; and
• The manner in which advisory opinions will be made available to the public.

Under section 1128D(b)(5)(B), the OIG is required to issue an advisory opinion to a party by not later than 60 days after receiving the request for the opinion and to charge the requesting party a fee that is equal to the costs the Secretary incurs in responding to the request.

The OIG's procedures for advisory opinions are set forth in 42 CFR part 1008. They were published as an interim final rule with comment period on February 19, 1997 (62 FR 7350). In section III. of this preamble, we discuss each of the elements required by section 1128D(b)(5)(A) (for the OIG's regulations). Many of our procedures are based on those articulated in the OIG regulations.

II. Provisions of the Interim Final Rule with Comment Period

A. Overview of the advisory opinion requirement

This interim final rule with comment period creates regulations at sections 411.370 through 411.389 that establish procedures for the advisory opinions described in section 1877(g)(6). These advisory opinions will provide the public with meaningful advice regarding whether, based on specific facts, a physician's referrals for a designated health service (other than a clinical laboratory service) are prohibited by the referral provisions in section 1877. The advisory opinion process will be meaningful to any parties who are interested in learning whether a particular business arrangement involving a physician (or a physician's immediate family member) will result in the physician being prohibited from making certain referrals under the Medicare program. This process also could prove significant to parties who are interested in the status of a physician's referrals under the Medicaid program. That is because the FFP provision in section 1903(s) of the Act depends upon whether a

physician's referrals would be prohibited under the Medicare rules if the Medicare program covered a designated health service in the same manner as it is covered under the State Medicaid plan.

In an advisory opinion, we will restate the material facts known to us, present our analysis, and provide conclusions about how we believe the law applies to the facts presented. We will base our analysis on our interpretation of the provisions in section 1877.

Section 1877(g)(6) requires advisory opinions only on the issue of whether a referral relating to designated health services (other than clinical laboratory services) is a prohibited referral under section 1877. If a physician has an unexcepted financial relationship with an entity, as defined by the statute and our regulations, then that physician's referrals for designated health services for a Medicare patient would be prohibited, regardless of the intent of any of the parties involved in the arrangement. Thus, our advisory opinions will be fact-based, and will contain no discussions about what we believe the parties knew when they entered into the arrangement or what they may have intended.

While section 1877 is primarily a payment ban that is effective regardless of the intent of the parties involved, there are additional sanctions under section 1877(g)(3) and (g)(4) that include elements of knowledge or intent. Section 1877(g)(4), in fact, imposes a penalty for certain referrals that might not otherwise be prohibited, if the parties involved in an arrangement have a particular purpose in mind. This provision applies to any physician or other entity that enters into an arrangement or scheme (such as a cross-referral arrangement) that the physician or entity knows or should know has a principal purpose of ensuring referrals by the physician to a particular entity that, if the physician directly made referrals to that entity, would be in violation of section 1877. Sanctions under this provision include potentially significant civil money penalties and possible exclusion from the Medicare and other health care programs.

We do not believe that section 1877(g)(6) requires us to express any opinion about what the parties to an arrangement knew or intended, for purposes of any of the sanctions in section 1877(g) (3) and (4). Even if we wished to comment on any intent-based aspect of the referral provisions, we believe that it is not practical for us to make an independent determination of the subjective intent of the parties based

only upon written materials that have been submitted by the requestor. While we expect requestors to submit complete written descriptions of their arrangements and transactions, along with relevant portions of documents, these materials do not afford a satisfactory basis upon which we could make a reliable determination of subjective intent.

Section 1877(g)(6)(A) states that an advisory opinion shall be binding on the Secretary and on the party or parties requesting an opinion. It is also our view that an advisory opinion may legally be relied upon only by the requestors.

We believe that advisory opinions are capable of being misused by persons *not* a party to the transaction in question in order to inappropriately escape liability. Advisory opinions are intended only to address the facts of a particular arrangement. A third party may implement an arrangement that appears similar to the arrangement described in the advisory opinion, but the third party may introduce *additional* factors that may make a difference in the outcome of an advisory opinion.

As set forth below, this interim final rule with comment period has been developed primarily to address the following issues:
• The procedure to be followed by a party applying for an advisory opinion.
• The procedure we will follow in responding to a request.
• The interval within in which we will respond to a request for an advisory opinion.
• The reasonable fee we will charge to the party requesting an advisory opinion.
• The manner in which we will make advisory opinions available to the public.

This final rule with comment period does not address the substance or the content of advisory opinions issued by us.

B. Responsibilities of outside parties seeking advisory opinions

1. Who can request an advisory opinion

Any individual or entity may submit a request to us for a written advisory opinion about whether a physician's referral relating to a designated health service, other than a clinical laboratory service, is prohibited under section 1877. We anticipate that most requests will involve financial relationships that involve health care business arrangements. Therefore, for purposes of this discussion, we will generally use the term "arrangement" to refer to the factual circumstances that are involved

Federal Register / Vol. 63, No. 6 / Friday, January 9, 1998 / Rules and Regulations **1649**

in a request for an advisory opinion, even though some requests might involve facts that are not related to a business arrangement.

As indicated above, the advisory opinion process is designed to provide authoritative guidance to participants in particular arrangements. Therefore, the arrangement in question must either be in existence at the time of the request for an advisory opinion or, with respect to prospective arrangements, there must be a good faith intention to enter into the described arrangement in the near future. (With respect to prospective conduct, we are stating that the requestor can declare the intention to enter into the arrangement contingent upon receiving a favorable advisory opinion from us or from both us and the OIG.)

Requestors who are not individuals are required to disclose certain ownership information, so that we can check to ensure that the matter which is the subject of the advisory opinion request is not under current investigation. We are also requiring that requestors inform us, to the best of their knowledge, about whether the arrangement involved in the request is the subject of any current investigations.

2. Matters not subject to an advisory opinion

As explained above, even if a party requests it, we will not address the issue of whether fair market value was, or will be, paid or received for any goods, services, or property or the issue of whether an individual is a bona fide employee within the requirements of section 3121(d)(2) of the Internal Revenue Code of 1986.

In addition, we do not believe that it is appropriate to provide advisory opinions to persons *not* involved in the arrangement in question. For example, we believe that a description of a competitor's arrangement is not the proper subject of an advisory opinion since the participants to the particular transaction would not be involved in the request. A party to an actual arrangement—either existing or about to be entered into—is in a position to provide full and complete information regarding the facts in question. By contrast, third parties are not in a position to provide a reliable statement about the facts of a particular arrangement in which the third party is not a participant. In addition, it is unclear who would be bound by an advisory opinion on an arrangement that does not involve the requestor.

Similarly, we do not believe it is appropriate to provide advisory opinions on hypothetical or generalized

arrangements. Section 1877(g)(6) requires the Secretary to issue advisory opinions concerning "whether a referral relating to designated health services (other than clinical laboratory services) is prohibited under this section." (Emphasis added.) We interpret this provision to mean a specific referral involving a physician in a specific situation. We also believe there are reasons to avoid opinions on generalized arrangements. Because of the complexity of the business arrangements that exist in today's health care community, physician referral cases are not likely to be the same in all material respects. The introduction by a party of any *additional* factors could make a material difference in the resulting opinion. We believe it would not be possible for an advisory opinion to reliably identify all the possible hypothetical factors that might lead to different results.

3. Initiating the process for an advisory opinion

A requestor must submit a written request for an advisory opinion in order to initiate the process. The request must clearly and thoroughly present a complete description of the situation that is the subject of the advisory opinion. The request should include all facts that would be relevant in determining whether a particular situation could result in a physician's referrals being prohibited under section 1877. To the extent that the request provides the necessary information in a clear and orderly manner, we will be better able to process it.

We are requiring any submission to include copies of all relevant documents or relevant portions of documents, such as financial statements, contracts, leases, employment agreements and court documents (requestors may withhold irrelevant portions), as well as descriptions of any other arrangements or relationships that may affect the documents or our analysis. In addition, the submission should include a narrative description of the arrangement. In making the request, a requestor must include the identities (including names and addresses) of the requestor and all other actual and potential parties to the arrangement, to the extent known to the requestor. In addition, the request must include the Taxpayer Identification Number (TIN) of the requestor. The Debt Collection Improvement Act of 1996 (section 31001 of Public Law 104–134) requires agencies to collect the TIN from all persons or businesses "doing business with a Federal agency." (See 31 U.S.C. 7701(c).) We believe that requesting,

receiving, and paying for our work on an advisory opinion fits into the category of "doing business with a Federal agency." Therefore, a request for an advisory opinion must include the TIN of the requestor. The TIN will be used for purposes of collecting and reporting on any delinquent amounts arising out of the requestor's failure to render proper payment for the advisory opinion. In addition to the above information, we are also requiring the requestor to identify a designated contact person who will be available to communicate with us.

We are also requiring that requestors make two certifications as part of their request for an advisory opinion. If the requestor is an individual, the individual must sign the certification; if the requestor is a corporation, it must be signed by the Chief Executive Officer, or a comparable officer; if the requestor is a partnership, it must be signed by a managing partner; and, if the requestor is a limited liability company, the certification must be signed by a managing member. The responsible individual must certify that all of the information provided as part of the request is true and correct, and constitutes a complete description of the facts regarding which an advisory opinion is being sought, to the best of the requestor's knowledge. If the request relates to prospective conduct, the regulations state that the request must also include a certification that the requestor intends in good faith to enter into the arrangement described in the request. A requestor may make this certification contingent upon receiving a favorable advisory opinion from us or from both us and the OIG.

While all submissions should include the above categories of information, we cannot in these interim final regulations provide complete details on exactly what information a requestor must provide. We anticipate that we will receive requests that involve a wide variety of business arrangements, some of which may be quite complex. At a minimum, any request must describe the entities and parties involved in an arrangement, the specific terms of the arrangement, and the direct or indirect relationship between the physician (or a physician's immediate relative) and any entity that furnishes designated health services. Requestors should also include any information they believe demonstrates that the arrangement meets one of the exceptions to the referral prohibition.

We are soliciting public comment and input on any other types of information that a requestor should routinely provide and intend to address this point

1650 Federal Register / Vol. 63, No. 6 / Friday, January 9, 1998 / Rules and Regulations

further in any revised final rulemaking. In the interim, prior to submitting a request for an advisory opinion, *we strongly advise* that a requestor contact us to inquire about the information HCFA will need to process a request of the type the requestor intends to submit. Inquiries can be made by telephoning Joanne Sinsheimer at (410) 786–4620. We may, depending on the subject matter of the inquiry, informally provide parties with preliminary questions to help them structure their requests. Our goal is to help ensure that the requests include the factual information we will need to respond to them. Requestors should (but are not required to) answer these questions in their requests for an advisory opinion. If the information we need is in the first submission, we will be better able to render a prompt, concise, and appropriate advisory opinion. We welcome comments on this approach.

The regulation also requires that a requestor inform us about whether the parties involved in the request have also asked for or are planning to ask for an advisory opinion on the arrangement in question from the OIG under section 1128D(b) of the Act. We plan to routinely exchange information with the OIG on requests that we receive and on our intended responses. We plan, in particular, to establish a system that will help guarantee adequate coordination when parties have asked for opinions from both us and the OIG.

4. Fees charged to requesting parties

There is no express authority for us to charge a user fee to individuals who request an advisory opinion under section 4314 of the Balanced Budget Act of 1997. However, in the absence of express authority for this particular purpose, we can rely on the authority for collecting such a fee provided by the Independent Offices Appropriations Act of 1952 (IOAA), 31 U.S.C. 9701. That statute generally governs Federal agencies' imposition and collection of user fees. In § 9701(a), the Congress expressed its intent that each service or thing of value provided by a Government agency to a person is to be self-sustaining to the extent possible. Section 9701(b) authorizes agencies to prescribe regulations establishing the fee for a service or thing of value provided by the agency. The fee must be "fair" and based on the cost to the government of providing the service or thing, the value of the service or thing to the recipient, public policy or interest served, and other relevant facts. 31 U.S.C. 9701(b).

In 1974, the Supreme Court ruled that the user fee statute must be read narrowly as authorizing not a "tax" (which may be levied only by Congress and need not relate to benefits bestowed on the taxpayer), but a "fee" for a particular benefit. *National Cable Television Ass'n, Inc. v. United States,* 415 U.S. 336 (1974) (FCC had authority to impose fees; costs that inure to the public's benefit should not be included in the fee imposed). In a companion case, *Federal Power Commission v. New England Power Company,* 415 U.S. 345 (1974), the Court opined that the Office of Management and Budget (OMB) had properly construed the user fee statute in a 1959 circular, which stated that a reasonable charge "should be made to each identifiable recipient for a measurable unit or amount of government service or property from which he derives a special benefit." *Id.* at 349. The OMB Circular A–25 was revised in 1993, and currently provides under the heading "General policy" that a user charge "will be assessed against each identifiable recipient for special benefits derived from Federal activities beyond those received by the general public." 58 FR 38142, 38144. The language of currently applicable OMB guidance to agencies about when a "special benefit" will be considered to accrue for purposes of imposing a charge is virtually identical to that cited by the Court with approval. *Id.* at 349, fn. 3.

More recent appellate court decisions addressing agencies' authority to impose user fees similarly examine the extent to which there is a "*specific* service that confers a *special* private benefit on an *identifiable* beneficiary." *Seafarers Int'l Union of N. Am. v. Coast Guard,* 81 F.3d 179, 184 (D.C. Cir. 1996) (emphasis in original). *See, also, Engine Mfrs. Ass'n v. EPA,* 20 F.2d 1177 (D.C. Cir. 1994) and *Central & Southern Motor Freight Tariff Ass'n v. United States,* 777 F.2d 722 (D.C. Cir. 1985). We believe that the advisory opinions we must provide under section 4314 fall squarely into this category. That is, they are an "extra" service that an interested party can request from the Secretary, they relate to the party's own, unique situation, and they are binding on the Secretary and the requesting party alone, with no general application.

Section 411.372(b)(9) requires that a requestor make payment for an advisory opinion directly to us. We believe that HCFA has the authority to both collect and retain the fees. Annual appropriations acts have since 1996 authorized our retention of otherwise authorized user fees, and this authority would apply to all user fees we are authorized to collect. The retention language appears in the most recent appropriations act, enacted on November 13, 1997, Public Law 105–78, in the paragraphs covering appropriations for our program management. This language states that, in carrying out titles XVIII and XIX of the Act, the Secretary is authorized to use a specific amount of money that will be transferred from the Federal Hospital Insurance and the Federal Supplementary Medical Insurance Trust Funds, together with "such sums as may be collected from authorized user fees and the sale of data, which shall remain available until expended. * * *."

Since section 1877(g)(6) of the Act requires that we take into account the OIG regulations implementing section 1128D(b)(5), we have modeled our user fee on the fee that appears in those regulations. Under section 1128D(b)(5)(A)(iv), the OIG regulations must provide for a "reasonable fee" to be charged to the party requesting an advisory opinion. Section 1128D(b)(5)(B)(ii) requires that requestors be charged a fee equal to the costs incurred by the Department in responding to the request.

We have adopted the "actual cost" fee from the OIG regulations. Section 411.375(b) of our regulations indicates that in determining the actual costs, we will factor in the salary, benefits, and overhead costs of policy analysts, attorneys, and others who may work on analyzing requests and writing advisory opinions, including administrative and supervisory support for these individuals. Because we expect that requests may range widely in their complexity, we do not believe it is possible to calculate or accurately estimate the cost of providing an advisory opinion in advance. In fact, the OIG has interpreted section 1128D(b)(5)(B)(ii) to require a fee that represents the *actual* costs that it has incurred in processing each individual request. We are also reflecting this concept in our regulations.

We have included in our regulations the OIG's requirement that, once the advisory opinion process is complete, either because we have issued the opinion or the request has been withdrawn, the requestor is responsible for paying an amount equal to the costs incurred by the Government in responding to the request.

Although we cannot reliably project the processing costs in advance, we can make broad estimates that may be of use to prospective requestors. We estimate that, currently, the actual cost of processing a request, including salaries, benefits and overhead, would be approximately $75 an hour. We must include in our estimate the time of technical staff, attorneys, supervisors, and support staff, as well as others with whom we may consult on various issues.

The time it will take us to process a request will depend on the complexity of the request and the quality of the submission. Simple requests might only take a few hours. For example, a request concerning whether a physician can refer patients to his wife, who works for a physical therapy facility, may take approximately 3 hours to analyze and produce a written opinion. On the other hand, a request involving the application of the physician referral rules to a large, multi-party, intricate business arrangement may take us in excess of 40 hours to fully analyze and produce a written advisory opinion.

We believe that it is reasonable to expect that requests for an advisory opinion will, at present, cost at least $250 for initial processing. It will take time for us to carefully read and analyze every request for an advisory opinion and to ensure that we have accurately understood all the material facts in each request. Accordingly, the regulations provide for a nonrefundable payment of $250 that must accompany any request for an advisory opinion that we receive through the end of 1998. Once we have gained experience in estimating the resources we will need and have factored in any inflation in our costs, we may need to revise our initial fee through a program issuance. We expect to revise the fee periodically after December 31, 1998.

Because we do not believe that we can accurately estimate our costs in advance for a particular request, we intend to try to accommodate requestors who may want to limit the costs of receiving an advisory opinion. The regulations provide that requestors may designate a "triggering dollar amount" in their requests for an advisory opinion. If we calculate that the cost of processing a request has reached, or is likely to exceed, that triggering amount, we will stop processing the request and promptly notify the requestor. The requestor may then decide to either authorize us to continue or withdraw the request. We believe we will be able to more accurately reflect costs in advance once we have gained experience. In the interim, this triggering mechanism should be useful in helping to ensure that requestors do not pay costs far in excess of what they expect to pay when they submit their requests.

Section 411.375(c)(4) of the regulations specifically indicates that, while a requestor may withdraw a request for an advisory opinion at any time, he or she will be responsible for any costs we incurred in processing the request before it was withdrawn.

When we have completed the advisory opinion as discussed below, or the requestor has withdrawn the request, we will calculate the total costs that we incurred in processing the request. In calculating this amount, we will take into account any previous payments associated with the request, such as the initial $250 fee, and then notify the requestor of the amount he or she still owes. Once the requestor has paid the full cost, we will release the opinion to the requestor.

We believe that our approach for payment and release will be sufficient for the vast majority of requests for advisory opinions. However, we also believe that we need an additional procedure for cases in which the request will necessitate that we acquire expert advice. We may, for example, need to consult with accountants or with business professionals in order to better understand complex financial relationships.

Because such expert reviews will entail additional time and expense, we believe that we should treat differently any request that requires outside consultation rather than just a standard application of the governing law to a given set of facts. If we determine that we require an expert opinion, we will obtain an estimate for the costs of the opinion and provide the requestor with that estimate. The requestor may then decide to either pay the estimated cost of the expert review or withdraw the request. If the requestor pays the estimated cost, we will promptly refer the matter to the expert for review. Once the outside expert has provided us with the review, we will continue the advisory opinion process by applying the expert evaluation to the legal questions at issue. If the expert evaluation ultimately costs more than the estimated cost, we will bill the requestor for the additional expense as part of the Department's overall costs in responding to the request. These additional costs will be included when we determine whether we are approaching a requestor's "triggering dollar amount."

We intend to begin processing requests as soon as we receive them. However, although we will be charging user fees for the cost to the Government for responding to these requests, we will not be adding staff until we determine the volume of requests and the complexity of the legal issues and fact patterns. Once we have had some experience processing requests for advisory opinions, we intend to

reconsider the method described in this section for calculating fees. We are specifically soliciting comments on our methodology for determining costs.

C. HCFA's responsibilities

1. Reviewing requests for advisory opinions

Once we receive a request for an advisory opinion, we will promptly examine it to determine if it appears to contain sufficient information for us to form the basis for an informed advisory opinion. (Generally speaking, a request is most likely to be sufficient if the requestor sought our advice before submitting a formal request, and the request contains responses to any preliminary questions we may have posed at that time.) If a request does not appear to us to be sufficient, we will promptly notify the requestor about the additional information we need. On the other hand, if the request appears to be sufficient, we will accept the request. In all cases, we will either ask for additional information or accept the request within 15 working days after we receive the request. If we have requested additional information and the requestor resubmits the advisory opinion request, we will assess the resubmission within 15 working days to determine whether it can be accepted or whether we still need further information. At the point when we accept the request, we will notify the requestor by U.S. mail of the date of our acceptance.

We believe that this approach will provide us with a reasonable amount of time to identify requests that do not contain sufficient information. We are limiting the time period for this initial assessment in order to ensure that we promptly process requests that appear to be complete. We are interested in public comments on whether we have developed an appropriate method for screening advisory opinion requests before we accept them.

Even in situations in which we have accepted a request, we reserve the right to later determine that we need additional information. If we decide that additional information is necessary, we will notify the requestor in the same manner as we would notify a requestor before accepting a request. The time period between when we notify the requestor about the additional information we need and when we receive the requested information will not be counted as part of the time within which we must issue an opinion.

Because we believe that we may need to make fact-intensive inquiries in order to render many advisory opinions, we

1652 Federal Register / Vol. 63, No. 6 / Friday, January 9, 1998 / Rules and Regulations

anticipate that we may need to request additional information from many requestors. In responding, the requestor should provide us with the necessary information and include with it a certification from the same individual who certified the original request for an advisory opinion (or, if the requestor is an entity, from an individual who is in a comparable position).

2. Timeframe for issuing advisory opinions

Section 1128D(b)(5)(B) of the Act requires that the OIG issue an advisory opinion within 60 days after it has received the request for the opinion. The OIG has reflected this timeframe in its regulations at 42 CFR 1008.43. Because section 1877(g)(6) does not impose any deadline, we have established our own 90-day timeframe for most requests. In addition, for requests that we determine, in our discretion, involve complex legal issues or highly complicated fact patterns, we reserve the right to issue an advisory opinion within a reasonable timeframe. We have created this timeframe based upon our perception that we will receive many requests for advisory opinions and that a large percentage will involve complex fact patterns. This perception is based on the quantity and the nature of phone calls we have received, on a daily basis, over many years. We believe that the number of requests will be affected by the fact that the referral provisions in section 1877 apply to many parties because they can be triggered regardless of the intent of the parties. In addition, if an arrangement involves a physician who has a problematic financial relationship with an entity that furnishes designated health services, the parties must know that the arrangement meets an exception before that physician can refer. We have also based our timeframe on staffing limitations.

Although we will be charging user fees for the cost to the Government for responding to these requests, we will not be adding staff until we determine the volume of requests and the complexity of the legal issues and fact patterns.

Once we have had some experience processing requests for advisory opinions, we intend to reevaluate the timeframe to ensure that it is fair and to determine whether more staff is necessary. We are specifically soliciting comments on this issue.

We intend to begin processing requests as soon as we receive them. Once we receive a request that appears to meet all the submission criteria, we will promptly accept the request and

our 90-day period for issuing an opinion will begin. We will send the advisory opinion to the requestor by regular U.S. mail by the end of the 90-day period and once the requestor has paid all the required fees.

We believe that under certain circumstances the running of our 90-day period for issuing an opinion should be tolled (suspended). The suspended periods will only reflect time when we cannot work on analyzing the request. If we notify a requestor that the costs have reached, or are likely to exceed, the triggering amount designated by that requestor, we will stop processing the request until the requestor instructs us to continue. Similarly, if we notify a requestor of the need for, and estimated cost of, an outside expert opinion on a nonlegal issue, the regulations state that we will stop processing the request until the requestor pays the estimated cost and the outside expert provides its opinion. Likewise, in those instances in which we request additional information from the requestor that we believe is necessary for us to issue the advisory opinion, we will stop processing the opinion until we receive the additional information.

The time period for issuing an advisory opinion does not include the time after we notify the requestor that the advisory opinion is complete and the requestor must pay the full balance due for the cost of the opinion.

While we intend to issue advisory opinions within 90 days of receiving the request, we do not believe that the 90-day time period should include delays in the processing of the request that are not within our control. With the exception of the delay that occurs while we wait for a necessary outside expert opinion, all of the possible events that can suspend the period are under the exclusive control of the requestor. We believe that for the vast majority of advisory opinion requests, the 90-day period will only be suspended for those periods during which the requestor has not paid a required fee or has not provided the information we need to process the request.

We will issue an advisory opinion to the requestor after we have considered the complete description of all the facts the requestor has provided to us. In the opinion, we will restate the material facts known to us, present our analysis, and provide conclusions about how we believe the law applies to the facts presented to us.

3. Dissemination of advisory opinions

Section 1128D(b)(5)(A)(v) requires that the OIG's regulations describe the manner in which advisory opinions will

be made available to the public. We have adopted the OIG's policy as follows: As set forth in § 411.384(b) of these regulations, once we issue an advisory opinion to a requestor, we will promptly make a copy of that opinion available for public inspection (in Room 309–G of the Department's offices at 200 Independence Avenue, SW., Washington, DC (phone: 202–690–7890)) during our normal hours of operation and on our web site (http://www.hcfa.gov/regs/aop/). We also anticipate that commercial publishers and trade groups are likely to make advisory opinions widely available to interested members of the public. We welcome public comments and additional suggestions about disseminating advisory opinions to the public.

We will make available documents that are related to a request for an advisory opinion and have been submitted to us and any related internal government documents, to the extent we are required to do so by the Freedom of Information Act (FOIA) (5 U.S.C. 552). If a requestor provides information it believes is not subject to disclosure under FOIA, such as items that the requestor believes are trade secrets or privileged and confidential commercial or financial information, the requestor should identify this information in the manner described in 45 CFR 5.65 (c) and (d). The requestor's assertions about the nature of the information, however, are not controlling.

In addition, although a document may be exempt from disclosure under FOIA, facts reflected in that document may become part of the advisory opinion that HCFA will provide to the public. We will describe the material facts of the arrangement in question in the body of each advisory opinion, which will be made fully available to the public. To the extent that it may be necessary to reveal specific facts that could be regarded as confidential information, we believe we have the authority to do so under sections 1106(a) and 1877(g)(6) of the Act. We do not intend to release any such facts unless we believe it is necessary to do so.

4. Rescission of an advisory opinion

Section 411.382 reserves our right to rescind or revoke an advisory opinion after we issue it, in limited circumstances. For example, we can rescind an opinion if we learn after issuing it that the arrangement in question may lead to fraud and abuse. In such a situation, we will notify the requestor that we have rescinded and make the notice available to the same extent as an advisory opinion. The requestor would not be subject to sanctions for any actions it took prior to the notice of rescission, if the requestor relied in good faith on the advisory opinion (unless we establish that the requestor failed to provide us with material information when it submitted the request for the opinion) and where the parties promptly discontinue the action upon receiving notice that we have rescinded or revoked our approval. We would also allow the parties to discontinue the action within what we believe is a reasonable "wind down" period, if we believe that the business arrangement is one that cannot be discontinued immediately. We are specifically soliciting comments on whether this approach reasonably balances the Government's need to ensure that advisory opinions are legally correct and the requestor's interest in finality.

5. Scope and effect of advisory opinions

Section 411.387 of these regulations addresses the scope and effect of advisory opinions. When we issue an advisory opinion under this process, it is legally binding on the Department and the requestor, but only with respect to the specific conduct of the particular requestor. Section 1877(g)(6)(A) requires only that an advisory opinion issued by the Secretary be binding upon the Secretary and the party or parties requesting the opinion. In light of this provision, the Department is not legally bound with respect to the conduct of a third party, even if the conduct of that party appears similar to the conduct of the requestor. Thus, under these regulations, no third parties are bound by nor may they rely upon an advisory opinion. Each advisory opinion will apply legal standards to a set of facts involving certain known persons who provide specific statements about key factual issues. A third party may create a look-alike arrangement, but any *additional* characteristics could lead to an unfavorable opinion. Therefore, by their very nature, advisory opinions cannot be applied generally.

We believe that even if a party has received a favorable advisory opinion from us regarding a particular arrangement, the Government is not totally prevented from commencing an action against a party to that arrangement. For example, this could occur if a requestor has failed to disclose a material fact. In any such action under sections 1128, 1128A or 1128B of the Act, an individual or entity who has requested and received an advisory opinion from us regarding the arrangement in question may seek to introduce the advisory opinion into evidence in the proceeding.

III. Regulatory Impact Analysis

We have examined the impact of this rule as required by Executive Order 12866 and the Regulatory Flexibility Act (RFA) (Pub. L. 96–354). Executive Order 12866 directs agencies to assess all costs and benefits of available regulatory alternatives and, when regulation is necessary, to select regulatory approaches that maximize net benefits (including potential economic, environmental, public health and safety effects, distributive impacts, and equity). The RFA requires agencies to analyze options for regulatory relief of small businesses. For purposes of the RFA, most hospitals, and most other providers, physicians, and health care suppliers are small entities, either by nonprofit status or by having revenues of $5 million or less annually.

Section 1102(b) of the Social Security Act requires us to prepare a regulatory impact analysis for any proposed rule that may have a significant impact on the operations of a substantial number of small rural hospitals. This analysis must conform to the provisions of section 603 of the RFA. For purposes of section 1102(b) of the Act, we define a small rural hospital as a hospital that is located outside a Metropolitan Statistical Area and has fewer than 50 beds.

This rule establishes procedures for us to receive, review, and respond to requests for advisory opinions on the issue of whether a physician's referrals for certain designated health services are prohibited under section 1877 of the Social Security Act. This rule does not address the substance of section 1877 nor the substance or content of the advisory opinions we may issue in the future. Any effect an advisory opinion may have on the behavior of health care providers is the result of the substantive content of section 1877 and of the advisory opinions themselves, and not this rule.

Parties interested in advisory opinions will incur certain costs in requesting the opinions. However, it is the law that allows us to require that requestors pay cost-based fees for advisory opinions. This rule merely lays out procedures for paying the costs.

Estimated number of respondents: Many individuals and entities that provide certain designated health services that may be paid for by Medicare or Medicaid could potentially have questions regarding the referral provisions in section 1877.

We estimate that, within the last year, we received an average of eight telephone calls each day regarding the physician self-referral provisions. We believe that some percentage of calls involved issues and situations about which the callers would be unlikely to request written advisory opinions. Nevertheless, we believe that we can use the number of inquiries as a basis for estimating the number of requests we are likely to receive for advisory opinions. Using this basis, we estimate that 200 physicians, health care entities, and other entities or individuals will request advisory opinions within the first year following publication of this rule. We also anticipate that the number of requests will decline in subsequent years, unless there are significant changes in the law. The costs to these requestors will vary depending on the complexity of each request. Compared, however, to the costs of seeking private legal advice, we believe that the fees charged for our review will not be substantial, and in many cases will not exceed the $250 minimum payment.

Obviously, the actual number of requests could be larger since, for the first time, formal written opinions are available. Conversely, the numbers could be smaller for a combination of many unquantifiable reasons, such as the desire not to subject an arrangement to official scrutiny.

Under the Regulatory Flexibility Act (5 U.S.C. 601–612), if a rule has a significant economic effect on a substantial number of small businesses, the Secretary must specifically consider the effects of the rule on small business entities and analyze regulatory options that could lessen the impact of the rule. As stated above, this rule does not address the substance of section 1877 of the Act or the substance of advisory opinions that may be issued in the future. It describes the *process* by which an individual or entity may receive an opinion about how section 1877 applies to particular business practices. The aggregate economic impact of this rulemaking on small business entities should, therefore, be minimal.

Thus, we have concluded, and the Secretary certifies, that this final rule will not have a significant economic impact on a substantial number of small business entities, and that a regulatory flexibility analysis is not required for this rulemaking.

In accordance with the provisions of E.O. 12866, this regulation was reviewed by the Office of Management and Budget.

1654 Federal Register / Vol. 63, No. 6 / Friday, January 9, 1998 / Rules and Regulations

IV. Authority for an Interim Final Rule with Comment Period, and Waiver of Delayed Effective Date

We ordinarily publish a general notice of proposed rulemaking in the **Federal Register** and invite public comment on the proposed rule. That rule would have included a reference to the legal authority under which we are proposing it, and the terms and substance of the proposed rule or a description of the subjects and issues involved. Further, we generally provide for final rules to be effective no sooner than 30 days after the date of publication unless we find good cause to waive the delay.

In order to implement the provisions in section 1877(g)(6) in a timely manner, section 1877(g)(6)(C) gives us the authority to promulgate regulations that take effect on an interim basis after notice and pending opportunity for public comment. We have chosen to exercise this authority for the following reasons. We believe that the statutory requirement that we accept requests for advisory opinions that are submitted on or after November 4, 1997, makes it imperative that, by that date, we have in place specific procedures to address how we will receive and process advisory opinion requests. It would be contrary to the public interest for us to receive and process advisory opinions without first setting forth procedural guidelines. We also believe that the 60-day period for public comment established by this interim final rule will protect the public's interest in this rulemaking, while providing us with additional input and recommendations, without unduly delaying the advisory opinion process. We are therefore publishing the advisory opinion procedures as an interim final rule with comment period. We also find that for good cause it would be against the public interest to delay the effective date of this rule. We will respond to all appropriate and relevant public comments that we receive during the 60-day comment period, and we will make any necessary revisions to these regulations through a revised final rule.

V. Collection of Information Requirements

In order to provide appropriate advisory opinions, we will need certain information from the parties who request advisory opinions. Sections 411.372, 411.373, and 411.378 of this interim final rule contain information collection requirements that require approval by OMB. We are required to solicit public comments under section 3506(c)(2)(A) of the Paperwork Reduction Act of 1995. Specifically,

comments are invited on (1) whether the proposed collection of information is necessary for the proper performance of the functions of the agency, including whether the information will have practical utility; (2) the accuracy of the estimate of the burden of the proposed collection of information; (3) ways to enhance the quality, utility and clarity of the information collected; and (4) ways to minimize the burden of the collection of information on respondents, including through the use of automated collection techniques or other forms of information technology.

We are requesting an emergency review of this interim final rule with comment period. In compliance with section 3506(c)(2)(A) of the Paperwork Reduction Act of 1995, we are submitting to OMB the collection of information requirements described below for emergency review. We are requesting an emergency review because the collection of this information is needed before the expiration of the normal time limits under OMB's regulations at 5 CFR part 1320, to ensure compliance with section 1877(g)(6)(D) of the Act, which was added by section 4314 of the Balanced Budget Act of 1997. Section 1877(g)(6)(D) requires us to respond to requests for advisory opinions that are submitted after November 3, 1997. We cannot reasonably comply with normal clearance procedures because of the statutory deadline and public harm is likely to result if the agency cannot provide for advisory opinions.

We are providing a 3-day public comment period from the date of publication of this interim final rule, with OMB review and approval 4 days from the date of publication, and a 180-day approval. During this 180-day period, we will publish a separate **Federal Register** notice announcing the initiation of an extensive 60-day agency review and public comment period on these requirements. We will submit the requirements for OMB review and an extension of this emergency approval.

Title: HCFA Advisory Opinion Procedure.

Summary of the collection of information: Section 4314 of Public Law 105–33, in establishing section 1877(g)(6) of the Act, requires the Department to provide advisory opinions to the public regarding whether a physician's referrals for certain designated health services are prohibited under the other provisions in section 1877 of the Act. These regulations provide the procedures under which members of the public may request advisory opinions from HCFA. Because all requests for advisory

opinions are purely voluntary, respondents will only be required to provide information to us that is relevant to their individual requests.

The following discussion describes the aggregate effect of the collections of information included in the text of this interim final rule.

Respondents: The "respondents" for the collection of information described in these regulations will be self-selected individuals and entities that choose to submit requests for advisory opinions to HCFA. We anticipate that the respondents will include health care providers of many types, from physicians who are sole practitioners to large diversified publicly-traded corporations.

Estimated number of respondents: 200. This estimate is based on the number of telephone calls we have received regarding the physician referral provisions.

Estimated number of responses per respondent: 1.

Estimated total annual burden on respondents: We believe that the burden of preparing a request for an advisory opinion will vary widely depending upon the size and complexity of the business transactions in question. We estimate that the average burden for each submitted request for an advisory opinion will be in the range of 2 to 40 hours. We further believe that the burden for most requests will be closer to the lower end of the range, with an average burden of 10 hours per respondent. Total burden for this proposed information collection is estimated to be 2000 hours.

We are requiring that requests for advisory opinions involve existing conduct, or conduct in which the requestor intends to engage. We anticipate that most requests will involve business arrangements into which the requesting party intends to enter. Because the facts will relate to business plans, we believe the requesting party in many cases will already have collected and analyzed all or almost all of the information we will need in order to review the request. Therefore, in order to request an advisory opinion, the requestor will most likely simply need to compile for our examination information that the requestor has already collected and reviewed. In some cases, however, the requestor may need to expend a more significant amount of time in order to submit information relating to a complex arrangement that involves a large number of parties.

Comments on this information collection should be sent to both:

Health Care Financing Administration, Office of Information Services, Information Technology Investment Management Group, Division of HCFA Enterprise Standards, Attn: HCFA–1902–IFC, Room C2–26–17, 7500 Security Boulevard, Baltimore, MD 21244–1850

and

Allison Herron Eydt, HCFA Desk Officer, Office of Management and Budget, Room 10235, New Executive Office Building, 725 17th Street, NW, Washington, D.C. 20503.

You may also fax comments on these paperwork reduction requirements to the Health Care Financing Administration at (410) 786–1415 and to Ms. Eydt at (202) 395–6974. All comments should refer to file code HCFA–1902–IFC.

To be considered, you must submit comments on these paperwork reduction requirements to the individuals listed above within 3 days after this interim final rule is published in the **Federal Register**.

List of Subjects in 42 CFR Part 411

Administrative practice and procedures, Fraud, Grant programs—health, Health facilities, Health professions, Medicaid, Medicare, Penalties.

42 CFR part 411 is amended as set forth below:

PART 411—EXCLUSIONS FROM MEDICARE AND LIMITATIONS ON MEDICARE PAYMENT

1. The authority citation for part 411 continues to read as follows:

Authority: Secs. 1102 and 1871 of the Social Security Act (42 U.S.C. 1302 and 1395hh).

2. Sections 411.370, 411.372, 411.373, 411.375, 411.377 through 411.380, 411.382, 411.384, and 411.386 through 411.389 are added to subpart J to read as follows:

§ 411.370   Advisory opinions relating to physician referrals.

(a) *Period during which HCFA will accept requests.* The provisions of §§ 411.370 through 411.389 apply to requests for advisory opinions that are submitted to HCFA after November 3, 1997, and before August 21, 2000, and to any requests submitted during any other time period during which HCFA is required by law to issue the advisory opinions described in this subpart.

(b) *Matters that qualify for advisory opinions and who may request one.* Any individual or entity may request a written advisory opinion from HCFA concerning whether a physician's referral relating to designated health services (other than clinical laboratory services) is prohibited under section 1877 of the Act. In the advisory opinion, HCFA determines whether a business arrangement described by the parties to that arrangement appears to constitute a "financial relationship" (as defined in section 1877(a)(2) of the Act) that could potentially restrict a physician's referrals, and whether the arrangement or the designated health services at issue appear to qualify for any of the exceptions to the referral prohibition described in section 1877 of the Act.

(1) The request must involve an existing arrangement or one into which the requestor, in good faith, specifically plans to enter. The planned arrangement may be contingent upon the party or parties receiving a favorable advisory opinion. HCFA does not consider, for purposes of an advisory opinion, requests that present a general question of interpretation, pose a hypothetical situation, or involve the activities of third parties.

(2) The requestor must be a party to the existing or proposed arrangement.

(c) *Matters not subject to advisory opinions.* HCFA does not address through the advisory opinion process—

(1) Whether the fair market value was, or will be, paid or received for any goods, services, or property; and

(2) Whether an individual is a bona fide employee within the requirements of section 3121(d)(2) of the Internal Revenue Code of 1986.

(d) *Facts subject to advisory opinions.* HCFA considers requests for advisory opinions that involve applying specific facts to the subject matter described in paragraph (b) of this section. Requestors must include in the advisory opinion request a complete description of the arrangement that the requestor is undertaking, or plans to undertake, as described in § 411.372.

(e) *Requests that will not be accepted.* HCFA does not accept an advisory opinion request or issue an advisory opinion if—

(1) The request is not related to a named individual or entity;

(2) HCFA is aware that the same, or substantially the same, course of action is under investigation, or is or has been the subject of a proceeding involving the Department of Health and Human Services or another governmental agency; or

(3) HCFA believes that it cannot make an informed opinion or could only make an informed opinion after extensive investigation, clinical study, testing, or collateral inquiry.

(f) *Effects of an advisory opinion on other Governmental authority.* Nothing in this part limits the investigatory or prosecutorial authority of the OIG, the Department of Justice, or any other agency of the Government. In addition, in connection with any request for an advisory opinion, HCFA, the OIG, or the Department of Justice may conduct whatever independent investigation it believes appropriate.

§ 411.372   Procedure for submitting a request.

(a) *Format for a request.* A party or parties must submit a request for an advisory opinion to HCFA in writing, including an original request and 2 copies. The request must be addressed to: Health Care Financing Administration, Department of Health and Human Services, Attention: Advisory Opinions, P.O. Box 26505, Baltimore, MD 21207.

(b) *Information HCFA requires with all submissions.* The request must include the following:

(1) The name, address, telephone number, and Taxpayer Identification Number of the requestor.

(2) The names and addresses, to the extent known, of all other actual and potential parties to the arrangement that is the subject of the request.

(3) The name, title, address, and daytime telephone number of a contact person who will be available to discuss the request with HCFA on behalf of the requestor.

(4) A complete and specific description of all relevant information bearing on the arrangement, including—

(i) A complete description of the arrangement that the requestor is undertaking, or plans to undertake, including: the purpose of the arrangement; the nature of each party's (including each entity's) contribution to the arrangement; the direct or indirect relationships between the parties, with an emphasis on the relationships between physicians involved in the arrangement (or their immediate family members who are involved) and any entities that provide designated health services; the types of services for which a physician wishes to refer, and whether the referrals will involve Medicare or Medicaid patients;

(ii) Complete copies of all relevant documents or relevant portions of documents that affect or could affect the arrangement, such as personal services or employment contracts, leases, deeds, pension or insurance plans, financial statements, or stock certificates (or, if these relevant documents do not yet exist, a complete description, to the best of the requestor's knowledge, of what these documents are likely to contain);

(iii) Detailed statements of all collateral or oral understandings, if any; and

(iv) Descriptions of any other arrangements or relationships that could affect HCFA's analysis.

(5) Complete information on the identity of all entities involved either directly or indirectly in the arrangement, including their names, addresses, legal form, ownership structure, nature of the business (products and services) and, if relevant, their Medicare and Medicaid provider numbers. The requestor must also include a brief description of any other entities that could affect the outcome of the opinion, including those with which the requestor, the other parties, or the immediate family members of involved physicians, have any financial relationships (either direct or indirect, and as defined in section 1877(a)(2) of the Act and § 411.351), or in which any of the parties holds an ownership or control interest as defined in section 1124(a)(3) of the Act.

(6) A discussion of the specific issues or questions the requestor would like HCFA to address including, if possible, a description of why the requestor believes the referral prohibition in section 1877 of the Act might or might not be triggered by the arrangement and which, if any, exceptions to the prohibition the requestor believes might apply. The requestor should attempt to designate which facts are relevant to each issue or question raised in the request and should cite the provisions of law under which each issue or question arises.

(7) An indication of whether the parties involved in the request have also asked for or are planning to ask for an advisory opinion on the arrangement in question from the OIG under section 1128D(b) of the Act (42 U.S.C. 1320a-7d(b)) and whether the arrangement is or is not, to the best of the requestor's knowledge, the subject of an investigation.

(8) The certification(s) described in § 411.373. The certification(s) must be signed by—

(i) The requestor, if the requestor is an individual;

(ii) The chief executive officer, or comparable officer, of the requestor, if the requestor is a corporation;

(iii) The managing partner of the requestor, if the requestor is a partnership; or

(iv) A managing member, if the requestor is a limited liability company.

(9) A check or money order payable to HCFA in the amount described in § 411.375(a).

(c) *Additional information HCFA might require.* If the request does not contain all of the information required by paragraph (b) of this section, or, if either before or after accepting the request, HCFA believes it needs more information in order to render an advisory opinion, it may request whatever additional information or documents it deems necessary. Additional information must be provided in writing, signed by the same person who signed the initial request (or by an individual in a comparable position), and be certified as described in § 411.373.

§ 411.373 Certification.

(a) Every request must include the following signed certification: "With knowledge of the penalties for false statements provided by 18 U.S.C. 1001 and with knowledge that this request for an advisory opinion is being submitted to the Department of Health and Human Services, I certify that all of the information provided is true and correct, and constitutes a complete description of the facts regarding which an advisory opinion is sought, to the best of my knowledge and belief."

(b) If the advisory opinion relates to a proposed arrangement, in addition to the certification required by paragraph (a) of this section, the following certification must be included and signed by the requestor: "The arrangement described in this request for an advisory opinion is one into which [the requestor], in good faith, plans to enter." This statement may be made contingent on a favorable advisory opinion, in which case the requestor should add one of the following phrases to the certification:

(1) "if HCFA issues a favorable advisory opinion."

(2) "if HCFA and the OIG issue favorable advisory opinions."

§ 411.375 Fees for the cost of advisory opinions.

(a) *Initial payment.* Parties must include with each request for an advisory opinion submitted through December 31, 1998, a check or money order payable to HCFA for $250. For requests submitted after this date, parties must include a check or money order in this amount, unless HCFA has revised the amount of the initial fee in a program issuance, in which case, the requestor must include the revised amount. This initial payment is nonrefundable.

(b) *How costs are calculated.* Before issuing the advisory opinion, HCFA calculates the costs the Department has incurred in responding to the request.

The calculation includes the costs of salaries, benefits, and overhead for analysts, attorneys, and others who have worked on the request, as well as administrative and supervisory support for these individuals.

(c) *Agreement to pay all costs.* (1) By submitting the request for an advisory opinion, the requestor agrees, except as indicated in paragraph (c)(3) of this section, to pay all costs the Department incurs in responding to the request for an advisory opinion.

(2) In its request for an advisory opinion, the requestor may designate a triggering dollar amount. If HCFA estimates that the costs of processing the advisory opinion request have reached or are likely to exceed the designated triggering dollar amount, HCFA notifies the requestor.

(3) If HCFA notifies the requestor that the actual or estimated cost of processing the request has reached or is likely to exceed the triggering dollar amount, HCFA stops processing the request until the requestor makes a written request for HCFA to continue. If HCFA is delayed in processing the request for an advisory opinion because of this procedure, the time within which HCFA must issue an advisory opinion is suspended until the requestor asks HCFA to continue working on the request.

(4) If the requestor chooses not to pay for HCFA to complete an advisory opinion, or withdraws the request, the requestor is still obligated to pay for all costs HCFA has identified as costs it incurred in processing the request for an advisory opinion, up to that point.

(5) If the costs HCFA has incurred in responding to the request are greater than the amount the requestor has paid, HCFA, before issuing the advisory opinion, notifies the requestor of any additional amount that is due. HCFA does not issue an advisory opinion until the requestor has paid the full amount that is owed. Once the requestor has paid HCFA the total amount due for the costs of processing the request, HCFA issues the advisory opinion. The time period HCFA has for issuing advisory opinions is suspended from the time HCFA notifies the requestor of the amount owed until the time HCFA receives full payment.

(d) *Fees for outside experts.* (1) In addition to the fees identified in this section, the requestor also must pay any required fees for expert opinions, if any, from outside sources, as described in § 411.377.

(2) The time period for issuing an advisory opinion is suspended from the time that HCFA notifies the requestor that it needs an outside expert opinion

Federal Register / Vol. 63, No. 6 / Friday, January 9, 1998 / Rules and Regulations **1657**

until the time HCFA receives that opinion.

§ 411.377   Expert opinions from outside sources.

(a) HCFA may request expert advice from qualified sources if HCFA believes that the advice is necessary to respond to a request for an advisory opinion. For example, HCFA may require the use of accountants or business experts to assess the structure of a complex business arrangement or to ascertain a physician's or immediate family member's financial relationship with entities that provide designated health services.

(b) If HCFA determines that it needs to obtain expert advice in order to issue a requested advisory opinion, HCFA notifies the requestor of that fact and provides the identity of the appropriate expert and an estimate of the costs of the expert advice. As indicated in § 411.375(d), the requestor must pay the estimated cost of the expert advice.

(c) Once HCFA has received payment for the estimated cost of the expert advice, HCFA arranges for the expert to provide a prompt review of the issue or issues in question. HCFA considers any additional expenses for the expert advice, beyond the estimated amount, as part of the costs HCFA has incurred in responding to the request, and the responsibility of the requestor, as described in § 411.375(c).

§ 411.378   Withdrawing a request.

The party requesting an advisory opinion may withdraw the request before HCFA issues a formal advisory opinion. This party must submit the withdrawal in writing to the same address as the request, as indicated in § 411.372(a). Even if the party withdraws the request, the party must pay the costs the Department has expended in processing the request, as discussed in § 411.375. HCFA reserves the right to keep any request for an advisory opinion and any accompanying documents and information, and to use them for any governmental purposes permitted by law.

§ 411.379   When HCFA accepts a request.

(a) Upon receiving a request for an advisory opinion, HCFA promptly makes an initial determination of whether the request includes all of the information it will need to process the request.

(b) Within 15 working days of receiving the request, HCFA—

(1) Formally accepts the request for an advisory opinion;

(2) Notifies the requestor about the additional information it needs, or

(3) Declines to formally accept the request.

(c) If the requestor provides the additional information HCFA has requested, or otherwise resubmits the request, HCFA processes the resubmission in accordance with paragraphs (a) and (b) of this section as if it were an initial request for an advisory opinion.

(d) Upon accepting the request, HCFA notifies the requestor by regular U.S. mail of the date that HCFA formally accepted the request.

(e) The 90-day period that HCFA has to issue an advisory opinion set forth in § 411.380(c) does not begin until HCFA has formally accepted the request for an advisory opinion.

§ 411.380   When HCFA issues a formal advisory opinion.

(a) HCFA considers an advisory opinion to be issued once it has received payment and once the opinion has been dated, numbered, and signed by an authorized HCFA official.

(b) An advisory opinion contains a description of the material facts known to HCFA that relate to the arrangement that is the subject of the advisory opinion, and states HCFA's opinion about the subject matter of the request based on those facts. If necessary, HCFA includes in the advisory opinion material facts that could be considered confidential information or trade secrets within the meaning of 18 U.S.C. 1095.

(c)(1) HCFA issues an advisory opinion, in accordance with the provisions of this part, within 90 days after it has formally accepted the request for an advisory opinion, or, for requests that HCFA determines, in its discretion, involve complex legal issues or highly complicated fact patterns, within a reasonable time period.

(2) If the 90th day falls on a Saturday, Sunday, or Federal holiday, the time period ends at the close of the first business day following the weekend or holiday;

(3) The 90-day period is suspended from the time HCFA—

(i) Notifies the requestor that the costs have reached or are likely to exceed the triggering amount as described in § 411.375(c)(2) until HCFA receives written notice from the requestor to continue processing the request;

(ii) Requests additional information from the requestor until HCFA receives the additional information;

(iii) Notifies the requestor of the full amount due until HCFA receives payment of this amount; and

(iv) Notifies the requestor of the need for expert advice until HCFA receives the expert advice.

(d) After HCFA has notified the requestor of the full amount owed and has received full payment of that amount, HCFA issues the advisory opinion and promptly mails it to the requestor by regular first class U.S. mail.

§ 411.382   HCFA's right to rescind advisory opinions.

Any advice HCFA gives in an opinion does not prejudice its right to reconsider the questions involved in the opinion and, if it determines that it is in the public interest, to rescind or revoke the opinion. HCFA provides notice to the requestor of its decision to rescind or revoke the opinion so that the requestor and the parties involved in the requestor's arrangement may discontinue any course of action they have taken in accordance with the advisory opinion. HCFA does not proceed against the requestor with respect to any action the requestor and the involved parties have taken in good faith reliance upon HCFA's advice under this part, provided—

(a) The requestor presented to HCFA a full, complete and accurate description of all the relevant facts; and

(b) The parties promptly discontinue the action upon receiving notice that HCFA had rescinded or revoked its approval, or discontinue the action within a reasonable "wind down" period, as determined by HCFA.

§ 411.384   Disclosing advisory opinions and supporting information.

(a) Advisory opinions that HCFA issues and releases in accordance with the procedures set forth in this subpart are available to the public.

(b) Promptly after HCFA issues an advisory opinion and releases it to the requestor, HCFA makes available a copy of the advisory opinion for public inspection during its normal hours of operation and on the DHHS/HCFA web site.

(c) Any predecisional document, or part of such predecisional document, that is prepared by HCFA, the Department of Justice, or any other Department or agency of the United States in connection with an advisory opinion request under the procedures set forth in this part is exempt from disclosure under 5 U.S.C. 552, and will not be made publicly available.

(d) Documents submitted by the requestor to HCFA in connection with a request for an advisory opinion are available to the public to the extent they are required to be made available by 5 U.S.C. 552, through procedures set forth in 45 CFR part 5.

(e) Nothing in this section limits HCFA's obligation, under applicable

1658 Federal Register / Vol. 63, No. 6 / Friday, January 9, 1998 / Rules and Regulations

laws, to publicly disclose the identity of the requesting party or parties, and the nature of the action HCFA has taken in response to the request.

§411.386 HCFA's advisory opinions as exclusive.

The procedures described in this subpart constitute the only method by which any individuals or entities can obtain a binding advisory opinion on the subject of a physician's referrals, as described in §411.370. HCFA has not and does not issue a binding advisory opinion on the subject matter in §411.370, in either oral or written form, except through written opinions it issues in accordance with this subpart.

§411.387 Parties affected by advisory opinions.

An advisory opinion issued by HCFA does not apply in any way to any individual or entity that does not join in the request for the opinion. Individuals or entities other than the requestor(s) may not rely on an advisory opinion.

§411.388 When advisory opinions are not admissible evidence.

The failure of a party to seek or to receive an advisory opinion may not be introduced into evidence to prove that the party either intended or did not intend to violate the provisions of sections 1128, 1128A or 1128B of the Act.

§411.389 Range of the advisory opinion.

(a) An advisory opinion states only HCFA's opinion regarding the subject matter of the request. If the subject of an advisory opinion is an arrangement that must be approved by or is regulated by any other agency, HCFA's advisory opinion cannot be read to indicate HCFA's views on the legal or factual issues that may be raised before that agency.

(b) An advisory opinion that HCFA issues under this part does not bind or obligate any agency other than the Department. It does not affect the requestor's, or anyone else's, obligations to any other agency, or under any statutory or regulatory provision other than that which is the specific subject matter of the advisory opinion.

(Catalog of Federal Domestic Assistance Program No. 93.773, Medicare—Hospital Insurance; and Program No. 93.774, Medicare—Supplementary Medical Insurance Program)

Dated: December 2, 1997.

Nancy-Ann Min DeParle,

Administrator, Health Care Financing Administration.

Dated: December 30, 1997.

Donna E. Shalala,

Secretary.

[FR Doc. 98–270 Filed 1–5–98; 8:45 am]

BILLING CODE 4120–01–P